One Hundred Years of Game Theory

In the winter of 2021, the Swedish Nobel Foundation organized a Nobel symposium "One Hundred Years of Game Theory" to commemorate the publication of famous mathematician Émile Borel's "La théorie du jeu et les équations intégrales à noyau symétrique." The symposium gathered roughly forty of the world's most prominent scholars with backgrounds ranging from the mathematical foundations of game theory to its applications in economics, political science, computer science, biology, sociology, and other fields. *One Hundred Years of Game Theory* brings together their writings to summarize and put in perspective the main achievements of game theory in the last 100 years. They address past achievements, taking stock of what has been accomplished and contemplating potential future developments and challenges. Offering cross-disciplinary discussions between eminent researchers, including five Nobel laureates, one Fields medalist, and two Gödel prize winners, the contributors provide a fascinating landscape of game theory and its wide range of applications.

Mark Voorneveld is a professor in the Department of Economics at the Stockholm School of Economics. His research is mostly in game theory and its applications in economics.

Jörgen W. Weibull is Professor Emeritus at the Stockholm School of Economics. He has taught game theory at many universities around the world. In his research he has made contributions to political economy, to the modeling of social norms and moral values, to evolutionary game theory, and to noncooperative game theory.

Tommy Andersson is a professor in the Department of Economics at Lund University. His research focuses on mechanism and market design. He is currently the president of the Society for Economic Design (2023–present) and a member of the Prize Committee for the Alfred Nobel Memorial Prize in Economic Sciences (2019–present).

Roger Myerson is David L Pearson Professor of Global Conflict Studies in the Harris School of Public Policy at the University of Chicago. He has written about game theory, information economics, and comparative political institutions. In 2007 he was awarded the Nobel Memorial Prize in Economic Sciences for contributions to mechanism design theory, which analyzes rules for coordinating economic agents efficiently when they have different information and difficulty trusting each other.

Jean-François Laslier is a senior researcher at the Centre National de la Recherche Scientifique (CNRS) and a professor at the Paris School of Economics. His work interests include games and social choice theory and political science. He does research on democracy, in particular on voting rules and citizens' behavior.

Rida Laraki is Director of the Moroccan Center for Game Theory at the University Mohammed VI Polytechnique (UM6P), Rabat, Morocco. He is a multidisciplinary researcher whose work includes stochastic games, voting design, economic theory, optimization, and multiagent learning. He is the coauthor of *Majority Judgment: Measuring, Ranking, and Electing* (2011).

Yukio Koriyama is Full Professor of Economics at the École Polytechnique in France. His research interests include game theory and its application to political economy.

ECONOMETRIC SOCIETY MONOGRAPHS SERIES

The Econometric Society is an international society for the advancement of economic theory in relation to statistics and mathematics. The Econometric Society Monographs series is designed to promote the publication of original research contributions of high quality in mathematical economics and theoretical and applied econometrics.

Books in the Series

Victor Chernozhukov, Johannes Hörner, Eliana La Ferrara, & Iván Werning, *Advances in Economics and Econometrics: Twelfth World Congress, Vols. I & II*, 2025

T. Strzalecki, *Stochastic Choice Theory*, 2025

C. Hsiao, *Analysis of Panel Data, 4th edn*, 2022

D. M. Kreps, *The Black–Scholes–Merton Model as an Idealization of Discrete-Time Economies*, 2019

W. Thomson, *How to Divide When There Isn't Enough: From Aristotle, the Talmud, and Maimonides to the Axiomatics of Resource Allocation*, 2019

O. Compte & A. Postlewaite, *Ignorance and Uncertainty*, 2018

I. Molchanov & F. Molinari, *Random Sets in Econometrics*, 2018

B. Honoré, A. Pakes, M. Piazzesi, & L. Samuelson (eds.), *Advances in Economics and Econometrics: Eleventh World Congress, Vols. I & II*, 2017

S. Maurer, *On the Shoulders of Giants: Colleagues Remember Suzanne Scotchmer's Contributions to Economics*, 2017

C. P. Chambers & F. Echenique, *Revealed Preference Theory*, 2016

J.-F. Mertens, S. Sorins, & S. Samir, *Repeated Games*, 2015

C. Hsiao, *Analysis of Panel Data, 3rd edn*, 2014

C. Cameron & P. Trivedi, *Regression Analysis of Count Data, 2nd edn*, 2013

A. Harvey, *Dynamic Models for Volatility and Heavy Tails, with Applications to Financial and Economic Time Series*, 2013

D. Acemoglu, M. Areilano, & E. Dekel (eds.), *Advances in Economics and Econometrics: Theory and Applications, Tenth World Congress, Vols. I, II, & III*, 2013

M. Fleurbaey & F. Maniquet, *A Theory of Fairness and Social Justice*, 2011

R. Vohra, *Mechanism Design: A Linear Programming Approach*, 2011

(*Continued after the Index*)

One Hundred Years of Game Theory

A Nobel Symposium

Edited by

MARK VOORNEVELD
Stockholm School of Economics

JÖRGEN W. WEIBULL
Stockholm School of Economics

TOMMY ANDERSSON
Lund University

ROGER MYERSON
University of Chicago

JEAN-FRANÇOIS LASLIER
Paris School of Economics

RIDA LARAKI
University Mohammed VI Polytechnique

YUKIO KORIYAMA
École Polytechnique

CAMBRIDGE
UNIVERSITY PRESS

CAMBRIDGE
UNIVERSITY PRESS

Shaftesbury Road, Cambridge CB2 8EA, United Kingdom

One Liberty Plaza, 20th Floor, New York, NY 10006, USA

477 Williamstown Road, Port Melbourne, VIC 3207, Australia

314–321, 3rd Floor, Plot 3, Splendor Forum, Jasola District Centre, New Delhi – 110025, India

103 Penang Road, #05–06/07, Visioncrest Commercial, Singapore 238467

Cambridge University Press is part of Cambridge University Press & Assessment, a department of the University of Cambridge.

We share the University's mission to contribute to society through the pursuit of education, learning and research at the highest international levels of excellence.

www.cambridge.org
Information on this title: www.cambridge.org/9781009686082

DOI: 10.1017/9781009686044

When citing this work, please include a reference to the DOI 10.1017/9781009686044

First published 2026

A catalogue record for this publication is available from the British Library

A Cataloging-in-Publication data record for this book is available from the Library of Congress

ISBN 978-1-009-68608-2 Hardback
ISBN 978-1-009-68606-8 Paperback

Contents

Preface

On December 19, 1921, the eminent mathematician Emile Borel published a paper that laid the foundation of modern game theory and thereby offered a new framework for theoretical analysis of strategic interactions between rational decision makers.

The centennial of this paper offered an appropriate occasion for asking questions about where we may look for the next intellectual breakthroughs that will be fundamental for the social sciences, computer science, and biology. What are the most promising future directions for applications of game-theoretic analysis? What other kinds of mathematical models have the potential to become as fruitful for these academic disciplines as game theory has turned out to be? What are the most important future challenges and applications? The Swedish Nobel Foundation organized a Nobel symposium on "One Hundred Years of Game Theory" in December 2021 to consider such questions, and this book is the result.

In the century since Borel's publication, the toolbox of game theory has been significantly enhanced, and game-theoretic analysis has flourished in many disciplines, including economics, mathematics, computer science, biology, political science, sociology, and philosophy. Game theory has become a lingua franca, a unifying methodological framework to address interactions between multiple agents that helps integrate these diverse fields. Major contributions that extended the methods and applications of game theory have on several occasions been recognized by an award of the Alfred Nobel Memorial Prize in Economic Sciences.

The December 2021 Nobel symposium featured sessions on the early history of game theory, the mathematics of game theory, biology and population dynamics, computer science, economics and institutional design, individual behavior in strategic interactions, political science, and the development of human society through history. In each area, a distinguished group of contributors was asked to offer a broad perspective that would be of interest to a wide readership from all these areas, as well as to newcomers with broad curiosity about scientific ideas.

These sessions correspond to the parts in this collection. Each part in its turn starts off with a brief general introduction to the topic of its separate chapters.

The aim of the symposium was not primarily to focus on past achievements but to reflect on future developments, with hope that younger scholars may find inspiration to become engaged in an exciting field of research. In this book, the contributions from this historic symposium are made available to readers throughout the world. Nobel symposium 176 "One Hundred Years of Game Theory" was funded by the Nobel Foundation and organized by the editors of this book. It took place on December 17-19, 2021, in Stockholm, Sweden. The Nobel Symposia Identification belongs to the Nobel Foundation.

PART I

THE EARLY HISTORY OF GAME THEORY FROM BOREL

1

Introduction to Part I

Françoise Forges

Around 1994, a number of scientific events were motivated by the 50-year anniversary of game theory, making it start with the first edition of von Neumann and Morgenstern's famous book *Theory of Games and Economic Behavior* (TGEB). And here we are, less than 30 years after, to celebrate 100 years of game theory, going back to a note that Borel wrote in 1921. This chapter will show us that considering Borel as a genuine founder of game theory is not artificial at all.

As Laurent Mazliak explains in the first chapter of this part, "The Games of Borel and Chance," Borel was interested in the interaction of strategic decision makers, who can make use of their *skill*, namely their "ability to make the most of the elements provided by chance." What Borel had in mind when referring to "skill" remains a bit vague but goes apparently beyond the use of randomized strategies that are symmetrically accessible to all players, the only use to be put forward by von Neumann (see, e.g., bluffing in poker or the well-known anecdote about Sherlock Holmes in TGEB).

While Borel did not formalize his notion of skillfulness and had apparently no intention to model general abstract games, he explicitly said (in the preface to Borel, 1938) that "to deal with economic questions satisfactorily, a place must be made for probability and psychology." As well understood by Guilbaud (1949), whose role is emphasized by Laurent Mazliak, Borel's contributions, like those of von Neumann and Morgenstern later, offered a definite renewal of economic thinking. The expression "psychological games" appears explicitly in Fréchet's English translation of several articles of Borel (including the 1921 one) in *Econometrica* in 1953. It is very tempting to relate these thoughts with recent themes like mechanism or information design (see Part V) – in which indeed economic actors make the optimal use of random events – or psychological games as they are analyzed today (see Dufwenberg, 2008). To mitigate such easy speculations, the notion of *belief*, which has become central in contemporary game theory, does not appear as such in Borel's heuristics. As Laurent Mazliak explains, Borel indeed combines a subjective interpretation of probability *à la* de Finetti with an objective view, motivated by applications of probability theory to scientific knowledge (see also Galavotti, 2019; Mazliak and Sage, 2022).

The second chapter of this part, by Robert Leonard, "Von Neumann, Morgenstern and Their Creation of Game Theory, 1900–1960," puts the elaboration of TGEB in context. He goes back to early work on chess, like Zermelo's 1913 article or the much less well-known book by Lasker (1907). Like the first author, he gives an account of Borel and von Neumann's exchanges on the minimax theorem during the 1920s. This second article confirms one of Laurent Mazliak's concluding remarks, namely that while Borel and von Neumann were both eager to contribute to political and social life, their approaches were complementary. Borel was skeptical about abstract models that would require sophisticated tools or become computationally complex. By contrast, von Neumann was confident that a mathematical theory could be built to usefully describe and advise society.

Indeed, von Neumann and Morgenstern conceived their book as a "manifesto for new mathematics demanded by the analysis of social interaction." They elaborated a quite general model of extensive form games. More importantly, as Robert Leonard recalls, they wanted to capture an ambitious notion of "standard of behavior." This led them to introduce the model of *coalitional games* (or "cooperative games"), with the understanding that players can make side payments. They proposed their notion of stable sets, known today as von Neumann and Morgenstern's solution. Coalitional games were very popular until the 1970s. Even if they are not a main topic of this symposium, they are still alive today (see, e.g., Alvin Roth's chapter in Part V).

As Robert Leonard explains, mathematical methods appeared as quite successful during the Second World War, which guaranteed support to research in game theory right after, for example, at Princeton or at the RAND Corporation. These institutions hosted the game theorists of the next generation, among which were Shapley and of course Nash, whose work, according to Roger Myerson (the third contributor of this part), marked a turning point in the history of economic thought.

Before telling us about Nash's tremendous achievements, Roger Myerson's chapter, "Borel and the Foundation of Game Theory," identifies three fundamental ideas of game theory that are already in the 1921 paper. A first idea is the already mentioned concept of randomized strategy. Another contribution of Borel (1921) is the expected payoff criterion, which, as pointed out by Roger Myerson, is carefully formulated in terms of winning probabilities. The perhaps most important idea, which was fully endorsed by von Neumann, is that strategic interaction can be analyzed in normal form games, in which players make independent choices. However, as noted by Roger Myerson, von Neumann did not go on with this view when he focused on coalitional games – with transferable utility – to analyze situations with more than two players. One has to wait for the fundamental contributions of Nash to recover fully consistent models. A first key is that all players' choices, including those about commitment and side payments, can be described in the extensive form. A second key is that a general solution concept, the Nash equilibrium, applies to every normal form game, possibly derived from a complex extensive form.

Summing up, the session on the history of game theory tells us about the "roots" of the discipline, from Borel to Nash, from 1921 to about 1960. The rest of this volume describes some parts of the "trunk" of game theory but, most importantly, its "foliage."

1.1 REFERENCES

E. Borel. La théorie du jeu et les équations intégrales à noyau symétrique. *Comptes Rendus Hebdomadaires des Séances de l'Académie des Sciences, Paris*, 173:1304–1308, 1921.

E. Borel. *Traité du calcul des probabilités et de ses applications. Tome IV: Applications diverses et conclusion. Fasc. 2: Applications aux jeux de hasard. Cours professé à la faculté des sciences de Paris, Rédigé par* J. Ville. *XI + 122p*. Paris: Gauthier-Villars, 1938.

M. Dufwenberg. Psychological games. In *The New Palgrave Dictionary of Economics*, vol. 6. New York: Palgrave Macmillan, 2008.

M. C. Galavotti. Pragmatism and the birth of subjective probability. *European Journal of Pragmatism and American Philosophy*, 11(1):1–13, 2019.

G.-T. Guilbaud. La théorie des jeux. Contributions critiques à la théorie de la valeur. *Economie appliquée*, 2:275–319, 1949.

E. Lasker. *Kampf*. New York: Lasker's, 1907.

L. Mazliak and M. Sage. Altered States, Borel and the probabilistic approach to reality. In P. Cantù and G. Schiemer, eds., *Logic, Epistemology, and Scientific Theories: From Peano to the Vienna Circle*. New York: Springer, 2022.

E. Zermelo. Uber eine Anwendung der Mengenlehre auf die Theorie des Schachspiels. *Proceedings of the Fifth International Congress of Mathematicians*, 1913.

2

The Games of Borel and Chance

Laurent Mazliak

Almost 100 years ago to the day,[1] on December 19, 1921, the mathematician Émile Borel (1871–1956) presented to the Paris Academy of Sciences a note entitled "Game theory and integral symmetric kernel equations" (Borel, 1921). Borel, then just fifty years old, was a true star of the world mathematical scene. He had been elected a member of the Academy a few months earlier. It was the first time in his abundant production that the title of a paper explicitly referred to the theory of games. This note was soon followed by a few other mathematical publications: three other notes to the Academy (Borel, 1924a; Borel, 1926; Borel, 1927) and a presentation at the congress of the French Association for the Advancement of Sciences (Borel, 1923). Finally in 1938 a fascicle (Borel, 1938) of the *Treaty of the calcul of probabilities and its applications*, a large encyclopedic enterprise launched by Borel at the beginning of the 1920s,[2] was devoted to the "Applications of probability calculus to games of chance." It was in fact Jean Ville (1910–1989), a student of Borel at the Ecole Normale Supérieure, who was then preparing a thesis criticizing the theory of collectives of Richard von Mises,[3] who took notes of the lectures on the topic of games that Borel was teaching during the academic year 1936–1937 at the Sorbonne.

One can see, therefore, that the 1921 note seems to have given Borel the initial impetus to deepen his views on games. Most often the mathematical formalization of his ideas was hardly Borel's central preoccupation, especially in areas where the audience he judged most important to reach was all but limited to the restricted circle of professional mathematicians. Notes to the Paris Academy of Sciences, papers whose required brevity just allowed Borel to expose main ideas and sketches of methods, thus suited him perfectly, often without him feeling it necessary, contrary to what other scientists systematically did, to extend the note by a detailed article. The fact that many of Borel's ideas

[1] Remark by editors: The talk on which this chapter is based took place on December 17, 2021.
[2] On the treaty and its history, see Bustamante et al. (2015)
[3] The thesis was defended in 1939 and published as Ville (1939). On Ville, see Shafer (2009).

remained somewhat imprecise (for others than himself) did not really help, as one might easily guess, to disseminate the results Borel wanted to publicize.

So what does Borel (1921) contain? The fundamental aspect that Borel wants to highlight is that in the classic situations of his former probabilistic studies, the games subject to a calculation of probabilities, such as coin tossing, were based on pure randomness. However, for Borel, the most interesting game situations were at a higher level of complexity, taking into account the actions of players whose skill must therefore combine with the elements provided by chance (such as a distribution of cards) in order to obtain victory. In this type of situation, the researcher must be interested in the actions selected by the players at each point in the game.

Obviously, if a particular choice of action is uniformly better than any other one, any player is sure to win against any other choice made by the other players. But such a situation occurs only with oversimplified games, and this certainty of winning annihilates in fact any interest for the game. In *real* games, such a case cannot happen: the game is too complex to allow the determination of a secure strategy. This is even true in games where randomness plays no role (at least after it has been decided which player starts) such as checkers or chess: it is in the complexity of elaborating strategies that the interest resides. Therefore, in real complex games, the players must distribute their selection of actions over the various possibilities.

Borel considers the simplest case of a game between two players A and B, each of them being able to choose her or his actions in a finite set of possibilities $C_1, C_2, \ldots, C_n$. An $n \times n$ matrix

$$\begin{pmatrix} 1/2+\alpha_{11} & 1/2+\alpha_{12} & \ldots & 1/2+\alpha_{1n} \\ 1/2+\alpha_{21} & 1/2+\alpha_{22} & \ldots & 1/2+\alpha_{2n} \\ \ldots & \ldots & \ldots & \ldots \\ 1/2+\alpha_{n1} & 1/2+\alpha_{n2} & \ldots & 1/2+\alpha_{nn} \end{pmatrix}$$

gives the probabilities for player A to win the game: α_{ij} is a number between $-1/2$ and $1/2$ and $1/2+\alpha_{ij}$ indicates the probability that A wins, knowing that A chose the strategy C_i and B the strategy C_j.

Borel further asks that $\alpha_{ii} = 0$ be true so that the same choice of strategy by both players results in a "neutralization" and that $\alpha_{ij} = -\alpha_{ji}$ so that the situation of A and B is symmetrical. The strategy of the players is represented by a distribution of probability over the various actions. One assumes that player A chooses strategy C_i with probability p_i and player B chooses C_j with probability q_j. Under these conditions, the probability for A to win the game is given by $1/2 + \alpha$, where

$$\alpha = \sum_{i=1}^{n} \sum_{k=1}^{n} \alpha_{ik} p_i q_k$$

and the game is fair if $\alpha = 0$. Borel wonders if it is still possible for player A to choose a strategy, that is, a probabilistic distribution of the actions

$p_1, p_2, \ldots, p_n$ such that whatever the strategy $q_1, q_2, \ldots, q_n$ chosen by B (and which A ignores), the game is favorable to him. In the case of $n = 3$, Borel asserts that this is clearly not the case and that each player has the opportunity to counter the other's strategy and thus make the game fair. He also asserts, without giving any details, that it is easy to see that if n is greater than 3, this equilibrium situation only holds for particular values of α_{ij}.

In his conclusion, Borel shares his thoughts on the interest he sees in addressing this type of problem (Borel, 1921).

> The problems of probability and analysis that one might ask about the art of war or economic and financial speculations are not without analogy with the problems relating to games, but with a much higher degree of complication in general.... The only advice that the researcher can give, in the absence of any psychological information, to player A whose opponent B seeks to use the preceding remarks, is to vary his game in such a way that the probabilities of his various ways of playing are never well defined for an outside observer.

How can one explain that Borel got involved in this type of question at this moment of his life? It seems necessary for that to comment a little on the amazing career of this singular mathematician. Born in 1871 in the south of France (with the year of the symposium, 2021, also marking the 150th anniversary of his birth), after exceptionally brilliant studies and after a PhD defended in 1894, Borel became known as a first-rank analyst, a specialist in function theory. He introduced radically new methods such as the summation of divergent series and above all a concept of measure of linear sets, which paved the way for Henri Lebesgue, his junior by four years, and his construction in 1900 of an integral that would conquer the world in only fifteen years.[4] The year 1905 was a fundamental step in the mathematical life of Borel who resolutely engaged in research in probability theory. I cannot detail here the underlying reasons for this choice;[5] let me just say that it was the convergence of three observations that led him to this decision:

1. The probabilistic approach provides a way to get around a Cantor-style approach based solely on internal logic that Borel, after having been a resolute Cantorian, now treated with defiance.[6]
2. The probabilistic approach has become essential in modern physics and in particular in the kinetic theory of gases.[7]
3. The probabilistic approach provides a means of scientifically apprehending the question of risk, which is at the heart of any reflection on social progress

[4] On the history of Lebesgue's integral and its conquest of the world in an amazingly short time, see Hawkins (2001).

[5] On this point, consult Mazliak and Sage (2022), Durand and Mazliak (2011), and Bru and Bru (2018).

[6] See Mazliak and Sage (2022).

[7] In 1906, Borel (1906) published the first mathematical systematic approach of the Maxwell-Boltzmann law. Borel extended his views in the book Borel (1914b). See also Bustamante De la Ossa (2019) for the connection between Borel and physics.

in modern, urban, and industrial society, in accordance with the radical-socialist political line to which it was close.

Borel therefore began an abundant production of work around these three directions. The foundation in 1905 of a monthly magazine, the aptly named *Revue du mois*, with his wife allowed him for several years to present his conception of the calculus of probabilities and its importance for the scientific education of the citizen. His most famous book, *Le hasard* (Borel, 1914a), the first edition of which in 1914 was to be followed by many others, presented this conception to a large (but cultivated) readership.

Borel's thoughts, however, could have remained confined to the inner circle of the public revolving around the academic scene if a major event did not propel them into a whole new dimension. The First World War was for him the occasion of unprecedented upheaval. Hired as a volunteer in 1915, Borel was quickly called in by Paul Painlevé (1863–1933), another mathematician who had been in politics for several years and was the current Minister of Public Instruction, to head the brand new department of inventions in favor of national defense. This entity, created to coordinate the scientific mobilization of the whole country in order to provide combatants with new technologies, gave Borel the opportunity to develop his undeniable qualities as an organizer and planner. This role also gave him the opportunity to test on a large scale the establishment of a "large numbers policy," revealing once again the importance of a rational approach to risk and statistical questions. It also confronted him with problems of strategic decision-making that can be considered as the sources of the subsequent development of operational research, such as the questions of locating enemy batteries by sound, where the positioning of listening stations is crucial, or the organization of transatlantic convoys during the extreme submarine warfare launched by Germany in 1917.[8]

Borel emerged from the conflict with the definitive conviction of an imperative need to improve the scientific culture of the masses on questions about risk estimation and, in particular, to transmit on a large scale the bases of the calculus of probabilities. In 1920 he decided to give up the chair of Theory of Functions he had held since 1909 (when it had been created for him) to take that of Calculus of Probabilities and Mathematical Physics. Deciding not to remain confined to the academic sphere, Borel in turn became involved in active politics: In 1924 he became a deputy for Aveyron, his department of birth in the south of the Massif Central, mayor of his birth city of Saint-Affrique and even Minister of the Navy for a few months in 1925. But above all, he acted concretely in the institutional sphere for the creation of two places that became the main elements for the transmission of the mathematics of randomness in Paris: the Institute of Statistics of the University of Paris in 1922 and the Institut Henri Poincaré in 1928.[9]

[8] On these questions, see Kirby (2003).

[9] On these points, see Catellier and Mazliak (2012) and Cléry (2020).

We can therefore see quite clearly how a systematic approach to the question of strategic games fits into the Borelian trajectory. In addition, two observations can be made.

The preparation of his new courses at the Sorbonne after 1920 led Borel to review the work of his predecessors, and in particular the book Bertrand (1889) published by Joseph Bertrand in 1889, in which Bertrand made a brief study of baccarat strategy. In his intervention at Association Francaise pour L'avancement des Sciences (AFAS) in 1923, Borel wrote:

> The only author who has studied a particular case of the problem we envisage is Joseph Bertrand, in the passage of his Calcul des Probabilités that he devotes to drawing for five in the game of baccarat. He there distinguishes clearly between the mathematical side and the psychological side of the problem; because he asks, for one thing, whether it is to the advantage of the punter to draw for five when the banker knows the punter's manner of playing, and for another thing, whether it is to the punter's advantage to draw for five letting the banker believe, if the punter can, that it is not his custom to do so. He also raises the same questions for not drawing for five. But, as will be seen from what follows, this study is extremely incomplete.[10]

An original hypothesis that does not seem to have been emphasized enough to explain Borel's conception of action was his cultural background inherited from his Protestant upbringing. Borel's father was a pastor of the Reformed Church in France, and his birthplace Saint-Affrique was an important mountain refuge for the Calvinists fleeing the bloodthirsty fury of the dragonnades sent by Louis XIV after the revocation of the Edict of Nantes in 1685. In his celebrated 1905 book, the sociologist Max Weber (1905) had underlined the connections between Protestantism and the entrepreneurial spirit at the foundation of capitalism. Although some aspects of Weber's analysis have subsequently been disputed, the attention paid by Protestant education to action in the material transformation of the world is not in doubt. As the philosopher Ellul wrote,

> Another consequence of the same dogma [of predestination] is the utilitarian nature of Calvinist ethics. There is no possible conflict between the individual and ethics. A man convinced of his salvation attests to this salvation by the objective results of his action. It is not a question of gratuitous actions to praise God abstractly, but to achieve useful and positive objectives; [as Weber puts it] "an idea exalted the Calvinist: that which God, in creating the world including the social order, had to objectively conceive ways to celebrate His glory; that He must have wanted not the creature for himself, but the ordering of the created subject according to His will. This is why unleashed by the doctrine of predestination, the active energies of the chosen one were transformed into efforts to rationalize the world". Unleashed? Yes, since the individual no longer had to seek

[10] Borel (1923), p. 79. On Bertrand's approach to baccarat, one can consult the interesting and very recent study by Ethier (2024). Ethier observes besides that contrary to Borel's assertion, some precursors to Bertrand may be found, especially by the engineer Albert Badoureau (1853–1923), on which one can consult Crovisier (2017).

> his salvation: if he was predestined, he was saved or lost for all eternity, without being able to change anything. So he could "take care of the world below." And [Weber's] work leads us to a final effect of the doctrine of predestination: rationalization. Calvinist theology is rigorously rational. Man's behavior must be so too and his action on the world, because anything that escapes this rigor is ultimately a kind of idolatry of the flesh. Any human relationship must be rationalized to escape sentimentalism, etc. But this rationalization must be understood: it is not a rationalism, it is not a final rationalization of reason. In reality, the life of the Christian is rationalized in relation to a single goal: to increase the glory of God on earth. It is from this end that a vigorous rationalization takes place. We must then annihilate the instinctive and spontaneous enjoyment, put order in individual behavior, establish a method of action in the world (but this, together with the idea of vocation, means: method in the work, in the economic behavior). The methodical regulation of personal life is the surest ethical expression of the belief in predestination. And this regulation involves both persons subject to our authority, and also that of social and economic structures.[11]

While Borel clearly distanced himself from any religious commitment, his attachment to his origins is obvious and his taste for concrete action, as well as a certain reiterated mistrust for speculative philosophy,[12] are probably a legacy of the latter. In 1937 Borel wrote a small entertaining note for the *Mercure de France*, entitled "Praise of the game," where, in the form of a pastiche of philosophical dialogue between three people, he exposed the role he attributed to the gambling phenomenon and the importance of its study for social progress. He thus put into the mouth of the mathematician Eudoxus, whom it is not difficult to see to be an image of himself, the following words:

> I take it easy on the risk appetite that manifests itself in those who expose small amounts of money to gambling. They know very well that in the fight over the issues, intelligence and attention are not enough, if the cards are not favorable; this uncertainty is even a large part of the pleasure they get from gambling. It is therefore certain that gambling contributes to maintaining and developing a taste for risk in men. It is a question of whether it is good or bad. For my part, I think it is a great favor that the game is doing to men in this way. Much of the great progress of mankind is due to the liking for risk. In order to make the generous gift of this progress to all their fellow human beings, men have risked their fortune, their peace of mind, their health and their lives against a magnificent stake: the hope of making their dream come true. (Borel, 1937b, pp. 280–281)

While this statement is not in itself particularly original, it takes a singular turn in its concomitance with Borel's permanent desire to think about the collective. The philosophy of Borel as a man of action is that society allows each of its members the full realization of their individuality in a framework where collective solidarity in the face of risks, rationalized through the use of scientific tools, allows the blows of fate to be limited. One recognizes here the assertions that underlie the entire political approach defended by the

[11] Ellul (1964), p. 9.

[12] See for instance his comments on Couturat (Borel, 1907).

radical-socialist and solidarist thinkers with whom Borel had socialized since his youth, among whom a certain number were linked to the protestant milieu.[13]

After his 1921 note (Borel, 1921), in his aforementioned short notes to the Academy and in his presentation to the AFAS, Borel deepened the situation of the first note and asserted, still without much detail, that it was possible to extend the result of "balanced" games[14] to cases when the number of actions available to both players equal first to 5 and then to 7. But he continued to raise doubts about the validity of the result for a general n.[15]

It is indeed slightly surprising to see that, for instance, Borel decided to include a supplementary note on games in the second edition of his textbook on probability (Borel, 1924b), in which he mostly reported the contents of what he wrote in 1921, with the noticeable difference that now the doubt about the validity was not beyond $n = 3$ actions but $n = 5$ (a case that he treated in 1924 through a slightly different formulation than he had in 1921 as a system of linear inequations [Borel, 1921; 1924b]). As mentioned previously, he indeed reiterated his doubts about the general validity of the possibility of a fair game.

How can one understand what Borel had in mind with this kind of (unproved) assertion? Dell'Aglio (1995) proposes a very convincing interpretation. Borel had no intention of dealing with an abstract theory of games and always kept real games in his mind. In a real game, it is compulsory to take into account an interaction between the two players: the probability distribution of the various actions quantifies the skillfulness (*habileté*) of the players to guess the strategy of their adversary. In 1938 Borel found it necessary to give some information about what he had in mind with this rather vague concept of *habileté*. He wrote:

> What do we mean by a player's "skill"? It is his or her ability to make the most of the elements provided by chance. A more detailed study ... will enable us to highlight in this skill two distinct factors: firstly, an exact knowledge of all the possible combinations that the game presents, and of their respective probabilities; secondly, the aptitude of the player to mislead his adversary on his intentions or on certain facts, such as the value of his own play. (Borel, 1938, p.x)

Borel had always been a supporter of a subjective interpretation of probability, except in the case when this probability is close to 0 or 1,[16] so that

[13] See for instance Rigoulot (2009).

[14] Here I use the term *balanced* only to refer to the type of situation Borel studied in his first note, as described previously. F. Forges informed me that the word has acquired technical contents in the context of cooperative game theory.

[15] Borel (1927), p. 54.

[16] On the Borelian version of Cournot's principle, see Martin (1994). The important question of Borel's position concerning the interpretation of probabilities has been addressed in many works (see for example Galavotti, 2005, pp. 191 ff). In the way that Borel had been qualified – ironically – as a *semiconstructivist* by Brouwer in connection with his refusal of a purely logical

the probabilities entering into the description of one player's strategy reflect their understanding (or guess) of what the other player will do. In a real game the number of available strategies is very high, and this is an obstacle to the possibility of a truly fair game: A perfect symmetry between two players is simply impossible because one of the two players is necessarily more skillful than the other.

In 1928 von Neumann asked Borel to present a note to the Academy, soberly entitled "On game theory" (von Neumann, 1928a), where he presented for the first time in France the so-called minmax theorem published the same year in an article in the journal *Matematische Annalen* (von Neumann, 1928b), in which he intended to give a final answer, for any n, to the question of fairness of play that Borel had considered. Von Neumann's note, though also laconic, thus clearly wanted to stand out against Borel's doubts about the general validity of the result in his former notes. Von Neumann besides did not hide that he had read Borel's notes while asserting that he had been interested in this type of question independently from his French colleague.[17]

It was Borel who presented the note to the Academy, but oddly he did not seem to pay much attention to it. When at the International Congress of Mathematicians in Oslo in 1936, Borel chose as the topic for his talk "Some remarks on the application of the calculus of probabilities to games of chance" (Borel, 1937a) and exposed some extensions of his results to the case of asymmetric games, he mentioned that he had been informed during the congress of the existence of von Neumann's article (von Neumann, 1928b; though this paper appeared eight years earlier and was directly connected to the aforementioned note [von Neumann, 1928a] that Borel himself had presented to the Academy). Maybe with a touch of annoyance (this is what Robert Leonard suggests),[18] Borel added that he had not had time to study it. Borel also added with a touch of irony that even if the theorem of the minmax was always true in theory, in the case where the number of possible actions of the players is very large, its practical interest is null considering the complexity of the necessary calculations.

In the fascicle of the treaty devoted to games of chance published two years later (Borel, 1938), Borel did not fail to include Ville's note,[19] which proposed

or totally constructive approach to mathematical objects, one can say of him that he was a semisubjectivist in his conception of probabilities, leaving room for an objective part linked to the principle of Cournot. This point seemed fundamental to him in order to place statistical physics, in particular the kinetic theory of gases, of which he was the first mathematician to attempt a purely mathematical synthesis in Borel (1906) on solid foundations. One can find in Bustamante et al. (2015) some comments on the last fascicule of the *Traité*, where Borel makes a comparative assessment between the various interpretations of the concept of probability, an assessment which gave rise the following year to the very profound article by Cavaillès (1940). On this subject, see in particular Sinaceur (2018).

[17] For a more detailed analysis on this point, see Leonard (2010), p. 57ff.

[18] Leonard (2010), p. 71, note 32.

[19] Ville (1938). Ville's note was translated into English and commented in Ben-El-Mechaiekh and Dimand (2010).

a relatively elementary proof of von Neumann's minmax theorem by methods of convex analysis. Nevertheless, Borel added again a note[20] in which he reiterated in detail his "pessimism" (the word was used by Guilbaud[21]) about the practical interest of the result:

> One only needs to think for a moment to realize that, even for a relatively simple game like the *écarté*, even if we believe we can take into account certain remarks made by the best players which would allow some actions to be ruled out because they would with certainty be too unreasonable, there are still such a large number of variables left that the task alone of writing the equations, let alone solving them, appears to be absolutely intractable.[22]

It seems to me important to mention that one must not see in Borel's commentary a negative judgment on the mathematical result as such (which he himself qualifies as an "important theorem").[23]

Between the two mathematicians, it was in fact a bit of a dialogue of the deaf. Dell'Aglio (1995) formulates as follows the fundamental difference between Borel's and von Neumann's points of view:

> It is again important to note the essential diversity between Borel and von Neumann's approaches to the idea of game. Unlike the Hungarian mathematician, Borel had no intention to define a game *ex novo* by means of a definite set of axioms but only to modify an already known notion. The most evident reason for this statement is given by the fact that, in Borel's work, there could be no game theory without the consideration of the essentially probabilistic concept of mixed strategy; this concept was in fact introduced by the French mathematician in 1921 and was to play a central role in all his subsequent works. In other words, according to Borel, the extension of the concept of game intrinsically corresponded to the randomization of the concept of strategy, reflecting the consideration of the intervention of the players' "habileté." ... This was essentially the opposite of von Neumann's work.[24]

Contrary to Borel, in von Neumann's conception of the game, the idea of an interaction between the two players is totally absent. The axiomatic presentation of the game is seen as an objective presentation of a reality in which psychology is excluded altogether, and this purely mathematical approach indeed simplified the question and allowed von Neumann to formulate and obtain a general theorem that considered Borel's skepticism as irrelevant to an applied mathematical research. If a result turned out to be impossible to use, it lost most of its credibility in Borel's eyes. Besides, Borel was also always reluctant to resort to sophisticated proofs in applied mathematics. This attitude of Borel (quite usual with him) sometimes evoked incomprehension from various colleagues. One of the most famous cases is that of the French

20 Borel (1938), p. 115ff.
21 Guilbaud (1952), p. 108, note 1.
22 Borel (1938), p. 115.
23 Borel (1938), p. 115.
24 Dell'Aglio (1995), p. 10.

probabilist Paul Lévy. After obtaining his fundamental proof of the central limit theorem through the use of characteristic functions,[25] Lévy was scandalized by a criticism of Borel asking whether the use of such sophisticated mathematics was justified to obtain a result that an elementary reasoning made it possible to obtain.[26]

All this said, Borel's notes would have in fact probably disappeared in the mists of prehistory if in 1953 Maurice Fréchet had not suddenly decided to publish an English translation of various works by Borel (1921, 1923, 1927) in an article (Fréchet, 1953) in the journal *Econometrica*.[27] This article had the slightly provocative title "Émile Borel, initiator of the theory of psychological games[28] and its application," accompanied by a virulent commentary in which, though not denying the difficultly contestable priority of von Neumann in the proof of the minmax theorem, Fréchet nevertheless seemed to consider that Borel's obtention of the result for $n = 3$, 5, or 7 (an assertion in itself not absolutely justifiable, as we have seen) had been the decisive step to "initiate" a theory that von Neumann and Morgenstern had in fact only extended ("far beyond the pioneering notes of Émile Borel," admitted Fréchet).[29] However, Fréchet concluded his paper with a slightly depreciative commentary on von Neumann and Morgestern's (1944) book:

> Important as the contribution of von Neumann and Morgenstern is, we must however consider it as falling within the progressive mathematical evolution of the theory. Their work is neither a beginning nor an end. We must not, indeed, adopt the disdainful attitude of these two authors for the work of the great initiators of mathematical economics – an attitude in which an exception is made in favor of the Austrian school, but an exception of which one senses a sentimental origin. The objections made to the work of their predecessors are of the same nature as

[25] In Lévy (1922).

[26] Borel wrote a sentence of this kind in Borel and Deltheil (1923). In the preface of Lévy (1925), Lévy left for once the traditional polished language of academic works to explicitly express how he was shocked by Borel's attitude. On the complicated relation between Borel and Lévy, see for instance Cléry (2020), p. 97ff.

[27] The question of priority between Borel and von Neumann in the creation of game theory has been studied in depth in several works – see for instance Dell'Aglio (1995), Kjeldsen (2001), or Leonard (2010). Kjeldsen (2001) contains in particular a refined analysis of von Neumann's proof of the minmax theorem and an interpretation of von Neuman's conception of its role. On the contrary, Guilbaud's rôle in this story seems to have been minimized by Kjeldsen or Leonard, but it did not escape Dell'Aglio (1995) or more recently Tazdaït (1923), who presents a detailed account of Guilbaud's aims in promoting the importance of game theory for economics in the 1950s in France.

[28] Thanks to F. Forges, I learned that there exists nowadays a concept of *psychological games* with a precise technical meaning. In Dufwenberg's entry for the *New Palgrave Dictionary of Economics*, by Durlauf and Blume (2008), the author presents this concept, originally developed in Geanakoplos et al. (1989) as a game in which utilities are defined on beliefs (about actions and beliefs), as well as on which actions are chosen. Dufwenberg comments that the term "game with belief-dependent motivation" would probably be more descriptive.

[29] Fréchet (1953), p. 121.

> those that can be presented against any theory. No theory takes everything into account; there will always be a more complete one; but the early one will retain its value as a less refined approximation. That, indeed, is what will happen to the work of von Neumann and Morgenstern itself; it will one day be obsolete, but it will certainly remain in the history of economic science (associated with the pioneering notes of Borel) as having contributed with clear results and opened new horizons.[30]

Fréchet's article cut von Neumann to the quick. He asked for a right of reply in the form of a communication (von Neumann, 1953) following Fréchet's paper, in which he disputed point by point Fréchet's assertions, claiming the total and autonomous authorship of the minmax theorem, obtained besides, according to him, in complete independence from Borel. Von Neumann was all the more confident to assert that Borel had himself questioned the validity of the result in his notes on the year 1920. Above all, von Neumann insisted on making the general minmax theorem the true foundation of game theory, so that this foundation could absolutely not be attributed to Borel. Fréchet was not ready to accept von Neumann's assertions (he probably had prepared himself for von Neumann's violent reaction). He added after von Neumann's note a somewhat caustic postnote in which he mentioned that "relying above all on examination of Borel's notes, the reader will judge."[31]

When he learned of Fréchet's intentions, Borel himself became alarmed. In a letter dated May 7, 1952,[32] he wrote to Fréchet that although he had studied the same question as von Neumann, he had not demonstrated, *nor even suspected*, the minimax theorem and asked him to be cautious. Borel added that, to his knowledge, it was René de Possel who had first made the minimax theorem known in France. It remains to be understood why Fréchet had nevertheless decided to launch a frontal attack on von Neumann's book. The source seems to have been the writing by the statistician and economist Georges-Théodule Guilbaud (1912–2008) of what was probably the first review in France of von Neumann and Morgenstern (1944). I cannot give much detail here about this original and important actor of the development of the theory of economics in France.[33] Let me only mention that after having discovered statistics under the teaching of Georges Darmois (1888–1960) at the Ecole Normale Supérieure in 1932, he became a teacher of mathematics in secondary schools. Member of a Christian movement of resistance during the Occupation of France in Dijon, he also gave lectures in philosophy of science at the local university. After the war, he was appointed as a researcher at the newly created Institut de science économique appliquée (ISEA) in Paris.

[30] Fréchet (1953), pp. 123–124.
[31] Fréchet (1953), p. 126.
[32] Archives Académie des Sciences de Paris. Fonds Fréchet AS67J86.
[33] For more about him, consult the special issue of the journal *Mathématiques et sciences humaines*, 183 (Fall 2008).

In fact, Guilbaud's 1949 contribution, in the words of the author, is not precisely a review. Guilbaud mentions that he has not the strength to face the immensity of the scope covered by the book:

> This work will have only one thing in common with an honest review: to encourage the direct reading of the work. But I will not restrict myself to a complete review of the subjects covered in this book; and, on the contrary, I will not limit myself either to the points of view of our two authors, thinking I am doing well by situating some elements of their work in a larger context, and showing a kind of continuity (dialectic, if one wants to speak thus, but not illusory) between the new homo oeconomicus and the old one.[34]

It was Guilbaud who seems to have first mentioned Borel's role in the mathematical approach to games mixing chance with the skill of players. He even reports the way in which Borel expressed, in the preface to Borel's 1938 work, the importance he envisaged for game theory as a source of economic thinking:

> The problems encountered in game theory in which the skill of the player comes into consideration present many analogies to those which arise in the study of economic phenomena. To be able to deal with economic questions satisfactorily, a place must be made for probability and psychology: the study of games of chance and psychology will therefore constitute a useful basis for this study.[35]

Fréchet himself mentions[36] that it was Guilbaud who introduced him to Borel's notes, whereas the literature on games did not generally exhibit works prior to von Neumann (1928b). It is undoubtedly this absence of Borel in what was becoming the official historiography of game theory that pushed Fréchet to take up the pen, in a rather aggressive tone. It seems to me, moreover, that Fréchet's caustic remark on the *sentimental weakness* that had urged von Neumann and Morgenstern to put a particular emphasis on the Austrian school is not without resonating with the way in which, in the mid 1930s, considering the exaggerated role taken by the logical empiricism of the Circle of Vienna in the philosophy of science, Fréchet partly united with the criticism formulated by Ferdinand Gonseth's idoneism.[37]

What conclusions can be drawn from this story that I have just outlined? First of all, we can undoubtedly recognize that Borel clearly perceived the importance of taking into account a complexification of the gambling model based only on randomness, which was generally the only one considered in the context of probabilistic studies. If, on the other hand, it seems somewhat exaggerated to attribute to Borel the idea of the minmax that von Neumann managed to identify, it is also true that he nevertheless considered mixed

34 Guilbaud (1949), p. 276.

35 Guilbaud (1949), p. 285, note 3.

36 Fréchet (1953), p. 95.

37 On this, and in particular on the use of Gonseth's idoneism by Destouches and Mariani for a new interpretation of quantum mechanics, I mention for information Eckes and Mazliak (2023).

strategies and raised the question of a fair game and that it cannot be excluded that reading Borel's notes motivated von Neumann in his formal research. Borel and von Neumann's attitudes reveal how complementary their approaches to the role and practice of applied mathematics were different. Besides, the controversy launched by Fréchet was less of a sterile priority conflict or a mere manifestation of French nationalism or hostility toward American domination at the time when the Marshall Plan was in its full development. In his very recent work Tazdaït (1923), after describing in detail the controversy, explains that it has been more consequential than what may be thought at first glance. In the first place, (Tazdaït, 1923, p. 52) observes that after the publication of Fréchet (1953), Borel's notes on game theory were more or less systematically mentioned in the English-language literature on the topic. But more important, in a mathematical context dominated by the Bourbaki group, whose lack of attraction toward probability (to put it mildly) is well-known, the emphasis put on the works of a French mathematician of the recent past was a powerful tool in the hands of Guilbaud and the economist Henri Guitton (1904–1992) to convince French politicians of the necessity for a deep transformation of the syllabus of economics in France in the 1950s.[38]

2.1 REFERENCES

H. Ben-El-Mechaiekh and R. W. Dimand. Von Neumann, Ville, and the minimax theorem. *International Game Theory Review*, 12(2):115–137, 2010.

J. Bertrand. *Calcul des probabilités*. Paris: Gauthier-Villars, 1889.

E. Borel. Sur les principes de la théorie cinétique des gaz. *Ann. Sci. Éc. Norm. Supér.*, 3(23):9–32, 1906.

E. Borel. La logique et l'intuition en mathématiques. *Rev. de métaphys. et de morale*, 15:273–283, 1907.

E. Borel. *Le Hasard*. Paris: Librairie Félix Alcan. Nouvelle collection scientifique, 1914a.

E. Borel. *Introduction géométrique à quelques théories physiques*. Paris: Gauthier-Villars, 1914b.

E. Borel. La théorie du jeu et les équations intégrales à noyau symétrique. *Comptes Rendus Hebdomadaires des Séances de l'Académie des Sciences, Paris*, 173:1304–1308, 1921.

E. Borel. Sur les jeux où interviennent le hasard et l'habileté des joueurs. *Association francaise pour l'avancement des Sciences*, 47:79, 1923.

E. Borel. Sur les jeux où le hasard se combine avec l'habilité des joueurs. *Comptes Rendus Hebdomadaires des Séances de l'Académie des Sciences, Paris*, 178:24–25, 1924a.

E. Borel. Elements de la théorie des probabilités, 3ième édition. Paris: J. Hermann, VII u. 266 S., 1924b.

E. Borel. Un théorème sur les systèmes de formes linéaires à déterminant symétrique gauche. *Comptes Rendus Hebdomadaires des Séances de l'Académie des Sciences, Paris*, 183:925–927, 1926.

[38] On this point, see Tazdaït (1923), chapter 3.

E. Borel. Sur les systèmes de formes linéaires a déterminant symétrique gauche et la théorie générale du jeu. *Comptes Rendus Hebdomadaires des Séances de l'Académie des Sciences, Paris*, 184:52–54, 1927.

E. Borel. Quelques remarques sur l'application du calcul des probabilités aux jeux de hasard. *Comptes Rendus du Congrès International des Mathématiciens Oslo, 1936*, 2:187–190, 1937a.

E. Borel. Eloge du jeu. *Mercure de France*, 275:290–301, 1937b.

E. Borel. *Traité du calcul des probabilités et de ses applications. Tome IV: Applications diverses et conclusion. Fasc. 2: Applications aux jeux de hasard. Cours professé à la faculté des sciences de Paris, Rédigé par* J. Ville. *XI + 122p*. Paris: Gauthier-Villars, 1938.

E. Borel and R. Deltheil. *Probabilités erreurs*. Paris: A. Colin (Collectio Armand Colin, section de mathématiques, Nr. 34.), VI u. 197 S. 8°, 1923.

M.-F. Bru and B. Bru. *Les jeux de l'infini et du hasard. Vol. 1. Les probabilités dénombrables à la portée de tous. Vol. 2. Les probabilités indénombrables à la portée de tous. Annexes et appendices*. Besançon: Presses Universitaires de Franche-Comté, 2018.

M.-C. Bustamante, M. Cléry, and L. Mazliak. Le *Traité du calcul des probabilités et de ses applications*: Étendue et limites d'un projet borélien de grande envergure (1921–1939). *North-West. Eur. J. Math.*, 1:111–167, 2015.

M. C. Bustamante De la Ossa. *À l'aube de la théorie des quanta. Notes inédites d'Émile Borel sur un cours de Paul Langevin au Collège de France (1912–1913)*, vol. 105. Turnhout: Brepols, 2019.

R. Catellier and L. Mazliak. L'émergence de la statistique probabiliste française. Borel et l'Institut Henri Poincaré dans les années 1920. *Rev. Hist. Math.*, 18(2):271–335, 2012.

J. Cavaillès. Du collectif au pari. *Revue de Métaphysique et de Morale*, 47:139–163, 1940.

M. Cléry. *La théorie des probabilités et l'Institut Henri Poincaré (1918–1939): Construction d'un champ probabiliste parisien et pratique d'un transfert culturel*. Paris: These, 2020.

J. Crovisier. Les loisirs de l'ingénieur des mines Badoureau à Amiens. *Verniana*, 10:191–206, 2017.

L. Dell'Aglio. Divergences in the history of mathematics: Borel, von Neumann and the genesis of game theory. *Rivista di Storia della Scienza*, 2:1–45, 1995.

A. Durand and L. Mazliak. Revisiting the sources of Borel's interest in probability: Continued fractions, social involvement, Volterra's Prolusione. *Centaurus*, 53(4):306–332, 2011.

S. Durlauf and L. Blume. *The new Palgrave dictionary of economics*, 2nd ed. New York: Palgrave Macmillan, 2008.

C. Eckes and L. Mazliak. Les Entretiens de Morgat: Nouvelles perspectives historiques sur une contre-offensive francophone en réponse aux positivismes logiques (1935–1948). *Philosophia Scientiae*, 27:129–162.

J. Ellul. Max Weber, l'éthique protestante et l'esprit du capitalisme. *Bulletin SEDEIS*, 905:4–17, 1964.

S. N. Ethier. Bertrand's analysis of baccarat. In L. A. Petrosyan, V. Mazalov, and N. A. Zenkevich, eds., *Frontiers of Dynamic Games*. Cham, Switzerland: Birkhäuser, 2024.

M. Fréchet. Commentary on the three notes of Émile Borel. *Econometrica*, 21:118–124, 1953.

M. C. Galavotti. *Philosophical introduction to probability*, vol. 167. Stanford, CA: Center for the Study of Language and Information (CSLI Publications), 2005.

J. Geanakoplos, D. Pearce, and E. Stacchetti. Psychological games and sequential rationality. *Games Econ. Behav.*, 1(1):60–79, 1989.

G.-T. Guilbaud. La théorie des jeux: Contributions critiques à la théorie de la valeur. *Economie Appliquée*, 2:275–319, 1949.

G. T. Guilbaud. Les problèmes de partage. *Economie Appliquée*, 5:93–137, 1952.

T. Hawkins. *Lebesgue's theory of integration: Its origins and development*. Providence, RI: American Mathematical Society (AMS) Chelsea, 2001.

M. W. Kirby. *Operational Research in War and Peace*. London: Imperial College Press, 2003.

T. H. Kjeldsen. John von Neumann's conception of the minimax theorem: A journey through different mathematical contexts. *Arch. Hist. Exact Sci.*, 56(1):39–68, 2001.

R. Leonard. *Von Neumann, Morgenstern, and the Creation of Game Theory: From Chess to Social Science, 1900–1960*. Cambridge: Cambridge University Press, 2010.

P. Lévy. Sur la détermination des lois de probailité par leurs fonctions caractéristiques. *C. R. Acad. Sci., Paris*, 175:854–856, 1922.

P. Lévy. *Calcul des probabilités. VIII + 352 S.* Paris: Gauthier-Villars, 1925.

T. Martin. La valeur objective du calcul des probabilités selon Cournot. *Mathématiques et Sciences humaines*, 127:5–17, 1994.

L. Mazliak and M. Sage. Altered states, Borel and the probabilistic approach to reality. In P. Cantù and G. Schiemer, eds., *Logic, Epistemology, and Scientific Theories: From Peano to the Vienna Circle*. Cham, Switzerland: Springer, 2022.

P. Rigoulot. Protestants and the French nation under the Third Republic: Between recognition and assimilation. *National Identities*, 11:45–57, 2009.

G. Shafer. The education of Jean André Ville. *Electronic Journal for History of Probability and Statistics*, 5(1):50, 2009. Id/No 6.

H. Sinaceur. Cavaillès et le calcul des probabilités. *Cahiers Philosophiques*, 155:47–64, 2018.

T. Tazdaït. *La science est un jeu. Théorie des jeux dans la France des années 1950*. Paris: Classiques Garnier, 1923.

J. Ville. Sur la théorie générale des jeux où intervient l'habileté des joueurs. In Borel (1938), 105–113, 1938.

J. Ville. *Étude critique de la notion de collectif*. Monographies des probabilités. Publiées par Émile Borel. Fasc. 3. Paris: Gauthier-Villars, 1939.

J. von Neumann. Sur la théorie des jeux. *C. R. Acad. Sci., Paris*, 186:1689–1691, 1928a.

J. von Neumann. Zur Theorie der Gesellschaftsspiele. *Mathematische Annalen*, 100:295–320, 1928b.

J. von Neumann. Communication on the Borel notes. *Econometrica*, 21:124–127, 1953.

J. von Neumann and O. Morgenstern. *Theory of games and economic behavior*. Princeton, NJ: Princeton University Press, 1944.

M. Weber. *Die protestantische Ethik und der "Geist" des Kapitalismus*. Berlin: Archiv für Sozialwissenschaft und Sozialpolitik (1905), 1905.

3

Von Neumann, Morgenstern and Their Creation of Game Theory, 1900–1960

Robert Leonard

3.1 INTRODUCTION

At the end of the 1930s, the Hungarian mathematician, John von Neumann (1903–1957) and Viennese economist Oskar Morgenstern (1902–1977) found themselves together at Princeton and thrown into a collaboration that neither would have predicted several years earlier. The result was their *Theory of Games and Economic Behavior* (1944), which proved to be one of the century's seminal books in social science, affecting various fields of economics, political science, philosophy and evolutionary biology, and providing a new field of mathematics proper.

Their collaboration was improbable in two senses. First, it occurred only because the events of history had seen Oskar Morgenstern 'cast up', as it were, at Princeton in 1938, forced to change country and begin a new career in the US. Second, being himself neither a mathematician nor a mathematical economist, Morgenstern's intellectual and scientific profile was not that of a likely co-author of a new, highly technical theory of strategic interaction. He himself was well aware of this, and privately he would later express surprise that this life-changing undertaking with von Neumann ever happened. Von Neumann, on the other hand, was quite different: having arrived at Princeton from Germany in 1931, he was widely recognized as one of the period's outstanding mathematicians, known for his seminal contributions to the theory of sets, the foundations of mathematics and the foundations of quantum mechanics, to name just a few areas. He was the technical contributor in the partnership. And yet, without the presence and stimulus provided by Morgenstern, the 'theory of games' would not have come to fruition.

In the following, drawing mainly on Leonard (2010), I tell in highly condensed form the story of how von Neumann and Morgenstern were brought together to write the *Theory of Games*. I consider von Neumann's early involvement in games before his emigration, Morgenstern's curious career in inter-war Vienna and their unlikely collaboration as exiles at Princeton during World War II. I conclude with the effect of war and Cold War on the reception of their research.

3.2 *HOMO LUDENS*: VON NEUMANN'S WORK ON GAMES BEFORE 1931

Before becoming a mathematician, the Hungarian-Jewish von Neumann showed early signs of exceptional brilliance: a photographic memory that allowed him to recite by heart entire sections of novels and other reading, some strange grasp of mental calculation that allowed him to multiply five- and six-digit numbers in his head and an encyclopedic memory that allowed him to gain a vastly detailed knowledge of military history. Years later, he would astonish Americans such as Abraham Flexner with his great knowledge of the American Civil War, and when he left for England as a naval consultant in 1943, it was with a volume of Gibbon's *The Decline and Fall of the Roman Empire* under his arm.

Educated largely by private tutors at home, von Neumann enrolled in mathematics at the University of Budapest in 1921, thereafter returning only to take exams. He spent two years studying physics at the University of Berlin and working on a range of topics, including set theory and foundations and the mathematical foundations of quantum mechanics. At the Swiss Federal Institute of Technology in Zurich, he took a degree in chemical engineering – largely under pressure from his banker father to become something more sensible than a mathematician – before reverting to type and becoming a postdoctoral student under Hilbert at Göttingen in 1926–1927.

It was in the intense atmosphere of Hilbert's Göttingen that von Neumann was led to the consideration of games. The influences were several. At the most general level, Göttingen was pervaded by a belief in the pre-established harmony between mathematics and the world, which the mathematician could potentially uncover. Mathematics was fruitfully applied there to a range of fields, including quantum mechanics, relativity and the kinetic theory of gases and, at a further remove, areas such as insurance and psycho-physics (colour perception). Much of this work involved the axiomatic approach, with the field under examination in question being characterized by plausible sets of axioms, checked for completeness and consistency, and used as the basis for theoretical elaboration. There was also the distinctly modern, Hilbertian perception that the mathematical formalism itself was a potentially rich source of truths about the world: let the mathematics speak, one might say, and things will be revealed to you. This attitude is key to understanding von Neumann's attitude to games, especially in his work at Princeton a decade later.

At a more particular level, there was the interest among continental mathematicians at the time in games, and particularly in the game of chess, which had enjoyed great cultural prominence since the late nineteenth century. Chess was of interest to novelists such as Nabokov, whose first book, *The Luzhin Defence*, was about a chessplayer who marries beyond his station and, retreating into his mind, begins to see the social world in terms of a chess-game, eventually losing his sanity. A 1925 Russian silent film, *Shakhmatnaya Goryachka*, or *Chess Fever*, was about a player who attempts to play both black and white, thereby threatening his own mental stability. The game was also of interest to psychologists, with an early contribution, based on surveys of chess players from French psychologist Alfred Binet (1894) and a more substantial contribution in 1927 from Russian psychologists Djakow and colleagues (1927), based on experiments conducted with chess-masters participating in the Moscow tournament two years previously.

A key figure who straddled the worlds of German mathematics and chess was Emanuel Lasker (1868–1941). Taught by Max Noether and Hilbert, he worked on the theory of abstract vector spaces before turning to chess in order to support himself financially. Dislodging Wilhelm Steinitz, he became world chess champion in 1894 and held the title for a remarkable twenty-seven years. Lasker wrote extensively not only about chess strategy but about the application of strategic ideas to areas such as military encounters and economic life. His 1907 book, *Kampf*, or *Struggle*, developed in discursive terms notions of strategy, dominance and equilibrium, and came close to the idea of a mixed strategy. The great Lasker was known to everyone interested in chess in early twentieth-century Europe, and I believe that von Neumann read him.

Drawing closer still to the mathematicians, chess was the subject of a series of papers by a series of mathematicians, with all of whom von Neumann was familiar. The first of these was by Ernst Zermelo, a former student of Hilbert, who had worked at Göttingen from 1897 till 1910, when he moved to Zurich. In his highly abstract, set-theoretic paper of 1913, Zermelo showed, first, that a player is in a winning position if and only if the set of all sequences of moves that guarantee a player can win is non-empty and, second, that it is possible to determine the number of moves necessary to ensure a win. Two refinements of Zermelo's paper were made after the Great War by Hungarian mathematicians well-known to von Neumann. Thanking the latter for his help, Dénes König (1927) proved that the number of moves with which a player in a winning position could force a victory was finite, and Lászlo Kalmár (1928–1929) showed that if it was possible for a player to force a win, then this could be done without the recurrence of any position.

The final element of the background for von Neumann's own contribution was the series of papers on the mathematics of games during the 1920s by Émile Borel in France. As Laurent Mazliak shows in this chapter, these were concerned with the generic two-person, zero-sum game, and asked whether it was always possible for a player to hold the expected gain of his opponent to zero by means of a suitably chosen mixed strategy. While Borel showed that this was possible for the sequence of games he examined, he surmised that it did not hold as a general rule for all such games. Although von Neumann would not cite Borel in his own 1928 paper, he was forced to address the matter many years later in a priority debate raised by Maurice Fréchet (1953) in the columns of *Econometrica*. There, von Neumann's discussion suggests that he was, indeed, familiar with Borel's work from the 1920s.

In his own paper, first presented in 1926 and published in 1928, von Neumann provides a long and very difficult proof of the existence of a minimax equilibrium in the generic two-person, zero-sum game. Chess, baccarat and poker were cited as examples of such games. Interestingly, given the background, von Neumann says that the existence of an equilibrium shows that 'psychological' questions no longer matter: 'It makes no difference which of the two players is the better psychologist, the game is so insensitive that the result is always the same' (1928, p. 23). He also notes the similarity between the game player, seeking to maximize a gain, and the absolutely selfish 'homo oeconomicus' of classical economics. Finally, he draws the paper to a close with a discussion of the three-player, zero-sum game, where coalitions of two players against one become possible. The question of which coalitions would actually form, he says, marks the reintroduction into the game of something that was completely eliminated from the balanced, two-person game, namely (Laskerian) 'struggle'. Von Neumann surmises that the analysis could be extended to games of four or more players, leading eventually to a satisfactory general theory.

With that, however, von Neumann essentially dropped game theory. Believing his chances of secure employment in German academia to be slim because of his Jewish background, he soon accepted a part-time appointment at Princeton Mathematics, 'rescued', as it were, by the geometer and topologist Oswald Veblen (1880–1960), the man who would become his American 'godfather'. In 1933, von Neumann and Veblen were, in turn, 'poached' by Abraham Flexner for the nearby and newly created Institute for Advanced Study, along with another recent exile, the physicist Albert Einstein. In the course of the 1930s, even if he continued to flee the humid summers of the eastern US, von Neumann became thoroughly settled at Princeton, embracing American life fully: large house, large cars (driven badly) and a full social life.

3.3 AUSTRIAN MAVERICK: OSKAR MORGENSTERN IN INTER-WAR VIENNA

Oskar Morgenstern was an economist trained in the non-mathematical, Austrian tradition. After a Rockefeller Foundation traveling scholarship for the period 1925–1928, which took him to London, Rome, Harvard and Columbia, he returned to Vienna, where he completed his *Habilitation* thesis on the impossibility of economic forecasting. Thoroughly 'Austrian' in outlook, it emphasized the complexity of economic events and the fact of unceasing change in real commercial life (Morgenstern, 1928).

Had Morgenstern remained an 'Austrian economist', like most of his mentors and peers, he would have been easier to categorize and describe. He did not, however, and this makes him elusive and difficult to capture. His key formative influences were two: Ludwig von Mises (1881–1973) and Hans Mayer (1879–1955). As is well-known, von Mises was a committed liberal, implacably opposed to all efforts at socialization or economic planning, the futility of which he believed to be demonstrated by economic theory. His article of 1920 on the impossibility of nationalization of the means of production is one of his best-known contributions. Mises was sceptical too of the value of mathematical economics, believing that the most significant economic insights were obtained through simple introspection, not through mathematical exploration. He also believed that mathematical economics offered an unduly 'mechanical' representation of a field that was, in its essence, not at all mechanical (see von Mises, 1933). Along with Hayek, Haberler, Machlup and other contemporaries, Morgenstern was a member of Mises' famous private seminar, a lively gathering place that had a huge formative influence on many Austrians of that generation.[1] For a while, Morgenstern went along with Mises' incessant blending of economics and politics, but by the mid-1930s, was distancing himself from this, becoming increasingly convinced of the need to separate the two.

If Hans Mayer is altogether less well-known than Mises, it is because of his collaboration with the Nazis on the eve of the annexation of Austria by the Third Reich in 1938. In particular, Mayer signed a letter inviting all Jewish members to leave the National Economic Association. Because of this, and because he stayed in Vienna during and after the war, Mayer was viewed for many decades as *persona non grata* among the influential Austrian exiles. Indeed, it was not until the early 1990s that some of his important essays were translated into English. All that being said, he was a lasting influence on Morgenstern, in particular through his Austrian critique of neoclassical equilibrium theory. In a long paper of 1932, Mayer set out his main criticism of the work of Cournot, Jevons, Edgeworth, Walras and Pareto. Any properly 'causal-genetic' theory of economic activity, said Mayer, would have to take account of the fact that preferences were in constant evolution. No sooner was a particular want satisfied than a new one emerged, so that the utility function could never be regarded as stable. All mechanical representations of equilibrium based on given utility functions were thus inadequate. They failed to account for the central Austrian emphases of causality and the passage of time.[2]

Morgenstern's first engagement with mathematical economics was thus a critical one. Although primarily a research director in Vienna, he was particularly interested in the philosophical foundations of neoclassical equilibrium theory and took the time to write about it. Thus, in a well-known paper of 1935, 'Perfect Foresight and Economic Equilibrium', he criticized the lack of specificity concerning the knowledge and foresight of the neoclassical agent. Sometimes nothing was said about the agent's capacities; other times it was blithely assumed that he had 'perfect foresight', which implied that agents could all 'outpredict' each other, leaving no possibility of equilibrium.

1 Parenthetically, it should also be noted that this seminar allowed Morgenstern to occasionally express a private disdain for his Jewish colleagues, an attitude that was not then uncommon in Austria. While this did not affect him profesionally, it is indicative of the 'distance' he would travel in order to become a close friend of von Neumann.

2 It is worth noting that, in order to illustrate the unknowable complexity of economic life, Mayer turned to the chess metaphor: just as the result of the game could not be known before it was played, so too was economic interaction a discovery process, unknowable in advance and inadequately captured by equilibrium analysis. It was a use of the chess metaphor quite removed from that of the Hungarian mathematicians.

Guided by such questions, and perhaps uniquely among the Viennese economists, Morgenstern began to actively seek the company of mathematicians and gradually develop an admiration for their way of thinking. In particular, he formed influential relationships with both Karl Menger (1902–1985), the mathematician son of the founding Austrian economist, who ran an important seminar in Vienna, and his gifted student, Abraham Wald (1902–1950), who worked in general equilibrium theory. Morgenstern began to regret his inadequate training in mathematics and, in the mid-1930s, took tutorials from Wald.

Karl Menger was a crucial influence on the evolving Morgenstern. In the charged political context of inter-war Vienna, Menger was critical of Mises' lack of rigour and of the ease with which he drew political conclusions from his economics. Menger's attitude reinforced Morgenstern's belief that it was necessary to 'purify' economics, through the application of truly rigorous methods. Another conduit for Menger's influence was provided by his 1934 book, *Morality, Decision and Social Organization*, which was his response to the political violence and civil war that marked Vienna in the first months of that year. Considering hypothetical agents who adhered to various ethical norms, Menger examined the possible formation of socially compatible groups: a social geometry, as he called it. Morgenstern saw in this the glimmer of a response to his 'perfect foresight' problem, and it was one of the things he was thinking about when he arrived at Princeton in 1938.

Unlike many Viennese intellectuals, Morgenstern left the country quite late. Hayek was gone by 1931, Mises by 1934, and most of the Jewish economists left very quickly thereafter. Abraham Wald got out late, and then only by the skin of his teeth. Not being Jewish, Morgenstern was not under the same pressures, but he chose to leave nonetheless. Indeed, already in the mid-1930s, he was sending out feelers to Abraham Flexner at the Institute for Advanced Study, to see whether he could be accommodated there.

3.4 'A MYSTERIOUS MAN': COLLABORATION AT PRINCETON

Von Neumann appears to have been brought back to game theory, not by Morgenstern primarily but by his observation of political events in Europe in the late 1930s. A close observer of politics, by the mid-1930s he was already predicting a full-scale war. In his correspondence with Hungarian colleagues such as physicist Rudolf Ortvay, he reveals himself to be concerned with the rationality of the behaviour of Mussolini and Hitler, in contrast with Ortvay's emphasis on Freudian, non-rational factors. His observation of European politics was further intensified by a twist in his personal life. In 1937, his wife, Mariette, left him for a graduate student in physics at Princeton, and von Neumann, in order to arrange a new marriage with Klára 'Klari' Dán, found himself spending several months in Hungary in 1938. His correspondence at this time shows him to have been particularly affected by changes in the social order in Hungary, where resurgent anti-Semitism found expression in new discriminatory laws. Watching this from Budapest, or Lake Balaton, or from short visits elsewhere in Europe, von Neumann was struck by this 'internal Nazification' of the country, and it appears to have been this intensive discussion of rationality and pathology, or politics and social relations, that brought him back to the renewed exploration of coalitional games and their possible equilibria.[3]

Morgenstern, at a Princeton he found somewhat provincial, was keen for European company, which he sought out at the Institute. Drawing on the ability he had developed in Vienna to engage with mathematicians, he presented von Neumann with his ideas about perfect foresight and interaction and found a sympathetic ear. Like other 'interlocutors', such as mathematics student Israel Halperin, Morgenstern sat willingly with von Neumann while he ploughed through the detailed and, be it said, rather tedious analysis of stable coalition formation in games of increasing numbers of players. The two men reinforced each other in their critique of standard neoclassical theory, which von Neumann had long regarded as primitive – the mere counting of equations and unknowns. Already in 1934, he had written to Flexner: 'I have the impression that [economics] is not yet ripe ... not yet fully enough understood ... to be reduced to a small number of fundamental postulates – like geometry or mechanics' (John von Neumann to Abraham Flexner, 25 May 1934).

In an unpublished 1941 paper on 'Maxims of Behavior', Morgenstern continued to try to develop, in discursive, non-formal fashion, Mengerian ideas about interacting agents. By 1942, he found himself writing an introductory chapter to The *Theory of Games and Economic Behavior*, which was at once a harsh critique of mathematical economics as it stood and a manifesto for a new mathematics demanded by the analysis of social interaction. Throughout this time, as he drew closer to von Neumann and observed other mathematicians, such as Hermann Weyl, Morgenstern gave vent privately to criticism of his own field: 'Economists simply don't know what science means. I am quite disgusted with all of this rubbish. – I am more and more of the opinion that Keynes is a scientific charlatan, and his followers not even that' (Oskar Morgenstern, diary, April–May 1942). He regretted having studied philosophy rather than mathematics, and in time would describe Hayek as a 'propaganda economist'.

In the finally published *Theory of Games and Economic Behavior*, von Neumann portrays game theory as an example of modern, Hilbertian mathematics. Invoking Hilbert's (1899) *Grundlagen der Geometrie*, chapter 2 describes the game in axiomatic form, discussing the completeness, freedom from contradiction and independence of those axioms. That a game can be thus 'axiomatised' shows that it 'is possible to describe and discuss mathematically human actions in which the main emphasis lies on the psychological side' (von Neumann and Morgenstern, 1944, pp. 76–77). In chapter 3 the minimax theorem is proved using not von Neumann's Göttingen proof but a variant of Jean Ville's elementary proof of 1938, using the theory of convex sets. The

[3] On the late 1930s and the influence of politics on von Neumann's return to game theory, see Leonard (2010), chapter 9.

succeeding chapters of the book go through the zero-sum game with three, four and more players, examining the various possibilities for stable coalition formation with compensations (side payments). Each game is described in terms of its characteristic function, which indicates the maximal payoff available to each possible coalition. In chapter 9, von Neumann moves to the 'general game', where the zero- or constant-sum restriction has been dropped.

The solution 'concept' offered by von Neumann is that of the 'stable set', which describes the ensemble of alternative achievable coalitions in a particular game. A stable set is characterised by the fact that (a) member coalitional outcomes do not dominate each other and (b) all non-member outcomes are dominated by at least one coalition within. The fact that even simple games admit a number of stable sets, each containing possibly an infinite number of outcomes, does not appear to have perturbed von Neumann, intent as he was on providing a mathematical treatment of social coalition formation. Throughout the book, he provides a sophisticated, and creatively opportunistic, theoretical justification of his mathematical procedure, here invoking criteria of empirical plausibility, there turning to strictly mathematical and/or aesthetical criteria, as the occasion demands.[4] When the book appeared in 1944, von Neumann's approach was utterly unlike anything seen previously in the field of economics beforehand, and even today, although still making for a rebarbative read, it remains an extraordinary intellectual tour de force.

For the next ten years, von Neumann defended the stable set solution as providing insight into social arrangements. For example, in 1953, Harold Kuhn wrote to him, asking about the possibility of subjecting the stable-set solution to experimental testing, such as was beginning to take place at the RAND Corporation. Von Neumann replied:

> I think that nothing smaller than a complete social system will give a reasonable 'empirical' picture. Here, over relatively long periods of time, one can meaningfully assert that the 'system' has not changed, while the positions of various participants within it may have changed many times. This would seem to me to the analogue of a single solution and an 'exploration' of the imputations that belong to it. After relatively long times, there occur discontinuous changes, 'revolutions' which produce a different 'system'. (Von Neumann to H. Kuhn, 14 April 1953)

As for John Nash, it is well-known that von Neumann showed little appreciation for his 'equilibrium point', as the Nash equilibrium was originally known. While Nash (1950) sought a solution that had the same elegance as von Neumann's minimax theorem, and achieved it by applying a fixed-point theorem to a game in which coalition formation was ruled out, von Neumann found this result to be trivial. Given the latter's background, it is easy to understand why he found the formation of social coalitions and alliances to be essential to game theory. This tension between him and the young tyro

[4] For an exploration of von Neumann's presentation and justification of his theory, see Leonard (2010), especially chapter 10.

seems to have persisted for a while. At a 1955 conference at Princeton, Nash challenged von Neumann on the capaciousness of the stable-set concept, which even in simple games permitted an inordinately large number of results. To Nash, von Neumann retorted, 'This result was not surprising in view of the correspondingly enormous variety of observed stable social structures; many differing conventions can endure, existing today for no better reason than that they were here yesterday' (Von Neumann in Wolfe, 1955, p. 25).

3.5 CONFLICT AND ANXIETY: GAME THEORY IN WAR AND COLD WAR

In order to understand the terms on which game theory entered the American research community in the late 1940s to early 1950s, it is important to understand not so much von Neumann's *Mitteleuropean* bid to understand social arrangements as his involvement as a mathematician-advisor in the war itself. Already in the midst of his collaboration with Morgenstern, he was being called away on missions in order to provide mathematical advice on matters such as ballistics and ammunitions testing at places such as the Aberdeen Proving Ground in Pennsylvania. In 1943, progress on their joint manuscript was delayed when von Neumann was called away to England for several months as an advisor to the Navy. He became increasingly solicited and increasingly peripatetic. Some of his work involved game theory. For example, Philip Morse, the director of the Anti-submarine Warfare Operations Research Group, operating off New England, reports that von Neumann was providing game-theoretic advice on military encounters such as the confrontation between a spotter plane and an enemy submarine – where the former is trying the maximize the probability of contact while the latter is trying to minimize it (see Morse, 1948). Soon, von Neumann was active at Los Alamos, where he not only worked on the problem of securing a uniform detonation of the plutonium core in the atomic bomb but was one of the few civilian members of the inside committee that selected the target cities in Japan.

If it would be difficult to overstate von Neumann's role as a military advisor during the war, he was also part of a broader involvement by mathematicians in such work, under the auspices of the Applied Mathematics Panel. For example, at centres such as the Statistical Research Group – Columbia, mathematicians such as Princeton's John Williams (1909–1964) and exile Abraham Wald worked alongside economists, including Milton Friedman, on problems of targeting and ammunitions testing. Others worked overseas with the Office of Strategic Services, as the forerunner of the Central Intelligence Agency (CIA) was called.

It was on foot of such engagements that the RAND Corporation was set up in 1947, with the involvement of the Douglas Aircraft Co. and the US Air Force. Among the first people brought in were operations researchers and game theorists, including John Williams, Merrill Flood (1908–1991), Melvin Dresher (1911–1992) and a young Lloyd Shapley (1923–2016), all there to provide advice on a likely future aerial conflict with the USSR. John Nash, too, was an occasional visitor. The links were strong with Princeton, where both Albert Tucker (1905–1995) and his protégé Harold Kuhn, along with Morgenstern himself, were actively involved in military consulting activities, especially with the Office of Naval Research. In the early years at RAND, as Shapley and Dresher developed models of bomber-fighter encounters, there was great hope that game theory would provide technical, quantitative solutions to concrete military problems. In time, however, as the anticipation of imminent war gave way to Cold War, it was not so much the technical models that prevailed as the use of game theory as a conceptual, qualitative guide to thought – best epitomized, perhaps, in the work of another influential RAND visitor, Tom Schelling (1960), in *The Strategy of Conflict*.

In the late forties and early fifties, von Neumann was a towering influence at RAND. His occasional visits were anxiously awaited, and researchers would queue up outside his office in order to seek advice on particular technical problems. Invariably, as he had done with colleagues such as Kakutani at Princeton during the war, he was able to quickly solve problems that had stumped mere earthlings for much longer. By 1953, however, von Neumann had become a member of the Atomic Energy Commission, which carried him to a higher level than the Air Force, and he ceased to visit RAND. By all accounts, his bellicosity grew and he became an advocate of a first strike with the hydrogen bomb against the Soviet Union, an attitude that cost him his friendship with his American mentor, Veblen. His friend Stan Ulam, who had also been deeply involved at Los Alamos, attributed von Neumann's harsh reasoning to his overly game-theoretic view of the world. When von Neumann contracted bone cancer in the mid-1950s, possibly through his exposure to nuclear testing, he had a long and painful death, surrounded by military personnel at Walter Reed Army Medical Center in Bethesda, Maryland, lest he reveal state secrets in his delirium. Morgenstern's path was less dramatic. He stayed at Princeton till retirement, supervising capable students and remaining actively involved alongside Harold Kuhn in advising the 'military-industrial complex', a world far removed from the Vienna he had left behind.

3.6 REFERENCES

A. Binet. *Psychologie des grands calculateurs et joueurs d'échecs*. Paris: Slatkin, 1894. Republished in 1981 with an introduction by François Le Lionnais.

I. N. Djakow, N. W. Petrowski and P. A. Rudik. *Psychologie des Schachspiels*. Berlin: Walter de Gruyter & Co., 1927.

M. Fréchet. Émile Borel, initiator of the theory of psychological games and its application. *Econometrica*, 21(1):95–96, 1953.

D. Hilbert. *Grundlagen der Geometrie*. Festschrift zur Feier der Enthüllung des Gauss-Weber-denkmals in Göttingen. Leipzig: B. G. Teubner, 1899.

L. Kalmár. Zur Theorie der abstrakten Spiele. *Acta Litterarum ac Scientiarum, Regiae Universitatis Hungaricae Francisco-Josephinae, Sectio: Scientiarum Mathematicarum*, 4:65–85, 1928/29. Translated as 'On the Theory of Abstract Games'.

D. König. Über eine Schlussweise aus dem Endlichen ins Unendliche. *Acta Litterarum ac Scientiarum, Regiae Universitatis Hungaricae Francisco-Josephinae, Sectio: Scientiarum Mathematicarum*, 3:121–30, 1927. Translated as 'On a Method of Conclusion from the Finite to the Infinite'.

E. Lasker. *Kampf*. New York: Lasker's Publishing Co., 1907. Reprinted in 2001 by Berlin-Brandenburg in Potsdam, with foreword by Lothar Schmidt.

R. Leonard. *Von Neumann, Morgenstern, and the Creation of Game Theory: From Chess to Social Science, 1900–1960*. Cambridge: Cambridge University Press, 2010.

H. Mayer. Der Erkenntniswert der funktionellen Preistheorien. In H. Mayer, ed., *Die Wirtschaftstheorie der Gegenwart*, pp. 147–239b. Vienna, 1932. Translated and reprinted as 'The cognitive value of functional theories of price, critical and positive investigations concerning the price problem', in I. Kirzner, ed., *Classics in Austrian Economics: A Sampling in the History of a Tradition*. London: William Pickering, 1994. pp. 55–168.

K. Menger. *Moral, Wille und Weltgestaltung. Grundlegung zur Logik der Sitten*. Vienna: Julius Springer, 1934. Translated (1974) as *Morality, Decision and Social Organization: Towards a Logic of Ethics*.

O. Morgenstern. *Wirtschaftsprognose: Eine Untersuchung ihrer Voraussetzungen und Möglichkeiten*. Vienna: Springer, 1928.

O. Morgenstern. Vollkommene Voraussicht und wirtschaftliches Gleichgewicht. *Zeitschrift für Nationalökonomie*, 6(3):337–57, 1935. Translated by Frank Knight (mimeographed University of Chicago). Reprinted as 'Perfect foresight and economic equilibrium', in Schotter (1976), pp. 169–183.

O. Morgenstern. *Quantitative Implications of Maxims of Behavior*. Unpublished manuscript, Princeton University, 1941.

P. M. Morse. Mathematical problems in operations research. *Bulletin of the American Mathematical Society*, 54(7):602–621, 1948.

J. F. Nash. Equilibrium points in *n*-person games. *Proceedings of the National Academy of Sciences*, 36:48–49, 1950.

T. Schelling. *The Strategy of Conflict*. Cambridge, MA: Harvard University Press, 1960.

L. von Mises. Economic calculation in the socialist commonwealth. In F. A. Hayek, ed., *Collectivist Economic Planning*. New York: Augustus M. Kelley, 1920.

L. von Mises. *Epistemological Problems of Economics*. Princeton: Van Nostrand, 1933.

J. von Neumann. Zur Theorie der Gesellschaftsspiele. *Mathematische Annalen*, 100:295–320, 1928. Translated by S. Bargmann as 'On the Theory of Games and Strategy', in A. W. Tucker and R. D. Luce, eds., *Contributions to the Theory of Games*, vol. 4. Princeton, NJ: Princeton University Press, 1959, pp. 13–42.

J. von Neumann and O. Morgenstern. *Theory of Games and Economic Behavior*. Princeton, NJ: Princeton University Press, 1944.

P. Wolfe. *Report of an Informal Conference on Recent Developments in the Theory of Games*. Princeton, NJ: Princeton University, 1955.

E. Zermelo. Über eine Anwendung der Mengenlehre auf die Theorie des Schachspiels. In *Proceedings of the Fifth International Congress Mathematicians*, pp. 501–504. Cambridge: Cambridge University Press, 1913. Translated as 'On an application of set theory to the theory of the game of chess' in U. Schwalbe and P. Walker, 'Zermelo and the Early History of Game Theory', *Games and Economic Behavior*, 34:123–137.

4

Borel and the Foundation of Game Theory

Roger Myerson

4.1 BOREL'S FUNDAMENTAL INSIGHTS IN THE THEORY OF GAMES

Nineteenth-century economic theorists used mathematical optimization models to develop a deeper understanding of the rational determinants of supply and demand in markets, and game theory follows naturally from such rational choice theory. In 1838, Augustin Cournot studied competitive supply decisions by modeling firms as profit maximizers, and to analyze a market with a small number of profit-maximizing suppliers, he developed models that introduced game-theoretic analysis into the literature of modern economic theory. In the decades after Cournot, other economists developed models of utility-maximizing consumers to explain demand, but the application of these rational-maximizer models was generally limited to the analysis of supply and demand in markets. When economists studied Cournot's oligopoly game, its assumption of simultaneous independent decision-making was viewed as a seriously restrictive theoretical assumption, because real oligopolists might consider how their actions could influence their competitors' future behavior. So Cournot and his successors did not perceive, as we do now, that such game-theoretic models could provide a general theoretical framework for analyzing competitive behavior, not only in markets but also in any kind of economic, political, or social institutions.

The breakthrough came with a paper that Émile Borel presented to the French Académie des Sciences a century ago, on December 19, 1921. Borel approached the study of games with a mathematician's instinct for generalization and with a particular focus on questions of probability theory. In the first few paragraphs of this short paper, Borel provided three fundamental insights that have been essential to the development of modern game theory.

First, Borel introduced the basic concept of strategic normalization of extensive games, which enables us to interpret one-stage simultaneous-move strategic-form games as general models for any kind of competitive interaction. The key idea was the modern game-theoretic concept of strategy, which was introduced by Borel almost too quickly. In his first paragraph, Borel tells us that in his game model, each of the given alternatives that a player can choose is to be interpreted as a 'method of play' or 'a code that determines for every possible circumstance what the person should do.' Thus, when we assume that the players will make independent choices among their given alternatives, that does not mean that the game will not involve opportunities for players to influence each other, because a player's alternatives in our analysis could represent strategic plans that could include the player's plans for observable actions that might influence others' subsequent behavior and also could include the player's plans for his own subsequent responses to observed prior actions of others. John von Neumann began his 1928 paper by developing this idea more fully, with an explicit definition of extensive-form games, which can then be reduced to strategic form, but the basic idea was right there in the first paragraph of Borel's 1921 paper.

In his second paragraph, Borel introduced the idea of a randomized strategy, because he understood that there are games where a rational player should not behave in a way that is perfectly predictable by others. Probability theory had developed from the analysis of games where uncertainty is generated by dice and cards. But Borel recognized that in competitive games, a significant component of a player's uncertainty could also be generated by the strategic behavior of other players. Borel introduced randomized strategies as a basic model of how a player could create uncertainty about his behavior.

In his third paragraph, Borel applied the criterion of expected payoff maximization to analyze each player's optimal response to his opponent's randomized strategy. Borel was able to completely justify this criterion, decades before von Neumann and Morgenstern published their axiomatic derivation of expected utility, because he assumed that a player's payoff for any strategy pair was measured in terms of the player's probability of winning the game, so that the expected payoff from a randomized strategy would correspond to the player's ex ante probability of winning. This idea is actually implicit in our standard justification of expected-payoff maximization for general von Neumann–Morgenstern utility scales, where an individual's utility for any given outcome can be quantified as the probability p such that the individual would be indifferent between this outcome and a simple lottery that gives probability p of the best possible outcome and probability $1 - p$ of the worst possible outcome.

Using a linear transformation of such win-probability payoffs in a symmetric two-player game that will have one winner, Borel (1921) analyzed symmetric two-person zero-sum games. He suggested that our analysis should began by iteratively eliminating certain "bad" strategies, which were weakly dominated in the game. He then asserted that, for any symmetric two-person zero-sum game where each player has three undominated strategies, we can find a randomized strategy such that each player can guarantee himself the fair expected payoff of 0. In the same paragraph, however, Borel also claimed that this result could not be generalized to larger games where players have more than three strategies.[1] So in 1921, Borel correctly asserted that the minimax theorem, which von Neumann would prove in 1928, was true for three-by-three symmetric games, but Borel also wrongly claimed that this theorem was false for larger games.[2]

4.2 FURTHER DEVELOPMENT OF THESE INSIGHTS BY VON NEUMANN AND NASH

In von Neumann's 1928 paper, before proving the minimax theorem, he began by formally developing the idea of strategic normalization that Borel had sketched in 1921. Von Neumann explicitly developed a general mathematical notation for describing multistage games in extensive form, and then he showed how any such game can be represented within the simpler class of models that we now call *strategic-form games*, where the players' alternatives are strategies for how to play the multistage extensive game. Because these strategies could be chosen by the players before they begin their interactions, there is no loss of generality in assuming that the players make their strategic choices independently. Thus a reader of von Neumann's paper could not miss the point that Borel made almost too quickly in 1921: that the analysis of one-stage games where players act independently can offer a general framework for analyzing rational behavior in any kind of competitive interactions. But this argument for the general assumption of independent strategic decisions was later obscured by von Neumann's subsequent emphasis on coalitional analysis for games with more than two players, and so it remained for John Nash (1950, 1951) to formulate the basic principles of equilibrium analysis for general games.

The fact that ex ante strategic optimization imposes no conditions on a player's responses to zero-probability events means that some Nash equilibria of the strategic-form game might involve behavior that is recognizably irrational in the extensive form, and so game theorists subsequently developed refined equilibrium concepts for analysis of dynamic games in extensive form.[3] But Borel's mathematical ability to see great potential generality in the simple structure of one-stage strategic-form games was essential to the development of game theory. We had to understand equilibrium analysis in strategic form

[1] In the 1953 English translation of Borel (1921) by Leonard J. Savage, the impossibility claim is misprinted as being for games with more than seven strategies. Perhaps Savage was influenced by his reading of Borel's subsequent 1927 paper, but the reference to seven-by-seven games has no precedent in Borel's 1921 paper.

[2] Both claims were asserted without proof in 1921. In a subsequent 1924 paper, Borel gave a proof of his correct assertion about three-by-three games and was more careful to indicate the hypothetical nature of his claim about larger games. Weinstein (2022) insightfully analyzes what Borel might have been thinking when he claimed that it seemed easy to disprove the minimax theorem. Weinstein observes that in a subsequent 1926 paper, Borel explicitly considered a conjecture that every symmetric two-person zero-sum game would have a randomized equilibrium in which all pure strategies yield the expected payoff 0, but counterexamples to this conjecture can indeed be found even among four-by-four games with no dominated strategies.

[3] A key advance was the introduction of sequential equilibrium by Kreps and Wilson (1982).

before we could develop other refinements and generalizations in the much more complicated structures of extensive-form games.

From von Neumann's proof of the minimax theorem for two-person zero-sum games and Nash's subsequent proof of equilibrium existence for general games, we know that for any finite game, it is possible to make probabilistic predictions about the players' behavior such that each player can know what is predicted for others and rationally behave according to prediction him- or herself. As remarked by von Neumann in 1953, Borel's conjecture that many finite games would not have such probabilistic equilibria would have meant the impossibility of game theory as we know it. In his pioneering work to demonstrate the power of admitting probabilities into our descriptions of rational competitive behavior, Borel nonetheless believed that there would be some games where even the mathematics of probability would be inadequate to describe the degree of unpredictability that rational behavior would require.

This belief was based on Borel's perception that in many real games, misleading others about one's strategy can be an essential component of skillful play. The best poker players may be particularly good at deceiving others when they bluff, but modern game-theoretic analysis has generally avoided any assumption that one player can systematically fool the others. If game theory taught that one player should bluff in some manner X when he has a weak hand, then the teachings of game theory would equally warn others of the possibility that this action X might indicate a weak hand. A general theory of games that is applicable to all players' decision problems cannot promise special analytical advantages to any one player.

In essence, the successful development of game theory for social science has been based on two fundamental assumptions: that players are rational agents who act to maximize their expected payoff given their information and that players are intelligent enough to know everything about their situation that the game theorist knows.[4] To satisfy this intelligence assumption, game theorists must assume that their model of a game is common knowledge among its players. These assumptions of rationality and intelligence together lead us to Nash's concept of equilibrium. A complete probabilistic prediction about how the players should behave in a game could be rationally fulfilled by each player, when he or she intelligently understands the predicted behavior of others, only if the prediction is a Nash equilibrium.[5]

4 One can argue that in biological applications, a human game theorist could have a more sophisticated understanding of a game than the animals or genes that play it. But in social science, game theory models are formulated by academic theorists to describe the behavior of practical men and women of the world. People tend to be appropriately skeptical of theoretical arguments about markets or politics that depend on professional experts missing something about their business that is supposedly clear to academic theorists.

5 Aumann (1987) has cogently argued for the more general concept of correlated equilibrium as a fundamental implication of Bayesian rationality. The argument for Nash equilibrium depends on the assumption that all opportunities for the players to communicate or share information have been included in the extensive game model, so that their preplay strategic decisions must be independent.

With this analytical methodology, even if it cannot suggest how a skillful player could fool others, game theory has substantial value for helping people understand how a change in the rules of a game could cause the players' behavior to change when they have learned how to compete under the new rules. Much work in social science is aimed at helping us better understand the institutions of our society, so that we can better evaluate proposals for institutional reform, but reforming an institution means changing the rules of the game that people in the institution will play. Before the rules have changed, when nobody has had any experience with the proposed new rules, it may be unclear how the players' strategies might change, and game theory gives us tools to probe these questions. We want to predict how individuals may behave in the institution when the reformed rules have become familiar to them and they have an intelligent understanding of their new competitive environment. When the goal of our analysis is to identify institutional reforms that could increase people's welfare, it is helpful to assume that each individual always acts rationally to maximize his or her own welfare, so that we can separate arguments for reforming the institution from arguments for better education of individuals. Thus the fundamental assumptions of game theory are well suited to such questions, and the generality of game theory's mathematical framework has meant that it can be applied to help analyze proposals for reforming the rules of any kind of institution or organization in society.

4.3 UNDERSTANDING THE EQUILIBRIUM COORDINATION PROBLEM AFTER NASH

The early work of Borel and von Neumann focused on two-person zero-sum games, where one player's gain would always equal the other player's loss. In a two-person zero-sum game, a player's equilibrium strategies are also *maximin* strategies that guarantee this player's expected payoff could not be less than his or her expected payoff in equilibrium, even if the other player did not act according to the equilibrium. In a two-person zero-sum game, if (a_1, a_2) and (b_1, b_2) are two different Nash equilibria, then these equilibria must be equivalent (in the sense that each player i gets the same expected payoff $u_i(a_1, a_2) = u_i(b_1, b_2)$ in both equilibria), and these equilibria will also be interchangeable (in the sense that (a_1, b_2) and (b_1, a_2) are also Nash equilibria). However, these properties do not hold in more general games.

In general, a game could have many different equilibria that would yield different payoffs for the players. Such multiplicity of equilibria was initially seen as a disadvantage of Nash's solution concept, because it implies that rational players' behavior may not be uniquely determined by the economic structure of the game.[6] But Thomas Schelling (1960) suggested that the existence of games with

[6] At one point, Luce and Raiffa (1957, p. 104) even suggested that the multiplicity of equilibria in games like the Battle of Sexes game, along with the uniqueness of a noncooperative equilibrium for finitely repeated Prisoners' Dilemma games, might 'sound a death knell' for Nash equilibrium as a principal solution concept for general games. Their concerns about how to interpret

multiple equilibria is a pervasive fact of life that needs to be studied and understood. In many games, there may be Nash equilibria that yield strictly lower expected payoffs for all players than other Pareto-superior Nash equilibria, and then all players would prefer to coordinate on one of these Pareto-superior equilibria. So games with multiple equilibria can be useful models for analyzing a society's need for coordination. This fundamental coordination problem could not be recognized as long as game theorists only studied two-person zero-sum games.

Thus Schelling taught game theorists to see commitment and coordination as fundamental social problems. Here the commitment problem is that people cannot be expected to behave in ways that are not part of a Nash equilibrium, and the coordination problem is that people may need guidance in focusing on an equilibrium that is better for them. Schelling argued that such coordination can be provided by any publicly observed aspect of the social or physical environment that tends to focus people's attention on one particular equilibrium. So Nash's theory of equilibria can be a framework for understanding the vital role of culture, tradition, and leadership in coordinating people's strategic expectations.[7]

In particular, the basis of power in society may be found in a socially recognized leader's ability to designate focal equilibria, which then become self-fulfilling directives. The leader's basic choice set is among alternative equilibria in games that have multiple equilibria. Benefits of holding such focal power can be derived from the leader's ability to induce social coordination on equilibria that are more favorable to the interests of the leader or the leader's clients.

Game theorists generally assume that players have consistent strategic expectations, because intelligent players should understand any predictions that we make about behavior in their game. Although methodological concerns may have led us to this assumption, it is often reasonable to assume such consistency of beliefs in a well-ordered society that has coordinating leadership, where people can expect each other to comply with strategic norms that have been designated by recognized leaders in their domain of authority. But this argument suggests questions about whether perhaps we should admit a possibility of finding some inconsistency of beliefs in divided societies where rival groups are fighting for supreme power.

Borel's 1921 paper was written in the aftermath of the First World War, and he expressed some hope that game-theoretic analysis could contribute to our understanding of the problems of war. Today there is an extensive literature on game theory and armed conflict, which is reviewed in this volume by James Fearon. Here we may just observe that when we understand war as a struggle for power over the designation of focal equilibria, then game-theoretic

the multiplicity of equilibria in coordination games were answered by Schelling (1960), and their concerns about the equilibrium analysis of finitely repeated Prisoners' Dilemma games were answered by Kreps and colleagues (1982).

7 An extensive review of these points is in Myerson (2009).

principles of equilibrium selection may differ, depending on whether the players begin the game in a state of war or peace.[8] Peace is a relationship between nations that have a mutually accepted framework for resolving disputes and maintaining consistent strategic expectations in transactions between them, but war means that the adversaries cannot agree about how to coordinate on equilibria that might be better for them all. So Pareto-inferior equilibria may be more tenable predictions in game models about the potential duration of a war, which is assumed to exist at the start of the game, than in game models about the onset of war, where it is assumed that the players start with peaceful leadership.

4.4 REFERENCES

R. J. Aumann. Correlated equilibrium as an expression of Bayesian rationality. *Econometrica*, 55(1):1–18, 1987.

E. Borel. La théorie du jeu et les équations intégrales à noyau symétrique. *Comptes Rendus Hebdomadaires des Séances de l'Académie des Sciences, Paris*, 173:1304–1308, 1921.

E. Borel. Sur les jeux où le hasard se combine avec l'habilité des joueurs. *Comptes Rendus Hebdomadaires des Séances de l'Académie des Sciences, Paris*, 178:24–25, 1924.

E. Borel. Un théorème sur les systèmes de formes linéaires à déterminant symétrique gauche. *Comptes Rendus Hebdomadaires des Séances de l'Académie des Sciences, Paris*, 183:925–927, 1926.

E. Borel. Sur les systèmes de formes linéaires a déterminant symétrique gauche et la théorie générale du jeu. *Comptes Rendus Hebdomadaires des Séances de l'Académie des Sciences, Paris*, 184:52–54, 1927.

A. Cournot. *Recherches sur les Principes Mathématiques de la Theorie des Richesses.* Paris: Hachette, 1838. English translation by N. T. Bacon, 1927. Researches into the Mathematical Principles of the Theory of Wealth. New York: MacMillan.

J. D. Fearon. Rationalist explanations for war. *International Organization*, 49(3):379–414, 1995.

D. M. Kreps and R. Wilson. Sequential equilibria. *Econometrica*, 50(4):863–894, 1982.

D. M. Kreps, P. Milgrom, J. Roberts, and R. Wilson. Rational cooperation in the finitely repeated prisoners' dilemma. *Journal of Economic Theory*, 27(2):245–252, 1982.

R. Luce and H. Raiffa. *Games and Decisions.* New York: Wiley, 1957.

R. B. Myerson. Learning from Schelling's Strategy of Conflict. *Journal of Economic Literature*, 47(4):1109–1125, 2009.

R. B. Myerson. Game theory and the First World War. *Journal of Economic Literature*, 61(2):716–735, 2023.

J. F. Nash. Equilibrium points in *n*-person games. *Proceedings of the National Academy of Sciences*, 36:48–49, 1950.

J. F. Nash. Non-cooperative games. *Annals of Mathematics*, 54(2):286–295, 1951.

T. Schelling. *The Strategy of Conflict.* Cambridge, MA: Harvard University Press, 1960.

[8] See Fearon (1995) and Myerson (2023), where principles of equilibrium selection in war-onset models and war-duration models are discussed.

J. von Neumann. Zur Theorie der Gesellschaftsspiele. *Mathematische Annalen*, 100:295–320, 1928.

J. von Neumann. Communication on the Borel notes. *Econometrica*, 21:124–127, 1953.

J. Weinstein. On a mistranslation of a mistake about minimax, 2022. https://sites.wustl.edu/weinstein/files/2023/06/borel-correction.pdf.

PART II

MATHEMATICS OF GAME THEORY AND ITS FOUNDATIONS

5

Introduction to Part II

Bernhard von Stengel

Pierre-Louis Lions' chapter "On Mean Field Games" gives a review of the current state of mean field games (MFGs), which he pioneered. The approach is inspired by the mean field theory in physics and probability theory of interacting particles, where the effect of other particles is approximated by a single averaged effect. MFG theory studies interactions in large populations modeled by a continuum of agents. In an MFG model, each agent acts rationally, taking into account the state of the population (assumed to be known in a symmetric manner by all agents), and the state of the population evolves according to the individual decisions.

The individual agent's dynamics are typically (particularly in the presence of noise) modeled as a stochastic differential equation, called the Master Equation. It is intrinsically infinite-dimensional, because the variation of the state x involves a probability measure m, where x and m are the two central variables in any MFG model. MFG theory is mathematically complex, but Lions carefully introduces the main components of the Master Equation to give the reader a first understanding of what it is about. At the same time, the text gives a survey of the state of the art in MFG theory, with current challenges, and describes some applications where the MFG model seems particularly adequate.

Sylvain Sorin's chapter "Value and Equilibrium" explores the different strands of the theory of two-player zero-sum games and equilibrium concepts for general multiplayer games. The conventional viewpoint is that equilibrium is an extension of the concept of value (and its associated optimal strategies) to non-zero-sum games, and the value just a special case of an equilibrium payoff. However, as argued by Sorin, a number of important concepts apply only to one of these concepts.

The article gives a high-level survey of the history and important mathematical activities in the two areas. The nonuniqueness of Nash equilibrium has led the development of a plethora of selection criteria. Of these, strategic and dynamic stability (see also the chapter by Robert Wilson) have motivated the study of the equilibrium manifold and Nash dynamics. This research has no equivalent for zero-sum games with a unique value. The value concept, on the other hand, extends to approachability questions of vector payoffs and operator approaches. They can be applied to repeated games, also with incomplete information. Some of these are unilateral security concepts that do not apply to non-zero-sum games.

Some concepts bridge the two theories. For example, correlated equilibrium, which generalizes Nash equilibrium, is characterized by linear inequalities like the minimax theorem. It appears as a natural solution concept in certain learning dynamics. Overall, Sorin's survey gives an excellent overview of classic and current challenges in the mathematics of noncooperative game theory.

Robert Wilson gives a survey of important current issues about "Refinements of Nash Equilibrium." Refinement concepts aim to select among the typically large number of Nash equilibria of a game only those that fulfill certain criteria of being "reasonable" in some sense. Many refinements do so by proposing a certain robustness against perturbations of the strategies or of the game parameters. While this is a fruitful approach, "perturbations are mathematical artefacts used to identify refinements with desirable properties, but they are not intrinsic to a fundamental theory of rational decision making in multi-person situations" (Govindan and Wilson, 2016). In contrast, the concept of strategic stability, pioneered by Kohlberg and Mertens (1986), is based on behavioral axioms, namely admissibility (no player uses a weakly dominated strategy), backward induction, invariance of embedding (to exclude framing effects), and independence of irrelevant alternatives. As Govindan and Wilson have shown in their work, these axioms characterize strategically stable sets of equilibria for extensive-form games with perfect recall and generic payoffs. While this is a set-valued concept, the genericity assumption implies that the resulting payoffs are unique.

A mathematically challenging extension is to games with nongeneric payoffs. Wilson concludes with a discussion of the behavioral challenges posed by the axiomatic approach for predicting strategic behaviors, in particular the absence of framing effects. The emerging "economic engineering" discipline of market design will need new connections from theory to practice.

5.1 REFERENCES

S. Govindan and R. B. Wilson. *Nash Equilibrium, Refinements Of.* In *The New Palgrave Dictionary of Economics*. London: Palgrave Macmillan, 2016.

E. Kohlberg and J.-F. Mertens. On the strategic stability of equilibria. *Econometrica*, 54(5):1003–1037, 1986.

6

On Mean Field Games

Pierre-Louis Lions

We briefly survey the state of the art for mean field games (MFGs) without entering any technical/mathematical detail. We review both the existing mathematical results and the modeling toolbox. We also mention a few applications. After describing a new numerical approach, we conclude with a few perspectives.

6.1 INTRODUCTION

MFG theory is a mathematical framework to describe/model dynamical equilibria for large (interacting) populations. It is also a toolbox allowing one to construct MFG models, analyze them and make numerical simulations of their solutions.

J-M. Lasry and the author coined the terminology "mean field games" (see Lasry and Lions, 2006a,b; 2007) and introduced the "Master Equation," which is in general an infinite-dimensional equation (described in detail later in this chapter), designed to help obtain some of the important mathematical building blocks of the theory (Hilbertian formulation, monotone MFG, etc.; see Lions 2006–2012). MFG models often (but not always) combine two facts: (i) Each agent/player anticipates rationally taking into account the state of the population and (ii) the state of the population evolves according to the individual decisions. Note that all members of the population, taken to be a continuum, share the same information about the state of the population. Let us also mention that in many cases, but not always, MFG models can be obtained by taking the limit, as N goes to $+\infty$, of N-players, Nash equilibria.

At this point, we wish to emphasize the fact that there have been many important works in economics that can be interpreted as MFG models, although to the best of our knowledge most deal with situations where the Master Equation can be reduced to finite-dimensional problems (thanks to the lack of common noise/risk described later). A remarkable exception is the article by Krusell and Smith (1998) in which the occurrence of shocks precludes any finite-dimensional reduction. For this model, our toolbox allows us to write down the equation (Master Equation) corresponding to the situation considered therein and to explain why solutions should be close to the explicit solutions in the deterministic case if the amount of "noise" is small, a fact that is consistent with the conclusions obtained numerically in the paper.

There have been in the last fifteen years many works on MFG models both on the theoretical side (maths) and on the applications side. The latter is not surprising since there are many areas where dynamical equilibria for large populations play an important role. Let us mention a few: economics (obviously!), finance, crowd motion, traffic, digital advertising (ads), cryptocurrencies, cybersecurity, machine learning, epidemiology, telecommunication networks and more generally all kinds of networks (social, computer). We briefly mention some examples in Section 6.5.

Finally, let us recall that the outcome of MFG models concern the dynamics of populations and is not concerned with potential erratic individual behaviors (unless they are statistically meaningful). These models can be seen as a decision support tool for policymakers, decision makers, regulatory bodies and others.

In Section 6.2, we briefly explain the form of the so-called Master Equations, which are nonlinear infinite-dimensional partial differential equations. Potential reductions to finite dimensions are treated in Section 6.3. Section 6.4 is devoted to a review of the MFG toolbox, both in mathematical terms and from the modeling viewpoint. We briefly discuss in Section 6.5 a few applications, while we attempt in Section 6.6 to describe a new numerical procedure to compute MFG equilibria. And we conclude with a few perspectives in Section 6.7.

Let us warn the reader that some formulae in the next section (where we introduce the Master Equation) may seem heavy on the technical side, but we shall try to explain how the various mathematical components/blocks appear.

6.2 PRESENTATION OF THE MASTER EQUATION

For the sake of simplicity, we shall only consider finite horizon problems, and the horizon is denoted by $T(\in]0,\infty[)$. Also, we emphasize the fact that in order to describe in a simpler way some mathematical properties, we "reverse" time (i.e., change the time variable t in $T-t$) and we write the equations on a time interval $t \in (0,T)$. (Note that we chose for this presentation a "continuous time.") In the simplest cases (single population), the unknown function of the equation denoted by U, which can be thought as a "value function," is a real valued function that depends on two (sets of) variables denoted by (i) $x \in \mathbb{R}^d$ (if the state space of the members of population is continuous and finite-dimensional), which corresponds to the description of the state of a generic agent/individual, and (ii) $m \in \mathcal{M}$, where $\mathcal{M}$ is the space of bounded nonnegative measures on $\mathbb{R}^d$. Note that when the total size of the population is fixed, one can restrict after an obvious normalization m to belong the space $\mathcal{P}$ of probability measures on $\mathbb{R}^d$.

Then, MFG dynamical equilibria lead to the following type of equation:

$$\frac{\partial U}{\partial t} + D + T + N = 0\,. \tag{6.1}$$

The block D corresponds to decision, T to transport and N to noise. Before writing the typical precise mathematical formulations, let us explain how each block arises naturally. First, D corresponds to the decisions made by a generic agent that depend on the state of the population and which clearly affect its state x. A simple example, but not the only possibility, is to assume that the decisions are made by a dynamic minimization procedure or in other words through optimal control. The block D then typically corresponds to (Hamilton–Jacobi) Bellman-like nonlinear equations such as "$\sup_\alpha\{-b_\alpha.\partial_x u - f_\alpha\}$," where b_α corresponds to the (deterministic part of the) dynamics, f_α is the cost/criterion function used to evaluate the choices made and the sup is taken over all admissible values of the controls/decisions. Of course, b_α and f_α are functions of (at least) x *and* m. And f_α is real valued while b_α takes values in $\mathbb{R}^d$. We denote by $\partial_x u$ the gradient vector whose components are $\frac{\partial u}{\partial x_i}$ $(1 \le i \le N)$ and $y.z = \sum_{i=1}^d y_i z_i$ if $y, z \in \mathbb{R}^d$. This example (and many others) lead to the following formula:

$$D = H(x, m, \partial_x u), \tag{6.2}$$

where H – often called the Hamiltonian – is convex in $\partial_x u$ in the above Bellman-like example but is not necessarily so in MFG equilibria. The Bellman rule yields an optimal control $\alpha^*(x, m, \partial_x u)$. Typically, in the provided example, the optimal dynamic b_{α^*} is given by $\partial_p H(x, m, p)$ at $p = \partial_x u$.

Next, let us discuss the T block. The individual actions modify the state of the population. The simplest (but not the only) case is when the modification of the population solely results from the individual actions (in a deterministic situation). In that case, the population measure is transported by the dynamics above namely the vector field b_{α^*}. Mathematically, an infinitesimal variation of the state $x+(\Delta t)b_{\alpha^*}$ modifies the measure m as follows: $\int \varphi(x)(m+\Delta m) \simeq \int m\varphi(x+(\Delta t)b_{\alpha^*}) \simeq \int m\varphi + \Delta t m b_{\alpha^*}.\partial_x\varphi = \int m\varphi - \Delta t \partial_x.(b_{\alpha^*}m)\varphi$, the last equality being obtained by a simple integration by parts. Hence, $\Delta m = -\partial_x.(b_{\alpha^*}m)$. And the T term naturally becomes

$$T = \langle \partial_m U, -\partial_x.(b_{\alpha^*}m)\rangle \tag{6.3}$$

(i.e., the derivative of U with respect to m in the direction $(-\partial_x.(b_{\alpha^*}m))$ we identified previously).

The provided heuristic derivations assumed that there was no noise, no source of randomness. If we go back to the dynamics of a generic agent, we may also (and often need to in realistic situations) assume that the agent's dynamics involve some noise or randomness. As a particular example, let us consider the case where these noises are Brownian motions. If we consider that the members of this large population are undistinguishable, then there are two types and only two types of noises: idiosyncratic noises (i.e., Brownian motions that are independent from one agent to the other ones) and a common noise that affects all agents (i.e., another Brownian motion independent from the previous ones, which is the same for all agents). Let us denote by at and bt their respective variance (a, b given nonnegative parameters). This leads by Itô's formula and the same transportation argument as before to the following:

$$N = -\frac{a+b}{2}\partial_x^2 U + \langle \partial_m u, \left(-\frac{a+b}{2}\partial_x^2 m\right)\rangle + b\langle \partial_x.\partial_m U, \partial_x m\rangle, \tag{6.4}$$

where $\partial_x^2 = -\sum_{i=1}^d \frac{\partial^2}{\partial_{x_i}^2}$ and the last term, which is a consequence of the fact that all agents and the population are submitted to the same Brownian motion, thus creating this extra term in Itô's formula, really means

$$\sum_{i=1}^d \langle \partial_{x_i} \partial_m u, \partial_{x_i} m\rangle.$$

In conclusion, one example of the MFG Master Equation in a simple continuous setting (continuous state space, continuous time, Brownian noises, etc.) is given by the following equation:

$$\begin{aligned} \frac{\partial U}{\partial t} &+ H(x, m, \partial_x U) - \frac{a+b}{2}\ \partial_x^2 U + \langle \partial_m U, -\partial_m.(B(x, m, \partial_x U)m \\ &- \frac{a+b}{2}\ \partial_x^2 m\rangle + b\langle \partial_x.\partial_m U, \partial_x m\rangle = 0 \end{aligned} \tag{6.5}$$

for some function B, which in the example provided was given by $\partial_p H$. Of course, this equation has to be complemented by an initial condition (in fact a terminal condition since we reversed time) like

$$U\mid_{t=0} = U_0(x, m) \ \text{ for all } x, m. \tag{6.6}$$

Just like Bellman's equation, at least superficially, with several forms depending on the model assumptions, MFG equations may "look different" depending, in particular, on the noise structure. For instance, and this is the case in the model of Krusell and Smith (1998), let us briefly consider the case when the entire population may switch between two states by a Poisson process with intensity $\lambda > 0$. In that case, we are naturally led to two value functions $U^1(x, m, t)$, $U^2(x, m, t)$ (which correspond to the two possible states of the population), solving

$$\begin{cases} \frac{\partial U^1}{\partial t} + H^1 + \langle \partial_m U^1, -\partial_x(B^1 m)\rangle + \lambda(U^1 - U^2) = 0 \\ \frac{\partial U^2}{\partial t} + H^2 + \langle \partial_m U^2, -\partial_x(B^2 m)\rangle + \lambda(U^2 - U^1) = 0. \end{cases} \tag{6.7}$$

6.3 FINITE REDUCTIONS

There are two main cases when the Master Equations become or can be reduced to finite-dimensional equations, making the resulting equations more amenable to both mathematical analysis and numerical computations.

The first case is when the state space is a finite set, say $\{1, \ldots, k\}$. In that case the x-dependence of the value function U becomes an index U^i $(1 \leq i \leq k)$. Next, the measure m describing the population simply becomes a point y in $\mathbb{R}^k$, whose coordinates correspond to the size of the population in state i. For the sake of simplicity, we will ignore the possible sign restrictions on the coordinates y_i $(1 \leq i \leq k)$. The partial derivative in m becomes the usual partial derivative with respect to y_i $(1 \leq i \leq k)$, and the Master Equation becomes

$$\frac{\partial U^i}{\partial t} + (B.\partial_y)U^i = A^i, \tag{6.8}$$

where A and B are (given) functions of $(y, U) \in \mathbb{R}^k \times \mathbb{R}^k$ into $\mathbb{R}^k$, with an initial condition

$$U^i \mid_{t=0} = U_0^i \quad \text{on } \mathbb{R}^k \tag{6.9}$$

for some (given) functions U_0^i from $\mathbb{R}^k$ into $\mathbb{R}^k$.

This set of equilibrium equations is a nonlinear first-order system that in the mathematical nomenclature is a nonconservative hyperbolic system. Let us emphasize the fact that prior to the introduction of the MFG equations, little was known mathematically on such systems.

The other case when we are able to write down finite-dimensional equations is the case when there is no common noise (i.e., $b = 0$ in formula (6.4) and (6.5)). In that case, we may integrate the equation (6.5) along "the characteristics in m" (i.e., the transportation flow),

$$-\frac{\partial m}{\partial t} + \partial_x (Bm) - \frac{a}{2}\, \partial_x^2 m = 0 \quad \text{for } x \in \mathbb{R}^d,\ t \in [0, T], \tag{6.10}$$

with a "terminal" condition (really an initial condition on the state of the population because of the time reversal convention)

$$m \mid_{t=T} = m_0 \quad \text{on } \mathbb{R}^d \tag{6.11}$$

and the equation for the value becomes

$$\frac{\partial u}{\partial t} + H - \frac{a}{2}\partial_x^2 u = 0 \quad \text{for } x \in \mathbb{R}^d, t \in [0, T] \tag{6.12}$$

with

$$u \mid_{t=0} = U_0(x, m(0)) \quad \text{on } \mathbb{R}^d. \tag{6.13}$$

Note that formulae (6.10) to (6.13) provide a backward–forward system of equations: the "backward" (remember, time reversal ...!) decision equation (6.12) (like in dynamic programming) and the "forward" evolution equation (6.10) for the state of the population. Once again, this type of problem was, prior to MFG theory, rather new from a mathematical perspective, with almost no mathematical tools or theories available.

The connections between such "backward–forward" systems and the infinite-dimensional equation are summarized by the following facts, where we assume that we can solve "nicely" both sets of equations:

$$U(x, m(t)) = u(x, t) \text{ for } 0 \leq t \leq T,\ x \in \mathbb{R}^d. \tag{6.14}$$

In particular: $U(x, m_0, T) = u(x, T)$ for $x \in \mathbb{R}^d$. In other words, the reconstruction of the full value function U requires one to solve (6.10) to (6.13) for all m_0. Let us emphasize the fact that this "backward–forward" formulation breaks the time consistency, which is obvious at the infinite-dimensional level (an evolution equation!), at least unless some further global analysis is performed at the finite-dimensional level. By time consistency, we mean the following formal property, reminiscent of dynamic programming: Let $T_1, T_2 > 0$ and denote by $T = T_1 + T_2$. The solution U of (6.5) at time T is also obtained by solving (6.5) on $[0, T_1]$, which yields a value function U^1 at time T_1, and then solving (6.5) again on $[0, T_2]$ (or on $[T_1, T]$, if we were to deal with time-dependent data), with an initial condition given by $U^1(T_1)$.

6.4 THE TOOLBOX

MFG equations are not simple objects from a mathematical point of view, but thanks to many contributions worldwide, a global understanding is now available, although several interesting questions are still open.

Since MFG models aim to describe the dynamics of a population (taking into account the individual rational decisions), one of the two sets of variables (state variables) is obviously a measure on the states of the agents (a probability measure when the total number of players does not vary). Hence, MFG equations are equations set on the space of measures (and on the state space), obviously an infinite-dimensional space. In other words, the infinite-dimensional character is an intrinsic fact.

As seen in the previous section, the reduction to finite-dimensional equations is possible only (essentially) in two cases: (i) There is no common noise, only idiosyncratic ones, in which case it suffices to study a coupled system of a backward (Hamilton–Jacobi) Bellman-like equations corresponding to the optimal decisions of the agents and a forward Fokker–Planck-like equation corresponding to the evolution of the measure describing the state of the population, or (ii) the state space of agents is a finite set, in which case the Master Equation reduces to a nonlinear system of first-order partial differential equations.

The space of probability of (say) measures has a complex mathematical structure ("lots of corners!"), and we showed how to recast the Master Equation on the linear space of random variables. Parts of the available mathematical theory concern (i) the local well-posedness of the Master Equation; (ii) the global existence of solutions; (iii) the identification of regularity/uniqueness regimes; (iv) the rigorous derivation of MFG from N-player Nash equilibria; (v) numerical methods in the finite-dimensional cases, at least when the dimension is small; (vi) how to recover "particle-like" or "agent-based" equations from MFG by letting the intertemporal preference rate go to $+\infty$; (vii) necessary and sufficient conditions for a MFG to be deduced from a centralized optimal control problem; and (viii) planning and transitions from one state of the population to another (possibly stationary equilibria). Some of the existing mathematical theory can be found in the work of Lions (2006–2012) and in the book by Carmona and Delarue (2018).

Let us give at this point one (and only one!) sample of the existing mathematical theory for the Master Equation (6.5). We assume that all the given data $(H.B)$ are smooth functions without being specific, for the sake of simplicity, about which precise type of regularity is required. The equation (6.5) is shown to be well posed (i.e., in terms of existence, uniqueness of solutions) locally in time (with a Cauchy–Lipschitz-like result), and globally under some monotonicity–convexity conditions, namely H is assumed to be convex in $p(= \partial_x u)$ and the monotonicity condition reads

$$\int (U(x,m_1) - U(x,m_2))d(m_1 - m_2) \geq 0. \tag{6.15}$$

This type of result was first shown by Lions (2006–2012), mostly in the so-called Hilbertian formula. More information is provided by Cardaliaguet and colleagues (2019) and Bertucci (2021).

In order to be a little more precise, let us mention a very recent study of (6.5) by Bertucci and colleages (2024), where we prove, among other facts, that there exists a maximal time $0 < T_0 \leq \infty$ such that, for all $T \in [0, T_0[$, if $U_0 \in X$, then there exists a unique solution U of (6.5) bounded in X. Furthermore, if $T_0 < \infty$, considering the case in general, $\|U\|_X$ goes to infinity as T goes to T_0. The space X consists of those functions on $\mathbb{R}^d \times \mathcal{P}(\mathbb{R}^d)$ such that $\partial_x U$ is Lipschitz in (x, m), where $\mathcal{P}$ is endowed with the Monge–Kantorovich–Wasserstein metric (i.e., the $W^{-1,1}$ Sobolev norm, if we were to work in $\mathcal{M}$ instead of $\mathcal{P}$). Let us point out that if one knows that $T_0 < \infty$ in general and that $T_0 = +\infty$ (global well-posedness) in the monotone (convex) regime and in some other very particular cases, we are far from understanding completely when T_0 is finite or not!

6.5 A FEW APPLICATIONS

As explained in the introductory Section 6.1 there are numerous applications of MFG models to many different fields. We are going to mention here just a few without entering any detailed explanation. The only common feature of these examples is that they all have been studied by our group with various collaborators/experts from these fields. Let us mention that, as usual in mathematical modeling, the quality and relevance of the results (the output) depend on the quality and relevance of the modeling assumptions (the input), and not on the mathematical tools that are being used. Here, like everywhere else, the famous GIGO principle ("Garbage In, Garbage Out") applies!

Let us begin with a few examples from economics. First of all, macroeconomics is an obvious candidate for applications in view of the Krusell and Smith (1998) model and various works for "heterogeneous agent" models – see, for instance, Aiyagari (1994) and Huggett (1993), among others. We have studied these models (and others) and have shown what the MFG toolbox can offer for such models. We refer the reader to Achdou and colleagues (2014); Achdou et al. (2022b).

Another application we wish to mention concerns the oil industry. Global models (called Edmond models) have been developed by Achdou and colleagues (2022a). In particular, the model "Edmond 2" is an attempt to study the oil industry, with its price dynamics, production for the Organization of Petroleum Exporting Countries (OPEC) and outside OPEC, investments, market shares, storage and so forth, and to explain the articulations between dynamics, the agent's decisions and their strategic interactions. It is a recursive midterm model (with a typical horizon of five years). In order to limit the complexity of the model, although many extensions can be developed without difficulty, we chose to take into account a major cartel-like player (OPEC+) and three "MFG crowds": consumers (summarized by the law of offer and demand), producers outside OPEC with simplified "reactive" decisions and speculative storage players (arbitragists). Let us emphasize the fact that the major player has strategic advantages when the level of storage is minimal or maximal: At the minimal level it "controls" prices that can be high and make a profit, and at the maximal level it also "controls" prices that can be low and recover market shares. Hence, we should expect trends pushing toward the minimal level or the maximal one, thus creating cycles and singularities due to the competition of the two trends. In other words, we should expect that the major player's strategy should be discontinuous. Edmond 2 does indeed reproduce such expected behaviors, agreeing well with the observations on market shares and providing a good representation of the critical periods 2015–2016 and 2020–2021 (a brutal drop of the prices and postcrisis dynamics).

Concerning financial applications, let us mention our work on high-frequency trading (in Lachapelle et al., 2016), This is an MFG model with several populations, including high-frequency traders and institutional investors, and we show various phenomena such as the efficiency of price formation and benefits for the high-frequency traders but not for the other populations.

Bertucci and colleagues (2022, 2024a) studied cryptocurrencies and in particular Bitcoin mining (involving a population of miners) and the proof-of-work consensus algorithm, taking into account various factors such as technological progress. And we obtain various information such as the total computational power devoted to mining the blockchain. Finally, an application of MFG models to mobile telecommunication networks (crowd of devices) has been proposed by Bertucci and colleagues (2018).

6.6 NUMERICAL SIMULATIONS

As mentioned previously, (rigorous) numerical methods have been developed in situations where the Master Equations may be reduced to a finite-dimensional system of equations. But these methods rely on traditional (numerical partial differential equation [PDE] methods) and thus can only be used if the dimension (of the state space) is not large (with three or four at most).

There are currently a few attempts to solve the Master Equation (in infinite dimensions) using (artificial) neural nets. Y. Achdou, J-M. Lasry and the author are currently developing a general method "hybrid-DN2A" (hybrid dynamical neural net algorithms), which combines the computational power of neural nets with our mathematical understanding of MFG equations. In particular, it relies upon the so-called localization principle that results from the Master Equation and can be seen as the extension to populations of the famous optimality principle in the dynamic programming theory, due to R. Bellman (for one agent). Our preliminary results indicate that the method is efficient at least when we expect solutions to have a "low complexity" (regularity or a small number of "hidden/unknown descriptive" variables). It has already provided numerical computations of the Master Equation for the Krusell–Smith model or for Bitcoin mining models (see the previous section).

6.7 A FEW PERSPECTIVES

Let us first indicate a few directions that our group is or will be working on:

- Partial observation/information (shared by all agents) in particular situations where the decision process only involves aggregate quantities known to all agents but the agents do not fully observe the state of the population
- Hierarchy of populations, multilevel populations, graphs of populations (for instance, customers, store managers, headquarters).
- Extending hybrid-DN2A to more complex equilibria, the first step being to consider situations where we expect singularities

This brief list is by no means exhaustive. There are many more challenging and relevant issues to be investigated concerning both the mathematical aspects and the modeling features of MFGs. From a mathematical perspective, let us mention the important issue of what happens when uniqueness is lost and singularities appear (both happen at the same time, as mentioned previously). How can we define solutions globally? What can we say about the set of solutions/equilibria? Can one distinguish between equilibria through additional game rules when encountering singularities? Some answers have been given in very particular examples, but no general theory is available.

From the modeling perspective, many interesting questions have been raised by the participants of the Colloquium. They include the possibility of incorporating in the theory multitime scales in a multipopulation context (note that the Edmond models described previously include a particular case of two time scales) or bounded rationality effects.

6.8 REFERENCES

Y. Achdou, C. Bertucci, J.-M. Lasry, P.-L. Lions, A. Rostand and J. Scheinkman. A class of short-term models for the oil industry that accounts for speculative oil storage. *Finance and Stochastics*, 26(3):631–669, 2022a.

Y. Achdou, F. J. Buera, J.-M. Lasry, P.-L. Lions and B. Moll. Partial differential equation models in macroeconomics. *Philosophical Transactions of the Royal Society A: Mathematical, Physical and Engineering Sciences*, 372(2028):20130397, 2014.

Y. Achdou, J.-M. Lasry and P.-L. Lions. Work in preparation on the Krusell–Smith model. Technical report, 2022b. https://arxiv.org/abs/2211.07698.

S. R. Aiyagari. Uninsured idiosyncratic risk and aggregate saving. *Quarterly Journal of Economics*, 109(3):659–684, 1994.

C. Bertucci. Monotone solutions for mean field games master equations: Finite state space and optimal stopping. *Journal de l'École polytechnique — Mathématiques*, 8:1099–1132, 2021.

C. Bertucci, L. Bertucci, J.-M. Lasry and P.-L. Lions. A mean field game approach to Bitcoin mining. *SIAM Journal on Financial Mathematics*, 15:960–987, 2024a.

C. Bertucci, K. Bertucci, J.-M. Lasry and P.-L. Lions. How resilient is the bitcoin protocol? Technical Report 3907822, University of Paris, Dauphine Research Paper, 2022.

C. Bertucci, J.-M. Lasry, and P.-L. Lions. On Lipschitz solutions of mean field games master equations. *Journal of Functional Analysis*, 287(5):110486, 2024.

C. Bertucci, S. Vassilaras, J.-M. Lasry, G. S. Pascho, M. Debbah and P.-L. Lions. Transmit strategies for massive machine-type communications based on mean field games. In *The 2018 Fifteenth International Symposium on Wireless Communication Systems (ISWCS)*, pp. 1–5, 2018.

P. Cardaliaguet, F. Delarue, J.-M. Lasry and P.-L. Lions. The master equation and the convergence problem in mean field games. Vol. 201 of *Annals of Math Studies*. Princeton, NJ: Princeton University Press, 2019.

R. Carmona and F. Delarue. *Probabilistic Theory of Mean Field Games with Applications I–II*. Springer, Berlin: Springer, 2018.

M. Huggett. The risk-free rate in heterogeneous-agent incomplete-insurance economies. *Journal of Economic Dynamics and Control*, 17(5):953–969, 1993.

P. Krusell and A. Smith Jr. Income and wealth heterogeneity in the macroeconomy. *Journal of Political Economy*, 106(5):867–896, 1998.

A. Lachapelle, J.-M. Lasry, C.-A. Lehalle and P.-L. Lions. Efficiency of the price formation process in presence of high frequency participants: A mean field game analysis. *Mathematics and Financial Economics*, 10(3):223–262, 2016.

J.-M. Lasry and P.-L. Lions. Jeux à champ moyen. i – le cas stationnaire. *Comptes Rendus Mathematique*, 343(9):619–625, 2006a.

J.-M. Lasry and P.-L. Lions. Jeux à champ moyen. ii – horizon fini et contrôle optimal. *Comptes Rendus Mathematique*, 343(10):679–684, 2006b.

J.-M. Lasry and P.-L. Lions. Mean field games. *Japanese Journal of Mathematics*, 2:229–260, 2007.

P.-L. Lions. Courses at College de France (Paris) from 2006 to 2012. Technical report, 2006–2012.

7

Value and Equilibrium

Sylvain Sorin

In this chapter, we compare the two basic concepts of minmax value and equilibrium points in terms of

- definitions, properties and interpretation;
- tools used in the existence proofs; and
- developments and applications, in particular for repeated games.

This will lead us to question the approach asserting the following viewpoint:

- equilibrium as extension of the value paradigm to non-zero-sum games; and
- value as a special case of equilibrium payoff for zero-sum games.

We claim that many important properties apply only to one of these concepts.

7.1 BASIC CONCEPTS

We first recall the framework and definition of these fundamental notions: value and equilibria.

7.1.1 Value

The minmax theorem allows one to evaluate some interactive situations of pure conflict by a *number*: the *value* of the game. Formally a function f from a product set $X \times Y$ to $\mathbb{R}$ defines a *two-person zero-sum game*, with *strategy* set X and *payoff* function f for player 1 (resp. Y and $-f$ for player 2).

The number $\underline{v} = \sup_{x\in X} \inf_{y\in Y} f(x, y)$ is the largest amount that player 1 can guarantee, and similarly $\overline{v} = \inf_{y\in Y} \sup_{x\in X} f(x, y)$ for player 2. The *minmax theorem* gives conditions under which the game has a *value*, v, namely

$$\underline{v} = \overline{v} = v. \tag{7.1}$$

See Borel (1921). In this case, v is a natural and unique evaluation – in the payoff space – of the interaction. Associated notions are the *duality gap*: $\delta = \overline{v} - \underline{v}$ and the *gap function* $\phi(x, y) = \sup_X f(., y) - \inf_Y f(x, .)$.

An equivalent formulation of (7.1) takes the duality form that for any $a \in \mathbb{R}$:

$$\forall y \in Y, \exists x \in X, \quad f(x,y) \geq a \Rightarrow \exists x \in X, \forall y \in Y, \quad f(x,y) \geq a. \qquad (7.2)$$

7.1.2 Equilibria

A Nash equilibrium (Nash, 1950) describes some joint behavior of players in a game exhibiting a robustness property. Consider a *strategic game* G defined by a set I of *players*, a set S^i of *strategies* for each $i \in I$, and a *payoff mapping* g from $S = \Pi_{i=1}^{I} S^i$ to $\mathbb{R}^I$. A *Nash equilibrium* is a profile of strategies $s \in S$ where no player can gain by changing his or her strategy:

$$g^i(t^i, s^{-i}) \leq g^i(s), \quad \forall t^i \in S^i, \quad \forall i \in I. \qquad (7.3)$$

Alternatively, a profile t *eliminates* a profile s if there exists a player $i \in I$ with $g^i(t^i, s^{-i}) > g^i(s)$. Let $E(t) \subset S$ be the set of profiles *not eliminated* by t. An equilibrium is then a profile in $\cap_{t \in S} E(t)$. This formulation is in the spirit of an equilibrium being a "rational" rule of behavior.

The minimal hypotheses used to sustain this concept are as follows:

- s is public knowledge;
- each player i knows his or her best reply correspondence BR^i (where $BR^i(s^{-i}) = \{s^i \in S^i; g^i(s^i, s^{-i}) \geq g^i(t^i, s^{-i}), \forall t^i \in S^i\}$); and
- each player i is rational.

The associated scenario is as follows: a profile s is suggested to all players, and each player i plays the corresponding component s^i if and only if $s^i \in BR^i(s^{-i})$.

At this level, no player knows whether the suggestion s is an equilibrium or not, and no notion of "credible threat" applies since i does not know g^j, for $j \neq i$. This leads to two interpretations (see the discussion by Kuhn et al., 1996). The first one (proposal) is that the only acceptable public proposals are equilibria; the second one (norm) involves a norm of behavior, namely a profile of strategies used repeatedly in the past, under the hypotheses that (1) the history available to the players includes the strategies and is public knowledge and (2) the structure of the interaction is stationary (a repeated game with short-lived players). Note that in this case the players, assuming a rational behavior of their opponents, will deduce that s is an equilibrium.

A related procedure with a dynamical aspect was suggested by Nash in his thesis (Nash, 1950b), under the name "mass action": The players are facing a stationary process (play generated by a population) and can identify their best replies; hence rest points will be equilibria.

The standard hypotheses under which the equilibrium concept is currently used are

- common knowledge of the game parameters; and
- common knowledge of rationality of the players.

The main issue is then a choice of which equilibrium is selected. This interpretation (rational prediction) was also suggested by Nash in his thesis (Nash, 1950b), but he added a uniqueness requirement to justify the play of an equilibrium.

Even in the case of uniqueness, the argument leading to an equilibrium may be problematic. A basic example is the following game from Aumann and Maschler (1972):

	L	R
T	$(2,0)$	$(0,1)$
B	$(0,1)$	$(1,0)$

Here, for both players, equilibrium payoff and value coincide. The only equilibrium is $x^1 = (1/2,1/2), x^2 = (1/3,2/3)$ with payoff $(2/3,1/2)$. For player 1 the minmax strategy $y^1 = (1/3,2/3)$ is also a best reply to x^2, but in addition it guarantees $2/3$. An analogous property holds for player 2, and no strong argument supports the use of x in a one-shot game.
A condition like "unique best reply" is needed to enforce the equilibrium play.

On the other hand, if the players share information on their payoffs, some Nash equilibria are nonjustifiable (see, e.g., Laraki et al., 2019):

	L	R
T	$(0,0)$	$(10,0)$
B	$(1,1)$	$(0,1)$

If player 2 (a dummy player who is indifferent about his or her two actions) knows player 1's payoff and knows that player 1 knows this fact, he will play L (to enforce B) and so the (T,R) equilibrium does not make sense. The only justifiable equilibrium is (B,L).

7.2 TOOLS IN THE EXISTENCE PROOFS

We now briefly describe the different tools used in the existence proofs.

7.2.1 Value

The initial proof of the minmax theorem is due to von Neumann (1928). f is a bilinear function on a product of simplices corresponding to the mixed extension of a game with finitely many choices for each player.

Actually von Neumann shows the existence of a *saddle point* for f, $(x^*,y^*) \in X \times Y$ with

$$f(x,y^*) \leq f(x^*,y^*) \leq f(x^*,y) \quad \forall (x,y) \in X \times Y,$$

with (x^*,y^*) being a fixed point of the best reply correspondence or a zero of the gap function ϕ.

The first proof using the separation property of disjoint convex sets is due to Ville (1938); see von Neumann and Morgenstern, 1944, 3rd ed., 1953, p. 154, n. 1.

7.2.1.1 *Alternative Proofs of the Minmax Theorem*

As already noticed by Kuhn (2003) in his lecture notes from 1953, a large variety of proofs are available, among which are

- induction on the size of the game (see Loomis, 1946);
- the Fourier elimination procedure (in finite dimension) and alternative lemma, along with duality for linear programming;
- separation in $\mathbb{R}^n$ (or more generally projection in Hilbert spaces);
- unilateral procedure in discrete time following Blackwell (1956);
- continuous time dynamics (see Brown and von Neumann, 1951);
- fictitious play in discrete and continuous time (see Brown, 1951; Robinson, 1951);
- replicator dynamics or, more generally, no-regret dynamics (see Hofbauer, 2018).

7.2.1.2 *General Formulation of the Minmax Theorem*

A useful and standard statement of the minmax theorem is the following:

Theorem 7.1 (Sion (1958)). *Let $G = (X, Y, f)$ be a zero-sum game satisfying*

(a) *X and Y are convex subsets of a topological vector space;*
(b) *X or Y is compact;*
(c) *for each y in Y, $f(., y)$ is quasiconcave and upper semicontinuous in x, and for each x in X, $f(x, .)$ is quasiconvex lower semicontinuous in y.*

Then G has a value.

Note that the hypotheses involve geometrical and topological properties on the strategy sets and the payoff function.

An optimal strategy $x^* \in X$ for player 1, which satisfies a unilateral property, namely guaranteeing the value, $f(x^*, y) \geq v, \forall y \in Y$, exists under a compactness assumption on X, and similarly for player 2. The basic tool used in the proof is the Hahn-Banach separation theorem via the intersection lemma; see Berge (1966, p. 172).

7.2.2 Equilibria

The first proof of existence for finite games was provided by Nash (1950); it used the Nash map and Brouwer's fixed-point theorem. A general version is as follows:

Theorem 7.2 (From Nash (1951), Glicksberg (1952), and Fan (1952)). *Let S^i be a compact convex subset of a topological vector space, and g^i be continuous on S and quasiconcave w.r.t. s^i, for all $i \in I$. Then the set of equilibria is compact and nonempty.*

The proof relies on Kakutani's fixed-point property (Kakutani, 1941), applied to the best reply correspondence. Alternatively, equilibria are the zeroes of the Nikaido map,

$$\Phi(s) = \sum_i [\sup_{S^i} g^i(., s^{-i}) - g^i(s)].$$

Notice that again the hypotheses involve geometrical and topological properties on strategy sets and payoff functions. The main difference with Theorem 7.1 is that joint continuity is required.

Conversely, McLennan and Tourky (2005) use the existence of Nash equilibria for two-person finite games to prove Kakutani's fixed-point theorem.

7.3 EXTENSIONS AND APPLICATIONS

7.3.1 Equilibrium

We identify here four different fields where research has been extremely active and productive.

7.3.1.1 Equilibrium Refinement

The literature on this topic, which aims at reducing the equilibrium set, is huge and diverse by its approaches and domains of applications (extensive or normal form games). Let us mention, among others,

- perfect equilibria, see Selten (1975) and Harsanyi and Selten (1988);
- proper equilibria, see Myerson (1978);
- sequential equilibria, see Kreps and Wilson (1982);
- persistent equilibria, see Kalai and Samet (1984);
- stable equilibria, see Kohlberg and Mertens (1986) and Mertens (1989; 1991);
- divine equilibria, see Banks and Sobel (1987);
- essential equilibria, see Govindan and Wilson (2005); and
- the surveys by van Damme (2002) and Hillas and Kohlberg (2002).

A related area analyzes games with signals and the associated notion of conjectural equilibrium (where the information after a play is consistent with the anticipation; see, e.g., Fudenberg and Levine, 1993).

7.3.1.2 *Manifold of Equilibria*

This area corresponds to the study of the graph E of the equilibrium correspondence over the space Γ of games (in the finite case),

$$E = \{(x, G);\ x \text{ equilibrium of } G, G \in \Gamma\},$$

and was introduced by Kohlberg and Mertens (1986). A first property they prove is that E is homeomorphic to Γ.

Define a Nash field Φ as a continuous map from $\Gamma \times S$ to S such that the fixed points of $\Phi(G, .)$ are the equilibria of G. Given a component of equilibria, its index is constant among Nash fields and is equal to the local degree of the projection map from E to Γ; see DeMichelis and Germano (2000; 2002) and also Govindan and Wilson (1997a,b).

7.3.1.3 *Supergames*

This field is devoted to the analysis of the set of equilibria of a repeated game with complete information. Basic results extend the "Folk theorem" asserting that "the set of equilibrium payoffs of the supergame are the feasible individually rational payoffs" to the framework of perfect equilibria; see Aumann and Shapley (1994) and Rubinstein (1994). Then follows a large and important literature involving variations on the payoffs: finite/discounted/uniform, equilibrium selection, games with signals, and various duration of the players. See, for instance, Abreu and colleagues (1990), Fudenberg and Levine (1994), Fudenberg and Maskin (1986), Benoit and Krishna (1985), Sorin (1992), Gossner (1995), and the book by Mailath and Samuelson (2006).

A closely related area studies the impact of perturbation/reputation effects on repeated interactions; see the Kreps et al. (1982) and Aumann and Sorin (1989).

7.3.1.4 *Games with a Large Number of Players: Population and Nonatomic Games*

Extension of Nash equilibria appears in the analysis of congestion modeling involving a crowd of players (Wardrop, 1952) and for general nonatomic games (Schmeidler, 1973; Mas-Colell, 1984). The model of population games is fundamental in biology (Maynard-Smith, 1982), with specific concepts like the Evolutionary Stable Strategy (Taylor and Jonker, 1978).

The basic results in this field can be found in the work of Hofbauer and Sigmund (1998), with a more recent presentation by Sandholm (2011). Let us also mention mean field games that study anonymous differential games with a continuum of players (Lasry and Lions, 2007; see also Chapter 6 in this volume).

7.3.2 Value

We describe here three fields where the analysis in terms of value has been particularly efficient.

7.3.2.1 *Alternative/Dual Statements*

This corresponds to properties that extend statement (7.2). A typical example is the approachability theory of Blackwell (1956) for games with vector payoffs, where f maps $X \times Y$ to $\mathbb{R}^n$. The basic duality takes the form

$$\forall y \in Y, \exists x \in X \quad f(x,y) \in W \Rightarrow \exists x \in X, \forall y \in Y, \quad f(x,y) \in W, \tag{7.4}$$

which is the alternative for half spaces W.

When applied to a repeated game it leads, in the case of a convex domain D, to the duality property: approachability versus excludability. In fact, if player 2 cannot force some set W disjoint from D, player 1 can inductively mimic a viable trajectory that generates a sequence of payoffs such that the average converges to D. In the more general case with signals on the outcomes, necessary and sufficient conditions of this kind for approachability are available (see Perchet, 2011).

7.3.2.2 *Operator Approach and Recursive Formula*

This domain analyzes the extension of the recursive structure for discounted stochastic games introduced by Shapley (1953).

For a general repeated game, the natural state space is given by the consistent probabilities on the universal belief space Ω (Mertens and Zamir, 1985; Mertens et al., 2015). A profile of one-stage strategies defines an information structure, and the signals allow one to compute the transition kernel on this state space Ω.

When the minmax theorem holds, the repeated game G has the same value as an auxiliary game G' where the one-stage strategies are announced. However, in G' a basic recursive formula on the value function as a function on Ω is available (Mertens et al., 2015, theorem IV.3.2).

This tool is fundamental to study asymptotic properties of the value but also regularity aspects and the link between discrete and continuous time approach (the Hamilton–Jacobi equation).

7.3.2.3 *Uniform and Asymptotic Criteria*

The analysis of zero-sum repeated games can be divided into

- an *asymptotic approach* that is concerned with the limit properties of the value function as the (expected) duration of the game goes to infinity, like existence of $\lim v_n$ (an n-stage game) or $\lim v_\lambda$ (a λ-discounted game);

- a *uniform approach* based on robustness properties of strategies in any game with long duration, leading to the notion of uniform maxmin and minmax (where the existence has to be proved), and of uniform value v_∞ when they coincide.

In particular, the existence of a uniform value implies the existence of an asymptotic value and their equality.

7.3.3 Comments

Note that the topics in Section 7.3.1 are trivial or vacuous when applied to the value of zero-sum games. On the other hand, there are no properties equivalent to those in Section 7.3.2 for equilibria of non-zero-sum games.

The viewpoint described in Section 7.3.2.1 is in the spirit of the basic approach of Blackwell and Girshik (1954) and applies as well to calibration procedures (see, e.g., Cesa-Bianchi and Lugosi, 2006, and Section 7.4.2 of this chapter) or to the link between α and β characteristic functions. The minmax theorem is one example of a duality result: expressing a property from two perspectives (achieve or defend an amount).

Section 7.3.2.2 has no counterpart in non-zero-sum games. Strategies have to be specified on (private) histories, not on Ω, and this prevents the emergence of a recursive structure. In addition, the "value operator" exhibits monotonic aspects (with respect to the payoff or the strategy spaces) that are crucial to deducing regularity aspects and analyzing limit behavior. One cannot establish similar properties for equilibria in non-zero-sum games. Also concerning Section 7.3.2.3, there are no analogous results in the non-zero-sum case. See Aumann and Maschler (1995) for incomplete-information games and Sorin (1986) for stochastic games.

7.4 SOME LINKS

We describe here two important connections between equilibrium and value.

7.4.1 Variational Inequalities

The equilibrium condition (7.3) for smooth concave payoff functions takes the form

$$\langle \nabla_i g^i(s), s^i - t^i \rangle \geq 0 \qquad \forall t^i \in S^i, \forall i \in I, \tag{7.5}$$

where $\nabla_i g^i$ denotes the gradient of g^i w.r.t. s^i.

More generally, for a vector field F on a compact convex set Z, one introduces the sets of internal solutions,

$$\langle F(z), z - z' \rangle \geq 0 \quad \forall z' \in Z,$$

and external solutions,

$$\langle F(z'), z - z' \rangle \geq 0 \quad \forall z' \in Z,$$

and for continuous fields the existence of an internal solution is equivalent to the fixed-point theorem, while external solutions may no exist.

The field is dissipative if

$$\langle F(z') - F(z), z - z' \rangle \geq 0 \quad \forall z, z' \in Z.$$

For dissipative continuous fields, there is equivalence between internal and external solutions of variational inequalities, and an existence proof is available via the minmax theorem (Minty, 1967). A basic example corresponds to $F = (\nabla_1 f, -\nabla_2 f)$ for smooth concave/convex zero-sum games (Rockafellar, 1970). This property has fundamental applications in the study of no-regret dynamics (Sorin, 2024).

A complementary perspective on the difference between fixed-point and minmax approaches for variational inequalities is discussed in a recent article by Foster and Hart (2021, sections III.D and VII).

7.4.2 Correlated Equilibria

Correlated equilibria correspond to equilibria of a game extended by an information structure (Aumann, 1974). Hart and Schmeidler (1989) proved existence by identifying the set of correlated equilibrium distributions as the set of optimal strategies in an associated two-person zero-sum game.

In repeated games, several learning procedures based on the no-regret property converge to the set of optimal strategies in zero-sum games (Hannan, 1958). A refinement asking for internal versus external consistency (Hart and Mas-Colell, 2013; Foster and Vohra, 1999) allows one to prove that if every player uses such a procedure, then all accumulation points of the empirical joint distribution of moves are correlated equilibria.

Note that one obtains convergence of the *average behavior* to the set of *correlated equilibria* under a profile of algorithms satisfying a *unilateral property* (equivalent to calibration).

7.5 RESEARCH DIRECTIONS

7.5.1 General Theory of Two-Person Zero-Sum Games

In the spirit of Sections 7.3.2.2 and 7.3.2.3, the aim is to build a comprehensive theory that includes stochastic aspects, incomplete information, and signals (Mertens et al., 2015), and develops the link with differential games and games in continuous time (Laraki and Sorin, 2015).

7.5.2 Equilibria as Solutions of Variational Inequalities

The objective here is to extend and generalize the results of Section 7.3.1.2 to the framework of Section 7.4.1. Games will appear there as special vector fields that decompose in the sense that

$$\langle \phi(z), v \rangle = \sum_{i \in I} \langle \phi^i(z), v^i \rangle, \quad z, v \in Z, \tag{7.6}$$

and the manifold solutions are defined on the vector space $\{\phi(.) + v, v \in Z\}$.

7.5.3 Nash Fields and Dynamic Stability

The analysis of the dynamical system $\dot{s}_t = \Phi(G, s_t)$, Φ being a Nash field, is of utmost importance, especially concerning its asymptotic properties. In particular, one can observe that attractors may not consist of subsets of fixed points (Shapley, 1964). The link with discrete time-related dynamics is also of interest, in the spirit of Benaïm and colleagues (2005; 2006).

7.6 SUMMARY

To summarize, it appears that value and equilibria are quite different concepts with specific properties and fields of application. They correspond to two approaches that are complementary and cannot be reduced to each other.

A typical example is the uniform approach for zero-sum games with lack of information on one side: an optimal strategy of the informed player is the celebrated splitting strategy, while an optimal strategy of the uninformed player relies on the approachability of an orthant. These are unilateral guarantees rather than equilibrium properties.

On the other hand, there are similar aspects of zero-sum games and certain classes of non-zero-sum games, mainly potential games (Monderer and Shapley, 1996) or dissipative games, in particular in terms of learning dynamics.

7.7 REFERENCES

D. Abreu, D. Pearce, and E. Stacchetti. Toward a theory of discounted repeated games with imperfect monitoring. *Econometrica*, 58(5):1041–1063, 1990.

R. J. Aumann. Subjectivity and correlation in randomized strategies. *Journal of Mathematical Economics*, 1(1):67–96, 1974.

R. J. Aumann and M. Maschler. Some thoughts on the minimax principle. *Management Science*, 18(5):P54–P63, 1972.

R. J. Aumann and M. Maschler. *Repeated Games with Incomplete Information*. Cambridge, MA: MIT Press, 1995.

R. J. Aumann and L. S. Shapley. Long-term competition – a game-theoretic analysis. In N. Megiddo, ed., *Essays in Game Theory: In Honor of Michael Maschler*, pp. 1–15. New York: Springer, 1994.

R. J. Aumann and S. Sorin. Cooperation and bounded recall. *Games and Economic Behavior*, 1(1):5–39, 1989.
J. S. Banks and J. Sobel. Equilibrium selection in signaling games. *Econometrica*, 55(3):647–661, 1987.
M. Benaïm, J. Hofbauer, and S. Sorin. Stochastic approximations and differential inclusions. *SIAM Journal on Control and Optimization*, 44(1):328–348, 2005.
M. Benaïm, J. Hofbauer, and S. Sorin. Stochastic approximations and differential inclusions, Part II: Applications. *Mathematics of Operations Research*, 31(4):673–695, 2006.
J.-P. Benoit and V. Krishna. Finitely repeated games. *Econometrica*, 53(4):905–922, 1985.
C. Berge. *Espaces Topologiques, Fonctions Multivoques*. Paris: Dunod, 1966.
D. Blackwell. An analog of the minimax theorem for vector payoffs. *Pacific Journal of Mathematics*, 6(1):1–8, 1956.
D. Blackwell and M. Girshik. *Theory of Games and Statistical Decisions*. New York: Wiley, 1954.
E. Borel. La théorie du jeu et les équations intégrales à noyau symétrique gauche. *C.R.A.S.*, 173:1304–1308, 1921.
G. W. Brown. Iterative solution of games by fictitious play. In T. C. Koopmans, ed., *Activity Analysis of Production and Allocation*. New York: Wiley, 1951.
G. W. Brown and J. von Neumann. Solutions of games by differential equations. In H. Kuhn and A. Tucker, eds., *Contributions to the Theory of Games (AM-24), Vol. I*, pp. 73–80. Princeton, NJ: Princeton University Press, 1951.
N. Cesa-Bianchi and G. Lugosi. *Prediction, Learning, and Games*. Cambridge: Cambridge University Press, 2006.
S. DeMichelis and F. Germano. On the indices of zeros of Nash fields. *Journal of Economic Theory*, 94(2):192–217, 2000.
S. DeMichelis and F. Germano. On (un)knots and dynamics in games. *Games and Economic Behavior*, 41(1):46–60, 2002.
K. Fan. Fixed-point and minimax theorems in locally convex topological linear spaces. *Proceedings of the National Academy of Sciences*, 38(2):121–126, 1952.
D. P. Foster and R. Vohra. Regret in the on-line decision problem. *Games and Economic Behavior*, 29(1):7–35, 1999.
D. Foster and S. Hart. Forecast hedging and calibration. *Journal of Political Economy*, 129(12):3447–3490, 2021.
D. Fudenberg and D. K. Levine. Steady state learning and Nash equilibrium. *Econometrica*, 61(3):547–573, 1993.
D. Fudenberg and D. K. Levine. Efficiency and observability with long-run and short-run players. *Journal of Economic Theory*, 62(1):103–135, 1994.
D. Fudenberg and E. Maskin. The folk theorem in repeated games with discounting or with incomplete information. *Econometrica*, 54(3):533–554, 1986.
I. L. Glicksberg. A further generalization of the Kakutani fixed point theorem, with application to Nash equilibrium points. *Proceedings of the American Mathematical Society*, 3(1):170–174, 1952.
O. Gossner. The folk theorem for finitely repeated games with mixed strategies. *International Journal of Game Theory*, 24:95–107, 1995.
S. Govindan and R. Wilson. Equivalence and invariance of the index and degree of Nash equilibria. *Games and Economic Behavior*, 21(1):56–61, 1997a.

S. Govindan and R. Wilson. Uniqueness of the index for Nash equilibria of two-player games. *Economic Theory*, 10:541–549, 1997b.

S. Govindan and R. Wilson. Essential equilibria. *Proceedings of the National Academy of Sciences*, 102(43):15706–15711, 2005.

J. Hannan. Approximation to Bayes risk in repeated plays. In M. Dresher, A. W. Tucker, and P. Wolfe, eds., *Contributions to the Theory of Games (AM-39), Vol. III*, pp. 97–140. Princeton, NJ: Princeton University Press, 1958.

J. Harsanyi and R. Selten. *A General Theory of Equilibrium Selection in Games*. Cambridge, MA: MIT Press, 1988.

S. Hart and A. Mas-Colell. *Simple Adaptive Strategies: From Regret-Matching to Uncoupled Dynamics*. Singapore: World Scientific Publishing, 2013.

S. Hart and D. Schmeidler. Existence of correlated equilibria. *Mathematics of Operations Research*, 14(1):18–25, 1989.

J. Hofbauer Minmax via replicator dynamics. *Dyn. Games Appl.*, 8:637–640, 2018.

J. Hillas and E. Kohlberg. Foundations of strategic equilibrium. In R. Aumann and S. Hart, eds., *Handbook of Game Theory with Economic Applications*, vol. 3, ch. 42, pp. 1597–1663. Amsterdam: Elsevier, 2002.

J. Hofbauer and K. Sigmund. *Evolutionary Games and Population Dynamics*. Cambridge: Cambridge University Press, 1998.

S. Kakutani. A generalization of Brouwer fixed point theorem. *Duke Mathematical Journal*, 8(3):457–459, 1941.

E. Kalai and D. Samet. Persistent equilibria in strategic games. *International Journal of Game Theory*, 8:129–144, 1984.

E. Kohlberg and J.-F. Mertens. On the strategic stability of equilibria. *Econometrica*, 54(5):1003–1037, 1986.

D. M. Kreps, P. Milgrom, J. Roberts, and R. Wilson. Rational cooperation in the finitely repeated prisoners' dilemma. *Journal of Economic Theory*, 27(2):245–252, 1982.

D. M. Kreps and R. Wilson. Sequential equilibria. *Econometrica*, 50(4):863–894, 1982.

H. Kuhn, J. Harsanyi, R. Selten, J. Weibull, E. van Damme, J. F. Nash, and P. Hammerstein. The work of John Nash in game theory. *Journal of Economic Theory*, 69:153–185, 1996.

H. M. Kuhn. Lectures on the theory of games. Vol. 37 of *Annals of Mathematics Studies*. Princeton, NJ: Princeton University Press, 2003.

R. Laraki, J. Renault, and S. Sorin. *Mathematical Foundations of Game Theory*. New York: Springer, 2019.

R. Laraki and S. Sorin. Advances in zero-sum dynamic games. In P. Young and S. Zamir, eds., Handbook of Game Theory, vol. IV, ch. 2, pp. 27-93. Amsterdam: Elsevier, 2015.

J.-M. Lasry and P.-L. Lions. Mean field games. *Japanese Journal of Mathematics*, 2:229–260, 2007.

L. H. Loomis. On a theorem of von Neumann. *Proceedings of the National Academy of Sciences*, 32(8):213–215, 1946.

G. J. Mailath and L. Samuelson. *Repeated Games and Reputations: Long-Run Relationships*. Oxford: Oxford University Press, 2006.

A. Mas-Colell. On a theorem of Schmeidler. *Journal of Mathematical Economics*, 13(3):201–206, 1984.

A. McLennan and R. Tourky. From imitation games to Kakutani. Technical report, Department of Economics, University of Pennsylvania, 2005.

J.-F. Mertens. Stable equilibria: A reformulation. Part I. Definitions and basic properties. *Mathematics of Operations Research*, 14(4):575–625, 1989.

J.-F. Mertens. Stable equilibria: A reformulation. Part II. Discussion of the definition, and further results. *Mathematics of Operations Research*, 16(4):694–753, 1991.

J.-F. Mertens, S. Sorin, and S. Zamir. *Repeated Games*. New York: Cambridge University Press 2015.

J.-F. Mertens and S. Zamir. Formulation of Bayesian analysis for games with incomplete information. *International Journal of Game Theory*, 14:1–29, 1985.

G. J. Minty. On the generalization of a direct method of the calculus of variations. *Bulletin of the American Mathematical Society*, 73(3):315–321, 1967.

D. Monderer and L. S. Shapley. Potential games. *Games and Economic Behavior*, 14(1):124–143, 1996.

R. Myerson. Refinements of the Nash equilibrium concept. *International Journal of Game Theory*, 7:73–80, 1978.

J. Nash. Non-cooperative games. *Annals of Mathematics*, 54(2):286–295, 1951.

J. F. Nash. Equilibrium points in *N*-person games. *Proceedings of the National Academy of Sciences*, 36(1):48–49, 1950a.

J. F. Nash. Non cooperative games. Technical report, PhD thesis, Princeton University, 1950b.

V. Perchet. Approachability of convex sets in games with partial monitoring. *Journal of Optimization Theory and Applications*, 149:665–677, 2011.

J. Robinson. An iterative method of solving a game. *Annals of Mathematics*, 54(2):296–301, 1951.

R. Rockafellar. Monotone operators associated with saddle-functions and minmax problems. In F. Browder, ed., *Nonlinear Functional Analysis*, vol. 18 of *Proceedings of Symposia in Pure Math*, pp. 241–250. Providence, RI: American Mathematical Society, 1970.

A. Rubinstein. Equilibrium in supergames. In N. Megiddo, ed., *Essays in Game Theory: In Honor of Michael Maschler*, pp. 17–28. New York: Springer, 1994.

W. Sandholm. *Population Games and Evolutionary Dynamics*. Cambridge, MA: MIT Press, 2011.

D. Schmeidler. Equilibrium points of nonatomic games. *J. Stat. Phys.*, 7:295–300, 1973.

R. Selten. Re-examination of the perfectness concept for equilibrium points in extensive games. *International Journal of Game Theory*, 4:25–55, 1975.

L. S. Shapley. Stochastic games. *Proceedings of the National Academy of Sciences*, 39(10):1095–1100, 1953.

L. S. Shapley. Some topics in two-person games. In M. Dresher, L. Shapley, and A. W. Tucker, eds., *Advances in Game Theory*, vol. 52 of *Annals of Mathematical Studies*, pp. 1–28. Princeton, NJ: Princeton University Press, 1970.

M. Sion. On general minimax theorems. *Pacific Journal of Mathematics*, 8(1):171–176, 1958.

Maynard Smith. *Evolution and the Theory of Games*. Cambridge: Cambridge University Press, 1982.

S. Sorin. Asymptotic properties of a non-zero-sum stochastic game. *International Journal of Game Theory*, 15:101–107, 1986.

S. Sorin. Repeated games with complete information. In R. Aumann and S. Hart, eds., *Handbook of Game Theory with Economic Applications*, vol. 1, ch. 4, pp. 71–107. Amsterdam: Elsevier, 1992.

S. Sorin. No-regret algorithms in on-line learning, games and convex optimization. *Mathematical Programming, Series B*, 203:645–686, 2024.

P. D. Taylor and L. B. Jonker. Evolutionary stable strategies and game dynamics. *Mathematical Biosciences*, 40(1):145–156, 1978.

E. van Damme. Strategic equilibrium. In R. Aumann and S. Hart, eds., *Handbook of Game Theory with Economic Applications*, vol. 3, ch. 41, pp. 1521–1596. Amsterdam: Elsevier, Elsevier, 2002.

J. Ville. Sur la théorie générale des jeux où intervient l'habileté des joueurs. In É. Borel, ed., *Traité du Calcul des Probabilités et de ses Applications IV*, pp. 105–113. Paris: Gauthier-Villars, 1938.

J. von Neumann. Zur Theorie des Gesellschaftsspiele *Math. Ann.*, 100:295–320, 1928.

J. von Neumann and O. Morgenstern. *Theory of Games and Economic Behavior*. Princeton, NJ: Princeton University Press, 1944.

G. Wardrop. Some theoretical aspects of road traffic research. *Proc. Inst. Civ. Eng.*, 1:325–362, 1952.

8

Refinements of Nash Equilibrium

Robert Wilson

This volume celebrates 100 years of game theory since the seminal article by Émile Borel (1921), and arrives 80 years after a formal mathematical apparatus of game theory was proposed by von Neumann and Morgenstern (1944). Their book was soon followed by the basic definition of equilibrium proposed by John Nash (1950). Nash's criterion for equilibrium has been the primary tool for predicting strategies and outcomes of games with rational players.

But Nash equilibrium is a weak criterion for games with dynamic interactions and/or private information among the players. Stronger criteria called *equilibrium refinements* are intended to remedy deficiencies that stem from these features. Kohlberg and Mertens (1986) and Hillas and Kohlberg (2002) discuss the motives for refinements.

After a summary of the main refinements, this chapter reports progress on characterizing the strongest refinement, called stability, via axioms that express basic properties of rational behavior.[1]

8.1 OVERVIEW OF REFINEMENTS

The main refinements divide into those that select isolated equilibria and those that select connected subsets of equilibria. First we describe the main single-valued refinements.

Refinements in this group exclude Nash equilibria that violate principles of decision theory. For extensive-form games with perfect recall, subgame perfect and sequential equilibria enforce the principle of backward induction, as in dynamic programming, and Bayes' rule of conditional probability. Sequential equilibrium can be strengthened further to ensure forward induction, which requires that at each information set the player acting there assigns positive probability only to other players' optimal strategies (if any) that reach this information set. A consistency condition for players' probability assessments

[1] I am deeply grateful to Srihari Govindan for decades of joint work, including on the topics in this chapter.

requires further that they are limits of conditional probabilities implied by perturbed strategies that can reach any part of the game tree. The weaker version, called *perfect-Bayesian equilibrium*, omits consistency at the risk of violating subgame perfection.

Other refinements enforce the principle of admissibility, which excludes use of weakly dominated strategies, and conditional admissibility, which requires admissibility of continuations from information sets. Even stronger is the iteration of admissibility as dominated strategies are excluded. In increasing strength, the main refinements in this group are perfect, quasiperfect, and proper equilibria. Each obtains a corresponding version of admissibility by requiring that an equilibrium of the given game is the limit of selected equilibria for a sequence, converging to the given game, of nearby games obtained by perturbing players' strategies toward some mixed strategy. Thus each requires that, for *some* sequence of perturbations, the limit and equilibrium operations commute.

These two approaches are related. If players' payoffs are generic, then iterated admissibility implies subgame perfection. A quasiperfect equilibrium is sequential, and a proper equilibrium of the normal form induces a sequential equilibrium of every extensive form with that normal form.

But single-valued refinements are inherently limited. Examples show that admissibility and iterated elimination of dominated strategies can be inconsistent, and a sequential equilibrium can be inconsistent with invariance to deletion of redundant strategies. This suggests that a refinement should select a set of equilibria, provided the set is connected and includes equilibria selected by single-valued refinements. Set-valued refinements are especially relevant when extensive-form payoffs are generic, since then all equilibria in a component yield the same outcome – that is, same distribution over terminal nodes of the game tree.

Set-valued refinements aim for more stringent selections. One might want a 'truly perfect' equilibrium, in that it is the limit of equilibria for *every* shrinking sequence of strategy perturbations. For a set-valued refinement, the analog is that every nearby game has a nearby equilibrium, where a game is nearby if all strategies are perturbed toward mixed strategies.[2] Geometrically, this requires a neighborhood of the origin in the space of perturbations of players' strategies to be the projection of a connected neighborhood of the selected set in the graph of the equilibrium correspondence over this space of perturbations. However, an example shows that this is insufficient if one wants a selected set to include an equilibrium satisfying backward induction, such as a sequential equilibrium.

To remedy this deficiency, Jean-François Mertens (1989; 1991) defined a *stable* set of equilibria by adding the requirement that the topological degree of

[2] As shown by Govindan and Wilson (2005), with payoff perturbations the analog of truly perfect is an essential component of the Nash equilibria (i.e., its topological index is nonzero), but this is too weak a refinement because an essential component can include inadmissible equilibria.

the projection map is not zero.[3] This implies that a selected set is *strategically stable* in that it is truly perfect and, due to Mertens' added requirement of non-zero-degree, includes a proper equilibrium that induces a sequential equilibrium of every extensive form with the same normal form.

Moreover, stable sets satisfy all the desirable structural properties that have been proposed (cf. Hillas and Kohlberg, 2002). *Admissibility, conditional admissibility*, and *iterated admissibility* that exclude weakly dominated strategies are all satisfied. *Invariance* requires exclusion of equilibria that depend on using pure strategies that are redundant in that all players' payoffs are replicated by some other (possibly mixed) strategy. Because invariance implies dependence only on the "reduced" normal form of the game obtained by excluding redundant strategies, it requires inclusion of an equilibrium for every extensive form with that reduced normal form. *Forward induction* is satisfied by invariant sequential equilibria. *Decomposition* requires that the refinement of the equilibria of a game that consists of two independent games should consist of the refinements of the two constituent games. *Small worlds* requires that a refinement should be not be affected by adding other players whose presence and actions are irrelevant for the players in the original game. *Player splitting* requires that a refinement not be affected by splitting a player into agents such that no path through the game includes actions of two agents. *Ordinality* is essentially the requirement that, like Nash equilibria, a refinement should depend only on players' best-reply correspondences.

These properties suggest that stable sets are a nearly complete solution to the problem of refining Nash equilibrium and thus close to an ultimate expression of the implications of rationality in multiplayer games. However, the purely mathematical definition of a stable set has been a major impediment to its adoption in the social sciences. Refinements that select stable sets need to be justified by the properties of rational behavior that imply it.

8.2 AXIOMS FOR STABILITY

We now describe axioms that are properties of refinements that select stable sets and, conversely for extensive-form games with perfect recall and generic payoffs, *imply* that a selected set is stable. These results were proved for two-player games by Govindan and Wilson (2012) using axioms A, B, and C, and using axiom D, extended to more players by Govindan and Wilson (2025).

The first two axioms invoke properties of equilibria selected by single-valued refinements using criteria from individual decision theory.

[3] When the dimensions of the domain and range are equal, this can be loosely stated as requiring that the projection map cannot be deformed to one that is not surjective while still surjective onto the boundary of the neighborhood. Equivalently, the projection map has a point of coincidence, with every continuous map having the same domain and range. This assures the existence of a fixed point that is a proper equilibrium. Finding or verifying that a set of equilibria is stable is a nontrivial computational problem that we do not address here. See Wilson (1992) for a partial solution.

A. Admissible strategies. This first axiom requires that for each equilibrium in a set selected by a refinement, no player uses a weakly dominated strategy.

B. Backward induction. This axiom requires that some equilibrium in a set selected by a refinement is consistent with backward induction by each player. One could require only a sequential equilibrium, but to be consistent with axiom A, one insists on a quasiperfect equilibrium, which for each player at each information specifies an admissible continuation strategy. Although this is a single equilibrium, genericity of payoffs implies that all other equilibria in the same component of equilibria have the same outcome.

The last two axioms state properties of Nash equilibria that are inherited by stable sets of Nash equilibria. Each specifies how a given game G can be embedded within a class of "larger" games that can have more strategies and players. Each invokes a projection map π that translates strategies in the larger game $\tilde{G}$ to strategies in G. The axiom requires that if E is the operation of computing an equilibrium, then π and E commute ($E \circ \pi = \pi \circ E$), which says that the selected sets of equilibria of $\tilde{G}$ translate to selected sets of equilibria of G. Implications of these commutative properties of Nash equilibria, now applied to selected sets of Nash equilibria, dispense with consideration of perturbed games and instead require consistency between a refinement's selection for the given game G and its selections for larger games $\tilde{G}$ in which G is embedded. Definitions of the two classes of larger games are deferred until after the statements of the axioms.

C. Invariance to embedding. This stronger version of small worlds excludes framing effects. It does so by requiring that the set selected for a larger game in which the given game is embedded translates to the set selected for the given game.

D. Independence of irrelevant alternatives. This variant of admissibility requires that the set selected for a game that is larger by giving a player an additional strategy, strictly dominated for him or her, translates to the set selected for the original game.

For the class of games in extensive form with perfect recall and generic payoffs, these four axioms imply that a set of equilibria selected by a refinement is a stable set. Moreover, this stable set is a component of the Nash equilibria in admissible strategies that contains a proper equilibrium, which induces a sequential equilibrium satisfying forward induction for every extensive form with the same normal form.

This characterization of stable sets of equilibria invokes the general principle that a refinement of Nash equilibrium should inherit the basic structural properties of Nash equilibrium. One might insist on inheritance of structural properties other than axioms C and D, but these suffice for the class of games assumed here.

Axioms A and B are about each player's behavior, in that each avoids weakly dominated strategies and each uses strategies consistent with dynamic optimization. Axioms C and D are cast as statements of collective behavior, but in each case they are implemented by individual behaviors. Axioms C and D are obtained when each player is immune to framing effects and the addition of strictly dominated strategies for other players.

We now specify axioms C and D in detail.

8.2.1 Axiom C: Invariance to Embedding

A game G is *embedded* in a game $\tilde{G}$ with the same players as in G (called insiders) and possibly other players (called outsiders), if two conditions are met for each insider:

(1) There is a one-to-one relation, independent of outsiders' strategies, between a subset of his or her pure strategies in $\tilde{G}$ and his or her pure strategies in G.
(2) His or her payoff from a profile of all players' pure strategies in $\tilde{G}$ is the same as his or her payoff in G from the insiders' corresponding pure strategies in G.

Axiom C asserts that if G is embedded in $\tilde{G}$, then a selected set of equilibria of G is the same as the translation via (1) of the selected set of equilibria of $\tilde{G}$.

The behavioral implication of axiom C is that because translates of an insider's pure strategies are still available when outsiders are present, and their payoffs are the same (independent of outsiders' actions), his or her rational behavior in the two games should be the same after filtering out noise from outsiders' behaviors observed by insiders. A subtle aspect is that an insider's pure strategy in $\tilde{G}$ that is not translated by (1) to a pure strategy in G translates to a payoff-equivalent mixed strategy in G because outsiders' actions in $\tilde{G}$ provide implicit randomization, as viewed in G. Thus a mixed strategy in G might be implemented by a pure strategy in $\tilde{G}$ that conditions on observations of outsiders' actions.

8.2.2 Axiom D: Independence of Irrelevant Alternatives

In this case, the game $\tilde{G}$ is obtained from G by adding *strictly* dominated strategies for some players. Thus, for each player, his or her simplex Σ of mixed strategies in G is a face of his or her simplex $\tilde{\Sigma}$ of mixed strategies in $\tilde{G}$, and a mixed strategy $\tilde{\sigma} \in \tilde{\Sigma}$ can be translated to the mixed strategy $\sigma \in \Sigma$ that is $\tilde{\sigma}$ conditional on no added dominated strategy actually being used. In its weakest version, the axiom is applied only to cases in which players' best replies are not affected by others' use of added dominated strategies with sufficiently small probabilities:

(*) Players' best replies in $\tilde{G}$ are the same as their best replies to their best replies in G when the added dominated strategies are used with sufficiently small probabilities.[4]

This condition limits the effect of an added strictly dominated strategy of one player on the best replies of other players. Axiom D asserts that if $\tilde{G}$ is obtained from G by adding strictly dominated strategies for some players, then a selected set of equilibria of $\tilde{G}$ projects to a selected set of equilibria of G.

The behavioral implication of axiom D is that each player expects dominated strategies to not be used, and even if they are used with small probabilities, then there is no effect on his or her best-reply strategies.

The gist of the mathematical argument for selecting stable sets is that because they are allowed to be sets of equilibria rather than singletons, they can be selected to be truly perfect and satisfy all the desired structural properties, and because of the non-zero-degree condition, they contain equilibria that satisfy backward and forward induction in every extensive form with the same normal form. The role of the axioms is to show that the mathematical definition of a stable set is implied by rational behavior of each player individually. This provides some justification for using stable sets in social science applications.

8.3 EXTENSIONS

The characterization reported herein is an initial step toward a full axiomatic development. Its extension will depend on progress with two basic mathematical problems. (1) Extensions to games with nongeneric payoffs are challenging because the space of perturbations of strategies need not have the same dimension as the neighborhood of the selected set in the graph of equilibria. (2) Hillas and Kvasov (2020) provide natural extensions of sequential equilibrium and other refinements to games with imperfect recall, but these extensions require strategy spaces larger than the space of behavioral strategies.

8.3.1 Infinitely Repeated Games

The previous discussion pertains to games with finite sets of strategies. The many "folk theorems" for games that are infinite repetitions of a stage game show that nearly any outcome can result from Nash equilibria, which suggests that refinements are needed to narrow predictions.

Govindan and Wilson (2011) suggest a method for refinements of the Nash equilibria of infinitely repeated games: One invokes a refinement for finite approximations of the infinite game and then identifies a refinement of the infinitely repeated game as the limit of the refined equilibria of its finite approximations. For example, if perfect recall is replaced by finite recall, then each

4 The strongest version omits condition (*), and then the refinement that selects all essential components of equilibria satisfies axiom D.

infinite path of play eventually cycles, which enables standard refinements to be applied, such as subgame perfection. In the repeated prisoners' dilemmas, with alternating moves, generic stage-game payoffs, and payoffs that are the average of stage-game payoffs on each path of play, finite recalls imply that each subgame has a unique payoff distinct from its subgame-perfect equilibria, so the limits of equilibria as the recalls increase refine the folk theorem.

A related result by Binmore and Samuelson (1992) shows that when players' strategies must be implemented by finite automata, the refinement that selects evolutionarily stable equilibria yields cooperative outcomes.

8.3.2 Learning in Repeated Games with Random Matching

We focus here on strategic stability and do not address criteria for dynamic stability of steady states of learning processes, nor other dynamic adjustment processes. A different perspective is provided in Chapter 22 in this volume, by Drew Fudenberg, who reports results about models of a large renewing population of players who are randomly matched repeatedly to play a stage game. Starting from a prior about the distribution of others' behaviors, but naively assuming it is constant, each player learns by optimally experimenting via his or her own strategies. As players' expected lifetimes grow, and they become more patient, their behaviors converge to a steady state. If the prior is diffuse, then such a steady state is a Nash equilibrium of the stage game and is called *patiently stable*. Thus at a patiently stable steady state, each player solves the statistical decision problem of identifying the limiting distribution of others' behaviors. This distribution need not satisfy backward induction for the stage game because experimentation far from the equilibrium path of play need not be sufficient to discover all opportunities; also, strategies that are dominated in the stage game can be used for experimentation in the dynamic game. This suggests a refinement of patiently stable equilibria in which players invoke rational behavior to restrict the supports of their priors, so that if steady states still exist, then they inherit some features of the refinements discussed in this chapter.

8.3.3 Nonrational Theories

Axioms A and B, admissibility and backward induction, have been criticized by Gul (1996), among others, who argue that common knowledge of rationality cannot be sustained at every information set (but common belief can be; cf. Feinberg, 2005). Axiom D, invariance to the addition of strictly dominated strategies, is not controversial. Axiom C, invariance to embedding, is vulnerable to criticism based on experimental and empirical studies in cognitive psychology (e.g., Kahneman, 2003) that emphasize the prevalence of framing effects. Because the chief effect observed in experiments is dependence on the player's perceived status quo or other reference point, a more descriptive behavioral analog of game theory could allow such preferences for some possible types of each player, akin to the way irrational types are modeled in game-theoretic studies of reputation in Kreps and Wilson (1982). Nevertheless, axiom C cannot be valid for rational types, because the frame created by an embedding alters the behavior of the frame-sensitive types.[5]

8.4 DISCUSSION

Game theory originated in the study of strategic behavior. It predicts social outcomes from agents' common knowledge of the game and of their rational behavior. With these (perhaps rare) ingredients, it is a conceptual framework for studies of what individual rationality might imply about social interactions. Refinements attempt to sharpen predictions derived from Nash equilibria by imposing more stringent conditions. Axiomatic characterization of the strongest refinement, stability, clarifies what rationality might entail. As yet it has not received an epistemic formulation based on common knowledge, nor on common belief (i.e., with no truth axiom), as in Feinberg (2005), which has been done for weaker refinements like backward induction.

A persistent issue is whether refinement is more than a philosophical exercise, since there is scant evidence that the stronger refinements are more accurate predictors in practice and ample evidence of behavioral departures from elementary decision theory. Even as a philosophical exercise, is refinement necessary? Kohlberg and Mertens (1986) and Hillas and Kohlberg (2002) argue at length, illustrated with many examples, that the seven structural properties listed in Section 8.2 are necessary to have a coherent theory of rational behavior.

Axiom C adds another perspective. Because it is satisfied by Nash equilibria, the issue is whether axiom C should be imposed on a refinement of Nash equilibrium. Without axiom C, equilibria of iterated embeddings of the original game G (i.e., of the games obtained from G after multiple consecutive embeddings) can translate to all equilibria of the original game G. Thus a refinement needs to inherit the "invariance to embedding" property of Nash equilibria if it is to yield sharper predictions than the Nash equilibrium. Further, axiom C is perhaps an intrinsic aspect of rationality because otherwise "rationality" allows players to have frame-sensitive preferences, as discussed in Section 8.3.3, contrary to standard decision theory.

Game-theoretic models have been useful tools for studying the implications of agents' rationality in social interactions. But such models are merely test beds for predicting strategic behaviors. They give only rough guidance for practical design of institutions and markets. These emerging "engineering" disciplines need more codified translations from theory to practice than can be achieved by the present reliance on scattered experimental and empirical evidence, as outlined by Roth and Wilson (2019).

[5] Gul and Pesendorfer (2006) show for one model of reference-dependent preferences that repeated reframing can violate the transitivity of preferences.

8.5 REFERENCES

K. G. Binmore and L. Samuelson. Evolutionary stability in repeated games played by finite automata. *Journal of Economic Theory*, 57(2):278–305, 1992.

E. Borel. La théorie du jeu et les équations intégrales à noyau symétrique gauche. *C.R.A.S.*, 173:1304–1308, 1921.

Y. Feinberg. Subjective reasoning – dynamic games. *Games and Economic Behavior*, 52(1):54–93, 2005.

S. Govindan and R. Wilson. Essential equilibria. *Proceedings of the National Academy of Sciences*, 102(43):15706–15711, 2005.

S. Govindan and R. Wilson. Uniqueness of payoffs from subgame perfect equilibria of the reciprocity game. Technical report, University of Rochester, 2011.

S. Govindan and R. Wilson. Axiomatic equilibrium selection for generic two-player games. *Econometrica*, 80(4):1639–1699, 2012.

S. Govindan and R. B. Wilson. Axiomatic equilibrium selection: The case of generic extensive form games. 2025. https://doi.org/10.48550/arXiv.2504.16908.

F. Gul. Rationality and coherent theories of strategic behavior. *Journal of Economic Theory*, 70(1):1–31, 1996.

F. Gul and W. Pesendorfer. The revealed preference implications of reference dependent preferences. Technical report, Princeton University, 2006.

J. Hillas and E. Kohlberg. Foundations of strategic equilibrium. In R. Aumann and S. Hart, eds., *Handbook of Game Theory with Economic Applications*, vol. 3, ch. 42, pp. 1597–1663. Amsterdam: Elsevier, 2002.

J. Hillas and D. Kvasov. Backward induction in games without perfect recall. *Games and Economic Behavior*, 124:207–218, 2020.

D. Kahneman. Maps of bounded rationality: Psychology for behavioral economics. *American Economic Review*, 93(5):1449–1475, 2003.

E. Kohlberg and J.-F. Mertens. On the strategic stability of equilibria. *Econometrica*, 54(5):1003–1037, 1986.

D. M. Kreps and R. Wilson. Sequential equilibria. *Econometrica*, 50(4):863–894, 1982.

J.-F. Mertens. Stable equilibria: A reformulation. Part I. Definition and basic properties. *Mathematics of Operations Research*, 14(4):575–625, 1989.

J.-F. Mertens. Stable equilibria: A reformulation. Part II. Discussion of the definition, and further results. *Mathematics of Operations Research*, 16(4):694–753, 1991.

J. F. Nash. Equilibrium points in *N*-person games. *Proceedings of the National Academy of Sciences*, 36(1):48–49, 1950.

A. E. Roth and R. B. Wilson. How market design emerged from game theory: A mutual interview. *Journal of Economic Perspectives*, 33(3):118–43, August 2019.

J. von Neumann and O. Morgenstern. *Theory of Games and Economic Behavior*. Princeton, NJ: Princeton University Press, 1944.

R. Wilson. Computing simply stable equilibria. *Econometrica*, 60(5):1039–1070, 1992.

PART III

POPULATION DYNAMICS, LEARNING, AND BIOLOGY

9

Introduction to Part III

Lawrence Blume

The three chapters in this part, by Michihiro Kandori, Olof Leimar, and Karl Sigmund, discuss biology and population dynamics in game theory. The chapters concern models of strategy adaptation – process models. Such models have refined our understanding of Nash and other equilibrium concepts, and the evolution of population shares through time is itself an object of interest from the perspectives of biological reproduction and learning human (and artificial) agents.

Dynamics came early to the analytical development of game theory. Brown and von Neumann (1950) used a dynamic model to demonstrate the existence of a value for finite zero-sum games. Nash (1951) used a discrete-time version of the same dynamic to demonstrate the existence of a (Nash) equilibrium point. Nash reports that this proof is a "considerable improvement over [the PNAS 1950] version and is based directly on the Brouwer theorem."[1]

Fictitious play, introduced by Brown (1949) and analyzed by Robinson (1951), was conceived as an algorithm for finding the value of two-person zero-sum games. Today we read it as an early learning model. Nash may have had a population version of fictitious play in mind when he wrote about the "mass action" interpretation of equilibrium: "To assume, as we did, that [the participants] accumulated empirical evidence on the pure strategies at their disposal is to assume that those playing in position i learn the numbers $p_{i\alpha}(s)$."[2]

Although the purpose of these dynamical systems was to shed light on static equilibrium concepts, concerns with process were important in the prehistory of game theory through the present day. In economic analysis, the most well-known early discussions of equilibration processes is Cournot's (1838) discussion of best-response dynamics and Edgeworth's (1881) recontracting process, from which developed the core of a cooperative game. Similarly, evolutionary game theory has a prehistory in the work on frequency-dependent

[1] The Brown–von Neumann–Nash (BNN) idea traveled beyond game theory. Using the BNN formalism as a price adjustment process, Nikaido (1959) proved the existence of competitive equilibrium in an excess-demand based model.

[2] Nash (1950, p. 22).

selection by Poulton (1884), on polymorphism in moths, and Düsing (1884) and Fisher (1930), on the sex ratio. The work of R. A. Fisher and Sewall Wright largely concerns perturbations around an equilibrium, but the problem was understood to be inherently dynamic and sophisticated dynamic models were available to biologists from the early fifties.[3] Although these writers did not conceive of the problem in game-theoretic terms, it is easy to read game theory into frequency-dependent models.

The modern development of process models begins with Taylor and Jonker's (1978) replicator dynamic. Their first result concerned the connection between its equilibrium states and the static evolutionarily stable strategy (ESS) equilibrium concept. Hofbauer and colleagues (1979) finally showed that every ESS is locally asymptotically stable. But other questions remained: What happens when there is no ESS? What about those asymptotically stable states that are not ESSs? These questions have been addressed, and other dynamics have since emerged: the projection dynamic, various imitation dynamics, the Smith dynamic, perturbed best response, no-regret dynamics, and so on.[4] Those of the most biological interest are surveyed by Sigmund's contribution.

These dynamic models provide new ways of looking at equilibrium. Consider matching pennies. The fictitious play of two people converges to the unique solution of the game. Replicator dynamics do not converge, but the time averages of the replicator path do converge to the solution. This is a novel interpretation of equilibrium. The connection between time averages of replicators and the limit behavior of best-response dynamics has been developed by Hofbauer and colleagues (2009).[5]

Formal models of the evolutionary dynamics of plant and animal populations are often indistinguishable from learning or other adaptive behavior models in human populations; thus evolutionary and epistemic game theory intersect. In the late 1950s and early 1960s, there was an outpouring of experimental research by social psychologists on the prisoners' dilemma and similar 2×2 games, appearing in places such as the *Journal of Conflict Resolution* and the *Journal of Abnormal and Social Psychology*. Some of this had to do with learning: for instance, consider Rapoport and Chammah (1965a; 1965b). This work appears to have had little influence on later work by game theorists and behavioral economists. Deschamps (1975) treats fictitious play as a learning model in Cournot duopoly. Smale (1980) develops a general model of learning rules based on *payoff* averaging, which he applies to the prisoner's dilemma. The modern interest in learning and adaptation seems to begin with

3 Düsing's and Fisher's insight was that to understand the sex ratio, one had to look to the grandchildren. For sophisticated dynamic models, see Feller (1951).

4 Sandholm (2010) describes these and others, and provides a useful classification scheme.

5 In many learning models, the time average of the marginal distribution of strategies may converge for all players, and the joint distribution time average may exhibit crossplayer dependence. Furthermore, although the distribution of individuals' average play may converge to equilibrium strategies, their payoffs need not. See Jordan (1993) for these and other convergence problems.

Fudenberg and Kreps (1988).[6] Kandori surveys and critiques this literature. He argues that research into learning models suffers for a lack of contact with empirical research.

As Kandori observes, the social sciences have imported and reinterpreted biological population models. There has also been a flow of ideas in the other direction. Models with origins in the social sciences have proven to be useful for biologists. For example, signaling games (sender–receiver games), introduced in Lewis (1969), have been important in economics and finance since the eighties. They have made their way into biology in the work of Grafen (1990) and Maynard Smith (1991).

Leimar surveys applications of game theory to biology. He shows how Maynard Smith and Price's (1973) ESS has informed several areas of biological research. This success, he says, is not replicated by process models. He suggests there are gains unrealized by ignoring these methods.

Despite the research interest in learning models, Leimar's critique applies to economics as well. The failure to make empirical use of process models is an epistemological failure for economics. In economics it is often the case that causal claims are established by reference to an equilibrium model (e.g., "The wheat price fell because of abundant rain this year"). Weather shifts a supply curve, and demand is downward-sloping. Although we do not explicate them, we imagine the processes that bring equilibrium about. But when the equilibrium concept is, for instance, Nash, when there are several equilibria, when equilibrium involves randomization, and when equilibrium has to be justified by particular beliefs about off-path play, equilibrium alone may not make a compelling causal claim. We should reach to process models to evaluate equilibrium causal claims, but this is beyond the current state of the art. We need two things: First, as described by Karl Sigmund, we need a richer set of process models that can be adapted to more situations. Second, we need the development of statistical techniques for bringing these models to data. I hope we do not have to wait for *Two Hundred Years of Game Theory* for these advances.

9.1 REFERENCES

G. W. Brown. Some notes on computation of games solutions. Technical Report Report P-78, RAND Corporation, 1949.

G. W. Brown and J. von Neumann. Solutions of games by differential equations. In H. Kuhn and A. Tucker, eds., *Annals of Mathematical Studies*, vol. 24, pp. 73–79. Princeton, NJ: Princeton University Press, 1950.

A. A. Cournot. *Recherces sur les principes mathématiques de la théorie des richesses.* Paris: Hachette, 1838.

[6] These papers are concerned with learning in a given game. Crawford (1974) and Rapoport (1966) consider games with unknown payoffs. Crawford shows that mixed equilibria are unstable for a wide class of learning rules.

V. Crawford. Learning the optimal strategy in a zero-sum game. *Econometrica*, 42:885–891, 1974.
R. Deschamps. An algorithm of game theory applied to the duopoly problem. *European Economic Review*, 6:187–194, 1975.
C. Düsing. *Die Regulierung des Geschlechtsverhältnisses bei der Vermehrung der Menschen, Tiere und Pflanzen*. Jena, Germany: Gustav Fischer, 1884.
F. Y. Edgeworth. *Mathematical Psychics: An Essay on the Application of Mathematics to the Moral Sciences*. London: Kegan Paul & Co., 1881.
W. Feller. Diffusion processes in genetics. In J. Neyman, ed., *Proceedings of the Second Berkeley Symposium on Mathematical Statistics and Probability*, pp. 227–246. Berkeley: University of California Press, 1951.
R. A. Fisher. *The Genetical Theory of Natural Selection*. Oxford: Clarendon Press, 1930.
D. Fudenberg and D. Kreps. A theory of learning and experimentation in games. 1988. https://scholar.harvard.edu/files/fudenberg/files/theory_of_learning_working_paper_1988.pdf.
A. Grafen. Biological signals as handicaps. *Journal of Theoretical Biology*, 144:517–546, 1990.
J. Hofbauer, P. Schuster, and K. Sigmund. A note on evolutionary stable strategies and game dynamics. *Journal of Theoretical Biology*, 81:609–612, 1979.
J. Hofbauer, S. Sorin, and Y. Viossat. Time-average replicator and best-reply dynamics. *Mathematics of Operations Research*, 34:263–269, 2009.
J. Jordan. Three problems in learning mixed-strategy Nash equilibria. *Games and Economic Behavior*, 5:368–386, 1993.
D. Lewis. *Convention: A Philosophical Study*. Cambridge, MA: Harvard University Press, 1969.
J. Maynard Smith. Honest signaling: The Sir Phillip Sydney game. *Animal Behavior*, 42:1034–1035, 1991.
J. Maynard Smith and G. R. Price. The logic of animal conflict. *Nature*, 246:15–18, 1973.
J. Nash. Non-cooperative games. *Annals of Mathematics*, 54:286–295, 1951.
J. F. Nash. Non-cooperative games. Unpublished PhD thesis, Princeton University, 1950.
H. Nikaido. Stability of equilibrium by the Brown–von Neumann differential equation. *Econometrica*, 27:654–671, 1959.
E. B. Poulton. Notes upon, or suggested by, the colours, markings, and protective attitudes of certain lepidopterous larvae and pupae, and of a phytophagous hymenopterous larva. *Transactions of the Entomology Society of London*, 27–60, 1884.
A. Rapoport. *Two-Person Game Theory: The Essential Ideas*. Ann Arbor: University of Michigan Press, 1966.
A. Rapoport and A. Chammah. Sex differences in factors contributing to the level of cooperation in the prisoner's dilemma game. *Journal of Personality and Social Psychology*, 2:831–838, 1965a.
A. Rapoport and A. Chammah. *The Prisoner's Dilemma: A Study in Conflict and Cooperation*. Ann Arbor: University of Michigan Press, 1965b.
J. Robinson. An iterative method of solving a game. *Annals of Mathematics*, 54:296–301, 1951.

W. H. Sandholm. *Population games and evolutionary dynamics*. Cambridge, MA: MIT Press, 2010.

S. Smale. The prisoner's dilemma and dynamical systems associated to non-cooperative games. *Econometrica*, 48:1617–1634, 1980.

P. D. Taylor and L. B. Jonker. Evolutionarily stable strategies and game dynamics. *Mathematical Biosciences*, 40(1–2):145–156, 1978.

10

Adjustment Dynamics for Human Players

Michihiro Kandori

ABSTRACT

In this chapter, I point out that there is a fundamental difficulty associated with the formal study of dynamic adjustment processes toward a Nash equilibrium in the context of social and economic problems (i.e., for human players). This difficulty has created an unfortunate dichotomy of researchers and has hindered progress in this area of research. I suggest, with a couple of examples, that a promising way to overcome this problem is to strengthen the empirical side of research on adjustment dynamics.

10.1 THE FUNDAMENTAL DIFFICULTY AND UNFORTUNATE DICHOTOMY OF RESEARCHERS

The concept of Nash equilibrium plays a key role in game theory, and therefore it is vital to understand how players come to play a Nash equilibrium. There are several ways to answer this question, but a prominent possibility is that a Nash equilibrium emerges via a dynamic adjustment process. If players accumulate experience in the same game or similar games, they learn what others do and which strategies fare well, and in the end (if the process ever converges) they would end up playing a Nash equilibrium.

The history of the research on adjustment dynamics dates back to as early as 1949 when Brown proposed fictitious play as an algorithm to find a Nash equilibrium (Brown, 1949). This area of research had a big impact around 1970,

I would like to thank Larry Blume, Mayuko Nakamaru, Ryoji Sawa, Ken-Ichi Shimomura, Dai Zusai, and an anonymous referee for their valuable comments and suggestions. Helpful discussion by my TA Ryo Shirakawa and the members of my reading group on dynamics is also gratefully acknowledged. I am also extremely grateful to Bill Sandholm, a leading figure in this field of research who sadly left us in 2020, for his helpful discussion with me about the general convergence properties of dynamics for zero-sum two-person games. I would like to dedicate this article to his memory. This work was supported by JSPS KAKENHI Grants JP20H00609, JP21K01399, and JP21H04979.

when biologists started to employ game theoretic ideas to study evolutionary dynamics and its convergent point, a stable Nash equilibrium called an evolutionary stable strategy (ESS; Maynard Smith, 1974). This inspired economists to formally analyze adjustment dynamics in the late 1980s, and evolutionary game theory then became a hot research topic. Various deterministic and stochastic dynamics were proposed and their properties examined. In the 1990s, the behavioral approach to dynamic adjustment processes was born, where the focus is to come up with parsimonious models that closely reproduce human subjects' adjustment behavior in lab experiments. Around the year 2000, game theoretic ideas were actively introduced in computer science and engineering, where adjustment dynamics and learning algorithms play a key role.

Rather than providing a comprehensive overview of those developments, here I focus on one conceptual issue that I view as crucial to advance this area of research: How should we formulate adjustment dynamics?[1] This is not an issue in biology because the adjustment dynamics there are undoubtedly driven by natural selection and mutations. In computer science and engineering, the answer to the question is also uncontroversial because adjustment dynamics and learning rules are directly designed and programmed by researchers. In contrast, in social and economic problems, *researchers have not yet reached a consensus on how adjustment dynamics should be formulated*. In this chapter, I will point out the fundamental difficulty associated with this issue and then explain how the difficulty has badly hindered the progress of research in this area. Finally, I will suggest a possible way to overcome the difficulty.

Let me make my point by means of a simple example. A well-established stylized fact is that people do play mixed-strategy Nash equilibria in zero-sum two-person games where the outcome is binary (win or lose). Instances include a card game (O'Neill, 1987), tennis serves (Walker and Wooders, 2001), and penalty kicks in soccer games (Palacios-Huerta, 2003). As there is no theoretical result that shows the Nash equilibrium in those games is derived via rational reasoning, if human players behave according to a Nash equilibrium strategy, it must have been achieved as a result of dynamic adjustment.

So, what does the existing research on dynamics tell us? A general, unifying condition for convergence to an equilibrium in such games has not yet been obtained, but it is known that best response dynamics and fictitious play do converge.[2] Now focus on a particular case of Matching Pennies (Table 10.1). Figure 10.1 depicts the associated state space. A point in this diagram may represent the current distribution of strategies in player 1's population and in player 2's, when we consider the best response dynamics. A point in the diagram

[1] Bill Sandholm's ambitious textbook (2010) provides a comprehensive overview of the field, encompassing both deterministic and stochastic dynamics.

[2] Sandholm (2010) and (2015) show that a general condition on dynamics, called *positive correlation*, plus various additional conditions guarantee the convergence of dynamic adjustment processes toward a Nash equilibrium in zero-sum two-person games.

TABLE 10.1 *Matching Pennies*

1\2	H	T
H	1, −1	−1, 1
T	−1, 1	1, −1

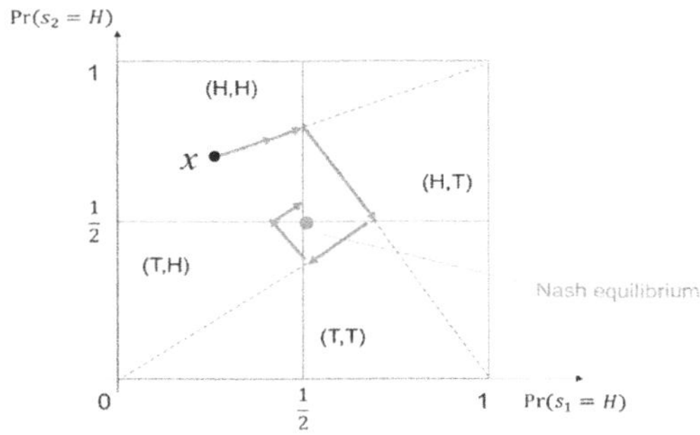

FIGURE 10.1 Best response dynamics in Matching Pennies.

can also be interpreted as the beliefs of players in the fictitious play model, which represent the past empirical frequencies of strategies of a pair of players who repeatedly play this game.

Figure 10.1 shows the best reply profile for each subset of the state space. For example, in the upper-left square, the best reply profile is (H, H), and if the current state is x, the state under the best response dynamics and fictitious play gradually moves toward (H, H), the upper-right corner of the state space, as indicated by the arrow in the diagram. Following this kind of argument, we can see that the state eventually converges to the midpoint, which is the mixed-strategy Nash equilibrium.

So far, so good. But if we view fictitious play as a learning process of players, it raises the following concern: When the current state is x at time t, where t is large, both players are going to play H for a rather long time. This is implausible, because sooner or later player 2 must realize that the opponent continues to play H and therefore would like to switch to T (so that she can win). In other words, player 2 is highly likely to deviate from fictitious play if the opponent mechanically sticks to the fictitious play adjustment process.

Let me explain what is happening here. Human players are intelligent, unlike animals (in biological applications) or machines (in engineering applications). Therefore, if players are mechanically following certain adjustment rules, sooner or later one might detect the opponent's adjustment rule and switch to the best or a better reply. In summary, adjustment dynamics are subject to potential instability if players are human. This is a *valid concern about ad-hoc adjustment rules* (rules that are not optimal, given what others do) imposed on human behavior, and such a concern never arises in biological or engineering applications.

The fundamental difficulty associated with this observation is that it is *logically impossible to wipe out this concern on a purely theoretical basis*. The only way to completely eliminate the concern is to look at a profile of adjustment processes that are free from the potential instability (i.e., the processes where switching to another adjustment rule is unprofitable for each player). In other words, the only way to eliminate the concern is to assume a Nash equilibrium in the dynamic adjustment game.[3] However, this contradicts the whole purpose of studying adjustment dynamics. To explain how a Nash equilibrium of a given game emerges over time, one should not assume a Nash equilibrium in a more complicated game of dynamic adjustment.

In summary, the fundamental difficulty is that *adjustment processes are subject to potential instability if players are human* and that it is impossible to eliminate this concern on a theoretical basis. This difficulty has created an *unfortunate dichotomy of researchers* that has badly hindered the progress of research in this area. On the one hand, there are researchers on dynamics who pay due attention to the importance of dynamic adjustment processes but do not fully address the valid concern about the potential instability issue. I am under the impression that some researchers, especially in disciplines other than economics, such as physics, biology, engineering, and sociology, when they come to analyze *human* adjustment processes for social problems, might not fully realize the importance of the valid concern about the potential instability. On the other hand, we have the skeptics. A group of researchers, probably including a nonnegligible fraction of economists, shy away from or even dismiss the research on adjustment dynamics because of the concern about the ad-hocness and potential instability of adjustment processes. For a long time, economists have fought against various ad-hoc approaches and have achieved commendable success by adopting a logically consistent, non-ad-hoc methodology based on the unifying principle of rationality. Anything ad hoc is regarded as faulty, and not without good reason. In my opinion, the flip side of the coin of this success story is that one of the most fundamental questions in game theory, that of how a Nash equilibrium emerges via an adjustment process, has not received its due attention in the field of economics.

How can we overcome the difficulty and the unfortunate dichotomy of researchers? First, the best way to overcome the skepticism about the research on adjustment dynamics is to present convincing empirical evidence. Second, the key question of how dynamic adjustment processes for human players should be formulated can only be answered empirically. In summary, what we need to do is to strengthen the empirical side of research on adjustment dynamics.

In what follows, I will present some promising observations about what empirical study can offer.

[3] The notion of perfect foresight dynamics by Matsui and Matsuyama (1995) provides a definition of Nash equilibria in a class of dynamic adjustment games. Sáez-Martí and Weibull (1999) examine what happens if clever agents try to outsmart naive players who play myopic best reply.

10.2 CONVINCING EMPIRICAL EVIDENCE

In this section, I will present some convincing empirical evidence to show that the research on adjustment dynamics is valuable.

10.2.1 Convergence

A leading "success story" of dynamic adjustment would be traffic allocation. Drivers try to go from their origins to destinations as fast as they can, and their strategies specify which route to choose. How fast one can go depends on how congested one's route is. This "congestion game" has a highly nontrivial Nash equilibrium, but empirical research has shown that the actual traffic allocation is reasonably close to the Nash equilibrium. Panel (a) of Figure 10.2 shows the Nash equilibrium traffic allocation around a midsized city in Japan (with thicker lines representing more traffic), and panel (b) compares the actual versus Nash equilibrium traffic allocation (with each dot in this diagram representing a segment of the routes). As you can see, the Nash equilibrium prediction fares reasonably well. It is a priori obvious that the Nash allocation is not achieved by ex-ante superrational reasoning of the drivers in this city, and that it must have been achieved via their trial-and-error dynamic adjustment of which route to choose. It is by no means obvious if such a process ever converges, but the theoretical research reveals that the congestion game is a potential game, and dynamic adjustment does converge to the Nash equilibrium under a fairly weak condition.[4] Note that, this concerns a significant problem in our society.[5]

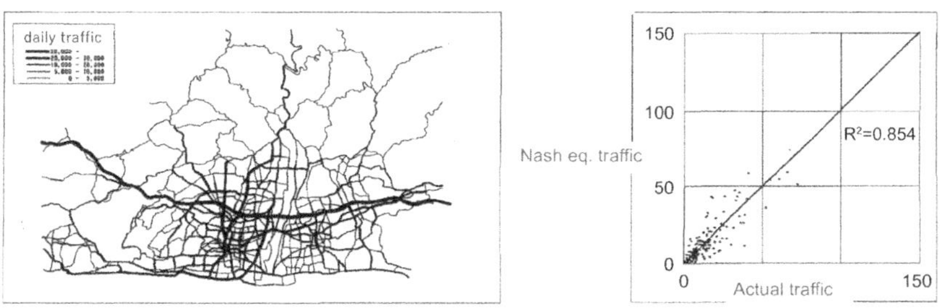

(a) (b)

FIGURE 10.2 Traffic allocation, Hamamatsu city, Japan.
Source: Japan Society of Civil Engineers (2003).

4 Research in civil engineering by Wardrop (1952) provides the key insights into the traffic allocation game. Sandholm (2001) shows that any "positively correlated dynamic," whose condition is much weaker than "switching to a better reply," converges to the Nash equilibrium.

5 Colin Camerer (in Chapter 24 of this volume), reports another "success story," namely the rough "empirical convergence" of field data to the mixed Nash equilibrium of a Poisson game model of the so-called LUPI game ("lowest unique positive integer").

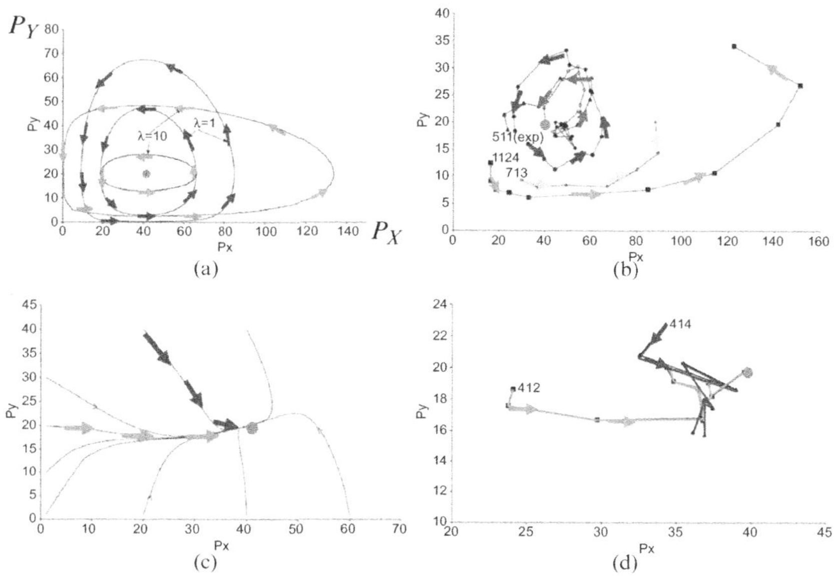

FIGURE 10.3 Multimarket price adjustment.

10.2.2 Nonconvergence and Cycles

Anderson and colleagues (2004) analyzed multimarket price adjustment in lab experiments. There are three goods, X, Y, and money, and players have utility functions over the consumption of those three goods. They come with initial holdings of those goods and exchange the goods in markets. The benchmark theoretical dynamics are given by the textbook model of price adjustment, where the price of good X or Y increases (decreases) when there is an excess demand (supply). In other words, the rate of change in the price (dp/dt) in each market is proportional to the excess demand. The authors chose special utility functions and initial endowments for which the theoretical price adjustment process is cyclical, as depicted in panel (a) of Figure 10.3. The shape of the cycle depends on the relative speed of price adjustment in markets for X and Y, and the figure presents two cases. In the lab, subjects traded their goods under basically the same rules as in the New York Stock Exchange. They could post any selling or buying order (such as "selling two units of good X at price 10") at any moment in time, and they could also take any outstanding selling or buying orders at any time. The dynamics of the average trading prices are shown in panel (b) of Figure 10.3, and they closely follow the theoretical prediction: Price trajectories cycle and the direction of movement is counterclockwise.

For another specification of utility functions and endowments, the theoretical price adjustment converges to the equilibrium, as is shown in panel (c) of Figure 10.3. And, again, the lab data (shown in panel (d)) are amazingly close

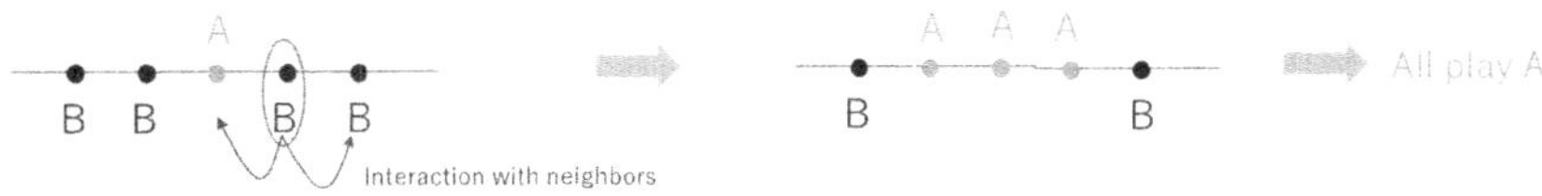

FIGURE 10.4 Local interaction.

to the theoretical prediction. This is not just a coincidence. Goeree and Lindsay (2016) replicated the counterclockwise cyclical movement in their lab experiments.

10.2.3 Equilibrium Selection: Risk Dominance

This work is in the field of biology, but I hope similar findings can be obtained for human adjustment processes. When there are multiple Nash equilibria, one can sometimes predict which one arises by analyzing dynamic adjustment processes. For example, one of the prominent findings in evolutionary game theory in economics is that a risk-dominant equilibrium emerges under certain conditions. Consider a game with two strategies, *A* and *B*, where "everyone plays *A*" and "everyone plays *B*" are both Nash equilibria. *A* is called a risk-dominant strategy if *A* is the unique best reply when at least half of the opponents play *A*. Risk-dominant equilibrium turned out to be the unique outcome of various adjustment dynamics, and Kandori and colleagues (1993) were some of the first to show it under a slight possibility of repeated random choice in the long run. The same selection result when players have local interaction was proved by Ellison (1993). Let me explain the basic logic behind Ellison's result. Figure 10.4 illustrates a simple case, where players are located on a line. The circled player, who is currently choosing *B*, interacts with her two neighbors. Since half of her opponents play *A* and *A* is risk dominant, she would like to switch to *A* in the next round. As the figure shows, this creates a "domino effect" and eventually everyone ends up playing *A*, as long as at least one player initially chooses *A*.

The work of Chao and Levin (1981) can be regarded as striking empirical evidence of the basic logic of Ellison's result.[6] They analyzed a type of bacteria (*Escherichia coli*) that comes in two types, *A* and *B*. *A* produces a toxic substance, and *B* is sensitive to the toxin. Because producing the toxin is costly, *A* has a smaller reproduction rate, but the toxin can interfere with the reproductive success of type *B*. When those two types are cultured in liquid that is constantly shaken, the situation is characterized by uniform random matching. In this case, the outcome depends on the initial condition, as shown in panel (a) of Figure 10.5. It shows that *A* fares better (has more offspring) when the fraction of *A* is more than 2 percent. This means that *A* is (very strongly) risk

[6] Ellison used this "domino effect" logic to show that convergence to the stochastically stable outcome does not take a long time when players are located on a line. More general analysis of the domino effect was provided by Morris (2000).

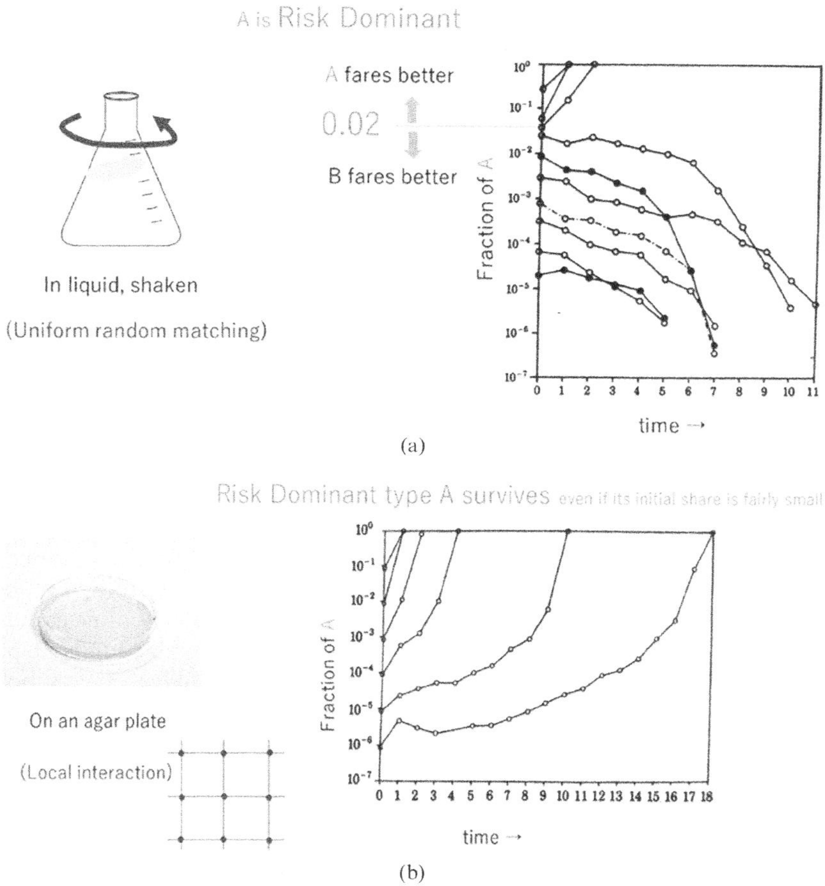

FIGURE 10.5 Random matching versus local interaction.
Source: Chao and Levin (1981); image of agar plate in (b) courtesy of Lilly_M, CC BY-SA 3.0 via Wikimedia Commons.

dominant. In contrast, if the two types are grown on agar plates, the situation is characterized as (two-dimensional) local interaction. Panel (b) of Figure 10.5 shows that in that case, the risk dominant *A* type survives even if its initial share is fairly small, as is predicted by the local interaction model.[7]

10.3 PRELIMINARY EMPIRICAL EVIDENCE ON THE NATURE OF HUMAN ADJUSTMENT PROCESSES

Now I turn to some preliminary empirical findings about the nature of adjustment dynamics for human players. Here I report some laboratory experimental

[7] Iwasa and colleagues (1998) provide an alternative model of dynamics on the agar plates.

1 \ 2	K	1	2	3
K	1, −1	−1, 1	−1, 1	−1, 1
1	−1, 1	−1, 1	1, −1	1, −1
2	−1, 1	1, −1	−1, 1	1, −1
3	−1, 1	1, −1	1, −1	−1, 1

(a) O'Neill game

	Player 1	Player 2
Nash equilibrium	**0.4**	**0.6**
Human subjects	0.41	0.59
EWA	0.39	0.61
EWA vs BR-EWA	0.24	0.76
Human vs BR-EWA	0.85	0.15

(b) Winning rates

FIGURE 10.6 Adjustment dynamics in O'Neill's game: Human versus programmed.

results I and my collaborators have obtained about a two-person zero-sum game with binary outcomes. As I mentioned, O'Neill (1987) discovered that subjects' behavior in his lab experiment about a rather complicated card game is very close to the mixed Nash equilibrium. Panel (a) of Figure 10.6 shows the payoff table of the card game, and in the unique mixed-strategy equilibrium of this game, each player chooses *K* (a King card) with probability 0.4 and each number card (1, 2, and 3) with probability 0.2. The equilibrium winning rate is 0.4 for the row player and 0.6 for the column player. I was able to replicate O'Neill's finding in a large data set I have collected through my online game theory course.[8] In the data set, 2,589 pairs played the game for 30 rounds. In panel (b), the second row shows the winning rates in my data set. The subjects' behavior is pretty close to the Nash equilibrium, and by inspecting the payoff table, one can see that it is highly unlikely that the subjects managed to compute the equilibrium. They must have learned, in some way, to play the mixed-strategy equilibrium. To discover their adjustment behavior, we estimated a leading learning model in behavioral economics called experience-weighted attraction (EWA; Camerer and Ho, 1999), which is basically a convex combination of fictitious play and reinforcement learning. The third row of panel (b) of Figure 10.6 reports the implied winning rates of the estimated EWA model, and it shows that the subjects' behavior is reasonably well replicated by the estimated model.

We then computed the dynamic best reply to the estimated EWA strategy in the 30-round repetition of the card game. The fourth row of panel (b) shows the implied winning rates where player 1 uses the estimated EWA strategy while player 2 adopts the dynamic best reply to the estimated EWA. As you can see, if the opponent is using EWA, one can gain substantially by switching from EWA to the best reply. The gain is substantial (winning rate increases from 0.61 to 0.76), and therefore the concern about the ad-hocness of the adjustment process is a real issue here. Finally, I conducted an experiment where subjects played against a computer program that plays the dynamic best reply to the estimated EWA. The result is reported in the bottom row of (b), and it is revealing. Against a computer programmed to play the best reply to EWA, human players no

[8] *Welcome to Game Theory* at Coursera, www.coursera.org/learn/game-theory-introduction.

longer used the estimated EWA-like behavior and acted very differently so as to exploit the program. The computer program, which is supposed to outsmart human players, fared miserably.

Those results indicate the following. First, human players do have some capacity to detect the opponent's behavior pattern and adjust their own behavior accordingly. Second, human players often stick to adjustment processes even though there is a substantial gain from switching to a better reply.

Call a profile of adjustment processes *compatible* if no one wants to deviate to another adjustment rule *in the field or in an experiment*. Even though a profile of adjustment rules actually admits some positive gain from deviation, human players in reality may not deviate (and therefore the profile is compatible) because of cognitive limitation or by some behavioral biases. As we have seen, fictitious play for Matching Pennies is apparently incompatible, and the EWA profile seems compatible. In contrast, the profile (EWA and best reply to EWA) turned out to be incompatible.

10.4 CONCLUSION: PROMISING RESEARCH DIRECTIONS

Given these observations, I would suggest the following agenda of potentially promising research directions. This would help us address the concern about the ad-hocness of adjustment processes and dissolve the unfortunate dichotomy of researchers. My suggestion is to bridge the gap between the top-down theoretical approach on dynamic adjustment, which has been a dominant mode of research, and the recent bottom-up research by behavioral economists. First, we need more empirical research to discover the nature of actual adjustment behavior in various social and economic problems. Logically speaking, this is the only way to address the valid concern about ad-hocness. Empirics should encompass not only laboratory experimental data but also field data on significant economic or social issues, as was suggested by the traffic allocation example. Once we have a better idea about the nature of dynamic adjustment processes actually adopted by human players, we could go about theorizing why a particular mode of adjustment behavior is prevalent (despite its potential instability). This amounts to identifying which processes are compatible and understanding why. Human adjustment is not completely mechanical, and players think strategically to some extent. Formulating such a mental process and coming up with models that fit the empirical data can be achieved through active feedback between bottom-up empirical research and top-down theoretical research.

Let me summarize. Adjustment dynamics are subject to potential instability if players are human. Because of this, some researchers are skeptical about research on adjustment dynamics for social and economic problems. To convince skeptics about the importance of adjustment dynamics and find out what the right adjustment dynamics for human players are, we need to strengthen the empirical side of research on adjustment dynamics. By doing so, I hope we can take ourselves one step closer to the answer to one of the most fundamental questions in game theory: how players come to play a Nash equilibrium.

10.5 REFERENCES

C. M. Anderson, C. R. Plott, K.-I. Shimomura, and S. Granat. Global instability in experimental general equilibrium: The Scarf example. *Journal of Economic Theory*, 115(2):209–249, 2004.

G. W. Brown. Some notes on computation of games solutions. Technical Report Report P-78, RAND Corporation, 1949.

C. Camerer and T.-H. Ho. Experience-weighted attraction learning in normal form games. *Econometrica*, 67(4):827–874, 1999.

L. Chao and B. R. Levin. Structured habitats and the evolution of anticompetitor toxins in bacteria. *Proceedings of the National Academy of Sciences USA*, 78(10):6324–6328, 1981.

G. Ellison. Learning, local interaction, and coordination. *Econometrica*, 61(5):1047–1071, 1993.

J. K. Goeree and L. Lindsay. Market design and the stability of general equilibrium. *Journal of Economic Theory*, 165:37–68, 2016.

Y. Iwasa, M. Nakamura, and S. A. Levin. Allelopathy of bacteria in a lattice population: Competition between colicin-sensitive and colicin-producing strains. *Evolutionary Ecology*, 12:785–802, 1998.

Japan Society of Civil Engineers. *Guidebook on Traffic Demand Forecasting. Volume I: Application of User Equilibrium Assignment Technique*. Tokyo: Japan Society of Civil Engineers, 2003. ISBN 4-8106-0407-1 (in Japanese).

M. Kandori, G. J. Mailath, and R. Rob. Learning, mutation, and long run equilibria in games. *Econometrica*, 61(1):29–56, 1993.

A. Matsui and K. Matsuyama. An approach to equilibrium selection. *Journal of Economic Theory*, 65(2):415–434, 1995.

J. Maynard Smith. The theory of games and the evolution of animal conflicts. *Journal of Theoretical Biology*, 47(1):209–221, 1974.

S. Morris. Contagion. *The Review of Economic Studies*, 67(1):57–78, 2000.

B. O'Neill. Nonmetric test of the minimax theory of two-person zerosum games. *Proceedings of the National Academy of Sciences USA*, 84(7):2106–2109, 1987.

I. Palacios-Huerta. Professionals play minimax. *Review of Economic Studies*, 70(2):395–415, 2003.

M. Sáez-Martí and J. W. Weibull. Clever agents in Young's evolutionary bargaining model. *Journal of Economic Theory*, 86:268–279, 1999.

W. H. Sandholm. Potential games with continuous player sets. *Journal of Economic Theory*, 97(1):81–108, 2001.

W. H. Sandholm. *Population Games and Evolutionary Dynamics*. Cambridge: MIT Press, 2010.

W. H. Sandholm. Population games and deterministic evolutionary dynamics. In P. Young and S. Zamir, eds., *Handbook of Game Theory with Economic Applications*, vol. 4, ch. 13, pp. 703–778. Amsterdam: Elsevier, 2015.

M. Walker and J. Wooders. Minimax play at Wimbledon. *American Economic Review*, 91(5):1521–1538, 2001.

J. G. Wardrop. Some theoretical aspects of road traffic research. *Proceedings of the Institution of Civil Engineers*, 1(3):325–362, 1952.

11

Game Theory in Biology

Ideas, Successes, and Challenges

Olof Leimar

ABSTRACT

Game theory in biology emerged as a theoretical and modelling approach to the evolutionary study of behaviour and other phenotypes. It was inspired by the prominence of game theory in economics. In this chapter, I give a perspective on the influence of economic thinking on biology. Which ideas were applied from economics and the social sciences to biology, how were they modified, which biological phenomena were they applied to, and what are the successes, challenges, and possible future of the field? I focus on two of the earliest applications of game theory in biology, namely sex-ratio theory and animal contests.

11.1 EARLY ARTICLES ON GAME THEORY IN BIOLOGY

Evolutionary geneticists knew about the status of game theory in economics and were inspired to apply the theory to biology. The early articles by biologists (Fisher, 1958; Lewontin, 1961; Hamilton, 1967; Maynard Smith, 1972, 1974, 1976; Maynard Smith and Price, 1973) understood game theory in economics to be primarily about zero-sum games, with minimax as the important solution concept. A possible reason (suggested to me by Peter Hammerstein) for these authors seemingly not being aware of the Nash equilibrium concept is that biologists learned about game theory mostly from reading the early chapters of works like Luce and Raiffa (1957) and Rapoport (1966), where the minimax concept is dealt with. Except for Fisher, biologists were not insiders to game theory. Nevertheless, the interest in and status of game theory in the social sciences led biologists to attempt to apply it to evolutionary biology.

R. A. Fisher contributed to the formal study of strategies in card games (the game 'Le Her'; Fisher, 1934). He used the minimax solution concept to show that players should randomise their moves at certain positions in the game.

This work was supported by a grant from the Swedish Research Council. I thank Larry Blume, Peter Hammerstein, Christer Wiklund, and an anonymous referee for helpful comments.

This result aligned with Fisher's great interest in randomisation, primarily as a tool for experimentalists to eliminate non-causal correlations. In a 1934 paper he argued that players could use randomisation to avoid exploitation by others who learn about their strategy. Much later he suggested that predator-prey interactions could be studied with game theory (Fisher, 1958), using similar ideas as in his analysis of the card game. He gave polymorphic Batesian mimicry as a possible example. Batesian mimicry is named after the nineteenth-century naturalist Henry Walter Bates. It denotes harmless species that have evolved a resemblance to poisonous or otherwise harmful species, referred to as models, thereby gaining protection from predators that have learned to avoid the model species. The mimicry is polymorphic when only part of a population has the mimetic phenotype. Fisher noted that such polymorphism reduced the chances that a predator would learn that a Batesian mimic is in fact suitable to eat and therefore attack it. Fisher was likely thinking of polymorphic mimicry either in the African butterfly *Papilio dardanus* or in the Asian butterfly *Papilio polytes*, both studied by Fisher's ecological geneticist colleagues, such as Cyril Clarke, Philip Sheppard, and E. B. Ford. Fisher's idea of a prey randomising its phenotype to counter predators is intriguing but somewhat fanciful, because a predator interacts with prey as a group or category that it learns about. One might compare this with the discussion of polymorphic Batesian mimicry by Wright (1977), which mentions frequency-dependent selection but does not go into ideas about randomisation.

Lewontin (1961) made an ambitious but seemingly failed attempt to apply game theory to games against 'nature', as an approach to the study of genetic adaptation of populations to different environments. The approach was criticised by Maynard Smith (1972, 1974, 1976), who pointed out that 'nature' is not a player in a game, in the sense of having an interest in maximising a payoff, and that Lewontin's reasoning implicitly appealed to group or species selection.

Discussions about how natural selection might act on the ratio of the two sexes in a population (i.e., the sex ratio) go back at least to Darwin's work on sexual selection (Darwin, 1871). A seeming difficulty is that a mother could have the same reproductive success regardless of the sex of her offspring (the problem was analysed by Fisher, 1930). Hamilton (1967) greatly improved the understanding of sex-ratio evolution by adapting the early work by Fisher (1930) to a number of different situations and mechanisms of sex determination. Many of his examples dealt with sex-ratio strategies of egg-laying females of species of parasitoid wasps. He described his approach as an application of game theory, mentioning minimax strategies and zero-sum games, but he did not cite any works on game theory. For his first solved example of an evolutionary equilibrium, he introduced the terminology of an 'unbeatable strategy', giving the verbal description that 'the Y chromosome that produces [the equilibrium strategy] has a selective advantage over any other, whatever the current gene frequency'. This appears to be correct for the example in question, but it is in general a needlessly strong requirement. The equilibrium sex-ratio strategies found by Hamilton (1967) were convergence-stable strict Nash equilibria, and this seems to be a suitable criterion for the situations he studied.

The main issue raised in the early game-theoretical works by Maynard Smith (1972, 1974, 1976) and Maynard Smith and Price (1973) was whether non-dangerous fighting behaviour could be explained by individual selection, without appeals to 'the good of the species' or to group selection. Appeals to the good of the species were commonly made by prominent ethologists (for instance by Lorenz, 1963) and other biologists, but such ideas appear not to have been put forward by evolutionary geneticists. Maynard Smith was an evolutionary geneticist who had insights into the thinking and observations by ethologists, placing him in a good position to investigate evolutionary explanations of non-dangerous fighting.

Maynard Smith (1972) introduced the term *evolutionarily stable strategy (ESS)* and gave the definition 'a strategy qualifies as an ESS if, in a population in which most individuals adopt it, there is no alternative strategy which will pay better'. This resembles the idea of a Nash equilibrium, but Maynard Smith was apparently not aware of this. He noted that payoffs in a game should represent contributions to fitness (i.e., contributions to reproductive success) and that a general characteristic of a game is that the success of a strategy depends on how others behave. The current definition of an ESS first appeared in Maynard Smith and Price (1973), presumably motivated by the need for a solution criterion for mixed strategies in the war-of-attrition model that was introduced at the end of that article.

Maynard Smith and Price (1973) are often cited as finding a mixed ESS of the Hawk–Dove game (I have done this myself several times), but this is not really correct and is an oversimplification of how the Hawk–Dove game came to be used to model fighting behaviour. The Hawk–Dove game, which is similar in terms of payoffs to the game of chicken, was first used by Maynard Smith (1976) to model symmetric contests and by Maynard Smith and Parker (1976) to model contests with a role asymmetry, such as owner–intruder. In this game there are two actions, Hawk and Dove, corresponding to dangerous and non-dangerous behaviour, and the contest is over a resource of value V. In a Hawk–Hawk contest, the individual who is injured first withdraws, paying a cost C, and the other wins and gains the resource. It is random which of the opponents wins. In Hawk–Dove and Dove–Hawk contests, the individual using Hawk wins the resource without cost for the loser, and for a Dove–Dove contest one of the opponents, at random, wins the resource, without cost for the loser.

The main biological conclusion of Maynard Smith and Price (1973) was that a strategy they referred to as 'retaliator' (starting with non-dangerous behaviour and escalating if the opponent uses dangerous behaviour) is an ESS and might explain the occurrence of non-dangerous fighting by animals such as males of red deer and bighorn sheep. As described by Maynard Smith (1976), Price's contribution to the paper was the idea that some form of retaliator strategy could explain non-dangerous fighting without the need to appeal to group selection. One might then ask how Price, not a biologist, came to his idea.

The likely answer identifies a little noted but probable link between Maynard Smith's early work on game theory and the social sciences. Thus an inspiration for the retaliator strategy might have been game-theory analyses of conflicts between nations in the Cold War era. An example of such work is Schelling (1960), in which retaliation and its possible role in inhibiting escalation plays a prominent role. (As an aside, retaliation was mentioned as a contribution by Schelling for his 2005 prize in Economic Sciences.) Price was familiar with the thinking of Cold War intellectuals, having worked on the Manhattan Project and at the Argonne National Laboratory, and as the author of an unpublished book manuscript on the Cold War (Harman, 2010). Price's entry into game theory in biology came in 1968, when he submitted a manuscript with the title 'Antlers, intraspecific combat, and altruism' to the journal *Nature* (Harman, 2010, 2011). The manuscript was reviewed by Maynard Smith and was rejected for being too long. It was never published but appears to have influenced Maynard Smith's thinking about game theory and animal contests. In his first essay on the topic (Maynard Smith, 1972), he started by giving a description of antler fighting in red deer stags. While in hindsight the significance of retaliation in promoting non-dangerous fighting is somewhat uncertain (as discussed later), Price's idea is still striking. The insight that mutual deterrence through retaliation might obviate the need for group selection in explanations of non-dangerous animal contests gave a new direction to animal behaviour research.

The game analysis by Maynard Smith and Price (1973) was criticised in a short note by Gale and Eaves (1975). The strategies and the game studied by Maynard Smith and Price (1973) were not specified in full detail, perhaps creating confusion. Maynard Smith (1982) corrected and clarified the analysis, again suggesting that a retaliator strategy could provide an explanation for non-dangerous fighting behaviour. There are, nevertheless, reasons to doubt that Price's idea of a retaliator strategy is the best explanation of such behaviour. The idea of assessment of fighting ability, put forward by Parker (1974), is likely to be more important. In spite of some weaknesses in the formulation and game-theory analysis, Maynard Smith and Price (1973) provided much inspiration for game theory in biology. Sigmund (2005) gives another perspective on Maynard Smith's contribution to the field, complementing my presentation here.

11.2 SEX-RATIO THEORY

Sex-ratio theory is often cited as one of the most successful applications of game theory in biology. To a large extent it was developed without direct reference to game theory. Fisher (1930) did not mention game theory or cite any previous work on sex ratios, but it is likely that he was aware of the biologist Düsing (1884), who performed a mathematical analysis of sex ratios using grandoffspring as a measure of the success of a strategy (see Edwards, 2000). This same reasoning was used by Shaw and Mohler (1953), who cited Fisher

(1930) but, like Fisher, did not make an explicit connection to game theory. As further illustration, Charnov (1982) is the author of an influential textbook on sex allocation that uses the approach of Shaw and Mohler (1953). The book has Maynard Smith (1976) as the only reference to game theory.

From this it seems that Hamilton (1967) was the first to see a strong connection between sex-ratio evolution and game theory. This might be because Hamilton (1967) studied situations like those of two parasitoid wasp females directly playing against each other when laying eggs in the same insect host. Hamilton referred to this as a 'gamelike element' and contrasted it with the assumptions made by Fisher (1930). It would seem that the playing-the-field situations common in sex-ratio games, in which the payoff to a strategy is determined by the population frequencies of the sexes, made biologists less inclined to think in terms of game theory.

Concerning empirical success, sex-ratio theory has been tested in many situations, ranging from experimental evolution of sex ratios in Atlantic silverside (*Menidia menidia*) fish (Conover and Van Voorhees, 1990) to several decades of observation of year-to-year breeding sex-ratio fluctuations in catches of shrimp (*Pandalus jordani*) off the US West Coast (Charnov and Groth, 2019). Overall, sex-ratio theory has had great success, but there are also sex-allocation phenomena where it has been less successful in explaining observations. An example is the much studied question of whether mothers in better versus worse phenotypic conditions should prefer to produce sons or daughters (Trivers and Willard, 1973).

11.3 ANIMAL CONTESTS

Maynard Smith and Parker (1976) noted that contestants could use a clear-cut asymmetry to settle a conflict without fighting. They gave role-asymmetric ESSs for the war-of-attrition game (Maynard Smith, 1974) and the Hawk–Dove game (with $V < C$), as examples. They suggested that an owner–intruder asymmetry could settle contests where an owner of a territory is challenged by an intruder, such that the intruder yields to the owner. This attracted interest by empiricists who saw an opportunity to test the theory. Davies (1978) did this in a field experiment with males of the speckled wood butterfly (*Pararge aegeria*), performed in Wytham Woods near Oxford. Speckled wood males often perch on vegetation in pools of sunlight on the forest floor, referred to as *sunspot territories*, where they look for and pursue flying females. Sometimes another male flies through or lands in the sunspot, in which case an aerial contest can occur, with the males chasing each other in circling flight. By capturing the sunspot owner in a butterfly net, waiting until another male occupied the territory, and then releasing the previous owner, Davies (1978) found that the new owner invariably won the resulting brief interaction. He concluded that an owner–intruder convention determined the outcome. This seeming success for game theory in providing a simple and novel explanation for animal contest observations was, however, not confirmed in subsequent work. Instead, observations on the same species showed that when a sunspot owner temporarily left his territory, for instance to engage in mating, and another male moved into the sunspot, the previous owner typically recaptured the territory after a longer or shorter aerial contest (Wickman and Wiklund, 1983).

It is commonly observed that owners tend to win contests against intruders, in speckled woods as well as in other species, but the main explanation is likely to be that owners either have higher fighting ability or are more motivated, in the sense of estimating the higher fitness benefits of territory possession. For instance, an experiment in a large outdoor cage showed that a speckled wood male's recent experience of encountering females in a sunspot strongly influences his likelihood of winning a territorial contest by making him persist for longer (Bergman et al., 2010). The result is qualitatively in accordance with an ESS of the so-called war of attrition with random rewards (Bishop et al., 1978).

As mentioned, Parker (1974) argued that assessment of fighting ability, where a contestant gives up if it has estimated itself as weaker, could be a reason for low-cost contests. There is a wealth of empirical evidence for assessment in animal fighting (Hsu et al., 2006; Arnott and Elwood, 2009), including the contests between red deer males that were used as illustration by Maynard Smith (1972, 1976). There are several elements of these contests that likely serve to assess relative fighting ability (Clutton-Brock and Albon, 1979; Clutton-Brock et al., 1979). Contests typically start with bouts of roaring, where the roaring rate as well as the depth of the pitch of the sound can indicate a male's size and strength. A contest sometimes ends after roaring, but roaring is more often followed by a parallel walk, where males have the opportunity to estimate and compare their relative size, vigour, and condition. If neither withdraws, there is a physical fight where they lock antlers and attempt to push each other back, ending with one male being driven backwards and fleeing. Also, if a male slips and stumbles during fighting, his opponent tries to horn him in the flank or neck. Although there are notable costs, both loss of condition and direct injuries (Clutton-Brock et al., 1979), males can withstand the activity over several yearly mating seasons, typically being most successful between ages five and ten. Geist (1966) gives a valuable perspective on such contests and on the evolutionary history of horn-like organs, like antlers in deer. These organs probably originated as offensive weapons and then evolved to become more defensive, by blocking and neutralising attacks. Geist's view partly supports and partly contradicts (see Geist, 1974; Maynard Smith, 1979) the interpretation of non-dangerous fighting by Maynard Smith (1972) and Maynard Smith and Price (1973).

The process of forming estimates of relative fighting ability has been incorporated into the sequential assessment game (Enquist and Leimar, 1983). In this model, the true relative fighting ability of a pair is normally distributed, and contestants obtain a sequence of observations of this variable plus independent errors. Using the concept of a sufficient statistic, it turns out that an ESS can be found among strategies that base the decision to continue or give up on the current sample mean and the number of observations so far

(Enquist and Leimar, 1983). A one- or low-dimensional sufficient statistic will usually not exist for general fighting interactions, but the sequential assessment game can be adapted to situations with an owner–intruder asymmetry (Leimar and Enquist, 1984) and variation in estimates of the value of winning (Enquist and Leimar, 1987).

Very dangerous or even lethal fights occur in nature. Honeybee queens that emerge in the same colony illustrate this. The queens are close relatives, being half- or full sisters, but still fight to the death for possession of the colony (Gilley, 2001). The life cycle of honeybee queens and their colonies explains the extreme phenomenon. A queen has no reproductive future without her colony, and sharing by swarming and splitting the colony only occurs when an established queen disperses and founds a new colony with part of her workers, leaving newly emerging queens to fight over the remaining colony. It is instructive to compare this with the aim by Maynard Smith and Price (1973) to explain non-dangerous fighting behaviour. Observations like those on honeybee queens give an idea of when game theory ought to predict dangerous fights. The fitness value of a contested resource generally influences the costs of contests, as is found for the ESSs of many models, including the Hawk–Dove game. Hammerstein and Riechert (1988) performed the first game-theory analysis of contests using empirical estimates of fitness costs and benefits over the life histories of females of the territorial spider *Agelenopsis aperta*. Enquist and Leimar (1990) used similar ideas to work out game-theory predictions for fatal fighting by taking into account how fitness increments accumulate over a life cycle. There is also a successful test of predictions on whether a contest ends with lethal injury or with the giving up of a contestant, using males of the bowl and doily spider that engage in contests over difficult-to-find and therefore high-value female webs (Leimar et al., 1991). The test involved the fitting of parameters of a sequential assessment game with the risk of fatal injury and experimental observations. More generally, limited reproductive prospects beyond the current interaction are characteristic of dangerous contests in nature. Such observations illustrate how game theory has contributed to the study of animal fighting behaviour by explaining when dangerous fighting is to be expected, in this way extending the seminal work by Maynard Smith and Price (1973).

11.4 CHALLENGES AND FUTURE PROSPECTS

Game theory in biology often assumes that organisms can use any information available to them to achieve the goal of high reproductive success. The assumption largely corresponds to ideas about rationality in game theory in economics. Just as is the case in that field, there are good reasons to question and modify such assumptions in biology. It is helpful to start with a general distinction between 'small worlds' and 'large worlds', which comes from theories of decision-making under ignorance (Savage, 1972; Binmore, 2009; Savage used the term 'grand world'). Adapted to biology, a small world could refer to a decision maker in a simple environment, where in principle all fitness-relevant states and state transitions of the environment can be assumed as known or somehow fully represented by the individual. If there is imperfect information, the assumption would be that prior distributions of environmental states and state transitions have realistic innate representations in decision makers, together with a calculus of computing posterior distributions given observations. In large worlds, on the other hand, such assumptions would be unrealistic, and this might often be the case for the real world.

The number of different circumstances encountered by organisms is often vast. Especially for social interactions, where the decision-making machineries of social partners form an important part of the environment, the idea of a large world could be relevant. Although one can argue that it is enough that organisms have characteristics (psychological and physiological traits) that permit evolution to reach an equilibrium that corresponds to a proper Bayesian analysis of a well-defined situation, this possibility seems unlikely to significantly reduce the difficulty. In the real world, organisms might instead rely on simpler strategies that work reasonably well in many circumstances, without necessarily being fully optimal in all or even most circumstances.

Similar ideas have been influential in economic game theory and are often discussed under the rubric of bounded rationality, but game theory in biology is less developed in this regard. It follows that game theory in biology might profit from examining large-worlds models, as argued by McNamara and Leimar (2020). This certainly holds for social interactions where individuals vary in their characteristics and should take this into account when making decisions. The modelling approach could make use of the well-established idea that concrete behavioural mechanisms are fundamental elements of the evolutionary study of behaviour (McNamara and Houston, 2009). So, while game theory in biology has been slow in incorporating behavioural mechanisms, biology in general has a long and successful history of investigating the mechanistic aspects of behaviour. Starting with the work by Pavlov (1927) on associative learning in dogs, the fields of experimental psychology, animal cognition, and more recently neuroscience have become major branches of biology. Game theory in biology could make use of this.

Returning to the topic of animal contests, it is striking that there are very few thoroughgoing small-worlds analyses of situations where contestants learn about each other's characteristics, with the sequential assessment game (Enquist and Leimar, 1983) as possibly the only example. Considering the wealth of phenomena and issues raised about animal contests, for instance different suggestions of precisely what individuals gain information about when interacting (Arnott and Elwood, 2009), or how one should interpret the range of different aggressive behaviour patterns (such as the ones described for red deer males), it is unlikely that modellers would succeed in working out the needed small-worlds models. It also seems unlikely that evolution could have given rise to equilibria of small-worlds models in highly complex social environments. (It is not even clear that such models and equilibria typically exist.)

The difficulties become even greater for situations with social hierarchies and social-dominance relations in group-living animals, where individuals need to take into account a network of relations and interactions between group members. Such social situations represent a widespread category of contests, including those between red deer males.

An attractive possibility is to use modern reinforcement-learning theory (Sutton and Barto, 2018) as an inspiration for behavioural mechanisms. Learning plays an important role in game theory in economics (Fudenberg and Levine, 1998), and ideas about learning in animal psychology and neuroscience could play similar roles in biology. In this way one can, for instance, investigate the evolution of social hierarchy formation (Leimar, 2021). To appreciate the kinds of questions that could be examined in this way, potentially contributing to the general aim by Maynard Smith and Price (1973) to explain lower-cost contests, one can note that in many group-living animals both males and females form social hierarchies, but there is much less aggression in interactions between females versus males (Stockley and Bro-Jørgensen, 2011; Clutton-Brock and Huchard, 2013a,b). This could be studied with game-theory models that incorporate the required behavioural mechanisms. The future might tell how successful such approaches to game theory in biology can be, and it seems like a worthwhile challenge.

11.5 REFERENCES

G. Arnott and R. W. Elwood. Assessment of fighting ability in animal contests. *Animal Behaviour*, 77(5):991–1004, 2009.

M. Bergman, M. Olofsson, and C. Wiklund. Contest outcome in a territorial butterfly: The role of motivation. *Proceedings of the Royal Society B: Biological Sciences*, 277(1696):3027–3033, 2010.

K. Binmore. *Rational Decisions*. Princeton, NJ: Princeton University Press, 2009.

D. T. Bishop, C. Cannings, and J. Maynard Smith. The war of attrition with random rewards. *Journal of Theoretical Biology*, 74(3):377–388, 1978.

E. L. Charnov. *The Theory of Sex Allocation*. Princeton, NJ: Princeton University Press, 1982.

E. L. Charnov and S. D. Groth. Fluctuating age distributions and sex ratio tracking in a protandrous shrimp. *Evolutionary Ecology Research*, 20(5):523–535, 2019.

T. Clutton-Brock and E. Huchard. Social competition and its consequences in female mammals. *Journal of Zoology*, 289(3):151–171, 2013a.

T. Clutton-Brock and S. Albon. The roaring of red deer and the evolution of honest advertisement. *Behaviour*, 69(3):145–170, 1979.

T. H. Clutton-Brock and E. Huchard. Social competition and selection in males and females. *Philosophical Transactions of the Royal Society B: Biological Sciences*, 368(1631):20130074, 2013b.

T. H. Clutton-Brock, S. D. Albon, R. M. Gibson, and F. E. Guinness. The logical stag: Adaptive aspects of fighting in red deer (*Cervus elaphus* L.). *Animal Behaviour*, 27:211–225, 1979.

D. O. Conover and D. A. Van Voorhees. Evolution of a balanced sex ratio by frequency-dependent selection in a fish. *Science*, 250(4987):1556–1558, 1990.

C. Darwin. *The Descent of Man, and Selection in Relation to Sex*. London: John Murray, 1871.

N. B. Davies. Territorial defence in the speckled wood butterfly (*Pararge aegeria*): The resident always wins. *Animal Behaviour*, 26:138–147, 1978.

C. Düsing. *Die Regulierung des Geschlechtsverhältnisses bei der Vermehrung der Menschen, Tiere und Pflanzen*. Jena, Germany: Gustav Fischer, 1884.

A. W. F. Edwards. Carl Düsing (1884) on the regulation of the sex-ratio. *Theoretical Population Biology*, 58(3):255–257, 2000.

M. Enquist and O. Leimar. Evolution of fighting behaviour: Decision rules and assessment of relative strength. *Journal of Theoretical Biology*, 102(3):387–410, 1983.

M. Enquist and O. Leimar. Evolution of fighting behaviour: The effect of variation in resource value. *Journal of Theoretical Biology*, 127(2):187–205, 1987.

M. Enquist and O. Leimar. The evolution of fatal fighting. *Animal Behaviour*, 39(1):1–9, 1990.

R. A. Fisher. *The Genetical Theory of Natural Selection*. Oxford: Clarendon Press, 1930.

R. A. Fisher. Randomisation, and an old enigma of card play. *The Mathematical Gazette*, 18:294–297, 1934.

R. A. Fisher. Polymorphism and natural selection. *Journal of Ecology*, 46(2):289–293, 1958.

D. Fudenberg and D. K. Levine. *The Theory of Learning in Games*. Cambridge, MA: MIT Press, 1998.

J. S. Gale and L. J. Eaves. Logic of animal conflict. *Nature*, 254(5499):463, 1975.

V. Geist. The evolution of horn-like organs. *Behaviour*, 27(1-2):175–214, 1966.

V. Geist. On fighting strategies in animal combat. *Nature*, 250(5464):354–354, 1974.

D. C. Gilley. The behaviour of honey bees (*Apis mellifera ligustica*) during queen duels. *Ethology*, 107:601–622, 2001.

W. D. Hamilton. Extraordinary sex ratios. *Science*, 156(3774):477–488, 1967.

P. Hammerstein and S. E. Riechert. Payoffs and strategies in territorial contests: ESS analyses of two ecotypes of the spider *Agelenopsis aperta*. *Evolutionary Ecology*, 2(2):115–138, 1988.

O. Harman. *The Price of Altruism*. New York: W. W. Norton, 2010.

O. Harman. Birth of the first ESS: George Price, John Maynard Smith, and the discovery of the lost 'Antlers' paper. *Journal of Experimental Zoology Part B: Molecular and Developmental Evolution*, 316B(1):1–9, 2011.

Y. Hsu, R. L. Earley, and L. L. Wolf. Modulation of aggressive behaviour by fighting experience: Mechanisms and contest outcomes. *Biological Reviews of the Cambridge Philosophical Society*, 81(1):33–74, 2006.

O. Leimar. The evolution of social dominance through reinforcement learning. *The American Naturalist*, 197(5):560–575, 2021.

O. Leimar and M. Enquist. Effects of asymmetries in owner–intruder conflicts. *Journal of Theoretical Biology*, 111(3):475–491, 1984.

O. Leimar, S. Austad, and M. Equist. A test of the sequential assessment game: Fighting in the bowl and doily spider *Frontinella pyramitela*. *Evolution*, 45(4):862–874, 1991.

R. C. Lewontin. Evolution and the theory of games. *Journal of Theoretical Biology*, 1(3):382–403, 1961.

K. Lorenz. *Das sogenannte Böse*. Wien: Dr. G. Borotha, 1963.

R. D. Luce and H. Raiffa. *Games and Decisions*. New York: Wiley, 1957.

J. Maynard Smith. *On Evolution*. Edinburgh: Edinburgh University Press, 1972.

J. Maynard Smith. The theory of games and the evolution of animal conflicts. *Journal of Theoretical Biology*, 47(1):209–221, 1974.

J. Maynard Smith. Evolution and the theory of games. *American Scientist*, 64(1):41–45, 1976.

J. Maynard Smith. Game theory and the evolution of behaviour. *Proceedings of the Royal Society of London: Series B, Biological Sciences*, 205(1161):475–488, 1979.

J. Maynard Smith. *Evolution and the Theory of Games*. Cambridge: Cambridge University Press, 1982.

J. Maynard Smith and G. A. Parker. The logic of asymmetric animal contests. *Animal Behaviour*, 24(1):159–175, 1976.

J. Maynard Smith and G. R. Price. The logic of animal conflict. *Nature*, 246:15–18, 1973.

J. M. McNamara and A. I. Houston. Integrating function and mechanism. *Trends in Ecology & Evolution*, 24:670–675, 2009.

J. M. McNamara and O. Leimar. *Game Theory in Biology: Concepts and Frontiers*. Oxford: Oxford University Press, 2020.

G. A. Parker. Assessment strategy and the evolution of fighting behaviour. *Journal of Theoretical Biology*, 47(1):223–243, 1974.

I. P. Pavlov. *Conditioned reflexes: An investigation of the physiological activity of the cerebral cortex*. Oxford: Oxford University Press, 1927.

A. Rapoport. *Two-Person Game Theory: The Essential Ideas*. Ann Arbor, MI: University of Michigan Press, 1966.

L. J. Savage. *The Foundation of Statistics*. New York: Dover Publications, 1972.

T. C. Schelling. *The Strategy of Conflict*. Cambridge, MA: Harvard University Press, 1960.

R. F. Shaw and J. D. Mohler. The selective significance of the sex ratio. *The American Naturalist*, 87(837):337–342, 1953.

K. Sigmund. John Maynard Smith and evolutionary game theory. *Theoretical Population Biology*, 68(1):7–10, 2005.

P. Stockley and J. Bro-Jørgensen. Female competition and its evolutionary consequences in mammals. *Biological Reviews*, 86(2):341–366, 2011.

R. S. Sutton and A. G. Barto. *Reinforcement Learning: An Introduction*, 2nd ed. Cambridge, MA: MIT Press, 2018.

R. L. Trivers and D. E. Willard. Natural selection of parental ability to vary the sex ratio of offspring. *Science*, 179:90–92, 1973.

P.-O. Wickman and C. Wiklund. Territorial defence and its seasonal decline in the speckled wood butterfly (*Pararge aegeria*). *Animal Behaviour*, 31(4):1206–1216, 1983.

S. Wright. *Evolution and the Genetics of Populations, Vol. 3*. Chicago: University of Chicago Press, 1977.

12

The Dynamics of Evolutionary Game Theory

Karl Sigmund

The best seller *The Selfish Gene* (Dawkins, 1976) acquainted a wide audience with the concept of an "evolutionarily stable strategy" (Maynard Smith, 1974; Maynard Smith, 1982). It also popularized the term *replicator*. This explains why the first dynamics of evolutionary game theory, introduced in the late seventies by Taylor and Jonker (1978), was named "replicator dynamics" by Schuster and Sigmund (1983). Not only did it model the action of selection on the frequencies of behavioral programs (i.e., strategies), but important special cases of these dynamics had also been studied, with no games in mind, in fields as diverse as population ecology, population genetics, and molecular evolution. The replicators there were organisms, genes, and molecules, respectively.

With time, it became clear that the replicator equation was only one of a quickly growing family of game dynamics (Weibull, 1995; Hofbauer and Sigmund, 1998; Gintis, 2000; Cressman, 2003; Nowak, 2006; Sandholm, 2010). There are many ways to classify them: for instance, discrete time versus continuous time dynamics, well-mixed populations with random encounters versus structured populations with local interactions, and so forth. We focus on the continuous-time well-mixed case, which behaves best, from the game theory viewpoint, and start by discriminating between polymorphic and monomorphic population models. This dichotomy corresponds, very roughly, to deciding between an ecological or an evolutionary population dynamics model.

In the "ecological" approach, a certain number of types of players is given, each type with its (pure or mixed) strategy, and the relative frequencies of the types change with time in response to their payoff, which in turn depends on the frequencies. To mention only the most popular of these dynamics,

1. Replicator dynamics
2. Best-reply dynamics (and smoothed versions thereof)

I would like to thank Hannelore De Silva, Josef Hofbauer, Michihiro Kandori, and an anonymous referee for their valuable comments and suggestions.

3. Brown–von Neumann–Nash dynamics
4. Payoff projection dynamics

For the sake of simplicity, we will only consider symmetric games with a finite number of strategies n. Then the equations appear as follows.

For the replicator dynamics,

$$\dot{x}_i = x_i(P_i - \overline{P}) \tag{12.1}$$

on the unit simplex Δ_n. Here $x_i(t)$ is the frequency of players of type i at time t, $P_i(x)$ is the expected payoff of such a player when the population state is x, and $\overline{P} = \sum x_i P_i$ is the average payoff in the population. The per capita growth rate of type i is given by how much it fares better or worse compared to the average payoff.

For the best-reply dynamics,

$$\dot{x} \in BR(x) - x, \tag{12.2}$$

where $BR(x)$ is the set of best replies to state x. If this set is not a singleton, then the right-hand side is multivalued and (12.2) is a differential inclusion. Solutions are Lipschitz functions satisfying (12.2) for almost all t. If the payoff function P is linear in x, the orbits are piecewise linear. This differential inclusion can be approximated by various "smoothed best-reply dynamics" such as, for instance, the logit dynamics $\dot{x}_i = N^{-1} \exp\left(\varepsilon^{-1} P_i\right) - x_i$, where N is a normalization factor. This yields an ordinary differential equation that approaches (12.2) for $\varepsilon \to 0$.

For the Brown–von Neumann–Nash dynamics,

$$\dot{x}_i = P_{i+} - x_i \sum P_{j+}, \tag{12.3}$$

where $P_{i+} = \max\{P_i - \overline{P}, 0\}$ is the so-called excess payoff for i. This is arguably the oldest game dynamics, used by Brown and von Neumann (1950) in their proof of the minimax theorem for zero-sum games, and by Nash (1950) to prove the existence of equilibria.

For the payoff projection dynamics,

$$\dot{x}_i = P_i - \frac{1}{n} \sum P_j \tag{12.4}$$

(with, for $x_i = 0$, the right-hand side modified in a way to be explained presently, such that orbits cannot leave the simplex Δ_n). The vector field is the orthogonal projection of the payoff vector on the tangent space of Δ_n, and it indicates the direction of the maximal feasible increase in payoff by a small minority slightly stepping away from the mean (Sandholm, 2010). The boundary condition introduces a discontinuity, which entails that trajectories can merge and thus cannot be uniquely extended backward in time.

In contrast to the "ecological" approach illustrated by these examples, the "evolutionary" approach assumes a monomorphic population, whose strategy is given by some continuous real-valued trait $z \in \mathbb{R}^n$. The underlying idea is that from time to time, a small dissident population with a slightly different trait y invades. If it does better, it becomes the new resident population. If not, it vanishes. In evolutionary biology, this leads to a "trait substitution sequence" powered by rare mutations that, if successful, replace the resident. In learning theory, we may assume that a random deviation is imitated by all if successful. With $W(y, z)$ denoting the payoff for a player with trait y in a population of z-players, the vector field $\dot{z}_i = \frac{\partial}{\partial y} W(y, z)$ (evaluated for $y = z$) points into the direction of maximal payoff increase for the deviation and defines the half-space where dissidents can invade. This is called the *canonical equation of adaptive dynamics*. The solution approximates the path $z(t)$ of a monomorphic population under selection and (very rare) mutation; alternatively, it mimics learning by (very occasional) trial and error. It helps to think of a homogenous population with trait z exploring its immediate neighborhood by sending out "scouts" with slightly different trait values y, and then imitating the scout who fared best.

If the trait z is constrained to some subspace, the dynamics must be restricted accordingly, by projecting onto the tangent cone of feasible directions. In particular, if the components of z are the probabilities of a mixed strategy, then $W(y, z)$ is the inner product $y \cdot P(z)$ and the trait evolves in the interior of the simplex Δ_n according to (12.4). Up to a change in velocity, this means $\dot{x}_i = \sum_j (P_i - P_j)$. On the boundary of Δ_n, the right-hand side must be modified to prevent orbits from leaving the simplex (see Sandholm, 2010): If $x_k = 0$ *and* $\dot{x}_k < 0$, all summation terms on the right-hand side containing P_k must be deleted (in particular, the modified vector field satisfies $\dot{x}_k = 0$ and $\sum \dot{x}_j = 0$).

Interestingly, if the metric used in Δ_n is not Euclidean but a Riemannian metric known in population biology as a Shashahani metric, one obtains the replicator equation (12.1) (Hofbauer and Sigmund, 1998). Thus the same equation can be encountered both in the polymorphic model, which describes a (usually mixed) population consisting of a given set of different types, and in the monomorphic setup, where it is the (usually mixed) strategy that evolves (see also Börgers and Sarin, 1997).

For all decent game dynamics, Nash equilibria are fixed points. For some, as for instance the payoff projection dynamics (12.4) or the related target projection dynamics (Tsakas and Voorneveld, 2009), they are exactly the fixed points. For others, such as replicator dynamics, there exist fixed points that are not Nash. The so-called folk theorem for the replicator dynamics states that every (Lyapunov) stable fixed point is a Nash equilibrium; so is every fixed point that is the limit of an orbit in the interior of Δ_n, and all strict Nash equilibria are asymptotically stable. The same results hold for any "imitation dynamics" $\dot{x}_i = x_i g_i(x)$ with $\sum g_i = 0$, with (for the last statement) the proviso that it is payoff monotonic: $g_i > g_j$ if and only if $P_i > P_j$.

Since the notion of evolutionarily stable strategy, or ESS, stood at the beginning of the population viewpoint in game theory, it also yielded the first test object for game dynamics. Let us assume for simplicity that the payoff is linear (i.e., $P(x) = Ux$ for some $n \times n$ matrix U). A strategy $\hat{p}$ is said to be an ESS if a "resident" population using $\hat{p}$ cannot be invaded by a "dissident" minority using some other strategy, in the sense that (i) p-players do not do better than $\hat{p}$-players, against $\hat{p}$ (this is the Nash equilibrium condition; $p \cdot U\hat{p} \leq \hat{p} \cdot U\hat{p}$), and (ii) in case they do equally well, $\hat{p}$ fares better than p against p (this is the "stability condition"; from $p \cdot U\hat{p} = \hat{p} \cdot u\hat{p}$ and $p \neq \hat{p}$ follows $\hat{p} \cdot Up > p \cdot Up$). Some games have no ESS, and sometimes a game admits several ESS (which then must be on the boundary of Δ_n). For payoff functions that are nonlinear, a localized version is used: $\hat{p}$ is a local ESS if $\hat{p} \cdot P(p) > p \cdot P(p)$ for all $p \neq \hat{p}$ in some neighborhood of $\hat{p}$. In the linear case, this is equivalent to (i) and (ii) provided previously.

In the original definition by Maynard Smith, the dynamics describing the invasion by the dissident were not specified explicitly. But if we apply, for instance, the replicator equation to the two "types" using $\hat{p}$ and p, respectively, then the ESS condition is equivalent to the condition that if the frequency of the "invader" p is initially small, it converges to 0.

For linear games, every ESS is an attractor for the replicator dynamics (Hofbauer et al., 1979). It is even a global attractor if it is in the interior of Δ_n. The same result holds for the other dynamics (12.2), (12.3) and (12.4) (see Hofbauer, 2011). On the other hand, there exist games with a Nash equilibrium that is asymptotically stable and even globally attracting for the replicator equation, but which is not an ESS (Zeeman, 1980; Cressman and Tao, 2014). It was shown by Cressman (1992) that a strategy $\hat{p}$ is an ESS if and only if it is strongly stable in the following sense. Let $p(1), \ldots, p(N) \in \Delta_n$ be any N strategies whose convex hull contains $\hat{p}$. Consider a population consisting of types i using strategies $p(i)$, and whose frequencies x_i evolve according to the replicator equation. If the mean strategy in the population, which is given by $\sum x_i p(i) = p(x)$, converges to $\hat{p}$ for $t \to +\infty$ whenever the initial value of $p(x)$ is sufficiently close to $\hat{p}$, then $\hat{p}$ is said to be strongly stable.

In the case of a monomorphic population evolving in a continuous trait space, any local ESS is a fixed point of the canonical equation of adaptive dynamics. If the payoff $W(y, z)$ is linear in y (i.e., of the form $y \cdot P(z)$), then a local ESS in the interior of Δ_n is attracting (Hofbauer and Sigmund, 1998). For other payoff functions, however, it need not be (Eshel, 1983; Nowak, 1992). A strategy is said to be convergence stable if it is an asymptotically stable fixed point of the canonical equation of adaptive dynamics. There exist locally stable ESS that are not convergence stable. In this case, the local ESS, while safe from future change because it is uninvadable by nearby strategies, is not a likely outcome of past adaptations: A population close by can evolve *away* from it. These results show that evolutionary stability alone does not suffice to capture the long-term behavior.

An important motivation of game dynamics is equilibrium selection. In many games, there are several Nash equilibria and even ESS. Some look more reasonable than others, but criteria of rationality are notoriously hard to agree upon. Dynamics offers simple means to weigh the importance of various equilibria

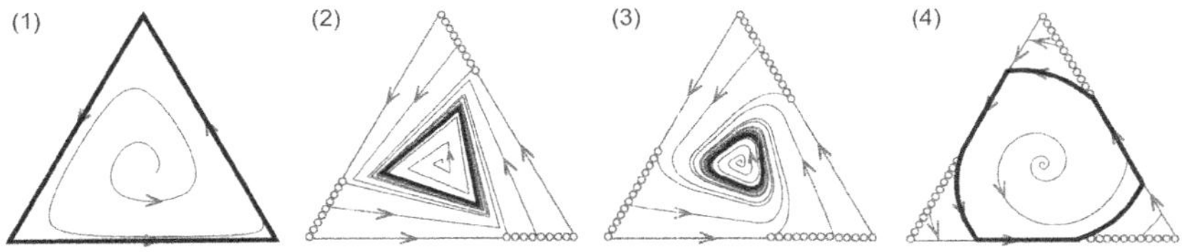

FIGURE 12.1 Rock-Paper-Scissors with (1) replicator, (2) best reply, (3) Brown–von Neumann–Nash, and (4) payoff projection dynamics. The bold line is the long-term outcome. The empty dots mark the boundary points of the state simplex Δ_3, where missing strategies can invade.

(for instance, various notions of stability, the size of the basins of attraction, etc.) and to discard spurious equilibria.

For many dynamics and for many games, the long-term outcome is not an equilibrium at all, but a periodic or chaotic attractor. Such outcomes offer a real enrichment of game theory, which was overly fixated on equilibria for a long time.

Let us consider, for instance, a cyclically symmetric Rock-Paper-Scissors game where the loss is twice as costly as the gain (see Hofbauer, 2011). In this case, the strategy $(1/3, 1/3, 1/3)$ is the only Nash equilibrium. However, it is unstable for each of the game dynamics (12.1)–(12.4). No orbit (apart from the equilibrium itself) remains close-by. This, however, is almost the only prediction on which these dynamics agree. It is an instructive exercise to compare their long-term attractors (see Figure 12.1).

The orbits of the replicator equation (12.1) converge to the boundary of Δ_n. The attractor is a so-called heteroclinic cycle. It consists of (i) the three vertices of the simplex, which are fixed points (and more precisely saddle points of (12.1) but not Nash equilibria), and (ii) the edges joining them. Asymptotically, the orbits from the interior will remain for a long time in the vicinity of one vertex, then quickly move over to the vicinity of the next vertex, remain there for a much longer time, then move over to the next, and so on. To an observer, it will look, most of the time, as if just one of the strategies is played in the population – but it can be suddenly replaced and is impossible to predict.

The orbits of the best-reply dynamics (12.2) converge to a limit cycle in the interior of Δ_n. It consists of a closed, piecewise linear orbit, the so-called Shapley triangle. Along this orbit, the maximal payoff achieved by a strategy is 0, which is higher than the payoff achieved at equilibrium.

The orbits of the Brown–von Neumann–Nash dynamics (12.3) converge to a limit cycle that looks like a more rounded version of the Shapley triangle. So does any smooth version of the best-reply dynamics, such as the logit dynamics. For both (12.2) and (12.3), all three strategies will coexist permanently in the long run.

The orbits of the payoff projection dynamics (12.4) also converge to a limit cycle, but this cycle consists of three segments on the edges of the boundary of

Δ_n, connected by three curved lines in the interior of Δ_n. To an observer, the population plays sometimes two, sometimes all three strategies. Periodically, one of them is eliminated in turn, only to reappear later.

While the unique Nash equilibrium in this example never attracts any orbit, it attracts all time averages $\frac{1}{T}\int_0^T x(t)\,\mathrm{d}t$, with $T \to +\infty$, for (12.2), (12.3), and (12.4) alike. However, it does not attract the time averages of the orbits of the replicator equation (12.1). Remarkably, these time averages converge to the Shapley triangle (see Gaunersdorfer and Hofbauer, 1995).

It should not be thought that this example is merely a mathematical curiosity. There exist several experimentally tested real-life interactions with the Rock-Scissors-Paper structure, ranging from bacteria (Kerr et al., 2002) to lizards (Sinervo and Lively, 1996) to humans (Semmann et al., 2003; Lahkar, 2011).

Does it make sense to test which are the "right" dynamics in a specific setup? Addressing such a question by field observations seems hopeless. In a game lab experiment studying social learning (Cason et al., 2014), the closest fit was obtained by none of the above dynamics but by a discrete-time best-reply model displaying undampened oscillations (Bednarik and Hofbauer, 2017).

Nonequilibrium outcomes are not a peculiarity of these or those specific dynamics. They may occur for any myopic adjustment dynamics (MADs). According to Swinkels (1993), these dynamics are defined, for linear games with payoff matrix U, by the property that $\dot{x} \cdot Ux \geq 0$, with equality only at the fixed points. Whenever this property holds, the population evolves in the direction of a local improvement of the payoff for those who move first. The dynamics (12.1)–(12.4) are all MADs. For each MAD, there exists open sets of games and initial states such that the long-term outcome approaches no equilibrium (see Hofbauer, 2011).

On the other hand, if $\hat{x}$ is an interior Nash equilibrium, then the dynamics heading straight toward it, namely $\dot{x}_i = \hat{x}_i - x_i$, are MADs if and only if $\hat{x}$ is an ESS. Furthermore, whenever the game is a partnership game (i.e., the payoff matrix U is symmetric), the mean payoff $x \cdot Ux$ never decreases along a trajectory of MADs, and every trajectory converges to a convex set of Nash equilibria. More generally, there exist large classes of games for which every reasonable dynamic converges to an equilibrium (see Sandholm, 2010).

Evolutionary game dynamics shift the perspective away from equilibria and also from rationality. For instance, a hallmark of rational play is the elimination of dominated strategies. If there is a pure strategy i that is strictly dominated by strategy y (in the sense that $P_i(x) < y \cdot P(x)$ for all $x \in \Delta_n$), then x_i converges to 0 for (12.1) and (12.3) but not necessarily for (12.2) and (12.4) (see Hofbauer and Weibull, 1996; Berger and Hofbauer, 2008).

Game dynamics can be "innovative," in the sense of allowing new strategies to arise. If not, then the boundary of the state space is invariant. (This is the case for the replicator dynamics and more generally for all imitation dynamics, which are entirely based on selecting among existing strategies.) Innovative dynamics can introduce new strategies into the population, by mutation, trial and error, or migration. More importantly, new strategies can be adopted by intelligent behavior, such as motivates the best-reply dynamics.

All deterministic dynamics rely on an underlying stochastic process, which describes how individuals in the population adopt and update strategies. This adjustment can occur through inheritance, and in this biological range of applications, evolutionary game dynamics is nothing but a branch of frequency-dependent selection. If one interprets the payoff $P_i(x)$ for type i as its "fitness," that is, as its reproductive success, then its population size $N_i(t)$ grows according to $\dot{N}_i(t) = N_i P_i$, which implies the replicator equation (12.1) for the relative frequencies x_i.

It must be stressed that this approach assumes "like begets like" – in other words, clonal reproduction. With sexually replicating species, genes are inherited by both father and mother. If the genetic locus determines a trait whose payoff is independent of the state of the population, then the classical selection equation of population dynamics, which describes the frequencies of the alleles of that locus, is a replicator equation. The "strategies" of the parents are the alleles that they contribute to the offspring. Not surprisingly, the underlying "game," namely mating, is a partnership game, and the average fitness in the population never decreases.

However, in the more interesting case that the trait is a behavioral strategy whose success depends on the coplayers, the complexity in the dynamics of both the genes and the strategies increases considerably. It depends on the intricacies of the genotype-phenotype map, on (genetic) dominance effects between alleles, on whether fitness operates via mortality or fertility, and so forth. If, as is commonly the case, *several* genetic loci determine the behavioral trait, then recombination between the loci introduces further complications. Models show that this can effectively counteract strategic predictions (Hofbauer and Sigmund, 1998). Neglecting such effects is termed the "phenotypic gambit." It often works, which is a pragmatic justification (see McNamara and Leimar, 2020). The phenotypic gambit seems hard to avoid, as soon as one studies organisms that are more complex than viruses or bacteria.

The updating of strategies can also occur through learning. This is the usual scenario for modeling human behavior. It also applies to many interactions among nonhuman populations, as for instance in the habitat selection game. Here individuals can gain information by sampling patches or else by sampling the strategies of other individuals. The two methods lead to different dynamics but the same asymptotic outcome: a Nash equilibrium, namely the ideal free distribution (see Krivan et al., 2008).

There exists a vast literature on possible learning mechanisms, through imitation, reinforcement, regret, belief-updating, and so forth. A general ansatz for models based on myopic decision-making is the input–output equation $\cdot x_i = \sum_j \left[x_j f_{ij}(x) - f_{ji}(x) x_i\right]$, where $f_{ij}(x)$ is the rate at which players using strategy j switch to i. If, for instance, $f_{ij}(x) = x_i\,[K + P_i(x)]$, or $f_{ij}(x) = x_i\,\left[[K - P_j(x)\right]$, or

$f_{ij}(x) = x_i\left[P_i(x) - P_j(x)\right]_+$ (where K is any constant to make the expressions positive), we obtain the replicator equation (12.1). The factor x_i indicates the probability that type i is randomly sampled as a model for potential imitation. The same expressions, with x_i replaced by $(nx_j)^{-1}$, leads to the payoff projection dynamics (12.4). This switching rate is driven by "insecurity": The fewer there are of the own type j, the more ready j-players are to update their strategy (see Sandholm, 2010).

Some mechanisms, for instance experience-weighed attraction (EWA; see Camerer and Ho, 1999; Pangallo et al., 2022), combine learning processes such as fictitious play and reinforcement learning. They are often empirically successful. Even for scenarios where the Nash equilibrium is dynamically unstable, they may offer support for an equilibrium prediction of the time averages.

For example, in a Rock-Scissors-Paper game, as considered previously (see Figure 12.1), the best-reply dynamics cycle along the Shapley triangle, and its time average converges to a point that (if the game is not cyclically symmetric) may be different from the Nash equilibrium, although often close by. It is called a time-averaged shapley polygon (TASP; see Benaïm et al., 2009). The time averages of the orbits of the replicator equation also converge to the Shapley triangle; however, the time averages *of the time averages* do not converge to a point. Similarly, in discrete-time stochastic fictitious play, where players play with a high probability of the best response to the mean strategy (averaged over *all* previous rounds), the strategies approach the Shapley triangle, while their time average will not converge. If the players, however, place a higher weight on more recent rounds, as in EWA, then almost all time averages converge to TASP, although the orbits keep cycling. An observation of the time limit, for such a learning rule, may wrongly conclude that play has converged to equilibrium.

So far, we have focused on players randomly matched with each other. In real life, most interactions are local, restricted to neighbors. Game dynamics in structured populations has been studied intensively in the last decades. It introduces the perspective of statistical mechanics and leads to outcomes that can sharply disagree with predictions of classical game theory (see Nowak and May, 1992; Blume, 1993). Here again, the updating mechanisms can get the upper hand. It is significant that a substantial part of game theory in structured populations is published in physics journals, with only modest impact on economic thinking.

The main open issue in game dynamics is the adjustment process itself. How does it lead to equilibrium? Does it lead to equilibrium at all? It is interesting that in population ecology, cycles have been in the focus of attention from the very start of Lotka's and Volterra's pioneering work, in spite of the fact that empirical support for such cycles was originally weak. In contrast to ecology, in game theory, cycles and other aspects of nonequilibrium dynamics have remained a relatively minor concern.

As Kandori has indicated in Chapter 10 an adjustment rule can be viewed as a strategy in its own right and can itself be adjusted by intelligent players. This chimes in with Émile Borel's demand that "a place must be made for probability *and* psychology" (my italics; see Mazliak's Chapter 2). It is this psychological aspect, the greater or smaller "habilité" of human players, that makes predictions about adjustment difficult. The profusion of learning mechanisms vindicates the variety of game dynamics currently offered.

A classical quote from the eminent geneticist Theodosius Dobzhanski is that "nothing in biology makes sense except in the light of evolution." Some of this sentiment applies to game theory too; the idea of players stepwise adjusting their strategies is certainly fundamental. However, we must be aware of the risk that the mechanisms of adaptation (inheritance, learning, contact networks, and so forth) can counteract the "sense" provided by game theory. This is where we have to borrow from biology and extend the selectionist "phenotypic gambit" to a more general "strategic gambit," in the hope that the intricacies underlying adjustment processes do not unduly interfere with the game theoretic perspective. A closer connection between empirical work and dynamical models is certainly needed.

To sum up, the basic paradigm shift behind evolutionary game dynamics consists in adopting a population viewpoint: Instead of considering two fully rational players trying to outguess each other, it considers large populations where players meet (often randomly), engage in a game according to their behavioral programs, and do so with more or less success, high payoff being translated into a spreading of the program. A population perspective is a key ingredient of the theory of natural selection, ever since Darwin. It is not by accident that evolutionary game theory was introduced by one of the foremost theoretical biologists, John Maynard Smith, and anticipated by two others, namely Fisher (1958) and Hamilton (1967).

This makes it all the more surprising that around 1950 already, John Nash had used the same ideas, proposing a game theory based on "mass action" rather than rationality. Players who are selected at random from their respective populations "accumulate empirical evidence on the pure strategies at their disposal" (see Nash, 1996, p. 32). Nash did not explicitly model a learning process but used three versions of game dynamics for his three proofs of the existence of Nash equilibria (namely, Brown–von Neumann–Nash, best reply, and smoothed best reply; see Hofbauer, 2001, for more details). In the same vein, Brown's venerable method of fictitious play can be seen as an anticipation of best-response dynamics (Sorin, 2011).

It took some thirty years before the game theoretic ideas of Émile Borel became known to a wider audience, with the publication of the seminal book by John von Neumann and Oskar Morgenstern. Similarly, it took thirty years for the evolutionary approach of Brown, von Neumann, and Nash to be taken up by a wider community. By now, a substantial set of potential updating mechanisms has been modelled and analyzed via game dynamics. Large as it is, it is yet unlikely to capture the full range of intelligent (and stupid) behavior used by human players. A closer relation between the dynamics of nonequilibrium play and empirical data on adaptation and learning is sorely needed. This is a topic where psychology and economics can fruitfully join hands.

12.1 REFERENCES

P. Bednarik and J. Hofbauer. Discretized best-response dynamics for the rock-paper-scissors game. *Journal of Dynamics and Games*, 4:75–86, 2017.

M. Benaïm, J. Hofbauer, and E. Hopkins. Learning in games with unstable equilibria. *Journal of Economic Theory*, 144:1694–1709, 2009.

U. Berger and J. Hofbauer. Irrational behavior in the Brown–von Neumann–Nash dynamics. *Games and Economic Behavior*, 56:1–6, 2008.

L. E. Blume. The statistical mechanics of strategic interaction. *Games and Economic Behavior*, 5:387–424, 1993.

T. Börgers and R. Sarin. Learning through reinforcement and replicator dynamics. *Journal of Economic Theory*, 77:1–14, 1997.

G. W. Brown and J. von Neumann. Solutions of games by differential equations. In H. Kuhn and A. Tucker, eds., *Annals of Mathematical Studies*, vol. 24, pp. 73–79. Princeton, NJ: Princeton University Press, 1950.

C. Camerer and T.-H. Ho. Experience-weighted attraction learning in normal form games. *Econometrica*, 67(4):827–874, 1999.

T. N. Cason, D. Friedman, and E. Hopkins. Cycles and instability in a rock-paper-scissors population game: A continuous time experiment. *Review of Economic Studies*, 81:112–136, 2014.

R. Cressman. *The Stability Concept of Evolutionary Game Theory*. Berlin: Springer, 1992.

R. Cressman. *Evolutionary Dynamics and Extensive Form Games*. Cambridge: MIT Press, 2003.

R. Cressman and Y. Tao. The replicator equation and other game dynamics. *PNAS*, 111:10810–10817, 2014.

R. Dawkins. *The Selfish Gene*. Oxford: Oxford University Press, 1976.

I. Eshel. Evolutionary and continuous stability. *Journal of Theoretical Biology*, 103:99–111, 1983.

R. A. Fisher. Polymorphism and natural selection. *Journal of Ecology*, 46(2):289–293, 1958.

A. Gaunersdorfer and J. Hofbauer. Fictitious play, Shapley polygons and the replicator equation. *Games and Economic Behavior*, 11:279–303, 1995.

H. Gintis. *Game Theory Evolving*. Princeton: Princeton University Press, 2000.

W. D. Hamilton. Extraordinary sex ratios. *Science*, 156(3774):477–488, 1967.

J. Hofbauer. From Nash and Brown to Maynard Smith: Equilibria, dynamics, and ESS. *Selection*, 1:81–88, 2001.

J. Hofbauer. Deterministic evolutionary game dynamics. In K. Sigmund, ed., *Evolutionary Game Dynamics*, pp. 61–79. AMS Symposia in Applied Mathematics. Providence, RI: American Mathematical Society, 2011.

J. Hofbauer, P. Schuster, and K. Sigmund. A note on evolutionary stable strategies and game dynamics. *Journal of Theoretical Biology*, 81:609–612, 1979.

J. Hofbauer and K. Sigmund. *Evolutionary Games and Population Dynamics*. Cambridge: Cambridge University Press, 1998.

J. Hofbauer and J. W. Weibull. Evolutionary selection against dominated strategies. *Journal of Economic Theory*, 71:558–573, 1996.

B. Kerr, M. A. Riley, M. W. Feldman, and B. J. M. Bohannan. Local dispersal promotes biodiversity in a real-life game of rock-paper-scissors. *Nature*, 418:171–174, 2002.

V. Krivan, R. Cressman, and C. Schneider. The ideal free distribution: A review and synthesis of the game-theoretic perspective. *Theoretical Population Biology*, 73:403–425, 2008.

R. Lahkar. The dynamic instability of dispersed price equilibria. *Journal of Economic Theory*, 146:1796–1827, 2011.

J. Maynard Smith. The theory of games and the evolution of animal conflicts. *Journal of Theoretical Biology*, 47(1):209–221, 1974.

J. Maynard Smith. *Evolution and the Theory of Games*. Cambridge: Cambridge University Press, 1982.

J. M. McNamara and O. Leimar. *Game Theory in Biology: Concepts and Frontiers*. Oxford: Oxford University Press, 2020.

J. F. Nash Jr. Equilibrium points in *N*-person games. *PNAS*, 36:48–49, 1950.

J. F. Nash Jr. *Essays on Game Theory*. Worcester: Edward Elgar, 1996.

M. A. Nowak. An evolutionarily stable strategy may be inaccessible. *Journal of Theoretical Biology*, 142:237–241, 1992.

M. A. Nowak. *Evolutionary Dynamics*. Cambridge, MA: Harvard University Press, 2006.

M. A. Nowak and R. May. Evolutionary games and spatial chaos. *Nature*, 359:826–829, 1992.

M. Pangallo, J. B. T. Sanders, T. Galla, and J. Doyne Farmer. Towards a taxonomy of learning dynamics in 2×2 games. *Games and Economic Behavior*, 132:1–21, 2022.

W. H. Sandholm. *Population Games and Evolutionary Dynamics*. Cambridge, MA: MIT Press, 2010.

P. Schuster and K. Sigmund. Replicator dynamics. *Journal of Theoretical Biology*, 100:533–538, 1983.

D. Semmann, H. J. Krambeck, and M. Milinski. Volunteering leads to rock-paper-scissors dynamics in a public goods game. *Nature*, 425:390–393, 2003.

M. Sinervo and C. M. Lively. The rock-paper-scissors game and the evolution of alternative male strategies. *Nature*, 380:240–243, 1996.

S. Sorin. On some global and unilateral adaptive dynamics. In K. Sigmund, ed., *Evolutionary Game Dynamics, AMS Symposia in Applied Mathematics*, pp. 81–109. Providence, RI: American Mathematical Society, 2011.

J. M. Swinkels. Adjustment dynamics and rational play in games. *Games and Economic Behavior*, 5:455–484, 1993.

P. D. Taylor and L. B. Jonker. Evolutionarily stable strategies and game dynamics. *Mathematical Biosciences*, 40(1–2):145–156, 1978.

E. Tsakas and M. Voorneveld. The target projection dynamic. *Games and Economic Behavior*, 67:708–719, 2009.

J. W. Weibull. *Evolutionary Game Theory*. Cambridge, MA: MIT Press, 1995.

E. C. Zeeman. Population dynamics from game theory. In Z. Nitecki and C. Robinson, eds., *Global Theory of Dynamical Systems, Lecture Notes in Mathematics 819*, pp. 471–497. Berlin: Springer, 1980.

PART IV

COMPUTER SCIENCE

13

Introduction to Part IV

Felix Brandt and Éva Tardos

In some sense the disciplines of computer science and game theory can be considered siblings because they share one of their founding fathers. John von Neumann initiated the formal study of games together with Oscar Morgenstern and their joint book *Games and Economic Behavior*, which appeared in 1944 (von Neumann and Morgenstern, 1944). Together with others such as Alan Turing and Charles Babbage, von Neumann is also considered one of the pioneers of computer science. Shortly after the publication of *Games and Economic Behavior*, von Neumann laid out the details of the first electronic and binary computer (von Neumann, 1945) and foresaw the importance of polynomial-time algorithms (von Neumann, 1953). To this date, students of computer science learn about the von Neumann computer architecture.

The purpose of this book is to celebrate 100 years of game theory. *Algorithmic game theory* has been an active subarea for at least twenty of them (Nisan et al., 2007). While it is impossible to pinpoint the exact origin of computational analyses of game-theoretic problems, there are notable examples of pioneering papers that brought techniques and insights from computer science to game theory. One of the earliest such examples is a paper by Donald Knuth, Christos Papadimitriou, and John Tsitsiklis on the complexity of iterated dominance (Knuth et al., 1988), but there have been even earlier precursors with a computational flavor such as the stable marriage algorithm, proposed by David Gale and Lloyd Shapley (Gale and Shapley, 1962). The strong connection between zero-sum games and linear programming, which is almost as old as game theory itself, constitutes another example (Vajda, 1956).

Nowadays, the computational perspective on game-theoretic problems is ubiquitous. Next to algorithmic game theory, related interdisciplinary areas such as *algorithmic mechanism design* or *computational social choice* are flourishing, and there are numerous regular international conferences such as the *ACM Conference on Economics and Computation* (since 1999), the *Conference on Web and Internet Economics* (since 2005), and the *Symposium on Algorithmic Game Theory* (since 2008), as well as a dedicated journal, the *ACM Transactions on Economics and Computation* (since 2013).

But algorithmic game theory is not all about algorithms and complexity. The algorithmic game theory community works to apply concepts from game theory to many areas of computer science from traffic routing through designing cryptocurrency systems and many others. The community also considers the applications of computer science notions in game theory, such as modeling users as learners or quantifying the efficiency of game theoretic outcomes via approximation ratios. On top of that, computer scientists have embraced the axiomatic approach of economic theory. For example, none of the papers in Part IV is exclusively concerned with computational questions.

Part IV consists of six papers that were presented in two sessions, demonstrating the breadth and maturity of research at the intersection of computer science and game theory.

The paper by **Constantinos Daskalakis** challenges one of the most basic assumptions of game theory, namely that each player's utility function is linear in his or her strategy. While there have been generalizations to concave utility functions, very little progress has been made for nonconcave utility functions because concavity is essential for the existence of Nash equilibria. Motivated by applications in machine learning, Daskalakis introduces the class of differentiable games, proposes the notion of local Nash equilibria (which are guaranteed to exist in differentiable games), and discusses their computational intractability even in two-player zero-sum games.

Edith Elkind's paper is concerned with multiwinner elections, an emerging topic in the area of computational social choice. Much of the classic literature in social choice theory deals with functions that map ordinal preferences over candidates to a winning candidate or perhaps a ranking of the candidates. The goal of multiwinner elections is to select a fixed-size set of candidates: a committee. This gives rise to new rules as well as new axioms. Elkind's piece focuses on the case of approval-based preferences and axioms capturing the idea of proportional representation.

The contribution by **Felix Brandt** shows how the theory of symmetric two-player zero-sum games, which was initiated by Borel in 1921, can be used for randomly selecting an alternative based on quantified pairwise comparisons between alternatives. He points out desirable properties satisfied by the equilibrium distribution and gives examples of where these distributions arise as the limit of simple dynamic processes that have been studied across various disciplines, such as population biology, quantum physics, and machine learning.

Paul Milgrom describes the successful application of advances in practical truthful mechanisms design to a large-scale computationally hard problem: the US Federal Communications Commission's (FCC's) 2016–2017 incentive auction, which reallocated tens of billions of dollars of radio spectrum resources from use in television broadcasting to higher-use uses in mobile broadband. The mechanism used was an impressive combination of advances in efficiently solving NP-hard resource allocation problems (in most cases) and in new mechanism design that is simple to implement and adapts well to limited computation capacity. The auction resulted in repurposing 84 megahertz of spectrum and yielded $19.8 billion in revenue.

Nash equilibria of games have been classically used as the default solution concept: the expected outcome of strategic interaction. In the last twenty years, it was realized there are no efficient algorithms that find Nash equilibria in general games, yet there was some remaining hope that repeated interaction of the players will help them eventually find an equilibrium (even if not efficiently). To date no learning dynamics have been identified that provide such guarantees. **Jason Milionis**, Christos Papadimitriou, Georgios Piliouras, and Kelly Spendlove report on impossibility results, showing that there is a positive measure of games where no dynamics are guaranteed to converge to Nash equilibria or even to an approximate version of equilibria. The result shatters the a common defense of using Nash equilibria as the default solution concept for all games.

Tuomas Sandholm gives an extensive overview of techniques and algorithms for representing and solving large imperfect-information extensive-form games and reports on recent breakthroughs that have been achieved for the game of poker. These breakthroughs were made possible by advances in three key areas: (i) game abstraction (i.e., the systematic construction of significantly smaller extensive-form games that are strategically similar to the original game), (ii) equilibrium-finding algorithms, and (iii) solving subgames during gameplay in much finer abstractions than would be possible in advance. A new proposal put forward in Sandholm's paper involves reasoning about games whose rules are modeled via a programming language.

The talk by Tim Roughgarden on the axiomatic study of transaction fee mechanisms for cryptocurrencies is, unfortunately, not included in this book.

13.1 REFERENCES

D. Gale and L. S. Shapley. College admissions and the stability of marriage. *American Mathematical Monthly*, 69(1):9–15, 1962.

D. E. Knuth, C. H. Papadimitriou, and J. N. Tsitsiklis. A note on strategy elimination in bimatrix games. *Operations Research Letters*, 7(3):103–107, 1988.

N. Nisan, T. Roughgarden, É. Tardos, and V. Vazirani. *Algorithmic Game Theory*. Cambridge: Cambridge University Press, 2007.

S. Vajda. *Theory of Games and Linear Programming*. New York: John Wiley & Sons, 1956.

J. von Neumann. First draft of a report on the EDVAC. Technical Report Report P-78, University of Pennsylvania, 1945.

J. von Neumann. A certain zero-sum two-person game equivalent to the optimal assignment problem. In H. W. Kuhn and A. W. Tucker, eds., *Contributions to the Theory of Games (AM-28), Volume II*, pp. 5–12. Princeton, NJ: Princeton University Press, 1953.

J. von Neumann and O. Morgenstern. *Theory of Games and Economic Behavior*. Princeton, NJ: Princeton University Press, 1944.

14

Nonconcave Games

A Challenge for Game Theory's Next 100 Years

Constantinos Daskalakis

A pervasive assumption in game theory is that players' utilities are concave, or at least quasiconcave, with respect to their own strategies. While mathematically instrumental, enabling the existence of many kinds of equilibria in many kinds of settings, (quasi)concavity of payoffs is too restrictive an assumption. For the same reasons that (quasi)concavity utilities can only go so far in capturing single-agent optimization problems, they can only go so far in modeling the considerations of an agent in a strategic interaction. Besides, the study of games with nonconcave utilities is increasingly coming to the fore as deep learning ventures into multiagent learning applications. In this article, we study which types of equilibria exist in such games, and whether they are computationally tractable, proposing paths for game theory and multiagent learning in the next 100 years.

14.1 A CENTURY OF (QUASI)CONCAVE GAMES

Convexity plays a central role in optimization. If your optimization problem can be fruitfully posed as a convex minimization – equivalently, a concave maximization – problem, over some convex set, this is a cause for celebration. A large gamut of optimization methods readily becomes available to you. These methods are versatile, accommodating different types of access to your objective and constraints and providing various tradeoffs between quality of optimization and use of computational resources. Additionally, convex programming duality provides a framework for gaining a deeper understanding of your problem.

Convexity has also played a key role in the development of equilibrium theory. Von Neumann's minimax theorem (von Neumann, 1928) establishes equilibrium existence in two-player zero-sum games under the assumption that each player's payoff is concave with respect to their own strategy – and, equivalently, that their cost is convex with respect to their own strategy. Under this assumption, computing equilibrium is in fact equivalent to convex programming (Dantzig, 1951; Adler, 2013; Brooks and Reny, 2023), which makes the convex optimization toolkit readily available for equilibrium computation. It also enables a game-theoretic perspective to influence computation theory and has motivated important developments at the interface of game theory, machine learning, and optimization; see, for example, works by Cesa-Bianchi and Lugosi (2006), Shalev-Shwartz (2012), Bubeck and Cesa-Bianchi (2012), and Hazan (2016).

The assumption that a player's payoff is concave, or at least quasiconcave, with respect to their own strategy percolates through the foundations of game theory and economic theory. It is crucial in establishing generalizations of the minimax theorem (see, e.g., Fan, 1953; Sion, 1958), the existence of Nash equilibrium (Nash, 1950), and the existence of several other equilibrium notions in noncooperative games (see, e.g., Osborne and Rubinstein, 1994). For instance, the following is a general family of noncooperative games, with coupled strategy constraints and concave utilities, for which a Nash equilibrium is guaranteed to exist.

Definition 14.1 (**Concave Games (Debreu, 1952; Rosen, 1965)**). A n-player *continuous concave game* has a finite number, n, of players, indexed by $1, \ldots, n$. Each player, i, may choose some strategy $x_i \in \mathcal{S}_i \subseteq \mathbb{R}^{d_i}$, where d_i is the dimensionality of her strategy space and the joint strategy profile $(x_1, \ldots, x_n)$ is constrained to lie in $\mathcal{R} \subseteq \mathcal{S}_1 \times \cdots \times \mathcal{S}_n$, where $\mathcal{R}$ is convex and compact. The payoff to each player, i, is determined by some function $u_i : \times_j \mathcal{S}_j \to [-1, 1]$ of the joint strategy profile $x = (x_1, \ldots, x_n)$, which is continuous and is also concave in x_i for all x_{-i}.

It is clear that the provided definition captures normal form games by taking x_i to be the mixed strategy of player i, specializing $\mathcal{R}$ to be a product of the players' mixed strategy simplices and taking each player's payoff to be a multilinear function of the mixed strategies. Thus the following theorem generalizes Nash's.

Theorem 14.1 (**Debreu (1952); Rosen (1965)**). *A continuous concave game has a Nash equilibrium, namely some strategy profile $x^* = (x_1^*, \ldots, x_n^*) \in \mathcal{R}$ such that, for all i, $u_i(x^*) = \max\{u_i(x) \mid x = (x_i, x_{-i}^*) \in \mathcal{R}\}$.*

The aforementioned family of concave games can, in fact, be expanded to accommodate quasiconcave utilities and even more general coupled constraints over player strategies and still maintain the existence of Nash equilibrium (Harker, 1991), but let us skip this generalization here to avoid overloading our notation.

Beyond the study of noncooperative games, quasiconcavity of payoffs is a very common assumption in economic theory and is crucial for many results, including showing the existence of a competitive equilibrium in exchange economies; see the work of Arrow and Debreu (1954) and McKenzie (1954), and the ensuing literature.

Ultimately, (quasi)concavity of payoffs is key for setting up the fixed point formulations used to show the existence of various kinds of equilibria. It is

TABLE 14.1 *The matching pennies game*

	Heads	Tails
Heads	(+1/2, −1/2)	(−1/2, +1/2)
Tails	(−1/2, +1/2)	(+1/2, −1/2)

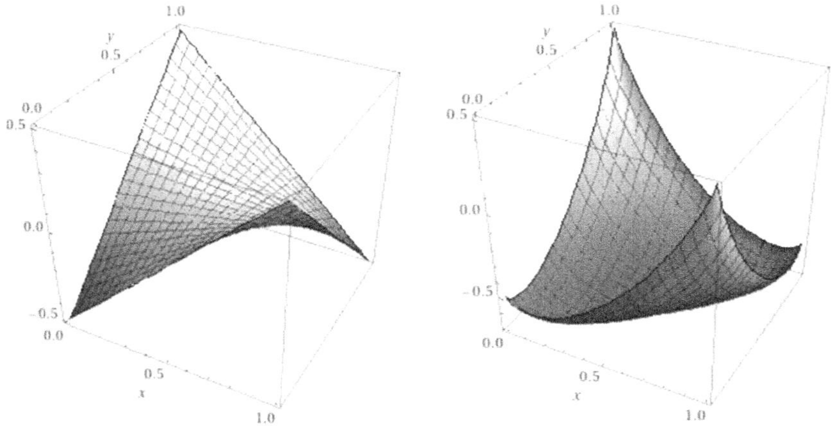

(a) StandardMatching Pennies

(b) Matching Pennies with Entropy Rewards and Costs

FIGURE 14.1 On the left, we see the payoff to the column player (a.k.a. the cost to the row player) in the matching pennies game of Table 14.1 as a function of the Heads probabilities x and y of the row and column players, respectively. The unique Nash equilibrium is $(x^*, y^*) = (1/2, 1/2)$. On the right, we see the payoff to the column player in a modified zero-sum game where the row player is additionally rewarded for a high-entropy mixed strategy, while the column player is penalized for a high-entropy mixed strategy, resulting in the column player receiving the payoff $(x + y - 2xy - \frac{1}{2}) - \frac{1}{2}H(x) - \frac{1}{2}H(y)$, where H is the entropy function. This function is not concave/quasiconcave in y, and the game has no Nash equilibrium.

also unavoidable, in general, as without this property equilibrium existence breaks, even in very simple games. Figure 14.1(a) shows the payoff to the column player (a.k.a. the cost to the row player) in the matching pennies game of Table 14.1, as a function of the Heads probabilities x and y of the row and column players, respectively. The unique equilibrium of this game is, of course, $(x^*, y^*) = \left(\frac{1}{2}, \frac{1}{2}\right)$. In Figure 14.1(b), we see the payoff to the column player in a modified zero-sum game where the row player is additionally rewarded from a high-entropy strategy, while the column player is penalized from a high-entropy strategy. In the resulting game, the column player's payoff is not concave/quasiconcave in y, and the game has no Nash equilibrium.

While mathematically instrumental, enabling the existence of many kinds of equilibria in many kinds of settings, concavity or quasiconcavity of payoffs is unfortunately too restrictive an assumption. For the same reasons that (quasi)concave utilities can only go so far in modeling single-agent decision-making, they can also go so far in modeling the considerations of an agent in a strategic interaction. Motivated by considerations such as concave production costs arising from economies of scale, the study of exchange economies with violations of (quasi)concave utilities/(quasi)convex costs has received some but not much study since the early days; see, for example, works by Graaff (1957), Bator (1957), Koopmans (1957), Farrell (1959), Rothenberg (1960), Starr (1969), and Papadimitriou and Wilkens (2011). Similarly, noncooperative games with non(quasi)concave utilities have also received some but not much study in recent works; see for example, the work of Ratliff and colleagues (2016). Ultimately, the lack of progress on these fronts is not because of lack of interest in nonconcave settings, but because these are incompatible with equilibrium existence. And without guaranteed existence of equilibria, the value of equilibrium analysis gets diminished.

14.2 THE DAWN OF NONCONCAVE GAMES

14.2.1 Embracing Nonconvexity in Machine Learning

Considerations of mathematical elegance, sharpness of prediction, and computational tractability had steered models of single-agent decision-making in the safe harbor of convex programming formulations for decades. Yet the avoidance of nonconvexity has recently landed on its face, with the advent of deep learning, and the breakthroughs it has delivered in many heretofore impenetrable problems in the field of artificial intelligence.

Deep learning has not shied away from formulating problems as nonconvex optimization problems. It has also not shied away from targeting approximate locally optimal, as opposed to globally optimal, solutions for these problems. While the latter are intractable, the former are easily attainable via lightweight optimization methods such as gradient descent (see, e.g., Ge et al., 2015; Lee et al., 2016; Allen-Zhu and Li, 2018). Whether, why, and under what conditions locally optimal solutions selected by gradient descent-based methods result in good models is still not fully understood, despite extensive study. Yet deep learning's attitude of embracing nonconvexity has led the field to groundbreaking advances in important learning challenges such as speech and image recognition, text generation, protein folding, automated translation, and more.

In recent years, deep learning has been rapidly expanding its scope to the domain of game theory, energizing the importance of studying *nonconcave games*. Indeed, many outstanding challenges in this field, such as training deep neural networks that are robust to adversarial attacks, training generative adversarial networks (GANs), and multiagent reinforcement learning (MARL), are born as multiplayer games with utility functions that are not concave (or even quasiconcave) in players' strategies, as players in these games choose parameters in deep neural networks and their utilities are functions of these neural networks. It seems that applications of nonconcave games will explode in a near future where complex agents using deep neural network models learn, make decisions, and receive rewards in a shared environment, whose state might also be affected by their decisions.

Unfortunately, embracing nonconvexity hits a wall on the multiagent front. It hits a wall as soon as we step away from single-agent settings, considering how to train two agents with nonconcave payoffs in a zero-sum interaction. Indeed, as illustrated earlier with the simple example of Figure 14.1(b), such games may not have Nash equilibria. Without much clarity about the target solution concept, practitioners have still been trying to train agents in nonconcave games by having them perform gradient ascent procedures in tandem to maximize their individual payoffs (and, equivalently, gradient descent procedures to minimize their individual losses). Unlike single-agent settings, however, gradient descent is not effective in such settings. It commonly exhibits unstable, oscillatory, or divergent behavior, and the quality of the solutions encountered in the course of training can be poor (see, e.g., Goodfellow, 2016; Metz et al., 2017; Daskalakis et al., 2018; Mescheder et al., 2018; Daskalakis and Panageas, 2018; Mazumdar et al., 2020; Adolphs et al., 2019). For example, training GANs, which are formulated as two-player zero-sum nonconcave games, is, at this point, more engineering than science, with rounds and rounds of fine-tuning before they can be reasonably trained, and even when they appear to be reasonably trained, we lack formal guarantees about the quality of samples they produce – on the contrary, they commonly fail to pass basic statistical tests of quality (see, e.g., Arora et al., 2018). The emerging importance of nonconcave games, and the practical frustration with solving them is the starting point of our investigation.

Question 1. Is there a theory of nonconcave games? What solution concepts are meaningful, universal, and tractable?

14.2.2 Nonconcave Games and Local Nash Equilibria

Motivated by the emerging applications of nonconcave games in machine learning, such as those discussed in the previous section, we propose a formal model of continuous games, dropping the concavity assumption from Definition 14.1 and adding differentiability, in accordance with the types of games arising in those applications.[1] We'll focus our attention to simultaneous games, although

[1] Some families of deep neural networks are nondifferentiable at a measure zero set of points. We could extend our exposition here to accommodate this by using subdifferentials. To avoid the unnecessary complexity that this would entail, we assume differentiability everywhere. Moreover, as noted earlier, we may consider even more general coupled constraints over player strategies. Our results can be extended to the types of coupled strategies considered by Harker (1991), but we skip such generalizations to avoid overloading our notation.

sequential games are also well-motivated and can be studied through a lens similar to the one used in our exposition; for some recent pursuits in this direction, see, for example, work by Jin and colleagues (2020), Fiez and colleagues (2020), and Mangoubi and Vishnoi (2021).

Definition 14.2 (Differentiable/Smooth Games). A n-player *differentiable game* is a simultaneous game with n players, indexed by $1, \ldots, n$. Each player, i, may choose some strategy $x_i \in \mathcal{S}_i \subset \mathbb{R}^{d_i}$, where d_i is the dimensionality of her strategy space, and the joint strategy profile $(x_1, \ldots, x_n)$ is constrained to lie in $\mathcal{R} \subset \mathcal{S}_1 \times \cdots \times \mathcal{S}_n$, where $\mathcal{R}$ is convex and compact. The payoff to each player, i, is determined by some function $u_i : \times_j \mathcal{S}_j \to [-1, 1]$ of the joint strategy profile $x = (x_1, \ldots, x_n)$, whose gradient with respect to x_i is continuous. We will refer to $\sum_i d_i$ as the *dimensionality of the game*. Moreover, we will call a differentiable game *smooth* if the gradient of u_i with respect to x_i is L_i-Lispchitz with respect to the ℓ_2 norm. In this case, we will refer to $\max_i L_i$ as the game's *smoothness*.

As illustrated in Figure 14.1(b), in the absence of concave utilities, a game may not have any Nash equilibrium. It can also be shown that checking if a game has one is NP-hard, even if the game is two-player zero-sum (Daskalakis et al., 2021). In accordance with the turn to local optimality driving recent advances in deep learning, we also advocate a turn to a notion of local Nash equilibrium, which we will argue exists exists in every differentiable game.

Definition 14.3 (Local Nash Equilibrium). Consider a differentiable game as in Definition 14.2. A strategy profile $x^* = (x_1^*, \ldots, x_n^*) \in \mathcal{R}$ is a *(first-order) local Nash equilibrium* iff for all i:

$$x_i^* = \Pi_{\mathcal{R}(x_{-i}^*)}\big(x_i^* + \nabla_{x_i} u_i(x_i^* \,;\, x_{-i}^*)\big), \tag{14.1}$$

where $\mathcal{R}(x_{-i}^*) = \{x_i \mid (x_i \,;\, x_{-i}^*) \in \mathcal{R}\}$ and $\Pi_{\mathcal{R}(x_{-i}^*)}(\cdot)$ is the ℓ_2 projection onto the set $\mathcal{R}(x_{-i}^*)$. A strategy profile $x^* = (x_1^*, \ldots, x_n^*) \in \mathcal{R}$ is an *ε-approximate local Nash equilibrium* iff for all i:

$$\left|\left|x_i^* - \Pi_{\mathcal{R}(x_{-i}^*)}\big(x_i^* + \nabla_{x_i} u_i(x_i^* \,;\, x_{-i}^*)\big)\right|\right|_2 \leq \varepsilon. \tag{14.2}$$

Intuitively, a first-order local Nash equilibrium x^* comprises strategies that satisfy a weak form of local optimality, assuming that each player has a myopic view of their utility as a function of their own strategy, consistent with a first-order Taylor approximation. This assumption fits well with the type of function access (through value and gradient value queries) that is practically available to agents in complex settings, such as those motivating our discussion. When the players have such a myopic view of their payoffs, Condition (14.1) captures that player i is playing a best response to his or her opponents' strategies.

Accordingly, Condition (14.2) captures that the player is playing an approximate best response. While the players would not be able to tell from first-order approximations to their utilities, their local Nash equilibrium strategies may, of course, be suboptimal for their true utilities. The following proposition characterizes how suboptimal players' utilities might be at an (approximate) local Nash equilibrium when considering deviations within a small ball around the local Nash equilibrium strategies. It says that the amount by which the utility might increase under small deviations is second order; namely deviations at small distance δ from a local Nash equilibrium can only give $\frac{L}{2}\delta^2$ payoff improvements, where L is the smoothness of the game (i.e., a bound on the Lipschitz constant of the gradients of the payoffs). Deviations around an ε-approximate local Nash equilibrium can benefit by an additional $\varepsilon\delta$.

Proposition 14.1 (Local Payoff Near Optimality). Consider a smooth game such that, for all i, $\nabla_{x_i} u_i(x_i\ ;\ x_{-i})$ is L-Lipschitz continuous with respect to the ℓ_2 norm. If $x^* = (x_1^*, \ldots, x_n^*)$ is a local Nash equilibrium of this game, then for all i

$$u_i(x^*) \geq u_i(x_i\ ;\ x_{-i}^*) - \frac{L}{2}||x_i - x_i^*||_2^2, \text{ for all } x_i \in \mathcal{R}(x_{-i}^*).$$

If x^* is an ε-approximate local Nash equilibrium of the game, then for all i

$$u_i(x^*) \geq u_i(x_i\ ;\ x_{-i}^*) - \varepsilon||x_i - x_i^*||_2 - \frac{L}{2}||x_i - x_i^*||_2^2, \text{ for all } x_i \in \mathcal{R}(x_{-i}^*).$$

Importantly, local Nash equilibria exist, under the assumption that the gradients of the payoff functions are continuous, as per the following proposition.[2]

Proposition 14.2 (Existence of Local Nash). Every differentiable game has at least one local Nash equilibrium.

Proof of Proposition 14.2: Consider the mapping $F : \mathcal{R} \to \mathcal{R}$, defined as follows:

$$x \mapsto \Pi_{\mathcal{R}}\left(\begin{bmatrix} x_1 + \nabla_{x_1} u_1(x) \\ \vdots \\ x_n + \nabla_{x_n} u_n(x) \end{bmatrix}\right).$$

The mapping is continuous because for all i, it is assumed that $\nabla_{x_i} u_i(x)$ is continuous, and because the ℓ_2 projection to a convex and compact set is continuous.

[2] We note that the local Nash equilibrium Condition (14.1) can be written as a quasivariational inequality problem (Bensoussan and Jacques-Louis, 1973), so a proof of Proposition 14.2 can alternatively be pursued by appealing to existence theorems for quasivariational inequalities; see, for example, the work of Chan and Pang (1982) and Harker (1991). We stick to our proof here using Brouwer's fixed point theorem, as it is simple and self-contained.

Given the continuity of F and the convexity and compactness of $\mathcal{R}$, it follows from Brouwer's fixed point theorem that F has a fixed point $x^* = F(x^*)$.

We will argue that for all i, Eq. (14.1) holds for the fixed point x^* of F. Indeed, denote by

$$z^* = \begin{bmatrix} x_1^* + \nabla_{x_1} u_1(x^*) \\ \vdots \\ x_n^* + \nabla_{x_n} u_n(x^*) \end{bmatrix}.$$

Because $x^* = \Pi_{\mathcal{R}}(z^*)$, we have by the properties of the ℓ_2 projection that

$$\langle z^* - x^*, x^* - y \rangle \geq 0, \forall y \in \mathcal{R}.$$

For an arbitrary $x_i \in \mathcal{R}(x_{-i}^*)$, plugging $y = (x_i \, ; \, x_{-i}^*)$ into the above inequality, we get that

$$\langle \nabla_{x_i} u_i(x^*), x_i^* - x_i \rangle \geq 0.$$

Thus we have

$$\langle \nabla_{x_i} u_i(x^*), x_i^* - x_i \rangle \geq 0, \forall x_i \in \mathcal{R}(x_{-i}^*),$$

which is tantamount to Eq. (14.1). □

We remark that the development of this section assumes that players are myopic, having a first-order understanding of their payoffs around the equilibrium, which is motivated by the value and gradient value access to the payoffs that is practically available in the deep learning applications motivating our discussion. The local Nash equilibrium concept of Definition 14.3 reflects that such myopic players are best responding. If the players have a richer local understanding of their utilities (e.g., if they have higher-order access to their payoffs), it would be appropriate to incorporate that richer player's knowledge into refined local Nash equilibrium concepts. We note, however, that improperly doing so might break equilibrium existence, even at the second order. This can be seen by considering a two-player zero-sum game, where the row chooses $x \in [0,1]$, the column player chooses $y \in [0,1]$, and the column's payoff is $(x+y-2xy-\frac{1}{2})-\frac{1}{2}x^2-\frac{1}{2}y^2$. In this game, the second-order view of the utilities incurs no information loss. So second-order local Nash equilibria correspond to Nash equilibria, but this game has no Nash equilibria!

14.3 THE COMPLEXITY OF LOCAL NASH EQUILIBRIA

As discussed in the previous section, first-order local Nash equilibria are guaranteed to exist in all differential games, making them a reasonable first cut at a solution concept. We say "first cut," as one might be dissatisfied with the first-order best-response nature of the solution concept. As discussed at the end of last section, one might want to incorporate richer understanding that players might have about their utilities to remove some first-order local Nash equilibria from consideration, ideally not eliminating them all. Regardless of what equilibrium refinement one might want to pursue, it is reasonable to ask at this point whether the weak solution concept of first-order local Nash equilibrium, which is guaranteed to exist, is also tractable, as any refinement would be at least as hard to compute.

Question 2. Are local Nash equilibria tractable?

As noted in Section 14.2.1, practical experience with nonconcave games considered in deep learning applications reveals that gradient descent-based methods have a real challenge converging, necessitating hyperoptimized training frameworks to get any reasonable performance. It is justified to wonder if there is some lingering intractability explaining this phenomenon. It turns out that this is indeed the case.

Theorem 14.2 (Daskalakis et al. (2021)). *Any method, which accesses players' payoffs in a smooth differentiable game through value queries and gradient value queries, needs a number of queries that is exponential in at least one of $1/\varepsilon$, the smoothness of the game, or the dimensionality of the game to compute an ε-approximate first-order local Nash equilibrium. This is true even if the game is a two-player zero-sum game.*

This exponential number of queries is in sharp contrast to single-agent nonconcave maximization (i.e., the restriction of Definition 14.3 to $n = 1$), where first-order approximate local maxima can be found using only a polynomial number of queries (polynomial in $1/\varepsilon$ and the smoothness). In fact, a stronger intractability result actually holds subject to a widely held complexity-theoretic assumption. Unless the complexity class PPAD[3] collapses to the class P of polynomial-time solvable problems, no method can compute local Nash equilibria in polynomial time, even if it has exact knowledge of the players' payoffs (rather than just first-order query access to them).

Theorem 14.3 (Daskalakis et al. (2021)). *Unless* P = PPAD, *no method can compute an ε-approximate first-order local Nash equilibrium of a smooth differentiable game in time polynomial in $1/\varepsilon$ and the game's smoothness and dimensionality. In particular, the problem is* PPAD*-complete. This is true even if the game is a two-player zero-sum game.*

In other words, computing local Nash equilibria in smooth differentiable games, even in two-player zero-sum ones, is exactly as hard as computing Brouwer fixed points of Lispchitz functions and computing mixed Nash equilibria in general-sum normal-form games (Daskalakis et al., 2009; Chen et al., 2009),

[3] The complexity class PPAD was introduced by Papadimitriou (1994) and used by Daskalakis and colleagues (2009) and Chen and colleagues (2009) to characterize the complexity of computing a mixed Nash equilibrium in normal-form games. See also Daskalakis (2018) for a recent survey of PPAD, and its uses and relationship to problems in topology, combinatorics, optimization, and game theory.

and is at least as hard as any other problem in the class PPAD. For a discussion of PPAD, its relationship to complexity theory, and the complexity of topological problems, see, for example, the work of Daskalakis (2018).

Intuition for Intractability. It is worth providing some intuition about the intractability results of this section and comparing these to nonconvex minimization/nonconcave maximization where similar intractability does not arise.

Question 3. Why is it that local optima in optimization problems are tractable but local Nash equilibria in multiplayer nonconcave games, even in two-player zero-sum ones, are intractable?

To answer this question, it is illustrative to compare differentiable two-player *common-interest* games, in which two players share an objective that they both want to minimize, to differentiable two-player *zero-sum* games, in which one player wants to minimize an objective that the other player wants to maximize. Approximate local Nash equilibria in a common-interest game are the same as approximate local minima of the shared cost function, and these are tractable, as noted previously. On the other hand, approximate local Nash equilibria in a zero-sum game are intractable, as per the above theorems. Why are local Nash equilibria in these two families of games so different in complexity? To shed some light on this, in Figure 14.2(a) we show what a better-response sequence of moves may look like in a two-player common-interest game, where one player controls moves along the horizontal axis, the other player controls moves along the vertical axis, and both players want to minimize a shared cost function. Because the game is common-interest, it is clear that the shared cost must decrease along a better response sequence. Indeed, a horizontal move only makes sense for the horizontal player if it decreases the shared cost, and a vertical move only makes sense if it decreases the shared cost. Thus a better response sequence makes progress toward a local minimum. In particular, if we normalize the shared cost function to lie in $[-1, 1]$, as in Definition 14.2, and only take steps that improve the shared cost by at least ε, then the number of steps until we find an ε-approximate local minimum is $O(1/\varepsilon)$.

In zero-sum games, however, the situation is much trickier. First, a sequence of better-response moves may actually be cyclic, as shown at the top right of Figure 14.2(b). Second, the payoff values along a better response sequence may repeat. As a result, payoff values along a better-response sequence do not reveal whether or not the sequence is cyclic. And even if it is noncyclic, we gain no information by querying the payoff function along the sequence about how far from the end of the sequence the query was made.

This apparent lack of much information gain about the location of local Nash equilibria when querying the payoff function of a zero-sum game lies at the heart of what makes local Nash equilibria so much more difficult than local minima/local maxima. To turn this intuition into an intractability proof, what we would like to do is to hide an exponentially long, better-response path with

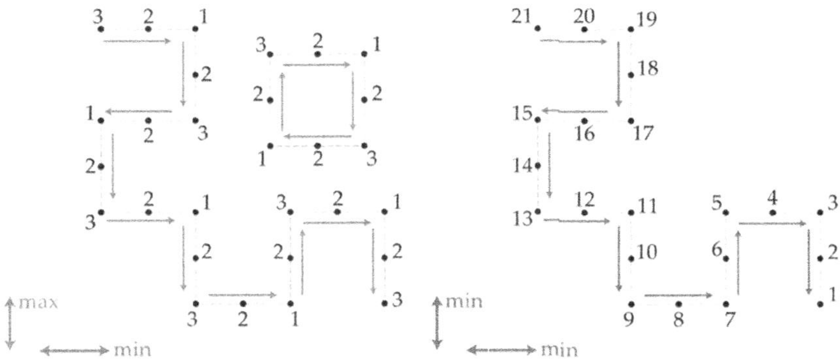

(a) A better-response path in a common interest game.

(b) A better-response path and a better-response cycle in a zero-sumgame.

FIGURE 14.2 An illustration of better-response move sequences in a two-player common-interest game (on the left) and a zero-sum game (on the right), where one player is choosing strategies on the horizontal axis and the other player is choosing strategies on the vertical axis. In both cases, the values shown represent the cost (i.e., minus the payoff) of the horizontal player. The vertical player shares the same cost on the left and has the opposite cost on the right.

recycled payoff values, like the one shown in Figure 14.2(b), within some ambient space so that querying the payoff function along the path or in the ambient space provides very little information about the location of local Nash equilibria. However, we do not see how to implement such a construction directly but use the complexity-theoretic machinery of PPAD, establishing Theorem 14.3 first and exploiting special properties of that construction to obtain Theorem 14.2 as a corollary. See the writings of Daskalakis and colleagues (2021) for the details.

14.4 PHILOSOPHICAL COROLLARY AND WAYS FORWARD

Motivated by emerging, multiagent applications in deep learning, we discussed the importance of nonconcave games, and specifically those of the differentiable kind, captured by Definition 14.2. As we noted, these games may have no Nash equilibria, and this prompted us to study what might be plausible solution concepts to target in these games. Motivated by the practical consideration that agents have restricted access to their payoff functions, typically via value and gradient value queries, in the complex settings motivating our study, we proposed the notion of first-order local Nash equilibrium of Definition 14.3, which are points where all players are best responding to their opponents' strategies, as far as the first-order Taylor approximation to their payoff functions can tell.

Local Nash equilibria are a natural generalization to the game-theoretic setting of local optima, whose computation in single-agent problems has been driving the spectacular progress that deep learning has made in the past decade.

Importantly, local Nash equilibria are guaranteed to exist, and their universality is appealing to theorists and practitioners alike.

Unfortunately, Theorems 14.2 and 14.3 of the previous section preclude the existence of some variant of gradient descent – or subject to the widely held complexity-theoretic assumption that $\mathtt{P} \neq \mathtt{PPAD}$ the existence of any algorithm – computing local Nash equilibria efficiently in general differentiable games.

In the balance, our results establish the existence of a methodological roadblock in extending the deep learning to multiagent settings. While postulating a complex parametric model for a learning agent and training this model using gradient descent has been a successful framework in single-agent settings, choosing complex models for a bunch of different agents and having them train their models via competing gradient descent-based procedures is just not going to work, even in two-agent zero-sum settings, even if one were to compromise with the solution concept of first-order local Nash equilibrium.

Our work advocates that progress in multiagent learning will be unlocked by modeling and methodological insights, as well as better clarity about the types of solutions that are useful and attainable, obtained by combining the perspectives of game theory and economics with those of machine learning and optimization. We conclude with some musings on where to go from here.

14.4.1 Asymptotic Local Nash Equilibrium Convergence in General Nonconcave Games

While local Nash equilibria are intractable in general games, it is still worth identifying iterative procedures whose steps are efficiently computable and which exhibit guaranteed asymptotic convergence to local Nash equilibrium. Since local Nash equilibria are fixed points of a continuous map (see Proposition 14.2), one may try to obtain such procedures by translating to the setting of differentiable games and optimizing the steps of iterative fixed point computation algorithms. We have recently pursued this avenue of research, proposing second-order methods that exhibit guaranteed asymptotic convergence to local Nash equilibria in smooth differentiable games (Daskalakis et al., 2022a). Our work advances a recent line of work proposing methods that attain local convergence (Jin et al., 2020; Fiez et al., 2020; Fiez and Ratliff, 2020; Wang et al., 2020). It is important to identify beyond-worst-case assumptions under which asymptotically convergent methods become computationally efficient, a direction that is underexplored.

14.4.2 Nonconcave Games with Tractable Equilibria, Stochastic Games, and MARL

The intractability results that we presented are worst case. It is plausible that vast families of nonconcave games have tractable local Nash equilibria or even global Nash equilibria. If those families are expressive enough to capture broad types of multiagent interactions, they would go a long way to alleviate the impact of our intractability results.

On this front, a prominent family of games to study are *stochastic games*. These are games where two or more agents interact and receive payoffs over multiple stages, or indefinitely, in some environment whose state gets updated at every stage, depending on the actions chosen by the agents, whose payoff functions are also state-dependent. These games, defined in Shapley's foundational work (Shapley, 1953), have received broad study in game theory literature (see, e.g., Solan and Vieille, 2015, for a recent review) and have found many applications due to their generality and versatility (see, e.g., Neyman and Sorin, 2003). Among these, of prominent importance is their application to *multiagent reinforcement learning* (MARL) – see, for example, work by Littman (1994), Hu and Wellman (2003), Busoniu and colleagues (2008), and Zhang and colleagues (2021). In this application, the stochastic game's state transitions and payoffs are not known to the players a priori, so the equilibrium has to be *learned* through interaction.

Since Shapley's work, a compelling notion of equilibrium considered in stochastic games are stationary Markov-Nash equilibria – that is, Nash equilibria in strategies (a.k.a. policies) that depend on the current state of the game but not on the stage count or the history of play so far (hence both *stationary* and *Markovian*). In terms of their stationary Markov strategies, player utilities in a stochastic game are nonconcave. Yet, under broad conditions (e.g., future payoff discounting and a finite number of states), stationary Markov-Nash equilibria exist; see, for example, work by Shapley (1953), Takahashi (1962), and Fink (1964), and an overview of such results in Solan and Vieille (2015). In fact, in the two-player zero-sum case, it is even known that the minimax theorem holds with respect to stationary Markov strategies (Shapley, 1953).

On the computation front, many works have studied the challenge of computing or learning Nash equilibria in stochastic games. Most of the focus has been on efficient computation and learning of (approximate) Nash equilibria in two-player zero-sum stochastic games (see, e.g., Brafman and Tennenholtz, 2002; Wei et al., 2017; Xie et al., 2020; Zhang et al., 2020; Sidford et al., 2020; Bai and Jin, 2020; Daskalakis et al., 2020; Bai et al., 2020; Liu et al., 2021; Tian et al., 2021; Baudin and Laraki, 2022a,b; and their references). Some of these works provide decentralized learning procedures via which the players of a zero-sum stochastic game efficiently converge to approximate stationary Markov minimax equilibria. Those learning procedures are decentralized in that the players are not allowed to communicate but only interact in the game by each employing some strategy and observing their own sequence of rewards and the game's state transitions.

Beyond these results, however, our understanding is lagging. First, there is still mystery surrounding whether exact stationary Nash equilibria of two-player zero-sum stochastic games can be computed efficiently when the discount factor is very close to 1 (Condon, 1992; Daskalakis and Papadimitriou, 2011). Beyond the two-player zero-sum case, stochastic games have intractable equilibria, since they are more expressive than normal-form games (Daskalakis et al., 2009; Chen et al., 2009). Can local Nash equilibria be computed/learned efficiently in this case? Alternatively, can the weaker solution concept of (coarse) correlated equilibrium be computed/learned efficiently, and what kinds of correlation among agents' strategies allow for efficient computation?

Some recent works have studied the computation and learning of (coarse) correlated equilibria in multiplayer stochastic games. These works target *nonstationary* (coarse) correlated equilibria, which are easy to compute using backward induction if the game is known. So they provide decentralized algorithms for *learning* approximate nonstationary (coarse) correlated equilibria. However, these works require either exponential time, in the number of players, to converge, or they compute equilibria that are *non-Markovian* (Liu et al., 2021; Song et al., 2022; Jin et al., 2021; Mao and Başar, 2023).

In very recent work (Daskalakis et al., 2022b), we address some of the outstanding questions about (coarse) correlated equilibrium computation and learning in these games. We show that focusing on nonstationary equilibria is in general unavoidable, as stationary Markov coarse correlated equilibria are intractable, namely PPAD-hard, even when the game has two players and the discount factor is 1/2 (i.e., the game is expected to last for two rounds).[4] This is quite surprising, as coarse correlated equilibrium computation in normal-form games is very tractable. Complementing our intractability results, we also provide decentralized procedures for efficiently learning nonstationary Markov coarse correlated equilibria, whose running time is polynomial in the number of players.

On the front of (coarse) correlated equilibrium learning in stochastic games, there is a lot more work to be pursued. First, it is important to provide simpler alternatives to the methods obtained in recent work. Moreover, in many games, the state/action spaces are infinite, but we are interested in strategies that are expressible compactly by a policy in some class of functions, which map states to (distributions over) actions taken at those states. Which types of equilibria exist and how is their computational and learning complexity affected by the choice of the policy class? We will touch upon this kind of questions in the next section, but specialized work should be done for this important class of games.

4 See also Jin and colleagues (2022) for a weaker version of this claim. We also note that both Daskalakis and colleagues (2022b) and Jin and colleagues (2022) show intractability results for a type of stationary Markov coarse correlated equilibrium wherein the correlation of players' actions is independent across stages and states of the game, and moreover the recommendations from the correlation device are revealed to the players step by step, as they reach a new state at each stage of the game, similar to the notion of extensive-form correlated equilibrium proposed in von Stengel and Forges (2008) for extensive-form games. The complexity of the alternative solution concept of strategic-form coarse correlated equilibrium in stationary Markov strategies still remains open.

Finally, it is important to study the aforementioned problems with learning and computation of equilibria in stochastic games with incomplete information. Their special case of extensive-form games have played a central role in recent practical developments in human-level Poker-playing algorithms (Brown and Sandholm, 2018, 2019). In these games, it is known how to compute Nash equilibria in the two-player zero-sum case (Koller et al., 1996; von Stengel, 2007). Nash equilibria are intractable in the general case (Daskalakis et al., 2009; Chen et al., 2009), and there is an active line of investigation on different notions of correlated equilibrium (von Stengel and Forges, 2008) and its computation and learning (see, e.g., Huang and von Stengel, 2008; Celli et al., 2020, and their references). It is worth pursuing these directions further and generalizing our existing understanding of general stochastic games with incomplete information.

14.4.3 Convexification and Global Equilibria

In many settings, the strategies available to players in a differentiable game correspond to a vector of parameters indexing a function from some function class. In deep learning applications, these could be the parameters of some deep neural network model. In multiagent reinforcement learning, as discussed in the previous section, these could be indexing a parametric policy in a stochastic game with an infinite number of states and actions.

Making this perspective explicit, we might consider the following generalization of differentiable games. Each player, i, may choose a function from some (potentially infinite and potentially nonparametric) function class $\mathcal{F}_i$, or a distribution over elements of $\mathcal{F}_i$, and the payoff to each player for a given pure strategy profile is determined by some function $u_i : \times_j \mathcal{F}_j \to \mathbb{R}$. Since these games generalize differentiable games, pure Nash equilibria are not guaranteed to exist, motivating our interest in local pure Nash equilibria, as discussed earlier in this chapter. If we do not want to give in to local optimality, we might alternatively turn to convexification approaches, considering mixed Nash or correlated equilibria in these games. Under what conditions are mixed Nash or correlated equilibria guaranteed to exist in infinite games? And under what conditions are they efficiently learnable?[5]

A recent line of work (Rakhlin et al., 2015; Hanneke et al., 2021; Daskalakis and Golowich, 2022) makes progress on these questions by developing equilibrium existence results and no-regret online learning algorithms converging to equilibrium, under necessary conditions about the complexity of

[5] We note that in many applications the strategies available to players are not necessarily from a compact set; thus we cannot apply known results to show that a mixed Nash equilibrium exists (Glicksberg, 1952) and even show that a finitely supported Nash equilibrium exists if the compactly supported game has extra structure (Dresher et al., 1950; Parrilo, 2006; Stein et al., 2008).

the game's strategy sets and utility functions.[6] Under these assumptions, it has been shown that the minimax theorem holds in the two-player zero-sum setting, and approximate coarse correlated equilibria (of arbitrary approximation) exist in the multiplayer/general-sum setting. Moreover, decoupled online learning procedures have been obtained that the players can employ to converge to these kinds of equilibria, or to guarantee small regret against worst-case adversaries. Naturally, the rates of convergence depend on the complexity of the function classes, but their time dependence in the context of games can match the fast rates known in finite games (Daskalakis and Golowich, 2022).

Going forward, it is also important to obtain conditions under which correlated equilibria and Nash equilibria exist. Especially for the latter it seems that entirely different techniques might be needed. Finally, it is important to identify settings where the convergence rates to equilibrium, in terms of the complexity of the game's strategy sets and utility functions, can be improved.

14.5 ACKNOWLEDGEMENTS

This work was supported by National Science Foundation (NSF) Awards CCF-1901292, DMS-2022448, and DMS-2134108; a Simons Investigator Award; the Simons Collaboration on the Theory of Algorithmic Fairness; a Defence Science and Technology (DSTA) grant; and the DOE PhILMs project (DE-AC05-76RL01830). We thank Noah Golowich and Manolis Zampetakis for providing feedback on earlier drafts.

14.6 REFERENCES

I. Adler. The equivalence of linear programs and zero-sum games. *International Journal of Game Theory*, 42(1):165–177, 2013.

L. Adolphs, H. Daneshmand, A. Lucchi, and T. Hofmann. Local saddle point optimization: A curvature exploitation approach. In *Proceedings of the Twenty-Second International Conference on Artificial Intelligence and Statistics (AISTATS)*, 2019.

Z. Allen-Zhu and Y. Li. Neon2: Finding local minima via first-order oracles. *Proceedings of the Thirty-Second Annual Conference on Neural Information Processing Systems (NeurIPS)*, 2018.

S. Arora, A. Risteski, and Y. Zhang. Do GANs learn the distribution? Some theory and empirics. In *Proceedings of the Sixth International Conference on Learning Representations (ICLR)*, 2018.

K. J. Arrow and G. Debreu. Existence of an equilibrium for a competitive economy. *Econometrica*, 22(3):265–290, 1954.

[6] Generalizing Rakhlin and colleagues (2015); Hanneke and colleagues (2021), in Daskalakis and Golowich (2022), we assume, roughly speaking, that for each player i, the function class $\mathcal{F}_i^{u_i} = \{\times_{j \neq i} \mathcal{F}_j \ni f_{-i} \mapsto u_i(f_i\,;\, f_{-i}) \mid f_i \in \mathcal{F}_i\}$ has bounded sequential fat-shattering dimension at all scales. This is a necessary assumption to avoid the two-player zero-sum game, wherein whoever says the largest number receives one dollar from the other player, which has no ε-approximate mixed Nash equilibria for any $\varepsilon < 1$ (Hanneke et al., 2021).

Y. Bai and C. Jin. Provable self-play algorithms for competitive reinforcement learning. In *Proceedings of the Thirty-Seventh International Conference on Machine Learning (ICML)*, 2020.

Y. Bai, C. Jin, and T. Yu. Near-optimal reinforcement learning with self-play. In *Proceedings of the Thirty-Fourth Annual Conference on Neural Information Processing Systems (NeurIPS)*, 2020.

F. M. Bator. The simple analytics of welfare maximization. *American Economic Review*, 47(1):22–59, 1957.

L. Baudin and R. Laraki. Fictitious play and best-response dynamics in identical interest and zero-sum stochastic games. In K. Chaudhuri, S. Jegelka, L. Song, C. Szepesvari, G. Niu, and S. Sabato, eds., *Proceedings of the Thirty-Ninth International Conference on Machine Learning*, vol. 162 of *Proceedings of Machine Learning Research*, pp. 1664–1690. 2022a.

L. Baudin and R. Laraki. Smooth fictitious play in stochastic games with perturbed payoffs and unknown transitions. In *Proceedings of the Thirty-Sixth Conference on Neural Information Processing Systems (NeurIPS 2022)*, 2022b.

A. Bensoussan and L. Jacques-Louis. Nouvelle formulation de problèmes de contrôle impulsionnel et applications. *Comptes Rendus des Séances de l'Académie des Sciences*, 276:1189–1192, 1973.

R. I. Brafman and M. Tennenholtz. R-MAX: A general polynomial-time algorithm for near-optimal reinforcement learning. *Journal of Machine Learning Research*, 3(October):213–231, 2002.

B. Brooks and P. J. Reny. A canonical game – nearly 75 years in the making – showing the equivalence of matrix games and linear programming. *Economic Theory Bulletin*, 11:171–180, 2023.

N. Brown and T. Sandholm. Superhuman AI for heads-up no-limit poker: Libratus beats top professionals. *Science*, 359(6374):418–424, 2018.

N. Brown and T. Sandholm. Superhuman AI for multiplayer poker. *Science*, 365(6456):885–890, 2019.

S. Bubeck and N. Cesa-Bianchi. Regret analysis of stochastic and nonstochastic multi-armed bandit problems. *Found. Trends Mach. Learn.*, 5(1):1–122, 2012.

L. Busoniu, R. Babuska, and B. De Schutter. A comprehensive survey of multiagent reinforcement learning. *IEEE Transactions on Systems, Man, and Cybernetics, Part C (Applications and Reviews)*, 38(2):156–172, 2008.

A. Celli, A. Marchesi, G. Farina, and N. Gatti. No-regret learning dynamics for extensive-form correlated equilibrium. In *Proceedings of the Thirty-Fourth Annual Conference on Neural Information Processing Systems (NeurIPS)*, 2020.

N. Cesa-Bianchi and G. Lugosi. *Prediction, Learning, and Games*. Cambridge: Cambridge University Press, 2006.

D. Chan and J. S. Pang. The generalized quasi-variational inequality problem. *Mathematics of Operations Research*, 7(2):211–222, 1982.

X. Chen, X. Deng, and S.-H. Teng. Settling the complexity of computing two-player Nash equilibria. *Journal of the ACM (JACM)*, 56(3):1–57, 2009.

A. Condon. The complexity of stochastic games. *Information and Computation*, 96(2):203–224, 1992.

G. B. Dantzig. A proof of the equivalence of the programming problem and the game problem. In T. C. Koopmans, ed., *Activity Analysis of Production and Allocation*. New York: Wiley, 1951.

C. Daskalakis. Equilibria, fixed points, and computational complexity: Nevanlinna Prize lecture. In *Proceedings of the International Congress of Mathematicians: Rio de Janeiro 2018*, pp. 147–209. Singapore: World Scientific, 2018.

C. Daskalakis, D. Foster, and N. Golowich. Independent policy gradient methods for competitive reinforcement learning. In *Proceedings of the Thirty-Fourth Annual Conference on Neural Information Processing Systems (NeurIPS)*, 2020.

C. Daskalakis, P. W. Goldberg, and C. H. Papadimitriou. The complexity of computing a Nash equilibrium. *SIAM Journal on Computing*, 39(1):195–259, 2009.

C. Daskalakis and N. Golowich. Fast rates for nonparametric online learning: From realizability to learning in games. In *Proceedings of the Fifty-Fourth Annual ACM SIGACT Symposium on Theory of Computing (STOC)*, 2022.

C. Daskalakis, N. Golowich, S. Skoulakis, and M. Zampetakis. Sperner continuous dynamics: Guaranteed convergence to local minimax equilibrium in nonconvex-nonconcave games. *arXiv preprint*, 2210.09769, 2022a.

C. Daskalakis, N. Golowich, and K. Zhang. The complexity of Markov equilibrium in stochastic games. *arXiv preprint*, arXiv:2204.03991, 2022b.

C. Daskalakis, A. Ilyas, V. Syrgkanis, and H. Zeng. Training GANs with optimism. In *Proceedings of the Sixth International Conference on Learning Representations (ICLR)*, 2018.

C. Daskalakis and I. Panageas. The limit points of (optimistic) gradient descent in min-max optimization. In *Proceedings of the Thirty-Second Annual Conference on Neural Information Processing Systems (NeurIPS)*, 2018.

C. Daskalakis and C. Papadimitriou. Continuous local search. In *Proceedings of the Twenty-Second Annual ACM-SIAM Symposium on Discrete Algorithms (SODA)*, 2011.

C. Daskalakis, S. Skoulakis, and M. Zampetakis. The complexity of constrained min-max optimization. In *Proceedings of the Fifty-Third Annual ACM SIGACT Symposium on Theory of Computing (STOC)*, 2021.

G. Debreu. A social equilibrium existence theorem. *Proceedings of the National Academy of Sciences (PNAS)*, 38(10):886–893, 1952.

M. Dresher, S. Karlin, and L. S. Shapley. Polynomial games. In *Contributions to the Theory of Games I*, vol. 24, pp. 161–180. Princeton, NJ: Princeton University Press, 1950.

K. Fan. Minimax theorems. *Proceedings of the National Academy of Sciences*, 39(1):42–47, 1953.

M. J. Farrell. The convexity assumption in the theory of competitive markets. *Journal of Political Economy*, 67(4):377–391, 1959.

T. Fiez, B. Chasnov, and L. Ratliff. Implicit learning dynamics in Stackelberg games: Equilibria characterization, convergence analysis, and empirical study. In *Proceedings of the Thirty-Seventh International Conference on Machine Learning (ICML)*, 2020.

T. Fiez and L. J. Ratliff. Local convergence analysis of gradient descent ascent with finite timescale separation. In *Proceedings of the Eighth International Conference on Learning Representations (ICLR)*, 2020.

A. M. Fink. Equilibrium in a stochastic n-person game. *Journal of Science of the Hiroshima University, Series A-I (Mathematics)*, 28(1):89–93, 1964.

R. Ge, F. Huang, C. Jin, and Y. Yuan. Escaping from saddle points: Online stochastic gradient for tensor decomposition. In *Proceedings of the Twenty-Eighth Annual Conference on Learning Theory (COLT)*, 2015.

I. L. Glicksberg. A further generalization of the Kakutani fixed point theorem, with application to Nash equilibrium points. *Proceedings of the American Mathematical Society*, 3(1):170–174, 1952.

I. Goodfellow. NIPS 2016 tutorial: Generative Adversarial Networks. *arXiv preprint*, arXiv:1701.00160, 2016.

J. d. V. Graaff. *Theoretical Welfare Economics*. Cambridge: Cambridge University Press, 1957.

S. Hanneke, R. Livni, and S. Moran. Online learning with simple predictors and a combinatorial characterization of minimax in 0/1 games. In *Proceedings of the Thirty-Fourth Conference on Learning Theory (COLT)*, 2021.

P. T. Harker. Generalized Nash games and quasi-variational inequalities. *European Journal of Operational Research*, 54(1):81–94, 1991.

E. Hazan. Introduction to online convex optimization. *Foundations and Trends in Optimization*, 2(3-4):157–325, 2016.

J. Hu and M. P. Wellman. Nash Q-learning for general-sum stochastic games. *Journal of Machine Learning Research*, 4(November):1039–1069, 2003.

W. Huang and B. von Stengel. Computing an extensive-form correlated equilibrium in polynomial time. In *Proceedings of the Fourth International Workshop on Internet and Network Economics (WINE)*, 2008.

C. Jin, Q. Liu, Y. Wang, and T. Yu. V-Learning: A simple, efficient, decentralized algorithm for multiagent RL. *arXiv preprint*, arXiv:2110.14555, 2021.

C. Jin, P. Netrapalli, and M. I. Jordan. What Is Local Optimality in Nonconvex-Nonconcave Minimax Optimization? In *Proceedings of the Thirty-Seventh International Conference on Machine Learning (ICML)*, 2020.

Y. Jin, V. Muthukumar, and A. Sidford. The complexity of infinite-horizon general-sum stochastic games. *arXiv preprint*, arXiv:2204.04186, 2022.

D. Koller, N. Megiddo, and B. von Stengel. Efficient computation of equilibria for extensive two-person games. *Games and Economic Behavior*, 14(2):247–259, 1996.

T. C. Koopmans. *Three Essays in the State of Economic Science*. New York: McGraw-Hill, 1957.

J. D. Lee, M. Simchowitz, M. I. Jordan, and B. Recht. Gradient descent only converges to minimizers. In *Proceedings of the Twenty-Ninth Annual Conference on Learning Theory (COLT)*, 2016.

M. L. Littman. Markov games as a framework for multi-agent reinforcement learning. In *Proceedings of the Eleventh International Conference on Machine Learning (ICML)*, 1994.

Q. Liu, T. Yu, Y. Bai, and C. Jin. A sharp analysis of model-based reinforcement learning with self-play. In *Proceedings of the Thirty-Eighth International Conference on Machine Learning (ICML)*, 2021.

O. Mangoubi and N. K. Vishnoi. Greedy adversarial equilibrium: An efficient alternative to nonconvex-nonconcave min-max optimization. In *Proceedings of the Fifty-Third Annual ACM SIGACT Symposium on Theory of Computing (STOC)*, 2021.

W. Mao and T. Başar. Provably efficient reinforcement learning in decentralized general-sum Markov games. *Dynamic Games and Applications*, 13(1):165–186, 2023.

E. Mazumdar, L. J. Ratliff, and S. S. Sastry. On gradient-based learning in continuous games. *SIAM J. Math. Data Sci.*, 2(1):103–131, 2020.

L. McKenzie. On equilibrium in Graham's model of world trade and other competitive systems. *Econometrica*, 22(2):147–161, 1954.

L. Mescheder, A. Geiger, and S. Nowozin. Which training methods for GANs do actually converge? In *Proceedings of the Thirty-Fifth International Conference on Machine Learning (ICML)*, 2018.

L. Metz, B. Poole, D. Pfau, and J. Sohl-Dickstein. Unrolled generative adversarial networks. In *Proceedings of the Fifth International Conference on Learning Representations (ICLR)*, 2017.

J. F. Nash. Equilibrium points in n-person games. *Proceedings of the National Academy of Sciences*, 36(1):48–49, 1950.

A. Neyman and S. Sorin, eds. *Stochastic games and applications*, vol. 570. Amsterdam: Springer Science & Business Media, 2003.

M. J. Osborne and A. Rubinstein. *A Course in Game Theory*. Cambridge, MA: MIT Press, 1994.

C. H. Papadimitriou. On the complexity of the parity argument and other inefficient proofs of existence. *J. Comput. Syst. Sci.*, 48(3):498–532, 1994.

C. H. Papadimitriou and C. A. Wilkens. Economies with non-convex production and complexity equilibria. In *Proceedings of the Twelfth ACM Conference on Electronic Commerce (EC)*, 2011.

P. A. Parrilo. Polynomial games and sum of squares optimization. In *Proceedings of the Forty-Fifth IEEE Conference on Decision and Control*, 2006.

A. Rakhlin, K. Sridharan, and A. Tewari. Online learning via sequential complexities. *J. Mach. Learn. Res.*, 16:155–186, 2015.

L. J. Ratliff, S. A. Burden, and S. S. Sastry. On the characterization of local Nash equilibria in continuous games. *IEEE Transactions on Automatic Control*, 61(8):2301–2307, 2016.

J. B. Rosen. Existence and uniqueness of equilibrium points for concave n-person games. *Econometrica*, 33(3):520–534, 1965.

J. Rothenberg. Non-convexity, aggregation, and Pareto optimality. *Journal of Political Economy*, 68(5):435–468, 1960.

S. Shalev-Shwartz. Online learning and online convex optimization. *Foundations and Trends in Machine Learning*, 4(2):107–194, 2012.

L. S. Shapley. Stochastic games. *Proceedings of the National Academy of Sciences*, 39(10):1095–1100, 1953.

A. Sidford, M. Wang, L. Yang, and Y. Ye. Solving discounted stochastic two-player games with near-optimal time and sample complexity. In *Proceedings of the Twenty-Third International Conference on Artificial Intelligence and Statistics (AISTATS)*, 2020.

M. Sion. On general minimax theorems. *Pacific Journal of Mathematics*, 8(1):171–176, 1958.

E. Solan and N. Vieille. Stochastic games. *Proceedings of the National Academy of Sciences*, 112(45):13743–13746, 2015.

Z. Song, S. Mei, and Y. Bai. When can we learn general-sum Markov games with a large number of players sample efficiently? In *Proceedings of the Tenth International Conference on Learning Representations (ICLR)*, 2022.

R. M. Starr. Quasi-equilibria in markets with non-convex preferences. *Econometrica*, 37(1):25–38, 1969.

N. D. Stein, A. Ozdaglar, and P. A. Parrilo. Separable and low-rank continuous games. *International Journal of Game Theory*, 37(4):475–504, 2008.

M. Takahashi. Stochastic games with infinitely many strategies. *Journal of Science of the Hiroshima University, Series A-I (Mathematics)*, 26(2):123–134, 1962.

Y. Tian, Y. Wang, T. Yu, and S. Sra. Online learning in unknown Markov games. In *Proceedings of the Thirty-Eighth International Conference on Machine Learning (ICML)*, 2021.

J. von Neumann. Zur Theorie der Gesellschaftsspiele. *Mathematische Annalen*, 100:295–320, 1928.

B. von Stengel. Equilibrium computation for two-player games in strategic and extensive form. In N. Nisan, T. Roughgarden, É. Tardos, and V. V. Vazirani, eds., *Algorithmic Game Theory*, ch. 3, pp. 53–78. Cambridge: Cambridge University Press, 2007.

B. von Stengel and F. Forges. Extensive-form correlated equilibrium: Definition and computational complexity. *Mathematics of Operations Research*, 33(4):1002–1022, 2008.

Y. Wang, G. Zhang, and J. Ba. On solving minimax optimization locally: A follow-the-ridge approach. In *Proceedings of the Eighth International Conference on Learning Representations (ICLR)*, 2020.

C. Wei, Y. Hong, and C. Lu. Online reinforcement learning in stochastic games. In *Proceedings of the Thirty-First Annual Conference on Neural Information Processing Systems (NeurIPS)*, 2017.

Q. Xie, Y. Chen, Z. Wang, and Z. Yang. Learning zero-sum simultaneous-move Markov games using function approximation and correlated equilibrium. In *Proceedings of the the Thirty-Third Annual Conference on Learning Theory (COLT)*, 2020.

K. Zhang, S. M. Kakade, T. Basar, and L. F. Yang. Model-based multi-agent RL in zero-sum Markov games with near-optimal sample complexity. In *Proceedings of the Thirty-Fourth Annual Conference on Neural Information Processing Systems (NeurIPS)*, 2020.

K. Zhang, Z. Yang, and T. Başar. Multi-agent reinforcement learning: A selective overview of theories and algorithms. *Handbook of Reinforcement Learning and Control*, pp. 321–384. Cham, Switzerland: Springer, 2021.

15

Fairness in Approval-Based Multiwinner Voting

Edith Elkind

Social choice is the science of group decision-making, and voting theory – the study of methods for aggregating individual preferences into a collective decision – is a prominent research direction in this field. Historically, much of the research in social choice focused on settings where the voters rank the available alternatives, and the goal is to either select a single winning alternative or to aggregate the individual rankings into a joint one. Indeed, the two famous impossibility results in this field – one by Arrow (1951) and one by Gibbard and Satterthwaite (1973; 1975) – consider, respectively, rank aggregation and single-winner voting. Accordingly, the nascent computational social choice community, which studies algorithmic challenges that arise in preference aggregation scenarios (Brandt et al., 2016), initially focused on these models as well. For instance, it was shown that computing the output of the Kemeny rank aggregation rule is NP-hard (Dwork et al., 2001) and that several prominent single-winner rules (such as, e.g., single transferable vote and ranked pairs) are hard to manipulate (Bartholdi et al., 1989; Parkes and Xia, 2012).

However, more recently, many researchers in the computational social choice community shifted their attention from single-winner voting to multiwinner voting (i.e., settings where the goal is to select a fixed-size set of winners, usually called a *committee*). There are several reasons for this shift. Throughout this chapter, we will briefly discuss some of them and offer pointers to the literature.

15.1 ALGORITHMIC COMPLEXITY OF MULTIWINNER VOTING

An overwhelming majority of appealing single-winner rules admit polynomial-time winner determination algorithms. In contrast, there are important multiwinner rules, such as, for instance, the Chamberlin–Courant rule (Chamberlin and Courant, 1983), the Monroe rule (Monroe, 1995), and proportional approval voting (PAV) (Thiele, 1895; Laslier and Sanver, 2010), for which winner determination is NP-hard (Procaccia et al., 2008; Lu and Boutilier, 2011; Aziz et al., 2015).[1]

[1] The proofs of these hardness results assume that both the number of voters and the number of candidates are unbounded. Indeed, for all multiwinner voting rules, winner determination

For concreteness, here we give a formal definition of the Chamberlin–Courant rule. This is a committee selection rule that operates on ranked ballots. Given an election with a set of candidates C, $|C| = m$, a set of voters $[n] = \{1, \ldots, n\}$, where each voter i reports a ranking v_i of all candidates in C, and a target committee size k, it outputs a set of size-k subsets of C, which are called the *winning committees*.

Definition 15.1 (Chamberlin–Courant). The *α-Chamberlin–Courant rule*, where $\alpha = (\alpha_1, \ldots, \alpha_m)$ is a vector of positive reals satisfying $\alpha_1 \geq \cdots \geq \alpha_m$, $\alpha_1 \neq \alpha_m$, assigns a score $\text{score}_\alpha(i, S)$ to every voter i and every size-k committee $S \subseteq C$. The score $\text{score}_\alpha(i, S)$ is set to α_j, where j is the highest position of a candidate in S in the ranking v_i. The output of the rule is the set of all size-k committees that maximize $\text{score}_\alpha(1, S) + \cdots + \text{score}_\alpha(n, S)$.

Informally, under the Chamberlin–Courant rule, each voter is assumed to evaluate a committee based on how much she likes her favorite member of this committee: If a voter ranks an element of S first, she contributes α_1 to the score of S, and if she ranks the elements of S in the last k positions, she contributes α_{m-k+1} to its score. This voting rule captures natural combinatorial problems: For instance, given a graph, we can construct an election where voters correspond to edges, candidates correspond to vertices, and each edge ranks the two incident vertices in top-two positions. Then if $\alpha = (1, 1, 0 \ldots, 0)$, a committee that scores n corresponds to a vertex cover; by tweaking this simple argument, we can show that winner determination under this rule is NP-hard for many choices of α, including $\alpha = (m-1, m-2, \ldots, 0)$ (the so-called Borda score vector, which was used in the original definition of the rule).

Now, arguably, the most important computational question associated with a voting rule is the complexity of winner determination, and if the rule is known to be NP-hard, there are many fruitful directions an algorithms researcher can explore, such as considering approximation, fixed-parameter tractability, and the complexity of evaluating the rule on restricted preference domains. For instance, there is a rich literature that concerns the complexity of the Chamberlin–Courant rule for various restricted preference domains, such as single-peaked (Betzler et al., 2013), single-crossing (Skowron et al., 2015), and group-separable preferences (Faliszewski et al., 2020), as well as preferences that are single-peaked on a cycle (Peters and Lackner, 2020), single-peaked on a tree (Peters et al., 2022), or single-crossing on a tree (Constantinescu and Elkind, 2021), with further results for preferences that are nearly single-peaked or nearly single-crossing (Misra et al., 2017); we refer the reader to a survey by Faliszewski et al. (2017) for further tractability results for this rule.

is easy if the number of candidates is bounded by a constant, as one can evaluate all potential committees one by one; assuming that the number of voters is bounded by a constant typically leads to polynomial-time algorithms as well, though proofs are often nontrivial (see, e.g., Yang and Wang, 2018).

Of course, if a rule is polynomial-time computable, there are other algorithmic questions one could ask, such as regarding the complexity of various forms of strategic behavior. However, such questions are clearly not as central to the task of preference aggregation as winner determination. Moreover, the relationship between the practical problem of understanding strategic behavior and the formal models of manipulation, control, and bribery (the three forms of strategic behavior that are extensively studied in the computational social choice literature; see, e.g., the surveys by Conitzer and Walsh, 2016; Faliszewski and Rothe, 2016) is quite complex. Indeed, these formal models typically presuppose that the strategic party has complete knowledge of the preferences of nonstrategic voters (and, in case of bribery, also the cost of changing these preferences in a certain way), and this is definitely not the case in most real-life scenarios that involve strategic actors. In contrast, the practical challenge of winner determination is precisely captured by its mathematical formulation: We simply need to apply a well-defined rule to a given set of ballots. This makes the topic of multiwinner voting attractive to researchers who are primarily interested in algorithms and complexity analysis, rather than developing and justifying new models.

15.2 VOTING RULE DESIGN

A complementary reason to study multiwinner voting is that historically this topic has received far less attention from the (noncomputational) social choice community. Hence there are important open questions in this field that are not computational at all and concern, for example, axiomatic characterizations of existing rules, as well as possibility and impossibility results. There is also room for designing new (families of) voting rules.

15.2.1 Committee Scoring Rules

A prominent example here is the family of *committee scoring rules* (Elkind et al., 2017), which are multiwinner analogs of positional scoring rules: While a positional scoring rule assigns points to each candidate based on that candidate's position in the votes, a committee scoring rule assigns points to each committee based on the positions of the committee members in the votes. More formally, a committee scoring rule for choosing k candidates out of m is defined by a mapping $f_{k,m}$ that assigns a numerical value to each size-k subset I of $\{1, \ldots, m\}$. Given an n-voter election over m candidates, in which each voter submits a ranking of all m candidates, and a committee S, $|S| = k$, the score of S is computed as

$$\sum_{i=1}^{n} f_{k,m}(I_{S,i}),$$

where $I_{S,i}$ is the set of positions of candidates in S in the ranking of voter i. The voting rule then outputs the committees with the highest score. The functions

$f_{k,m}$ are required to satisfy basic monotonicity constraints, so that if it is clear from voter i's ranking that she prefers committee S to committee S', then she assign a higher score to S.

On the one hand, this family of rules is flexible enough to capture a diverse range of well-known multiwinner voting rules, including, for instance, the multiwinner extensions of classic single-winner rules, such as Plurality and Borda, as well as the Chamberlin–Courant rule. On the other hand, it is structured enough to admit axiomatic characterization results, both for the entire family of rules (Skowron et al., 2019; this result can be seen as an extension of Young's characterization of positional scoring rules [Young, 1975] to the multiwinner domain) and for specific rules within the family (Faliszewski et al., 2019).

15.2.2 Proportionality Axioms in Approval-Based Voting

Another example of axiomatic approach to understanding multiwinner voting rules that originated in the computational social choice community is the family of *justified representation* axioms (Aziz et al., 2017; Sánchez-Fernández et al., 2017). These axioms apply in the setting of multiwinner voting with approval ballots and aim to capture the idea of *proportional representation*: Every group of voters that is sufficiently large and cohesive should be represented in the committee. In the stronger variants of this axiom, this requirement is made quantitative: A sufficiently large and sufficiently cohesive group may "deserve" not one but multiple representatives.

Definition 15.2. An instance of *committee selection problem with approval ballots* is given by a set of *candidates* C, $|C| = m$; a set of *voters* $[n] = \{1, \ldots, n\}$; a list of *approval ballots* $\mathcal{A} = (A_1, \ldots, A_n)$, where $A_i \subseteq C$ for each $i \in [n]$; and the target committee size k, $1 \leq k \leq m$. A *committee selection rule* $\mathcal{R}$ maps an instance $\mathcal{I} = \langle C, [n], \mathcal{A}, k\rangle$ to a nonempty collection of size-k subsets of C, denoted by $\mathcal{R}(\mathcal{I})$; the elements of this collection are called the *winning committees under* $\mathcal{R}$.

Given that there are k slots in the committee, it is reasonable to expect that a group of voters of size n/k that jointly approves some candidate can demand to be represented in the committee. There are different interpretations of what it means for a group of voters to be represented; the weakest of them simply requires that at least one voter in the group should approve at least one committee member.

Definition 15.3 (Justified Representation). Given an instance $\mathcal{I} = \langle C, [n], \mathcal{A}, k\rangle$ of the committee selection problem with approval ballots, we say that a group of voters $N' \subseteq [n]$ is *cohesive* if $\cap_{i\in N'} A_i \neq \varnothing$. A committee $W \subset C$ is said to provide *justified representation (JR)* for $\mathcal{I}$ if for every cohesive group of voters N' such that $|N'| \geq n/k$ there exists a voter $i \in N'$ such that $A_i \cap W \neq \varnothing$. A committee selection rule $\mathcal{R}$ is said to *satisfy JR* if for every instance $\mathcal{I}$ every committee in the set $\mathcal{R}(\mathcal{I})$ provides JR.

The definition of justified representation does not appear to be particularly demanding, as illustrated by Example 15.1.

Example 15.1. Consider a twelve-voter instance with $C = \{c_1, \ldots, c_8\}$ and $k = 4$, where $A_1 = A_2 = \{c_1\}$, $A_3 = \{c_1, c_2, c_3\}$, $A_4 = \cdots = A_7 = \{c_4, c_5, c_6, c_7\}$, and $A_8 = \cdots = A_{12} = \{c_4, c_5, c_6, c_8\}$. Voters 1, 2, and 3 form a cohesive group of size 3, and voters 4, …, 12 form a cohesive group of size 9. Committees $W_1 = \{c_1, c_4, c_5, c_6\}$ and $W_2 = \{c_2, c_3, c_4, c_8\}$ both provide JR for this instance. Note that W_2 does not contain the candidate c_1 that is jointly approved by voters 1, 2, and 3; nevertheless, it provides JR by virtue of containing at least one (in fact, two) approved candidates of voter 3.

However, perhaps surprisingly, there are prominent examples of approval-based committee selection rules that fail this axiom. To make this claim precise, we will now define two families of approval-based committee selection rules and discuss their behavior with respect to justified representation.

Definition 15.4. A *Thiele rule* for selecting a k-member committee is defined by a vector of nonnegative weights $\mathbf{w} = (w_1, \ldots, w_k)$ with $w_1 = 1$; we denote this rule by $\mathbf{w}$-Th. Given an instance $\mathcal{I} = \langle C, [n], \mathcal{A}, k\rangle$ of the committee selection problem with approval ballots and a committee $S \subseteq C$, $|S| = k$, it computes the score of S as

$$w(S) = \sum_{i\in[n]} \sum_{j=1}^{|S\cap A_i|} w_j$$

and outputs the set of all committees with the highest score.

A *sequential Thiele rule* for selecting a k-member committee is also defined by a vector of nonnegative weights $\mathbf{w} = (w_1, \ldots, w_k)$ and is denoted by $\mathbf{w}$-seqTh. Given an instance $\mathcal{I} = \langle C, [n], \mathcal{A}, k\rangle$ of the committee selection problem with approval ballots, it forms a size-k committee in k steps. It starts by setting $S = \varnothing$ and then, at each of the k iterations, adds to S a candidate $c \in C \setminus S$ that maximizes the quantity $w(S \cup \{c\}) - w(S)$ (breaking ties arbitrarily).

Intuitively, under a Thiele rule a voter is assumed to derive a utility of w_1 from having one approved candidate in the committee, a utility of $w_1 + w_2$ from having two approved candidates in the committee, and so forth, with the marginal utility of the jth additional candidate being w_j; it is typically assumed that $w_1 \geq \cdots \geq w_k$.

The family of Thiele rules was proposed by the Danish statistician Thorvald N. Thiele in the beginning of the twentieth century (Thiele, 1895) and was briefly used in Sweden. However, for many choices of the weight vector $\mathbf{w}$, these rules are computationally intractable (as was informally observed by Thiele himself, with a formal proof provided more than a century later by Aziz et al., 2015). The sequential Thiele rules were proposed as a way to mitigate these computational complexity barriers, as they are, by construction, efficiently computable.

However, computational tractability comes at a cost: A **w**-Th rule satisfies the JR axiom as long as $w_i \leq 1/i$ for each $i = 1, \ldots, k$, while, on the other hand, a **w**-seqTh rule satisfies the JR axiom if and only if $\mathbf{w} = (1, 0, \ldots, 0)$ (Aziz et al., 2017). However, setting $\mathbf{w} = (1, 0, \ldots, 0)$ results in an unappealing voting rule: In particular, this rule does not distinguish between a committee containing just a single approved candidate of each voter and a committee containing several approved candidates for each voter.

To formally capture this objection, we need a stronger variant of the JR axiom. Here we describe two such axioms: Both are based on the idea that very large, very cohesive groups of voters "deserve" several representatives.

Definition 15.5 (Proportional/Extended Justified Representation). Consider an instance $\mathcal{I} = \langle C, [n], \mathcal{A}, k\rangle$ of the committee selection problem with approval ballots. Given a group of voters $N' \subseteq [n]$ and a positive integer ℓ, we say that N' is *ℓ-large* if $|N'| \geq \ell \cdot \frac{n}{k}$, and we say that N' is *ℓ-cohesive* if $|\bigcap_{i\in N'} A_i| \geq \ell$. A committee $W \subset C$ is said to provide *proportional* (respectively, *extended*) *justified representation (PJR/EJR)* for $\mathcal{I}$ if for every $\ell = 1, \ldots, k$ and every ℓ-large, ℓ-cohesive group of voters N' it holds that the set W contains at least ℓ candidates from $\bigcup_{i\in N'} A_i$ (respectively that $|W \cap A_i| \geq \ell$ for some $i \in N'$). A committee selection rule $\mathcal{R}$ is said to *satisfy PJR/EJR* if for every instance $\mathcal{I}$ every committee in the set $\mathcal{R}(\mathcal{I})$ provides PJR/EJR.

These definitions are significantly more demanding than the definition of JR.

Example 15.2. Consider again the instance described in Example 15.1. Observe that voters 4, …, 12 form a 3-large, 3-cohesive group. Consider the committee $W_3 = \{c_1, c_4, c_7, c_8\}$. This committee contains three candidates in $\bigcup_{i=4,\ldots,12} A_i$, and it can be verified that it provides PJR for this instance. However, it fails to provide EJR, as no voter from the 3-large, 3-cohesive group {4, …, 12} approves three committee members. In contrast, $W_4 = \{c_1, c_4, c_5, c_7\}$ contains three candidates approved by voter 4 and can be shown to provide EJR.

The definition of extended justified representation was proposed by Aziz and colleagues (2017), and proportional justified representation was subsequently defined by Sánchez-Fernández et al. (2017). It can be verified that for $\ell = 1$ both definitions collapse to the definition of justified representation. Moreover, if a committee contains ℓ approved candidates of some voter $i \in N'$, then it contains at least ℓ candidates in the set $\bigcup_{i\in N'} A_i$, and therefore any committee that provides PJR also provides EJR (while the converse can be shown to be false).

These definitions enable us to formulate why the sequential Thiele rule with $\mathbf{w} = (1, 0, \ldots, 0)$ is unappealing: This rule fails PJR (and hence, a forteriori, EJR). Indeed, these axioms are quite demanding even when we consider the nonsequential rules: Among all **w**-Th rules, the only rule that satisfies either PJR or EJR is the proportional approval voting rule (PAV), which corresponds to the harmonic weight vector $\mathbf{w} = (1, 1/2, 1/3, \ldots)$; for EJR, this was proved by Aziz and colleagues (2017), and subsequently Sánchez-Fernández and colleagues (2017) observed that this remains true for PJR. We will now prove one-half of this result – namely that the PAV rule satisfies the EJR axiom.

Theorem 15.1. *The PAV rule satisfies EJR.*

Proof: Consider an instance $\mathcal{I} = \langle C, [n], \mathcal{A}, k \rangle$ of the committee selection problem with approval ballots. Let W be a committee with the maximum PAV score, and suppose for the sake of contradiction that W does not provide EJR. This means that there is a positive integer ℓ, $\ell \leq k$, and an ℓ-large, ℓ-cohesive group of voters N' such that for each $i \in N'$ we have $|A_i \cap W| < \ell$. Consider some candidate $a \notin W$ jointly approved by all voters in N'. Since each of these voters currently approves at most $\ell - 1$ candidates in W, if we could add a to W, this would increase the PAV score of W by at least $|N'| \cdot \frac{1}{\ell} \geq n/k$. We will now argue that we can identify a voter $b \in W$ such that replacing b with a results in an increase of the PAV score, a contradiction for the choice of W.

Given a candidate $c \in W$, we define the *marginal utility* of c to voter i, denoted by $mu(c, i)$, to be 0 if $c \notin A_i$ and $1/|W \cap A_i|$ otherwise; this is the difference between i's contribution to the PAV score of W and her contribution to the PAV score of $W \setminus \{c\}$. Let $mc(c) = \sum_{i \in N} mu(c, i)$ be the *marginal contribution* of c to W; if we remove c from W, the PAV score of W decreases by $mc(c)$. By construction, for each $i \in N$ such that $W \cap A_i \neq \varnothing$, we have

$$\sum_{c \in W} mu(c, i) = |W \cap A_i| \cdot \frac{1}{|W \cap A_i|} = 1;$$

if $W \cap A_i = \varnothing$, then $\sum_{c \in W} mu(c, i) = 0$. Consequently, we have

$$\sum_{c \in W} mc(c) = \sum_{c \in W} \sum_{i \in N} mu(c, i) = \sum_{i \in N} \sum_{c \in W} mu(c, i) \leq n.$$

This inequality is strict if and only if $W \cap A_i = \varnothing$ for some $i \in [n]$. From this, we can conclude that there is a candidate $b \in W$ with $mc(b) \leq n/k$.

Suppose we have $mc(b) < n/k$ for some $b \in W$. Then replacing b with a strictly increases the PAV score, and we are done. It remains to consider the possibility that $mc(c) = n/k$ for all $c \in W$; note that this implies that $W \cap A_i \neq \varnothing$ for all $i \in [n]$. Pick a voter $i \in N'$ and consider a candidate $b \in W \cap A_i$. As i approves at most $\ell - 1$ candidates in W, she approves at most $\ell - 2$ candidates in $W \setminus \{b\}$, so the marginal utility of a to i with respect to $W' = (W \setminus \{b\}) \cup \{a\}$ is at least $\frac{1}{\ell - 1}$. Hence, the marginal contribution of a to W' is at least

$$(|N'| - 1) \cdot \frac{1}{\ell} + \frac{1}{\ell - 1} \geq n/k + \frac{1}{\ell(\ell - 1)}.$$

Thus, in this case, too, replacing b with a increases the PAV score of W. □

Theorem 15.1 characterizes the PAV rule in the class of all Thiele rules. However, it is disappointing from an algorithmic perspective: The outputs of the PAV rule are NP-hard to compute. It is therefore natural to ask if the PJR and EJR axioms are compatible with polynomial-time computability.

The first result of this type was obtained for the PJR rule: Brill and colleagues (2017) show that a variant of the voting rule that was proposed by Thiele's contemporary, Edward Phragmén (1894), is polynomial-time computable and satisfies PJR. Briefly, under the sequential Phragmén rule, voters continuously earn "money," which they use to "purchase" candidates one by one, with each candidate having a unit cost that needs to be shared by the voters who approve this candidate. At each iteration, the rule selects a candidate so as to minimize the maximum cumulative payment, over all voters. Thus this voting rule can be thought of as a myopic load-balancing procedure. However, unfortunately, as shown by Brill and colleagues (2017), no known variant of Phragmén's rule satisfies EJR.

Aziz and colleagues (2018) then observed that revisiting the proof of Theorem 15.1 offers us a path toward a solution. Effectively, this proof describes an iterative procedure for finding a committee that provides EJR: Given a committee W, check if there is a pair of candidates $b \in W$, $a \notin W$ such that the committee $(W \setminus \{b\}) \cup \{a\}$ has a higher PAV score than W, and, if so, replace b with a; repeat until the PAV score of W cannot be improved in this manner. The proof shows that when this local search algorithm stops, the resulting committee provides EJR.

There is a problem, however: While it is clear that our local search algorithm eventually converges (as each step increases the PAV score), it is not clear if it converges in polynomially many steps. To resolve this issue, we need to take an even closer look at the proof of Theorem 15.1. In that proof, we have shown that the PAV score of $W' = (W \setminus \{b\}) \cup \{a\}$ is strictly higher than that of W. However, it can be shown that this argument actually establishes a stronger result: The difference between the PAV scores of W' and W is at least $\frac{1}{k^2}$. This is immediate for the case where the marginal contribution of every candidate in W is exactly n/k, as we show that in this case replacing b with a increases the PAV score by at least $\frac{1}{\ell(\ell-1)} \geq \frac{1}{k^2}$; the case where $mc(b, W) < n/k$ requires a bit more effort, so we omit the argument.

Thus we can modify our local search procedure to only look for swaps that increase the PAV score by at least $\frac{1}{k^2}$; the proof of Theorem 15.1 shows that when no such swaps are available, the current committee provides EJR. To bound the running time of the modified algorithm, it suffices to observe that the maximum PAV score of any committee is at most $n(1 + \cdots + 1/k)$ and hence the modified local search algorithm stops after $O(nk^2 \log k)$ swaps. As each swap can be implemented in $O(nm^2)$ time, this establishes that the modified local search algorithm runs in time $O(n^2 m^2 k^2 \log k)$ and finds a committee that provides EJR. (Aziz et al., 2018, employ more careful analysis to show that it suffices to consider swaps that improve the PAV score by at least a factor of $\frac{n}{k^2}$, which leads to better running time.)

While we have accomplished our goal of identifying a polynomial-time algorithm that provides EJR, the solution offered by the modified local search algorithm is not fully satisfactory: In particular, if it were implemented in practice, it may be difficult to explain to the voters why we may stop the procedure even if there exists another swap that can improve the PAV score (by an amount that is less than $1/k^2$). Also, it is difficult to analyze this procedure from an axiomatic perspective.

This issue is partially addressed by Aziz and colleagues (2018), who put forward an alternative voting rule that can be executed in polynomial-time and satisfies EJR. This is an iterative rule that adds candidates to the committee one by one; it starts by assigning each voter a weight of 1 and modifies the voters' weights after each step, reducing a voter's weight when their approved candidate is added to the committee. However, this rule is perhaps too complex to be practical.

A more appealing solution was recently proposed by Peters and Skowron (2020), who defined a new approval-based voting rule, which they called Rule X. Under this rule, each voter is endowed with one unit of money, and voters "buy" k candidates one by one. The price of each candidate is n/k, and when a candidate c is bought, its price is shared among the voters who approve c but typically in a nonuniform way. Specifically, at each step we look for the smallest value of q such that there exists a candidate c with the property that we can share the price of c (i.e., n/k) among the voters who approve c so that each voter contributes at most q. Once we have computed q, we add the respective candidate to the committee. This rule is very similar in spirit to the sequential Phragmén rule; the primary difference is that the voters receive their endowments up front rather than earning them continuously.

Rule X is quite intuitive, and it is not hard to verify that it is polynomial-time computable. Moreover, Peters and Skowron (2020) establish that it satisfies EJR, as well as two additional axioms defined in their work, namely, priceability and laminar proportionality; in contrast, PAV does not satisfy either of these two axioms.

To conclude this section, we mention that the EJR axiom is very similar in spirit to a core stability condition in a cooperative game associated with the committee selection problem. Specifically, imagine a game where each of the n voters is endowed with one unit of money and each candidate costs n/k. If a committee W is selected, the utility of each voter is $|W \cap A_i|$. Now, suppose a committee W is selected; we say that a group of voters N' has a *deviation* if they can pool their money and purchase a subset of candidates W' (we allow W' to have a nonempty intersection with W), such that each voter in N' prefers W' to W. A committee is in the *core* if no group of voters has a deviation.

Recall that the definition of EJR was formulated in terms of ℓ-large, ℓ-cohesive groups of voters who do not have ℓ representatives in the current committee. The reader can verify that any such group corresponds to a deviation, as defined in the previous paragraph. This means that if a committee is in the core, then it also provides EJR. However, Aziz and colleagues (2017) show that the converse is not true. In fact, it remains an open problem whether every instance of the committee selection problem with approval ballots has a nonempty core. Partial progress on this question includes positive results for restricted preference domains (Brill et al., 2020; Pierczyński and Skowron, 2021) and for *approximate core*, where we only allow deviations that increase the utility of each deviator by a certain factor (Jiang et al., 2020; Munagala et al., 2021).

15.3 PARTICIPATORY BUDGETING

We have argued that multiwinner voting is an appealing research area because of its algorithmic richness and opportunities for voting rule design and axiomatic analysis. Another reason to study multiwinner voting is its relevance to the very practical problem of *participatory budgeting* (Shah, 2007). In participatory budgeting, a local government has to select a subset of projects from a given list based on residents' preferences; each project has a cost, and there is an overall budget constraint, so that the total cost of the selected projects cannot exceed the budget. The voters are asked to report their preferences over the projects (e.g., they may be asked to indicate which of the projects they approve or describe their "ideal" budget allocation), and then a budget-feasible allocation is selected based on voters' reports.

Designing a good participatory budgeting procedure is a very challenging problem: Eliciting the voters' preferences is far from trivial, there may be complicated dependencies among the projects, and one needs to distinguish between all-or-nothing projects (e.g., installing new lights along a path) and projects that admit partial implementation (allocating funding to road repair); we refer the reader to a survey by Aziz and Shah (2021). In particular, the committee selection problem can be viewed as a special case of the participatory budgeting problem: We can associate each candidate with a unit-cost project, assume that voters have approval preferences (so, in particular, they are indifferent among all projects that they approve), and set the budget to be equal to the target committee size.

As a consequence, algorithms, voting rules, and axioms developed in the context of multiwinner voting serve as a useful starting point in the analysis of participatory budgeting. Indeed, there are already a number of papers that make this connection explicit. For instance, Fluschnik and colleagues (2019) consider the complexity of an extension of the Chamberlin–Courant rule to the participatory budgeting setting in the utilitarian model (i.e., where each voter reports her utility for each project) and use techniques developed for the Chamberlin–Courant rule (such as fixed-parameter analysis and algorithms for restricted domains) to obtain positive algorithmic results. For approval ballots, Talmon and Faliszewski (2019) describe how to extend several committee selection rules and axioms for these rules to the domain of participatory budgeting. Another example is the work of Peters and colleagues (2021), who formulate a variant of the extended justified representation axiom for the participatory budgeting setting and propose a variant of Rule X that satisfies this axiom. We believe that this research agenda has a potential to contribute to the widespread adoption of democratic budget allocation.

15.4 OPEN PROBLEMS

To conclude, we will now list several open problems associated with the task of finding representative committees and budgets. The most prominent one is that of determining whether every instance of the committee selection problem with approval ballots has a nonempty core. Another challenge is to develop a characterization of the class of voting rules that satisfy the JR axiom; the same question can be asked for PJR and EJR. Further afield, it would be interesting to explore whether the justified representation axioms can be adapted to a setting where some of the candidates/projects are incompatible (as may be the case in many participatory budgeting applications).

15.5 REFERENCES

K. J. Arrow. *Social Choice and Individual Values*. New York: John Wiley and Sons, 1951.

H. Aziz, M. Brill, V. Conitzer, E. Elkind, R. Freeman, and T. Walsh. Justified representation in approval-based committee voting. *Social Choice and Welfare*, 48(2):461–485, 2017.

H. Aziz, E. Elkind, S. Huang, M. Lackner, L. Sánchez-Fernández, and P. Skowron. On the complexity of extended and proportional justified representation. In *Proceedings of the Thirty-Second AAAI Conference on Artificial Intelligence (AAAI)*, 2018.

H. Aziz, S. Gaspers, J. Gudmundsson, S. Mackenzie, N. Mattei, and T. Walsh. Computational aspects of multi-winner approval voting. In *Proceedings of the Fourteenth International Conference on Autonomous Agents and Multiagent Systems (AAMAS)*, pp. 107–115, 2015.

H. Aziz and N. Shah. Participatory budgeting: Models and approaches. In T. Rudas and G. Péli, eds., *Pathways between Social Science and Computational Social Science*, pp. 215–236. Amsterdam: Springer, 2021.

J. J. Bartholdi, C. A. Tovey, and M. A. Trick. The computational difficulty of manipulating an election. *Social Choice and Welfare*, 6(3):227–241, 1989.

N. Betzler, A. Slinko, and J. Uhlmann. On the computation of fully proportional representation. *Journal of Artificial Intelligence Research*, 47:475–519, 2013.

F. Brandt, V. Conitzer, U. Endriss, J. Lang, and A. Procaccia. *Handbook of Computational Social Choice*. Cambridge: Cambridge University Press, 2016.

M. Brill, R. Freeman, S. Janson, and M. Lackner. Phragmén's voting methods and justified representation. In *Proceedings of the Thirty-First AAAI Conference on Artificial Intelligence (AAAI)*, pp. 406–413, 2017.

M. Brill, P. Gölz, D. Peters, U. Schmidt-Kraepelin, and K. Wilker. Approval-based apportionment. In *Proceedings of the Thirty-Fourth AAAI Conference on Artificial Intelligence (AAAI)*, pp. 1854–1861, 2020.

B. Chamberlin and P. Courant. Representative deliberations and representative decisions: Proportional representation and the Borda rule. *American Political Science Review*, 77(3):718–733, 1983.

V. Conitzer and T. Walsh. Barriers to manipulation in voting. In F. Brandt, V. Conitzer, U. Endriss, J. Lang, and A. Procaccia, eds., *Handbook of Computational Social Choice*. Cambridge: Cambridge University Press, 2016.

A. C. Constantinescu and E. Elkind. Proportional representation under single-crossing preferences revisited. In *Proceedings of the Thirty-Fifth AAAI Conference on Artificial Intelligence (AAAI)*, pp. 5286–5293, 2021.

C. Dwork, R. Kumar, M. Naor, and D. Sivakumar. Rank aggregation methods for the web. In *Proceedings of the Tenth International ACM Conference on World Wide Web*, pp. 613–622. 2001.

E. Elkind, P. Faliszewski, P. Skowron, and A. Slinko. Properties of multiwinner voting rules. *Social Choice and Welfare*, 48(3):599–632, 2017.

P. Faliszewski, A. Karpov, and S. Obraztsova. The complexity of election problems with group-separable preferences. In *Proceedings of the Twenty-Ninth International Joint Conference on Artificial Intelligence (IJCAI)*, pp. 203–209, 2020.

P. Faliszewski and J. Rothe. Control and bribery in voting. In F. Brandt, V. Conitzer, U. Endriss, J. Lang, and A. Procaccia, eds., *Handbook of Computational Social Choice*. Cambridge: Cambridge University Press, 2016.

P. Faliszewski, P. Skowron, A. Slinko, and N. Talmon. Multiwinner voting: A new challenge for social choice theory. In U. Endriss, ed., *Trends in Computational Social Choice*, pp. 27–47. El Segundo, CA: AI Access, 2017.

P. Faliszewski, P. Skowron, A. Slinko, and N. Talmon. Committee scoring rules: Axiomatic characterization and hierarchy. *ACM Transactions on Economics and Computation (TEAC)*, 7(1):1–39, 2019.

T. Fluschnik, P. Skowron, M. Triphaus, and K. Wilker. Fair knapsack. In *Proceedings of the Thirty-Third AAAI Conference on Artificial Intelligence (AAAI)*, pp. 1941–1948, 2019.

A. Gibbard. Manipulation of voting schemes: A general result. *Econometrica: Journal of the Econometric Society*, pp. 587–601, 1973.

Z. Jiang, K. Munagala, and K. Wang. Approximately stable committee selection. In *Proceedings of the Fifty-Second Annual ACM Symposium on Theory of Computing (STOC)*, pp. 463–472, 2020.

J.-F. Laslier and M. R. Sanver. *Handbook on Approval Voting*. Amsterdam: Springer, 2010.

T. Lu and C. Boutilier. Budgeted social choice: From consensus to personalized decision making. In *Proceedings of the Twenty-Second International Joint Conference on Artificial Intelligence (IJCAI)*, vol. 11, pp. 280–286, 2011.

N. Misra, C. Sonar, and P. R. Vaidyanathan. On the complexity of Chamberlin–Courant on almost structured profiles. In *Proceedings of the Fifth International Conference on Algorithmic Decision Theory (ADT)*, pp. 124–138. Amsterdam: Springer, 2017.

B. L. Monroe. Fully proportional representation. *American Political Science Review*, 89(4):925–940, 1995.

K. Munagala, Y. Shen, K. Wang, and Z. Wang. Approximate core for committee selection via multilinear extension and market clearing. In *Proceedings of the*

Thirty-Third Annual ACM-SIAM Symposium on Discrete Algorithms (SODA), 2021.

D. C. Parkes and L. Xia. A complexity-of-strategic-behavior comparison between Schulze's rule and ranked pairs. In *Proceedings of the Twenty-Sixth AAAI Conference on Artificial Intelligence (AAAI)*, 2012.

D. Peters and M. Lackner. Preferences single-peaked on a circle. *Journal of Artificial Intelligence Research*, 68:463–502, 2020.

D. Peters and P. Skowron. Proportionality and the limits of welfarism. In *Proceedings of the Twenty-First ACM Conference on Economics and Computation (ACM-EC)*, pp. 793–794, 2020.

D. Peters, G. Pierczyński, and P. Skowron. Proportional participatory budgeting with cardinal utilities. In *Proceedings of the Thirty-Fifth Annual Conference on Neural Information Processing Systems (NeurIPS)*, 2021.

D. Peters, L. Yu, H. Chan, and E. Elkind. Preferences single-peaked on a tree: Multiwinner elections and structural results. *Journal of AI Research*, 73:231–276, 2022.

E. Phragmén. Sur une méthode nouvelle pour réaliser, dans les élections, la représentation proportionnelle des partis. *Öfversigt af Kongliga Vetenskaps-Akademiens Förhandlingar*, 51(3):133–137, 1894.

G. Pierczyński and P. Skowron. Core-stable committees under restricted domains. *arXiv preprint*, arXiv:2108.01987, 2021.

A. D. Procaccia, J. S. Rosenschein, and A. Zohar. On the complexity of achieving proportional representation. *Social Choice and Welfare*, 30(3):353–362, 2008.

L. Sánchez-Fernández, E. Elkind, M. Lackner, N. Fernández, J. Fisteus, P. B. Val, and P. Skowron. Proportional justified representation. In *Proceedings of the Thirty-First AAAI Conference on Artificial Intelligence (AAAI)*, 2017.

M. A. Satterthwaite. Strategy-proofness and Arrow's conditions: Existence and correspondence theorems for voting procedures and social welfare functions. *Journal of Economic Theory*, 10(2):187–217, 1975.

A. Shah. *Participatory Budgeting*. Washington, DC: World Bank Publications, 2007.

P. Skowron, L. Yu, P. Faliszewski, and E. Elkind. The complexity of fully proportional representation for single-crossing electorates. *Theoretical Computer Science*, 569:43–57, 2015.

P. Skowron, P. Faliszewski, and A. Slinko. Axiomatic characterization of committee scoring rules. *Journal of Economic Theory*, 180:244–273, 2019.

N. Talmon and P. Faliszewski. A framework for approval-based budgeting methods. In *Proceedings of the Thirty-Third AAAI Conference on Artificial Intelligence (AAAI)*, pp. 2181–2188, 2019.

T. N. Thiele. Om flerfoldsvalg. In *Oversigt over det Kongelige Danske Videnskabernes Selskabs Forhandlinger*, pp. 415–441. Copenhagen: Bianco Lunos Kgl. Hof Bogtrykkeri 1895.

Y. Yang and J. Wang. Parameterized complexity of multi-winner determination: More effort towards fixed-parameter tractability. In *Proceedings of the Seventeenth International Conference on Autonomous Agents and Multiagent Systems (AAMAS)*, pp. 2142–2144, 2018.

H. P. Young. Social choice scoring functions. *SIAM Journal on Applied Mathematics*, 28(4):824–838, 1975.

16

Stochastic Choice and Dynamics Based on Pairwise Comparisons

Felix Brandt

A recurring problem in various disciplines is of the following form: There is a set of alternatives and any pair of alternatives can be compared with each other. A pairwise comparison reveals which of the two alternatives is better than the other. Moreover, comparisons may be cyclic (a is better than b, which is better than c, which is better than a) and probabilistic (a beats b with probability $2/3$). Since none of the alternatives needs to be superior to all the other ones, central normative questions in this context concern which concepts are suitable to take over the role of the conventional notion of maximality and which axiomatic properties these concepts should satisfy. At the same time, one can consider dynamic processes in which a population of entities, each associated with an alternative, engages in pairwise interactions such that the loser of a pairwise comparison will be associated with the alternative of the winner. Descriptive questions in this context concern the resulting sequence of distributions and its convergence behavior.

The following is a list of six diverse areas where such questions have recently appeared.

Game playing (Balduzzi et al., 2018; Vinyals et al., 2019). When using machine learning to master difficult two-player games via self-play, large populations of bots compete with each other in pairwise matchups. Given the recorded wins and losses, how can a "universal sparring partner" be randomly selected such that, against any other bot, the expected number of wins is at least as large as the expected number of losses?

Voting (Brandl et al., 2016). There is a group of voters, each of which rank orders the set of available candidates. Which lotteries over the candidates satisfy desirable properties such as Condorcet consistency (a candidate that beats all other candidates in pairwise comparisons is selected with probability 1), population consistency (whenever two disjoint electorates agree on a lottery, this lottery should also be chosen for the union of both electorates), and independence of clones (the probability with which a candidate is selected is unaffected by introducing clone of other candidates)?

Machine learning (Dudik et al., 2015; Balsubramani et al., 2016). A company has several online ads targeted at different user groups. Each time a user visits a website, he is confronted with two ads and the website tracks which of the ads, if any, the user clicks on. Initially, no information on user behavior is available. Which randomly generated sequence of ads minimizes expected regret? Here, the regret of a sequence of ads is the maximal probability that a fixed sequence of identical ads is more successful in attracting clicks by a random user.

Opinion formation (Brandl and Brandt, 2024). There is a group of agents, each of which entertains one of many possible opinions. Agents come together in random pairwise interactions, in which they try to convince each other of their opinion. There are fixed probabilities with which one opinion beats another, and with some small probability, an agent randomly changes his opinion. What can be said about the distribution of opinions when running this process for a large number of rounds?

Population biology (Laslier and Laslier, 2017; Grilli et al., 2017). There is a continuum of individuals, which are assigned to some species, and for each pair of species there is a fixed probability with which one supplants the other. In each round, one individual dies and is replaced with an individual whose species is determined as the result of a competition based on pairwise random interactions: Three individuals are randomly selected and the winner of the comparison between the first two faces off against the third one. Against which distribution of species does this process converge?

Quantum physics (Knebel et al., 2015). There is a continuum of quantum particles, so-called bosons, which are assigned one of several possible quantum states. Bosons engage in pairwise random interactions, and there are fixed probabilities specifying with which probability a boson transitions from one state to the other when encountering another boson. What is the temporal average of quantum state distributions generated by this process in the limit?

As it turns out, the answers to *all* these questions are intimately connected to mixed equilibria of symmetric zero-sum games. That is precisely the class of games that Émile Borel's initial contribution to the theory of games, which is celebrated with this volume, was exclusively concerned with (Borel, 1921, 1953).

16.1 THE MODEL

Let A be a finite set of alternatives and $\Delta = \{p \in [0,1]^A : \sum_{x \in A} p_x = 1\}$ be the set of all lotteries over alternatives. The square matrix $M \in [0,1]^{A \times A}$ describes the pairwise comparisons between alternatives. For two alternatives x and y, $M_{xy} \in [0,1]$ says how much x is preferred to y ($1/2$ represents indifference).

By convention, $M_{xx} = 0$ and $M_{xy} + M_{yx} = 1$ for all $x, y \in A$. These numbers could, for example, be interpreted as dominance probabilities, relative strengths of pairwise comparisons, or as fractions of voters who prefer one alternative to another. I will refer to them as dominance probabilities here. The important special case where M is a binary matrix (i.e., all entries of M are either 0 or 1), corresponds to complete and antisymmetric relations and thus to tournament graphs. The matrix M induces a skew-symmetric matrix $\tilde{M} = M - M^\top$, (i.e., $\tilde{M}_{xy} = -\tilde{M}_{yx}$ for all $x, y \in A$).

16.2 MAXIMAL LOTTERIES

Obviously, there need not be a "maximal" alternative $x \in A$ in the sense that it defeats every other alternative with a comparison probability of at least 1/2 (i.e., $\tilde{M}_{xy} \geq 0$ for all $y \in A$). However, it follows from the minimax theorem (von Neumann, 1928) that there has to be a "maximal" lottery $p \in \Delta$ such that $p^\top \tilde{M} q \geq 0$ for all lotteries $q \in \Delta$ (i.e., p performs at least as well as any other lottery). This amounts to $\max_{p\in\Delta} \min_{q\in\Delta} p^\top \tilde{M} q = 0$, which holds because

$$\begin{aligned}\max_{p\in\Delta}\min_{q\in\Delta} p^\top \tilde{M} q &= \min_{q\in\Delta}\max_{p\in\Delta} p^\top \tilde{M} q = \min_{q\in\Delta}\max_{p\in\Delta} -q^\top \tilde{M} p \\ &= -\max_{q\in\Delta}\min_{p\in\Delta} q^\top \tilde{M} p = -\max_{p\in\Delta}\min_{q\in\Delta} p^\top \tilde{M} q,\end{aligned}$$

where the first equality follows from the minimax theorem and the second one from the skew-symmetry of $\tilde{M}$. In game-theoretic terms, $\tilde{M}$ can be interpreted as a symmetric zero-sum game. The value of any such game is 0, and the maximal lotteries described previously are the probability distributions of the maximin or Nash equilibrium strategies of $\tilde{M}$. It does not matter whether one takes the equilibrium strategies of the row or column player since the game is symmetric. In summary,

$$\text{a lottery } p \in \Delta \text{ is } \textit{maximal} \text{ if } p^\top \tilde{M} \geq 0,$$

and every comparison matrix M admits at least one maximal lottery.

Consider, for example, pairwise comparisons among three alternatives $A = \{a, b, c\}$ given in Figure 16.1. The matrix $\tilde{M}$ admits a unique maximal lottery $p = (1/6, 1/3, 1/2)^\top$ since

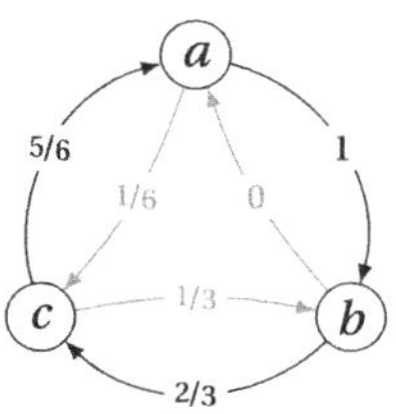

$$M = \begin{array}{c} \\ a \\ b \\ c \end{array}\!\!\begin{array}{c} \begin{array}{ccc} a & b & c \end{array} \\ \begin{pmatrix} 0 & 1 & 1/6 \\ 0 & 0 & 2/3 \\ 5/6 & 1/3 & 0 \end{pmatrix} \end{array} \quad \text{(comparison matrix)}$$

$$\tilde{M} = \begin{array}{c} \\ a \\ b \\ c \end{array}\!\!\begin{array}{c} \begin{array}{ccc} a & b & c \end{array} \\ \begin{pmatrix} 0 & 1 & -2/3 \\ -1 & 0 & 1/3 \\ 2/3 & -1/3 & 0 \end{pmatrix} \end{array} \quad (M - M^\top)$$

FIGURE 16.1 Example of a comparison matrix M (center), its corresponding directed graph (left), and the induced skew-symmetric matrix $\tilde{M}$ (right).

$$p^{\mathsf{T}}\tilde{M} = \begin{pmatrix} 1/6 \\ 1/3 \\ 1/2 \end{pmatrix}^{\mathsf{T}} \begin{pmatrix} 0 & 1 & -2/3 \\ -1 & 0 & 1/3 \\ 2/3 & -1/3 & 0 \end{pmatrix} = (0 \quad 0 \quad 0) \geq 0.$$

The term *maximal lottery* goes to back to Fishburn (1984), who introduced this concept in the context of social choice theory. The idea to circumvent the Condorcet paradox – which lies at the heart of Arrow's impossibility theorem – by introducing the notion of a randomized Condorcet winner can be traced back to Kreweras (1965). Maximal lotteries have been rediscovered several times under various names. Depending on whether the comparison matrix is binary, the support of maximal lotteries has been analyzed under the name *bipartisan set* (a term proposed by Roger Myerson) or *essential set* (Laffond et al., 1993; Dutta and Laslier, 1999). Felsenthal and Machover (1992) refer to maximal lotteries as the *game theory procedure*, and Rivest and Shen (2010) refer to them as the *game theory method*. More recently, maximal lotteries have been rediscovered again in machine learning, where they are called *von Neumann winners* in the context of dueling multi-armed bandits (Dudik et al., 2015; Balsubramani et al., 2016) or *Nash averaging* when evaluating the performance of players in round-robin tournaments (Balduzzi et al., 2018; Vinyals et al., 2019).

16.3 UNIQUENESS AND SUPPORT SIZE

Fisher and Ryan (1992) and Laffond et al. (1993) have shown independently that there is a *unique* maximal lottery when M is binary. This statement was strengthened by Laffond et al. (1997), who extended it to matrices whose entries are fractions with odd denominators. An even weaker sufficient condition based on congruencies was provided by Le Breton (2005). In a more abstract sense, maximal lotteries are almost always unique since the set of all matrices M that admit multiple maximal lotteries has measure zero and is nowhere dense in $[0, 1]^{A \times A}$. This follows from considering the dimension of the kernel of submatrices of $\tilde{M}$. Fisher and Reeves (1995) and Brandl (2017) analyzed the size of the support of maximal lotteries for random matrices. Under fairly general symmetric distributions of matrices, maximal lotteries randomize over half of the alternatives on average.

16.4 AXIOMATIC PROPERTIES

Maximal lotteries satisfy a number of axiomatic properties that are deemed desirable in various contexts. In the following, the maximal lottery ML probability of an alternative is the probability that a maximal lottery assigns to the alternative based on a given comparison matrix.

- Any alternative that defeats every other alternative with probability greater than 1/2 has ML probability 1. Such an alternative corresponds to a strict pure Nash equilibrium of $\tilde{M}$. Similarly, any alternative that is defeated by every other alternative with probability greater than 1/2 has ML probability 0 (Laffond et al., 1993; Laslier, 2000).

- A lottery that is maximal for two comparison matrices is also maximal for any convex combination of both matrices (Brandl et al., 2016; Brandl and Brandt, 2019).
- A lottery remains maximal when removing alternatives with ML probability 0 (Laffond et al., 1993; Laslier, 2000).
- A maximal lottery is unaffected by reducing the dominance probabilities of alternatives with ML probability 0. In particular, the dominance probabilities between two such alternatives are irrelevant (Laslier, 1997).
- When increasing the dominance probability of x against y, the ML probability of x relative to the ML probability of y does not decrease (Brandl et al., 2022).
- The ML probability of an alternative is unaffected by cloning other alternatives. More generally, maximal lotteries of comparison matrices that admit a substitution decomposition can be decomposed into the maximal lotteries of each component (Laffond et al., 1996; Laslier, 2000; Brandl et al., 2016).

In probabilistic social choice, some of these properties have been used to completely characterize maximal lotteries. There are characterizations using Arrow's independence of irrelevant alternatives and Pareto efficiency (Brandl and Brandt, 2020), as well as population consistency and composition consistency (Brandl et al., 2016), and Condorcet consistency and a strong version of Moulin's participation condition (Brandl et al., 2016).[1] The support of maximal lotteries has been characterized using axioms that prescribe consistency with respect to variable sets of alternatives (Laslier, 2000; Brandt et al., 2018). Moreover, versions of these axioms have been used to characterize Nash equilibrium in zero-sum games (Brandl and Brandt, 2019).

16.5 COMPUTATION AND DYNAMICS

Maximal lotteries correspond to equilibrium strategies of a zero-sum game and can thus be computed in polynomial time via linear programming. This entails a number of convenient technical properties (e.g., the set of maximal lotteries for a given comparison matrix is convex and the function that maps a comparison matrix to the corresponding set of maximal lotteries is upper-hemi-continuous). It follows from the well-known reduction from linear programs to symmetric two-player zero-sum games, due to Dantzig (1951), that deciding whether an action is played with positive probability in a symmetric zero-sum game is at least as hard as deciding feasibility of a linear program. The latter problem is known to be P-complete, which implies P-completeness of the former (see also Brandt and Fischer, 2008). As a consequence, *computing maximal lotteries belongs to the "hardest" problems that can be solved in polynomial time.*

[1] Note, however, that maximal lotteries violate strategy-proofness. In fact, only random dictatorships are strategy-proof and efficient (Gibbard, 1977; Hylland, 2005).

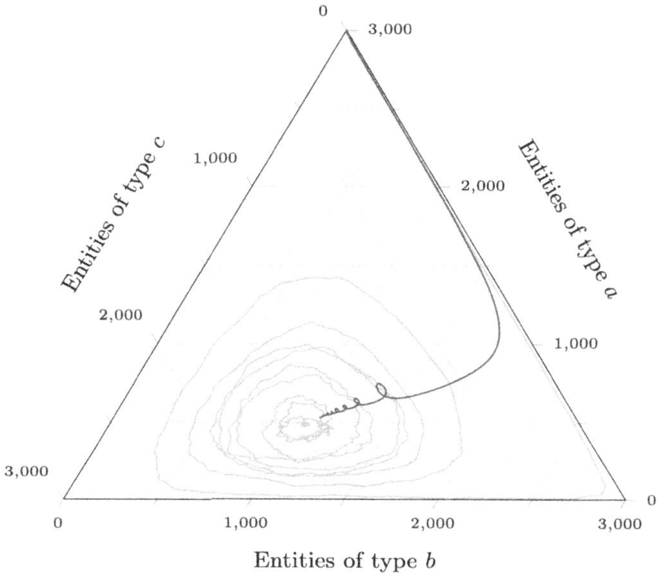

FIGURE 16.2 Simulation of a simple replacement process that approaches the unique maximal lottery of the comparison matrix M given in Figure 16.1. There are 3,000 entities, who are initially all of type a, and the process runs for 300,000 rounds. In each round, two random entities engage in a pairwise comparison with probability 0.98. With the remaining probability, the type of a random entity "mutates" to a random type. The light line depicts the distribution of types among the entities over time, while the dark line depicts the temporal average of type distributions until the given round. The type distribution corresponding to the maximal lottery is $(500, 1000, 2500)$.

As alluded to at the beginning of this essay, maximal lotteries emerge through several simple dynamic processes in which entities change their type based on the comparison matrix. These types of entities could be agents that entertain the same opinion, creatures that belong to the same species, or particles that are in the same quantum state. Let me here consider the discrete and probabilistic model proposed by Brandl and Brandt (2024), where there is a fixed finite number of entities, each of which belongs to some type. The initial distribution of types is irrelevant. Types correspond to alternatives and are thus elements of A. In each round of the process, two random entities come together and are randomly compared with respect to the dominance probabilities of the comparison matrix M. The entity of the inferior type is replaced with one of the superior type. Additionally, every now and then, the type of a random entity "mutates" to a random type.[2] It can be shown that *when the number of entities is sufficiently large and the process is run for sufficiently many rounds, the*

[2] Without these mutations, the distribution of types will eventually be degenerate with probability 1.

distribution of types among the entities is close to a maximal lottery of the comparison matrix with high probability.

As a consequence, the temporal average of type distributions converges to a lottery close to a maximal lottery with probability 1. Moreover, the probability that the distribution is close to a maximal lottery increases exponentially fast. Figure 16.2 shows an example run of this process for the comparison matrix given in Figure 16.1. The continuous and deterministic version of this process is related to the replicator equation in population dynamics and evolutionary game theory (see, e.g., Taylor and Jonker, 1978; Schuster and Sigmund, 1983; Hofbauer and Sigmund, 1998).

Apart from providing a strong argument for the natural emergence of maximal lotteries, this result is also of interest from a computational perspective. Since computing a maximal lottery is equivalent to solving a linear program, the process can be seen as a probabilistic algorithm that approximates a polynomial-time computable function represented by the comparison matrix. In contrast to traditional computing devices such as Turing machines, the dynamic process is based on unordered elementary entities that randomly interact according to very simple replacement rules.

16.6 OUTLOOK

In this essay, I gave several examples where equilibrium strategies of symmetric zero-sum games, whose study was initiated by Émile Borel, appear unexpectedly in diverse fields such as economics, computer science, biology, and physics. Some of the attractive properties of equilibrium distributions, such as their robustness with respect to clones, have been observed independently and repeatedly with different applications in mind. I believe this area offers a lot of potential for inter-disciplinary research, in particular, with respect to the recent developments in machine learning and dynamic processes.

16.7 ACKNOWLEDGMENTS

This chapter is based on work supported by the Deutsche Forschungsgemeinschaft under grants BR 2312/11-2 and BR 2312/12-1. I am grateful to Florian Brandl for many captivating discussions on maximal lotteries.

16.8 REFERENCES

D. Balduzzi, K. Tuyls, J. Perolat, and T. Graepel. Re-evaluating evaluation. In S. Bengio, H. Wallach, H. Larochelle, K. Grauman, N. Cesa-Bianchi, and R. Garnett, eds., *Advances in Neural Information Processing Systems*, vol. 31. Red Hook, NY: Curran Associates, 2018.

A. Balsubramani, Z. Karnin, R. E. Schapire, and M. Zoghi. Instance-dependent regret bounds for dueling bandits. In V. Feldman, A. Rakhlin, and O. Shamir, eds., *Twenty-Ninth Annual Conference on Learning Theory*, vol. 49 of *Proceedings of Machine*

Learning Research, pp. 336–360, Columbia University, New York, June 23–26. New York: PMLR, 2016.

E. Borel. La théorie du jeu et les équations intégrales à noyau symétrique gauche. *C.R.A.S.*, 173:1304–1308, 1921.

E. Borel. The theory of play and integral equations with skew symmetric kernels. *Econometrica*, 21(1):97–100, 1953.

F. Brandl. The distribution of optimal strategies in symmetric zero-sum games. *Games and Economic Behavior*, 104:674–680, 2017.

F. Brandl and F. Brandt. Justifying optimal play via consistency. *Theoretical Economics*, 14(4):1185–1201, 2019.

F. Brandl and F. Brandt. Arrovian aggregation of convex preferences. *Econometrica*, 88(2):799–844, 2020.

F. Brandl and F. Brandt. A natural adaptive process for collective decision-making. *Theoretical Economics*, 19:667–703, 2024.

F. Brandl, F. Brandt, and H. G. Seedig. Consistent probabilistic social choice. *Econometrica*, 84(5):1839–1880, 2016.

F. Brandl, F. Brandt, and C. Stricker. An analytical and experimental comparison of maximal lottery schemes. *Social Choice and Welfare*, 58(1):5–38, 2022.

F. Brandt, M. Brill, H. G. Seedig, and W. Suksompong. On the structure of stable tournament solutions. *Economic Theory*, 65(2):483–507, 2018.

F. Brandt and F. Fischer. Computing the minimal covering set. *Mathematical Social Sciences*, 56(2):254–268, 2008.

G. B. Dantzig. A proof of the equivalence of the programming problem and the game problem. In T. C. Koopmans, ed., *Activity Analysis of Production and Allocation*. New York: Wiley, 1951.

M. Dudik, K. Hofmann, R. E. Schapire, A. Slivkins, and M. Zoghi. Contextual dueling bandits. In P. Grunwald, E. Hazan, and S. Kale, eds., *Proceedings of the Twenty-Eighth Conference on Learning Theory*, vol. 40 of *Proceedings of Machine Learning Research*, pp. 563–587, Paris, France, July 3–6. Paris: PMLR, 2015.. PMLR.

B. Dutta and J.-F. Laslier. Comparison functions and choice correspondences. *Social Choice and Welfare*, 16(4):513–532, 1999.

D. S. Felsenthal and M. Machover. After two centuries, should Condorcet's voting procedure be implemented? *Behavioral Science*, 37(4):250–274, 1992.

P. C. Fishburn. Probabilistic social choice based on simple voting comparisons. *Review of Economic Studies*, 51(4):683–692, 1984.

D. C. Fisher and R. B. Reeves. Optimal strategies for random tournament games. *Linear Algebra and Its Applications*, 217:83–85, 1995. Proceedings of a Conference on Graphs and Matrices in Honor of John Maybee.

D. C. Fisher and J. Ryan. Optimal strategies for a generalized "scissors, paper, and stone" game. *The American Mathematical Monthly*, 99(10):935–942, 1992.

A. Gibbard. Manipulation of schemes that mix voting with chance. *Econometrica*, 45(3):665–681, 1977.

J. Grilli, G. Barabás, M. J. Michalska-Smith, and S. Allesina. Higher-order interactions stabilize dynamics in competitive network models. *Nature*, 548(7666):210–213, 2017.

J. Hofbauer and K. Sigmund. *Evolutionary Games and Population Dynamics*. Cambridge: Cambridge University Press, 1998.

A. Hylland. Strategy proofness of voting procedures with lotteries as outcomes and infinite sets of strategies. Technical report, Mimeo, 2005.

J. Knebel, M. F. Weber, T. Krüger, and E. Frey. Evolutionary games of condensates in coupled birth–death processes. *Nature Communications*, 6(1):6977, 2015.

G. Kreweras. Aggregation of preference orderings. In *Mathematics and Social Sciences*, vol. 1 of *Proceedings of the Seminars of Menthon-Saint-Bernard, France (1–27 July 1960) and of Gösing, Austria (3–27 July 1962)*, pp. 73–79, 1965.

G. Laffond, J. Lainé, and J.-F. Laslier. Composition-consistent tournament solutions and social choice functions. *Social Choice and Welfare*, 13(1):75–93, 1996.

G. Laffond, J. Laslier, and M. Le Breton. The bipartisan set of a tournament game. *Games and Economic Behavior*, 5(1):182–201, 1993.

G. Laffond, J.-F. Laslier, and M. Le Breton. A theorem on symmetric two-player zero-sum games. *Journal of Economic Theory*, 72(2):426–431, 1997.

B. Laslier and J.-F. Laslier. Reinforcement learning from comparisons: Three alternatives is enough, two is not. *The Annals of Applied Probability*, 27(5):2907–2925, 2017.

J.-F. Laslier. *Tournament Solutions and Majority Voting*. Amsterdam: Springer-Verlag, 1997.

J.-F. Laslier. Aggregation of preferences with a variable set of alternatives. *Social Choice and Welfare*, 17(2):269–282, 2000.

M. Le Breton. On the uniqueness of equilibrium in symmetric two-player zero-sum games with integer payoffs. *Économie Publique*, 17:187–195, 2005.

R. L. Rivest and E. Shen. An optimal single-winner preferential voting system based on game theory. In *Proceedings of the Third International Workshop on Computational Social Choice (COMSOC)*, pp. 399–410, 2010.

P. Schuster and K. Sigmund. Replicator dynamics. *Journal of Theoretical Biology*, 100(3):533–538, 1983.

P. D. Taylor and L. B. Jonker. Evolutionary stable strategies and game dynamics. *Mathematical Biosciences*, 40(1):145–156, 1978.

O. Vinyals, I. Babuschkin, W. M. Czarnecki, M. Mathieu, A. Dudzik, J. Chung, D. H. Choi, R. Powell, T. Ewalds, P. Georgiev, J. Oh, D. Horgan, M. Kroiss, I. Danihelka, A. Huang, L. Sifre, T. Cai, J. P. Agapiou, M. Jaderberg, A. S. Vezhnevets, R. Leblond, T. Pohlen, V. Dalibard, D. Budden, Y. Sulsky, J. Molloy, T. L. Paine, C. Gulcehre, Z. Wang, T. Pfaff, Y. Wu, R. Ring, D. Yogatama, D. Wünsch, K. McKinney, O. Smith, T. Schaul, T. Lillicrap, K. Kavukcuoglu, D. Hassabis, C. Apps, and D. Silver. Grandmaster level in StarCraft II using multi-agent reinforcement learning. *Nature*, 575(7782):350–354, 2019.

J. von Neumann. Zur Theorie der Gesellschaftsspiele. *Mathematische Annalen*, 100:295–320, 1928.

17

Truthful Mechanism Design for Computationally Hard Resource Allocation

Paul Milgrom

17.1 BEGINNINGS

One recent development in game theory and mechanism design, inspired by advances in computer science, has been to apply practical truthful mechanisms to large-scale computationally hard problems. A famous recent example was the Federal Communications Commission's (FCC's) 2016–2017 incentive auction, which reallocated tens of billions of dollars of radio spectrum resources from use in television broadcasting to higher-value uses in mobile broadband, incorporating rules based on a new class of truthful mechanisms introduced by Milgrom and Segal (2020).

The theory of truthful mechanisms for computationally hard problems began with a paper by computer scientists Lehmann and colleagues (2002) (cited hereafter as LOS). That paper inspired more research in the years that followed. Before this LOS paper, most research about truthful mechanisms with transferable utility was about mechanisms that optimized some objective. Most prominent among these were the Vickrey–Clark–Groves (VCG) mechanisms, which is the class of all truthful mechanisms that maximize total welfare, and Myerson's (1981) optimal auctions, which is the truthful mechanism that maximizes the seller's expected revenue for a particular class of auction environments with a single item for sale. In Myerson's paper, the optimal truthful mechanism is a threshold auction, which means that the winning bidder pays a price equal to the lowest bid that would still have been winning. Limiting attention to mechanisms in which losing bidders always pay zero, the Myerson threshold auction is the only expected-revenue-maximizing truthful auction.

LOS modeled auctions for resource allocation as a knapsack problem in which each item is owned by a different bidder. Bidder n enjoys a value v_n if its item is packed, where that value is private information that the auctioneer must ask the bidder to report. The size of each item, denoted by s_n, is assumed to be publicly observed. The general knapsack problem is NP-hard, but when the item sizes are small relative to the knapsack, there is a fast and easy way to find a good approximation of the optimal solution: the Dantzig greedy algorithm, which works like this: Arrange the items in order based on an index v_n/s_n, from largest to smallest, and pack the items in that order until some item does not fit. The greedy algorithm then terminates when either all items are packed or one is encountered that does not fit. If no item size is larger than a fraction α of the size of the knapsack, then this algorithm outputs an optimal package for the related problem in which the knapsack is smaller – just large enough to pack the selected items. The smaller knapsack is at least $1-\alpha$ of the size of the original knapsack, so the optimal value of the revised problem is at least a $1-\alpha$ fraction of that of the original problem.

Can this greedy algorithm be incorporated in a truthful mechanism? LOS showed that it can be by setting bidder's prices equal to their threshold prices, which are the smallest values that the winning bidders could report and still be packed. These prices are easy to compute, and one can show that if losing bidders are to pay zero, then the LOS knapsack-threshold auction is the only truthful auction that implements the greedy allocation.

As LOS noted, the same analysis can be applied to the problem of incorporating any monotonic algorithm in a truthful mechanism for the knapsack problem. To be *monotonic* means that for any values v_{-n} of the other participants, there is some threshold value $\bar{v}_n$ (possibly $\pm\infty$) such that n's item is packed if it exceeds $\bar{v}_n$ and is not packed if it is less than $\bar{v}_n$, a definition that allows ambiguity about what happens in the boundary case of $v_n = \bar{v}_n$ Monotonic algorithms include generalized greedy algorithms for problems with more complicated upper bounding constraints than the knapsack constraints. These operate by ordering the items according to some index and then packing them one at a time, from highest index to lowest, terminating when either all items are packed or it becomes infeasible to pack the next item, given the already-packed items. Such an algorithm is monotonic when each item's index is a nondecreasing function of its declared value, given all its other properties (such as its volume, weight, shape, priority labels, etc.). That explains why such an algorithm is known as monotonic.

We may say that a packing mechanism has the opt-out property if any participant reporting a zero value remains unpacked and pays a price of zero. Limiting attention to truthful mechanisms with the opt-out property, LOS found that no non-monotonic algorithm can be incorporated in such a mechanism. Notice that truthfulness and the opt-out property together imply that (i) no packed bidder ever pays a price higher than its true value (otherwise, it could increase its payoff by "opting out," that is, by untruthfully reporting a zero value) and (ii) every unpacked bidder pays exactly zero (otherwise, if the price were higher, then the bidder could profit by untruthfully reporting a value of zero; if lower – meaning that the auctioneer pays the bidder – then the zero-value bidder could profit by untruthfully reporting a value leading to the negative payment). With no threshold, there must be some v_{-n} and two values $v'_n < v_n$ such that bidder n is packed when the value profile is (v'_n, v_{-n}) but not when it is (v_n, v_{-n}). But then the mechanism cannot be truthful, because when the value profile is (v_n, v_{-n}), n would earn zero by reporting truthfully and at least $v_n - v'_n > 0$ by untruthfully reporting the lower value v'_n.

LOS explained that their result applies more generally to single-minded participants, for whom there are only two relevant outcomes: winning or losing; its item packed or not packed. The next important developmental step for this theory was to expand the result to apply to any finite number of different outcomes. This extension is important for many practical applications. For example, in a wholesale auto auction, a participant might win the red or brown Ford Mustang or both or neither; in a radio spectrum licensing auction, it might win between zero and five licenses in each of one hundred regions (6^{100} possibilities); in a team project with N tasks, a participant might be assigned any of the 2^N subsets of the collection of necessary tasks. Some of these applications raise important problems of how participants may communicate their values, but that is not the challenge I will address today (but see Milgrom, 2009, and Bichler et al., 2023).

The Saks-Yu theorem (2005) extends the LOS theory to any finite number of outcomes for each participant. Informally, it says that if the set of possible value vectors for each participant is a convex set, then an algorithm can be incorporated in a truthful mechanism if and only if the mechanism is monotonic for each pair of outcomes separately.

The formalism works as follows. Let $[K] \stackrel{\text{def}}{=} \{1, \ldots, K\}$ be a finite set of possible allocations that the algorithm might select. We assume that for each participant n, there is a vector v_n describing its values for each outcome: v_{nk} (sometimes written $v_n(k)$) denotes the value that n receives if the allocation is $k \in [K]$. The participant's possible value vectors are points $v_n \in V_n \subset \mathbb{R}_+^K$. An *allocation function* (e.g., allocation rule) is a mapping $A : \times_{n\in[N]} V_n \to [K]$, which maps each profile of participants' value vectors into a chosen allocation. A *mechanism* is a pair (A, P), where A is the allocation function and $P : \times_{n\in[N]} V_n \to \mathbb{R}^N$ is the payment rule, so that when the reported value profile is $v \in \times_{n\in[N]} V_n$, participant n pays $P_n(v)$. Adopting the language of algorithms, we sometimes call the argument v of the mechanism functions the *input* to the mechanism.

If participant n reports that her value vector is v'_n and others report values v_{-n}, then the mechanism will select the allocation $A(v'_n, v_{-n})$ and the participant will pay $P(v'_n, v_{-n})$. In a truthful mechanism, participant n earns her highest payoff by reporting truthfully, regardless of v_{-n}.

Definition 17.1. A mechanism is *truthful* if for all $v_{-n} \in V_{-n}$, all n and all $v_n, v'_n \in V_n$:

$$v_n\left(A(v'_n, v_{-n})\right) - P_n(v'_n, v_{-n}) \leq v_n\left(A(v_n, v_{-n})\right) - P_n(v_n, v_{-n}).$$

The left-hand side of the truthfulness inequality is the participant's payoff when her value is v_n and she reports that her value is v'_n. Her report v'_n becomes an input to the mechanism (A, P), which is shown on the left-hand side by the use of v'_n as one of the inputs to the two mechanism functions, leading to the outcome $A(v'_n, v_{-n})$ and payment $P_n(v'_n, v_{-n})$. The value to agent n of the outcome is then $v_n\left(A(v'_n, v_{-n})\right)$, and her payment is subtracted from that value to determine her net payoff from reporting v'_n. The right-hand side of the truthfulness inequality is similar, giving the payoff that participant n receives when she truthfully reports that her value vector is v_n. The truthfulness inequality asserts that participant n cannot increase her payoff above that from truthful reporting by instead reporting a value vector $v'_n \neq v_n$.

An allocation function A is *truthfully implementable* if there exists a payment rule P such that the mechanism (A, P) is truthful. The Saks–Yu theorem asserts that under its stated conditions, an allocation function is truthfully implementable if and only if it is weakly monotone, defined as follows.

Definition 17.2. The allocation rule $A : \times_{n\in[N]} V_n \to [K]$ is *weakly monotone* if for all $\bar{k} \in [K]$ and all value profiles v, v' such that $A(v) = \bar{k}$,

$$\left[(\forall k \in [K])\, v'_{n\bar{k}} - v'_{nk} \geq v_{n\bar{k}} - v_{nk}\right] \Rightarrow A(v'_n, v_{-n}) = \bar{k}.$$

Informally, weak monotonicity means monotonicity pairwise and can be read as if outcome $\bar{k}$ represents packed and k represents unpacked, but excluding the usual normalization that the payoff to being unpacked is zero. The left-hand side of the implication asserts that compared to the value profile v_n, profile v'_n leads n to be willing to pay a larger amount to bring about outcome $\bar{k}$ ("packed") rather than any outcome k ("unpacked"), and that this is true for all values of k. We say that changing the report from v_n to v'_n confirms the outcome compared to each other outcome. Weak monotonicity of A asserts that if whenever n changes her report to confirm the outcome selected by A, then the selection made by A also does not change.

Theorem 17.1 (Saks and Yu, 2005). *Suppose that K is finite and that for each participant n, V_n is convex. Then, A is truthfully implementable if and only if A is weakly monotone.*

We will limit our focus here to truthfully implementable algorithms. One interesting property of such algorithms is that much like the threshold auctions and the VCG mechanisms discussed previously, the payment rules that implement these algorithms are sharply limited.

Theorem 17.2. *Suppose that each set V_n is smoothly path connected and that (A, P) and (A, P') are both truthful mechanisms. Then there exist functions h_n : $\times_{j\neq n} V_j \to \mathbb{R}$ such that for all value profiles v and participants n, $P'_n(v_n, v_{-n}) \equiv P_n(v_n, v_{-n}) + h_n(v_{-n})$. In particular,*

$$P_n(v) = P'_n(v) \quad \Longrightarrow \quad h_n(v_{-n}) \equiv 0 \quad \Longrightarrow \quad P_n(v'_n, v_{-n}) \equiv P'(v'_n, v_{-n}).$$

PROOF: Let $w : [0,1] \rightarrow V_n$ be a smooth path from v_n to v'_n, which means that $w(0) = v_n$, $w(1) = v'_n$, and $(\forall s \in [0,1])$ $w'(s)$ exists. By the integral form envelope theorem of Milgrom and Segal (2002), any participant n's payoff must satisfy these two envelope formulas:

$$\begin{aligned}&(v_n(A(v_n, v_{-n})) - P_n(v_n, v_{-n})) - \left(v'_n\left(A(v'_n, v_{-n})\right) - P_n(v'_n, v_{-n})\right)\\&= \int_0^1 w'(A(w(s), v_{-n})\,ds\\&= \left(v_n(A(v_n, v_{-n})) - P'_n(v_n, v_{-n})\right) - \left(v'_n\left(A(v'_n, v_{-n})\right) - P'_n(v'_n, v_{-n})\right).\end{aligned}$$

Let $h_n(v_{-n}) \stackrel{\text{def}}{=} P'_n(v'_n, v_{-n}) - P_n(v'_n, v_{-n})$. Then, rearranging the first and last expressions provided yields $P'_n(v_n, v_{-n}) = P_n(v_n, v_{-n}) + h_n(v_{-n})$. □

What the preceding theorem teaches us is that in any truthful mechanism, the difference h_n between any two truthful payment functions P_n, P'_n cannot depend directly on n's report but only on others' reports v_{-n}. According to the second part of the theorem, if we require that the mechanism yields a zero payoff to the bidder with the lowest possible value, then the truthful payment rule accomplishing that is unique.

17.2 THE BROADCAST INCENTIVE AUCTION

During the Obama administration, the federal government conceived and executed its so-called Broadcast Incentive Auction, conducted by the FCC. The process was to consist of three parts. It would

- Acquire broadcast rights from a set of existing television broadcasters using a "reverse" auction (in which we seek the lowest prices from bidders).
- Reassign the stations that continued to broadcast to use a reduced set of frequencies ("channels") for television broadcast.
- Sell the spectrum that was cleared of television broadcasting to mobile broadband providers using a "forward" auction (in which we seek the highest prices from bidders).

This auction guided an historically complicated transaction, combining unprecedented computational, economic, and political challenges. Computationally, the first challenge was to check whether given a set of offers by stations to sell their rights, buying those would be sufficient to allow the remaining stations to continue to broadcast within a given set of channels. Checking that requires verifying whether there exists an assignment of channels to stations that satisfies the legal noninterference constraints. In a simplified but suggestive form, suppose we represent each of the roughly 2,500 TV stations by a node in a graph, and for edges in the graph, we create one between any pair of stations that cannot be assigned to the same channel without creating interference. There are hundreds of thousands of such edges in the actual graph. If these were the only constraints on channel assignment,[1] then the question of whether there exists a feasible assignment of channels from a fixed set to stations would be a graph coloring problem, equivalent to the problem of assigning colors to nodes in a graph such that no two connected nodes are of the same color. This problem is NP-complete, and its scale here is very large. No known algorithm can solve all such problems in polynomial time, so any practical implementation requires an approximation algorithm.

A second important algorithmic-design challenge was to use the bids to decide how many channels to clear. Increasing the number of such channels would require both buying more broadcast rights at a higher average cost and selling more mobile broadband rights but at a lower average price, which could increase or decrease total revenue from the sale. A firm requirement was that the cost of clearing spectrum in the reverse auction plus certain other costs must not exceed the revenue raised in the forward auction of mobile broadband rights. Including constraints on revenue and cost is a challenging requirement for truthful mechanisms. For example, it is known that there is no truthful mechanism for buying and selling efficiently that also ensures a balanced budget, and there is also no Bayesian truthful mechanism that does so (Myerson and Satterthwaite, 1983).

Another fact adding to the algorithmic and economic challenges was that the licenses being bought and sold were very heterogeneous. On the forward auction side, a mobile broadband license to serve Chicago, Illinois, is very different from a license to serve Dallas, Texas. On the side of the reverse auction, nearly every TV station broadcasts from a unique location, serves a unique set of viewers, and has unique protections against interference from other users, so there were no one-for-one substitutions among different stations in the problem of spectrum clearing. As between broadcast licenses and mobile broadband licenses, the engineering requirements are very different, even within a single limited area like Chicago. Broadcasting uses powerful signals emitted at high altitudes, such as the tops of tall buildings, to cover homes located as far as 200 miles from the broadcast tower. Those signals are quite strong near the broadcast tower and become weak near the edges of the broadcast area, where they need sensitive protection from interference. Mobile broadband uses much lower powered signals, including ones sent by handheld devices that have no fixed location. These require different solutions for protection from interference.

Yet another big challenge was a consequence of the law that authorized the auction, which specified that stations must have an option to swap broadcast rights in the UHF band for a payment plus a less valuable broadcast right in the upper or lower VHF band. Options to swap needed to be incorporated in the auction design.

[1] The constraints described here are the "co-channel" interference constraints, which account for a great majority of the constraints in assigning channels to stations but not the only ones.

For the rest of this paper, I set aside several of these complications. I suppress any discussion of the design of the forward auction, the algorithm to determine how many channels to clear, and bidders' options to swap for a VHF license, focusing instead on a simplified account of the reverse auction. Even with those omissions, the reverse auction design raised a new conceptual issue for economic and game-theoretic analysis.

Traditionally, a mechanism is analyzed as if it were chosen by the designer, and the resulting game is known by all the participants. For that to be true, participants need to know the mapping A from profiles of values to outcomes, but that was hardly possible. The software used for the NP-complete problem of checking the feasibility of assigning channels to stations without interference was developed by a CS team led by Kevin Leyton-Brown. The team worked continuously to improve algorithm performance, changing parameters and adding new features to the software until shortly before the actual auction (Newman et al., 2017). Because the algorithm runtime to completion is uncertain and the computer would sometimes time out on this NP-complete problem, performance also depends on how the runtimes for each problem are chosen. To understand the allocation rule completely, participants would need to understand not only the algorithm but also the runtime policy and how those affect the allocation function. Runtime policy, however, was not specified in advance but decided in real time during the auction, and algorithmic features evolved until late in the planning process. For these reasons, it was not plausible to suppose that the bidders could understand the allocation rule exactly or perhaps even approximately.

The design team, run through a consulting company called Auctionomics that I had cofounded, proposed that three critical requirements should guide the auction mechanism design. The rules should (i) ensure that the cost of the reverse auction could never exceed the available budget, which would be determined endogenously by the results of the forward auction; (ii) be robust to computational limits, accounting for the inevitable timeouts that would arise using any feasibility checking software and limited runtime; and (iii) be truthful for bidders, so that bidding would be easy despite the daunting complexity of the computations that bidders would be unlikely to understand. Secondary to those necessary properties, the mechanism also aimed to (iv) promote efficient allocations, selecting broadcasters to remain on air with the highest broadcast values, and (v) keep the costs of acquiring broadcast rights low. These last two objectives are not perfectly aligned, as the famous analysis of Myerson (1981) shows.

To guide the implementation, Milgrom and Segal (2020) introduced a new class of descending clock auctions. From a bidder's perspective (and excluding the swap options), these are easy to describe. In each round of the auction, a bidder sees a price. If it is the first round or if the price is lower than that of the previous round, the bidder can accept or reject the new price. If the bidder rejects, then it exits the auction and is guaranteed to be assigned a channel to continue broadcasting over the air. If the bidder accepts, then it remains "active" and may see a new, lower price in the next round. The auction ends in the first round when no bidder's price has changed. The auctioneer then buys each active bidder's rights at the last price quoted to that bidder. Formally, a descending clock auction uses any finite set of prices $\mathcal{P} \subset \mathbb{R}_+$, where $0 \in \mathcal{P}$. An auction using $\mathcal{P}$ is described by a function $p : H \to \mathcal{P}^N$ mapping the history of bidder decisions from every past round into a vector of prices for bidders in the current round, subject to the condition that a bidder's current round price is no higher than its previous round price. There are very many auctions in this class.

For such an auction, we defined a "truthful" strategy to mean one that accepts offers that are higher than the bidder's value of its broadcast rights and rejects lower offers. A bidder who accepts a price higher than its value never earns less than zero in the game and can earn only zero by rejecting that price. Similarly, a bidder who rejects an offer less than its value earns zero and can never earn more by accepting that offer.[2] Consequently, the truthful strategy is a dominant strategy. Remarkably, the preceding discussion implies that a participant in a descending clock auction knows that the mechanism is truthful even without knowing the function p, which is the rule used to decide how to determine price offers and when to terminate the auction. The bidders and the auctioneer know that the auction is truthful, even without knowing the complete auction rules!

Milgrom and Segal (2002) identified several key properties of the class of descending clock auction mechanisms. Importantly, the class meets three requirements described previously and still allows us to choose an auction that implements a generalized greedy algorithm for different objectives, so it can be approximately efficient or approximately expected-cost-minimizing. Here is a partial list of the important properties of the class.

1. *Every descending clock auction is truthful*, as explained previously. More strongly, every such auction is obviously strategy-proof in the sense of Li (2017) by a similar argument.
2. *Every descending clock auction can be adapted to limited computation capacity.* For if, in any round, the software times out when computing whether to reduce a bidder's price or what price to set, the algorithm can simply leave that price unchanged.
3. *Every descending clock auction can be extended to satisfy any positive budget without affecting its operation when budgets would anyway be satisfied.* To create the extension, we only need to modify p in rounds when it would specify that the auction ends but spending exceeds the budget. In such rounds, change the rule so that it reduces at least one active bidder's positive price to the next lower price in $\mathcal{P}$. Doing this as many times as necessary ensures that when the auction ends, the total expenditure will not exceed the positive budget.

[2] See Li (2017) for a set of closely related ideas, especially the concepts of "obviously dominant" strategies and "obviously strategy-proof" mechanisms.

4. *Every descending clock auction is weakly group strategy–proof.* This is a general property of obviously strategy-proof mechanisms, so it follows from property 1.
5. *If the set of possible station values is finite, then every generalized greedy algorithm to maximize the total value of the "packed" stations – those that continue to broadcast – is part of a descending clock auction.* This auction is constructed to reduce one station's price in each round and to set that the price so that the station will reject it and be packed if and only if one can infer that the algorithm would pack the station, given what has been revealed about the other stations.
6. *If the set of possible station values is finite, then every generalized greedy algorithm to minimize the total expected cost of acquisition is part of a descending clock auction.* By a modest extension of Myerson's analysis, minimizing expected acquisition costs is the same as minimizing the total virtual value of the purchased stations, which has the same solution as maximizing the total virtual value of the packed stations. Given any generalized greedy algorithm to approximate that, the corresponding descending clock auction can be created along the same lines as for the previous numbered property.
7. *Every descending clock auction preserves winner privacy.* This means that the only things one can infer about winners' values from the history of bids in the auction is that the values were low enough to result in those bidders becoming winners. They could be slightly lower or much lower, but no information about that is revealed.

17.3 INVESTMENTS IN APPROXIMATE MECHANISMS

The traditional computer science approach to mechanism design addresses what economists call *short-run problems*, in which the set of resources is given, and the only remaining question is how they should be allocated. In the long run, the resources are the result of investments made in anticipation of some future short-run allocation. For the VCG mechanisms, which implement efficient short-run decisions, Rogerson (1992) showed that any single investor's incentive to invest to change its own values for various outcomes preserves optimality. That is, the VCG mechanism with the investments that it elicits is efficient for the long-run problem as well.

More generally, one may wonder: Does good performance of an approximation algorithm for short-run problems imply similarly good performance for the corresponding truthful mechanism with endogenous investments? It turns out that it does not. To be precise, let us characterize the short-run performance λ_S of an algorithm by the worst-case ratio of the welfare produced by the algorithm to the maximal value. Similarly, the long-run performance λ_L is a worst-case ratio, where

- the numerator is the expected welfare, net of investment costs, when the investment is chosen to maximize the single investor's expected net payoff (net of its investment cost and short-run price); and

- the denominator is the expected welfare, net of investment costs, for a VCG mechanism when the investment is chosen to maximize this expectation.

The model assumes that in both the numerator and denominator, investments are made under uncertainty, described by a probability distribution $\mathbb{P}$ over the values of other participants, the value that will result from each investment alternative, and the feasible set that will apply to the future short-run problem. The long-run worst-case λ_L is the minimum of the described ratio over all possible probability distributions and investment costs. Akbarpour et al. (2022) have reported the following findings:

- For every truthful mechanism except the VCG mechanisms, there are instances (not necessarily worst-case ones) in which individually profitable investments in resources reduce the net value of the outcome. These instances correspond to negative externalities. When an investor makes an investment and changes its report, it may affect the outcomes that others experience. If the change in the investor's price does not reflect the opportunity cost its investment imposes on others, then total welfare can be reduced.
- There exist approximation algorithms for the knapsack problem with short-run worst-case ratios $\lambda_S \approx 1$ arbitrarily close to one such that the long-run performance ratio, accounting for investments and investment costs, is $\lambda_L = 0$. Informally, this means that even the most excellent approximation performance by an algorithm does not guarantee any nonzero performance by its mechanism when investments are possible.
- There is a necessary and sufficient condition for $\lambda_L = \lambda_S$, which is the certain kinds of negative externalities (ones that result from confirming changes in reports) always satisfy a certain bound.
- More tractably, when no negative externalities can result from confirming changes to a bidder's values, then $\lambda_L = \lambda_S$.

The cited paper also identifies several standard approximation algorithms that satisfy the externality conditions and others that do not, providing some partial guidance to market designers about how to design mechanisms that encourage good performance in both the short-run and the long-run. Many other questions remain. An especially pressing one is how to implement the communications needed for a practical market design.

17.4 REFERENCES

M. Akbarpour, S. D. Kominers, S. Li, and P. R. Milgrom. Investment incentives in near-optimal mechanisms. 2022.

M. Bichler, P. Milgrom, and G. Schwarz. Taming the communication and computation complexity of combinatorial auctions: The FUEL bid language. *Management Science*, 69:2217–2238, 2023.

D. Lehmann, L. I. Oćallaghan, and Y. Shoham. Truth revelation in approximately efficient combinatorial auctions. *Journal of ACM*, 49(5):577–602, 2002.

S. Li. Obviously strategy-proof mechanisms. *American Economic Review*, 107(11): 3257–3287, November 2017.

P. Milgrom. Assignment messages and exchanges. *American Economic Journal: Microeconomics*, 1(2):95–113, 2009.

P. Milgrom and I. Segal. Envelope theorems for arbitrary choice sets. *Econometrica*, 70:583–601, 2002.

P. Milgrom and I. Segal. Clock auctions and radio spectrum reallocation. *Journal of Political Economy*, 128:1–31, 2020.

R. B. Myerson. Optimal auction design. *Mathematics of Operations Research*, 6(1):58–73, 1981.

R. B. Myerson and M. A. Satterthwaite. Efficient mechanisms for bilateral trading. *Journal of Economic Theory*, 29(2):265–281, 1983.

N. Newman, A. Fréchette, and K. Leyton-Brown. Deep optimization for spectrum repacking. *Communications of the ACM*, 61:97–104, 2017.

W. P. Rogerson. Contractual solutions to the hold-up problem. *The Review of Economic Studies*, 59(4):777–793, 1992.

M. Saks and L. Yu. Weak monotonicity suffices for truthfulness on convex domains. pages 286–293, 2005.

18

Impossibility in Game Dynamics

Jason Milionis, Christos Papadimitriou, Georgios Piliouras, and Kelly Spendlove

Under which conditions do the behaviors of players, who play a game repeatedly, converge to a Nash equilibrium? If one assumes that the players' behavior is a discrete-time or continuous-time rule whereby the current mixed strategy profile is mapped to the next, this becomes a problem in the theory of dynamical systems. We apply this theory, and in particular the concepts of chain recurrence, attractors, and the Conley index, to prove a general impossibility result: There exist games for which any dynamics will fail to globally converge to the set of Nash equilibria. The games that help prove this impossibility result are degenerate, but we conjecture that an analogous result holds, under complexity assumptions, for nondegenerate games. We also prove a stronger result for approximate Nash equilibria: For a set of games of positive measure, there are no game dynamics that converge to the set of approximate Nash equilibria for some substantial approximation bound. These impossibility results also apply to dynamics with memory. We argue that these results further weaken the appeal of the Nash equilibrium as the solution concept of choice in game theory and discuss alternatives suggested by the dynamics point of view.

18.1 INTRODUCTION

The Nash equilibrium, defined and shown universal by John F. Nash in 1950 (Nash, 1950), is paramount in game theory, routinely considered as the default solution concept – "the fate and meaning of the game." Over the years – and especially in the past two decades, during which game theory has come under intense computational scrutiny – the Nash equilibrium has been noted to suffer from a number of disadvantages of a computational nature. There are no efficient algorithms for computing the Nash equilibrium of a game, and in fact the problem has been shown to be intractable (Daskalakis et al., 2006; Chen et al., 2006; Etessami and Yannakakis, 2007). Also, there are typically

Remark by editors: During the Nobel symposium, this chapter was presented by Christos Papadimitriou.

many Nash equilibria in a game, and the selection problem leads to conceptual complications and further intractability (see, e.g., Goldberg et al., 2013).

A common defense of the Nash equilibrium is the informal argument that "the players will eventually get there." However, no learning behavior has been shown to converge to the Nash equilibrium, and many *game dynamics* of various sorts proposed in the past have typically been shown to fail to reach a Nash equilibrium for some games. Intractability may already seem to suggest that it would be difficult for any behavior to converge to the Nash equilibria: How can the dynamics converge to the solution of the problem if the problem cannot be solved efficiently? It turns out that the long-term behavior of most natural and simple dynamics are not easy to predict analytically or simulate computationally. Hence the intractability of the Nash equilibrium leaves open the possibility of convergence. *A very natural question arises: Are there player dynamics that are guaranteed to converge to a Nash equilibrium in all games?*

Our main result is an impossibility theorem:

Main Result (Informal Statement). *There are games in which any dynamics fail to globally converge to the set of Nash equilibria.*

This is to say, we exhibit games in which any dynamics must possess long-term behavior that does not coincide with the set of Nash equilibria – in fact, as we shall see, even with the set of approximate Nash equilibria. Hence, in addition to its computational problems, the Nash equilibrium concept is plagued by a form of *incompleteness:* It is incapable of capturing the long-term behaviors of the players in all games.

Naturally, we need to clarify, (1) what do we mean by "dynamics" in this statement and (2) what is the definition of "fails to converge"?

Given a game, the deterministic way players move from one mixed strategy profile to the next can be formalized in the theory of dynamical systems as a continuous function φ assigning to each point x in the strategy space X and each time $t \geq 0$ a point $\varphi(t,x)$: the point where the players will be after time t. The curve $\varphi(t,x)$ parameterized by t is called the *trajectory* of x. Obviously, this function should satisfy $\varphi(t',\varphi(t,x)) = \varphi(t+t',x)$. This *continuous time dynamics* framework avails a rich analytical arsenal, which we exploit in this chapter.

In game theory, the dynamics of player behavior are also often described in terms of *discrete time*, say through a continuous function f mapping any strategy profile x to its value at the next time step, $f(x)$. Is our investigation excluding such dynamics? It turns out that it does not. In dynamical systems, the parallel narratives between continuous and discrete-time dynamics are known to be very rich, and our results are no exception: Our theorems hold, through a mirrored version of our proof, in the context of discrete time game dynamics. See the full version of the paper by Milionis and colleagues (2023) for a description of how this is done. Here we shall deal only with continuous time dynamics.

Implicit in these two formulations of dynamical systems are two basic assumptions we make about dynamics: *continuity* and *determinism*. Stochastic dynamics (e.g., Brownian motion or a discrete-time system in which $f(x)$ is a *distribution* of next points) are excluded. This is important because, as we shall see, there are stochastic dynamics that achieve an approximate Nash equilibrium, albeit after exponential expected time.

There is a third property we assume any reasonable dynamics to have, namely *Nash stationarity:* All Nash equilibria are fixed points of the dynamics. Mathematically, if x is a Nash equilibrium, then $\varphi(t, x) = x$ for all $t \geq 0$. Since the Nash equilibrium has everything we want in a strategy profile, it would be very strange for game dynamics to abandon it. As we shall see, a slightly weaker version of our theorem holds even in the absence of this assumption.

Finally, many known dynamics for games use *memory*, that is, the ability of players maintain and update commonly known, or private, values in some domain, presumably summarizing their experience so far. As we shall see, our results hold for such dynamics as well.

To summarize, "any dynamics" in the statement of the provided theorem assumes dynamics with three properties: *continuity, determinism, and Nash stationarity*. On the positive side, the dynamics can be either discrete time or continuous time, and use memory.

18.2 CONVERGENCE TO THE NASH EQUILIBRIA

Having outlined the assumptions of our result, we now turn to clarifying its conclusion: For a dynamical system φ and a game g, what does it mean for φ to (fail to) *converge* to $NE(g)$, the set of Nash equilibria of the game g?

In past work on the subject (Demichelis and Ritzberger, 2003; DeMichelis and Germano, 2000), φ is required to have as fixed points precisely the set $NE(g)$ – or it could be that the remaining fixed points can be perturbed away. Unfortunately, such requirements are insufficient criteria of convergence, as they allow *cycling*, a behavior that obviously means that not all trajectories converge to the Nash equilibria.

Dynamical systems theory provides an answer through the notions of *ω-limit sets* and *attractors*. Let X denote the set of all strategy profiles. For a point $x \in X$, the *ω-limit set* $\omega(x)$ captures the asymptotic behavior of the dynamics starting at x and informally can be considered as the set of points any neighborhood of which is visited infinitely often under the dynamics starting at x. This can be generalized to $\omega(Y)$ for a subset Y of X, which again stands for the destiny of the set Y under the dynamics.

Finally, an attractor A is a set that has a neighborhood U of itself such that $\omega(U) = A$. That is, the dynamics never leaves A and, in fact, has a neighborhood from which it converges to A.

At this point it is reasonable to suppose that a way to state our result is to say that for any dynamics $NE(g)$ is *not* an attractor of the dynamics. However, this statement is slightly too strong and decidedly too weak. To address the

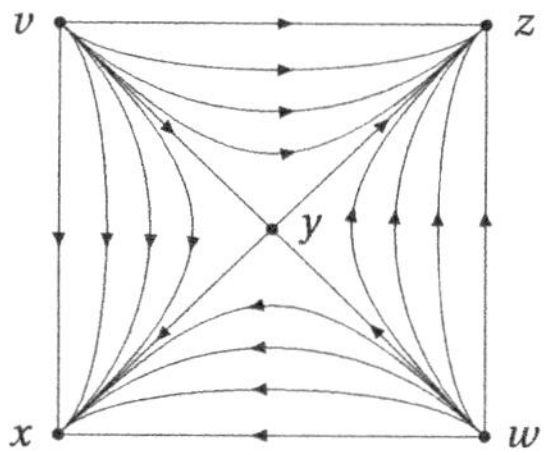

FIGURE 18.1 Phase space of a coordination game. The Nash equilibria of the game are the points x, y, z. The replicator dynamics have the Nash equilibria as fixed points, as well as the points v and w. In this case, the maximal attractor $\omega(X)$ is the disjoint union of the fixed points (the recurrent dynamics) and the connecting orbits (the transient dynamics) between the fixed points. The chain recurrent set $CR(\varphi)$ is precisely the set of fixed points.

weakness first, an attractor does draw the dynamics to it, but not necessarily from everywhere. Every attractor A has a *dual repeller* $R(A)$ such that $\omega(R(A))$ is *disjoint* from A: The points of $R(A)$ do not end up in A. Thus a more appropriate condition is to require that $NE(g)$ be a *maximal attractor* – that is, one whose dual repeller is empty.

But now the requirement has become a bit too strong: It turns out that the maximal attractor must then include orbits *connecting* Nash equilibria. For example, in the 2×2 coordination game (the symmetric game with unit payoff matrix), the natural replicator dynamics contains a trajectory leading from the unstable mixed Nash equilibrium y to each of the two pure Nash equilibria, x and z (see Figure 18.1). But since the unstable point *is* a Nash equilibrium, the motion to the pure Nash starts with zero speed. For any time $t > 0$, no matter how large, and any arbitrary point x' of such an orbit, we can find a point y', possibly arbitrarily close to the unstable Nash, such that $\varphi(t, y') = x'$. Hence these trajectories will also be a part of the attractor.

To make progress on our result, we must elaborate on the notions of recurrence and limit behavior and their connections to each other. This is a deep question, and it took close to a century to pin down. In the benign case of two dimensions (e.g., two-by-two games), the answer is quite simple: No matter the starting point, the dynamics will either converge to a point, or it will cycle. This is the Poincaré-Bendixson theorem from the beginning of the twentieth century (Hirsch et al., 2004), which states that the ω-limit set of any starting point in two-dimensions is either a fixed point or a cycle (or orbits connecting fixed points as in the 2×2 coordination game). The intuitive reason behind the theorem is that in two dimensions *trajectories cannot cross,* and this guarantees some measure of good behavior. Both fixed points and cycles are instances of *periodicity*, and in two dimensions all possible limit behaviors cannot be much more complicated. In three or more dimensions, however, dynamics can be chaotic, and hence simple concepts such as periodicity become insufficient as a conception of limit behavior and convergence.

Topologists strived for many decades, since the dawn of the twentieth century and the Poincaré-Bendixson theorem, to devise more general conception of periodicity that would restore the simplicity of two dimensions, and in the late 1970s they succeeded! The definition is simple (and has much computer science and game theory appeal). First, let us consider the slightly more general notion of *recurrent point*: an x such that $x \in \omega(x)$ (i.e., points that get arbitrarily close to where they started from infinitely often). Now, let us expand this notion as follows: A point x_0 is *chain recurrent* if for every $\epsilon > 0$ there is an integer n and a cyclic sequence of points $x_0, x_1, \ldots, x_n = x_0$ such that for each $i < n$, the dynamical system will bring point x_i *inside the* ϵ*-ball around* x_{i+1}. That is, the system, started at x_0, will cycle after $n - 1$ segments of dynamical system trajectory, interleaved with $< \epsilon$ jumps. Intuitively, it is as if an adversary manipulates the round-off errors of our computation to convince us that we are on a cycle!

Denote by $CR(\varphi)$ the set of all chain recurrent points of the system. The main result of this theory is a decomposition theorem due to Conley, called the Fundamental Theorem of Dynamical Systems, which states that any dynamical system φ, no matter where it is started, eventually ends up in $CR(\varphi)$, in fact drawn there by a Lyapunov function that remains constant on the chain recurrent set (Conley, 1978). In other words, the dynamics decompose into the chain recurrent set and a gradient-like/transient part and moreover $\omega(x) \subset CR(\varphi)$ for any starting point x, in full analogy with two-dimensional dynamics.

Now the technical statement of our main result becomes clear (stated for continuous-time dynamics):

Theorem 18.1. *There is a game g such that, for any dynamical system φ satisfying Nash stationarity, $NE(g)$ is not equal to $CR(\varphi)$.*

That is, some initial conditions will necessarily cause the players to cycle or converge to something that is not Nash. This is indeed what we prove.

18.3 OUTLINE OF THE PROOF

Very inspirational for our result was the work of Benaïm and colleagues (2012), wherein they make in passing a statement, without a complete proof, suggesting our main result that there are games g such that for all dynamics φ (in fact, a more general class of multivalued dynamics), $NE(g)$ is not equal to $CR(\varphi)$. The argument sketched in Benaïm and colleagues (2012) ultimately requires the development of a fixed-point index for components of Nash equilibria and its comparison to the Euler characteristic of the set of Nash equilibria. However, the argument is incomplete. Indeed, the reader is directed to two papers: Demichelis and Ritzberger, 2003; Demichelis and Sorin, 2003). Instead, in our proof we show that requiring that $NE(g)$ be a subset of $CR(\varphi)$ poses certain constraints on $NE(g)$. We then leverage an existing index theory more closely aligned to attractors: that of the *Conley index* (Conley, 1978), a theory which requires minimal technical assumptions on the space and dynamics.

Consider any dynamical system φ in the strategy space X of a game g. The dynamical system can be seen as acting on the whole space X: $\varphi(t, X)$ is how φ has transformed X by time t. Asymptotically, X will be transformed to $\omega(X)$, the maximal attractor. The Conley index of X is an algebraic description of the nature of the cycles in X, and is maintained through such a transformation – and in fact in the limit as well. Thus we are motivated to find a game g such that $NE(g)$ is unusual enough to force $\omega(X)$ to have Conley index different from that of X.

And this is exactly what we do. We use for this purpose a classical degenerate two-player game g with three strategies for each player – a variant of rock-paper-scissors attributed to Kohlberg and Mertens (1986). The game is symmetric and shown here:

$$g = \begin{pmatrix} 1,1 & 0,-1 & -1,1 \\ -1,0 & 0,0 & -1,0 \\ 1,-1 & 0,-1 & -2,-2 \end{pmatrix}. \tag{18.1}$$

The Nash equilibria of g form a continuum, namely a closed hexagonal curve in the four-dimensional space. Now suppose that $CR(\varphi)$ is a subset of $NE(g)$. Since all points of $NE(g)$ were assumed to be fixed points, it follows easily from the definition of chain recurrence that $CR(\varphi) = NE(g)$.[1] Thus $CR(\varphi)$ has a single component, and hence we can conclude (by a duality theorem for the chain recurrent set and lattice of attractors) that this component is the maximal attractor – a place where all of X ends up (see, e.g., Kalies et al., 2021, theorem 6).

We have reached the culmination of the proof: We calculate the Conley index of X and that of $NE(g)$. Now, the Conley index of an isolated invariant set is an algebraic description of the nature of the cycles of the set. Comparing X with $NE(g)$, we notice immediately that the former only has cycles that can be collapsed and vanish in the limit by becoming smaller and smaller, while $NE(g)$ *is by itself* a rigid cycle. Hence the Conley indices of the two are different, and this is a contradiction, which we reached by assuming that $NE(g)$ is a superset of $CR(\varphi)$, completing the proof of the main result. the papers by Milionis and colleages (2022, 2023). As noted previously, without Nash stationarity we can prove a slightly weaker notion of nonconvergence.

Corollary 18.1. *There is a game g such that for any dynamical system φ, $NE(G) \neq CR(\varphi)$.*

18.4 NONDEGENERATE

Now that we have proved the theorem, we can look for chinks on its armor. The theorem seems to be exploiting the degeneracy of the Kohlberg–Mertens game. Does it only hold for degenerate games – a class of measure zero in the space of all games? Also, what if we moderate our ambitions to only finding

[1] This is the only place in the proof where Nash stationarity is used; see Corollary 18.1.

an approximate equilibrium? And, finally, how about stochastic dynamics, or dynamics with memory? These are the subjects of the remaining sections.

We first show that indeed degeneracy is required for the negative result:

Theorem 18.2. *For any nondegenerate game g, there is a dynamical system φ_g converging to the game's Nash equilibria, such that the function $\varphi_g(x, t)$ is efficiently computable.*

Proof: Since g is nondegenerate, it has an odd number of isolated Nash equilibria (Shapley, 1974). Fix one such equilibrium and call it y. We next define φ_g in terms of y. We shall define it at an arbitrary point x implicitly, in terms of the direction of motion, and the speed of motion; if this is done, $\varphi_g(t, x)$ is easily computed through integration on t. The direction of motion is the unit vector of $y - x$: The dynamics heads to y. The speed of motion is defined to be $c \cdot D_g(x)$, where $c > 0$ is a constant, and by $D_g(x)$ we denote the *deficit at x:* the sum, over all players, of the difference between the best-response utility at x and the actual utility at x. It is clear that $D_g(x) \geq 0$, and it becomes zero precisely at any Nash equilibrium.

Now it is easy to check that φ_g is a well-defined dynamical system. Furthermore, since the underlying flow is acyclic in a very strong starlike sense, its chain recurrent set coincides with the set of its fixed points, which coincides with the set of Nash equilibria of g – since there is no opportunity to close extra chain recurrent cycles by ϵ jumps – completing the proof.[2] □

Note, however, that the algorithm for specifying φ_g requires finding y, a PPAD-complete (and FIXP-complete for more than two players) problem. Therefore, the calculation of φ of this dynamical system cannot be carried out in polynomial time, unless PPAD = P. We believe that the dependence is inherent:

Conjecture 18.1. The computational task of finding that from the description of a game g, either a degeneracy of g or an algorithm producing the direction of motion and speed of a dynamical system converging to the game's Nash equilibria is PPAD-hard (and FIXP-hard for three or more players).

Due to the same difficulties with the efficient simulation of dynamics mentioned previously, this conjecture is not a trivial corollary of the corresponding complexity results. We believe this is an important open question in the boundary between computation, game theory, and the topology of dynamical systems, whose resolution is likely to require the development of new complexity-theoretic techniques pertinent to dynamical systems.

[2] The simplicity of this idea leads to the natural question: Why does not this work with the game g of our impossibility theorem? The answer is tricky: The fact that the Nash equilibria of g are a ring means that any two points of the ring are connected via ϵ-jump paths and therefore close a cycle with the trajectory of a point ϵ near the ring: $CR(\varphi)$ will contain a straight line between the chosen equilibrium y and any point of the ring.

18.5 ϵ-APPROXIMATE NASH EQUILIBRIA

Next, it may seem plausible that the difficulty of designing dynamics that converge to Nash equilibria can be overcome when only ϵ-approximation is sought, for some $\epsilon > 0$. Recall that an ϵ-Nash equilibrium is a mixed strategy profile in which all players' utilities are within an additive $\epsilon > 0$ of their respective best response – here we assume that the utilities of the game are normalized to be in $[0, 1]$. We go on to show that our impossibility theorem extends to this case as well. Let us denote by $NE_\epsilon(g)$ the set of ϵ-approximate Nash equilibria of a game g. Finally, we assume ϵ-Nash stationarity (that is, all points in $NE_\epsilon(g)$) are fixpoints.

Theorem 18.3. *There is a game g that admits no dynamics φ such that $CR(\varphi)$ is a subset of $NE_\epsilon(g)$. In fact, the set of such games has positive measure.*

PROOF: Consider again the Kohlberg–Mertens game (Eq. 18.1). We claim that its set of ϵ-Nash equilibria $NE_\epsilon(g)$ is topologically equivalent to a torus for sufficiently small $\epsilon > 0$. To prove the claim, we subdivide the set of all strategy profiles into nine polytopes P^{ij} for all $i, j \in \{1, 2, 3\}$, where the polytope P^{ij} is the subset of the strategy space such that the best response of player 1 is i, and that of player 2 is j. Obviously, these regions can be defined by linear inequalities. Let P_ϵ^{ij} denote the intersection of P^{ij} and $NE_\epsilon(g)$; it can be defined by the linear inequalities defining P^{ij} plus the inequality stating that (x, y) is in $NE_\epsilon(g)$,

$$x^T M_1 y \geq (M_1 y)_i - \epsilon,$$

with a similar inequality for player 2.

Now it is clear that $NE_\epsilon(g)$ is the union of these nine manifolds. However, it is easy to check for the Kohlberg–Mertens game that strategies 2 and 3 are weakly dominated by the first strategy for the first player (and, by symmetry, also for the second player).

Hence all manifolds P_ϵ^{ij} are contained within P_ϵ^{11}. Thus $NE_\epsilon(g)$ is a connected, compact four-dimensional manifold (with boundary) that is homotopy equivalent to $NE(g)$ for a sufficiently small ϵ. Figure 18.2 shows a projection (in a particular direction in $\mathbb{R}^4$) of $NE_\epsilon(g)$ for $\epsilon = 0.09$. Computations performed using Mathematica show that $NE_\epsilon(g)$ is topologically equivalent to the torus up to at least $\epsilon = 0.27$ (when the utilities are normalized to $[0, 1]$), and it becomes homotopy equivalent to a ball for some ϵ very close to $\frac{1}{3}$.

Now, by assuming that $NE_\epsilon(g)$ is a subset of $CR(\varphi)$ for a dynamical system φ, we may reason similarly to the proof of Theorem 18.1 to show that there are no dynamics for g converging to $NE_\epsilon(g)$.

To show that the set of such games has positive measure, consider the approximation problem for an ϵ substantially smaller than the limit near 0.3 – say $\epsilon = 0.03$ – and all perturbations of the same game where each utility value of the normal form of g in (Eq. 18.1) is perturbed independently, so that the eighteen-dimensional vector of perturbations has norm $\frac{\epsilon}{c}$, for some appropriately large constant c. It is clear that this set of games has positive measure.

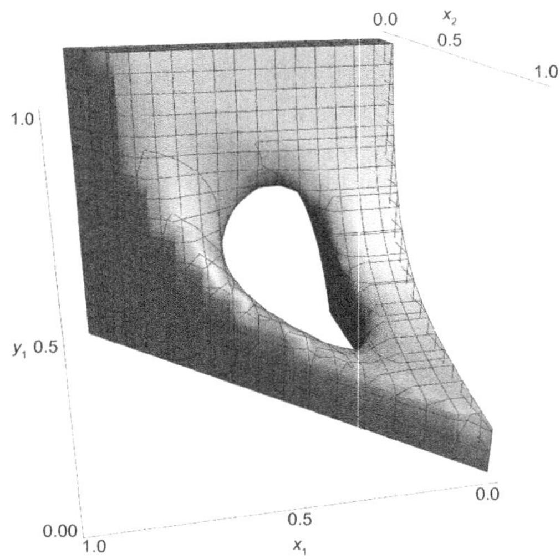

FIGURE 18.2 Three-dimensional projection of $NE_\epsilon(g)$ when g is the Kohlberg–Mertens game (Eq. 18.1) and utility-normalized $\epsilon = 0.09$. The object depicted is homotopy equivalent to S^1 (a circle).

Let us consider a game g' in this ball. First, it is self-evident that any equilibrium of g is an ϵ-equilibrium of g'; hence the set of $NE_\epsilon(g')$ contains $NE(g)$. Furthermore, it is also clear that any strategy profile that is *not* a 0.09-equilibrium of g is not in $NE_\epsilon(g')$. Thus $NE_\epsilon(g')$ is contained in $NE_{0.09}(g)$. It follows that $NE_\epsilon(g')$ is homotopy equivalent to the torus, and thus the argument provided holds for g', which completes the proof. □

Remark 18.1. A generic perturbation of the Kohlberg–Mertens game has a finite set of isolated Nash equilibria (and is nondegenerate), and we know from Theorem 18.2 that dynamics converging to the Nash equilibria do exist for this perturbed game. It may, therefore, appear surprising that we can prove a stronger impossibility result (positive measure of such games), despite the goal being more modest (just approximation instead of an exact equilibrium). The reason is that as soon as the sought approximation ϵ becomes much larger than the perturbation of the game (equivalently, the perturbation of the game being much smaller than the approximation), and it is required that all approximate equilibria be the only chain recurrent points of the dynamics, $NE_\epsilon(g)$ once again has a nontrivial Conley index, and our impossibility result once again applies.

18.6 STOCHASTIC DYNAMICS AND DYNAMICS WITH MEMORY

As we have remarked, our framework does not include stochastic dynamics – dynamics in which the next mixed strategy is a probabilistic distribution depending on the current one. In fact, it is trivial to see that there *are* stochastic dynamics guaranteed to converge to an ϵ-approximate Nash equilibrium, albeit in exponential expected time:

> *Choose a mixed strategy profile at random and check if it is an ϵ-approximate Nash equilibrium.*

In an interesting paper by Hart and Mas-Colell (2006), the authors present far more sophisticated stochastic dynamics, albeit in a constrained framework: Decisions are uncoupled – that is, each player has access to a memory and decides their next move in isolation, and each player only sees the actions (not mixed strategies) of the other players. In addition to some impossibility results (exploiting these constraints), they propose an exhaustive search allowing for convergence to approximate Nash equilibria; it is also exponentially slow to converge.

We suspect that a variant of our Conjecture 1 is afoot here:

Conjecture 18.2. Unless PPAD = P, any stochastic algorithm must take expected time exponential in $\frac{1}{\epsilon}$ to converge to an ϵ-approximate Nash equilibrium.

Finally, many repeated play behaviors proposed in the literature (including in the work by Hart and Mas-Colell, 2006, noted previously) utilize *memory:* a space of possible memories M that the players can consult and update. Let us assume for concreteness that $M = \mathbb{R}^m$, even though the same logic holds for other cases, such as discrete memories. The space of the dynamics now becomes $X \times M$. How about the set of Nash equilibria? It is not a loss of generality to assume that after reaching a Nash equilibrium, the players continue forever updating their memory – but not the strategies – in a way that effectively revisits (in the chain recurrent sense) all memory configurations. Hence convergence to the Nash equilibrium now becomes the requirement that $CR(\varphi)$ be a subset of $NE(g) \times M$, and our original proof applies.

18.7 CONCLUSION AND FUTURE WORK

We have identified mathematical reasons why no kind of repeated play can be guaranteed to globally converge to Nash equilibria for all games and from all initial strategy profiles. Moreover, this is true even when one relaxes the focus from Nash equilibria to approximate Nash equilibria, or allows the players to have memory. For nondegenerate games and stochastic dynamics, we believe that similar impossibility results are possible, this time established through arguments of computational complexity. We believe that these are exciting, difficult, and potentially productive conjectures in the theory of complexity, and very much worth pursuing.

In order to characterize the nature of convergence in game dynamics, we have relied on the concept of chain recurrence. As a tool for the analysis of game dynamics, however, chain recurrence has a fundamental shortcoming: It is not robust under perturbations. This lies in contrast to the nature of game dynamics, where the behavior of the players, *as well as the game itself*, are best thought to be rough approximations. In the words of Conley (1978), *"if such rough equations are to be of use it is necessary to study them in rough terms."* We believe that *robust* characterizations of game dynamics can be derived using the notion of *Morse decomposition* (Conley, 1978) – which coincides with the chain recurrent set for certain classes of well-behaved dynamics but in general is a more robust mathematical concept – and we plan to pursue this direction in the future.

If, in view of the present results, the Nash equilibrium seems unsatisfactory as a conception of the meaning and fate of the game, what is a better one? Two alternative directions have been suggested in recent work as worthy of study in this context. One is the concept of the *Markov–Conley chain (MCC*; Papadimitriou and Piliouras, 2019; Omidshafiei et al., 2019). Consider the directed graph whose nodes are all pure strategy profiles of the game, and there is a directed edge from node u to node v if v differs from u in one strategy and the utility of the corresponding player in v is no worse than that in u – that is to say, the better response graph. This directed graph can be considered as a Markov chain by breaking ties between players and moves uniformly at random. Consider now the ergodic components of this Markov chain (the sink of strongly connected components of the underlying directed graph) and call them the *Markov–Conley chains (MCCs)* of the game. Notice that when an MCC has a single node, it is a pure Nash equilibrium. Papadimitriou and Piliouras (2019) considered these objects a solution concept of the game that is compatible with dynamics. Each MCC of a game is a generalization of the pure Nash equilibrium – just like the mixed Nash equilibria of the game are. A similar solution concept has been proposed by Young (1993), albeit restricted to the case in which all MCCs are pure Nash. We believe that the MCCs of a game are an attractive alternative to Nash equilibria. Importantly for this consideration, it can be shown that any reasonable dynamics, if appropriately perturbed by arbitrarily small random noise, will eventually end up in one of the MCCs of the game (Papadimitriou and Piliouras, 2019; Omidshafiei et al., 2019).

A second alternative conception of the meaning of the game is this: Let us fix the dynamics – it has been argued that the replicator dynamics (Schuster and Sigmund, 1983) are an appropriate and natural choice, as, for example, they are invariant under positive linear transformations of the utilities. A game g can now be seen as a function mapping any initial strategy profile x to a distribution on strategy profiles $g(x)$ – namely, the limit distribution of the dynamics when started at x,

$$g : X \to \Delta_X,$$

where by Δ_X we denote all distributions over X. For example, if g is the 2×2 coordination game of Figure 18.1, then $g(x)$ is the pure Nash equilibrium closest to x – or the mixed Nash if the pure ones are equidistant. If g is the matching pennies game, $g(x)$ is a particular distribution, which can be computed explicitly, over all strategy profiles that have Kullback–Leibler divergence from the Nash equilibrium equal to that of x. We believe that this is a sensible and powerful way of redefining the meaning of a game. The downside here is that this map for general games is a computational challenge, which we plan to pursue in the future; there has been preliminary work on this calculation for certain simple games (Omidshafiei et al., 2019).

18.8 REFERENCES

M. Benaïm, J. Hofbauer, and S. Sorin. Perturbations of set-valued dynamical systems, with applications to game theory. *Dynamic Games and Applications*, 2(2):195–205, 2012.

X. Chen, X. Deng, and S.-h. Teng. Computing Nash equilibria: Approximation and smoothed complexity. In *2006 Forty-Seventh Annual IEEE Symposium on Foundations of Computer Science (FOCS '06)*, pp. 603–612. New York: IEEE Computer Society, 2006.

C. Conley. *Isolated Invariant Sets and the Morse Index*. Number 38 in Regional Conference Series in Mathematics. Providence, RI: American Mathematical Society, 1978.

C. Daskalakis, P. W. Goldberg, and C. H. Papadimitriou. The complexity of computing a Nash equilibrium. In *Proceedings of the Thirty-Eighth Annual ACM Symposium on Theory of Computing, STOC '06*, PP. 71–78. New York: Association for Computing Machinery, 2006.

S. DeMichelis and F. Germano. On the indices of zeros of Nash fields. *Journal of Economic Theory*, 94(2):192–217, 2000.

S. DeMichelis and K. Ritzberger. From evolutionary to strategic stability. *Journal of Economic Theory*, 113(1):51–75, 2003.

S. Demichelis and S. Sorin. Asymptotic stability for convex-valued differential inclusions. Preprint. 2003.

K. Etessami and M. Yannakakis. On the complexity of Nash equilibria and other fixed points (extended abstract). In *Proceedings of the Forty-Eighth Annual IEEE Symposium on Foundations of Computer Science, FOCS '07*, pp. 113–123. IEEE Computer Society, 2007.

P. W. Goldberg, C. H. Papadimitriou, and R. Savani. The complexity of the homotopy method, equilibrium selection, and Lemke-Howson solutions. *ACM Trans. Econ. Comput.*, 1(2):1–25, May 2013.

S. Hart and A. Mas-Colell. Stochastic uncoupled dynamics and Nash equilibrium. *Games and Economic Behavior*, 57(2):286–303, 2006.

M. W. Hirsch, S. Smale, and R. L. Devaney. *Differential Equations, Dynamical Systems, and an Introduction to Chaos*, 2nd ed. Vol. 60 in Pure and Applied Mathematics: A Series of Monographs and Textbooks. San Diego, CA: Academic Press, 2004.

W. D. Kalies, K. Mischaikow, and R. C. Vandervorst. Lattice structures for attractors III. *Journal of Dynamics and Differential Equations*, 34:1–40, 2021.

E. Kohlberg and J.-F. Mertens. On the strategic stability of equilibria. *Econometrica*, 54(5):1003, September 1986.

J. Milionis, C. Papadimitriou, G. Piliouras, and K. Spendlove. Nash, Conley, and computation: Impossibility and incompleteness in game dynamics. *arXiv preprint*, arXiv:2203.14129, 2022.

J. Milionis, C. Papadimitriou, G. Piliouras, and K. Spendlove. An impossibility theorem in game dynamics. *Proceedings of the National Academy of Sciences*, 120(41), e2305349120, 2023.

J. F. Nash. Equilibrium points in *N*-person games. *Proceedings of the National Academy of Sciences*, 36(1):48–49, 1950.

S. Omidshafiei, C. Papadimitriou, G. Piliouras, K. Tuyls, M. Rowland, J.-B. Lespiau, W. M. Czarnecki, M. Lanctot, J. Perolat, and R. Munos. α-Rank: Multi-agent evaluation by evolution. *Scientific Reports*, 9(1):9937, December 2019.

C. Papadimitriou and G. Piliouras. Game dynamics as the meaning of a game. *SIGecom Exch.*, 16(2):53–63, May 2019.

P. Schuster and K. Sigmund. Replicator dynamics. *Journal of Theoretical Biology*, 100(3):533–538, 1983.

L. S. Shapley. A note on the Lemke-Howson algorithm. *Mathematical Programming Studies*, 1:175–189, 1974.

H. P. Young. The evolution of conventions. *Econometrica*, 61(1):57–84, 1993.

19

The State of Representing and Solving Games

Tuomas Sandholm

19.1 INTRODUCTION

Game-theoretic solution concepts provide meticulous definitions of how rational parties should act. That has enabled humans to think rigorously about strategic interactions, leading to game theory revolutionizing many fields such as economics, political science, and biology. So far, game theory has mainly been used for reasoning by humans. The models have therefore been quite stylized and coarse: small enough for humans to solve in their heads or by paper and pen. The goal has been to draw insights from such models, which humans then judiciously apply to the drastically more complicated real world. The boundaries of game theory have thus been defined by the limits of humans.

However, many – arguably most – important game classes lie beyond those boundaries. There is now another, more nascent, use of game theory that goes beyond human intelligence. The game is computationally solved in its full detail – or else in a large, faithful abstraction thereof – as opposed to solving a small, stylized version to obtain insight for humans. Novel approaches, game representations, and algorithms have recently enabled game theory to advance significantly beyond its traditional boundaries in at least three broad categories of game.

- One such category is games that are simply too large for humans to solve. These include large, detailed models that are close to reality in games of practical importance, as well as many recreational games.
- A second category, introduced in the present paper, is a setup where the rules are provided in a programming language that is not executed but rather analyzed by a game-solving algorithm. This can make general-purpose game modeling significantly easier and more scalable.
- A third category is games where the rules exist but are not provided. This includes settings where the game is defined by a simulation – such as a war simulatiom, real-time strategy game, or trading simulation – or potentially even the real world.

Poker was the main game of interest to the early game theory pioneers (Borel and Ville, 1938; von Neumann and Morgenstern, 1947; Kuhn, 1950; Nash, 1950; Nash and Shapley, 1950). They focused on tiny artificial poker games that are solvable by hand. Poker has remained an active benchmark and research topic in game theory, operations research, applied mathematics, and artificial intelligence ever since. The most popular poker game played by people, no-limit Texas hold'em, served as the main challenge problem in imperfect-information game solving. In the two-player case, the game tree has 10^{165} nodes and 10^{161} information sets (Johanson, 2013). The milestone of superhuman play was recently reached both in the two-player (Brown and Sandholm, 2018) and multiplayer case (Brown and Sandholm, 2019b). The latter is the only superhuman milestone in any game beyond two-player zero-sum games. These breakthroughs were achieved using general-purpose game-theoretic algorithms – and not by earlier approaches such as strategies programmed by hand, machine learning from human play, simulation-based approaches, or opponent modeling and exploitation.

In Section 19.2, I will describe the main intellectual developments that made game solving possible at this scale. Over the last twenty years, the scalability of game solving has increased by numerous orders of magnitude – even controlling for the increase in the speed and storage of computers, the impacts of which have been modest compared to those of the algorithmic advances. Because most real-world games are multistep games of imperfect information, this paper will focus on such games. See Sandholm (2007, 2010, 2015b,a) for additional reviews. The state-of-the-art techniques for correlated equilibria and for team games are discussed in Section 19.5.

The state-of-the-art algorithms for perfect-information extensive-form games are based on neural network learning of node evaluations using Monte Carlo tree search both at training time and play time (Silver et al., 2018; Schrittwieser et al., 2020). For normal-form games, the state-of-the-art algorithms for the two-player zero-sum case (Brown and Sandholm, 2019a; Farina, Kroer, and Sandholm, 2021d) are discussed later in this paper, the state-of-the-art algorithm for the two-player general-sum case is a form of random restarting (Gatti, Patrini, Rocco, and Sandholm, 2012) on top of the pivoting algorithm of Lemke and Howson (1964), and the state-of-the-art algorithm for the multiplayer case is tree search that keeps splitting the probability space supplemented with subroutines for checking possible equilibrium existence in a given subspace (Berg and Sandholm, 2017).

Computational game solving has started to be fielded in games of real-world importance. In a subclass of Stackelberg games called security games, computationally generated strategies (Conitzer and Sandholm, 2006) have been used in a few notable applications such as allocation of airport canine units, air marshals, rail ticket inspectors, port patrol vessels, and antipoaching teams (Tambe, 2011; Yin et al., 2012; Sinha et al., 2018). In a different direction, large-scale Nash equilibrium finding has been productized in military applications, with the goal of deterrence as well as safety via avoiding irrationality.[1] Those products include portfolio and deployment planning for missile defense, base defense, and multidomain combat. They also include course-of-action generation for settings where the game rules are not provided and the game-solving algorithm only has access to a simulator. In this paper I will also draw from those experiences, especially when it comes to new ways of representing games. The effort of presenting the game to a solver must be low, and different settings require different representations. This makes game solving more scalable in terms of labor. It also enables game solving to be scalable through productization rather than being mere consulting. I expect these approaches to significantly amplify the real-world impact of game theory. Section 19.3 introduces a new game representation paradigm: using a programming language to define the game and reasoning about the program instead of executing it. Section 19.4 discusses a new methodology that finds game-theoretic strategies of provably low exploitability in settings where the rules are not provided in any form and the algorithm is only given simulator access to the game (Zhang and Sandholm, 2020a, 2021a).

In some cases, computationally-generated game-theoretic strategies also provide human-understandable insights. For example, humans have been able to copy, to an extent, the huge "overbets" and tiny "underbets" used by our our game-theoretically-generated superhuman AIs for no-limit Texas hold'em. In other cases, it is prohibitively complicated for humans to receive a description of the strategy, understand it, or memorize it. For example, our poker AIs use "donk betting," which humans have not been able to profitably incorporate into their play. In either case, the strategies can be executed by machine – or by having a machine advise the human(s) on how to execute the strategy action by action. While it has often been questioned whether game theory accurately *describes* how humans or animals behave, it is in this algorithm-powered setting that I foresee the *prescriptive* power of game theory come to unprecedented fruition.

19.2 DECLARATIVE GAME REPRESENTATIONS AND ALGORITHMS FOR THEM

Most of game theory has used *declarative game representations*, which describe the rules of the game without specifying a control flow for a computer to execute. The most common examples are the extensive form and normal form (Fudenberg and Tirole, 1991). General-purpose compact game representations have also been developed, such as graphical games (Kearns et al., 2001). *Game-class-specific* declarative representations have also been developed, for example, for game classes that generalize poker (Gilpin and Sandholm, 2007b). For poker games, they describe the number of cards in the deck, the number of rounds, how cards get revealed in each round, how betting is allowed in each

[1] Work conducted with my applied scientists and engineers at Strategy Robot Inc.

round, what is observed in each round, and so forth. These representations enable prohibitively large extensive-form game trees to be represented using a small number of parameters. Game-class-specific declarative representations have also been developed for military portfolio planning, acquisition, and deployment games.[1] Prior game-solving software packages have typically only supported the normal and/or extensive form. This has limited their usability and scalability. Thus they have not found many real-world uses.

The rest of this section describes the state-of-the-art modules that are combined to make solvers for declarative game representations. It focuses on extensive-form representations and application-class-specific representations, such as those that generalize poker.

19.2.1 Game Abstraction Algorithms and Game-Theoretically Sound Modeling

Real games are typically too large to tackle directly with an equilibrium-finding algorithm. A key to even getting started is *game abstraction* – that is, constructing a drastically smaller extensive-form game that is strategically similar (Sandholm, 2015a). This section will first discuss information abstraction, followed by action abstraction.

Perhaps surprisingly, it is possible to algorithmically construct a *lossless abstraction*, that is, a smaller game in which any Nash equilibrium is an exact Nash equilibrium for the original game (Gilpin and Sandholm, 2007b). The GameShrink algorithm takes as input the *signal tree*, a structure like the game tree but significantly smaller because it does not include the players' actions. It conducts a bottom-up pass in the signal tree to mark strategically isomorphic nodes. Two leaves are isomorphic for this purpose if their payoff vectors (one payoff per player) are the same. Two internal nodes are isomorphic if they are siblings and their children are isomorphic. Once the marking of isomorphisms up the tree is finished, GameShrink conducts a top-down pass in the signal tree to merge isomorphic nodes. GameShrink runs in $\tilde{O}(s^2)$ time and space, where s is the number of nodes in the signal tree. So, it typically runs in highly *sublinear* time and space in the size of the game tree because the signal tree is significantly smaller than the game tree in most nontrivial games. GameShrink enabled the exact solving (within machine precision) of Rhode Island hold'em, a two-player zero-sum benchmark introduced by Shi and Littman (2000) with 3.1 billion nodes in the game tree. To my knowledge, this is the largest imperfect-information game that has been exactly solved, and it is more than four orders of magnitude larger than the largest game solved previously (Koller and Pfeffer, 1995). GameShrink ran in less than a second on that game. The original game had 91,224,226 rows and columns in the *sequence-form linear program* (Romanovskii, 1962; Koller et al., 1996), which would have been prohibitive to solve. After running GameShrink, the resulting linear program had 1,237,238 rows and columns (50,428,638 nonzeros, that is, leaf nodes of the game tree). That linear program was then solved using CPLEX's barrier method in 8 days using 25 gigabytes of RAM.

On even larger games such as two-player no-limit Texas hold'em, reducing game size by two orders of magnitude via lossless abstraction is insufficient. Rather, *lossy abstraction* is additionally used to bring the game down to manageable size. With lossy abstraction, the equilibrium computed in the abstracted game does not generally yield an exact equilibrium for the original game. The first lossy abstractions for Texas hold'em poker were built by hand (Billings et al., 2003). Modern algorithms for generating lossy information abstractions for games operate on each agent's individual signal tree. The main ideas that have been developed for this include the following.

- One approach is to cluster states (e.g., in poker, possible combinations of private and public cards) according to strength defined as the probability of winning plus one-half the probability of tying against a uniform random draw of private signals for the opponent, assuming a uniform random rollout of the remaining public information; (Gilpin and Sandholm, 2006b; Zinkevich, Bowling, Johanson, and Piccione, 2007; Waugh, Zinkevich, Johanson, Kan, Schnizlein, and Bowling, 2009b). A better idea is *distribution-aware abstraction*: clustering states according to the distribution of payoffs over leaves under the states (Gilpin et al., 2007b; Gilpin and Sandholm, 2008; Johanson et al., 2013). However, even that is not ideal because it fails to capture that the information from chance may be revealed at differences paces and in different ways on different paths, and capturing that can be important for playing well. To address this, *potential-aware abstraction* was introduced (Gilpin, Sandholm, and Sørensen, 2007b). It starts by clustering the leaves. Then at the second-to-last level of the player's signal tree, it clusters states according to their transition probability vector to leaf clusters. Then at the third-to-last level of the player's signal tree, it clusters states according to their transition probability vector to the second-to-last level clusters, and so on.
- Originally, Euclidean distance was used as the metric for clustering states (Gilpin, Sandholm, and Sørensen, 2007b; Gilpin and Sandholm, 2008), but earth-mover's distance leads to better abstractions (Johanson et al., 2013; Ganzfried and Sandholm, 2014).
- One can use integer programming to decide how many children each node at a given level of the tree is allowed to have, so as to minimize a notion of error due to the clustering, subject to a given limit on the total number of child nodes (Gilpin and Sandholm, 2007a). The limit is selected based on the scalability of the equilibrium-finding algorithm that is used to solve the abstract game.
- Imperfect-recall games have largely been a curiosity in game theory. Here they find a computational use. It turns out that it is beneficial to have a player forget some of the past in order to computationally be able to afford a finer-grained abstraction of the present (Waugh et al., 2009b). Imperfect-recall

abstraction can also obviate the need for integer programs to determine how many children each node is allowed to have.

The current state-of-the-art abstraction algorithm does potential-aware, imperfect-recall abstraction with earth-mover's distance as the metric (Ganzfried and Sandholm, 2014). In distributed computing for equilibrium finding – for example, using counterfactual regret minimization (CFR) algorithms, discussed later – it is beneficial to keep each play-through on its own compute server and not to split any information sets across servers so that memory locations (variables specific to each information set) do not need to be locked across servers, which would cause significant waiting. This can be accomplished by dividing the game across servers based on information that is public among the players (Brown, Ganzfried, and Sandholm, 2015) – for example, the public cards on the table in the case of poker. This is the approach used in the abstraction module in the recent game-solving milestones where superhuman play was achieved for two-player (Brown and Sandholm, 2018) and multiplayer no-limit Texas hold'em (Brown and Sandholm, 2019b).

Action abstraction – that is, which of the actions of the game, or prototypical other actions, to include in the game abstraction – is still largely manual in practice. One significant exception is that when actions are scalars (e.g., bet sizes in poker), a vector of action sizes for the action abstraction can be optimized using gradient-based techniques with gradients that are estimated in a certain way (Brown and Sandholm, 2014). Furthermore, CFR can be carefully warm started from the abstraction used in the previous iteration. In large games this scales to optimizing up to two actions at a time, and that is what was used in the two-player no-limit Texas hold'em superhuman milestone (Brown and Sandholm, 2018).

A concern with the abstraction paradigm, even in the zero-sum setting, is that in games, unlike in single-agent settings, *abstraction pathologies* can arise: The strategy obtained from a finer abstraction can be more *exploitable*[2] than the strategy obtained from a coarser abstraction (Waugh et al., 2009a). Despite this, game abstraction with guaranteed low exploitability is possible (Sandholm and Singh, 2012; Lanctot et al., 2012; Kroer and Sandholm, 2014, 2015, 2016). The state of the art in lossy game abstraction with such bounds is a framework that supports both information abstraction and action abstraction via game tree topology changes (e.g., collapsing multiple actions into one abstract action) and information set changes (e.g., information coarsening) (Kroer and Sandholm, 2018). The theory provides for an exploitability bound based on the ϵ in the ϵ-equilibrium computed in the abstract game and certain differences between the payoffs and probabilities of the abstract game and the actual game model. The theory can be used before equilibrium finding by taking worst cases over the player's strategies when determining the differences.

[2] A strategy is exploitable by amount ϵ if its expected value against its best response is ϵ lower than the value of the game.

A tighter exploitability guarantee can be computed after equilibrium finding by using the computed strategies when determining the differences.

It occurred to me later that this framework can be used not only to bound the exploitability that stems from the difference between the game model and the abstraction, but also, for the first time in the history of game theory, to *soundly evaluate game modeling* – that is, to bound the exploitability that stems from the difference between reality and the game model, or even the difference between reality and the abstraction. While it is important in any modeling to understand the solution quality implications of the gap between reality and model, in game-theoretic modeling that is particularly important because intuitive notions of what makes for a better model do not always hold due to abstraction pathology.

One reason abstraction is so challenging is that the computed equilibrium strategies depend on the abstraction, but also what a good abstraction is depends on the equilibrium. After all, two states should fall in the same abstract bucket if the optimal action probabilities in them are (almost) the same. To cut through this chicken-and-egg problem, one can move away from the waterfall of abstraction first, followed by equilibrium finding. Instead, one can do *strategy-based abstraction* by abstracting, then solving, then changing the abstraction based on the computed strategies, and so on (Sandholm, 2010). This is essentially what one does in practice manually when building strong game-theory-based AIs. However, this process can be automated. The iterative action abstraction mentioned previously is an example of this. Another example is adding actions algorithmically to the action abstraction based on the computed equilibrium (Brown and Sandholm, 2015). This allows the program to begin equilibrium finding with a coarse abstraction, and then to insert actions at points that the strategy computed in the current abstraction deems important. The algorithm can quickly add actions to the abstraction while provably not having to restart the equilibrium finding.

19.2.2 Equilibrium-Finding Algorithms

I will now move to discussing the state of the art in how the abstracted game is solved. One can model two-player zero-sum extensive-form games using the *sequence form* where the variables are sequences of one player's actions, and the resulting bilinear saddle point problem for finding a Nash (minmax) equilibrium can be solved using a linear program (LP) that is of linear size in the size of the game tree (Romanovskii, 1962; Koller et al., 1996). The LP can be solved for ϵ-equilibrium in $O(\log(1/\epsilon))$ time and fast in practice using the barrier method. This is a reasonable approach for games with up to 10^8 leaves if one has about a week of time to compute (Gilpin and Sandholm, 2007b). It does not scale to larger games (without the game LP sparsification techniques discussed later) because the memory requirements of this second-order optimization method become prohibitive.

Better strategies can be created by using a significantly larger abstract game and solving it using scalable iterative first-order methods developed for extensive-form games, which do not use matrix inversion operations – that are memory intensive and slow – like second-order methods do. Also, they do not have to represent the sequence-form game matrix and conduct matrix-vector multiplications using it. Rather, these algorithms can be implemented to use only a traversal of the game tree to compute the needed quantities, such as gradients.

19.2.2.1 Offline First-Order Optimization Methods for Extensive-Form Games

Adapting and improving algorithms that converge in $O(1/\epsilon)$ iterations. The first custom equilibrium-finding algorithm for extensive-form games (Gilpin, Hoda, Peña, and Sandholm, 2007a; Hoda, Gilpin, Peña, and Sandholm, 2010) took equilibrium finding to a new level by solving poker game abstractions with 10^{12} leaves in the game tree (Gilpin, Sandholm, and Sørensen, 2007b). The algorithm is an adaptation and improvement of Nesterov's *excessive gap technique (EGT*; Nesterov, 2005a). EGT is a smoothing-based algorithm for nonsmooth convex optimization in settings where the spaces to optimize over are quite simple, such as the two players' simplices in normal-form games. EGT adds to each player i's nonsmooth optimization problem a smooth, strongly convex function with some multiplier μ_i, making the player's altered problem smooth and strongly convex, and thus easier to optimize over. At each iteration, EGT refines the player's strategies and decreases the amount of smoothing by decreasing μ_1 and μ_2. It finds an ϵ-equilibrium in $O(1/\epsilon)$ iterations.

EGT was generalized to extensive-form games by designing for a player's *treeplex* (i.e., sequence-form strategy polytope) appropriate *distance-generating functions (DGFs)* that define the distance between points (Gilpin, Hoda, Peña, and Sandholm, 2007a; Hoda, Gilpin, Peña, and Sandholm, 2010). A DGF can be used as the smoothing function in EGT if it is smooth, strongly convex, and supports fast computation of gradients and smoothed best responses. In addition, theoretically sound techniques were added to speed up EGT. First, EGT has a parameter τ that controls the speed of progress. The traditional way of setting τ is correct but overly conservative. Experimentally, an order of magnitude faster decrease in ϵ can be achieved by using a larger value for τ. Also, a sound way was developed for checking whether the algorithm took too large a step and, if so, using a smaller, safe step instead. Second, μ_1 and μ_2 typically become highly unbalanced, which causes EGT's progress to be unnecessarily slow. Experimentally, another order of magnitude decrease in ϵ can be achieved by balancing μ_1 and μ_2 every so many iterations. After the balancing, the values of μ_1 and μ_2 can often be further decreased soundly before continuing the main algorithm. Furthermore, a structured way of representing the payoff matrix was introduced, which drastically decreases the algorithm's memory footprint.

The technique has been successfully used to solve abstracted games on a shared-memory supercomputer for the Association for the Advancement of Artificial Intelligence (AAAI) Annual Computer Poker Competition. The technique has also been used for computation on a laptop. Furthermore, to my knowledge, it is the first extensive-form equilibrium-finding algorithm to have also been implemented on a graphics processing unit (GPU) (Kroer, Farina, and Sandholm, 2018).

There has been significant further progress on developing increasingly better DGFs that make the problem more strongly convex and thus require fewer iterations (Kroer, Waugh, Kılınç-Karzan, and Sandholm, 2020). The state-of-the-art DGF leads to a number of iterations that is polynomial in the depth of the game even if the tree is highly lop-sided (Farina, Kroer, and Sandholm, 2025). The DGFs can be used in other first-order methods than EGT as well, such as mirror prox. These EGT-based and mirror prox-based methods are among the fastest algorithms for extensive-form games in practice as well.

Developing an algorithm that converges in $O(\log(1/\epsilon))$ iterations. Gilpin, Peña, and Sandholm (2012) developed a gradient-based algorithm that converges to minmax equilibrium in $O(\log(1/\epsilon))$ iterations – that is, exponentially faster. (That complexity hides a game-dependent condition number.) It uses as a subroutine a procedure called SMOOTHING, a smoothing technique for nonsmooth convex optimization (Nesterov, 2005b). The algorithm is unlike EGT in that there is only one function that is being optimized and smoothed instead of two. Also unlike in EGT, the target ϵ needs to be specified in advance; it is used to set the constant μ that is used as the multiplier on the smoothing function. Unlike in EGT, μ does not change inside SMOOTHING. Gilpin and colleagues extended SMOOTHING to extensive-form games by developing a custom dynamic program. They then added an outer loop that decreases ϵ by a factor e between calls to SMOOTHING. The key was to prove that each such call to SMOOTHING uses only a constant number of first-order iterations (that is, gradient steps). It then follows immediately that the overall algorithm runs in $O(\log(1/\epsilon))$ iterations. Experiments on medium-sized games verified that the algorithm converges faster than EGT and the speed difference increases, the lower one wants the exploitability bound ϵ. The $O(\log(1/\epsilon))$ convergence rate matches the best-known convergence rate – that of interior point methods such as the barrier method. At the same time, this algorithm – being a first-order method – is scalable, while interior-point methods can be prohibitive in terms of memory usage.

19.2.2.2 Regret-Minimization Methods

The most popular, and currently fastest in practice, equilibrium-finding algorithms for large extensive-form games are based on regret minimization. Such algorithms – learning dynamics – adjust in various ways a player's strategy toward strategies that have positive regret (that is, strategies the player regrets having not played in the interaction so far). An algorithm is called a *regret minimizer* if it guarantees that the average regret approaches zero (that is, the cumulative regret is sublinear in the number of interactions). In self-play among regret minimizers, the empirical distribution of the joint actions converges to a coarse correlated equilibrium – a minmax equilibrium in two-player zero-sum games. A regret minimizer also learns to play a best response against any static opponent.

In practice, extensive-form games are too large to run regret minimization in the space of pure strategies because there is an exponential blowup when translating the game into normal form. The first algorithm to address this was *counterfactual regret minimization (CFR*; Zinkevich et al., 2007). It cuts through the exponential blowup by allowing each information set to have its own regret minimizer, typically *regret matching* (Hart and Mas-Colell, 2000). In self-play, the empirical distribution of the joint actions converges to a coarse correlated equilibrium. After $O(1/\epsilon^2)$ iterations, they have at most ϵ average regret, and in the two-player zero-sum setting, at most ϵ exploitability. Despite this poor worst-case speed, modern improvements over CFR are very fast in practice.

An early improvement was CFR^+, which changes three dimensions (Tammelin, 2014; Burch, Moravčík, and Schmid, 2019). First, each regret minimizer adjusts regrets of the actions that have negative cumulative regret to zero cumulative regret. Second, alternating updates between players are used instead of both players updating their regrets at each iteration. Third, the current action probabilities are counted toward the weighted average strategy by weighting them with the number of the current iteration. These changes together improve the speed of CFR by an order of magnitude. They enabled two-player limit Texas hold'em – that is, Texas hold'em where one can raise only a given amount at a time – to be solved near-optimally (Bowling, Burch, Johanson, and Tammelin, 2015). The game has 3.19×10^{14} information sets, and after lossless abstraction via suit isomorphism removal, it has 1.38×10^{13}. It is the smallest variant of poker actually played competitively by humans. It is, to my knowledge, the largest imperfect-information game solved to provable near-optimality.

A more general and faster – and still theoretically sound – improvement is *discounted CFR (DCFR*; Brown and Sandholm, 2019a). It is currently the fastest equilibrium-finding algorithm for many zero-sum games, both in the extensive and normal form. It has three parameters: α, β, and γ. At each iteration t, it deweights regrets by multiplying the positive cumulative regrets by $\frac{t^\alpha}{t^\alpha+1}$ and the negative cumulative regrets by $\frac{t^\beta}{t^\beta+1}$. It also adds the current action probabilities toward the weighted average action probabilities with weight $(\frac{t}{t+1})^\gamma$. All of these approaches allow one to assign more weight to more recent iterations that are likely better than earlier iterations. For example, with $\alpha = \frac{3}{2}$, $\beta = 0$, and $\gamma = 2$, DCFR is an order of magnitude faster than CFR^+.

It remains a mystery why offline first-order methods, which have significantly better worst-case convergence and would be allowed to optimize both players' strategy variables together, are not faster in practice than regret-based methods, which only look at a single player's decision problem at a time. I believe there is still room for improvement in the former. Starting to build a bridge in the other direction, *predictive* (a.k.a. *optimistic*) regret-minimization algorithms have been extended to extensive-form games (Farina, Kroer, and Sandholm, 2019c, 2021d; Farina, Kroer, Brown, and Sandholm, 2019a). These algorithms always offer the usual $O(1/\epsilon^2)$ convergence and enjoy faster convergence in practice if they are given a small amount of predictivity about what the payoffs in the next iteration will be, which is easy to achieve in self-play because we know the opponent. These predictive regret minimizers are the fastest algorithms for most two-player zero-sum games in practice (Farina, Kroer, and Sandholm, 2021d), but for poker-like games, DCFR is faster.

If the (abstracted) game is too large to traverse, one can use *stochastic* regret minimization. At the cost of less accurate regret updates, one samples the opponent and/or chance when conducting an iteration of a CFR-based algorithm. This can be done using *Monte Carlo CFR (MCCFR*; Lanctot, Waugh, Zinkevich, and Bowling, 2009; Gibson, Lanctot, Burch, Szafron, and Bowling, 2012) or newer variants (Farina, Kroer, and Sandholm, 2020b; Farina, Schmucker, and Sandholm, 2021e; Farina and Sandholm, 2021).

Farina, Kroer, and Sandholm (2019d) developed a calculus for constructing regret minimizers for composite convex sets that are obtained from convexity-preserving operations on simpler convex sets. Local regret minimizers for the simpler sets can be combined with additional regret minimizers into an aggregate regret minimizer for the composite set. Applied to the sequence-form decision space of the agents, it gives a significantly simpler understanding and proof of CFR. It also enables one to use different regret minimizers at different information sets. The approach also enables the construction of a CFR generalization for extensive-form games with general convex strategy constraints that can cut across decision points. The approach also applies to quantal response equilibrium and safe opponent exploitation (Farina, Kroer, and Sandholm, 2019b), welfare-maximizing extensive-form correlated and coarse correlated equilibrium in two-player extensive-form games in which such equilibria are computable in polynomial time (Farina and Sandholm, 2020; Farina, Bianchi, and Sandholm, 2020a), extensive-form-correlated and coarse-correlated equilibrium (not necessarily welfare-maximizing) in multiplayer games (Farina, Celli, Marchesi, and Gatti, 2022), team maxmin equilibria with a correlation device in certain zero-sum two-team games (Farina, Celli, Gatti, and Sandholm, 2021a), normal-form coarse correlated equilibrium in multiplayer games, learning a best response, and online play against an unknown opponent or environment.

19.2.2.3 *Warm Starting the Equilibrium Finding from Preexisting Strategies*

Regret-minimization algorithms are usually started from uniform strategies. Based on many negative experiences, it was believed that warm starting from better strategies does not work. However, it turns out that with special care, one can soundly warm start from any strategies – not just ones obtained using regret minimization – and the approach provably works even in extensive form (Brown and Sandholm, 2016). Those strategies can be handcrafted, strategies from a coarser abstraction, strategies from a different equilibrium-finding algorithm, and so forth. From just a strategy for each player, the method provably warm starts CFR to as many iterations as CFR would have taken to reach a strategy profile of the same quality, and does not alter the convergence rate guarantee of CFR. The key is to pretend that the input strategies came from CFR by not just setting the average strategies in CFR but also appropriately setting the number of iterations so far and the regrets.

19.2.2.4 *Dynamic, Temporary Pruning of the Tree*

One can speed up tree traversals by pruning subtrees that are reached only if someone makes a mistake. This is commonly done in perfect-information games. It is more challenging in iterative algorithms for solving imperfect-information games because actions that currently seem like mistakes may turn good in later iterations.

In CFR-like algorithms, one can temporarily prune an action that seems like a mistake in the sense that its cumulative regret is negative (Brown and Sandholm, 2017a, 2018, 2019b). One can further project how many iterations it would take at a minimum for its regret to turn positive. Then, if needed, the player's treeplex for such a subtree can be regenerated and its iterates caught up to the current iteration in one traversal by computing a *counterfactual best response (CBR*; "(like" a best response, except it maximizes value even at points that it does not reach due to its earlier actions) in the subtree against the opponent's average strategy over all iterations played so far, and setting cumulative regrets as if the player had played the CBR strategy throughout those iterations. In zero-sum games, the resulting algorithm expends only a logarithmic fraction of its effort on "irrational" parts of the game that are not reached by any CBR to any equilibrium. The pruning works with most parameter settings of DCFR, but not with CFR$^+$ because it never keeps negative cumulative regrets.

Pruning can also be used in other extensive-form algorithms, such as the offline first-order methods discussed previously (Brown, Kroer, and Sandholm, 2017). A threshold is set at every iteration, such that any action in a player's treeplex with probability below the threshold is set to zero probability. This enables sound pruning for the first time in a wide range of algorithms.

19.2.2.5 *Automated Game LP Sparsification*

Zhang and Sandholm (2020b) developed an algorithm for automatically sparsifying the sequence-form game matrix. For poker games, further structural properties can be leveraged for additional decomposition and matrix sparsification (Farina, Gatti, and Sandholm, 2021b; Farina and Sandholm, 2022). These techniques make the LP drastically smaller. That enables the scalable use of the barrier method, which converges rapidly, and the simplex method that finds exact solutions. It also supports various kinds of side constraint with which one can then ask research questions such as "What is the least exploitable pure strategy for this game?" Furthermore, the sparsification significantly speeds up parallel first-order game-solving algorithms, begetting state-of-the-art speed on a GPU.

19.2.3 Subgame Solving during Game Play

The single most important development in solving imperfect-information games over the last twenty years is subgame solving.[3] It enables subgames to be solved during game play in significantly finer abstractions than one could computationally afford to use when solving the full game in advance (Gilpin and Sandholm, 2006a). In perfect-information games, it is immediate that subgames can be solved independently, and algorithms for such games heavily exploit that fact. For example, chess engines conduct forward search from the current position. In imperfect-information games this is significantly more challenging because strategies need to be balanced across the game tree (e.g., in poker, it would be too predictable to always raise with strong hands and check with weak hands), so a subgame cannot be solved using information from the subgame alone. Despite this, game-theoretically sound (i.e., "safe," as described later) subgame solving is now possible.

To overcome the challenge, most subgame solving techniques leverage *blueprint strategies* for the players for the entire game, and subgame solving then uses a finer-grained abstraction in those parts of the game that are actually reached during play. Subgame solving also enables one to compute an abstraction specifically for the situation at hand – that is, an abstraction conditioned on the players' and nature's observed actions.

In principle, the blueprint strategies can come from any source. They can come from an abstraction that is coarse enough to support the entire game to be approximately solved, and any equilibrium-finding algorithm could be

[3] Here, the term *subgame* is used the way it is used in artificial intelligence. Unlike in the game theory literature, a subgame can start with an information set that contains multiple nodes. As in game theory, subgames are defined so that information sets do not cut across subgames. In other words, a subgame starts with the common-knowledge closure of the player's current information set – that is, the smallest set of nodes in which it is common knowledge that the current node belongs.

used to solve it (Gilpin and Sandholm, 2006a). The state of the art (Brown and Sandholm, 2019b) is to solve it using sampling akin to MCCFR (or newer variants; Farina, Kroer, and Sandholm, 2020b; Farina, Schmucker, and Sandholm, 2021e; Farina and Sandholm, 2021), but with dynamic pruning and DCFR for the regret updates. Or the blueprint strategies can come from solving the early part of the game for approximate equilibrium under the assumption that players follow given strategies in the latter part of game, such as default strategies (e.g., no betting in poker; Gilpin and Sandholm, 2006a) or strong strategies from prior AIs (Gilpin and Sandholm, 2007a). I coined the latter *bootstrapping with base strategies* (Sandholm, 2010). Or they could come from reinforcement learning or be crafted manually.

The first approaches to subgame solving derived the beliefs of the players for the beginning of the subgame from the blueprint strategies and the players' observations on the current path of play using Bayes' rule (Gilpin and Sandholm, 2006a, 2007a). This leads to fairly strong play in many games in practice, but it is *unsafe*: It can make a strategy more exploitable than the blueprint strategy (Ganzfried and Sandholm, 2015). For example, in the rock-paper-scissors game (where we can say that Player 1 moves first as long as Player 2 does not observe Player 1's move), if Player 1 plays scissors in the blueprint strategy with even slightly higher probability than rock and paper, Player 2's subgame solver would conclude that the best strategy is to play rock with probability one, which is obviously highly exploitable by Player 1 playing paper. In longer games, the unsafety can be mitigated by starting the subgame solve earlier in the tree than the current information set, while fixing our own strategy for that earlier part (Gilpin and Sandholm, 2007a; Brown and Sandholm, 2019b).

It turns out that in two-player zero-sum games, *safe* subgame solving is possible – that is, guaranteeing that the game-theoretic exploitability of the agent is no higher than that of the blueprint strategy and, in practice, significantly lower. The first step is to construct a model of the subgame, typically in a finer abstraction than the blueprint. Then, we give the opponent the conceptual choice to either best respond in the original game model against our blueprint strategy or play in the subgame model. Our subgame strategy is safe if for no type (that is, private information) that the opponent might have does the opponent prefer to choose the subgame model. One can compute our subgame strategy using this condition by constructing an *auxiliary game* that can be solved with any equilibrium-finding algorithm (Burch et al., 2014). A better approach that still satisfies the provided condition is to solve an auxiliary game that finds a strategy for us that maximizes the minimum (over opponent's types) difference between the opponent's best-response value against our blueprint and the opponent's payoff in the subgame model (Moravčík et al., 2016). The state of the art is to further take into account when computing those differences that for some types the opponent would have had to make mistakes to reach the current subgame, and in the subgame model we *can give back to the opponent those gifts* (Brown and Sandholm, 2017b, 2018).

This gives us a larger safe strategy space to optimize over in the subgame and better performance. This is called *reach max-margin subgame solving*. There are two further issues that the method has to address. First, the gifts calculated based on the blueprint might be inaccurate because other subgames emanating from sibling actions of the path's actions would have been tackled with subgame solving, rather than playing the blueprint strategy in them, had they been reached. This is handled safely by using any lower bound on the gifts. Second, each gift received on the path must be divided among its descendant subgames, for example using chance's probabilities, so not too much is returned to the opponent.

Subgame solving can be applied recursively every time it is our turn to move, by treating the previous subgame solution as the new blueprint strategy (Brown and Sandholm, 2017b). This has the advantage that as we get closer to the end of the game, increasingly finer-grained abstractions become computationally feasible to solve. If one uses the safe methodology described previously, this recursive approach is also safe.

Sometimes the opponent may play an action that is outside our action abstraction. The traditional approach has been to *reverse map* the action back into our action abstraction. Increasingly sophisticated reverse mapping techniques have been developed. Even with state-of-the-art reverse mapping (Ganzfried and Sandholm, 2013), this causes inaccuracy in our beliefs, as well as weaknesses that the opponent can exploit. This has been observed in practice in the competitions that I have organized pitting our AIs *Claudico* and *Libratus* against the best professional two-player no-limit Texas hold'em players. Subgame solving can obviate the need for reverse mapping. One can start the subgame solving earlier in the tree than the current information set while adding into the subgame model the opponent's action that was not in the original abstraction (Ganzfried and Sandholm, 2015; Brown and Sandholm, 2017b). This way missing actions can be added to the model at play time while, in the case of the safe subgame-solving techniques, still guaranteeing safety.

The previously noted subgame-solving techniques were the most important component techniques for achieving superhuman performance in two-player no-limit Texas hold'em (Brown and Sandholm, 2018). Those techniques solve the subgame all the way to the end of the game. In most large games this is computationally wasteful and thus prevents the use of even finer-grained abstractions. In other games this is downright infeasible computationally. In perfect-information games the standard approach is depth-limited subgame solving, where the subgame is searched to a shallower depth than the end of the game. At the point when a path is cut off in the search, an evaluation function is used to estimate the value of the leaf of the search. Again, imperfect-information games are more intricate. Here, leaves of the depth-limited subgame do not have values because if we change our strategy below some leaf, it may cause the opponent to want to deviate to a different strategy even in the earlier part of the tree, which changes the payoffs of the leaves. Nevertheless, depth-limited subgame solving is possible in a game-theoretically sound way (Brown, Sandholm, and Amos, 2018). The idea is that at each information set at the depth limit of the subgame, each player is provided with alternative *continuation strategies* for the rest of the game that she can choose among in her subgame strategy. With just one continuation strategy per player, this is essentially the same as bootstrapping with base strategies discussed previously. However, additional continuation strategies can be generated incrementally, for example, by alternating between solving the subgame with the current continuation strategy candidates, and then generating for some player her best-response continuation strategy and adding it to the pool of continuation strategy candidates for that player. This iteration leads to Nash equilibrium in two-player zero-sum games. In poker, four continuation strategies per player suffices for very strong play. This depth-limited subgame solving, applied recursively, was the key to achieving superhuman performance in six-player no-limit Texas hold'em, the most popular poker game in the world (Brown and Sandholm, 2019b).

Another way to accomplish, in effect, depth-limited subgame solving is to solve a large number of endgames, each of which starts with a randomly generated belief state, in advance (Moravčík et al., 2017). Then the main endgame solving is conducted in a way where a search path stops early if the node has a belief state close to one that has been solved in advance. This is very expensive computationally because a large number of belief states needs to be solved in advance. A more frugal approach has also been developed where the subgames to be solved are selected based on strategies computed for earlier parts of the game (Zarick et al., 2020). While this is an improvement down this avenue, it has not reached the level of *Libratus* (Brown and Sandholm, 2018).

Subgame solving techniques suffer from a weakness that precludes their use in games where the imperfect information is much greater than in poker: They require reasoning about the common-knowledge closure of the player's current information set – that is, the smallest set of states in which it is common knowledge that the current state belongs. Recently, *knowledge-limited subgame solving* was developed, which does not have this weakness (Zhang and Sandholm, 2021b). Here, information sets can cut across subgames. The approach can be unsafe but in practice that is rare. There are also ways of recovering various safety guarantees. A depth-limited version of the technique led to the first strong AI for the massive challenge problem *dark chess*, the most popular imperfect-information variant of chess – where common knowledge closures can include 10^{14} game tree or more.

19.2.4 Algorithms for Equilibrium Refinements

Nash equilibrium strategies do not necessarily play optimally after some player(s) have made mistakes: One just has to play well enough that those mistakes do not become profitable for the opponent. Equilibrium refinements have been designed to remedy such weaknesses. A key refinement for extensive-form imperfect-information games is *sequential equilibrium* (Kreps and Wilson, 1982). The main further refinements of it are *extensive-form trembling hand perfect equilibrium (EFPE*; Selten, 1975) and *quasi-perfect equilibrium (QPE*; van Damme, 1984). QPE is particularly appealing because it offers both sequential rationality and admissibility.

Even in the two-player zero-sum setting, EFPE and QPE have been too complex to compute in imperfect-information games beyond small ones. The best algorithm up to 2018 (Miltersen and Sørensen, 2010) is able to find a QPE in a game with 1,000 leaves and 550 information sets (Farina, Gatti, and Sandholm, 2018b). Then there was a scalability breakthrough. EFPE-style and QPE-style trembling can be modeled as *trembling linear programs* for a given trembling magnitude $\epsilon > 0$. As $\epsilon \to 0$, the path of the LP optimum approaches an EFPE or QPE, respectively. Farina, Gatti, and Sandholm (2018b), extending prior work by Miltersen and Sørensen (Miltersen and Sørensen (2010) and Farina and Gatti (2017), showed that there is a finite game-specific $\epsilon^* > 0$ such that for all $0 < \epsilon \leq \epsilon^*$, the optimal LP basis is stable (i.e., it stays the same). Intuitively, the same vertex of the LP – that is, the vertex where the same constraints are active – stays optimal although the constraints still keep changing so the vertex itself still keeps moving. The LP objective also still keeps changing. The analytical ϵ^* is so tiny that it would underwhelm a computer. Thus, trying to directly exploit the provided fact about ϵ^* is not practical. However, Farina, Gatti, and Sandholm (2018b) made a scalable algorithm that starts with some $\epsilon > 0$, and then repeatedly checks whether the basis is stable and, if not, decreases ϵ by a factor, say 1,000. To make this algorithm possible, they developed fast algorithms for (1) checking whether the LP basis is stable for a given ϵ, and (2) once a stable basis has been reached, computing the limit of the optimal LP solution as $\epsilon \to 0$. The newest version of the algorithm runs LP sparsification as a preprocessor before running the provided algorithm (Farina, Gatti, and Sandholm, 2021b). It finds exact EFPEs and QPEs for games with hundreds of millions of leaves on a laptop in one day.

19.3 EQUILIBRIUM FINDING FROM A GAME *PROGRAM*

A new setup, introduced in the present paper, is one where the game is provided in a programming language that a game-theoretic solver then *analyzes* rather than *executes*. Using a programming language can make general-purpose game modeling significantly easier and more scalable – by manual modelers and by software products that automatically output the game model. An imperative programming language for this has been developed.[1] Figure 19.1 shows a small example program in that language. For ease of learning to use it, that language is a subset of the broadly adopted Python programming language. However, it has certain additional structures at the end, such as those for describing the players' decision variables and utility, as well as (not in this example)

```
def equal(x, y):
    return (x-y) < 0.5 and (y-x) < 0.5

def utility(blue_choice, red_choice):
    z = 0 if equal(blue_choice, red_choice) else 2
    blue_win = ((equal(red_choice, 0) and equal(blue_choice, 1)) or
                (equal(red_choice, 1) and equal(blue_choice, 2)) or
                (equal(red_choice, 2) and equal(blue_choice, 0)))
    blue_win_value = 1 if blue_win else -1
    final = z if (z == 0) else blue_win_value
    return final
""
enum blue_choice: [0, 2]
""
enum red_choice: [0, 2]
""
""
""
utility(blue_choice, red_choice)
```

FIGURE 19.1 Rock-paper-scissors game expressed in the game programming language.

side constraints on combinations of variables, temporal indexing, and variable observability.

One could interpret or compile the language the traditional way for a computer to execute, in which case the solving algorithm would face the black-box setting described in the next section. That would not enable the solver to exploit all the structural knowledge present in the program. Therefore, we do not execute the program. Rather, our solving algorithms analyze it in their game-theoretic *reasoning*. For example, one subroutine that we developed *differentiates through the entire game* (utility as a function of the players' strategy variables). This is surprisingly scalable for the chosen subset of Python. We have several game-theoretic solving algorithms that use that gradient information.[4]

[4] In the *General Game Playing Competition (GGPC)*, the rules are provided to the playing programs as a logic program, which is a form of declarative programming language. Unlike the usual programming languages that are imperative, declarative programming languages do not associate a control flow with the program and are thus more like the declarative game representations discussed in Section 19.2, except more compact because game states are viewed as databases where certain facts are true. In the GGPC, the playing programs typically use the provided logic program for generating the legal moves and similar dynamics, so the representation is used more as a programming language in that sense than what I am describing in this section, where the input program is used as an input to reasoning, not execution. Their language was designed for perfect-information games. An extension exists for imperfect-information games, with logical expressions describing which players know which facts in which states (Genesereth and Thielscher, 2014). To my knowledge, no game-theoretic solving algorithms have been developed for it. So it remains to be seen whether logic programs will be useful for representing and solving such games.

19.4 WHAT IF THE RULES ARE NOT PROVIDED?

In the military course-of-action-generation applications,[1] the algorithm is not given rules of the game in any form but rather a simulator in which the algorithm can try to learn by playing the game repeatedly while controlling all the players. That black-box setup occurs also in real-time strategy games and trading simulations (Wellman, 2006; Vorobeychik et al., 2006; Lanctot et al., 2017; Tuyls et al., 2018; Areyan Viqueira et al., 2020). Settings may even arise where the rules are defined by the real world. That would lead to an analogous setup as long as the training phase is still essentially costless and the algorithm can control all the strategic players during that phase.

In this setting, the algorithm may never find out the game exactly. While deep reinforcement learning has yielded impressive demonstrations in this setting (Vinyals et al., 2019; Berner et al., 2019), such techniques lack the low-exploitability guarantee of game theory, even with infinite samples and computation. Furthermore, the standard method of evaluating a strategy's exploitability is to compute a best response to it. This assumes the game is known. So, with just a simulator, that method cannot evaluate exploitability, even after strategies have been computed.

There had been some work on algorithms with exploitability guarantees for black-box games (Lanctot, Waugh, Zinkevich, and Bowling 2009; Gatti and Restelli, 2011; Marchesi, Trovò, and Gatti, 2020; Zhou, Li, and Zhu, 2020; Farina, Schmucker, and Sandholm, 2021e; Farina and Sandholm, 2021). In each, the exploitability guarantee is vacuous unless the algorithm touches at least as many information sets as there are in the game. Furthermore, some of them, such as MCCFR, can take exponential time in the size of the game tree unless given additional information.

Recently, Zhang and Sandholm (2020a, 2021a) introduced an approach that provides exploitability guarantees – even zero exploitability – in black-box games without fully exploring the game tree, by producing a *certificate* that is often much smaller than the game. The certificate is a partially expanded game tree with bounds on each player's payoffs at the leaves of the expanded part; the certificate also includes the players' strategies for that part. A certificate can be verified in time linear in its size, without further knowledge about the game. Two-player perfect-information and normal-form games always have small certificates. Extensive-form games do not always have them, even in the two-player zero-sum case, but do in two-player games where the players do not observe too much. Even in the two-player zero-sum case, it is NP-hard to approximate the smallest certificate to within a logarithmic factor, and there are games where solving takes exponential time in the size of the smallest certificate. Nevertheless, they developed a sampling-based certificate-creation technique with convergence rate $\tilde{O}(N/\sqrt{T})$ to coarse correlated equilibrium in multiplayer extensive-form games, where N is the number of nodes in the expanded part of the game, which is typically a tiny portion of the full game, and T is the number of samples, where each sample is one play-through of the game. This rate is optimal for the setting. For the two-player zero-sum case, this offers the first game-solving algorithm with $\tilde{O}(N/\sqrt{T})$ exploitability. Experiments show that the methods construct certificates – even of exact equilibrium – while indeed exploring only a tiny portion of the game. The methods run quickly on a laptop on games with hundreds of thousands of nodes and even infinite games.

For even better computational scalability, I foresee that additional structural knowledge of the game should be leveraged. One example is knowing that certain chance probabilities are independent of other chance probabilities or player actions. Additional structure could include outside knowledge or common-sense knowledge such as "Gremlins in this game that keep biting my ankles will not turn into a nuclear bomb later on." Also, one could (first try to) solve the game under optimistic assumptions, such as "If the path of play reaches nuclear holocaust, at least one player has made a mistake."

19.5 CONCLUSIONS AND FUTURE RESEARCH

There has been dramatic progress in game solving over the last twenty years via a myriad of new ideas and techniques. That has enabled game theory to extend well beyond human intelligence. The game is computationally solved in its full detail – or in a large, faithful abstraction thereof – as opposed to solving a small, stylized variant manually to obtain insight for humans. I discussed three categories of games where such advances have occurred. One is games that are simply too large for humans to solve. Examples include our superhuman strategies for two-player and multiplayer no-limit Texas hold'em poker, as well as portfolio and deployment planning for missile defense and multidomain combat. The second category is a setup where the rules are provided in a programming language that is not executed but rather analyzed by a game-solving algorithm. The third category is games where the rules exist but are not provided. This includes settings where the game is defined by a simulation – such as a real-time strategy game, war simulation, or trading simulation – or potentially even the real world. For this category, methods that yield strategies with game-theoretic guarantees of low exploitability have been developed recently (Zhang and Sandholm, 2020a, 2021a). On the applied side, we have developed algorithms on top of military simulators that generate superhuman strategies for scenarios with 1,400 entities.[1]

The experiences covered in this paper point to several interesting directions for future research. For each of the three categories of game described previously, there is still significant room to develop algorithms for two-player zero-sum games that find better equilibrium approximations faster and with lower memory usage. For each of the three categories, there is also room for improved algorithms for non-zero-sum and multiplayer games. Even for normal-form settings, no algorithm that can find a Nash equilibrium for *all* such games in polynomial time in the game size can be expected (absent a surprising collapse in the hierarchy of computational complexity classes) (Daskalakis, Goldberg, and Papadimitriou, 2009; Chen, Deng, and Teng, 2009, Etessami and Yannakakis, 2010), and random normal-form games are hard in practice, even for the fastest current algorithms (Gatti, Patrini, Rocco, and Sandholm, 2012; Berg and Sandholm, 2017). However, there can be subclasses of such games for which this can be achieved. That said, it is not clear that one would even want to use a Nash equilibrium strategy, due to issues such as equilibrium selection. Perhaps more promising is to try to understand why algorithms like those that created superhuman strategies for multiplayer poker (Brown and Sandholm, 2019b) generate strategies that are so strong in practice. In external-regret-minimizing algorithms, the average of joint play converges to coarse correlated equilibria, which are a superset of Nash equilibria, so the equilibrium-selection problem could even be worse. However, do all coarse correlated equilibria play well in some sense in some game classes (though it is already known that in two-player zero-sum games they are min-max strategies)? Do the algorithms – at least for some game classes – actually satisfy some stronger equilibrium notion than coarse correlated equilibrium? For example, in normal-form games, coarse correlated equilibrium can prescribe play of strictly dominated strategies, but regret-minimization algorithms that assign zero probability to actions with negative regret remove all iteratively strictly dominated strategies (Gibson, 2014).

There is also a flurry of research on how to define and compute correlated equilibria in extensive-form games. There are four such equilibrium concepts, depending on whether the correlation device reveals to each agent recommendations up front or incrementally, and whether each agent has to decide whether or not to follow the recommendations before or after receiving them (Farina, Bianchi, and Sandholm, 2020a). For the case where the correlation device reveals up front and agents decide after receiving recommendations, it is unknown whether an equilibrium can be found in polynomial time, but for the other three concepts there is an algorithm that runs in polynomial time in theory (Huang and von Stengel, 2008) and there are uncoupled no-regret dynamics that converge (Farina, Celli, Marchesi, and Gatti, 2022). Finding an *optimal* (e.g., welfare-maximizing) equilibrium is NP-hard for all four concepts, even with just two players (von Stengel and Forges, 2008; Farina, Bianchi, and Sandholm, 2020a). For the three concepts, the currently fastest algorithms for finding an optimal equilibrium are either (1) based on a *correlation directed acyclic graph* representation that is exponential only in the greatest number of player private states (summed across all players) per public state (Zhang, Farina, Celli, and Sandholm, 2022a) or (2) based on custom column-generation approaches (Zhang, Farina, Celli, and Sandholm, 2022a). The former approach is faster in practice on problems for which that theoretical exponent is small.

More general equilibrium notions – *communication equilibria* (Forges, 1986) and *certification equilibria* (Forges and Koessler, 2005) – use a mediator that can both send and receive messages. Optimal equilibria in both notions can be computed in polynomial time (Zhang and Sandholm, 2022a), the latter under a natural additional assumption known in the literature. This is done by constructing a *mediator-augmented game* LP of polynomial size that explicitly represents the mediator's decisions and actions. This framework allows one to define an entire family of equilibrium concepts by varying the mediator's information partition, the players' ability to lie, and the players' ability to deviate.

Under this lens, the typical notions of correlated equilibria in extensive-form games discussed herein correspond to a mediator that has *imperfect recall*. So, at least among all these equilibrium notions, the hardness of computation is driven by the mediator's imperfect recall. Using a nonforgetful mediator both enables better equilibria and circumvents the computational complexity!

Another game class of significant recent interest is *team games*, where each player belongs to one of two teams and the members of a team receive the same payoffs. If the players on each team can share their information during the game, this is simply a two-player game. If the players on a team cannot share random numbers before the game, one is in the setting of *team-maxmin equilibrium* (von Stengel and Koller, 1997), which is peculiar in that the natural way of writing the problem of optimizing the players' joint strategy is not convex and the minmax theorem may not hold. The most interesting setting is *team-maxmin equilibrium with correlation device (TMECor*; Celli and Gatti, 2018; Farina, Celli, Gatti, and Sandholm, 2018a), where team members can correlate before the game but not during the game (except via their actions in the game) – such as in bridge, collusion in poker, communications-denied military settings, and coordinated swindling. These games are equivalent to two-player games of imperfect recall and are a special case of extensive-form correlated equilibrium. Recently a new representation was introduced for team-coordinated game-theoretic decision-making, the *team-belief-directed acyclic graph form* (Zhang, Farina, and Sandholm, 2023). At every time step, a team coordinator observes the information that is public to all members of the team and then decides on a prescription for all the possible states consistent with his or her observations. Similar to the approach of Carminati, Cacciamani, Ciccone, and Gatti (2021), this enables techniques for team games that have led to the main breakthroughs in nonteam games, such as abstraction, advanced extensive-form regret-minimization techniques, and subgame solving. However, the new representation can be exponentially smaller than that of Carminati and colleagues (2021) and can be viewed as a lossless abstraction of theirs into a directed acyclic graph. As in the LP-based algorithm of Zhang and Sandholm (2022b), the size of the representation is exponential only in the greatest number of player information sets per team public state. Using the new representation is the fastest approach for TMECor in practice on problems where the theoretical exponent is small. On other problems, custom column-generation approaches are fastest (Zhang, Farina, Celli, and Sandholm, 2022a).

Ultimately, the pudding is not in the proofs. The value of game theory will hinge on its impact on the world. It is via the algorithm-powered paradigm discussed in this paper that I foresee the prescriptive power of game theory coming to unprecedented fruition. Significant work needs to be done to apply computational game solving to additional games of importance. The direct application of equilibrium finding to real-world settings is still in its infancy. With the leaps in game representations and solving techniques from the last twenty years, I expect this paradigm to become extremely important in the future.

19.6 ACKNOWLEDGEMENTS

I thank Jörgen Weibull, Victor Lesser, Bengt Holmström, Christina Fong, Gabriele Farina, and Brian Zhang for helpful comments on drafts of this paper. This work is supported by the National Science Foundation under grants IIS-1718457, IIS-1901403, and CCF-1733556, and the US Army Research Office (ARO) under award W911NF2010081.

19.7 REFERENCES

E. Areyan Viqueira, C. Cousins, and A. Greenwald. Improved algorithms for learning equilibria in simulation-based games. In *Proceedings of the International Conference on Autonomous Agents and Multiagent Systems*, pp. 79–87, 2020.

K. Berg and T. Sandholm. Exclusion method for finding Nash equilibrium in multiplayer games. In *Proceedings of the AAAI Conference on Artificial Intelligence (AAAI)*, 2017.

C. Berner, G. Brockman, B. Chan, V. Cheung, P. Debiak, C. Dennison, D. Farhi, Q. Fischer, S. Hashme, C. Hesse, et al. Dota 2 with large scale deep reinforcement learning. *arXiv preprint*, arXiv:1912.06680, 2019.

D. Billings, N. Burch, A. Davidson, R. Holte, J. Schaeffer, T. Schauenberg, and D. Szafron. Approximating game-theoretic optimal strategies for full-scale poker. In *Proceedings of the International Joint Conference on Artificial Intelligence (IJCAI)*, 2003.

É. Borel and J. Ville. *Applications de la théorie des probabilités aux jeux de hasard*. Paris: Gauthier-Villars, 1938.

N. Brown, S. Ganzfried, and T. Sandholm. Hierarchical abstraction, distributed equilibrium computation, and post-processing, with application to a champion no-limit Texas Hold'em agent. In *Proceedings of the International Conference on Autonomous Agents and Multi-agent Systems (AAMAS)*, 2015.

N. Brown, C. Kroer, and T. Sandholm. Dynamic thresholding and pruning for regret minimization. In *Proceedings of the AAAI Conference on Artificial Intelligence (AAAI)*, 2017.

M. Bowling, N. Burch, M. Johanson, and O. Tammelin. Heads-up limit hold'em poker is solved. *Science*, 347(6218):145–149, 2015.

N. Brown and T. Sandholm. Regret transfer and parameter optimization. In *Proceedings of the AAAI Conference on Artificial Intelligence (AAAI)*, 2014.

N. Brown and T. Sandholm. Simultaneous abstraction and equilibrium finding in games. In *Proceedings of the International Joint Conference on Artificial Intelligence (IJCAI)*, 2015.

N. Brown and T. Sandholm. Strategy-based warm starting for regret minimization in games. In *Proceedings of the AAAI Conference on Artificial Intelligence (AAAI)*, 2016.

N. Brown and T. Sandholm. Reduced space and faster convergence in imperfect-information games via pruning. In *International Conference on Machine Learning (ICML)*, 2017a.

N. Brown and T. Sandholm. Safe and nested subgame solving for imperfect-information games. In *Proceedings of the Conference on Neural Information Processing Systems (NeurIPS)*, 2017b. First published at the AAAI-17 Workshop on Computer Poker and Imperfect Information Games, submitted November 4, 2016.

N. Brown and T. Sandholm. Superhuman AI for heads-up no-limit poker: Libratus beats top professionals. *Science*, 359(6374):418–424, 2018.

N. Brown and T. Sandholm. Solving imperfect-information games via discounted regret minimization. In *Proceedings of the AAAI Conference on Artificial Intelligence (AAAI)*, 2019a.

N. Brown and T. Sandholm. Superhuman AI for multiplayer poker. *Science*, 365(6456):885–890, 2019b.

N. Brown, T. Sandholm, and B. Amos. Depth-limited solving for imperfect-information games. In *Proceedings of the Conference on Neural Information Processing Systems (NeurIPS)*, 2018.

N. Burch, M. Johanson, and M. Bowling. Solving imperfect information games using decomposition. In *Proceedings of the AAAI Conference on Artificial Intelligence (AAAI)*, 2014.

N. Burch, M. Moravčík, and M. Schmid. Revisiting CFR+ and alternating updates. *Journal of Artificial Intelligence Research*, 64:429–443, 2019.

L. Carminati, F. Cacciamani, M. Ciccone, and N. Gatti. Public information representation for adversarial team games. In *NeurIPS Cooperative AI Workshop*, 2021.

A. Celli and N. Gatti. Computational results for extensive-form adversarial team games. In *Proceedings of the AAAI Conference on Artificial Intelligence (AAAI)*, 2018.

X. Chen, X. Deng, and S.-H. Teng. Settling the complexity of computing two-player Nash equilibria. *Journal of the ACM*, 56:1–57, 2009.

V. Conitzer and T. Sandholm. Computing the optimal strategy to commit to. In *Proceedings of the ACM Conference on Electronic Commerce (ACM-EC)*, 2006.

C. Daskalakis, P. W. Goldberg, and C. H. Papadimitriou. The complexity of computing a Nash equilibrium. *SIAM Journal on Computing*, 39(1):195–259, 2009.

K. Etessami and M. Yannakakis. On the complexity of Nash equilibria and other fixed points. *SIAM Journal on Computing*, 39(6):2531–2597, 2010.

G. Farina, T. Bianchi, and T. Sandholm. Coarse correlation in extensive-form games. In *Proceedings of the AAAI Conference on Artificial Intelligence (AAAI)*, 2020a.

G. Farina, A. Celli, N. Gatti, and T. Sandholm. *Ex ante* coordination and collusion in zero-sum multi-player extensive-form games. In *Proceedings of the Conference on Neural Information Processing Systems (NeurIPS)*, 2018a.

G. Farina, A. Celli, N. Gatti, and T. Sandholm. Connecting optimal ex-ante collusion in teams to extensive-form correlation: Faster algorithms and positive complexity results. In *Proceedings of the International Conference on Machine Learning*, 2021a.

G. Farina, A. Celli, A. Marchesi, and N. Gatti. Simple uncoupled no-regret learning dynamics for extensive-form correlated equilibrium. *Journal of the ACM* , article 41, 2022.

G. Farina and N. Gatti. Extensive-form perfect equilibrium computation in two-player games. In *Proceedings of the AAAI Conference on Artificial Intelligence (AAAI)*, 2017.

G. Farina, N. Gatti, and T. Sandholm. Practical exact algorithm for trembling-hand equilibrium refinements in games. In *Proceedings of the Conference on Neural Information Processing Systems (NeurIPS)*, 2018b.

G. Farina, N. Gatti, and T. Sandholm. *Trembling Linear Programs: Algorithm and Application to Equilibrium Refinements*. Manuscript, 2021b.

G. Farina, C. Kroer, N. Brown, and T. Sandholm. Stable-predictive optimistic counterfactual regret minimization. In *Proceedings of the International Conference on Machine Learning (ICML)*, 2019a.

G. Farina, C. Kroer, and T. Sandholm. Online convex optimization for sequential decision processes and extensive-form games. In *AAAI Conference on Artificial Intelligence*, 2019b.

G. Farina, C. Kroer, and T. Sandholm. Optimistic regret minimization for extensive-form games via dilated distance-generating functions. In *Proceedings of the Conference on Neural Information Processing Systems (NeurIPS)*, 2019c.

G. Farina, C. Kroer, and T. Sandholm. Regret circuits: Composability of regret minimizers. In *International Conference on Machine Learning*, pp. 1863–1872, 2019d.

G. Farina, C. Kroer, and T. Sandholm. Stochastic regret minimization in extensive-form games. In *Proceedings of the International Conference on Machine Learning (ICML)*, 2020b.

G. Farina, C. Kroer, and T. Sandholm. Better regularization for sequential decision spaces: Fast convergence rates for Nash, correlated, and team equilibria. *Operations Research* 73(5): 2430–2457, 2025.

G. Farina, C. Kroer, and T. Sandholm. Faster game solving via predictive Blackwell approachability: Connecting regret matching and mirror descent. In *Proceedings of the AAAI Conference on Artificial Intelligence (AAAI)*, 2021d.

G. Farina and T. Sandholm. Polynomial-time computation of optimal correlated equilibria in two-player extensive-form games with public chance moves and beyond. In *Proceedings of the Conference on Neural Information Processing Systems (NeurIPS)*, 2020.

G. Farina and T. Sandholm. Model-free online learning in unknown sequential decision making problems and games. In *Proceedings of the AAAI Conference on Artificial Intelligence (AAAI)*, 2021.

G. Farina and T. Sandholm. Fast payoff matrix sparsification techniques for structured extensive-form games. In *Proceedings of the AAAI Conference on Artificial Intelligence (AAAI)*, 2022.

G. Farina, R. Schmucker, and T. Sandholm. Bandit linear optimization for sequential decision making and extensive-form games. In *Proceedings of the AAAI Conference on Artificial Intelligence (AAAI)*, 2021e.

F. Forges. An approach to communication equilibria. *Econometrica*, 54:1375–1385, 1986.

F. Forges and F. Koessler. Communication equilibria with partially verifiable types. *Journal of Mathematical Economics*, 41(7):793–811, 2005.

D. Fudenberg and J. Tirole. *Game Theory*. Cambridge, MA: MIT Press, 1991.

S. Ganzfried and T. Sandholm. Action translation in extensive-form games with large action spaces: Axioms, paradoxes, and the pseudo-harmonic mapping. In *Proceedings of the International Joint Conference on Artificial Intelligence (IJCAI)*, 2013.

S. Ganzfried and T. Sandholm. Potential-aware imperfect-recall abstraction with earth mover's distance in imperfect-information games. In *Proceedings of the AAAI Conference on Artificial Intelligence (AAAI)*, 2014.

S. Ganzfried and T. Sandholm. Endgame solving in large imperfect-information games. In *Proceedings of the International Conference on Autonomous Agents and Multi-agent Systems (AAMAS)*, 2015. Early version presented at the AAAI-13 Workshop on Computer Poker and Imperfect Information.

N. Gatti, G. Patrini, M. Rocco, and T. Sandholm. Combining local search techniques and path following for bimatrix games. In *Proceedings of the Conference on Uncertainty in Artificial Intelligence (UAI)*, 2012.

N. Gatti and M. Restelli. Equilibrium approximation in simulation-based extensive-form games. In *Proceedings of the International Conference on Autonomous Agents and Multiagent Systems*, 2011.

M. Genesereth and M. Thielscher. *General Game Playing*. San Rafael, CA: Morgan & Claypool, 2014.

R. Gibson. *Regret Minimization in Games and the Development of Champion Multiplayer Computer Poker-Playing Agents*. PhD thesis, University of Alberta, 2014.

R. Gibson, M. Lanctot, N. Burch, D. Szafron, and M. Bowling. Generalized sampling and variance in counterfactual regret minimization. In *Proceedings of the AAAI Conference on Artificial Intelligence (AAAI)*, 2012.

A. Gilpin, S. Hoda, J. Peña, and T. Sandholm. Gradient-based algorithms for finding Nash equilibria in extensive form games. In *International Workshop on Internet and Network Economics (WINE)*, 2007a.

A. Gilpin, J. Peña, and T. Sandholm. First-order algorithm with $\mathcal{O}(\ln(1/\epsilon))$ convergence for ϵ-equilibrium in two-person zero-sum games. *Mathematical Programming*, 133(1–2):279–298, 2012. Conference version was presented at AAAI-08.

A. Gilpin and T. Sandholm. A competitive Texas Hold'em poker player via automated abstraction and real-time equilibrium computation. In *Proceedings of the National Conference on Artificial Intelligence (AAAI)*, 2006a.

A. Gilpin and T. Sandholm. A Texas Hold'em poker player based on automated abstraction and real-time equilibrium computation. In *Proceedings of the International Conference on Autonomous Agents and Multi-agent Systems (AAMAS)*, 2006b.

A. Gilpin and T. Sandholm. Better automated abstraction techniques for imperfect information games, with application to Texas Hold'em poker. In *Proceedings of the International Conference on Autonomous Agents and Multi-agent Systems (AAMAS)*, 2007a.

A. Gilpin and T. Sandholm. Lossless abstraction of imperfect information games. *Journal of the ACM*, 54(5), 2007b. An early version, 'Finding equilibria in large sequential games of imperfect information', appeared in the Proceedings of the ACM Conference on Electronic Commerce (EC), pp. 160–169, 2006.

A. Gilpin and T. Sandholm. Expectation-based versus potential-aware automated abstraction in imperfect information games: An experimental comparison using poker. In *Proceedings of the AAAI Conference on Artificial Intelligence (AAAI)*, 2008. Short paper.

A. Gilpin, T. Sandholm, and T. B. Sørensen. Potential-aware automated abstraction of sequential games, and holistic equilibrium analysis of Texas Hold'em poker. In *Proceedings of the AAAI Conference on Artificial Intelligence (AAAI)*, 2007b.

S. Hart and A. Mas-Colell. A simple adaptive procedure leading to correlated equilibrium. *Econometrica*, 68:1127–1150, 2000.

S. Hoda, A. Gilpin, J. Peña, and T. Sandholm. Smoothing techniques for computing Nash equilibria of sequential games. *Mathematics of Operations Research*, 35(2):494–512, 2010.

W. Huang and B. von Stengel. Computing an extensive-form correlated equilibrium in polynomial time. In *Proceedings of the International Workshop on Internet and Network Economics (WINE)*, 2008.

M. Johanson. Measuring the size of large no-limit poker games. Technical report, University of Alberta, 2013.

M. Johanson, N. Burch, R. Valenzano, and M. Bowling. Evaluating state-space abstractions in extensive-form games. In *Proceedings of the International Conference on Autonomous Agents and Multi-agent Systems (AAMAS)*, 2013.

M. Kearns, M. Littman, and S. Singh. Graphical models for game theory. In *Proceedings of the Conference on Uncertainty in Artificial Intelligence (UAI)*, 2001.

D. Koller, N. Megiddo, and B. von Stengel. Efficient computation of equilibria for extensive two-person games. *Games and Economic Behavior*, 14(2):247–259, 1996.

D. Koller and A. Pfeffer. Generating and solving imperfect information games. In *Proceedings of the Fourteenth International Joint Conference on Artificial Intelligence (IJCAI)*, 1995.

D. M. Kreps and R. Wilson. Sequential equilibria. *Econometrica*, 50(4):863–894, 1982.

C. Kroer, G. Farina, and T. Sandholm. Solving large sequential games with the excessive gap technique. In *Proceedings of the Conference on Neural Information Processing Systems (NeurIPS)*, 2018.

C. Kroer and T. Sandholm. Extensive-form game abstraction with bounds. In *Proceedings of the ACM Conference on Economics and Computation (EC)*, 2014.

C. Kroer and T. Sandholm. Discretization of continuous action spaces in extensive-form games. In *Proceedings of the International Conference on Autonomous Agents and Multi-agent Systems (AAMAS)*, 2015.

C. Kroer and T. Sandholm. Imperfect-recall abstractions with bounds in games. In *Proceedings of the ACM Conference on Economics and Computation (EC)*, 2016.

C. Kroer and T. Sandholm. A unified framework for extensive-form game abstraction with bounds. In *Proceedings of the Conference on Neural Information Processing Systems (NeurIPS)*, 2018.

C. Kroer, K. Waugh, F. Kılınç-Karzan, and T. Sandholm. Faster algorithms for extensive-form game solving via improved smoothing functions. *Mathematical Programming*, 179:385–417, 2020.

H. W. Kuhn. A simplified two-person poker. In H. W. Kuhn and A. W. Tucker, eds., *Contributions to the Theory of Games*, vol. 1 of *Annals of Mathematics Studies*, 24, pp. 97–103. Princeton, NJ: Princeton University Press, 1950.

M. Lanctot, R. Gibson, N. Burch, M. Zinkevich, and M. Bowling. No-regret learning in extensive-form games with imperfect recall. In *Proceedings of the International Conference on Machine Learning (ICML)*, 2012.

M. Lanctot, K. Waugh, M. Zinkevich, and M. Bowling. Monte Carlo sampling for regret minimization in extensive games. In *Proceedings of the Conference on Neural Information Processing Systems (NeurIPS)*, 2009.

M. Lanctot, V. Zambaldi, A. Gruslys, A. Lazaridou, K. Tuyls, J. Pérolat, D. Silver, and T. Graepel. A unified game-theoretic approach to multiagent reinforcement learning. In *Proceedings of the Conference on Neural Information Processing Systems (NeurIPS)*, 2017.

C. Lemke and J. Howson. Equilibrium points of bimatrix games. *Journal of the Society of Industrial and Applied Mathematics*, 12:413–423, 1964.

A. Marchesi, F. Trovò, and N. Gatti. Learning probably approximately correct maximin strategies in simulation-based games with infinite strategy spaces. In *Proceedings of the International Conference on Autonomous Agents and Multiagent Systems*, 2020.

P. B. Miltersen and T. B. Sørensen. Computing a quasi-perfect equilibrium of a two-player game. *Economic Theory*, 42:175–192, 2010.

M. Moravčík, M. Schmid, N. Burch, V. Lisý, D. Morrill, N. Bard, T. Davis, K. Waugh, M. Johanson, and M. Bowling. Deepstack: Expert-level artificial intelligence in heads-up no-limit poker. *Science*, 356:508–513, May 2017.

M. Moravčík, M. Schmid, K. Ha, M. Hladik, and S. Gaukrodger. Refining subgames in large imperfect information games. In *Proceedings of the AAAI Conference on Artificial Intelligence (AAAI)*, 2016.

J. Nash. *Non-cooperative Games*. PhD thesis, Princeton University, 1950.

J. Nash and L. Shapley. A simple three-person poker game. In H. W. Kuhn and A. W. Tucker, eds., *Contributions to the Theory of Games*, vol. 1, pp. 105–116. Princeton, NJ: Princeton University Press, 1950.

Y. Nesterov. Excessive gap technique in nonsmooth convex minimization. *SIAM Journal of Optimization*, 16(1):235–249, 2005a.

Y. Nesterov. Smooth minimization of non-smooth functions. *Mathematical Programming*, 103:127–152, 2005b.

I. Romanovskii. Reduction of a game with complete memory to a matrix game. *Soviet Mathematics*, 3, 1962.

T. Sandholm. Perspectives on multiagent learning. *Artificial Intelligence*, 171:382–391, 2007.

T. Sandholm. The state of solving large incomplete-information games, and application to poker. *AI Magazine*, 2010. Special issue on algorithmic game theory.

T. Sandholm. Abstraction for solving large incomplete-information games. In *Proceedings of the AAAI Conference on Artificial Intelligence (AAAI)*, 2015a. Senior Member Track.

T. Sandholm. Solving imperfect-information games. *Science*, 347(6218):122–123, 2015b.

T. Sandholm and S. Singh. Lossy stochastic game abstraction with bounds. In *Proceedings of the ACM Conference on Electronic Commerce (EC)*, 2012.

J. Schrittwieser, I. Antonoglou, T. Hubert, K. Simonyan, L. Sifre, S. Schmitt, A. Guez, E. Lockhart, D. Hassabis, T. Graepel, T. Lillicrap, and D. Silver. Mastering Atari, Go, chess and shogi by planning with a learned model. *Nature*, 588(7839):604–609, December 2020.

R. Selten. Reexamination of the perfectness concept for equilibrium points in extensive games. *International Journal of Game Theory*, 4:25–55, 1975.

J. Shi and M. Littman. Abstraction methods for game theoretic poker. In *CG '00: Revised Papers from the Second International Conference on Computers and Games*. London: Springer-Verlag, 2000.

D. Silver, T. Hubert, J. Schrittwieser, I. Antonoglou, M. Lai, A. Guez, M. Lanctot, L. Sifre, D. Kumaran, T. Graepel, T. Lillicrap, K. Simonyan, and D. Hassabis. A general reinforcement learning algorithm that masters chess, shogi, and go through self-play. *Science*, 362(6419):1140–1144, 2018.

A. Sinha, F. Fang, B. An, C. Kiekintveld, and M. Tambe. Stackelberg security games: Looking beyond a decade of success. In *International Joint Conference on Artificial Intelligence and the European Conference on Artificial Intelligence (IJCAI-ECAI)*, 2018.

M. Tambe. *Security and Game Theory: Algorithms, Deployed Systems, Lessons Learned*. Cambridge: Cambridge University Press, 2011.

O. Tammelin. Solving large imperfect information games using CFR+. *arXiv preprint*, arXiv:1407.5042, 2014.

K. Tuyls, J. Perolat, M. Lanctot, J. Z. Leibo, and T. Graepel. A generalised method for empirical game theoretic analysis. In *Proceedings of the International Conference on Autonomous Agents and Multiagent Systems*, 2018.

E. van Damme. A relationship between perfect equilibria in extensive form games and proper equilibria in normal form games. *International Journal of Game Theory*, 13:1–13, 1984.

O. Vinyals, I. Babuschkin, W. M. Czarnecki, M. Mathieu, A. Dudzik, J. Chung, D. H. Choi, R. Powell, T. Ewalds, P. Georgiev, et al. Grandmaster level in StarCraft II using multi-agent reinforcement learning. *Nature*, 575(7782):350–354, 2019.

J. von Neumann and O. Morgenstern. *Theory of Games and Economic Behavior*. Princeton, NJ: Princeton University Press, 1947.

B. von Stengel and F. Forges. Extensive-form correlated equilibrium: Definition and computational complexity. *Mathematics of Operations Research*, 33(4):1002–1022, 2008.

B. von Stengel and D. Koller. Team-maxmin equilibria. *Games and Economic Behavior*, 21:309–321, 1997.

Y. Vorobeychik, C. Kiekintveld, and M. Wellman. Empirical mechanism design: Methods, with application to a supply chain scenario. In *Proceedings of the ACM Conference on Economics and Computation (EC)*, 2006.

K. Waugh, D. Schnizlein, M. Bowling, and D. Szafron. Abstraction pathologies in extensive games. In *Proceedings of the International Conference on Autonomous Agents and Multi-agent Systems (AAMAS)*, 2009a.

K. Waugh, M. Zinkevich, M. Johanson, M. Kan, D. Schnizlein, and M. Bowling. A practical use of imperfect recall. In *Symposium on Abstraction, Reformulation and Approximation (SARA)*, 2009b.

M. Wellman. Methods for empirical game-theoretic analysis (extended abstract). In *Proceedings of the National Conference on Artificial Intelligence (AAAI)*, 2006.

Z. Yin, A. Jiang, M. Tambe, C. Kietkintveld, K. Leyton-Brown, T. Sandholm, and J. Sullivan. TRUSTS: Scheduling randomized patrols for fare inspection in transit systems using game theory. *AI Magazine*, 33:59–72, 2012.

R. Zarick, B. Pellegrino, N. Brown, and C. Banister. Unlocking the potential of deep counterfactual value networks. In *Proceedings of the Conference on Neural Information Processing Systems (NeurIPS)*, 2020.

B. H. Zhang, G. Farina, A. Celli, and T. Sandholm. Optimal correlated equilibria in general-sum extensive-form games: Fixed-parameter algorithms, hardness, and two-sided column-generation. In *Proceedings of the ACM Conference on Economics and Computation (EC)*, 2022a.

B. H. Zhang, G. Farina, and T. Sandholm. Team belief DAG: Generalizing the sequence form to team games for fast computation of correlated team max-min equilibria via regret minimization. In *Proceedings of the International Conference on Machine Learning (ICML)*, 2023.

B. H. Zhang and T. Sandholm. Small Nash equilibrium certificates in very large games. In *Proceedings of the Conference on Neural Information Processing Systems (NeurIPS)*, 2020a.

B. H. Zhang and T. Sandholm. Sparsified linear programming for zero-sum equilibrium finding. In *Proceedings of the International Conference on Machine Learning (ICML)*, 2020b.

B. H. Zhang and T. Sandholm. Finding and certifying (near-)optimal strategies in black-box extensive-form games. In *Proceedings of the AAAI Conference on Artificial Intelligence (AAAI)*, 2021a.

B. H. Zhang and T. Sandholm. Subgame solving without common knowledge. In *Proceedings of the Conference on Neural Information Processing Systems (NeurIPS)*, 2021b.

B. H. Zhang and T. Sandholm. Polynomial-time optimal equilibria with a mediator in extensive-form games. In *Proceedings of the Conference on Neural Information Processing Systems (NeurIPS)*, 2022a.

B. H. Zhang and T. Sandholm. Team correlated equilibria in zero-sum extensive-form games via tree decompositions. In *Proceedings of the AAAI Conference on Artificial Intelligence (AAAI)*, 2022b.

Y. Zhou, J. Li, and J. Zhu. Posterior sampling for multi-agent reinforcement learning: Solving extensive games with imperfect information. In *Proceedings of the International Conference on Learning Representations (ICLR)*, 2020.

M. Zinkevich, M. Bowling, M. Johanson, and C. Piccione. Regret minimization in games with incomplete information. In *Proceedings of the Conference on Neural Information Processing Systems (NeurIPS)*, 2007.

PART V

ECONOMICS AND INSTITUTIONAL DESIGN

20

Introduction to Part V

Tommy Andersson

Economics is a broad subject, and game theory has been applied in many subfields within the discipline. Part V covers two research fields in the economics literature. The first deals with the design of markets, marketplaces, and institutions, whereas the second more generally encompasses agent behavior and learning in games. These research strands are connected through game theory, for example, because much of the analysis of markets and marketplaces, as well as many analytical aspects of learning, relies on equilibrium analysis, making use of either Nash equilibrium (Nash, 1950) or one of its refinements.

All markets consist of customs, infrastructure, and rules through which information is exchanged and transactions are made among the participating agents. Different markets also have different purposes and tasks to accomplish, and the practice of market design aims to either repair existing but poorly functioning marketplaces or establish new marketplaces (Roth, 2018). Because there are many different "types" of marketplaces – including, for example, markets for financial assets, internet advertising, organ exchanges, school choice, and spectrum auctions – economists have studied markets not only theoretically and empirically, but also through the lens of a market designer. Both cooperative and noncooperative game theory have been key for designing and redesigning marketplaces, and for predicting and understanding the behavior of market participants, for example, in terms of how their strategies evolve over time in repeated interactions.

In Chapter 21, Alvin E. Roth introduces market design and describes how the field has evolved since the beginning of the 1950s, when the development of cooperative and noncooperative game theory started to accelerate. It is a fascinating development, and despite the wide breach between different "types" of markets, they often have similar objectives and structure. In fact, many of the most celebrated results in the literature (e.g., Ausubel and Milgrom, 2002; Gale and Shapley, 1962; Dubins and Freedman, 1981; Edelman et al., 2007;

Remark by editors: During the Nobel symposium, this session was chaired and introduced by Erik Maskin, Harvard University.

Roth, 1982a; Shapley and Scarf, 1974; Vickrey, 1961; Varian, 2007) can be formulated using concepts from both cooperative and noncooperative game theory. For example, the stability axiom (Shapley, 1955; Gale and Shapley, 1962) originates from cooperative game theory, and dominant strategy equilibrium is a solution concept from noncooperative game theory. Yet, and as illustrated by Roth, the two concepts are contained in many of the key findings in the literature, including, for example, general statements of the type "In the [X] model, when the direct mechanism using the [Y] algorithm is employed, it is a dominant strategy for players in the set [Z] to submit their true preferences, and the resulting outcome is [stable/in the core]."

As also discussed by Roth, there are many reasons why it is difficult to model and analyze larger economic environments in which marketplaces are designed to operate, for example, because strategy sets are large and hard for outsiders to observe and analyze. These obstacles also prevent market participants themselves from doing so. Consequently, market participants must learn how to engage in complicated environments. In this learning process, new strategies can be discovered. A similar observation was made by Susan Athey in the second talk of the session.[1] More precisely, even if game theory and mechanism design are essential for analyzing auction markets, some results, including the celebrated revenue equivalence theorem (Myerson, 1981; Vickrey, 1961), which roughly states that given certain conditions any two mechanisms that result in the same outcome also have the same expected revenue, are often not directly applicable in their original forms (e.g., because learning and experimentation play a role on these markets). For example, sponsored search auctions (i.e., ad space auctions) have become some of the more practically important topics in the economics of auctions (seminal contributions were made by, e.g., Athey and Ellison, 2011; Edelman et al., 2007; Varian, 2007). In the early days of online display advertising, ad space was sold to advertisers in second-price auctions (where the final price paid by the winner is determined by the second-highest bid). Over time, many ad-selling platforms in Google (Google Ad Manager, Google AdMob, Adsense, etc.) have switched their auctions from second price to first price (where the final price reflects the winning bid), even if they should theoretically result in identical revenues. Athey's own research has contributed to several strands of the auction literature, for example, related to marketplace design (Athey and Ellison, 2011; Abraham et al., 2020) and various empirical and econometric aspects of auctions (Agarwal et al., 2009; Athey et al., 2011; Athey and Haile, 2002, 2007; Athey and Nekipelov, 2010).

As remarked on in the literature, economic agents are often engaged in complicated dynamic environments that they somehow must learn. Because agents may differ in many aspects, for example if they are short-lived or long-lived, and if they are patient or inpatient, learning models have been developed to analyze a large variety of environments (Fudenberg and Levine, 2016). This is

[1] The talk by Susan Athey is, unfortunately, not included in this book.

also the point of departure in the chapter by Drew Fudenberg. When agents are short-lived, they have little chance to learn, so they play a best response to their priors. But if they are long-lived and impatient, they do learn the steady state path of play, but need not learn how opponents respond to deviations. In this case, any self-confirming equilibrium (Fudenberg and Levine, 1993b) in strategies that is not weakly dominated could arise. This calls for refinements of Nash equilibrium. To obtain such refinements, a vibrant literature has emerged where attention has been given to strategy profiles that arise in steady states in the limit where agents first become long-lived and then arbitrarily patient, the so-called patiently stable strategy profiles (see Fudenberg and Levine, 1993a,b). The basic learning model, introduced in the chapter by Fudenberg, is rich and has been adopted to provide many insightful results (e.g., that patiently stable profiles must be Nash equilibria [Fudenberg and Levine, 1993a] but need not satisfy backward induction [Fudenberg and Levine, 2006]). Fudenberg's chapter also contains extensive discussions on signaling games, alternative refinements of Nash equilibria, and how they relate to each other.

Both chapters in Part V give very nice and thoughtful introductions to their respective research fields. They are also forward looking in the sense that they outline future challenges and unsolved research problems where game theory will play a major role in finding the solution.

20.1 REFERENCES

I. Abraham, S. Athey, M. Babaioff, and M. Grubb. Peaches, lemons, and cookies: Designing auction markets with dispersed information. *Games and Economic Behavior*, 124:454–477, 2020.

N. Agarwal, S. Athey, and D. Yang. Skewed bidding in pay-per-action auctions for online advertising. *American Economic Review*, 99:441–447, 2009.

S. Athey and G. Ellison. Position auctions with consumer search. *Quarterly Journal of Economics*, 126:1213–1270, 2011.

S. Athey and P. A. Haile. Identification of standard auction models. *Econometrica*, 70:2107–2140, 2002.

S. Athey and P. A. Haile. Nonparametric approaches to auctions. In J. J. Heckman and E. E. Leamer, eds., *Handbook of Econometrics*, vol. 6A, ch. 60, pp. 3847–3965. London: Elsevier, 2007.

S. Athey, J. Levin, and E. Seira. Comparing open and sealed bid auctions: Evidence from timber auctions. *Quarterly Journal of Economics*, 126:207–257, 2011.

S. Athey and D. Nekipelov. A structural model of sponsored search advertising auctions. Paper presented at the Sixth Ad Auctions Workshop, 2010.

L. M. Ausubel and P. R. Milgrom. Ascending auctions with package bidding. *B.E. Journal of Theoretical Economics*, 1(1):1–44, 2002.

L. E. Dubins and D. A. Freedman. Machiavelli and the Gale–Shapley algorithm. *American Mathematical Monthly*, 88(7):485–494, 1981.

B. Edelman, M. Ostrovsky, and M. Schwarz. Internet advertising and the generalized second-price auction: Selling billions of dollars worth of keywords. *American Economic Review*, 97(1):242–259, 2007.

D. Fudenberg and D. K. Levine. Steady state learning and Nash equilibrium. *Econometrica*, 61:547–573, 1993a.

D. Fudenberg and D. K. Levine. Self-confirming equilibrium. *Econometrica*, 61:523–545, 1993b.

D. Fudenberg and D. K. Levine. Superstition and rational learning. *American Economic Review*, 96:630–651, 2006.

D. Fudenberg and D. K. Levine. Whither game theory? Towards a theory of learning in games. *Journal of Economic Perspectives*, 30(4):151–170, 2016.

D. Gale and L. S. Shapley. College admissions and the stability of marriage. *American Mathematical Monthly*, 69(1):9–15, 1962.

R. B. Myerson. Optimal auction design. *Mathematics of Operations Research*, 6(1):58–73, 1981.

J. Nash. Equilibrium points in *N*-person games. *Proceedings of the National Academy of Sciences*, 36(1):48–49, January 1950.

A. E. Roth. The economics of matching: Stability and incentives. *Mathematics of Operations Research*, 7:617–628, 1982.

A. E. Roth. Marketplaces, markets, and market design. *American Economic Review*, 108(7):1609–1658, July 2018.

L. Shapley and H. Scarf. On cores and indivisibility. *Journal of Mathematical Economics*, 1(1):23–37, 1974.

L. S. Shapley. Markets as cooperative games. *Rand Corporation Paper P-629*, 1955.

H. R. Varian. Position auctions. *International Journal of Industrial Organization*, 25(6):1163–1178, 2007.

W. Vickrey. Counterspeculation, auctions, and competitive sealed tenders. *Journal of Finance*, 16(1):8–37, 1961.

21

Game Theory and Practical Market Design

How Big, Unobserved Strategy Sets Brought Cooperative and Noncooperative Game Theory Together

Alvin E. Roth

21.1 INTRODUCTION

One relatively recent development related to the growth of practical market design is the need to deal with big strategy sets that may involve parts of the economic environment beyond the boundaries of individual marketplaces. A related matter is that in naturally occurring environments, strategies may be discovered in the course of play. Discovering new strategies is very much like inventing new technology or new game theory: All of these things can change the game in important ways. These issues blur the borders of what historically were regarded as separate domains of game theory, namely the theories of cooperative and noncooperative games.

21.2 SOME EARLY HISTORY

The basic model of two-person zero-sum games was laid out in a paper of Borel (1921/1953), and its theoretical foundation – the minimax theorem – was established by von Neumann (1928/1959) and further developed by von Neumann and Morgenstern (1944). But two-person games and the minimax theorem could hardly be the basis of a theory of games well suited to economics, which deals not only with dividing scarce resources among many more than two participants but also with making resources less scarce (i.e., with creating nonzero gains in welfare). So von Neumann and Morgenstern (1944) also proposed to model cooperative games in which players could form coalitions, while Nash (1950, 1951) formulated the now eponymous equilibrium notion for games with arbitrarily many players that became the basis of noncooperative game theory.

I had helpful conversations with Fuhito Kojima, Mike Ostrovsky, and Drew Fudenberg, and this chapter also owes a debt to the discussion of the history of game theory by Roth and Wilson (2019).

I was among the many students of game theory who first learned it not from these original sources but from the thrilling, lucid introduction and interpretation by Luce and Raiffa (1957).[1] What we learned is that there were two kinds of game theory, for two kinds of games. There were cooperative games, in which coalitions of players could make binding agreements, and there were noncooperative games, in which individual players chose independently from strategies available to them. The goal of the theory of cooperative games was to determine what outcomes would result from agreements, while the goal of the theory of noncooperative games was to determine what individual players would do (i.e., which strategies rational players would choose).

Cooperative games were modeled by a set $N = \{1, \ldots, n\}$ of players and a function v from coalitions of players (subsets of N) to sets of feasible outcomes. The interpretation of this model is that each coalition S could achieve for its members their payoffs at any outcome in the set of outcomes $v(S)$. Coalition S was said to be effective for the outcomes $v(S)$. von Neumann and Morgenstern focused on a particularly simple class of such games, games with "side payments," in which $v : 2^N \to \mathcal{R}$ (i.e., in which v associated with each coalition a real number, such that a coalition S could distribute payoffs summing to $v(S)$ among its members in any way that they agreed upon). A vector of outcomes $x = (x_1, \ldots, x_n)$ representing the payoffs to each player was said to dominate a vector $y = (y_1, \ldots, y_n)$ via the coalition S if $x_i > y_i$ for all i in S, and the coalition S is effective for its payoffs in x. von Neumann and Morgenstern (1944) used this notion of domination to define sets of outcomes that they called "solutions" to a game given by N and v: A solution is a set of outcomes such that no outcome in the set is dominated by any other and every outcome outside of the set is dominated by an outcome inside the set.[2] They placed great importance on the conjecture that at least one solution would exist for every game in the class of games (N, v) with side payments. But by the time this conjecture was disproved by Lucas (1968), who produced a ten-person game with no von Neumann–Morgenstern solution, it had already become clear that this kind of solution would be of at most limited use in economics.[3]

[1] I had a formal course in game theory in 1972, when Michael Maschler visited Stanford from the Hebrew University in Jerusalem, which was an early center of game theory research.

[2] Notice that a solution cannot be the empty set, since every outcome not contained in the solution must be dominated by some outcome in the solution.

[3] For example, Shapley (1959) produced a game in which any continuous curve – such as your signature – could occur as a distinct part of some von Neumann–Morgenstern solution, indicating that some solutions would have properties that couldn't be interpreted in any natural economic way. I later contributed (Roth, 1975, 1976) by defining a generalization of von Neumann–Morgenstern solutions that existed for all games (although it could be the empty set), but by then the die was cast – these kinds of "solutions" were too unpredictive, too difficult to work with, too hard to derive and test empirical predictions, and they have largely disappeared from the modern game theory literature, although sets of similar sorts are studied in graph theory and elsewhere (including combinatorial games such as Nim, by Roth [1978]).

But the set of undominated outcomes (i.e., outcomes not dominated by any other outcome) came to be called the core of the game. Related ideas had appeared earlier. For example, Edgeworth's contract curve (Edgeworth, 1881) is the core of the game defined by an exchange economy in which players have initial endowments of goods that they are free to keep or trade (see also Shapley, 1959). The core contains the competitive allocation and so is nonempty in games for which competitive equilibria exist.[4] Zhao (2018) nominates Shapley (1955), an unpublished working paper,[5] as the first paper to single out the core as a general game theoretic solution concept, and Bondareva (1963), Shapley (1967), and Shapley and Shubik (1975) have early papers focusing on the relationship between market games and the nonemptiness of the core. Two papers involving the core that turn out to be very important in the design of matching markets are Gale and Shapley (1962) and Shapley and Scarf (1974).

Gale and Shapley modeled a marriage game consisting of two disjoint sets of men and women, each of whom had preferences over the people of the opposite sex. Any man and woman could mutually agree to marry one another, and individuals could decide to remain single. The core of that game consists of matchings that are individually rational and pairwise stable: No one is married to an unacceptable mate, and there are no blocking pairs (coalitions) consisting of a man and a woman who are not matched to each other but would both prefer to be. Gale and Shapley showed that the core of the game is nonempty, for any preferences of the men and women. They did this by demonstrating a deferred acceptance (DA) algorithm that for any preferences would produce a matching in the core.[6]

4 Edgeworth (1881) sketched an argument showing that the contract curve shrinks to the competitive allocation as agents are replicated, and Aumann (1964) showed how, when perfect competition is modeled as an exchange economy with a continuum of traders (each of measure zero), then the core coincides with the set of competitive allocations.

5 When I began to study game theory in the 1970s, unpublished working papers formed a substantial "secret" subliterature of game theory. I recall once proving something about market games and communicating it to Bob Aumann, who replied that he thought it was already a known result and that I should check on that by "sending it to Lloyd [Shapley]." In due course I received a numbered copy of an unpublished Rand working paper, indicating that about two dozen copies had already been distributed, and among the many results that it contained was the one I had derived. That is how I became the $n+1^{st}$ person to know of this previously known result.

6 The marriage model is symmetric between men and women, but the DA algorithm is not, so it has two different forms. The man-proposing DA algorithm begins with each man proposing to his most preferred woman, and each woman who receives more than one acceptable proposal (i.e., from a man she prefers to be matched to, rather than remaining single) holds the most preferred proposal and rejects the rest. At any subsequent stage of the algorithm, each man rejected in the previous stage proposes to his most preferred acceptable woman who hasn't yet rejected him, and each woman holds the most preferred acceptable proposal she has so far received and rejects the rest. The algorithm stops when no more proposals are made, at which point each woman accepts the proposal if any that she is holding (i.e., acceptances) are "deferred" to the end (hence the name of the algorithm). The matching that results has the property that no man and woman who are not matched to one another would both prefer to

Shapley and Scarf modeled an exchange economy in which each of *n* traders has an initial endowment of one unit of an indivisible good, which they called a *house*, and each trader has preferences over all the houses (including their initial endowment). Trade must proceed without the use of any money: An outcome of the game is simply some permutation of the initial endowments. Shapley and Scarf showed that the core of this exchange economy is nonempty, for any preferences of the traders, by demonstrating a top trading cycles algorithm that for any preferences would produce an allocation in the core (i.e., an allocation that no coalition could have been improved upon by trading the initial endowments of coalition members among the coalition).[7]

I'll have more to say later about the core. But to continue with this history, it's fair to say that cooperative game theory fell out of fashion in the economics literature, perhaps in response to the "Nash program" of attempting to model all games in terms of the detailed strategies available to the players. (In this view, for example, if players are able to reach binding agreements, a strategic model should specify precisely which steps need to be taken by individuals to reach particular agreements, in what order, with what information available. See, for example, Kuhn [1950, 1953] for formulations of games in "extensive" form meant in principle to be able to capture such detail.[8]) The great game theory text by Fudenberg and Tirole (1991), for example, makes no mention of ideas like the core, perhaps because it was being taught more in connection with general equilibrium theory (see, e.g., Hildenbrand and Kirman, 1976).

The origins of mechanism design (from which market design derives much of its initial theoretical impetus) took this strategic approach (Hurwicz, 1960). The designer specifies a game in extensive form (typically a direct mechanism, in which players have a set of messages they can send to a centralized mechanism), which is itself designed so that the equilibria of the game it implements

be, and this means that it is in the core of the marriage game. Gale and Shapley also discussed the closely related "College admissions" model, in which the players are students and colleges and there is a many-to-one matching in which each college can admit a fixed number of students. See Roth (2008) for a history of the DA algorithm.

7 The top trading cycles algorithm discussed by Shapley and Scarf (1974), which they attributed to David Gale, begins by having each trader point to their most preferred house (and its owner). There must exist at least one cycle, in which everyone is pointing to their first choice, and everyone in this cycle receives their first choice and leaves the market. This is repeated among the remaining agents and houses (each agent points to their first choice among the remaining houses) until everyone has been assigned. (Some agents may point to their own house, forming a cycle of length 1, so this algorithm stops in at most *n* steps.)

8 In Roth (1991a) I had this to say about coalitional and strategic models: "A cynical observer might summarize the present situation by saying that the less detailed cooperative models, which try to represent a game without specifying all the rules, aspire to a spurious generality, while the non-cooperative, strategic models, which are analyzed as if they represented all the potential moves in a game, offer a spurious specificity when the game in question is a model of some observable situation. It will be largely an empirical matter to determine which aspects of games need to be modelled in detail in order to confidently draw which kinds of conclusions." That paper was part of a volume celebrating the 100th anniversary of the Royal Economic Society and the *Economic Journal*, whose founding editor in 1891 was none other than Edgeworth.

have a property specified by the designer. (Sometimes the equilibria of interest are ordinary Nash equilibria; sometimes they are subsets or generalizations of those.) The participants are assumed to have no other actions available to them inside or outside of the mechanism (i.e., the description of the mechanism is comprehensive).

But perhaps unexpectedly, today we are seeing the usefulness of hybrid theories that combine strategic equilibria and the core (i.e., elements of both noncooperative and cooperative game theory that make use of both strategic and coalitional models of a game).[9]

21.3 COOPERATIVE AND NONCOOPERATIVE GAME THEORY HAVE MERGED

Here's what a theorem mixing cooperative and strategic models looks like (typically combining the work of multiple authors):

> In the [X] model, when the direct mechanism using the [Y] algorithm is employed, it is a dominant strategy for players in the set [Z] to submit their true preferences, and the resulting outcome is [stable/in the core].

And here are some important specific theorems in that style.

1. Theorem: In the marriage model, when the direct mechanism using the DA algorithm is employed, it is a dominant strategy for the proposing players to submit their true preferences, and the resulting outcome is in the core of the game. (There exist no mechanisms that always produce stable matchings in stated preferences that make it a dominant strategy for all players to state their true preferences. But when the DA algorithm is used, at any equilibrium misrepresentation of preferences in which the proposing side plays its dominant strategy, the resulting outcome will be stable with respect to the true preferences as well as the stated preferences; Gale and Shapley, 1962; Dubins and Freedman, 1981; Roth, 1982a, 1984; Bergstrom and Manning, 1982.)
2. In the many-to-one "college admissions" model, when the direct mechanism using the student-proposing DA algorithm is employed, it is a dominant strategy for students to submit their true preferences, and the resulting outcome is pairwise stable (Gale and Shapley, 1962; Roth, 1985).
3. In the Shapley–Scarf housing exchange model, when the direct mechanism using the top trading cycle (TTC) algorithm is employed, it is a dominant

[9] I'm speaking of the core a little loosely here, whose definition in particular models depends on how the domination relation over outcomes is realized. Sometimes it would be more precise to speak of "pairwise stable matchings" if the coalitions that are being considered as potential blocking coalitions are only pairs of players. In models like the one-to-one marriage model, the set of pairwise stable matchings equals the core as conventionally defined, while in many-to-one matching models, they differ (see Roth and Sotomayor, 1990).

strategy for all players to submit their true preferences, and the resulting outcome is in the core (Shapley and Scarf, 1974; Roth, 1982b).

4. In the single-unit private value sealed bid auction, when the second-price algorithm is used, it is a dominant strategy for all bidders to state their true preferences, and the resulting outcome is in the core (Vickrey, 1961).
5. In a multiunit auction with heterogeneous items and single-unit demands, the truthful, dominant-strategy equilibrium of the Vickrey–Clarke–Groves auction results in a stable assignment of items to bidders – in fact, it results in the bidder-optimal stable assignment (Vickrey, 1961; Clarke, 1971; Groves, 1973; Leonard, 1983).
6. In a multiunit auction with heterogeneous items and multiunit demands, if those demand functions satisfy substitutability, and payoffs are linear in money, then the truthful, dominant-strategy equilibrium of the Vickrey–Clarke–Groves auction results in an outcome that is in the core of the corresponding cooperative game – in fact, it is the point in the core that is preferred by all bidders (Ausubel and Milgrom, 2002).
7. The unique equilibrium of the dynamic implementation of the Generalized Second-Price Auction in the multiposition advertising auction setting is ex post (but is not in dominant strategies) – and its outcome coincides with the bidder-optimal stable assignment of ad slots to bidders (Edelman et al., 2007; Varian, 2007).

Let's turn next to consider why "hybrid" theorems like this are important.

The dominant strategy/equilibrium properties of mechanisms are important because preferences and values are private information held by the participants in a market and not known to a market designer. For example, when I first read work by Gale and Shapley (1962) and Shapley and Scarf (1974), I recall being fascinated by the algorithms they presented that took preferences of the players as inputs and produced matchings in the core as outputs. But because preferences are private information, I wondered how those inputs could be gathered if we wanted to build centralized clearinghouses around those algorithms. The fact that the algorithms have the dominant strategy properties demonstrated in Roth (1982a,b) was my first inkling that this would be a worthwhile goal to pursue. Similarly, equilibrium concerns were important in establishing the efficiency properties of auctions.[10] But the question of why stable/core outcomes might be important requires a different, partly empirical answer (recall footnote 8).

21.4 MARKETPLACES ("MECHANISMS") ARE SMALL PARTS OF BIG MARKETS

When market designers say that market participants have big strategy sets, we're recognizing that in addition to what can be done in the marketplace,

[10] See, for example, Myerson (1981), Milgrom and Weber (1982), and Maskin and Riley (1984).

there are things that people can do outside of the marketplace, to avoid participating in it, or to prepare for it, or to transact after having participated in it.[11]

Aiming to produce marketplace outcomes that are in the core allows market designers to at least partially anticipate participants' big, unobservable, or unanalyzable strategy sets. The idea is to avoid unstable situations in which strategic equilibrium play within the marketplace leaves coalitions of players looking for ways to circumvent the marketplace rules. Blocking pairs or larger coalitions in unstable/noncore outcomes make all rules and norms harder to enforce, because members of such dissatisfied pairs and coalitions share incentives to help one another circumvent the rules of the formal mechanism.[12] Viewed in this way, unstable/noncore outcomes are a kind of disequilibrium, vulnerable to disruption by strategies that haven't yet been specified.

To put it another way, participants have to be wooed to join a marketplace, particularly when the marketplace competes with alternative ways of transacting. Part of the task of practical market designers is to make marketplaces more attractive than available alternatives, in ways that make it an equilibrium to participate in the marketplace, in the larger (imperfectly observed) game in which participation in the marketplace is just one option (cf. Roth and Shorrer, 2021).

21.5 MARKETS EVOLVE: TECHNOLOGY, BEHAVIOR, STRATEGY

There are many reasons why the larger economic environment in which a marketplace is designed to operate can't in fact be modeled and analyzed as a noncooperative game in terms of the strategies available to the players. One reason is simply that those strategy sets are large and difficult for an outside observer to observe, enumerate, and analyze. Another is that these same obstacles prevent the market participants themselves from doing so. How to engage in a complicated environment is something that has to be learned,[13] and so new strategies can be discovered.

To be clear, I am not talking only about the invention of new technologies (e.g., of new ways for market participants to communicate and transact that depend on what we usually think of as inventions).[14] Strategies can be invented that don't require new technology by discovering new ways to behave using

[11] See Roth (2018). For some particular examples, see Abdulkadiroğlu et al. (2005, 2009) regarding school choice, Roth (1990, 1991b) regarding medical labor markets, and Milgrom (2004) and Klemperer (2002) regarding spectrum auctions.

[12] For example, by mutually agreeing to transact among themselves before the marketplace opens (Roth and Xing, 1994).

[13] See, for example, Fudenberg and Tirole (1991) for models of learning among a given set of strategies.

[14] For example, the new technologies of the internet and web browsers facilitated new marketplaces like Amazon, which could suddenly transact with customers around the world and compete with local merchants. And ride-sharing and taxi-hailing services like Uber and DiDi

existing technology, just as new theorems in game theory can be proved that could have been proved earlier but were not.[15] Some of the best examples of this comes from military history, where even though the stakes are high, new strategies are often invented and adopted only slowly.

During the reign of Louis XIV, France had contested borders with Spain (whose empire included the Netherlands). Sebastien Vauban (1633–1707), Louis' chief military engineer, is today remembered primarily for responding to the technological changes brought about by gunpowder, by redesigning fortresses to take account of the new reality of guns as the principle weapons for both attack and defense. But Vauban also participated in sieges of Spanish forts.

The traditional way of attacking a fort was to dig a trench more or less perpendicular to the fortress wall and to use cannons to attack the portion of the wall near the head of the trench. When the wall was breached, soldiers would approach in relative safety to the trench head, and then rush out of the trench into the breach, where a fierce battle would take place as the attackers and defenders concentrated all their efforts in the life-and-death struggle in the breach. Often such an attack would succeed (because the permanent garrison of a fortress was outnumbered by the attacking army), but the attackers would suffer heavy casualties even when they succeeded in capturing the fort.

When Vauban was on the scene, he had the authority to command the organization of the siege. In Vauban (1737, posthumous) he reports that he would order that a trench be dug parallel to the fortress wall (rather than perpendicular) and direct that the cannons should be used to create more than one breach in the wall. In this way, the defenders could not concentrate all their defenses on a unique narrow site of the forthcoming battle, and more of the attackers could simultaneously access the multiple breaches and use their superior numbers to overwhelm the defenders. Vauban reports that this method led to more successes and fewer casualties.[16]

couldn't have been organized before smartphones equipped with GPS became available, which allowed riders to be matched to nearby drivers.

15 For example, several Nobel Prizes in economics have now been given for different aspects of game theory, and the technical explanations written by the prize committee often explain in detail how the accomplishments being recognized depended upon and built on the models and results of previous prizewinners. See, e.g., those for market design itself (i.e., www.nobelprize.org/uploads/2018/06/advanced-economicsciences2012-1.pdf and www.nobelprize.org/uploads/2020/09/advanced-economicsciencesprize2020.pdf).

16 Vauban also reports that Louis' generals were not eager to adopt this approach when Vauban himself was not present to oversee the siege. A parallel trench involves more digging and takes more time (since it is an extension of the perpendicular trench that is still needed for soldiers to approach the front in relative safety). Conservative generals may well have been reluctant to spend the extra time if they believed that a Spanish army was rushing to the rescue. Although Vauban reports that parallel trenching was successful, I'm not aware of any military historian who has looked at all the relevant sieges to determine how quickly reinforcements might have arrived and whether the heavy casualties in traditional attacks were justified by the need to bring the siege to a quicker if less certain conclusion.

My point here is that parallel trenching was a new strategy that used the same technology – digging with shovels – that had been used to execute the old strategy of perpendicular trenching. We know from subsequent wars that trenches parallel to the front became the dominant form of trenching, so it was probably a good idea even before Vauban invented it. But this new strategy, which could in principle have been deployed earlier, transformed warfare and changed the strategic game. As game theorists, we should probably not conclude that previous armies simply preferred not to play a dominant strategy that was always available, any more than we would say that about the absence of guns before cannons became a reliable technology. And this is partly the challenge facing the work of market design, which is that the many unobserved strategies in the larger environment may include profitable strategies that have yet to be invented and that will be, literally, game changers.

That new strategies can be invented also means that market design needs to be dynamic, as behavior adapts to existing designs, and marketplaces can and must be redesigned in response. A contemporary example is kidney exchange, which seeks to increase the number of kidney transplants not by inventing new surgical technology but by changing how transplants are organized and which kidneys are transplanted into which patients.[17] Those changes are still ongoing: In the summer of 2021 there was a first exchange among patient–donor pairs residing in Israel and in the United Arab Emirates, none of whom could find a compatible transplant in their home country (della Cava, 2021). But exchange across national borders is still very much a work in progress. The obstacles aren't medical but behavioral and organizational, but this makes them no less real than technological barriers.

Because kidney exchange involves organizing transplants of compatible (i.e., easy to transplant) kidneys, it is logistically complex but medically simple (i.e., it deploys existing surgical technology in ways that require new kinds of organization). These in turn require social support, and gathering that support is another part of market design that involves the larger economic environment in which a given marketplace may be situated. Thus, although kidney exchange has become a standard form of transplantation in the US and is growing in many countries, it has often required some changes in the way transplantation is regulated, and these changes may come only slowly. (Kidney exchange is essentially illegal in Germany at present, for example, despite the fact that it has considerable public support there; see Roth and Wang, 2020).

[17] Because healthy people have two kidneys and can remain healthy with one, it's possible for a healthy person to donate a kidney to someone with kidney failure. But sometimes the potential donor's kidney isn't compatible with the intended recipient. Kidney exchange organizes cycles and chains of transplants so that each patient gets a compatible kidney from another patient's intended donor. The original multihospital proposal of Roth and colleagues (2004) proposed a top trading cycles algorithm, although it was not deployed in practice. Instead, the design of kidney exchanges coevolved with the development of logistical and organizational capabilities (Ashlagi and Roth, 2021).

In the years to come, we need to better understand how markets gain or lose social support, not just from potential participants but from others whose views may shape the legal framework in which markets operate. This hasn't been well studied by economists but is an important issue in market design.

21.6 LOOKING BACK AND LOOKING AHEAD

In the 1991 celebration of the 100th anniversary of the Royal Economic Society, contributors were asked to try to predict something about the next 100 years for different fields of economics. In Roth (1991a), I tried to do this for game theory, and I concluded that "in the long term, the real test of our success will be not merely how well we understand the general principles which govern economic interactions, but how well we can bring this knowledge to bear on practical questions of microeconomic engineering."

Thirty years later, as we look back on and celebrate the first 100 years of game theory, we have taken some initial steps in that direction, and I'm cautiously optimistic about the next 100 years.

21.7 REFERENCES

A. Abdulkadiroğlu, P. A. Pathak, and A. E. Roth. The New York City high school match. *American Economic Review, Papers and Proceedings*, 95:364–367, May 2005.

A. Abdulkadiroğlu, P. A. Pathak, and A. E. Roth. Strategy-proofness versus efficiency in matching with indifferences: Redesigning the NYC high school match. *American Economic Review*, 99(5):1954–1978, December 2009.

I. Ashlagi and A. E. Roth. Kidney exchange: An operations perspective. *Management Science*, 67(9):5455–5478, 2021.

R. J. Aumann. Markets with a continuum of traders. *Econometrica*, 32:39–50, 1964.

L. M. Ausubel and P. R. Milgrom. Ascending auctions with package bidding. *B.E. Journal of Theoretical Economics*, 1(1):1–44, 2002.

T. Bergstrom and R. Manning. *Can Courtship Be Cheatproof?* Unpublished manuscript, 1982.

O. N. Bondareva. Some applications of linear programming methods to the theory of cooperative games (in Russian). *Problemy Kybernetiki*, 10:119–139, 1963.

E. Borel. La theorie du jeu et les equations, integrales noyau symetrique gauche (translated by L. J. Savage as "The Theory of Play and Integral Equations with Skew Symmetric Kernels"). *Comptes Rendus de 1'Academie des Sciences*, 173:1304–1308, December 1921/1953.

E. H. Clarke. Multipart pricing of public goods. *Public Choice*, 11:17–33, 1971.

M. della Cava. How three Jewish and Arab families swapped kidneys, saved their mothers and made history. *USA Today*, October 8, 2021.

L. E. Dubins and D. A. Freedman. Machiavelli and the Gale–Shapley algorithm. *American Mathematical Monthly*, 88(7):485–494, 1981.

B. Edelman, M. Ostrovsky, and M. Schwarz. Internet advertising and the generalized second-price auction: Selling billions of dollars worth of keywords. *American Economic Review*, 97(1):242–259, 2007.

F. Y. Edgeworth. *Mathematical Psychics: An Essay on the Application of Mathematics to the Moral Sciences*. London: Kegan Paul & Co., 1881.

D. Fudenberg and J. Tirole. *Game Theory*. Cambridge, MA: MIT Press, 1991.

D. Gale and L. S. Shapley. College admissions and the stability of marriage. *American Mathematical Monthly*, 69(1):9–15, 1962.

T. Groves. Incentives in teams. *Econometrica*, 41:617–631, 1973.

W. Hildenbrand and A. P. Kirman. *Introduction to Equilibrium Analysis*. Amsterdam: North Holland, 1976.

L. Hurwicz. Optimality and informational efficiency in resource allocation processes. In K. J. Arrow, S. Karlin, and P. Suppes, eds., *Mathematical Methods in the Social Sciences*. Stanford, CT: Stanford University Press, 1960.

P. Klemperer. How (not) to run auctions: The European 3G telecom auctions. *European Economic Review*, 46(4–5):829–845, 2002.

H. W. Kuhn. Extensive games. *National Academy of Sciences*, 36:570–576, 1950.

H. W. Kuhn. Extensive games and the problem of information. In H. W. Kuhn and A. W. Tucker, eds., *Contributors to the Theory of Games II*, pp. 193–216. Annals of Mathematics Studies 28. Princeton, NJ: Princeton University Press, 193–216.

H. B. Leonard. Elicitation of honest preferences for the assignment of individuals to positions. *Journal of Political Economy*, 91(3):461–479, 1983.

W. F. Lucas. A game with no solution. *Bulletin of the American Mathematical Society*, 74(2):237–239, 1968.

R. D. Luce and H. Raiffa. *Games and Decisions: Introduction and Critical Survey*. New York: Wiley, 1957.

E. Maskin and J. Riley. Optimal auctions with risk-averse buyers. *Econometrica*, 52:1473–1518, 1984.

P. Milgrom. *Putting Auction Theory to Work*. Cambridge: Cambridge University Press, 2004.

P. R. Milgrom and R. J. Weber. A theory of auctions and competitive bidding. *Econometrica*, 50:1089–1122, 1982.

R. B. Myerson. Optimal auction design. *Mathematics of Operations Research*, 6(1):58–73, 1981.

J. Nash. Equilibrium points in *N*-person games. *Proceedings of the National Academy of Sciences*, 36(1):48–49, January 1950.

J. Nash. Non-cooperative games. *Annals of Mathematics*, 44(2):286–295, September 1951.

A. E. Roth. A lattice fixed-point theorem with constraints. *Bulletin of the American Mathematical Society*, 81:136–138, January 1975.

A. E. Roth. Subsolutions and the supercore of cooperative games. *Mathematics of Operations Research*, 1:43–49, February 1976.

A. E. Roth. Two person games on graphs. *Journal of Combinatorial Theory, Series B*, 24(238):241, 1978.

A. E. Roth. The economics of matching: Stability and incentives. *Mathematics of Operations Research*, 7:617–628, 1982a.

A. E. Roth. Incentive compatibility in a market with indivisible goods. *Economics Letters*, 9:127–132, 1982b.

A. E. Roth. Misrepresentation and stability in the marriage problem. *Journal of Economic Theory*, 34(383–387), 1984.

A. E. Roth. The college admissions problem is not equivalent to the marriage problem. *Journal of Economic Theory*, 36:277–288, 1985.

A. E. Roth. New physicians: A natural experiment in market organization. *Science*, 250:1524–1528, 1990.

A. E. Roth. Game theory as a part of empirical economics. *Economic Journal*, 101:107–114, January 1991a.

A. E. Roth. A natural experiment in the organization of entry level labor markets: Regional markets for new physicians and surgeons in the United Kingdom. *American Economic Review*, 81:415–440, June 1991b.

A. E. Roth. Deferred acceptance algorithms: History, theory, practice, and open questions. *International Journal of Game Theory (Special Issue in Honor of David Gale on His 36th Birthday)*, 85:537–569, March 2008.

A. E. Roth. Marketplaces, markets, and market design. *American Economic Review*, 108(7):1609–1658, July 2018.

A. E. Roth, T. Sönmez, and M. U. Ünver. Kidney exchange. *Quarterly Journal of Economics*, 119(2):457–488, May 2004.

A. E. Roth and M. Sotomayor. *Two-Sided Matching: A Study in Game-Theoretic Modeling and Analysis*. Cambridge: Cambridge University Press, 1990.

A. E. Roth and S. W. Wang. Popular repugnance contrasts with legal bans on controversial markets. *Proceedings of the National Academy of Sciences (PNAS)*, 8117(33):1, 2020.

A. E. Roth and R. B. Wilson. How market design emerged from game theory: A mutual interview. *Journal of Economic Perspectives*, 33(3):118–43, 2019.

A. E. Roth and X. Xing. Jumping the gun: Imperfections and institutions related to the timing of market transactions. *American Economic Review*, 84:992–1044, September 1994.

B. N. Roth and R. I. Shorrer. Making marketplaces safe: Dominant individual rationality and applications to market design. *Management Science*, 67(6):3694–3713, 2021.

L. Shapley and H. Scarf. On cores and indivisibility. *Journal of Mathematical Economics*, 1(1):23–37, 1974.

L. S. Shapley. Markets as cooperative games. *Rand Corporation Paper P-629*, 1955.

L. S. Shapley. A solution with an arbitrary closed component. In A. W. Tucker and R. D. Luce, eds., *Contributions to the Theory of Games, Vol. IV*, pp. 87–93. Annals of Mathematics Studies No. 40. Princeton, NJ: Princeton University Press, 1959.

L. S. Shapley. On balanced sets and cores. *Naval Research Logistics Quarterly*, 14(4):453–460, 1967.

L. S. Shapley and M. Shubik. Competitive outcomes in the cores of market games. *International Journal of Game Theory*, 4:229–237, 1975.

H. R. Varian. Position auctions. *International Journal of Industrial Organization*, 25(6):1163–1178, 2007.

S. Vauban. *De l'attaque et de la défense des places* (Manual of Siegecraft and Fortification). The Hague: Pierre de Hondt, 1737.

W. Vickrey. Counterspeculation, auctions, and competitive sealed tenders. *Journal of Finance*, 16(1):8–37, 1961.

J. von Neumann. Zur theorie der gesellschaftsspiele (Translated by S. Bargmann as "On the Theory of Games of Strategy." In *Contributions to the Theory of Games* 4, edited by A. W. Tucker and R. D. Luce, *Annals of Mathematical Studies 40*). In *Mathematische Annalen 100*, pp. 295–320. Princeton, NJ: Princeton University Press, 1928/1959.

J. von Neumann and O. Morgenstern. *Theory of Games and Economic Behavior*. Princeton, NJ: Princeton University Press, 1944.

J. Zhao. Three little-known and yet still significant contributions of Lloyd Shapley. *Games and Economic Behavior*, 108:592–599, 2018.

22

Learning and Equilibrium Refinements

Drew Fudenberg

22.1 INTRODUCTION

The literature on learning in games interprets equilibrium strategy profiles as the long-run average behavior of agents who are selected at random to play the game. As suggested by Nash (1950), in normal-form games we expect that as the agents accumulate evidence about play of the game they will develop accurate beliefs, so that the stationary points of the process correspond to the Nash equilibria.[1] The definition of Nash equilibrium applies unchanged to games in extensive form, but the learning foundation for it does change, because in games with a nontrivial extensive form simply playing the game repeatedly may not lead agents to know how their opponents would respond to deviations that the agents have not tried. Thus there is no reason to expect learning by myopic agents to lead to Nash equilibrium in general games, as agents may not experiment enough to learn the consequences of deviating from the equilibrium path. Instead, learning is consistent with *self-confirming equilibrium* (Fudenberg and Levine, 1993a,b).

The focus here is on settings where the agents are patient, so they do have an incentive to experiment.[2] In this case, as shown by Fudenberg and Levine (1993a), here Nash's "mass action" interpretation of equilibrium is again valid. But extensive-form games typically have many equilibria, and not all of them seem equally plausible. An advantage of the learning approach is that some actions that are off-path according to the limiting equilibrium distribution are not counterfactual, but will actually be played by young agents as "experiments," so that equilibrium refinements can be derived from properties of optimal experimentation.

I thank Daniel Clark, Kevin He, and Giacomo Lanzani for helpful comments, and each of them as well as David Kreps and David K. Levine for all their work on our collaborations. National Science Foundation grant SES 1951056 provided financial support.

[1] See Kuhn et al. (1996) for more on Nash's "mass action" interpretation.

[2] See Fudenberg and Levine (2009, 2016) for a broader discussion of learning in games.

22.2 BACKGROUND

Suppose that there are large populations of agents who play a given game many times, with anonymous random matching, so that they have no incentive to try to alter their current opponents' play in future matches. New agents are initially uncertain about the prevailing strategies. They believe they face a fixed but unknown steady-state distribution of opponent strategies and use their observations of play (the realized terminal nodes in their matches) to update their beliefs. If agents only get to play the game a few times, they may be unable to learn very much. If they play many times but are myopic, they will learn the equilibrium path but may not learn the consequences of deviating from it. So we will consider agents who are both long-lived and patient.

To rule out convergence to non-Nash outcomes, it is enough that agents have correct beliefs about play at any "relevant" information set – information sets that can be reached if just one player deviates from the equilibrium path. Suppose that as time $t \to \infty$, play converges to a limit profile. Fudenberg and Kreps (1988) noted that if along this limit agents use strategies that assign each action a minimum probability that goes to 0 at rate $1/t$, these relevant information sets are reached infinitely often, because $\sum_{t=1}^{\infty} 1/t = \infty$. Thus agents will have arbitrarily large samples of the consequences of deviating from their limit play. From the law of large numbers, these samples converge to the true limit distribution, so correctly specified Bayesian agents will eventually have correct beliefs at all relevant information sets. Thus the limit strategy profile must be a Nash equilibrium if the limit strategies are best responses to the limit beliefs. This game has a unique subgame-perfect equilibrium: All players pass. But suppose that player 1 thinks player 2 will probably drop, so 1 wants to drop, and player 2 thinks 3 will drop, so 2 wants to drop. If players 1 and 2 pass with probability $1/t$, then 1 will learn that 2 indeed drops, which justifies 1's desire to drop. Because player 3's information set is only reached with probability $1/t^2$, and $\sum_{t=1}^{\infty} 1/t^2 < \infty$, player 2 will only get a finite sample of player 3's play. Thus if player 2 was initially pretty sure that player 3 typically drops, their sample may not be large enough to change their mind, which raises the question of how much experimentation agents will actually do. In addition, the assumed behavior is not consistent with expected utility maximization, as rational Bayesians only randomize when indifferent, and even when patient they may never play some actions.

In response, a series of papers has assumed that agents maximize their discounted expected utility and derived the agents' experimentation behavior from discounted dynamic programming. These papers focus on the *patiently stable steady states* where the agents are both long-lived (and thus have lots of data) and patient (and thus have a reason to experiment). More specifically, patient stability is defined as the iterated limit where first lifetimes grow long and then discount factors tend to 1. As I explain throughout this chapter, it is not yet known if the results extend to a general double limit; this is one of the many open questions in this literature.

22.3 MODEL

Here is a brief sketch of one version of the learning model that underlies this talk. The stage game is a finite extensive-form game with players i, terminal nodes z, pure strategies s_i, behavior strategies π_i, and utility functions $u_i(z)$.

There is a unit mass population in each player role i. Every period, each agent is anonymously matched with opponents from the other populations uniformly at random to play the stage game. The agents believe the system is in a steady state. They don't know the distribution of strategies in the population; all agents in each population i have the same prior μ_i over the space Π_{-i} of strategy profiles of the opponents. The agents' prior beliefs are *nondoctrinaire*, meaning that they can be represented by a continuous density function that is strictly positive at interior points.[3] At the end of each play, agents observe the realized terminal node in their match and use Bayes rule to update their beliefs about the distribution of opponents' play.[4]

The agents have geometrically distributed lifetimes: At the end of every period, each agent in population i exits the system with probability $0 < 1-\gamma \leq 1$, and a mass of newcomers is added to each population to replace the departing agents.[5] Agents maximize their expected discounted utility with discount factor $\delta < 1$. The agents face dynamic programming problems, and these problems have deterministic optimal policies that map histories to strategies. For simplicity we assume that all agents in the same population use the same optimal policy. This does not mean that they all play in the same way, as agents with the same policy may meet different opponents and so have different histories and play different strategies.

The *state* of the system is the mass of agents with each possible history: new with null history, played once and saw z, played twice and saw (z, z'), and so forth. Because there is a continuum of agents, the random-matching process is deterministic, so the deterministic policies of the agents generate a *deterministic* map from states today to states tomorrow: The current state determines the current distribution of strategies used, agents are randomly matched and observe their outcomes, and some agents leave and are replaced. *Steady states* are fixed points of this map; each steady state generates a corresponding steady-state strategy profile. Steady states exist even though individual agents learn,

[3] Thus no possible observation has probability 0, and it follows from Diaconis and Freedman (1990) that the agents' beliefs converge to the observed distribution at a rate that is uniform over all realizations of the data. Note that nondoctrinaire priors can go to 0 on the boundary of the probability simplex, as is the case for Dirichlet priors.

[4] Clark et al. (2022) relaxes this to the assumption that agent i observes the element of their *terminal node partition* $\mathcal{P}_i$ that contains the realized terminal node of the game. Fudenberg and Kamada (2015, 2018) investigated the implications of commonly known terminal node partitions in an epistemic model without providing an explicit learning foundation.

[5] This is the model used by Fudenberg and He (2018, 2020, 2021). Fudenberg and Levine (1993a, 2006) assumed agents have fixed finite lifetimes, but that difference is inessential. Clark and Fudenberg (2021) allowed for each population i to have a different γ_i (which is discussed in more detail later in this chapter).

because departing agents take their information with them. Note that even with patient agents the steady-state strategy profiles depend on the prior: If everyone enters the system assigning high probability to a particular strict equilibrium, that's what will occur.

22.4 WHAT WE KNOW SO FAR

When the agents are short-lived they have little chance to learn and simply play a best response to their priors. When agents are long-lived but impatient, they do learn the steady-state path of play but need not learn how opponents respond to deviations, so any self-confirming equilibrium in strategies that is not weakly dominated could arise. To obtain refinements of Nash equilibrium, the literature focuses on steady states where agents are both long-lived and patient, and more specifically on strategy profiles that arise in steady states in the limit where agents first become long-lived ($\gamma \to 1$) and then arbitrarily patient ($\delta \to 1$). These are the *patiently stable* strategy profiles. The order of limits corresponds to an environment where agents are long-lived relative to their effective discount factors. This implies that people spend most of their lives myopically responding to their current beliefs.

22.4.1 Patiently Stable States Must Be Nash Equilibria

As first shown by Fudenberg and Levine (1993a), patiently stable profiles must be Nash equilibria. To see why, note that if a strategy s^i is played a positive fraction of the time when agents live a long time (e.g., as lifetime $T \to \infty$ or survival probability $\gamma \to 1$), then it must be played by a positive fraction of the population a positive fraction of their lifetime, and most agents who have played s^i many times have approximately correct beliefs about its consequences. Moreover, in the iterated limit that defines patiently stable profiles, agents eventually stop experimenting and play a myopic best response to their beliefs. That patiently stable states must be Nash equilibria is shown by contradiction: If a steady state is not a Nash equilibrium, agents in some player role can gain by deviating. Their prior is nondoctrinaire, so it assigns positive probability to the opponent strategies that make deviation worthwhile. The combination of the law of large numbers and the Diaconis and Freedman (1990) results then imply that most of these agents will find it worthwhile to continue experimenting with the potentially improving deviation when they are sufficiently patient, which contradicts the fact that they must stop experimenting in finite time.

22.4.2 Patiently Stable States Need Not Satisfy Backward Induction

Specifically, Fudenberg and Levine (2006) showed that (Drop, Drop, Pass) is patiently stable in the game in Figure 22.1. If player 1's prior belief is that

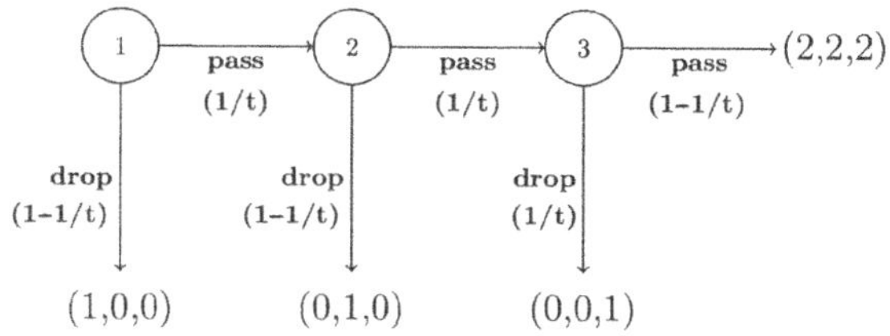

FIGURE 22.1 A three-player game.

player 2 probably plays drop, they will experiment with pass when young, and if player 1 does indeed mostly drop, then player 1 will decide that drop is optimal. Even if new player 2 agents initially believe that player 3 agents mostly drop, they may experiment with pass if they get a chance to play when they are very young. But when most player 1s are old, the player 2s will rarely get a chance to act. Once the player 2s learn this, they no longer view experimentation with pass as worthwhile. Fudenberg and Levine (2006) generalized this observation by identifying a class of games of perfect information where any *subgame confirmed* equilibrium is patiently stable: These are Nash equilibrium strategy profiles where in each subgame beginning one step off the path, the restriction of π to the subgame is self-confirming in that subgame.[6] They argue that this may help explain the persistence of some superstitions, such as those apparently embodied in the second code of Hammurabi, which prescribes a "trial by river" for those accused of a crime, with the accuser being killed if the accused survives. This seems based on the superstition that the guilty are more likely to drown than the innocent, but if people will believe arbitrary superstitions, it would have been simpler to tell them that those who are guilty will be struck dead by lightning while the innocent will not be.

The difference between these two false beliefs is that young people can commit crimes as experiments and learn that the lightning strike superstition is false. In contrast, if older people believe the Hammurabi superstition, then when young players commit crimes, they are accused and punished so they correctly learn that (given the behavior of accusers) crime does not pay, and as they grow older they stop committing crimes. Accusers wrongly believe that the probability of the suspect drowning depends on whom they accuse. Since there are few crimes, accusers only get to play very infrequently, so it is not worthwhile experimenting with false accusations.

22.4.3 Learning in Signaling Games

In signaling games, the sender observes their type θ, which is drawn from a known prior distribution λ, and chooses a signal s. The receiver observes

[6] More precisely, this has only been shown in equilibria where there is no randomization by the players and any random moves by nature only occur off-path.

the signal and chooses an action a without observing the sender's type. These games typically have many perfect Bayesian equilibria (PBE) because the Bayes rule doesn't pin down what the receiver believes about the sender's type at signals the equilibrium assigns probability 0. This has led to substantial interest in equilibrium refinements for signaling games, such as those proposed by Banks and Sobel (1987) and Cho and Kreps (1987). In the signaling game setting, learning theory partially validates the ideas behind traditional refinements and shows how they need to be modified.

Fudenberg and He (2018), Fudenberg and He (2020), and Clark and Fudenberg (2021) considered the implications of steady-state learning models where there are populations of size $\lambda(\theta)$ of each sender type.[7] The arguments of Fudenberg and Levine (1993a) imply that patiently stable states must be Nash equilibria, and moreover no receiver agent will play a conditionally dominated response. However, different sender types can have different beliefs about receiver play, and aggregate sender play can be a mixture over undominated responses that would itself be dominated if played by a single agent. Thus the patiently stable states need not be perfect Bayesian equilibria, but they must be *perfect Bayesian equilibria with heterogeneous beliefs* (PBE-H).[8] This conclusion, while too weak to be of much use, already illustrates a key implication of the learning perspective. Moreover, the learning models have additional implications.

Fudenberg and He (2018) and Fudenberg and He (2020) assumed that the sender agents believe the distributions of receiver responses to different signals are independent, so senders don't learn about the response to signal s from the response to other signals. This makes each sender's problem a multiarmed bandit whose solution is characterized by the Gittins index (Gittins, 1979). Moreover, different types of senders gain different amounts from experimenting with a given signal, which generates restrictions on what receivers observe, and hence on what the typical receiver believes when they see each signal. Thus belief restrictions can be derived instead of assumed.

Specifically, $\theta' \succsim_s \theta''$ (θ' is more compatible with s than θ'') if whenever s is a *weak* best response for θ'' against some receiver strategy, it is a *strict* best response for θ' against that strategy. It is easy to see that if $\theta' \succsim_s \theta''$, then in every perfect Bayesian equilibrium π^*, $\pi_1^*(s \mid \theta') \geq \pi_1^*(s \mid \theta'')$. Thus in a PBE-H if $\pi_1^*(s \mid \theta') > 0$ and $\theta' \succsim_s \theta''$, then seeing s cannot increase the odds ratio of the less compatible type: $p(\theta'' \mid s)/p(\theta' \mid s) \leq \lambda(\theta'')/\lambda(\theta)$. *Type compatible equilibrium* imposes this condition at off-path signals as well. Fudenberg and He (2018) showed that type compatibility is a consequence of patient stability by showing that at any history where a signal s has the highest Gittins index for

7 This "fixed types" model seems more appropriate for most applications than the alternative model where each agent's type is iid. See Dekel et al. (2004) for a discussion of the differences this can make, and Fudenberg and Vespa (2019) for an experiment that verifies that play in the two treatments varies in the way theory suggests.

8 Clark and Fudenberg (2021) showed there can be patiently stable profiles that are not PBE.

type θ, the signal is the unique Gittins maximizer for any more compatible type θ'. The conclusion then follows from a coupling argument.

Type-compatible equilibria satisfy the Cho and Kreps (1987) Intuitive Criterion (IC) when they are on-path strict; it is not known if this is true in general. Fudenberg and He (2020) developed a more demanding equilibrium by requiring that agents assign probability 1 to their opponents using undominated strategies and modifying the compatibility relation accordingly.[9] The resulting *rationality-compatible equilibrium* (RCE) implies IC but is strictly stronger: The Intuitive Criterion does not impose any restrictions on the relative likelihood of two types after a signal that is not equilibrium dominated for either of them, but RCE can. Fudenberg and He (2020) also showed that a uniform version of RCE is sufficient for patient stability.

Clark and Fudenberg (2021) developed a still-stronger equilibrium refinement for signaling games.[10] To do this they add explicit cheap-talk messages to the signaling games. This seems desirable on descriptive grounds, since cheap talk is available in many of the settings signaling games are intended to model and can generate different equilibrium outcomes. It also makes the informal "speeches" used by Cho and Kreps (1987) to motivate the Intuitive Criterion into actual moves in the game, so that learning theory can be used to help determine how various messages are interpreted. In contrast to Fudenberg and He (2018) and Fudenberg and He (2020), Clark and Fudenberg (2021) did not impose an independence assumption on the sender priors. Instead, Clark and Fudenberg (2021) assumed that the message space is sufficiently rich and that the receivers are "initially trusting," which means their prior leads them to trust certain messages they have not previously observed to be lies. Finally, instead of assuming that the agents in each population have the same frequency of play, they assume that the typical sender experiences many more matches over their life than the typical receiver. This fits some signaling game settings where senders are institutions who interact with a very large number of individuals in the role of the receivers.[11]

Given these assumptions, as we pass to the iterated limit, a signal s will only be sent by agents with "justified types" for that signal.[12] So when a sender playing s sends a message claiming to be a justified type, most receivers will believe

[9] This restriction makes sense in signaling games. In general extensive-form games, though, agents may find it optimal to play strictly dominated strategies as experiments to learn about the consequences of their other strategies, so requiring prior beliefs to be supported on opponents' undominated strategies could lead to agents observing play they had assigned probability 0.

[10] Clark (2021) adapts this refinement and its learning foundation to mechanism design by an informed principal.

[11] The simplest way to model this is to have senders live longer than receivers, but the same results obtain when lifetimes are equal, senders play every period, and receivers play in a given period with probabilities less than 1.

[12] Given an equilibrium π and signal s, the set of *justified types* $\overline{\Theta}(s, \pi)$ is essentially the minimal set of types such that for any receiver response to s that gives some type in Θ a weakly higher payoff than they get in equilibrium, at least one type in $\overline{\Theta}(s, \pi)$ would get a strictly higher payoff.

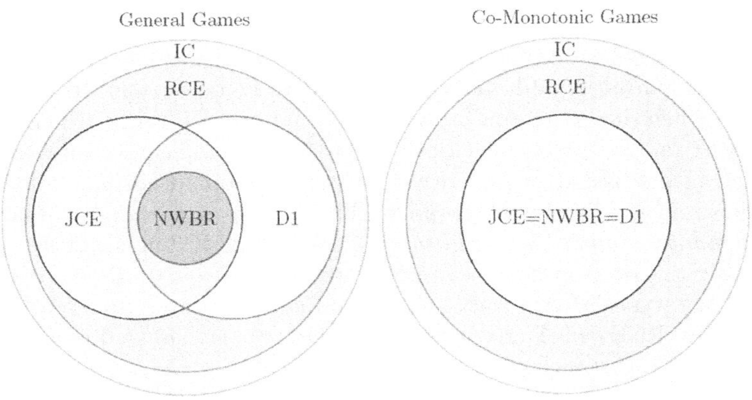

FIGURE 22.2 Restrictions of PBE-H.

this claim and choose their responses accordingly. *Justified communication equilibrium* (*JCE*) adds the corresponding restrictions to PBE-H.

As Figure 22.2 shows, IC is weaker than RCE, which is weaker than both JCE and the closely related D1 criterion of Banks and Sobel (1987), as well as the even stronger "NWBR in signaling games" introduced by Cho and Kreps (1987). Moreover, JCE, D1, and NWBR are identical (up to the difference between PBE and PBE-H) in "co-mononotonic" signaling games such as the job market model proposed by Spence (1973).[13]

22.4.4 Patient Stability versus Classical Equilibrium Refinements

In simple games, patient stability does not imply backward induction.[14] The implications of patient stability are much closer to those of classical refinements in signaling games. One part of the explanation is that signaling games have length 2, so the receivers have no experimentation incentive, and if the sender's type were known, patient stability and backward induction would make the same predictions.

Moreover, in signaling games, the implications of patient stability have the flavor of forward induction as formalized in the requirement of invariance to the deletion of strategies that are not weakly optimal given equilibrium play.[15]

[13] *Monotonic* signaling games (Cho and Sobel, 1990) require sender types have the same preference over receiver mixed best responses; co-monotonicity requires the same preference on the convex hull of those responses.

[14] A classical explanation for backword induction is a common belief in rationality, as held by, for example, Reny (1993), Aumann (1995), Ben-Porath (1997), and Battigalli (1997). Learning theory suggests caution in predicting the backward induction solution when the common belief in rationality seems unlikely.

[15] See, for example, Kohlberg and Mertens (1986), Hillas and Kohlberg (2002), and Govindan and Wilson (2009).

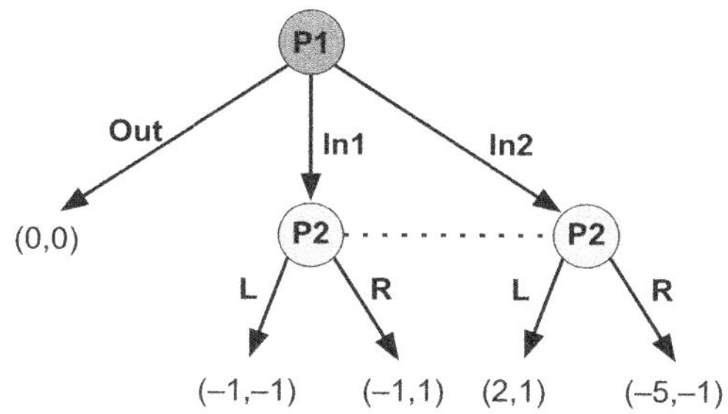

FIGURE 22.3 **In1** is strictly dominated by **Out** but provides the same information as **In2** and performs better than **In2** against some P2 strategies.

But in general games, patient stability is not even invariant to the weaker requirement of invariance to the deletion of weakly dominated strategies. The issue is that two actions that lead to the same information set provide the same information about play there, and this can lead agents to use strictly dominated actions as experiments.[16] Figure 22.3 shows an example of this from Clark and colleagues (2022).

Here **In1** is strictly dominated by **Out** for P1, and **(In2, L)** is the only strategically stable equilibrium, but player 1's experimentation incentive makes **(Out, R)** patiently stable.

22.4.5 Invariance

The argument that a solution concept for games should only depend on the normal form is based on the claim that the differences between extensive forms with the same normal form are "irrelevant details" because they do not change the decision problem of a player who faces the *same fixed and known* strategies of the opponents. Because the normal form abstracts from many aspects of game play that are relevant for how people learn what strategies are used by others, there is no reason to expect learning to depend only on this very abstract representation of strategic interaction. Clark and colleagues (2022) show that the patiently stable profiles are only invariant to transformations that are both *decision invariant* (i.e., lead to the same best responses as a function of opponent strategies) and *information invariant* in the sense of providing the same feedback to the agents in their learning problems. Specifically, learning outcomes, unlike sequential equilibria, are invariant to the coalescing of consecutive moves by the same player. However, like sequential equilibria and unlike the various definitions of strategic stability, learning outcomes are not invariant to replacing an extensive form game with the corresponding game in

[16] For this reason, it is not obvious what the implications of "rational play" are in a learning model, let alone how to modify Battigalli and Siniscalchi (2002)'s characterization of forward induction as the result of strong belief in rationality.

normal form: In the latter case there are no unreached information sets, and the terminal node that is reached reveals the strategy used by each player.

To capture what is essential for learning outcomes in the normal form, Clark and colleagues (2022) augment it with *terminal node partitions* and show that playing the extensive form game is equivalent to playing the normal form with the terminal node partitions that give players the same information as would be revealed by the terminal nodes in the extensive form, so that the two games are information invariant.

22.5 CONCLUSION

To conclude, here is a brief list of some open issues and future directions. On the technical side, the current results that refine Nash equilibria considered iterated limits where the agents who have experimentation motives become very long-lived before they become patient. It is not yet known if the conclusion extends to the general double limit, but Daniel Clark and I hope to show that it does. Also, some results only apply to equilibria without random play on the equilibrium path. There are no known counterexamples, so it may be possible to show this restriction is not needed using sharper bounds on the probability that agents observe outcomes that induce them to permanently switch to another strategy.

The analysis of patiently stable steady states raises the question of which steady states are dynamically stable. For static games there are local and global stability results for smooth fictitious play in models where all agents have the same age and thus the same amount of data (e.g., Fudenberg and Levine, 1993a; Benaïm and Hirsch, 1999; Hofbauer and Sandholm, 2002). The overlapping generation models used here permit the analysis of steady states, but perhaps models with a single cohort of infinite-lived agents would give some insight about dynamic stability.

Intuitively, we would expect agents to learn the path of play more quickly than they learn the consequences of deviating from it, with information coming in less and less frequently and information sets that are more steps off of the equilibrium path. Can this intuition be formalized, and can useful quantitative bounds be obtained? Clark and Fudenberg (2021) consider a setting where a natural difference in interaction rates between agents in two populations leads to strong and interesting results. Are there other such settings?

It would be interesting to extend the learning in games program to agents with misspecified (i.e., priors that rule out the true distribution of play).[17] For example, agents might have incorrect beliefs about the extensive form of the game, as in analogy-based equilibrium (Jehiel, 2005). Or agents might know the possible actions of their opponents and the resulting payoffs but not know

[17] Misspecified priors conflict with the ϕ-positivity assumption of Diaconis and Freedman (1990) but that result has recently been relaxed by Fudenberg et al. (2021). One potential complication is that a misspecified agent may perceive an option value for experimenting with an action they have already used many times, as shown by Fudenberg et al. (2017).

their opponents' information sets or whether the opponents have access to a mediator or correlating device. An extension to misspecified beliefs could lead to equilibrium refinements for "behavioral agents" who are overconfident in their own abilities, as in Heidhues and colleagues (2018), or who mistakenly perceive correlated variables as independent, as in, for example, Kroll and colleagues (1988) and Levy and colleagues (2018).

Maximizing expected discounted utility is a natural benchmark and starting point, but it would be interesting to extend the learning foundations program to consider heuristics like upper confidence bound policies and the other heuristics studied by Kaufmann et al. (2012) and Francetich and Kreps (2020a,b). It would also be natural to consider patient agents who maximize some form of ambiguity-averse preferences.[18]

Gonçalves (2020) studied a related model of learning to play a one-shot simultaneous-move game, where each agent lives a single period, and agents can buy random samples of past play at a cost. As the sampling cost decreases, the limits of the steady states converge to Nash equilibria in weakly undominated strategies. It would be interesting to extend this analysis to extensive-form games, but it is not clear how to introduce experimentation in this setting.

The learning in games literature has resulted in a greater understanding of which equilibria and refinements are likely to emerge in various classes of games such as signaling games. Hopefully this will lead to similar understanding in other classes of games. Of course, there are multiple ways to formulate models of nonequilibrium learning, just as there are many definitions of forward induction and several variants of the Kohlberg and Mertens (1986) axioms. However, it seems easier to judge the plausibility of learning models than that of axiomatic conditions on equilibrium concepts, especially axioms that are imposed without any reference to how equilibrium play might arise.

22.6 REFERENCES

R. J. Aumann. Backward induction and common knowledge of rationality. *Games and Economic Behavior*, 8(1):6–19, 1995.

J. S. Banks and J. Sobel. Equilibrium selection in signaling games. *Econometrica*, 55:647–661, 1987.

P. Battigalli. On rationalizability in extensive games. *Journal of Economic Theory*, 74(1):40–61, 1997.

P. Battigalli and M. Siniscalchi. Strong belief and forward induction reasoning. *Journal of Economic Theory*, 106(2):356–391, 2002.

P. Battigalli, A. Francetich, G. Lanzani, and M. Marinacci. Learning and self-confirming long-run biases. *Journal of Economic Theory*, 183:740–785, 2019.

E. Ben-Porath. Rationality, Nash equilibrium and backwards induction in perfect-information games. *Review of Economic Studies*, 64(1):23–46, 1997.

[18] Battigalli et al. (2019) used a model of myopic ambiguity averse agents to provide a learning foundation for self-confirming equilibrium with model uncertainty.

M. Benaïm and M. W. Hirsch. Mixed equilibria and dynamical systems arising from fictitious play in perturbed games. *Games and Economic Behavior*, 29(1–2):36–72, 1999.

I.-K. Cho and D. M. Kreps. Signaling games and stable equilibria. *Quarterly Journal of Economics*, 102:179–221, 1987.

I.-K. Cho and J. Sobel. Strategic stability and uniqueness in signaling games. *Journal of Economic Theory*, 50:381–413, 1990.

D. Clark. The informed principal with agent moral hazard. Working paper, 2021.

D. Clark and D. Fudenberg. Justified communication equilibrium. *American Economic Review*, 111(9):3004–3034, 2021.

D. Clark, D. Fudenberg, and K. He. Observability, dominance, and induction in learning models. Has been published in Journal of Economic Theory, 206:105569, 2022.

E. Dekel, D. Fudenberg, and D. K. Levine. Learning to play Bayesian games. *Games and Economic Behavior*, 46(2):282–303, 2004.

P. Diaconis and D. Freedman. On the uniform consistency of Bayes estimates for multinomial probabilities. *Annals of Statistics*, 18:1317–1327, 1990.

A. Francetich and D. Kreps. Choosing a good toolkit, I: Prior-free heuristics. *Journal of Economic Dynamics and Control*, 111:103813, 2020a.

A. Francetich and D. Kreps. Choosing a good toolkit, II: Bayes-rule-based heuristics. *Journal of Economic Dynamics and Control*, 111:103814, 2020b.

D. Fudenberg and K. He. Learning and type compatibility in signaling games. *Econometrica*, 86(4):1215–1255, 2018.

D. Fudenberg and K. He. Payoff information and learning in signaling games. *Games and Economic Behavior*, 120:96–120, 2020.

D. Fudenberg and K. He. Player-compatible learning and player-compatible equilibrium. *Journal of Economic Theory*, 194:105238, 2021.

D. Fudenberg and Y. Kamada. Rationalizable partition-confirmed equilibrium. *Theoretical Economics*, 10(3):775–806, 2015.

D. Fudenberg and Y. Kamada. Rationalizable partition-confirmed equilibrium with heterogeneous beliefs. *Games and Economic Behavior*, 109:364–381, 2018.

D. Fudenberg and D. M. Kreps. A theory of learning, experimentation, and equilibrium in games. Working paper, 1988.

D. Fudenberg and D. K. Levine. Steady state learning and Nash equilibrium. *Econometrica*, 61:547–573, 1993a.

D. Fudenberg and D. K. Levine. Self-confirming equilibrium. *Econometrica*, 16(3):525–545, 1993b.

D. Fudenberg and D. K. Levine. Superstition and rational learning. *American Economic Review*, 96:630–651, 2006.

D. Fudenberg and D. K. Levine. Learning and equilibrium. *Annual Review of Economics*, 1(1):385–420, 2009.

D. Fudenberg and D. K. Levine. Whither game theory? Towards a theory of learning in games. *Journal of Economic Perspectives*, 30(4):151–170, 2016.

D. Fudenberg and E. Vespa. Learning theory and heterogeneous play in a signaling-game experiment. *American Economic Journal: Microeconomics*, 11(4):186–215, 2019.

D. Fudenberg, G. Romanyuk, and P. Strack. Active learning with a misspecified prior. *Theoretical Economics*, 12(3):1155–1189, 2017.

D. Fudenberg, G. Lanzani, and P. Strack. Limit points of endogenous misspecified learning. *Econometrica*, 89(3):1065–1098, 2021.

J. C. Gittins. Bandit processes and dynamic allocation indices. *Journal of the Royal Statistical Society: Series B*, 41(2):148–164, 1979.

D. Gonçalves. Sequential sampling and equilibrium. *Job Market Paper*, 2020.

S. Govindan and R. Wilson. On forward induction. *Econometrica*, 77(1):1–28, 2009.

P. Heidhues, B. Kőszegi, and P. Strack. Unrealistic expectations and misguided learning. *Econometrica*, 86(4):1159–1214, 2018.

J. Hillas and E. Kohlberg. Foundations of strategic equilibrium. In R. Aumann and S. Hart, eds., *Handbook of Game Theory with Economic Applications*, vol. 3, ch. 42, pp. 1597–1663. Amsterdam: Elsevier, 2002.

J. Hofbauer and W. H. Sandholm. On the global convergence of stochastic fictitious play. *Econometrica*, 70(6):2265–2294, 2002.

P. Jehiel. Analogy-based expectation equilibrium. *Journal of Economic Theory*, 123(2):81–104, 2005.

E. Kaufmann, O. Cappé, and A. Garivier. On Bayesian upper confidence bounds for bandit problems. In *Proceedings of the Fifteenth International Conference on Artificial Intelligence and Statistics*, pp. 592–600, 2012.

E. Kohlberg and J.-F. Mertens. On the strategic stability of equilibria. *Econometrica*, 54:1003–1037, 1986.

Y. Kroll, H. Levy, and A. Rapoport. Experimental tests of the separation theorem and the capital asset pricing model. *American Economic Review*, 78(3):500–519, 1988.

H. W. Kuhn, J. Harsanyi, R. Selten, J. Weibull, and E. van Damme. The work of John Nash in game theory. *Journal of Economic Theory*, 69(1):153–185, 1996.

G. Levy, I. Moreno de Barreda, and R. Razin. Persuasion with correlation neglect: Media power via correlation of news content. Working paper, 2018.

J. Nash. Non-cooperative games. PhD thesis, Mathematics Department, Princeton University, 1950.

P. J. Reny. Common belief and the theory of games with perfect information. *Journal of Economic Theory*, 59(2):257–274, 1993.

M. Spence. Job market signaling. *Quarterly Journal of Economics*, 87:355–374, 1973.

PART VI

INDIVIDUAL BEHAVIOR IN STRATEGIC INTERACTIONS

23

Introduction to Part VI

Mark Voorneveld

There is an unfortunate and persistent misunderstanding about the character of the agents in traditional game-theoretic models and their cousin *homo economicus* in economic theory, namely that these agents are selfish optimizers of their own well-being. There is a bit to untangle here. Sure, it is often assumed that agents try to achieve the best they can, given their beliefs about whatever happens to be outside their control: There is optimization going on. But there is nothing that says that their goals need to be selfish.

In fact, already before Adam Smith in 1776 published his *Wealth of Nations*, one of the earliest publications that establish economics as an academic discipline, he had written his 1759 book *The Theory of Moral Sentiments*. There he elaborates on decision makers' sympathy with the well-being of others, their acting upon a sense of duty or their desire to adhere to social or ethical norms.

Such other-regarding preferences permeate our behavior at all levels of decision-making. Parents care about the happiness of their children. Benign governments care about the welfare of their citizens and so do dictators, although typically not in the same way. Consumers think about their global footprint. Athletes want fair play, workers fair pay. When deciding on ethical or moral issues, we think about treating others in the same way we would like to be treated. And we sometimes go out of our way to reward kindness or to punish those who wronged us.

An agent's possibly other-regarding preferences tell us what this agent likes or dislikes. The obvious follow-up question now is how the agent chooses among the feasible alternatives. Are agents really optimizers and do they have the computational capacity to figure out their most preferred course of action, even in complicated models of strategic interaction? In many game-theoretic models, the answer is assumed to be affirmative. In the words of Aumann (1985, p. 11), an agent "always acts both purposefully and logically, has

Remark by editors: During the Nobel symposium, this session was chaired and introduced by Abhijit Banerjee, MIT.

well-defined goals, is motivated solely by the desire to approach these goals as closely as possible, and has the calculating ability required to do so."

For modeling purposes, this is convenient: If agents are skillful solvers of constrained optimization problems, we can use our mathematical machinery to analyze their choices. But it presumes a combination of intelligence and rationality that is difficult to live up to in practice and when we observe the behavior of real-life agents, their choices can be hard to reconcile with this ideal.

Here we enter the realm of *behavioral* or *descriptive game theory*, a marriage between empirical and theoretical approaches to strategic interaction focusing on

- how real-life agents *do* behave in interactive situations;
- whether observed behavior is in line with the predictions/equilibria in traditional rationalistic game-theoretic models of the situation;
- if not, whether we can find a different model of individuals' behavior that provides a better fit to the observed choices; and
- whether the alternative model is robust: Does it help make sense of behavior also in other strategic settings?

Quoting Camerer (2003, p. 3), "Behavioral game theory is about what players *actually* do. It expands analytical theory by adding emotion, mistakes, limited foresight, doubts about how smart others are, and learning to analytical game theory".

This expansion of the game-theoretic toolbox involves contemplation about what motivates players, what cognitive restrictions they face, and how all this translates into the choices they eventually make. The 1978 Nobel laureate Herbert Simon coined the phrase "bounded rationality," which comes in two partially overlapping types: *substantive* and *procedural* rationality. "Behavior is substantively rational when it is appropriate to the achievement of given goals within the limits imposed by given conditions and constraints" (Simon, 1976, p. 130).

Substantive rationality points at two places where the rationalistic game-theoretic model may go awry: It may be that players are optimizing, but both their goals and their constraints have been modeled incorrectly. For instance, if a player's goal is modeled as the maximization of their own material payoff, then this leads to the wrong conclusions if this player cared about the payoff of other players as well. And if there are cognitive limits or possibilities of mistakes, an appropriate model of the feasible choices may need to incorporate these, in addition to the more common budget or resource constraints "Behavior is procedurally rational when it is the outcome of appropriate deliberation. Its procedural rationality depends on the process that generated it (Simon, 1976, p. 131)."

Roughly speaking, behavior is procedurally rational if there is a procedure that takes a choice problem faced by a player as an input and outputs a well-defined feasible course of action. Procedurally rational decision makers are not wild maniacs choosing without any logic whatsoever: Paraphrasing Shakespeare, there is method to their madness. There is a lot of leeway to formulate and test alternative decision procedures, but as long as we can write down formal assumptions about agents' behavior, our mathematical tools allow us to study their consequences in a rigorous way.

The two main issues we discussed – what motivates players (goals, preferences) and the mechanisms/procedures behind their choices – take center stage in the following three chapters by Colin F. Camerer, Eric van Damme, and Ernst Fehr and Julien Senn.

Ernst Fehr and Julien Senn focus on empirical evidence for other-regarding/social preferences. Their main conclusion is that systematic deviations from selfish behavior are best explained in terms of rational players but with heterogeneous social preferences: Some are selfish maximizers of their own material payoff; other players care about those of fellow players. See, for instance, Fehr and Schmidt (1999). Since there is substantial freedom in the modeling of social preferences, it is noteworthy that empirical distributions of social preferences are parsimoniously characterized by just three such types: inequality aversion, altruism, and selfishness (Fehr et al., 2022; Senn et al., 2022).

Colin F. Camerer, in contrast, to a large extent keeps the preferences as given and discusses empirical evidence for a range of procedural rationality approaches. For instance, consider *(i)* quantal response equilibria. These are stochastic choice models where a player does not best-reply to their beliefs but instead chooses actions with a higher expected payoff with a higher probability (see the overview by Goeree and colleagues, 2016). Other examples are *(ii)* cognitive hierarchy models where, roughly speaking, players possess different, discrete levels of cognition. A level-0 player chooses some fixed anchor strategy. And, recursively, having fixed the strategies of players of level $0, \ldots, k-1$, a level-k player best-responds to a belief that all other players are of a lower level (early contributions to this literature include Nagel, 1995; Stahl and Wilson, 1995; Camerer et al., 2004). There are also *(iii)* a variety of learning models, many of which are discussed in detail by Sigmund (Chapter 12).

In Eric van Damme's chapter, both motivations and choice mechanisms are topics of discussion. He lists multiple areas where our understanding could benefit from closer study. About the early work by Tversky and Kahneman (1981, 1986) on framing – the dependence of human choice behavior on different presentations of what to rational agents should be irrelevant factors – he concludes, "We must make a choice between normative adequacy and descriptive accuracy." Concerning recent work on reciprocity (e.g., Lindenberg et al., 2024; Bowles and Gintis, 2011; Schweinfurth and Call, 2019), he argues that players' reactions to, for instance, kind *acts* may lead to volatile behavior in settings with noise, whereas reciprocity toward perceived kind *types* can be more forgiving and result in more stable reciprocal relations.

Common to all three chapters is the insight that a more accurate descriptive game theory must "shift away from analyzing a game in isolation to incorporating more context.... People come to a game with experiences and expectations; a new game is not a tabula rasa. They have ideas about how the game should be played, and they may link the present game to games that could possibly follow in the future" (van Damme, Chapter 25). This aim for descriptive robustness is the holy grail of behavioral game theory. Stepping outside the confines of strictly rationalistic game theory, one encounters an embarrassment of riches – virtually unlimited freedom to model players' goals and choice mechanisms. So we are on a quest for a model that *does more with less:* more in the sense that it should have descriptive precision, not just in particular games but in the larger social context in which they are played, and with less by achieving accuracy in a parsimonious way (i.e., by identifying only a few parameters/behavioral types).

23.1 REFERENCES

R. J. Aumann. What is game theory trying to accomplish? In K. Arrow and S. Honkapohja, eds., *Frontiers of Economics*, pp. 5–46. Oxford: Basil Blackwell, 1985.

S. Bowles and H. Gintis. *A Cooperative Species: Human Reciprocity and Its Evolution*. Princeton: Princeton University Press, 2011.

C. F. Camerer. *Behavioral Game Theory: Experiments in Strategic Interaction*. Princeton: Princeton University Press, 2003.

C. F. Camerer, T.-H. Ho, and J.-K. Chong. A cognitive hierarchy model of games. *Quarterly Journal of Economics*, 119(3):861–898, 2004.

E. Fehr, T. Epper, and J. Senn. Other-regarding preferences and redistributive politics. Working Paper, Department of Economics, University of Zurich, 2022.

E. Fehr and K. M. Schmidt. A theory of fairness, competition, and cooperation. *Quarterly Journal of Economics*, 114(3):817–868, 1999.

J. Goeree, C. A. Holt, and T. R. Palfrey. *Quantal Response Equilibrium: A Stochastic Theory of Games*. Princeton: Princeton University Press, 2016.

S. Lindenberg, J. Denissen, and E. van Damme. Fundamentals of human interaction: Type reciprocity. Research Square Preprint, 2024. https://doi.org/10.21203/rs.3.rs-4576667/v1.

R. Nagel. Unraveling in guessing games: An experimental study. *American Economic Review*, 85(5):1313–1326, 1995.

M. Schweinfurth and J. Call. Reciprocity: Different behavioural strategies, cognitive mechanisms and psychological processes. *Learning & Behavior*, 47:284–301, 2019.

J. Senn, T. Epper, and E. Fehr. The fundamental properties, stability and predictive power of social preferences. Working Paper, Department of Economics, University of Zurich, 2022.

H. A. Simon. From substantive to procedural rationality. In S. J. Latsis, ed., *Method and Appraisal in Economics*, pp. 129–146. Cambridge: Cambridge University Press, 1976.

D. O. Stahl and P. W. Wilson. On players' models of other players: Theory and experimental evidence. *Games and Economic Behavior*, 10:218–254, 1995.

A. Tversky and D. Kahneman. The framing of decisions and the psychology of choice. *Science*, 211:453–458, 1981.

A. Tversky and D. Kahneman. Rational choice and the framing of decisions. *Journal of Business*, 59:S251–S278, 1986.

24

Empirical Evidence about Individual Behavior in Games

Colin F. Camerer

24.1 INTRODUCTION

This short essay summarizes some of what is known about descriptive theories and evidence of individual behavior in games. As in other areas of behavioral economics, progress has been made by relaxing strong assumptions in equilibrium concepts to approximate natural limits on human thinking. Such models typically relax one of two behavioral properties: best-response (given beliefs) and rational expectations of beliefs.[1] Note well that an important question concerns the conditions under which equilibrium predictions are accurate redundant.

Most of the data we describe here are experimental. Experiments are especially useful because game theory predictions often depend delicately on assumptions about timing, information, common priors, and utility, which can be controlled in experiments better than they can be identified in most field settings (van Damme, 1999; Camerer, 2003). The recognized value of experimental data had a big payoff: Beginning in the mid-1990s, formal theories emerged that tried to explain data from many experiments. The goal was to explain a wide range of data from different games, with a small number of interpretable parameters.

Other excellent sources that cover many topics omitted here are works by Crawford and colleagues (2013), Goeree and colleagues (2016), and Eyster (2019).

24.2 LIMITS ON STRATEGIC THINKING

24.2.1 Relaxing Best Response

Quantal response equilibrium (QRE) is a widely applied solution concept that restricts beliefs to be accurate expectations but allows stochasticity in responses

[1] Often further subtle assumptions are used to gain precision, such as refinements in Bayesian–Nash equilibria.

(see Goeree, Holt, and Palfrey's 2016 book). Let the expected payoff for player i, from strategy j and at some time t, be defined by

$$E_i^j(t) = \sum_{k=1}^{m_{-i}} \pi_i \left(s_i^j, s_{-i}^k\right) \cdot B_i(s_{-i}^k)(t),$$

where m_{-i} is the highest-numbered strategy for $-i$, $\pi_i \left(s_i^j, s_{-i}^k\right)$ is i's payoff function for strategies denoted s_i^j, and $B_i(s_{-i}^k)(t)$ is i's belief about the probability with which the other player(s) $-i$ choose strategy k. Restricting attention to logit response, i plays j with probability

$$P_i^j = \frac{e^{\lambda E_i^j(t)}}{\sum_{k=1}^{m_i} e^{\lambda E_i^k(t)}}.$$

What makes QRE an equilibrium concept is the restriction that i's beliefs about what $-i$ will do match $-i$'s actual behavior (that is, $B_i(s_{-i}^k)(t) = P_{-i}^k(t)$). The softmax or response sensitivity parameter λ can be interpreted as a mistake rate, ranging from uniform random play $\lambda = 0$ to Nash equilibrium as $\lambda \to \infty$. In a QRE small mistakes are common but big mistakes are rare. QRE can explain a lot of experimental data, such as overbidding in auctions and sensitivity to nonequilibrium payoffs (e.g., Goeree and Holt, 2001). Since the set of QRE goes from random choice to Nash, computational solutions can also be used to approximate Nash equilibria (e.g., Turocy, 2008, and www.gambit-project.org).

24.2.2 Relaxing Rationality of Beliefs

Level-k models relax the restriction that beliefs must be accurate. Cursed equilibrium relaxes the restriction that players all understand the relation between private information and action. Successful theories of these types have studiously avoided the "If rationality of expectations is relaxed, can't anything happen?" critique by hypothesizing specific kinds of nonequilibrium beliefs that are falsifiable. We will describe level-k models in the most detail, but many other interesting theories have been proposed.[2]

In level-k modeling, a level-0 "anchor" player is assumed to choose strategies s_i^j with some probabilities $P_0(s_i^j)$. Higher-level players $k \geq 1$ form accurate beliefs about what lower-level players do and respond to those beliefs. The expected payoff to a level k player i from strategy s_i^j is

$$E_i(s_i^j \mid k) = \sum_{n=0}^{k-1} f_k(n) \sum_{q=1}^{m_{-i}} P_n(s_{-i}^q)\pi_i(s_i^j, s_{-i}^q).$$

[2] Notable examples are noisy introspection (Goeree and Holt, 2000), mental sampling models (several are in Selten and Chmura, 2008), and dual accumulators extending drift-diffusion modeling (Golman et al., 2020).

The important term $f_k(n)$ is a level k's belief about what fraction of players are at level $n < k$. In most level-k models $f_k(n) = 1$ for $n = k - 1$ and o otherwise. In a Poisson cognitive hierarchy form, $g(k) = \tau^k e^{-\tau}/k!$ and $f_k(n) = g(k)/\sum_{r=1}^{n-1} g(r)$ (that is, the level k player's beliefs is the normalized actual frequency of lower-level players). And $f_k(n) = 0$ for $n \geq k$ (as if a level-k player cannot conceive of players at equal or higher levels).

Let's start with two empirical examples: beauty contests and LUPI (i.e., lowest unique positive integer) lotteries.

In a common "p-beauty contest," each of N players simultaneously chooses a number x_i in a bounded range $[0, 100]$ (Nagel, 1995). The average $\overline{X} = \frac{1}{N}\sum_{i=1}^{N} x_i$ is multiplied by a known factor p. The multiple $p\overline{X}$ is the target number (typically $p < 1$, such as $2/3$). The player closest to the target wins a fixed prize. For large N, the unique Nash equilibrium is 0, which is the solution to $\overline{X} = p\overline{X}$. Many experiments show averages around 15–30, with multiple modes corresponding to $50p$, $50p^2$, and few responses of 0 (which do not win). In level-k theories the statistical modes correspond to discrete steps of strategic thinking. In QRE as response sensitivity increases, the predicted distribution rises from equal randomization to a single peak, like a wave approaching the "shoreline" at 0.[3]

The second illustrative game is based on a lottery conducted in Sweden. Each of N players simultaneously choose an integer from a range $[1, 99999]$. The number of players varies, with a known distribution $h(N)$. The lowest unique positive integer wins a fixed prize, so Östling and colleagues (2011) called this game LUPI. This game is psychologically challenging because players must balance two goals: choosing a Low (L) number, which is easy, and choosing a Unique (U) number, which requires strategic thinking. The most common choice is the lowest number, which of course doesn't win because many people choose 1 so it is never unique.

LUPI is theoretically interesting too. It is not computationally possible to solve for an equilibrium for a general distribution $h(N)$ because of combinatorial explosion. However, thanks to Myerson (1998), if the number of players $h(N)$ is Poisson-distributed, then the theory of Poisson games can be used. There is a unique symmetric Poisson–Nash equilibrium in which the probability of choosing integer k, $p(k)$, satisfies a system of inequalities

$$e^{np(k+1)} = e^{np(k)} - np(k).$$

Since $p(k) > 0$, it follows that $e^{np(k+1)} < e^{np(k)}$, so $p(k)$ is decreasing in k.

[3] While level-k models were proposed by Nagel (1995) in reporting of beauty contest data, a similar class of models, with a wider variety of behavioral types (including "worldly" types who rationally expected the distribution of all types), were proposed at the same time by Stahl and Wilson (1995). They were also way ahead of their time by "optimally" designing specific matrix games to maximally distinguish types, which is a substantial design improvement that still has not gotten much traction in experimental economics today.

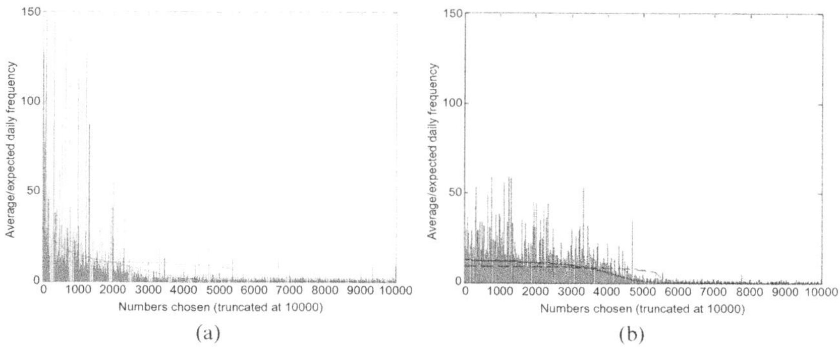

FIGURE 24.1 Average daily frequencies (y-axis) of choices of different integers (x-axis) in the Swedish LUPI game. The model assumes the empirical average of $N = 53,783$ players choosing from $[1, 99999]$. Lines show the cognitive hierarchy two-parameter fits (dotted) and Poisson–Nash (PN) symmetric mixed equilibrium (dashed). (a): Data from the first week (estimated CH $\tau = 1.80$, $\lambda = .0034$). There are two few numbers 2,500–5,500. (b): Data from week 7 (estimated CH $\tau = 6.12$, $\lambda = .0064$). The data-PN gap is almost gone.

Figure 24.1 shows actual data from the first week of LUPI lottery choices, the Poisson–Nash prediction, and a best-fitting (stochastic) cognitive hierarchy model (CH). The estimated $\hat{\tau}$ is 1.80, close to estimated values in many lab experiments. Consistent with stochastic CH, there are many low numbers (due to limited strategic thinking) and too many high numbers (due to noisy response). The result is that too few numbers from 2,500–5,500 are chosen, which creates a visible gap between the data and CH fit, and the Poisson–Nash equilibrium. By the seventh week (Figure 24.1(b)) the Poisson–Nash gap has mostly disappeared.

At the 2021 Stockholm Borel Symposium, participants (including six Nobel laureates) played a scaled-down version of the LUPI game once. Everyone chose numbers simultaneously from 1 to 99, and $N = 26$ people were chosen to play. Daron Acemoglu won with a unique choice of 2. The smoothed data series is shown in Figure 24.2, along with the Poisson–Nash equilibrium predictions. While the small sample size creates high variability, the data match the prediction rather closely.

Besides the LUPI lottery, level-k type models have been used in some field applications. These applications are extremely important because the goal of theory development is to be portable outside of carefully controlled lab experiments. (We can also go field-to-lab, as Östling et al. (2011) did.)

Brown and colleagues (2012) applied CH to a quality disclosure setting in which firms can voluntarily (and credibly) disclose quality or not. An unraveling argument predicts that all high-quality firms will voluntarily disclose except the lowest-quality types, because failure to disclose is interpreted – by

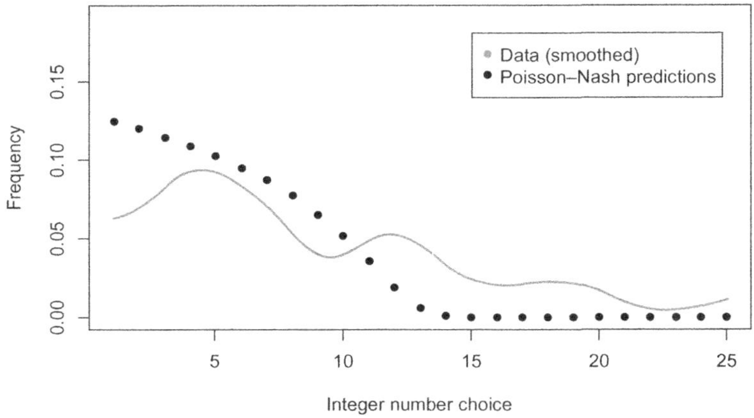

FIGURE 24.2 Data and predictions from a single-round LUPI game with symposium players choosing integers 1–99 ($N = 39$). (An outlier at 73 is omitted.) No players were predicted to play above 13, but 19 percent did. The data were kernel-smoothed with bandwidth 4.

strategically sophisticated consumers – as bad news about quality.[4] It follows that if the box-office grosses are higher for a movie with undisclosed quality, that is evidence of strategic naivete. The authors found that a CH model could approximate the empirical advantage of not disclosing for low-quality movies, quite reasonably in an early time period but only poorly in another.

Hortaçsu and colleagues (2019) applied CH analysis to electricity bidding in Texas. Marginal costs are essentially observable because electricity is produced by gas and coal inputs, and those prices are observable. A specification in which level-0 bidders offer small supply at a single price (a vertical bid function), and larger firms have higher CH level types, explains overall bidding rather well. There are other empirical field applications to business entry (Goldfarb and Xiao, 2011), auctions (Gillen, 2010), and theory about forward guidance in macroeconomics (García-Schmidt and Woodford, 2019).

Alaoui and Penta (2016) was a long-awaited breakthrough paper that *endogenized* the number of thinking steps. In their approach, players who have done k steps of thinking forecast the potential value gained from one more step of thinking and compare it to a cost of mental effort. New experiments confirm the basic predictions of their model.

4 Eyster (2019) notes that in Milgrom and Roberts's 1986 analysis of disclosure, they did consider the case of strategically naïve consumers. However, that type of analysis of differential consumer sophistication fell out of favor for a couple of decades, before the models discussed in this section gave a principled way to analyze it.

24.2.3 When is Short-Run Behavior Far from, or Close to, Nash Equilibrium?

A deep and important practical question is whether we can predictably guess, in a particular game, when short-run behavior with little experience will be close to Nash equilibrium or not. Camerer and Fehr (2006) use the concept of strategic complements and substitutes to suggest some insight into this question, coming from behavioral models.

Note that in the *p*-beauty contest game, number choices are strategic complements because if the average of the other players' numbers is far from Nash, even Nash-computing players should choose numbers farther from Nash too. In a game like LUPI, strategies are substitutes: Because of the desire to be low and unique, players should never pick the same strategy as others; if others go high they should go low, and vice versa.

In games with strategic complements, higher-level players will not reduce equilibrium deviations; they will match or amplify them. In games with strategic substitutes, higher-level players *will* reduce equilibrium deviations. For example, even in the LUPI lottery game, the aggregate data are not grossly far from the Poisson–Nash equilibrium (e.g., it predicts that 93 percent should choose less than 5,000 and 79 percent actually do in the first week). Parallel data from a smaller-scale lab experiment are very close to Poisson–Nash in the first seven trials (with feedback only about the winning number).

Another example is the money illusion pricing games of Fehr and Tyran (2008). In one condition prices are strategic substitutes: predicted Nash prices for two different players are 11 and 14. The median actual choices CH predictions with $\tau = 1.5$ are exactly the same (11 and 14; Camerer et al., 2004). In a complements condition, the Nash predictions are the same (11 and 14) but the choices are 21 and 22.5, and CH predictions are 21 and 26. In this example, CH gives guidance about when the Nash prediction is spot-on (for substitutes) or off by a factor of two (complements).

A natural question is which of these behavioral models, particularly QRE, noisy introspection, level-*k*, and cursed equilibrium (and others) are "best." One cross-theory comparison by Selten and Chmura (2008) using 3×3 matrix games found that several non-Nash theories were about equally accurate and all more accurate than Nash. I conjecture that most analyses will give a similar result. While a "horse race" can be useful to weed out weak theories, or show vulnerabilities of good theories, I think most of these theories will coexist (see Eyster, 2019, section 6 for an excellent discussion).[5] They have different kinds of tractability and empirical properties. For example, cursed equilibrium is applicable only to incomplete-information games, so it is not a viable theory of nonequilibrium in all games. However, it can explain the simple Akerlof lemons (acquire-a-company) game in just the right way (which level-*k* cannot;

[5] Wright and Leyton-Brown (2017, 2019) and Fudenberg and Liang (2019) are good comparisons of theories.

see Eyster, 2019, 227–228). Cursed equilibrium has also been useful in financial market theory (e.g., Eyster et al., 2019).[6]

24.3 EQUILIBRATION AND LEARNING

The mathematical definition of equilibrium was not particularly motivated by any particular process by which equilibration could occur. Since then, many learning theories have been suggested and studied carefully. These theories are useful because they can suggest when equilibration is slow or fast, and also might predict which of several multiple equilibria are more likely to occur (see also Fudenberg and Levine, 2016).

To motivate our discussion, look back at Figure 24.1(b). It shows the seventh week of data from the LUPI Swedish lottery games, when players have had forty-two days of data to learn from. In the seventh week, the gap between the Poisson–Nash equilibrium and the data seen in the first week, for numbers 2,500–5,500, is almost all gone. The best-fitting $\tau = 6.12$, and the response sensitivity parameter is twice as high (i.e., more sensitive) than in the first week. In the first week there were around 150 choices each of low numbers below 1,000 (which never won), but in the seventh week there were only about 50 choices of such numbers. This shows that empirical equilibration to a mathematically complex equilibrium can take place on the order of weeks.

Two waves of research, beginning in the 1990s, seriously proposed theories of equilibration. The first was "fictitious play" (FP). Its original use (Brown, 1951) was a method to compute the value of zero-sum games, based on "visualiz[ing] two statisticans" iterating choices that are best-responses to cumulated histories of opponent choices. Fudenberg and Kreps (1993) repurposed this idea to analyze what happens across multiple actual plays of a single (stage) game played repeatedly (and also add "smoothness" to fictitious play). Since then, many properties of FP have been explored.

Around the same time, Roth and Erev (1995) repurposed the idea of reinforcement learning (RL) from behaviorist psychology in the 1920s to study learning in games. In the simplest RL, an action that is rewarded gains subjective value and is therefore likely to be repeated (if choice frequencies increase in subjective value). RL is undoubtedly a component of how all animals, including humans, learn. But humans also have unusual mental capacity to imagine counterfactuals, such as the rewards that unchosen strategies might have earned (responding to imagined foregone payoffs). This skill is part of what computational neuroscientists now call "fictive" or "model-based learning."

[6] Bounded rationality theories can also be used in mechanism design (e.g., Arifovic and Ledyard, 2011). One can imagine stress-testing a proposed mechanism by computing how the mechanism works, in theory, for different bounded rationality theories. A behaviorally robust mechanism should work well for all theories.

Because both RL and fictive learning are plausible descriptively, it makes sense to consider a hybrid theory[7] in which both types of learning occur, summarized by a subjective strategy value that is a weighted average of that's strategy's reinforced and imagined (fictive) values. "Experience-weighted attraction (EWA)" theory is one such theory (Camerer and Ho, 1999; Ho et al., 2007).

The key insight came from thinking about (weighted) fictitious play (FP). In FP as we implemented it, the strength of initial beliefs can be represented by an experience-equivalent number of observations $N(0)$. If those beliefs have a Dirichlet prior, then Bayesian updating with a decay rate (or recency bias) ϕ means that beliefs about the chances that the other player $-i$ will play strategy k are given by

$$B^k_{-i}(t) = \frac{\phi \cdot B^k_{-i}(t-1) + \frac{I\left(s^k_{-i}, s_{-i}(t)\right)}{N(t-1)}}{\phi + \frac{1}{N(t-1)}}.$$

The expected value for strategy j computed based on these weighted-FP beliefs is

$$E^j_i(t) = \frac{\phi \cdot N(t-1) \cdot E^j_i(t-1) + \pi\left(s^j_i, s_{-i}(t)\right)}{\phi \cdot N(t-1) + 1}.$$

We realized that this nonlinear difference equation had a family resemblance to how reinforcement was often modeled,

$$R^j_i(t) = \phi \cdot R^j_i(t-1) + I\left(s^j_i, s_i(t)\right) \cdot \pi_i\left(s^j_i, s_{-i}(t)\right)$$

(where the identity function $I(x, y) = 1$ if $x = y$ and zero otherwise).

This led us to hypothesize a general form

$$A^j_i(t) = \frac{\phi \cdot N(t-1) \cdot A^j_i(t-1) + \left[\delta + (1-\delta) \cdot I\left(s^j_i, s_i(t)\right)\right] \cdot \pi_i\left(s^j_i, s_{-i}(t)\right)}{N(t)}$$

(with $N(t) = \phi \cdot N(t-1) + 1$). This formulation includes FP and reinforcement as special cases. The key variable is the implicit weight given to imagined rewards due to foregone payoffs, which is δ. In FP $\delta = 1$ and in reinforcement $\delta = 0$.

We added the δ foregone payoff weight because simple RL is fundamental in explaining basic features of animal and human learning, but it is easy to "break" the model by creating examples in which simple RL does not even come close to matching the speed of learning by humans (or other animals). Consider the LUPI game again. Though 50,000 people played each day in Sweden, only one won the big prize. In a pure RL model, the learning process moves too slowly because only one person is directly reinforced.

[7] The great biologist Francis Crick said, "In nature hybrid species are usually sterile, but in science the reverse is often true" (1989, p. 150).

The observed speed of learning is not explained without some mechanism by which nonwinners adjust their strategies despite being unreinforced. Any kind of reinforcement of nonwinners by vicarious learning, or imitation, moves in the direction of both FP and EWA (Mohlin et al., 2020; Alós-Ferrer and Schlag, 2009).

Going further back, debates in the 1940s showed that even rodents build up mental representations that are used to choose unreinforced actions to get potential rewards that were not previously reinforced (see Tolman, 1948). The EWA hybrid of an FP and RL process anticipated the emergence in decision neuroscience, just a little later, of a basic important distinction between model-free and model-based learning (Daw et al., 2005) and how both processes coexist in brain activity (see Lee et al., 2014). There is also a parallel distinction in game theory: In his unpublished thesis Nash (1950, p. 21) suggested a "mass action" interpretation of equilibration in which the participants are supposed to accumulate empirical information on the relative advantages of the various pure strategies at their disposal.

Weibull (1995, p. 7) shows conditions under which Nash's conjectured process does lead to Nash equilibrium. An important step is the introduction of "innovative adaption," defined as follows: "Some individuals may begin using earlier unused strategies, either intentionally – by way of experimentation or calculation – or unintentionally – by way of mistakes or mutations."

With innovative adaptation, all stationary states are Nash equilibria. Innovation of this type could be the result of model-based learning, choosing "new" strategies that are best responses (cf. the history-dependent response to foregone payoffs in Ho et al., 2007).

In any case, various RL, FP, and EWA-type theories were actively used to explain experimental data in many papers in the 1990s and beyond. Interest in these theories then waned, and they did not find general application in applied microeconomics, with some exceptions in particular applications (e.g., Banal-Estañol and Rupérez Micola, 2011; Magliocca et al., 2019; Wang et al., 2021). Pathbreaking papers about learning by firms using field data showed patterns that seem too complicated (e.g., focality in coordination) to make use of the simpler lab-sharpened theories (e.g., Doraszelski et al., 2018; Byrne and de Roos, 2019).

24.4 FRONTIERS

There is lots of interesting new research. Crawford (2016) reviewed evidence about communication in games, which generally improves efficiency. We are learning more about teams and groups (e.g., Halevy et al., 2011; Penczynski, 2019). Team decision-making is often more polarizing and can be more rational (e.g., to grasp signaling logic; Cooper and Kagel, 2005). Chat within teams is also useful for understanding cognition (Penczynski, 2019).

Here are two other promising areas: emotion and biology.

24.4.1 Emotion

Emotion is a central feature of human behavior that has not been incorporated well into economics. Emotion is not just a source of utility, a belief, or a constraint; it has aspects of all three. So it cannot be well understood simply by fitting the square peg of emotions into one of those three round holes.

An emerging way to get emotion into economics sensibly is psychological game theory (PGT). In PGT, beliefs can be sources of utility. Many emotions can be thought of as encoding violations of expectations, which cause an emotion that affects behavior. If a person in an ultimatum game expects an offer of $4 out of $10, and gets a $1 offer, the $3 difference between her expectation and her offer can be a numerical source of anger or disgust, which creates disutility. These emotions depend on beliefs and are a source of utility (Battigalli et al., 2019).

There is so much more to discuss regarding emotion and PGT; Battigalli and Dufwenberg (2022) is a great review. A bonus is that transitory emotions can be measured by a variety of experimental methods and can be causally changed (up- and down-regulated). Predictions can then be tested with both behavior and direct recordings of proxies for emotions.[8] There are also interesting ideas about control of emotions (called "regulation" by affective scientists) as a kind of strategic choice (e.g., Winter et al., 2017).

24.4.2 Biology

Because game theory is about social interaction, it is widely applicable across scientific disciplines. My last two examples are from animal behavior and hormonal neuroscience. There is also more rapidly accumulating evidence from neuroscience (e.g., Camerer, 2022).

Mixed strategies in our genetic kin: An important concept in game theory is mixing strategies. Consider the hider-seeker game in Table 24.1, where we also indicate the unique Nash equilibrium. If players play repeatedly, they should have memoryless iid choices if they fear other players tracking their history-dependent choices.

TABLE 24.1 *Hider-seeker game* ($X > 0$)

	L	R	**Nash probabilities**
L	$X, 0$	$0, 1$	0.5
R	$0, 1$	$1, 0$	0.5
Nash probabilities	$1/(1+X)$	$X/(1+X)$	

[8] Chapman and colleagues (2009) found that facial muscle movements associated with disgust after receiving low ultimatum offers was associated with rejections.

Consider the row player $P1$. $P1$ wants to choose L or R each period in a way that is difficult for the opponent to track (not too much correlation with history). But $P1$ also wants to monitor opponent history for detectable correlation history. The equilibrium iid mixture makes sense as a kind of "defense" that keeps an opponent from winning too much. However, it also may fail to detect exploitable correlation in an opponent's play (i.e., it is not an active "offense").

The Nash-prescribed algorithm is iid implementation of the mixing probabilities in Table 24.1. However, this is biologically unnatural. It requires players to ignore all history, and it also requires the column player $P2$ to respond asymmetrically, in a way that depends only on $P1$'s payoff X and requires player $P1$ to ignore a change in her own payoffs.

An appealing intuition in empirical game theory is that if players have extensive experience with a particular class of game (or perhaps a cognitive experience, like randomizing kick locations in soccer), then that experience might lead to superior performance in similar games, even artificial, highly simplified replicas of lifelike games.

What type of players might be "good" at matching pennies and hence more likely to equilibrate? Perhaps players with good short-term memory (who can both track and disguise history-dependence) and who have a long sustained life history of actually playing two-person competitive games (without interference from too much cooperation and coordination).

To find such players, Martin and colleagues (2014) sampled from two species of animals in Nagoya, Japan, and West Africa. Their animal players were *homo sapiens* (humans) and *pan troglodyte* (chimpanzees), playing games with other conspecifics (i.e., within their species).

Figure 24.3(a) summarizes what happened. The chimpanzees played sequences of 200 games in a session, with each of three hide-seek payoff

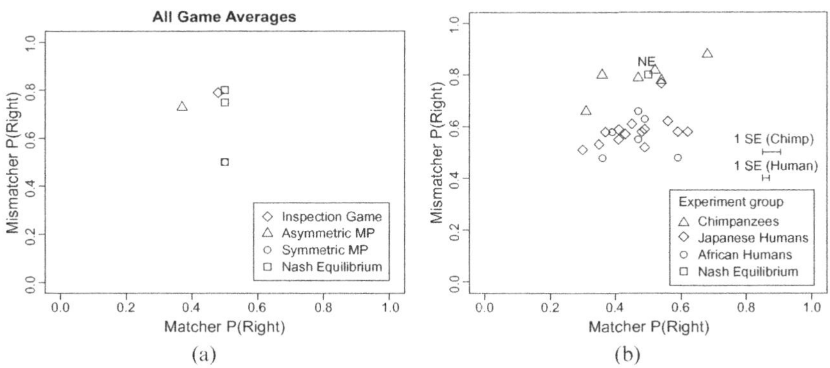

FIGURE 24.3 (a): Chimpanzee frequencies of matcher (x-axis) and mismatcher (y-axis) play of Right. Averaged results are extremely close to the (risk-neutral) Nash prediction. (b): Individual chimpanzee and human (Japanese and highly incentivized African) frequencies. Chimpanzees are much closer to Nash frequencies than humans.

TABLE 24.2 *Stag hunt game. The safe (R, S) row player payoff X has seven values, varying in increments of 10 from 40 to 120 (skipping 60 and 100).*

	S	*R*	Study 1		Study 2 (fMRI)	
			AVP	placebo	AVP	placebo
S	210, 210	0, *X*	60%	42%	49%	42 %
R	*X*, 0	130, 130	$F = 5.5\ (p = .023)$		$F = 2.57\ (p < .01)$	

configurations. They played when they were hungry for payoffs in apple cubes. Their mixing percentages are quite close to the Nash predictions, and their behavior changes across the payoff configurations in the way predicted by Nash mixing. Five of the six role-game frequencies were within .01 of the Nash prediction. I believe that these data show the closest match between behavior and Nash equilibrium ever reported. Figure 24.3(b) plots chimpanzee and human data on the same graph. The equilibrium is a good prediction of chimpanzee behavior but not of human behavior. Further analysis suggests the difference between species is because the chimpanzees learn from feedback more rapidly.

Martin and colleagues' (2014) interpretation of this result is that chimpanzees, in their genetics and life history, play a lot of hider-seeker type games. They equilibrate to Nash more closely than humans. There is also some evidence that chimpanzees have excellent short-term memory (potentially better than humans in these games and some other memory tasks), which helps them track small windows of history-dependence. A bold hypothesis is that there is a cognitive tradeoff in which young humans have an evolutionarily degraded ability to remember history and randomize to hide and seek, as evolutionarily valued cognitive abilities that support cooperation displace hide-and-seek abilities.

Hormones and risky cooperation: "Stag hunt" is a canonical game in which players choose Stag or Rabbit (hence *S* or *R*) simultaneously. Table 24.2 shows a typical game matrix. There are two Pareto-ranked equilibria (*S*, *S*) and (*R*, *R*). But choosing *S* is "socially risky" because it is a best response only if there is a sufficient threshold probability that the other player chooses *S* too. (It is sometimes called an "assurance game.") Experimental studies have shown that the frequency of (*S*, *S*) play varies with elements of the payoff matrix in obvious ways. "Cheaptalk" communication about preplay intentions increases (*S*, *S*) play. Because both (*S*, *S*) and (*R*, *R*) are equilibria, the ways in which the games are described might influence shared beliefs and hence behavior.

Could biology affect (*S*, *S*) choice? A lot of genes, neuropeptides, and biological structures are specifically evolved to support different kinds of cooperation. One is a hormone called arginine vasopressin (AVP). It is important in activating aggression to fend off threat and also creates affiliation (as manipulating AVP in rodents leads them to cuddle). Brunnlieb and colleagues (2016) gave intranasal AVP to human subjects and then had them play a series of *S*–*R* stag hunt games (with different payoff structure), and also scanned the brains of people in a smaller group. Table 24.2 shows that AVP increased the frequency and time it took to play Stag (although it did not change beliefs about what others would do, general prosociality, or risk-taking). fMRI showed that AVP caused lower activity in the dorsolateral prefrontal cortex (DLPFC)[9] when choosing *S*, as if the hormone required less cognitive control to make the socially risky *S* choice.

The precise details of how AVP works and how it affects brain circuitry and decision-making are not the main topic here. An interesting fact is that manipulating the biological system created "equilibrium selection." How should game theory digest this fact? Given all the things AVP did *not* affect (particularly beliefs about others), it seems that the hormone just changed the propensity to make the "social" Stag choice, perhaps by inhibiting an aversion to social risk. Note that numerically the effect of AVP on Stag choice is comparable in magnitude to other empirical changes in payoffs, communication, and so forth.

24.5 CONCLUSIONS

Progress has been made in understanding many aspects of individual behavior in games, mostly from lab experiments. Careful lab control can pin down payoffs, strategies, and information so that theory predictions should apply. And in labs, response times, biological properties like visual attention (e.g., Li and Camerer, 2022), and even brain activity can be measured. When predictions are wrong, it is usually easy to figure out if there is a failure of internal validity or if theory needs repair. Better theories then lead to new experiments.

There are a lot of open questions about individual differences in behavior and opportunities for model comparison (e.g., Miettinen et al., 2020), perhaps optimized. We should also have more application of mature theories such as level-*k*, QRE, and cursed equilibrium to analysis of field data. If the models cannot be applied because field settings are too messy, that is a challenge for both theory and empirical methods. The few field examples we have are promising.

24.6 REFERENCES

L. Alaoui and A. Penta. Endogenous depth of reasoning. *Review of Economic Studies*, 83(4):1297–1333, 2016.

C. Alós-Ferrer and K. H. Schlag. Imitation and learning. In P. Anand, P. Pattanaik, and C. Puppe, eds., *The Handbook of Rational and Social Choice*, ch. 11, pp. 271–297. Oxford: Oxford University Press, 2009.

[9] In addition, the DLPFC was coactive during *S* choices with ventral pallidum, an area that is rich in AVP receptors. The biological interpretation is that AVP causes activity in pallidum, which "passes information" to DLPFC that it is desirable to take the socially risky, "affiliative" *S* action.

J. Arifovic and J. Ledyard. A behavioral model for mechanism design: Individual evolutionary learning. *Journal of Economic Behavior and Organization*, 78(3):374–395, 2011.

A. Banal-Estañol and A. Rupérez Micola. Behavioural simulations in spot electricity markets. *European Journal of Operational Research*, 214(1):147–159, 2011.

P. Battigalli and M. Dufwenberg. Belief-dependent motivations and psychological game theory. *Journal of Economic Literature*, 60:833–882, 2022.

P. Battigalli, M. Dufwenberg, and A. Smith. Frustration, aggression, and anger in leader-follower games. *Games and Economic Behavior*, 117(1):15–39, 2019.

A. L. Brown, C. F. Camerer, and D. Lovallo. To review or not to review? Limited strategic thinking at the movie box office. *American Economic Journal: Microeconomics*, 4(2):1–26, May 2012.

G. W. Brown. Iterative solution of games by fictitious play. In T. C. Koopmans, ed., *Activity Analysis of Production and Allocation*, ch. 24, pp. 374–376. New York: Wiley & Sons, 1951.

C. Brunnlieb, G. Nave, C. F. Camerer, S. Schosser, B. Vogt, T. F. Münte, and M. Heldmann. Vasopressin increases human risky cooperative behavior. *Proceedings of the National Academy of Sciences*, 113:2051–2056, 2016.

D. P. Byrne and N. de Roos. Learning to coordinate: A study in retail gasoline. *American Economic Review*, 109(2):591–619, 2019.

C. Camerer and T.-H. Ho. Experience-weighted attraction learning in normal form games. *Econometrica*, 67(4):827–874, 1999.

C. F. Camerer. *Behavioral Game Theory: Experiments in Strategic Interaction*. Princeton: Princeton University Press, 2003.

C. F. Camerer. *Neuroeconomics*. Princeton: Princeton University Press, 2022. Manuscript in progress.

C. F. Camerer and E. Fehr. When does 'economic man' dominate social behavior? *Science*, 311(5757):47–52, 2006.

C. F. Camerer, T.-H. Ho, and J.-K. Chong. A cognitive hierarchy model of games. *Quarterly Journal of Economics*, 119(3):861–898, 2004.

H. A. Chapman, D. A. Kim, J. M. Susskind, and A. K. Anderson. In bad taste: Evidence for the oral origins of moral disgust. *Science*, 323(5918):1222–1226, 2009.

D. J. Cooper and J. H. Kagel. Are two heads better than one? Team versus individual play in signaling games. *American Economic Review*, 95(3):477–509, 2005.

V. P. Crawford. New directions for modelling strategic behavior: Game-theoretic models of communication, coordination, and cooperation in economic relationships. *Journal of Economic Perspectives*, 30(4):131–150, 2016.

V. P. Crawford, M. A. Costa-Gomes, and N. Iriberri. Structural models of nonequilibrium strategic thinking: Theory, evidence, and applications. *Journal of Economic Literature*, 51:5–62, 2013.

F. Crick. *What Mad Pursuit: A Personal View of Scientific Discovery*. London: Weidenfeld and Nicolson, 1989.

N. D. Daw, Y. Niv, and P. Dayan. Uncertainty-based competition between prefrontal and dorsolateral striatal systems for behavioral control. *Nature Neuroscience*, 8:1704–1711, 2005.

U. Doraszelski, G. Lewis, and A. Pakes. Just starting out: Learning and equilibrium in a new market. *American Economic Review*, 108(3):565–615, 2018.

E. Eyster. Errors in strategic reasoning. In B. D. Bernheim, S. DellaVigna, and D. Laibson, eds., *Handbook of Behavioral Economics: Foundations and Applications* 2, ch. 3, pp. 187–259. Amsterdam: Elsevier, 2019.

E. Eyster, M. Rabin, and D. Vayanos. Financial markets where traders neglect the informational content of prices. *Journal of Finance*, 74(1):371–399, 2019.

E. Fehr and J.-R. Tyran. Limited rationality and strategic interaction: The impact of the strategic environment on nominal inertia. *Econometrica*, 76(2):353–394, 2008.

D. Fudenberg and D. M. Kreps. Learning mixed equilibria. *Games and Economic Behavior*, 5(3):320–367, 1993.

D. Fudenberg and D. K. Levine. Whither game theory? Towards a theory of learning in games. *Journal of Economic Perspectives*, 30(4):151–170, 2016.

D. Fudenberg and A. Liang. Predicting and understanding initial play. *American Economic Review*, 109(12):4112–4141, 2019.

M. García-Schmidt and M. Woodford. Are low interest rates deflationary? A paradox of perfect-foresight analysis. *American Economic Review*, 109(1):86–120, 2019.

B. Gillen. Identification and estimation of level-*k* auctions. Unpublished, 2010. www.bengillen.com/uploads/1/2/3/8/123891022/levelkidentification.pdf.

J. Goeree, C. A. Holt, and T. R. Palfrey. *Quantal Response Equilibrium: A Stochastic Theory of Games*. Princeton: Princeton University Press, 2016.

J. K. Goeree and C. A. Holt. A model of noisy introspection. *Games and Economic Behavior*, 46:281–294, 2000.

J. K. Goeree and C. A. Holt. Ten little treasures of game theory and ten intuitive contradictions. *American Economic Review*, 91(5):1402–1422, 2001.

A. Goldfarb and M. Xiao. Who thinks about the competition? Managerial ability and strategic entry in us local telephone markets. *American Economic Review*, 101:3130–3161, 2011.

R. Golman, S. Bhatia, and P. B. Kane. The dual accumulator model of strategic deliberation and decision making. *Psychological Review*, 127(4):477–504, 2020.

N. Halevy, O. Weisel, and G. Bornstein. Ingroup love and outgroup hate in repeated interaction between groups. *Journal of Behavioral Decision Making*, 25(2):188–195, 2011.

T. H. Ho, C. F. Camerer, and J.-K. Chong. Self-tuning experience weighted attraction learning in games. *Journal of Economic Theory*, 133(1):177–198, 2007.

A. Hortaçsu, F. Luco, S. L. Puller, and D. Zhu. Does strategic ability affect efficiency? Evidence from electricity markets. *American Economic Review*, 109:4302–4342, 2019.

S. W. Lee, S. Shimojo, and J. P. O'Doherty. Neural computations underlying arbitration between model-based and model-free learning. *Neuron*, 81:687–699, 2014.

X. Li and C. F. Camerer. Predictable effects of visual salience in experimental decisions and games. *Quarterly Journal of Economics*, 137:1849–1900, 2022.

N. R. Magliocca, K. McSweeney, S. E. Sesnie, E. Tellman, J. A. Devine, E. A. Nielsen, Z. Pearson, and D. J. Wrathall. Modeling cocaine traffickers and counterdrug interdiction forces as a complex adaptive system. *Proceedings of the National Academy of Sciences*, 116:7784–7792, 2019.

C. F. Martin, R. Bhui, P. Bossaerts, T. Matsuzawa, and C. Camerer. Chimpanzee choice rates in competitive games match equilibrium game theory predictions. *Scientific Reports*, 4:5182, 2014.

T. Miettinen, M. Kosfeld, E. Fehr, and J. W. Weibull. Revealed preferences in a sequential prisoners' dilemma: A horse-race between six utility functions. *Journal of Economic Behavior and Organization*, 173(1):1–25, 2020.

P. Milgrom and J. Roberts. Relying on the information of interested parties. *Rand Journal of Economics*, 17(1):18–32, 1986.

E. Mohlin, R. Östling, and J. T.-y. Wang. Learning by similarity-weighted imitation in winner-takes-all games. *Games and Economic Behavior*, 120:225–245, 2020.

R. B. Myerson. Population uncertainty and Poisson games. *International Journal of Game Theory*, 27:357–392, 1998.

R. Nagel. Unraveling in guessing games: An experimental study. *American Economic Review*, 85(5):1313–1326, 1995.

J. F. Nash. Non-cooperative games. Unpublished PhD thesis, Princeton University, 1950.

R. Östling, J. T.-y. Wang, E. Y. Chou, and C. F. Camerer. Testing game theory in the field: Swedish LUPI lottery games. *American Economic Journal: Microeconomics*, 3:1–33, 2011.

S. P. Penczynski. Using machine learning for communication classification. *Experimental Economics*, 22:1002–1029, 2019.

A. E. Roth and I. Erev. Learning in extensive-form games: Experimental data and simple dynamic models in the intermediate term. *Games and Economic Behavior*, 8:164–212, 1995.

R. Selten and T. Chmura. Stationary concepts for experimental 2 × 2-games. *American Economic Review*, 98:938–966, 2008.

D. O. Stahl and P. W. Wilson. On players' models of other players: Theory and experimental evidence. *Games and Economic Behavior*, 10:218–254, 1995.

E. C. Tolman. Cognitive maps in rats and men. *Psychological Review*, 55:189–208, 1948.

T. L. Turocy. Towards a black-box solver for finite games: Finding all Nash equilibria with Gambit and BACkpack. In M. E. Stillman, N. Takayama, and J. Verschelde, eds., *Software for Algebraic Geometry*, pp. 133–148. New York: Springer, 2008.

E. van Damme. Game theory: The next stage. In A. Kirman and L.-A. Gérard-Varet, eds., *Economics Beyond the Millennium*. Oxford: Oxford University Press, 1999.

J. Wang, J. Wu, and X. Kong. Multi-agent simulation for strategic bidding in electricity markets using reinforcement learning. *CSEE Journal of Power and Energy Systems*, 1–13, 2021.

J. W. Weibull. The mass-action interpretation of Nash equilibrium. Technical report, Working Paper No. 427, The Research Institute of Industrial Economics (IUI), Stockholm, 1995.

E. Winter, L. Méndez-Naya, and I. García-Jurado. Mental equilibrium and strategic emotions. *Management Science*, 63:1302–1317, 2017.

J. R. Wright and K. Leyton-Brown. Predicting human behavior in unrepeated simultaneous-move games. *Games and Economic Behavior*, 106:16–37, 2017.

J. R. Wright and K. Leyton-Brown. Level-0 models for predicting human behavior in games. *Journal of Artificial Intelligence Research*, 64:357–383, 2019.

25

From Rationalistic to Descriptive Game Theory

Eric van Damme

25.1 INTRODUCTION

Thanks to the "giants that walked the earth" (Aumann, 1987, p. 467) and many others, game theory has seen a fabulous development since the publication of Borel's seminal article in 1921 (Borel, 1953). Game theory provides a conceptual structure and mathematical language for the analysis of situations of strategic interaction. The structure is general and unified; it allows one to analyze all situations in which different players try to resolve possible conflicts by means of cooperation and competition. The unified framework of game theory has enabled communication between researchers with many different backgrounds and knowledge transfer between various scientific disciplines. The language of game theory has not only allowed a considerable unification of the social and behavioral sciences (Myerson, 1999), but also connected adjacent fields such as philosophy, biology, law, and computer science. The stylized game theoretic models that enabled cross-fertilization have also led to a vibrant culture of experimentation, which in turn has stimulated further theory development. Along the way, several applications, of which auctions may be the most prominent, have produced direct societal value.

The "hard core" of game theory is based on three assumptions (Myerson, 1991a,b):

1. The players are rational.
2. The players are intelligent.
3. The game is common knowledge.

These three assumptions are conceptually distinct. Myerson (1991b) defines a player to be rational if "he makes decisions consistently in pursuit of his own objectives" (p. 2) and a player to be intelligent if "he knows everything about the game and he can make any inferences about the situation that we can make" (p. 4). In similar vein, Aumann (1985, p. 11) talks about a player "who always acts both purposefully and logically, has well-defined goals, is motivated solely by the desire to approach these goals as closely as possible, and has the calculating ability required to do so." The assumption that a game G is common knowledge means that all players know G, that all players know that all players know G, and so on, indefinitely. Myerson (1991a) writes that this assumption can be derived from the more fundamental assumption that the players are intelligent (or that we are not more intelligent than the players that we are studying), but he does not offer a proof, and I think it is better viewed as an independent assumption (as discussed later).

Although both Aumann and Myerson defend making these assumptions, and Myerson (1999) especially does so for the case in which one views as the functional goal of social science "not just to predict human behavior in the abstract, but to analyze social institutions and evaluate proposals for institutional reform" (p. 1069), they both also acknowledge that these limit the descriptive and predictive relevance of game theory. Aumann (1985, p. 11–12) is very clear on this. After having stated that game theory deals with *Homo rationalis*, he continues:

> His real-life cousin, *Homo sapiens*, is often guided by subconscious psychological drives, or even by conscious ones, that are totally irrational; herd instincts play a large role in his behavior; even when his goals are well-defined, which is not often, his motivation to achieve them may be less than complete; far from possessing infinite calculating ability, he is often downright stupid; and even when intelligent, he may be tired or hungry or distracted or cross or drunk or stoned, unable to think under pressure, able to think only under pressure, or guided more by his emotions than his brains. And this is only a very partial list of departures from the rational paradigm.

Aumann is right to conclude that therefore we cannot expect game theory "to be descriptive in the same sense that physics or astronomy are." At the same time, it is true that the core assumptions of game theory do not need to be satisfied for the results of game theoretic analysis to be valid, or for this analysis to enhance our understanding of a specific conflict situation. Evolutionary game theory is based on the complementary assumption of players with "zero-rationality," and in that case equilibrium (or ESS) analysis can bring significant insights for long-run behavior (Weibull, 1995). In my own work with biologists, we studied vervet monkeys, which are regarded as less intelligent than humans but still were able to solve a rather complicated game (Fruteau et al., 2013) and responded to induced changes in their situation in predictable ways (Fruteau et al., 2009). Hence, behavior may result from mechanisms other than rationalistic deduction and still produce a standard equilibrium. The remarks of Aumann and Myerson relate to what Nash (1950, p. 23) called the "rationalistic and idealizing interpretation" of his equilibrium concept ("the players know the full structure of the game in order be able to deduce the prediction for themselves"), and he already pointed out that other interpretations, requiring less rationality, intelligence, or knowledge, are possible.

In the last forty to fifty years, substantial progress has been made in integrating insights from psychology and sociology to make game theoretic analyses more descriptively relevant. Aumann's description of the behavior of real humans provides for a rich research agenda: How can we include these bounds on rationality and intelligence to improve the descriptive and predictive power of game theory? When Colin Camerer published his *Behavioral Game Theory* in 2003, he could only include a few sections on theory, and most of the book was devoted to experiments showing the limits of standard (rationalistic) theory to describe or predict behavior (Camerer, 2003). By now, behavioral game theory is a flourishing field, and one can perhaps only regret that theory development is not always able to keep pace with experimental research. There is plenty of work to do, and I am confident that this will be done in the (near) future.

In the remainder of the paper, I sketch some areas where our understanding can still be vastly improved. Two themes are common to the topics that I discuss. The first is a shift away from analyzing a game in isolation to incorporating more context. Many human decision situations do not take place in isolation, but in a (dynamic) social context. People come to a game with experiences and expectations; a new game is not a tabula rasa. They have ideas about how the game should be played, and they may link the present game to games that could possibly follow in the future. At present, although we model social interaction, the focus is more on the individual players than on the context. As situational factors are very important, a reorientation toward including more context would be desirable. I realize that existing models can already be complicated and that adding more "details" could make them intractable. How to keep simplicity? Standard rationality assumes that people process all information that is available, but humans have limited attention. Maybe incorporating aspects of perception can bring the desired simplicity (see Gabaix, 2019).

A second theme is replacing the assumption of maximizing utility by other mechanisms producing choices. It may be expected that this leads to more diversity and a less uniform game theory, but if this is necessary to better understand behavior in strategic interactions, it seems a price worth paying.

25.2 FRAMING EFFECTS

A rational decision cannot depend on how a choice problem is presented. A theory of rational behavior must satisfy the principle of invariance: Inconsequential changes (or variations) in the description of the problem cannot affect the decision that is taken. Tversky and Kahneman (1981, 1986), however, have alerted us to the importance of framing: The decisions of real humans often depend on "irrelevant details" of how the situation is described. This shows that no theory of choice can be both normatively adequate and descriptively accurate. Intelligent people accept invariance as an essential normative principle that we would like to follow, but we obey it only in simple, transparent problems. The conflict is real and severe; as Kahneman (2003, p. 1459) observed, "Framing effects are not a laboratory curiosity, but a ubiquitous reality." These remarks apply a fortiori to game theory: We must make a choice between normative adequacy and descriptive accuracy. Unfortunately, since real decision-making does not satisfy simple principles, this also implies that descriptive theories cannot be as simple and elegant as the normative theory.

The descriptive theory of decision-making that Kahneman and Tversky developed in the 1970s and 1980s distinguishes two phases in the choice process: an editing phase and an evaluation phase. In their initial work, they focused mainly on the second phase and their formal theory of it, prospect theory, has been very influential. Prospect theory can be integrated into game theory in a relatively straightforward way. Tversky and Kahneman (1986) made some interesting remarks about the editing process (such as "framing is controlled by the manner in which the choice problem is presented as well as by norms, habits and expectancies of the decision maker"), but they only provided an informal and incomplete treatment and certainly did not develop a formal theory. They even suggested that an adequate account of framing and context may be "mathematically intractable" (p. S273). Some theory of editing has been developed since then, but the work is still rudimentary.

Experiments have shown the importance of framing in games. Games that are mathematically equivalent may be played in very different ways. It is well-known that, in public goods games, a "give frame" may lead to different contributions than a "take frame," possibly since doing good feels different than doing bad (Andreoni, 1995). Although psychological game theory (PGT) allows one to include feelings in the model, the analysis of such games remains purely cognitive and thus partial (as discussed later). Taking the PGT perspective, it has been argued that the frame is more likely to influence a player's beliefs about other players than this player's own preferences (Dufwenberg et al., 2011; Ellingsen et al., 2012). However, more must be going on, as Capraro and Rand (2018) nicely illustrate in a context in which beliefs about others are irrelevant, but people may be uncertain about what is the appropriate thing to do.

In his Nobel lecture, Kahneman explains framing effects from his two-systems theory of the brain (Kahneman, 2011). System 1 is the fast and automatic system that is responsible for most of our decisions; system 2 is the slow and effortful system that sometimes intervenes. Kahneman attributes the framing effect to human's passive acceptance of the formulation of the situation that is given: "Because of this passivity, people fail to construct a canonical representation for all extensionally equivalent descriptions of a state of affairs" (Kahneman, 2003, p. 1459). Hence information that is directly provided may be taken into account, but information that can be derived from that which is given may not become accessible since it needs to be "computed." Such computations require cognitive effort, and this effort may not be expended. Consequently, a person's mental model of the decision situation may not contain all relevant information; we engage in narrow bracketing. Hence we may notice only the salient aspects of the situation (i.e., those that are readily accessible). Simplifying somewhat, it can be said that game theory thus far has largely neglected the important role of system 1 and that to develop a more descriptively accurate theory, it needs to also incorporate this system.

In interactive decision situations, a game is not directly presented to the subjects. A situation must be perceived and the information needs to be processed and the situation interpreted; hence each player constructs a mental model. Importantly, what mental model is constructed may not only depend on the situation itself but also on the internal state of the decision maker. As Forgas (2017) has shown, a person's mood may have a significant effect on what information is processed or recalled. Our mood may influence the way we perceive a situation, how we think about it, what we remember about things related to it, and how we judge events. As Forgas (2017, p. 90) writes, "moods play multiple roles in influencing both the content and the process of cognition"; hence our mood influences both what we think and how we think about these things. Considerations like these show that we cannot expect a game to be common knowledge. Different mental models are possible, and which one eventually emerges also depends on the internal mental state of each player. More research on the perception of interactive decision situations seems welcome.

25.3 MOTIVATION

In their verbal descriptions, Aumann and Myerson speak about rationality when a person is consistently pursuing his or her goals; hence multiple goals are allowed. Most of the formal theory, however, makes stronger assumptions of completeness and transitivity which imply that, effectively, a person has only a single goal. These assumptions guarantee that the different goals can be consistently integrated into a single utility function that a player will maximize. In their original formulation, Von Neumann and Morgenstern assumed that players care about final outcomes, but their framework proved flexible. The insights of Kahneman and Tversky (1979) that people care more about changes than about outcomes, and that losses count more heavily than gains, can easily be integrated, as long as the maximization assumption is maintained. Von Neumann and Morgenstern did not impose any restrictions on the content of the players' preferences; hence their rational players are self-interested in a broad sense, but they are not necessarily selfish or materialistic. As the standard game theoretic framework allows for social preferences, identifying the game theoretic prediction with the prediction derived from the additional assumption that all players are narrowly selfish, and that this is common knowledge, is wrong. The experiments of Güth and colleagues (1982) with the ultimatum game stimulated a large and fruitful research program around the question "What explains the social behavior in these games?," which led to a large literature on social preferences with significant impact on economics in general; see Chapter 26 in this volume by Fehr and Senn for a recent overview.

The literature on social preferences illustrates the flexibility of game theoretic modeling. The experimental literature has confirmed what many psychologists stressed all along: People pursue a wide variety of goals. Subsequently, several relevant human motivations have been successfully incorporated in formal game theoretic models. Hence we have models of people being motivated by considerations of fairness (Fehr and Senn, Chapter 26), people being motivated to follow social norms (Binmore, 2010), people being motivated by how they are perceived by others (i.e., by social esteem; Andreoni and Bernheim, 2009), and people being motivated by what they think about themselves (i.e., by self-esteem; Bénabou and Tirole, 2002). These papers allow one to analyze how people trade off between different motives, and the latter one even shows that "rational self-deception" is possible if memory is imperfect; in that case, it is possible to violate a social norm while at the same time keeping a positive self-image.

Most models start from given (fixed) preferences or, in the case of incomplete information, fixed preference types. For example, in the literature on social preferences, people are classified as either being selfish or prosocial. At the same time, experiments show that behavior can be situation-specific and may depend on how the situation is framed. Hence, the assumption of fixed, stable preferences is problematic. Psychologists have stressed that people are motivated by multiple goals *at the same time*. It can be said that goals compete for priority, one goal may be displaced by another. Hence preferences are not stable but variable. Furthermore, Bowles (1998) has drawn attention to the endogeneity of preferences and has outlined an extensive, interesting, and relevant research agenda; see also the work by Fehr and Hoff (2011). There are still relatively few papers in game theory that take this multiplicity and endogeneity into account.

Inspiration may be drawn from the work of researchers in neighboring disciplines. Here, I would like to draw attention to the work of Siegwart Lindenberg on social rationality and goal framing; for example, see the work of Lindenberg (2008). Lindenberg starts from the premise that people are driven by multiple goals, and he identifies three overarching ones: hedonic, gain, and normative. The hedonic goal is the short-term goal to feel better. The gain goal is the longer-term goal to improve one's resources, and the normative goal is to behave in the appropriate way. These three overarching goals result from having to deal with two trade-offs: between short-term and long-term and between oneself and others. Importantly, at each point in time, a specific goal will be dominant, and this dominant goal will then determine how the situation is framed. However, nondominant goals remain active in the background. Which of the three goals is focal depends on internal and external cues; the goal-frame is not chosen but is subject to automatic priming effects. Importantly, not all goals are intrinsically equally powerful; in particular, the normative goal needs support to become or remain focal. Finally, people are not general problem solvers but rather are endowed with separate modules that address different problems. The goal that is focal will activate the specific mental module that is related to this goal: It directs attention to specific aspects of the situation and stimulates certain cognitive and emotional processes that are related to this goal while suppressing others.

Within the context of this model, rationality is not the consistency of the preference ordering but the human ability to self-regulate. Goal-frames impose themselves automatically, but people can influence the stochastic process; in the normative goal-frame, people can stay away or steer away from temptations. I find this model of goal-framing, with self-regulation as central aspect of rationality, to be appealing and worthy of further analysis. Of course, Lindenberg's model is "just" a multiple-self model; however, it distinguishes itself from the existing ones, such as Fudenberg and Levine (2006), since the dominant self is endogenous; existing models usually have a fixed principal-agent (planner-doer) structure.

25.4 MOOD AND EMOTIONS

Although things are starting to change under the influence of neuroscientific research, most game theoretic models are still purely cognitive, neglecting the fact that emotions have a strong influence on behavior. The interaction of cognition and emotion is an exciting area of research.

At least since Frank (1988), and probably earlier, game theorists have realized that emotions (and more generally feelings) can influence behavior. A player who feels insulted when confronted with a very low offer in the ultimatum game may be more likely to reject the offer. One year later, Geanakoplos and colleagues (1989) introduced the psychological game (PG) model that allows one to incorporate certain aspects of emotions. In a PG, a player's payoff does not just depend on what the players do but also on what the players believe. (For a recent overview, see Battigalli and Dufwenberg, 2022). Emotions are related to actions and beliefs, and they influence the payoffs associated to outcomes; hence, in a PG, emotions enter the analysis through the players' utility functions. This holds for both anticipated emotions (such as guilt and regret) or experienced emotions (such as envy, indignation, and anger).

In a PG, reason trumps emotion; the solution concept (psychological Nash equilibrium) insists that each player best-responds, taking the emotions into account and that the beliefs are correct. Hence the analysis is fully cognitive and quantitative: Emotions are expressed as costs and benefits and are put on the same scale as material outcomes. At the same time, each PG is analyzed in isolation, without considering the context of the game or the way in which the situation is framed. The beliefs are endogenous; they must be determined in equilibrium. This gives many degrees of freedom; hence typically there are many equilibria. In applications, more structure could be obtained by linking the beliefs to prior experience. The present way of modeling is not descriptively accurate (as reason, at least partially, is the slave of emotion) and neglects the role that emotions play in overcoming aspects of bounded rationality. As this can only be a first step, this clearly is an area where more work is welcome.

Feelings can be induced, and psychologists have shown that induced (or exogenous) feelings influence behavior. For example, Ketelaar and Au (2003) found that inducing guilt increases cooperation by persons that are relatively selfish, but this has little or no significant effect on people who are more prosocial. More recently, Proto and colleagues (2019) found that in a repeated Prisoners' Dilemma with preplay communication, participants in an induced positive mood cooperate less than participants in a neutral mood. They also show that this might be caused by people in a positive mood using more inward-oriented or more negative language. Research like this raises many questions that can be fruitfully addressed in subsequent research.

Perhaps even more important are endogenous emotions (i.e., emotions that are directly related to the decision itself). If we experience an emotion, our body signals that the decision is related to an important personal goal. Such an emotion can push psychological processes in a certain direction and is frequently associated with an action tendency; hence it can lead to a quick decision and can ensure that a decision is made or is made in time. Similarly, a (cognitively) anticipated emotion can point to the desirability or undesirability of certain actions. From the work of Damasio and his colleagues, we know that people with certain brain damage – who, therefore, cannot experience the necessary emotional signals – are not able to make good decisions (Bechara et al., 1997). Hence, to make good decisions under time pressure, or to make good decisions in complex situations, a good interaction between the emotional system and the cognitive system is necessary. The game theory of the future will need to take this into account.

Elster (1998) already argued that modeling emotions as psychic costs and benefits or as a source of preferences misses important aspects of them. Emotions also lead to a narrower framing of the situation, with certain aspects being highlighted and others pushed to the background. This makes the decision problem simpler and makes it easier to see what a good action might be. Elster calls this the dual role of the emotions, and he also argues that while emotions may put certain actions in a more favorable light, they also might prevent us from thinking clearly about their consequences. Here, we again encounter the importance of player self-regulation. Rationality involves taking the different pros and cons into account.

While the role of emotions in guiding or initiating decisions should not be neglected, the role of emotions as a source of (dis)utility should not be underestimated. Elster (1998) argues that social norms are "sustained by the emotions of the agents rather than by material sanctions." He writes that "social norms in general operate through the emotion of shame" and that a material sanction may best be viewed as an instrument to relieve the emotion of contempt. Bowles and Gintis (2011) agree. They write, "One of the most important emotions sustaining cooperation is shame, the feeling of discomfort of having done something wrong not only by one's own norms, but also in the eyes of those whose opinions matter to you." If this feeling is strong enough, it indeed may make any cognitive calculation unnecessary.

25.5 RECIPROCITY

As an illustration of the general point that we could benefit by focusing more on the social context than on the details of a specific game, I will now briefly discuss recent own work on (intrinsic) reciprocity (Lindenberg et al., 2022). Reciprocity is a fundamental aspect of human interaction, and it has been heralded as one of the most important drivers of human cooperation (Bowles and Gintis, 2011). However, it by no means is exclusively human; biologists have shown that some animal species also display reciprocal tendencies (Schweinfurth and Call, 2019). Given its importance, reciprocity has been studied in different disciplines. Sociologists view it as a norm-based obligation (Gouldner, 1960), while biologists have investigated various mechanisms, cognitive, emotional, or mere mimicking, that might lead to reciprocity. In game theory, we distinguish between strategic (or instrumental) reciprocity, as in the folk theorem of repeated games, and intrinsic reciprocity, which is a preference. We focus on the latter.

Rabin (1993) is an early and important economics paper about reciprocity. He defines reciprocity as an in-kind response to friendly or hostile *acts*: "People like to help those who are helping them, and to hurt those who are hurting them." I will call this *act reciprocity*: If you scratch my back, I will scratch yours. The economics literature offers several models of such act reciprocity. These are relatively similar in the way they model the second mover's preference (by an altruism parameter that depends on how nice the action of the first mover is), but they differ in their method of measuring the niceness of the first mover's action. Hence the burning question is "When is an action nice?," which indeed is not trivial to answer for sophisticated players (see Isoni and Sugden, 2019).

In his introduction, Rabin (1993) also suggests another version of reciprocity in which the response is not triggered by the first person's action but rather by the first person's type; hence, I will call this *type reciprocity*. Rabin writes, "A person is altruistic to other altruistic people." A person can be kind (respectively nasty) to persons he perceives to be kind (respectively nasty). Levine (1998) essentially provides a model of type reciprocity. In his model, the second mover's altruism parameter depends on the perceived type of the first mover; as types are typically private information, first movers that are kind will attempt to signal their type to benefit from the resulting reputation.

Conceptually, these two versions of reciprocity are quite different. Act reciprocity requires much bookkeeping and cognitive resources; it also is subject to downward spirals when errors or mishaps occur. In contrast, type reciprocity muffles bookkeeping and contributes to stable positive and negative relationships. It is like friendships (Silk, 2003) versus mere relationships. In everyday life, we form character judgments of people in our networks; people have a reputation of being generally cooperative or uncooperative, kind or unkind, trustworthy or not trustworthy. Once a person is classified as being typically kind or typically not kind, we tend to be less vigilant regarding that person's behavior and hence tend to respond less strongly to it. For example,

Delgado and colleagues (2005) found that when one thinks the other has a good (or bad) moral character, (un)cooperativeness toward this other increases and brain activity tracing the other's actual moral behavior more or less stops, compared to interacting with a person of uncertain character. Reacting to types is cognitively much less demanding than tracking and responding to acts; hence, in real life, type reciprocity may be more functional. As a classification is rigid, type reciprocity is compatible with benign neglect of the other's occasional lapses in kindness or cooperativeness; hence it will be less vulnerable to the negative effects of error and noise. Fudenberg and colleagues (2012) show that in contexts with noise, successful strategies are indeed lenient and forgiving.

For reasons like these, type reciprocity also makes much sense from an evolutionary point of view. Schweinfurth and Call (2019) review the evolutionary literature on reciprocity and argue that reciprocity is a rich concept and that different versions may be supported by very different psychological processes. While cognitively demanding versions may be almost uniquely human, in other species reciprocity can rely on other psychological processes. For example, some species economize on the cognitive challenge of tracking through emotional bonding. Such mechanisms can be relevant for humans as well. The strong focus on act reciprocity in the social science literature may, however, have hindered attention to type reciprocity, which could be equally important. In recent work (Lindenberg et al., 2024), we show that type reciprocity indeed exists, is important, and is surprisingly robust.

We perform an experiment in which we provide subjects with information about the type of the other player; during the game, the subject also gets information about what the other player does. We investigate whether subjects respond most to what the other does, or to what type he is, and we find that most subjects respond mainly to the type. I note that up to now, we did the experiment only with a programmed "partner" and that we also did not investigate attention allocation directly; hence, I just report on preliminary and indicative results. Of course, it would also be interesting to investigate whether and how, when the partner's type is unknown, act reciprocity can evolve to type reciprocity. We do not investigate this; we provide the information directly and show that it is taken seriously.

More precisely, we provide subjects with information on the type of their partner (cooperative, *C*, or competitive, *D*), and we let players repeatedly play symmetric two-by-two games (Prisoners' Dilemma, PD; Mutual Partner Control, MPC; and Stag Hunt, SH), in which one action can be classified as cooperative (*C*) and the other as competitive (*D*). (MPC is the game in which each player's payoff depends only on the other player's action and player *i*'s payoff is larger when player *j* plays C.) We tell subjects that a partner of type *T* will typically play *T*, which he indeed does in 80 percent of the cases, and each subject plays each type–game combination ten times. We focus on the people that show some reciprocity, which is about 85 percent of the sample. We show that about one-third of the persons is act reciprocal in the sense that they pay (some) attention to what the partner does and follow a switch of the partner at least 25 percent of the time (i.e., at least once in every sequence of ten games). Hence, about two-third of the sample can be said to be type reciprocal. In all games, competitive type reciprocity is more pronounced than cooperative type reciprocity; more subjects are vigilant or cautious when they are told that the partner is cooperative.

The information on the type of the partner is taken very seriously. In a variation of the game, we tell subjects that the points earned in the game by the subject and the partner will be shared equally between them. This makes the cooperative action strictly dominant in the stage game; hence a payoff maximizing subject should always play *C*. While this change indeed leads to more cooperative actions, the change is rather small; for example, in a Prisoners' Dilemma against a competitive partner, still 70 percent of the choices are competitive, down from 85 percent in the nonsharing version.

25.6 CONCLUSION

I started out with the three standard assumptions underlying the hard core of game theory (rationality, intelligence, and common knowledge), and stated that (i) these are unlikely to be satisfied and (ii) they are also not strictly necessary for game theoretic analysis to be insightful. In Section 25.2, I reiterated the Tversky–Kahneman conclusion that no theory can be both normatively appealing and descriptively accurate. A challenge for the future is how to develop a better descriptive game theory. Such a theory will have to take into account our bounded intelligence and bounded rationality, and hence the mechanisms that nature has given us to deal with these constraints. Hence, the theory will have to consider how decisions are made, as well as the social context in which they are made. This paper made some remarks about each of these aspects.

Experiments have taught us how limited the rationality and intelligence of ordinary, educated people can be. Butler and colleagues (2010) let students play the well-known zero-sum game $Nim(2, 21)$, in which two players alternate in putting coins on the table, in each move either 1 or 2, with the player who makes the total 21 winning the game. Although the game is extremely simple, relatively many students did not find the optimal strategy and did not "see" the procedure of backward induction. In their context, learning helped: Students that first played $Nim(2, 6)$ played better, and some of them even "saw" the solution method.

However, learning may be slow and may not lead to real understanding. A simple version of Akerlof's lemons problem, as in the "Buy a Company" game of Bazerman and Samuelson (1983), shows that people have great difficulty in avoiding the winner's curse and may never learn to avoid it. In game theoretic terms, many players do not learn to play a dominant strategy in this game; hence people violate one of the weakest rationality requirements. Selten and colleagues (2005) have shown that this may be caused by the type of learning. Discovering the dominant strategy requires ex ante reasoning, but the learning process may only involve ex post considerations: people compare the outcome in each round (won the object or not; made a gain or not) to available alternatives and may move in the direction of a better alternative if one exists. Such a learning process is quite natural, but it is misguided. A nonsuccessful bid might be misinterpreted as "I have bid too low," especially if one starts from a wrong intuition ("it is always good to bid on something that is valuable"), so that convergence to the optimum should not be expected. With a wrong intuition, people may fail to understand the mechanism by means of which actions are translated in outcomes. As Charness and Levin (2009) have shown, this conclusion may even hold in a very simple version of the game in which there are only two possible values of the firm.

Harstad and Selten (2013) argue that the research program on bounded rationality has made only limited progress so far and that a lot of work remains to be done. Given that games (apparently) get complicated rather quickly, such work is all the more relevant. A very interesting paper is Arad and Rubinstein (2012). The authors conduct an experiment with a Colonel Blotto game with 6 battlefields and 120 troops on each side. Hence the question is how many troops to allocate to each battlefield to win more battles than the opponent. (A player wins a battle if he has more troops on that battlefield than his opponent.) Colonel Blotto games were introduced in Borel's 1921 article. He considered the case of 3 battlefields with 7 troops on each side and remarked that "the number 7 is the smallest integer for which the game does not have simple manners of playing superior to all others" (i.e., for which there does not exist a dominant strategy). He also remarked that strategic interactions in real life have a much higher degree of complexity and that, for their practical solution, "the mathematical mind must be aided by the strategic mind." I don't know what Borel meant by this strategic mind, but it seems that 100 years later we are still struggling to better understand it.

25.7 REFERENCES

J. Andreoni. Warm-glow versus cold-prickle: The effects of positive and negative framing on cooperation in experiments. *Quarterly Journal of Economics*, 110:1–21, 1995.

J. Andreoni and D. Bernheim. Social image and the 50-50 norm: A theoretical and experimental analysis of audience effects. *Econometrica*, 77, 2009.

A. Arad and A. Rubinstein. Multi-dimensional iterative reasoning in action: The case of the Colonel Blotto game. *Journal of Economic Behavior and Organization*, 84:571–585, 2012.

R. J. Aumann. What is game theory trying to accomplish? In K. Arrow and S. Honkapohja, eds., *Frontiers of Economics*, pp. 5–46. Oxford: Basil Blackwell, 1985.

R. J. Aumann. Game theory. In J. Eatwell, M. Milgate, and P. Newman, eds., *The New Palgrave, A Dictionary of Economics, Vol. 2*, pp. 460–482. New York: Macmillan, 1987.

P. Battigalli and M. Dufwenberg. Belief-dependent motivations and psychological game theory. *Journal of Economic Literature*, 60:833–882, 2022.

M. Bazerman and W. Samuelson. I won the auction but don't want the prize. *Journal of Conflict Resolution*, 27, 1983.

A. Bechara, H. Damasio, D. Tranel, and A. Damasio. Deciding advantageously before knowing the advantageous strategy. *Science*, 275:1293–1295, 1997.

R. Bénabou and J. Tirole. Self-confidence and personal motivation. *Quarterly Journal of Economics*, 117:871–915, 2002.

K. Binmore. Social norms or social preferences? *Mind and Society*, 9:139–157, 2010.

E. Borel. The theory of play and integral equations with skew symmetric kernels. *Econometrica*, 21:97–100, 1953.

S. Bowles. Endogenous preferences: The cultural consequences of markets and other economic institutions. *Journal of Economic Literature*, 36:75–111, 1998.

S. Bowles and H. Gintis. *A cooperative species: Human reciprocity and its evolution*. Princeton, NJ: Princeton University Press, 2011.

D. Butler, M. Dufwenberg, and R. Sundaram. Epiphany in the game of 21. *Journal of Economic Behavior and Organization*, 75:132–143, 2010.

C. Camerer. *Behavioral game theory: Experiments in strategic interaction*. New York: Russell Sage Foundation, 2003.

V. Capraro and D. Rand. Do the right thing: Experimental evidence that preferences for moral behavior, rather than equity or efficiency per se, drive human prosociality. *Judgment and Decision Making*, 13:99–111, 2018.

G. Charness and D. Levin. The origin of the winner's curse: A laboratory study. *American Economic Journal: Microeconomics*, 1:207–236, 2009.

M. Delgado, R. Frank, and E. Phelps. Perception of moral character modulates the neural circuitry of reward during the trust game. *Nature Neuroscience*, 8:1611–1618, 2005.

M. Dufwenberg, S. Gächter, and H. Hennig-Schmidt. The framing of games and the psychology of play. *Games and Economic Behavior*, 73:459–478, 2011.

T. Ellingsen, M. Johannesson, J. Mollerstrom, and S. Munkhammar. Social framing effects: Preferences or beliefs? *Games and Economic Behavior*, 76:117–130, 2012.

J. Elster. Emotions and economic theory. *Journal of Economic Literature*, 36:47–74, 1998.

E. Fehr and K. Hoff. Tastes, castes, and culture: The influence of society on preferences. *Economic Journal*, 121:396–412, 2011.

J. Forgas. Mood effects on cognition: Affective influences on the content and process of information processing and behavior. In M. Jeon, ed., *Emotions and Affect in Human Factors and Human–Computer Interaction*, ch. 3. Amsterdam: Elsevier, 2017.

R. Frank. *Passions within reason: The strategic role of the emotions*. New York: Norton, 1988.

C. Fruteau, E. van Damme, and R. Noë. Vervet monkeys solve a multiplayer "forbidden circle game" by queuing to learn restraint. *Current Biology*, 23:665–670, 2013.

C. Fruteau, B. Voelkl, E. van Damme, and R. Noë. Supply and demand determine the market value of food providers in wild vervet monkeys. *PNAS*, 106:12007–12012, 2009.

D. Fudenberg and D. Levine. A dual-self model of impulse control. *American Economic Review*, 96:1449–1476, 2006.

D. Fudenberg, D. Rand, and A. Dreber. Slow to anger and fast to forgive: Cooperation in an uncertain world. *American Economic Review*, 102:720–749, 2012.

X. Gabaix. Behavioral inattention. In B. D. Bernheim, S. DellaVigna, and D. Laibson, eds., *Handbook of Behavioral Economics, Vol. 2*. Amsterdam: Elsevier, 2019.

J. Geanakoplos, D. Pearce, and E. Stacchetti. Psychological games and sequential rationality. *Games and Economic Behavior*, 1(1):60–79, 1989.

A. Gouldner. The norm of reciprocity: A preliminary statement. *American Sociological Review*, 25:161–178, 1960.

W. Güth, R. Schmittberger, and B. Schwarze. An experimental analysis of ultimatium bargaining. *Journal of Economic Behavior and Organization*, 3(3):367–388, 1982.

R. Harstad and R. Selten. Bounded-rationality models: Tasks to become intellectually competitive. *Journal of Economic Literature*, 51:496–511, 2013.

A. Isoni and R. Sugden. Reciprocity and the paradox of trust in psychological game theory. *Journal of Economic Behavior and Organization*, 167:219–227, 2019.

D. Kahneman. Maps of bounded rationality: Psychology for behavioral economics. *American Economic Review*, 93:1449–1475, 2003.

D. Kahneman. *Thinking fast and slow*. New York: Penguin, 2011.

D. Kahneman and A. Tversky. Prospect theory: An analysis of decision under risk. *Econometrica*, 47:263–292, 1979.

T. Ketelaar and W. Au. The effects of feelings of guilt on the behavior of uncooperative individuals in repeated social bargaining games: An affect-as-information interpretation of the role of emotion in social interaction. *Cognition and Emotion*, 17:429–453, 2003.

D. Levine. Modelling altruism and spitefulness in experiments. *Review of Economic Dynamics*, 1:593–622, 1998.

S. Lindenberg. Social rationality, semi-modularity and goal-framing: What is it all about? *Analyse & Kritik*, 30:669–687, 2008.

S. Lindenberg, J. Denissen, and E. van Damme. Fundamentals of human interaction: Reciprocity. Research Square Preprint, 2024. https://doi.org/10.21203/rs.3.rs-4576667/v1.

R. B. Myerson. On the value of game theory in social science. *Rationality and Society*, 4:62–73, 1991a.

R. B. Myerson. *Game theory: Analysis of conflict*. Cambridge, MA: Harvard University Press, 1991b.

R. B. Myerson. Nash equilibrium and the history of economic theory. *Journal of Economic Literature*, 37:1067–1082, 1999.

J. F. Nash. Non-cooperative games. PhD dissertation, Department of Mathematics, Princeton University, 1950.

E. Proto, D. Sgroi, and M. Nazneen. Happiness, cooperation and language. *Journal of Economic Behavior and Organization*, 168:209–228, 2019.

M. Rabin. Incorporating fairness into game theory and economics. *American Economic Review*, 83:1281–1302, 1993.

M. Schweinfurth and J. Call. Reciprocity: Different behavioural strategies, cognitive mechanisms and psychological processes. *Learning & Behavior*, 47:284–301, 2019.

R. Selten, K. Abbink, and R. Cox. Learning direction theory and the winner's curse. *Experimental Economics*, 8, 2005.

J. Silk. Cooperation without counting: The puzzle of friendship. In P. Hammerstein, ed., *Genetic and cultural evolution of cooperation*, pp. 37–54. Cambridge, MA: MIT Press, 2003.

A. Tversky and D. Kahneman. The framing of decisions and the psychology of choice. *Science*, 211:453–458, 1981.
A. Tversky and D. Kahneman. Rational choice and the framing of decisions. *Journal of Business*, 59:S251–S278, 1986.
J. W. Weibull. *Evolutionary game theory*. Cambridge; MA: MIT Press, 1995.

26

Social Preferences and Strategic Interactions

Ernst Fehr and Julien Senn

ABSTRACT

A large share of individuals deviate from self-interested behavior in many "paradigmatic" games, but in many other strategic situations almost all individuals behave in a self-interested manner. Models with heterogeneous social preferences provide a unifying understanding for these seemingly contradictory facts by focusing on the interaction between agents with other-regarding and selfish preferences. This focus explains why and when selfish agents behave as if they were other-regarding, as well as why and when other-regarding agents behave as if they were selfish. This focus also helps understand (i) the importance of seemingly irrelevant institutional details, (ii) the role of contractual incompleteness for the behavioral relevance of social preferences, (iii) the role of social preferences for the prevalence of contractual incompleteness, and (iv) why social preferences are an important component in explaining key characteristics of the employment relation. More recent evidence suggests that the empirical distribution of social preferences can be parsimoniously characterized by a small number of preference types, which also have out-of-sample predictive power for important behaviors such as the demand for politically enforced redistribution.

26.1 INTRODUCTION

Individuals have social preferences if they care not only about their own material payoff but also about the material payoff allocated to relevant reference agents. In the 1980s and 1990s, behavioral experiments with "paradigmatic" one-shot games, such as the ultimatum and dictator game, the gift exchange game, the trust game, the third-party punishment game, or cooperation games, provided solid evidence indicating that a substantial number of people behave in other-regarding ways (i.e., that they have social preferences). Because these preferences often generate economic outcomes that radically differ from those the self-interest model predicts, this evidence was frequently interpreted as a refutation of game theory and rational decision-making. However, because game theory often makes sharp and refutable predictions in simple games, it is one of the most important tools in acquiring a deeper understanding of the properties and economic consequences of social preferences.

The combination of game theory with the assumption of (heterogenous) social preferences allowed us to understand the conditions under which social preferences are key for the outcome of strategic interactions and the conditions under which their influence is likely to be small. It turns out that seemingly innocuous institutional details are often relevant. In important institutional environments, a minority of agents with social preferences can have a disproportionately large influence on aggregate outcomes because they induce the selfish agents to mimic their behavior. However, in certain competitive situations, the reverse is also true: The selfish agents induce those with social preferences to behave as if they were completely selfish. It also turns out that social preferences are likely to be influential in situations characterized by incomplete contracts because informal, social-preference-driven rewards and sanctions play a key role in these situations. Moreover, these rewards and sanctions often render incomplete contractual arrangements much more efficient than predicted by the self-interest model, and therefore they greatly diminish the incentive to make contracts more complete.

We could not have acquired these insights without the tools of game theory, nor could we have gained these insights without identifying the empirical role of heterogeneous social preferences and integrating them into our models. In order to understand the limits of the self-interest model, we have to go beyond these limits (i.e., we must explicitly model heterogenous social preferences!). The empirical evidence from broad population samples, in fact, suggests that the majority of individuals have some form of social preference, while the selfish type constitutes "only" a substantial minority. These findings also have, for example, strong implications for people's demand for politically enforced redistribution. More generally, these findings suggest that social scientists should routinely consider heterogenous social preferences in their theoretical and empirical endeavors.

In the following discussion, we substantiate these claims with the help of theoretical insights and empirical findings from the literature, and we conclude this essay by pointing out important open problems.

26.2 EVIDENCE FOR SOCIAL PREFERENCES

The early empirical evidence for social preferences mainly comes from laboratory experiments. These experiments have a privileged status in rigorously documenting the existence of social preferences because they enable controlling for a host of potentially confounding factors that are difficult to account for in naturally occurring interactions. For example, the possibility of repeated interactions and reputation formation are potentially important confounds in nonexperimental settings. Although individuals in large societies frequently engage in one-shot interactions with strangers, it is difficult to completely rule out the expectation of repeated interactions or reputational gain in a natural environment. In contrast, laboratory experiments can easily implement anonymous one-shot interactions that leave no room for such expectations. In fact, some experimental designs even guarantee that subjects know that the experimenter will never learn of their individual decisions (Hoffman et al., 1996; Barmettler et al., 2012) or that the experimenter cannot know the identity of individual subjects (as in anonymous internet experiments). Thus even reputational issues vis-à-vis the experimenter can be completely ruled out.

Evidence in favor of social preferences therefore mainly comes from *one-shot, anonymously played*, paradigmatic experimental games such as the dictator game, the ultimatum game, the trust game, the gift exchange game, the third-party punishment game, the public good game (with and without punishment), and the contract enforcement game.

One of the earliest pieces of evidence in favor of social preferences comes from the bilateral ultimatum game (Güth et al., 1982; Henrich et al., 2001). In this game, selfish responders should never reject any positive amount of money. However, many responders reject substantial shares of the available bargaining pie. Likewise, a selfish "dictator" should never voluntarily transfer money to the recipient in the dictator game (Forsythe et al., 1994), but many "dictators" do so. Moreover, selfish trustees should never transfer money back to the investor in the trust game (Berg et al., 1995), but many trustees do so.

Similarly, a selfish agent should never reciprocate high wages offered by the principal with costly nonminimal effort levels in the gift exchange game (Fehr et al., 1993). Yet many agents behave in this reciprocal manner. In the third-party punishment game (Fehr and Fischbacher, 2004), a selfish third party should be indifferent with regard to how fairly a dictator treats a recipient in an *unrelated* dictator game, but in fact third parties display a substantial willingness to incur cost to punish unfair dictators if given a chance to do so. Similarly, a selfish third party should be indifferent with regard to other players' cooperation levels in an *unrelated* prisoners' dilemma game, but many third parties are willing to incur cost to punish unilateral free-riding in the prisoners' dilemma. "Second parties" (i.e., the parties whose payoff is negatively affected by free-riding) display an even stronger willingness to incur cost to punish free-riding in the prisoners' dilemma (Fehr and Fischbacher, 2004) and in public goods games (Fehr and Gächter, 2000; Fehr and Gächter, 2002), although a selfish "second party" would never punish in these cases. Finally, many principals in contract enforcement games (Fehr et al., 1997; Fehr and Gächter, 1998) incur costs to reward high-performing agents and to punish low-performing agents, although a selfish principal would never do so in this one-shot and anonymously played game.

Thus, taken together, there is a large body of evidence indicating substantial deviations from selfish behavior. Much of this evidence is consistent with the notion that a considerable share of the subjects cares for reciprocal fairness and/or equality and is willing to reciprocate kind behaviors with kind actions and unkind behaviors with unkind, punitive, actions.

26.3 EVIDENCE SEEMINGLY CHALLENGING THE EXISTENCE OF SOCIAL PREFERENCES

There is, however, also a considerable body of evidence in which experimental subjects display behaviors that appear very consistent with models that assume entirely self-interested subjects. Perhaps competitive experimental markets under the double auction institution (Smith, 1962) and under the posted offer institution (Davis and Holt, 1993) provide the most prominent examples of this. In competitive experimental double auctions with homogenous goods, prices and quantities quickly converge to the competitive equilibrium derived from the assumption of selfish preferences. Convergence to the "selfish" competitive equilibrium is also observed in posted offer markets, although it takes longer to reach the equilibrium. Convergence to the "selfish" equilibrium even occurs in those double auctions where one side of the market reaps all the gains from trade and the other side earns almost nothing (Holt et al., 1986).

Market games with responder competition also demonstrate the sometimes very limited influence of fairness motives on market outcomes.[1] Even if only one additional responder is added to the bilateral ultimatum game, the two competing responders are suddenly willing to accept much lower offers (Fischbacher et al., 2009) compared to the bilateral ultimatum game (see Figure 26.1). Moreover, in response to the responders' willingness to accept rather unfair offers, the proposers in the market game make very unfair offers. How can it be that the introduction of a little bit of competition on the responders' side induces subjects to accept unfair offers if they really care for fairness and equality? And why do fair-minded proposers, who make rather egalitarian offers in the bilateral ultimatum game, suddenly make very unfair offers in the market game?

Equally puzzling behavioral patterns have been observed in games with proposer competition. If only one competing proposer is added to the bilateral ultimatum game, the two competing proposers now make very high offers, allowing the responder to thus appropriate the lion's share of the bargaining pie (Fischbacher et al., 2009). In fact, Roth et al. (1991) show in four culturally very different countries that in market games with many proposers, the players in all countries very quickly converge to an outcome where the responder basically appropriates the whole bargaining pie, as the self-interest equilibrium predicts. Again, this raises the question of why the responders are willing to accept, and why proposers are willing to make, such unfair offers if they care for fairness and equality.

[1] In the market game with responder competition, the institutional rules are as follows: One proposer makes a take-it-or-leave-it offer (in terms of a proposed share of the bargaining pie) to the *n* responders who then observe the offer and simultaneously decide whether to accept or reject it. If all responders reject, all parties earn zero. If some responders accept the offer, a random device determines which responder receives the proposed share and which accepting responders receive nothing. If only one responder accepts, this responder receives the proposed share while the other responders receive nothing.

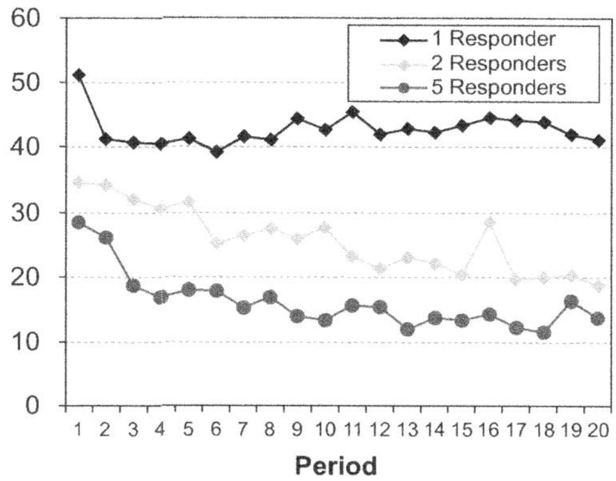

FIGURE 26.1 Responder share in the ultimatum game and in market games with responder competition. The figure shows data from Fischbacher and colleagues (2009). A large group of players is randomly rematched every period into smaller groups of players that play – depending on the treatment – either a bilateral bargaining game, a market game with two competing responders, or a market game with five competing responders. Players never know with whom they are matched, and the probability of meeting the same player is so low that players essentially repeatedly play a one-shot game with their current group members in each period.

The behavioral patterns observed in linear public good games with and without a punishment opportunity constitute similarly puzzling observations. In the linear game without a punishment opportunity, free-riding is a dominant strategy for selfish players in the one-shot game, while the total group payoff is maximized if all players contribute their whole endowment to the public good. Typically, after a few initial periods with relatively high contributions, cooperation rapidly deteriorates to low levels in repeated one-shot games with varying group members ("strangers") in each period (Andreoni, 1988; Croson, 1996). Interestingly, cooperation also declines to low levels in groups with stable group membership (e.g., for ten periods). Cooperation in Ambrus and Pathak (2011) declined literally to zero in period ten (i.e., no players contributed anything to the public good). Because there is strong evidence from other sources (Fehr and Gächter, 2002; Fehr and Fischbacher, 2004) that many subjects consider free-riding on others' contributions to be very unfair, the question arises about why cooperation nevertheless converges to extremely low levels.

26.4 RECONCILIATION: HETEROGENEOUS SOCIAL PREFERENCES IN STRATEGIC INTERACTIONS

How can we explain these seemingly contradictory patterns of behavior? Why is it the case that almost all subjects sometimes appear to be cooperative and behave in a fair-minded way (like in the public goods game with punishment opportunity), while almost all subjects in other situations behave in a noncooperative manner that appears consistent with the assumption that everybody is selfish (as in the public goods game without punishment opportunity)?

One possibility is to give up the assumption of rational, consistent, preferences and rely, instead, on the idea that subjects have developed situation-specific preferences or behavioral rules. For example, when one of us (Fehr) presented the evidence on market games with responder competition to psychologists or behavioral economists raised in the tradition of the "heuristics and biases" approach, the audience's typical reaction was to explain the lack of fair outcomes in market games by assuming that competition activates competitive preferences that overwhelm the fairness motive. The problem with these kinds of ad hoc explanations is, of course, the risk of providing superficial, "empty" rationales that explain "everything" as much as they explain "nothing," since *any* behavioral phenomenon can be "explained" by assuming some sort of situation-specific preference or rule.

Another strand of the literature (Binmore and Samuelson, 1994; Gale et al., 1995; Roth and Erev, 1995) has interpreted the evidence – such as rejections in the ultimatum game – as a form of boundedly rational rule-based behavior that emerges through learning processes such as reinforcement learning, for example. The problem with these approaches is that they only explain the behavior in the ultimatum game but do not provide a general model that can reconcile the evidence discussed previously in Sections 26.2 and 26.3. Similarly, the idea that subjects have selfish preferences but implement noisy (i.e., error-prone) best replies – which led to the notion of quantal response equilibria (McKelvey and Palfrey, 1995, 1998) – cannot achieve this reconciliation.[2]

Up until now, the only way of reconciling most of the evidence presented in Sections 26.2 and 26.3 has been to assume *heterogeneous* preferences for fairness/equity or reciprocity as, for example, in Fehr and Schmidt (1999) or Falk and Fischbacher (2006), while also maintaining the usual game theoretic approach of rational decision-making in strategic interactions. Here we will illustrate this approach – which relies on subjects' ability to perform backward induction – for some of the market and cooperation games discussed previously. But before we do so, which additional arguments speak in favor of capturing the deviations from self-interest as a social preference?

In this context, it is useful to emphasize that the existence of social preferences is always inferred from the last mover's behavior in simple one-shot games, such as the responder's rejection behavior in the ultimatum game, the agent's effort behavior in the gift exchange game, the trustee's back-transfers in the trust game, or the third party's action in the third-party punishment game. In these cases, the last mover does not have to make a complicated strategic decision requiring anticipation of how the other player will respond but only

[2] However, combining the notion of quantal response equilibria with heterogeneous social preferences can be a powerful explanatory tool, as shown by Goeree and Holt (2000) and Fischbacher et al. (2009).

determines the final payoff distribution from his or her action. In other words, the last mover's decision is extremely simple – for example, whether to accept or reject a 9:1 offer in the ultimatum game or whether to provide a high effort in the gift exchange game. This provides an a priori case that bounded rationality cannot play much of a role in these decisions.

In addition, the hallmark of a preference is that it incorporates the trade-offs between different goods, implying that behaviors associated with lower rewards or higher costs are less frequent. Research from dictator games with varying costs of giving (Andreoni and Miller, 2002; Fisman et al., 2007) has shown that individuals aptly make these trade-offs and that the behavior of the vast majority of subjects is close to utility maximization in the sense that they fully obey the generalized axiom of revealed preferences (GARP) or show only minor violations of GARP in terms of Afriat's (1972) Critical Cost Efficiency Index.[3]

Likewise, subjects in the domain of punishing behaviors respond to the pecuniary and nonpecuniary rewards and costs of punishment in ways that are consistent with a preference for reducing unfair players' income. In the ultimatum game, for example, the willingness to reject an unfairly low offer is much lower in those versions of the game where the proposer loses only part of his proposed share through a rejection (Bolton and Zwick, 1995; Suleiman, 1996). This indicates that the responders' motive is to reduce the proposers' income, and if the "reward" of a rejection in terms of a reduced proposer income is lower, then rejections become less frequent. Similarly, if the cost of punishing free riders increases, "second parties" reduce the frequency of punishing (Falk et al., 2005; Anderson and Putterman, 2006; Carpenter, 2007) – a behavior that is fully in line with a preference for punishing free riders.

Finally, there is also persuasive evidence indicating that subjects clearly understand the difference between situations where they can and where they cannot acquire a beneficial reputation. They tend to cooperate much more in gift exchange games with repeated interactions compared to one-shot gift exchange games (Gächter and Falk, 2002; Brown et al., 2004). Likewise, responders in repeated ultimatum games, where they can build a reputation for being a tough bargainer, display considerably higher minimum thresholds for accepting an offer compared to responders in one-shot ultimatum games (Fehr and Fischbacher, 2003). Thus subjects neither misperceive one-shot games as repeated games, nor do they misinterpret anonymous one-shot games as games in which one can acquire a reputation.

Overall, the evidence strongly suggests that the deviations from selfish behaviors observed in paradigmatic experimental games represent some form of a social preference. It may well be the case that these social preferences, or aspects thereof, are the result of an evolutionary process that led to a deeply seated "egalitarian ethos," as hypothesized by Boehm (1993; 2012)

[3] The Critical Cost Efficiency Index measures the amount by which each budget constraint must be adjusted in order to remove all violations of GARP.

and Acemoglu (Chapter 32). However, how does an approach relying on the combination of heterogenous social preferences and rationality *simultaneously* explain the fair-minded behaviors described in Section 26.2 and the rather selfish behaviors described in Section 26.3?

We only illustrate the explanatory power of models with heterogeneous social preferences that follow by providing the key intuition for understanding the data pattern observed in Figure 26.1.[4] The model is based on the notion of inequality aversion – the idea that a significant share of the people is willing to pay (i) to *reduce* the payoff of individuals who have a higher payoff and (ii) to *increase* the payoff of individuals who have a lower payoff.

It is easy to understand that if proposers in the ultimatum game anticipate that there is a significant share of responders who dislike inequality, proposers will need to make relatively high offers to induce responders to accept, which explains the relatively egalitarian outcomes in bilateral ultimatum games. Yet why can proposers enforce much lower offers if just one additional responder is added (Figure 26.1)? The reason is that even if both responders are very inequality averse but assign a sufficiently high probability to the possibility that the other player will accept a low offer, it is in the interest of each inequality-averse agent to accept the offer as well. This follows from the fact that if the other agent accepts, the inequality-averse agent can no longer avoid inequality by rejecting the offer.

The model also predicts the observation (see Figure 26.1) that an increase in the number of responders leads to further decreases in the responders' share because in a population with a given mix of selfish and inequality-averse agents, the probability that *at least one of the responders* will be selfish increases with the number of responders. This also means that the probability that at least one of the responders will accept low offers increases, which then induces even inequality-averse individuals to accept these offers too, because they can no longer "buy" equality with a rejection.

How can we discriminate between this explanation, which is based on the existence of stable social preferences across treatments and one that relies on treatment-specific rules or preferences? The key mechanism underlying the stable-social-preference explanation is *exclusively* based on responders' beliefs about how many other responders will reject low offers. If an inequality-averse subject believes that *all* other responders will reject a low offer, the subject should display a much higher willingness to reject the offer as well, because she then basically believes that a rejection will result in equality. Thus the question is then whether the changes in responders' beliefs across treatments are capable of *fully* explaining the treatment effects. Interestingly, this is exactly the pattern observed in the data. The treatment differences in responders' rejection behavior are no longer significant if one controls for the belief that all other

[4] For a more thorough explanation, we refer the interested reader to propositions 1–5 and sections V–VI in Fehr and Schmidt (1999). In addition, the reader may also consult Bolton (2000), Bolton (2000), and Dufwenberg et al. (2011).

responders will reject a given offer. In other words, the differences in responders' behavior across treatments is entirely due to different beliefs across the treatments, while there is no evidence that the responders' preferences change across treatments.

26.5 MORE GENERAL LESSONS: INSTITUTIONAL DETAILS AND THE INTERACTION BETWEEN DIFFERENT PREFERENCE TYPES

One of the most important implications of heterogeneous social preference models is that *the existence of inequality-averse or reciprocal agents often changes the incentives for the selfish agents to behave like an inequality-averse or reciprocal agent.* The existence of inequality-averse responders in the ultimatum game provides an incentive for selfish proposers to make offers that resemble those of fair-minded, inequality-averse proposers. Likewise, the existence of sufficiently reciprocal agents in the gift exchange game constitutes an incentive for selfish principals to make high wage offers. Or the existence of inequality-averse punishers in the public goods game with punishment opportunities provides an incentive for the selfish agents to cooperate (i.e., to behave like the inequality-averse agents). The incentive to build a reputation for having a social preference, instead of being known to be selfish, is another example of how the existence of social preference types affects the behavior of the selfish individuals. Thus, because the existence of social preference types often generates incentives for the selfish types to mimic the behavior of the social preference types, *even a minority of individuals with social preferences can have a disproportionately large influence on the aggregate outcome of games.*

Another important implication of heterogeneous social preference models is that *seemingly innocuous institutional and situational details are often decisive for who has an incentive to mimic whom.* This is, for example, the case in the sequentially played one-shot prisoners' dilemma with symmetric payoffs, where it is common knowledge that one agent is selfish and the other agent is inequality averse. If the selfish agent moves first in the sequential prisoners' dilemma, the unique equilibrium outcome is "cooperate, cooperate," while if the inequality-averse player moves first, the unique outcome is "defect, defect." The reason for this is that an inequality-averse second-mover will reciprocate the cooperative first move of a selfish first-mover, and the first-mover will anticipate this. In contrast, an inequality-averse first-mover will anticipate that a selfish second-mover will defect; hence the first-mover will also defect.

Another example is the market game with multiple responders. Assume that it is common knowledge that there is a single selfish responder but $n-1$ strongly inequality-averse responders. In this case, the single selfish responder suffices to induce all $n-1$ inequality-averse responders to accept every low but positive offer. In other words, a single selfish responder suffices to ensure a unique equilibrium outcome in which responders receive the minimum possible payoff.

The market game with responder competition suggests that even a little bit of competition can generate enormous competitive pressure that severely weakens responders' bargaining powers. Now let us consider the introduction of competing responders (i.e., competing agents) in the gift exchange game (Fehr and Falk, 1999). Recall that the proposer (i.e., the principal) in the bilateral version of this one-shot game makes a binding wage offer. If the agent accepts the offer, she is free to choose any effort level because *effort* is assumed to be *noncontractible*. In this game, even a selfish principal has an incentive to offer high wages if the agents reciprocate high offers with high effort. Importantly, this incentive does not vanish if additional competing agents are introduced to the game. Therefore, as shown in Fehr and Falk (1999), the introduction of competition has little effect on wage offers due to the existence of agents with social preferences. Note that if all players are completely selfish, the fact that effort is noncontractible does not affect the impact of competition because agents always choose the lowest possible effort level anyway.

The interplay between noncontractibility and social preferences can also be illustrated by adding the following moves to the simple bilateral one-shot gift exchange game: The principal can promise a *nonbinding bonus payment* together with the binding wage offer, after which the agent freely chooses his or her effort. Then the principal observes the effort and can freely decide on his actual bonus payment. In this setting, the existence of principals with social preferences constitutes powerful incentives for the agents to provide high effort levels (Fehr et al., 2007) because these principals will honor high effort with a high bonus. Again, the noncontractibility of bonus payments would have no effect in a world of only selfish individuals.

The provided considerations lead to the hypothesis that *noncontractibilities generate action opportunities that render social preferences more important*. The reason for this is that while selfish actors always choose the cost-minimizing action when they are free to choose, actors with social preferences are willing to incur cost to reward or punish the behavior of other individuals if noncontractibilities allow them to do so. This willingness to reward fair and punish unfair behavior, even though no contract prescribes or enforces such rewards and sanctions, has been shown to render incomplete contractual arrangements much more efficient than predicted by the self-interest model (Fehr et al., 1997; Fehr and Gächter, 1998; Fehr et al., 2007). Naturally, the trading parties have therefore strongly diminished incentives to render contracts more complete.

Moreover, in the presence of some noncontractibilities, social preferences may be the force that contributes to further incompleteness of the contract. Take, for example, the labor relation in which effort is typically not contractually determined and enforced. The workers' opportunity to inflict cost on the firm ex post by varying their effort levels may render it profitable for the firms to rigidly fix wages ex ante instead of introducing state-contingent wages (Fehr et al., 2011). If all workers were selfish, state-contingent wages would be the efficient solution, but in the presence of workers with social preferences, rigid wages can be more profitable because they prevent ex post haggling and dysfunctional cooperation choices by the workers. In this way, social preferences become an important component of explaining (i) the behavioral relevance of what Williamson called the "fundamental transformation" of relationships *after* a contract is concluded and (ii) the existence of perhaps the key aspect of labor relations – the presence of rigid, non-state-contingent wages.

Nevertheless, informal rewards and sanctions often do not guarantee that efficient effort or investment levels are obtained, and thus there still may exist an incentive to render contracts more complete. The literature mentions observable but unverifiable payoff-relevant information as a key obstacle for complete contracts (Grossman and Hart, 1986), because unverifiable information items cannot be the basis of enforceable contracts. However, Maskin and Tirole (1999) have challenged this rationale for contractual incompleteness. They show that it is possible to design a (subgame perfect implementation) mechanism that induces the trading parties to *publicly announce* the truth about the unverifiable information item. In fact, the Maskin–Tirole mechanism induces truth-telling as the *unique subgame perfect equilibrium* of the game induced by the mechanism. Thus contracts can now be based on true public announcements about previously unverifiable information such as an effort level, and remuneration can be credibly conditioned on the announced effort level. In other words, the mechanism basically removes contractual incompleteness and enables the realization of unexploited gains from trade.

This raises the question whether one could constrain the influence of social preferences by rendering incomplete contracts more complete through mechanisms such as those proposed by Maskin and Tirole (1999). While this might be possible, the mechanism assumes that trading parties are selfish, and recent evidence shows that the very existence of social preferences thoroughly undermines the functioning of the Maskin–Tirole mechanism (Fehr et al., 2021). In fact, incorporating negative reciprocity into the model leads to the conclusion that even very small amounts of negative reciprocity often suffice to undermine the mechanism. Thus, by rendering mechanisms that could remove contractual incompleteness inefficient, social preferences may contribute to the very noncontractibilities under which their influence on aggregate outcomes is large.

26.6 THE PROPERTIES, DISTRIBUTION, AND POLITICAL CONSEQUENCES OF SOCIAL PREFERENCES

The "paradigmatic" games mentioned in Section 26.2 are well-suited to document the existence of social preferences, but they are not ideal for identifying their precise properties. Fehr and colleagues (2022) propose an experimental paradigm that is better suited for identifying the properties of distributional social preferences. In their study, a decision maker (DM) has to allocate money between herself and an anonymous partner in different choice situations. In each choice situation, the DM faces seven different equidistantly placed money allocations that are located on a linear budget line with either a positive or a negative slope in the "other payoff (y) – own payoff (x)" space. These seven feasible allocations, labeled $(y_0, x_0), (y_1, x_1), \ldots, (y_6, x_6)$, are graphically presented to the subjects in a way that makes the distributional consequences of each allocation very transparent. The budget lines always cut through the forty-five-degree line in the (y, x)-space in their midpoint. That is, the DM can implement an allocation that equalizes payoffs ($x = y$), an allocation that favors him- or herself ($x > y$), or an allocation that favors the other individual ($x < y$).

Several important insights can be inferred from the DM's behavior in the different choice situations. Choice situations involving negatively sloped budget lines enable us to measure how much money the DM is willing to give up to *increase* the partner's payoff. The behavior associated with these budget lines thus informs us about the DM's altruism or advantageous inequality aversion. Positively sloped budget lines allow us to determine how much money the DM is willing to give up to *reduce* the partner's payoff (i.e., they inform us about the DM's disadvantageous inequality aversion or envy).

Figure 26.2 documents the distribution of social preferences based on the task described previously for a broad sample of the (adult) Swiss population that is roughly representative in terms of gender, age, and education.[5] The figure is based on each individual's modal decision for (i) the five positively sloped budget lines and (ii) the five negatively sloped budget lines. Allocations on each budget line are numbered with integers from 0 to 6, with 0 indicating an own-payoff-minimizing choice, 3 indicating a payoff-equalizing choice, and 6 indicating an own-payoff-maximizing choice.

The figure impressively shows that the vast majority of individuals' modal choices are payoff-equalizing or own-payoff maximizing. The modal choice of individuals located at (3, 3) is payoff-equalizing on *both* the negatively *and* the positively sloped budget lines, indicating a strong *desire to equalize payoffs*, even if that requires sacrificing money to reduce the partner's payoff. Because this behavior is predicted by models of inequality aversion (Fehr and Schmidt, 1999; Bolton, 2000), we label these individuals as *inequality averse*. The modal choice of individuals located at (6, 6) is the own-payoff maximizing allocation, regardless of the slope of the budget line; they can thus be labeled as *selfish*. Finally, the modal choice of individuals located at (3, 6) is payoff-equalizing on negatively sloped budget lines, but it is own-payoff maximizing on positively sloped budget lines. Because this behavior is consistent with models of altruistic social preferences (Andreoni and Miller, 2002; Charness and Rabin, 2002; Fisman et al., 2007; Alger and Weibull, 2013), we label these individuals as *altruistic*, as they are willing to sacrifice money to increase their partners'

[5] The sample is broadly representative of the German-speaking and the French-speaking parts of Switzerland, which make up more than 90 percent of the Swiss population. Figure 26.2 is based on the 467 panel subjects whose social preferences were measured in 2017 (see Fehr et al., 2022) and who also participated in another study involving social preference measurement in 2020 (see Senn et al., 2022).

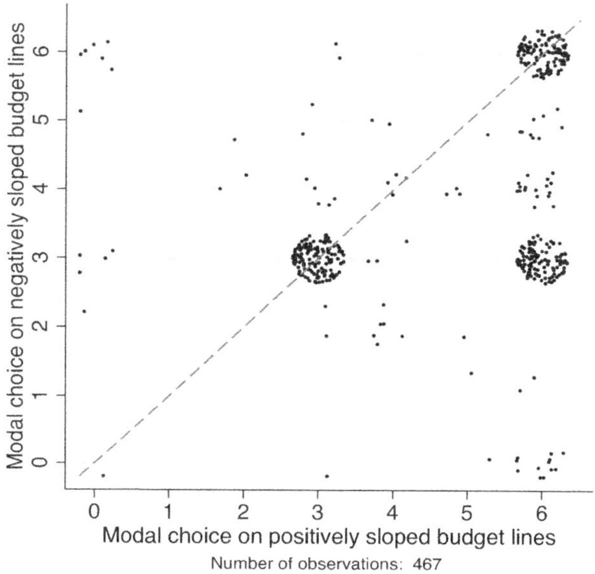

FIGURE 26.2 Descriptive evidence on the distribution of social preferences. The figure shows subjects' modal choices for the five positively sloped budget lines on the horizontal axis and for the five negatively sloped budget lines on the vertical axis. There are seven feasible allocations on each budget line. They are numbered with integers from 0 to 6, with 0 indicating an own-payoff-minimizing choice, 3 indicating a payoff-equalizing choice, and 6 indicating an own-payoff-maximizing choice. To make identical modal choices of individuals, visible dots are jittered.

payoffs (on negatively sloped budget lines) but are never willing to sacrifice money (on positively sloped budget lines) to decrease their partners' payoffs for the sake of equality.

These three behavioral agglomerations, which descriptively characterize the modal behavior of a vast number of subjects (roughly 80.7 percent in this sample), have a very clear interpretation in terms of social preferences. If subjects would have randomly chosen their allocations on each of the ten budget lines, the likelihood that 80 percent or more subjects would have had their modal choice located at one of the three behavioral agglomerations is vanishingly small, indicating that the observed pattern is very unlikely to be the product of chance.[6]

When we apply a more rigorous clustering technique – the Dirichlet Process Means clustering algorithm (Kulis and Jordan, 2012) – that takes *all* choices individuals make in this task into account (instead of only using the modal

[6] We simulated random choices for 467 subjects 1,000 times. In *none* of the 1,000 simulations, 80 percent or more subjects had their modal choices at one of the three behavioral agglomerations.

choice over positively or negatively sloped budget lines), we again find evidence that three classes of distinct social preferences with a clear behavioral interpretation exist: A large group of subjects are inequality averse, another large group is altruistic, and the remaining subjects are selfish. Moreover, the same three social preference types emerge in three further broad populations samples, comprising in total more than 2,000 individuals (Senn et al., 2022). In these Swiss data sets, the share of inequality-averse individuals varies between 45 and 53 percent, the share of altruistic individuals is between 30 and 42 percent, and the share of selfish individuals is between 10 and 25 percent. Finally, we find again the same three preference types (Epper et al., 2020) in an independent data set of roughly 3,600 Danish individuals aged between 32 and 42 years (that are representative for this age group and for people living in the Copenhagen area) with 37 percent inequality-averse subjects, 30 percent altruistic subjects, and 32 percent selfish subjects. Thus, taken together, a fairly robust picture emerges that suggests that the nonselfish types constitute a clear majority in broad populations samples, while the selfish type represents a substantial minority.

These facts further strengthen the conclusion that disregarding social preferences may severely inhibit the ability to understand important social, political, and economic phenomena. To illustrate this for the political realm, we shortly discuss the role of inequality aversion and altruism in the demand for redistribution. With a few exceptions (Fisman et al., 2017; Kerschbamer and Muller, 2020), the economic literature on the demand for redistribution has largely neglected the role of social preferences, such as inequality aversion and altruism in the demand for redistribution. This may perhaps be due to the difficulties of integrating the measurement of inequality aversion and altruism in survey studies on voters' support for redistribution. However, studying the demand for redistribution without explicitly accounting for individuals' social preferences for distributional outcomes is a bit like studying insurance markets without taking people's risk aversion into account.

In Fehr and colleagues (2022), we integrate inequality aversion and altruism in an otherwise standard political economy model for the demand for redistribution (Meltzer and Richard, 1981). The model predicts that inequality aversion and altruism will lead to an increase in support for redistribution, in particular among more affluent voters with higher incomes. Figure 26.3, which depicts subjects' average support for four redistributive policy proposals put to vote in Switzerland, shows that this prediction is nicely borne out by the data. Both inequality aversion and altruism, measured using the experimental paradigm described previously, lead to a substantial, income-dependent increase in support for redistribution relative to selfish individuals. In addition, these results indicate that experimental behavioral measures of inequality aversion and altruism can significantly deepen our understanding of phenomena outside the laboratory.

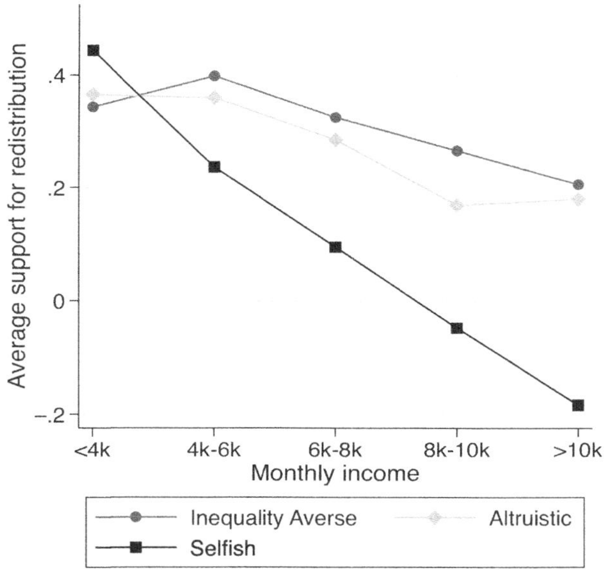

FIGURE 26.3 The role of social preferences in the support for redistribution. The figure is taken from Fehr et al. (2022). It shows individuals' support for redistributive proposals that were similar or identical to proposals that were up for vote in national plebiscites in Switzerland.

26.7 SUMMARY AND OPEN PROBLEMS

Taken together, the arguments in this essay can be summarized as follows. There is compelling evidence for systematic deviations from self-interested behavior in many "paradigmatic" games. These deviations can be best explained in terms of rational individuals with heterogenous social preferences. This explanation can, in particular, also clarify when and why social preferences affect the outcomes of games, as well as when and why they have little influence. Although the evidence from broad population samples suggests that a majority of individuals has social preferences, they can have decisive effects on equilibrium play even if only a minority of people have these preferences. Social preferences appear to play a particularly important role in environments with incomplete contracts that provide a range of noncontractual action opportunities for the involved parties. By undermining mechanisms that have been proposed as solutions for overcoming incomplete contracts, social preferences may further contribute to environmental conditions under which they have impact.

More recent evidence suggests that the experimentally elicited distribution of social preferences can be parsimoniously characterized by the existence of three distinct types of preferences in broad population samples: inequality aversion, altruism, and selfishness. Type-based social preference measures provide a deeper understanding of the support for redistribution because altruistic and inequality-averse individuals exhibit a much stronger, yet income-dependent, support for redistributive policy proposals.

Despite substantial progress in understanding the properties of social preferences and their consequences for strategic interactions, there are a number of exciting and important open problems. Social preferences are typically based on some sort of social comparison process, but the empirical identification of the relevant comparison subjects is still in its infancy – though see the work of Hvidberg and colleagues (2020) for an interesting recent study. Another question concerns the relationship between social preferences, which are a property of individuals, and social norms, which are a property of groups. To what extent are social preferences based on prevailing norms? To what extent do social norms generate behavioral regularities that are internalized over time as a social preference? And to what extent do social preferences help enforce social norms (Fehr and Schurtenberger, 2018; Ellingsen and Mohlin, 2019)?

In addition, we know very little about the formation of social preferences. There are only a few recent papers (Cappelen et al., 2020; Kosse et al., 2020) that indicate that educational practices shape children's social preferences, but there is still a large knowledge gap. More generally, one would like to know which features of our institutions and social interactions shape which aspects of social preferences. For example, there is a strong negative correlation between young Danish males' grade point average in the final school year and the strength of their aversion against disadvantageous inequality in the work of Epper and colleagues (2022). Perhaps, the experience of a history of "being behind" generates systematic "behindness aversion." This hypothesis could also explain why several papers (Fisman et al., 2015; Bruhin et al., 2019) observe much less "behindness aversion" in student populations compared to what is known from the general population. However, more (causal) evidence is needed to substantiate this hypothesis.

A related question is which aspect of social preferences is primarily shaped through cultural practices and can thus be changed in the short or medium run, and which aspect is deeply ingrained in human egalitarian evolutionary history, as described by Boehm (1993; 2012) and Acemoglu (Chapter 32). For example, the notion of intention-based reciprocity requires a high degree of perspective taking, which not all human beings may be capable of performing. In contrast, it requires less cognitive sophistication to notice if one gets less from a trade or a cooperative endeavor than one's partner, perhaps suggesting that inequality aversion represents a more primitive, and hence more deeply ingrained, evolutionary legacy.

Finally, another interesting question is whether a parsimonious characterization of the distribution of social preferences in terms of a small number of distinct types exists across several cultures and countries. Perhaps not all cultures are characterized by the same types. For example, some may exhibit envious types while others may not. It would, however, already be quite remarkable if the parsimony in terms of only a few existing types could be identified in several cultures. To study such questions, it would be desirable to develop cross-culturally reliable yet simple survey measures of inequality aversion and envy.

26.8 REFERENCES

S. Afriat. Efficiency estimation of production functions. *International Economic Review*, 13:568–598, 1972.

I. Alger and J. W. Weibull. *Homo moralis*: Preference evolution under incomplete information and assortative matching. *Econometrica*, 81:2269–2302, 2013.

A. Ambrus and P. Pathak. Cooperation over finite horizons: A theory and experiments. *Journal of Public Economics*, 95(7–8):500–512, 2011.

C. M. Anderson and L. Putterman. Do non-strategic sanctions obey the Law of Demand? The demand for punishment in the voluntary contribution mechanism. *Games and Economic Behavior*, 54:1–24, 2006.

J. Andreoni. Why free ride? Strategies and learning in public goods experiments. *Journal of Public Economics*, 37(3):291–304, 1988.

J. Andreoni and J. Miller. Giving according to Garp: An experimental test of the consistency of preferences for altruism. *Econometrica*, 70(2):737–753, 2002.

F. Barmettler, E. Fehr, and C. Zehnder. Big Experimenter is watching you! Anonimity and prosocial behavior in the laboratory. *Games and Economic Behavior*, 75(1):17–34, 2012.

J. Berg, J. W. Dickhaut, and K. A. McCabe. Trust, reciprocity, and social history. *Games and Economic Behavior*, 10(1):122–142, 1995.

K. Binmore and L. Samuelson. An economists perspective on the evolution of norms. *Journal of Institutional and Theoretical Economics; Zeitschrift für die Gesamte Staatswissenschaft*, 150(1):45–63, 1994.

C. Boehm. Egalitarian behavior and reverse dominance hierarchy. *Current Anthropology*, 34(3):227–254, 1993.

C. Boehm. *Moral origins: The evolution of virtue, altruism, and shame*. New York: Basic Books, 2012.

A. Bolton and G. E. Ockenfels. ERC: A theory of equity, reciprocity, and competition. *American Economic Review*, 90(1):166–193, 2000.

G. Bolton and R. Zwick. Anonymity versus punishment in ultimatum bargaining. *Games and Economic Behavior*, 10(1):95–121, 1995.

M. Brown, A. Falk, and E. Fehr. Relational contracts and the nature of market interactions. *Econometrica*, 72(3):757–780, 2004.

A. Bruhin, E. Fehr, and D. Schunk. The many faces of human sociality: Uncovering the distribution and stability of social preferences. *Journal of the European Economic Association*, 17(4):1025–1069, 2019.

A. Cappelen, J. List, A. Samek, and B. Tungodden. The effect of early-childhood education on social preferences. *Journal of Political Economy*, 127(7):2739–2758, 2020.

J. Carpenter. The demand for punishment. *Journal of Economic Behavior and Organization*, 62:522–542, 2007.

G. Charness and M. Rabin. Understanding social preferences with simple tests. *Quarterly Journal of Economics*, 117(3):817–869, 2002.

R. Croson. Partners and strangers revisited. *Economics Letters*, 53:25–32, 1996.

D. D. Davis and C. A. Holt. *Experimental economics.* Princeton, NJ: Princeton University Press, 1993.

M. Dufwenberg, P. Heidhues, G. Kirchsteiger, F. Riedel, and J. Sobel. Other-regarding preferences in general equilibrium. *Review of Economic Studies*, 78(2):613–639, 2011.

T. Ellingsen and E. Mohlin. Decency. Working paper, Stockholm School of Economics, 2019.

T. Epper, E. Fehr, H. Fehr-Duda, C. T. Kreiner, D. Lassen, S. Leth-Petersen, and G. N. Rasmussen. Time discounting and wealth inequality. *American Economic Review*, 110(4):1177–1205, 2020.

T. Epper, E. Fehr, K. B. Hvidberg, C. Thustrup Kreiner, S. Leth-Petersen, and G. N. Rasmussen. Preferences predict who commits crime among young men. *Proceedings of the National Academy of Sciences*, 119(6): e2112645119, 2022.

A. Falk, E. Fehr, and U. Fischbacher. Driving forces behind informal sanctions. *Econometrica*, 73(6):2017–2030, 2005.

A. Falk and U. Fischbacher. A theory of reciprocity. *Games and Economic Behavior*, 54(2):293–315, 2006.

E. Fehr, T. Epper, and J. Senn. Other-regarding preferences and redistributive politics. Working Paper, Department of Economics, University of Zurich, 2022.

E. Fehr and A. Falk. Wage rigidity in a competitive incomplete contract market. *Journal of Political Economy*, 107(1):106–134, 1999.

E. Fehr and U. Fischbacher. The nature of human altruism. *Nature*, 425(6960):785–791, 2003.

E. Fehr and U. Fischbacher. Third-party punishment and social norms. *Evolution and Human Behavior*, 25(2):63–87, 2004.

E. Fehr and S. Gächter. How effective are trust- and reciprocity-based incentives? In A. Ben-Ner and L. Putterman, eds., *Economics, Values and Organizations*. Cambridge: Cambridge University Press, 1998.

E. Fehr and S. Gächter. Cooperation and punishment in public goods experiments. *American Economic Review*, 90(4): 980–994, 2000.

E. Fehr and S. Gächter. Altruistic punishment in humans. *Nature*, 415:137–140, 2002.

E. Fehr, S. Gächter, and G. Kirchsteiger. Reciprocity as a contract enforcement device: Experimental evidence. *Econometrica*, 65(4):833–860, 1997.

E. Fehr, O. Hart, and C. Zehnder. Contracts as reference points: Experimental evidence. *American Economic Review*, 101(2):493–525, 2011.

E. Fehr, G. Kirchsteiger, and A. Riedl. Does fairness prevent market clearing: An experimental investigation. *Quarterly Journal of Economics*, 108(2):437–459, 1993.

E. Fehr, A. Klein, and K. M. Schmidt. Fairness and contract design. *Econometrica*, 75(1):121–154, 2007.

E. Fehr, M. Powell, and T. Wilkening. Behavioral constraints on the design of subgame-perfect implementation mechanisms. *American Economic Review*, 111(4):1055–1091, 2021.

E. Fehr and K. M. Schmidt. A theory of fairness, competition, and cooperation. *Quarterly Journal of Economics*, 114(3):817–868, 1999.

E. Fehr and I. Schurtenberger. Normative foundations of human cooperation. *Nature Human Behaviour*, 2(7):458–468, 2018.

U. Fischbacher, C. M. Fong, and E. Fehr. Fairness, errors and the power of competition. *Journal of Economic Behavior and Organization*, 72(1):527–545, 2009.

R. Fisman, P. Jakiela, and S. Kariv. Distributional preferences and political behavior. *Journal of Public Economics*, 155:1–10, 2017.

R. Fisman, P. Jakiela, S. Kariv, and D. Markovits. The distributional preferences of an elite. *Science*, 349(6254):aab0096, 2015.

R. Fisman, S. Kariv, and D. Markovits. Individual preferences for giving. *American Economic Review*, 97(5):1858–1876, 2007.

R. Forsythe, H. L. Horowitz, N. E. Savin, and M. Sefton. Fairness in simple bargaining games. *Games and Economic Behavior*, 6(3):347–369, 1994.

S. Gächter and A. Falk. Reputation and reciprocity: Consequences for the labour relation. *Scandinavian Journal of Economics*, 104(1):1–26, 2002.

J. Gale, K. Binmore, and L. Samuelson. Learning to be imperfect: The ultimatum game. *Games and Economic Behavior*, 8(1):56–80, 1995.

J. K. Goeree and C. A. Holt. Asymmetric inequality aversion and noisy behavior in alternating-offer bargaining games. *European Economic Review*, 44(4–6):1079–1089, 2000.

S. J. Grossman and O. D. Hart. The costs and benefits of ownership: A theory of vertical and lateral integration. *Journal of Political Economy*, 94(4):691–719, 1986.

W. Güth, R. Schmittberger, and B. Schwarze. An experimental analysis of ultimatium bargaining. *Journal of Economic Behavior and Organization*, 3(3):367–388, 1982.

J. Henrich, R. Boyd, S. Bowles, C. Camerer, E. Fehr, H. Gintis, and R. McElreath. In search of *Homo Economicus*: Behavioral experiments in 15 small-scale societies. *American Economic Review*, 91(2):73–78, 2001.

E. Hoffman, K. McCabe, and V. Smith. Social distance and other-regarding behavior in dictator games. *American Economic Review*, 86(3):653–660, 1996.

C. A. Holt, L. Langan, and A. P. Villamil. Market power in oral double auctions. *Economic Inquiry*, 24(1):107–123, 1986.

K. B. Hvidberg, S. Stantcheva, and C. Thustrup-Kreiner. Social position and fairness views. NBER Working Paper 28099, 2020.

R. Kerschbamer and D. Muller. Social preferences and political attitudes: An online experiment on a large heterogeneous sample. *Journal of Public Economics*, 182:104076, 2020.

F. Kosse, T. Deckers, P. Pinger, H. Schildberg-Horisch, and A. Falk. The formation of prosociality: Causal evidence on the role of social environment. *Journal of Political Economy*, 128(2):437–467, 2020.

B. Kulis and M. I. Jordan. Revisiting k-means: New algorithms via bayesian non-parametrics. In *Proceedings of the Twenty-Ninth International Coference on International Conference on Machine Learning*, pp. 1131–1138. Madison, WI: Omnipress, 2012.

E. Maskin and J. Tirole. Unforeseen contingencies and incomplete contracts. *Review of Economic Studies*, 66(1):83–114, 1999.

R. D. McKelvey and T. R. Palfrey. Quantal response equilibria for normal form games. *Games and Economic Behavior*, 10(1):6–38, 1995.

R. D. McKelvey and T. R. Palfrey. Quantal response equilibria for extensive form games. *Experimental Economics*, 1:9–41, 1998.

A. H. Meltzer and S. F. Richard. A rational theory of the size of government. *Journal of Political Economy*, 89(5):914–927, 1981.

A. E. Roth and I. Erev. Learning in extensive-form games: Experimental data and simple dynamic models in the intermediate term. *Games and Economic Behavior*, 8(1):164–212, 1995.

A. E. Roth, V. Prasnikar, M. Okuno-Fujiwara, and S. Zamir. Bargaining and market behavior in Jerusalem, Ljubljana, Pittsburgh, and Tokyo: An experimental study. *American Economic Review*, 81(5):1068–1095, 1991.

J. Senn, T. Epper, and E. Fehr. The fundamental properties, stability and predictive power of social preferences. Working Paper, Department of Economics, University of Zurich, 2022.

V. L. Smith. An experimental study of competitive market behavior. *Journal of Political Economy*, 70:111–137, 1962.

R. Suleiman. Expectations and fairness in a modified ultimatum game. *Journal of Economic Psychology*, 17:531–554, 1996.

PART VII

POLITICAL SCIENCE

27

Introduction to Part VII

Yukio Koriyama

Political science has been at the center of the application of game theory since its early years. Given the strategic nature of interaction in social decision-making, it is not surprising that game theory has become one of the main tools for analyzing such interactions as the influence of voters on collective decisions (Shapley and Shubik, 1954), the relationship between individual and group preferences (Downs, 1957), and the properties of mechanisms in political decision-making (Riker, 1962). Since the Cuban crisis of 1962, the importance of game-theoretic analysis of armed conflict has been widely recognized (Schelling, 1960, 1966). Why do armed conflicts occur, in spite of obvious common interests in avoiding military destruction? Game-theoretic analysis helps elucidate the nature of problems by highlighting the strategic structure underlying them, such as the prisoner's dilemma in arming competition, dynamic commitment problem, and bargaining with incomplete information in the use of violent force. Strategic choice of tariff policies has been formulated as a game between the governments (Johnson, 1953). Analysis of the strategic interaction between governments, interest groups, political parties, and legislators provides us with insights into important aspects of trade policy, such as the implementation of tariffs, cross-sectional trade protection (Grossman and Helpman, 1994), the inefficiency induced by noncooperative competitions, and the conditions for reaching international agreements to overcome such inefficiency.

In this part, three applications of game theory in political science are covered. The first one concerns political decision-making. The quality of collective decision-making hinges on the structure of the institution through which members' strategic incentives are induced. Therefore, the tools of game theory can provide insights into key questions concerning the design of the institutions that make decisions, such as voting committees or large elections. The second is about armed conflict. Game-theoretic analysis of arming competition, using

Remark by editors: During the Nobel symposium, this session was chaired and introduced by Torsten Persson, Institute for International Economic Studies (IIES), Stockholm University.

the contest success function, illustrates the underlying rationale for inefficient investment in self-defense, which is consistent with Thomas Hobbes' pessimism in an anarchical state. As for the use of violent force, costly conflicts may result from dynamic commitment problems. This class of models helps explain the characteristics of civil wars and the differences between them and interstate wars. The third is about trade policies. Various phenomena in trade, such as tariff setting and international protection of intellectual property, can be explained by game-theoretic models between governments. In addition, interest groups play a central role as they compete for favorable government treatment of the industries they represent in exchange for their contributions. Trade policies can also be instruments for political parties and legislators competing for power. The inefficiencies induced by such competition motivate the achievement of negotiated trade agreements.

In Chapter 28, David Austen-Smith offers an in-depth review of the literature on game-theoretic analysis of voting, from its earliest days (Shapley and Shubik, 1954; Riker, 1962). Both cooperative and noncooperative concepts are used to answer questions such as, How do candidates or parties propose alternatives to voters in strategic interactions? Why do voters vote? What are the implications of asymmetric information for candidates' and voters' incentives? Do prevoting deliberations improve information sharing? If so, through what type of rules? Sophisticated voters may act strategically (Farqhuarson, 1969). Therefore, the arguments conditional on being pivotal play a crucial role (Ordeshook and Palfrey, 1988). In the presence of private information, the mechanism design approach is highly appropriate, as voters' incentives can be heavily influenced by the decision rule. The analysis of information aggregation in large-scale elections (Feddersen and Pesendorfer, 1997) brings important insights to our understanding of representative democracy. Due to the nonexistence of a core and the cyclical structure of pairwise comparison, there may be a fundamental difficulty in the preference aggregation by majoritarian democracy in large-scale elections. Chapter 28 concludes with questions for future research: How does the limitation of preference/information aggregation in large-scale elections affect the stability of representative democracy? What are the determinants of the robustness of democratic norms (Acemoglu et al., 2012)? What is the role of the media in the presence of information asymmetry, particularly in ideological battles where information filtering can play an exacerbating role?

In Chapter 29, James D. Fearon reviews game-theoretic models of large-scale armed conflict. From the earliest years of its history, the analysis of military tactics has been at the heart of game theory's scope of application, as evidenced by Borel's (1921) mention of "*l'art de la guerre* (art of war)." Despite obvious common interests in avoiding the devastating consequences of military or economic destruction, we witness a large number of destructive armed conflict, such as interstate wars, civil wars, and internal disputes. The central question in this literature helps us understand why these conflicts occur. The literature has provided two classes of the models: the arming models, where inefficiency stems from exerting costly efforts to arm, and the violence models, where inefficiency stems from the actual use of force. In the former, inefficient use of resources in arms can be explained by the prisoner's dilemma induced by the structure of contest's success function (Haavelmo, 1954; Tullock, 2001). Even when zero investment in armaments by both parties is Pareto efficient, the profile is not maintained in Nash equilibrium because each party would prefer to deviate toward positive investment. In the latter, dynamic commitment problems may arise: In order to discourage the use of costly force by the opponent, each party may prefer to commit not to exploit the bargaining power obtained through the increase in coercive power, but such a commitment is not credible. This explains why civil conflicts tend to last a long time: Rebel groups are reluctant to accept a disarmament agreement, as they expect the government to renege on its decision. With regard to the analysis of bargaining with incomplete information, auction-type models, in which states' bids represent their willingness to run a disaster risk, are apt to take into account the intensity of preferences on the political issues at stake.

In Chapter 30, Gene M. Grossman reviews applications of game theory in trade policy. Since Johnson (1953), the formulation of government policy choices as a game and the application of equilibrium analysis have shed light on strategic interaction between governments, such as tariff setting (Dixit, 1987), international intellectual property protection (Grossman and Lai, 2004), and regulatory policy in the service of production delocation (Grossman and colleagues, 2021). Analysis of the role played by interest groups representing the industry or issue and competing for favorable treatment from government focused on *electoral motive* of political parties in early studies (Magee and colleagues, 1989). Grossman and Helpman (1994) developed the Protection for Sale (PFS) model, which features *influence motive* for campaign giving. By considering interest groups that propose a contribution schedule, they derive a modified Ramsey rule. In addition to its theoretical rigor and elegance, the model is appreciated for its ability to provide predictions for the cross-sectional structure of trade protection (Goldberg and Maggi, 1999). The analysis of strategic interactions between interest groups, political parties, and legislators has encompassed political campaigns, legislative bargaining, and legislative deliberations due to the potential use of trade policies as political instruments to compete for power. In particular, protectionist bias in majoritarian politics is identified in Grossman and Helpman (2005). The inefficiency generated in noncooperative equilibrium motivates the institutional design that aims to induce cooperative behavior through international trade agreements. Cooperative game theory can be helpful in identifying the type of institutions that enhance Pareto improvement, such as tariff quotas, voluntary export restrictions, and multilateral trade agreements.

Common to all three topics covered in this part is the fact that the concepts developed in both noncooperative and cooperative game theory are useful for the analysis of strategic interaction in political science. At the end of the chapter, each author provides a description of the main challenges we face for future research. A wide range of theoretical and empirical questions are still underexplored. We expect exciting new developments of game theory in political science over the next 100 years.

27.1 REFERENCES

D. Acemoglu, G. Egorov, and K. Sonin. Dynamics and stability of constitutions, coalitions, and clubs. *American Economic Review*, 102:1446–1476, 2012.

E. Borel. La théorie du jeu et les équations intégrales à noyau symétrique. *Comptes rendus de l'Académie des Sciences*, 173:1304–1308, 1921.

A. K. Dixit. Strategic aspects of trade policy. In T. Bewley, ed., *Advances in Economic Theory*. New York: Cambridge University Press, 1987.

A. Downs. An economic theory of political action in a democracy. *Journal of Political Economy*, 65(2):135–150, 1957.

R. Farqhuarson. *Theory of Voting*. New Haven, CT: Yale University Press, 1969.

T. J. Feddersen and W. Pesendorfer. Voting behavior and information aggregation in elections with private information. *Econometrica*, 65:1029–1058, 1997.

P. K. Goldberg and G. Maggi. Protection for sale: An empirical investigation. *American Economic Review*, 89(5):1135–1155, 1999.

G. M. Grossman and E. Helpman. Protection for sale. *American Economic Review*, 84(4):833–850, 1994.

G. M. Grossman and E. Helpman. A protectionist bias in majoritarian politics. *Quarterly Journal of Economics*, 120(4):1239–1282, 2005.

G. M. Grossman and E. L.-C. Lai. International protection of intellectual property. *American Economic Review*, 94(5):1635–1653, 2004.

G. M. Grossman, P. McCalman, and R. W. Staiger. The "new" economics of trade agreements: From trade liberalization to regulatory convergence? *Econometrica*, 89(1):215–249, 2021.

T. Haavelmo. *A Study in the Theory of Economic Evolution*. Amsterdam: North-Holland Publishing, 1954.

H. G. Johnson. Optimal tariffs and retaliation. *Review of Econoic Studies*, 21(2):142–153, 1953.

S. P. Magee, W. Brock, and L. Young. *Black Hole Tariffs and Endogenous Policy Theory*. Cambridge: Cambridge University Press, 1989.

P. C. Ordeshook and T. R. Palfrey. Agendas, strategic voting, and signaling with incomplete information. *American Journal of Political Science*, 32:441–466, 1988.

W. H. Riker. *The Theory of Political Coalitions*. New Haven: Yale University Press, 1962.

T. C. Schelling. *The Strategy of Conflict*. Cambridge, MA: Harvard University Press, 1960.

T. C. Schelling. *Arms and Influence*. New Haven, CT: Yale University Press, 1966.

L. S. Shapley and M. Shubik. A method of evaluating the distribution of power in a committee system. *American Political Science Review*, 48:787–792, 1954.

G. Tullock. Efficient rent seeking (first published 1980). In G. Tullock and A. Lockhard, eds., *Efficient Rent-Seeking*, pp. 3–16. Boston: Springer, 2001.

28

Game Theory in Political Science

Voting, Elections, and Information Aggregation

David Austen-Smith

Shapley and Shubik (1954) is the first game-theoretic paper published in a political science journal. Almost devoid of notation, the paper introduces the Shapley–Shubik Power Index to measure individual influence in voting games, illustrating the concept through several examples. Although important in its own right, perhaps the most significant consequence of the paper was that it was read by William H. Riker, who at the time was looking for a way to turn what passed for political science into a more rigorous positive discipline. He was already studying Arrow (1951), and the Shapley and Shubik paper led him to von Neumann and Morgenstern (1944). As a consequence, Riker published the seminal (cooperative) game-theoretic book in political science per se, *A Theory of Political Coalitions* (Riker, 1962). Riker (1992) tells this story and goes on to relate how game theory penetrated political science over the thirty years following publication of his book.

Since Riker's 1962 contribution, the rational choice and game-theoretic literature in political science has grown rapidly. Early contributions were largely cooperative game-theoretic, with noncooperative models currently predominant. Although the contributions cover a wide variety of subfields within political science, this essay is confined to game-theoretic models of preference and information aggregation through voting. For reasons of space, I focus almost exclusively on vote aggregation through plurality rule, under which the salient collective choice is determined by the alternative receiving the most votes. The normative aspiration underlying this aggregation mechanism is that it identifies and selects the best (information aggregation) available alternative for a majority of the electorate (preference aggregation). And in large democratic societies, the mechanism is typically implemented through representative democracy: Citizens elect candidates to represent their interests in a legislature that makes payoff-relevant policy decisions.

The relevant voting literature is considerable, and it is useful to distinguish models of electoral competition with a large number of voters n from models of committee decision-making with a small n. From a formal perspective, the key distinction is that in large n elections, the probability that an individual's vote changes the outcome (i.e., the individual's pivot probability) becomes negligible as n becomes large, whereas in small n committees, pivot probabilities are significant. From a substantive perspective, policy outcomes in modern representative democracies, as noted previously, do not solely depend on who occupies legislative offices (determined in large n elections) but also on the decisions made by those elected to the legislature (determined in small n committees). In principle, analyzing voting in an integrated framework (electoral and legislative decision-making) is most desirable. Here, however, I consider them – as does almost all of the literature – separately.[1]

28.1 ELECTORAL COMPETITION AND TURNOUT

28.1.1 A Benchmark Model of Elections

A principal goal of the theory of elections is to explain the alternatives strategically offered to voters by candidates or parties competing for electoral office. As such, the agenda confronting voters (i.e., candidates' policy platforms) is necessarily endogenous. In particular, given candidates' objectives and feasible policy sets, the alternatives offered by candidates depend, at least in part, on how they anticipate voters will respond.

The benchmark framework for modeling electoral competition is the two-candidate spatial model. There are two candidates A, B, along with n individual voters.[2] Available policies are alternatives in some convex and compact set $X \subset \mathbb{R}^k$ over which voters have preferences representable by continuous and strictly quasiconcave utilities. Candidates compete for a single office by committing to proposals (platforms) from X; individuals vote over the proposals, and the winning candidate's platform is given by plurality rule. Both candidates only value winning office and choose (and commit to) platforms to maximize their respective expected pluralities, given their opponent's platform and voter behavior. With only two alternatives proposed and costless voting, sincere voting is strategically rational: Voters vote sincerely for their most preferred platform, flipping a fair coin when indifferent.

Under complete information, this simple model defines a zero-sum game between the candidates. And since there is no abstention, individuals vote sincerely, and purely office-motivated, plurality-maximizing candidates offer policies strategically, the set of (weakly undominated) pure strategy Nash equilibria under majority rule coincides with the majority core. Unfortunately, the majority core is only guaranteed to be nonempty when the dimensionality of the policy space, k, is one (Plott, 1967), in which case we have the median

[1] Austen-Smith and Banks (1988) and Baron and Diermeier (2001) are exceptions.

[2] The literature with multiple candidates and varying electoral rules is extensive: In particular, see Cox (1987, 1990) and Myerson and Weber (1993). It is ignored here purely in the interest of space.

voter theorem: Candidates converge on the median voter's most preferred policy and all voters are indifferent between candidates. [3] In multidimensional policy spaces, the existence problem for pure strategy Nash equilibria is largely due to discontinuities in candidate payoff functions as majority preference switches between candidate platforms. Duggan and Jackson (2005) prove the existence of a mixed strategy equilibrium in multidimensional policy spaces by having indifferent voters make decisions deterministically in specific ways rather than randomly. Characterizing such equilibria, however, has proved elusive.[4] As a result, the prevailing approach to restoring continuity to support pure strategy equilibria with multidimensional policies is to assume probabilistic voting (Lindbeck and Weibull, 1987; Banks and Duggan, 2005), with the idiosyncratic stochastic component of any individual's decision independent of policy.

28.1.2 Turnout with Costly Voting

In the benchmark model, voting is costless, which as recognized by Downs (1957) finesses the turnout problem: If voting is costly and the likelihood of being the pivotal voter in a large election is negligible, why vote at all? Moreover, since candidate platform choice is conditional on the aggregate voter response, understanding turnout is fundamental to understanding the strategic provision of electoral policy alternatives.

There are a great many models aimed at solving the problem.[5] The seminal game-theoretic papers were written by Palfrey and Rosenthal (1983), who study a costly turnout game in which voters have strict preferences over two exogenously given (distinct) candidates, and Ledyard (1984), who builds a general spatial model of a two-candidate election with endogenous platform choice and costly voting. In both contributions, expected turnout and the probability of being pivotal are simultaneously determined in equilibrium. In the work of Palfrey and Rosenthal, turnout goes to zero as n increases, and according to Ledyard, candidates converge on the aggregate utility maximizing policy in

[3] Core nonexistence results, *mutatis mutandis*, extend to all strong simple rules in the spatial model (Schofield, 1984). Moreover, in higher dimensional spaces, core emptiness implies there exist majority preference (i.e., the majority sincere vote) cycles that cover the entire space (McKelvey, 1979; Schofield, 1983). Riker (1982) concluded from these results that unconstrained democratic politics were inherently unstable and furthermore that concepts of a "general will" or "the common good" widespread in the normative literature were basically vacuous, a heresy that continues to foster debate.

[4] McKelvey (1986) and Banks et al. (2002) show that the support of any mixed strategy equilibrium lies within the closure of the uncovered set: An alternative y is *covered* by an alternative x if x is strictly majority preferred to y and any alternative z that defeats x also defeats y; the *uncovered set* is the set of alternatives that are not covered (Miller, 1980). If the policy space X is finite, Laffond et al. (1993) prove the mixed strategy equilibrium is unique and symmetric: Both candidates adopt the same mixed strategy and thus ex ante the candidates are equivalent from a policy perspective, just as they are under the median voter theorem.

[5] See Feddersen (2004) for an excellent review of the literature here.

equilibrium and there is zero turnout. Feddersen (1992) analyzes a multidimensional spatial model with a large *n* electorate, plurality rule, and costly voting, but *no* candidates (equivalently, an uncountable number of candidates, one per possible policy). Instead of voting over a limited set of candidate proposals, individuals cast ballots by marking the policy they most prefer. There is no coordination among individuals, save that implicit in a Nash equilibrium. Not surprisingly, there are multiple (weakly undominant) pure strategy equilibria. What is surprising is that inter alia every equilibrium involves exactly two nonconvergent, centrally located policies receiving any votes. Furthermore, there is strictly positive voting and abstention.

Myerson (2000) develops a theory of Poisson voting games to study the relevance of individuals being unsure of the number of voters in any election and therefore the realized distribution of preferences.[6] Although the theory has been profitably used to study the comparative information aggregation properties of various sorts of voting rule (e.g., Bouton, 2013; Bouton and Castanheira, 2012), the application to turnout per se has been less successful. Myatt (2015) argues that turnout is better understood through aggregate uncertainty than through individual uncertainty about the number of voters.

Other approaches focus less on individual pivot decisions and more on the ability of groups of voters to coordinate behavior, subject to individual incentive compatibility conditions. Morton (1991) examines a group-mobilization model with coordination encouraged through group leadership and finds positive equilibrium turnout.[7] Feddersen and Sandroni (2006) and Coate and Conlin (2004) use Harsanyi's (1977) Rule Utilitarian perspective to develop noncooperative theories of group turnout in which "ethical" individuals receive a "warm-glow" payoff for acting to promote the utilitarian welfare principle of aggregate cost minimization. Unlike in the work of Harsanyi, the ethical rule for implementing the principle is endogenous and individuals have heterogenous preferences and voting costs. In equilibrium, there is high turnout and some individuals behave "ethically" by not voting.

In an earlier contribution, Feddersen and Pesendorfer (1996) pose the turnout problem more generally: If voting is costly, then why do so many people vote? If the response is that voting is not sufficiently costly, then why is there so much abstention? They develop a model with no voting costs and incomplete information regarding both the distribution of voter preferences and a decision-relevant state variable. In this model, they prove the existence of a "swing voter's curse": less informed indifferent voters strictly prefer to abstain, despite voting being costless. Furthermore, even when uncertain voters have a strict ex ante preference for one alternative over another, there can be substantial

[6] Earlier, Myerson and Weber (1993) provide an elegant and subtle theory of (pivotal) voting equilibria in a multicandidate model of elections with a fixed set of platforms and costless voting. Voters are fully strategic and equilibrium perceptions of candidates' chances of success are then driven by voters' strategic uncertainty.

[7] Groups may be defined by a shared identity, ethnicity, occupation, religion, and so forth.

abstention in equilibrium. Intuitively, the cost of casting a vote for a voter's less preferred candidate ex post is too high, even with no voting costs. Perhaps surprisingly in view of the pivotal voter considerations exploited in equilibrium, the swing voter's curse has been found in small n voting experiments (Battaglini et al., 2010). Nevertheless, a singular focus on policy and pivotal voting as motivating turnout in large n elections is insufficient.

Pivotal voter models can account for the observed comparative statics of turnout in elections but largely fail to account for levels of turnout. Indeed, zero turnout is the typical equilibrium outcome with large n elections, costly voting, and complete information. A promising approach to understanding both the comparative statics and levels of turnout, as remarked by Feddersen (2004), lies in developing richer models of mobilization and *intra*group coordination.

28.2 "SOPHISTICATED" (STRATEGIC) VOTING IN COMMITTEES

In committees with comparatively few individual voters, pivot probabilities are appreciable. As indicated earlier, with only two alternatives for consideration and plurality rule, an individual has a weakly undominated voting strategy: Vote sincerely. Committees, however, frequently have to make a collective choice from a finite set of three or more alternatives. Individuals vote sincerely in this case if their votes coincide with their preferences over the entire set of alternatives. But in this case, sincere voting is typically not a strategically rational decision under any (nondictatorial) voting rule. Nevertheless, sincere voting was a standard assumption in models of committee voting until Farqhuarson's *Theory of Voting* (1969).[8]

Unlike the existing voting literature at the time, Farquharson assumed individuals to be strategically rational and, for committee decisions over a given multistage agenda, defined "sophisticated [voting] strategies" as those surviving a successive elimination of dominated strategies in an n-person normal form representation of the agenda.[9] Using the extensive form representation of the agenda, McKelvey and Niemi (1978) provided a much simpler, backward induction algorithm for identifying strategically rational strategies and outcomes in binary voting games. Although occasionally resulting in different sets of sophisticated strategies, McKelvey and Niemi conjectured, and Gretlein (1980) proved that the set of "sophisticated outcomes" supported by Farquharson's sophisticated strategies necessarily coincided with those found through backward induction. McKelvey and Niemi's simpler methodology initiated a huge

[8] This volume was essentially written in 1958 as Farquharson's D.Phil. dissertation. It was first rejected for publication by Yale University Press in 1962, but later, with Shubik's help, Yale reversed its decision.

[9] In a multistage agenda, decision-making is constrained to follow some prespecified sequence of votes over the (finite) set of alternatives X. Prominent examples include *amendment* and *sequential elimination agendas*. An amendment agenda is of the form $\langle a$ vs b, winner vs $c, \ldots\rangle$, and a sequential elimination agenda is of the form $\langle[a$ vs $X\backslash\{a\}]$, if a STOP; if $X\backslash\{a\}$ then $[b$ vs $X\backslash\{a,b\}]$, if b STOP; if $X\backslash\{a,b\}$ then $[c$ vs $X\backslash\{a,b,c\}], \ldots\rangle$.

theoretical literature on sophisticated voting over various agenda forms (Miller, 1995; Laslier, 1997). Banks (1985) fully characterized the set sophisticated outcomes for binary amendment agendas–that is, agendas of the form $\langle a$ versus b, winner versus $c, \ldots\rangle$. Shepsle and Weingast (1984) consider sophisticated voting in the spatial voting model (with a continuum of possible alternatives) proving inter alia that any sophisticated outcome of an agenda starting with x, say y, cannot be covered by x (fn. [4]). If there is an agenda that leads from x to y, then there is a two-step agenda that leads from x to y (i.e., for some alternative z, the sophisticated outcome of agenda $\langle x, z, y\rangle$ is y).

The analytical focus in the literature is almost entirely on how the ordering of a given set of alternatives and the agenda form influence what outcomes can be supported as sophisticated outcomes. Largely absent is any serious consideration of exactly how the alternatives on an agenda get there. One possibility is that alternatives are proposed by members of the committee, as proposed by Austen-Smith (1987) and Duggan (2003). At least for amendment agendas with sequential proposals, Austen-Smith (1987) shows that strategic and sincere voting over the resulting agendas coincide. This result speaks to why empirical efforts to identify sophisticated voting in congressional committees have produced mixed results.

28.3 INFORMATION AGGREGATION

Games with incomplete information began to appear in political science journals during the latter half of the 1980s. The first regrettably overlooked and underappreciated application of incomplete information to voting in committees is Ordeshook and Palfrey (1988). To my knowledge, this paper was the first to identify the importance of individuals conditioning their voting strategies over a given agenda on the event of casting a pivotal vote. The paper was written to illustrate the use of Bayesian and, in particular, sequential equilibria in binary voting games through a series of explicitly worked examples. Each example involved three committee members with preferences private information, voting over a three alternative amendment agenda under majority rule. While the examples demonstrated that some of the established, complete information results regarding committee voting became suspect when there was incomplete information, the authors offered no more general results. Such results first appeared in Austen-Smith and Banks (1996) for committee voting and, independently, Feddersen and Pesendorfer (1996, 1997) for voting in elections. In both, voters have noisy private information about the relative value of two alternatives.[10] The motivating problem here is the robustness of Condorcet

[10] Austen-Smith and Banks' paper (1996) was stimulated by a two-alternative example of majority voting with incomplete information in Austen-Smith (1990). Feddersen and Pesendorfer (1998) explore jury voting under unanimity rule. Although not concerned with information aggregation, Banks (1990) provides a model of elections with incomplete information in which the candidates' types are their costs of lying with respect to implementing their electoral platforms.

Jury Theorem (1785) with Bayesian voters. Since these contributions, the literature on information aggregation in committee decisions and large elections have followed largely different paths.

28.3.1 Information Aggregation in Committees

The literature on (majoritarian) committee voting explores the role of prevote debate (typically but not exclusively modeled as cheap talk) in information aggregation with private values (where the common knowledge of common values case is trivial).[11] The distinction between debate here and the canonic expert advice framework is that all committee members have private information (independent and individually distributed [i.i.d.] signals from a common distribution) regarding the true state and all committee members vote after strategically sharing their information. The earliest models assumed a simple committee protocol for choosing between two alternatives: Committee members privately observe a noisy but informative signal regarding the state, then simultaneously announce a cheap talk message about their signals and, finally, the committee votes (Austen-Smith, 1990; Austen-Smith and Feddersen, 2005, 2006; Meirowitz, 2006, 2007).[12] The focus in this literature is the relationship between the voting rule and incentives to share information. The formal difficulty is that an individual's incentive to share private information is conditional on the event that their message is pivotal in influencing others' beliefs in debate sufficiently to affect the subsequent committee decision. Moreover, best-response voting strategies following debate are conditional on the event that their votes are pivotal, *given* updated beliefs induced by the realized debate. In equilibrium, both sets of pivotal conditions – message and vote – must be mutually consistent. Loosely speaking, the main finding is that while there exist conditions under which nonunanimity rules support full information sharing in debate, the same is not true of unanimity rule.

The intuition here is that committee members prefer to share information in debate when they believe that they will be in the de facto winning coalition as a result, but not otherwise. Given a fully revealing debate, postdebate best-response voting strategies are sincere (relative to beliefs), and under nonunanimous majoritarian voting rules, there can be multiple message-pivotal events for any individual. For some (nontrivial) information structures and some message-pivotal events, the individual's best-response message strategy is to reveal her signal truthfully; for other such events, dissembling is her best response. If, however, the voting rule requires unanimity to choose y over x, any committee member can guarantee x by exercising a veto. Therefore, her voting

[11] For current purposes, "majoritarian" is shorthand for any supermajority voting rule, from simple majority to unanimity. We also assume all committee members values are such that preferences over the alternatives are state dependent.

[12] Allowing individuals to send messages regarding their private values (biases) in addition to their signals does not affect what follows.

strategy is independent of her own signal and so, regardless of her signal, she always prefers to send the message that induces others to vote for y.

Identifying equilibria in collective choice with talk becomes less tedious with a mechanism design approach to deliberation in committees. Within a very general common values "jury" setting with voters having idiosyncratic "thresholds of doubt," Gerardi and Yariv (2007) prove that subject to the committee having at least five members, full information revelation in debate is achievable with unconstrained debate without a mediator. Moreover, this result holds for any majoritarian voting rule save the unamity rule. The key idea is that the mechanism makes voting unanimous, effectively removing the pivotal constraints on (weakly undominated) best-response voting strategies. Goeree and Yariv (2011) provide experimental evidence that unconstrained debate does elicit full revelation but observe that more restrictive deliberation protocols imply the voting rule is consequential – just how consequential is an open issue.[13]

28.3.2 Information Aggregation in Elections

Unlike the committee literature noted previously, issues around strategic communication are largely absent when we come to information aggregation in large elections. Here the focus is on the robustness of the original, remarkable Feddersen and Pesendorfer aggregation result (1997): In a large election with positively correlated voter preferences and uncertainty regarding a decision-relevant state variable, all information is aggregated in majority voting equilibrium in the sense that as the size of the electorate goes to infinity, the limiting final outcome coincides with the outcome under complete information. For any finite electorate, individual voters vote sincerely (relative to their beliefs), conditional on being pivotal. The aggregation result then follows from two properties of equilibria as the electorate becomes large: First, the proportion of voters voting informatively in equilibrium becomes vanishingly small (pivot probabilities go to zero), and second, the information reflected in the event of being pivotal approaches certainty (via the law of large numbers). Feddersen and Pesendorfer show (loosely speaking) that the second property goes to the limit faster than the first. Hence sufficiently large n, almost nobody is voting informatively in equilibrium, yet all information is aggregated. Inter alia, this result hinges on the positive correlation of preferences and uncertainty being only in regard to a single state variable.

There are several subsequent models that explore the extent to which alternative assumptions on preferences and the information structure affect preference aggregation in elections. The (currently) most general analysis of

[13] For an innovative dynamic model of debate with private values, see Chan and colleagues (2018). Hafer and Landa (2007) develop a very different model of deliberation in which individuals are endowed with "active" arguments of which they are aware and "latent" arguments of which they are unaware. Latent arguments need to be triggered by others making active arguments to become active and induce changes in belief.

the robustness problem is due to Barelli and colleagues (2021), who establish a necessary and sufficient property of the information structure for information aggregation in a given election. Essentially, the signal space must be "sufficiently rich" relative to the state space. In general, this property is unlikely to obtain. These results extend to elections with private values, multiple alternatives, and voting rules other than simple majority, and subsume existing specific results on environments where full information in an election fails. Nevertheless, the literature on information aggregation in elections provides an explanation for why democracies might function well, despite not all citizens being well informed. At the same time, asymmetric information provides opportunities for candidate manipulation of voters. Alonso and Camara (2016) use a Bayesian persuasion approach to investigate the extent to which a purely office-oriented politician can manipulate the electorate. They address both welfare implications of such manipulation (not good) and the majoritarian voting rule that minimizes the negative impact of manipulation (supermajoritarian).[14]

28.4 WHERE NEXT?

The core emptiness and global cycling theorems for the multidimensional spatial voting model (Plott, 1967; McKelvey, 1979; Schofield, 1983; among others) frustrated any hope of aggregating preferences through voting in a majoritarian democracy with a large electorate. Likewise, following the seminal contributions by Feddersen and Pesendorfer (1997, 1999), recent theorems on the general possibility of successful information aggregation in large electorates are negative (Mandler, 2012; Bhattacharya, 2013; Barelli et al., 2021). The implication of these two sets of results, at least for large majoritarian societies, is that both elections and information aggregation are necessarily subject to strategic manipulation. The situation is a little more promising for small committees. Although preference instabilities are inherent in almost any collective decision-making, prevote debate can ensure full information aggregation if the protocol is designed with sufficient care (Gerardi and Yariv, 2007). Game theory and mechanism design are thus natural frameworks within which to study politics. There are many open questions.

How does the failure of voting to aggregate either preferences or information in large elections affect the stability of representative democracy? What determines the robustness (or not) of democratic norms?[15] These questions appear especially salient when politics seems less about finding good policies and more about an 'us-versus-them' ideological battle. The rhetoric of tribalism threatens to undermine both policy debate and trust in democratic institutions, a concern

[14] A primitive example of Bayesian persuasion, albeit not by that name, is used in Austen-Smith (1998) to model lobbyists' strategic influence on a legislator's policy decision, conditional on being granted access to the legislator.

[15] Efforts to understand at least the stability of voting rules include Acemoglu et al. (2012), Aghion et al. (2004), and Barbera and Jackson (2004).

that is exacerbated by the considerable evidence of information filtering among voters. What is the impact of non-Bayesian voters in candidate competition and campaigns under uncertainty?[16] What is the role of the media in such elections?

Representative democracies, as observed previously, involve candidates for legislative office competing in large *n* elections and elected legislators choosing policies in small *n* committees. As of yet there are very few integrated models of such democracies. Most of the distinct literatures on elections and legislative decision-making therefore offer only a "partial equilibrium" understanding. Current electoral models implicitly assume an elected candidate has monopoly control over the final legislative policy. Does this matter? In a legislative election model with a multimember legislature, for instance, fully rational voters take account of the expected legislative policy consequences when voting in their respective constituency elections. Thus individuals' vote decisions depend in part on their expectations of the electoral outcomes in other constituencies (if any, which is typically the case), which in turn influences candidates' electoral platforms.

Electoral rules in the literature are typically assumed exogenous. Different rules induce different incentives and mostly distinct equilibrium outcomes. The comparative analysis of such rules then proceeds by comparing these outcomes against some given yardstick, such as a measure of citizen representation or the distribution of resources. Although almost all democracies use "first past the post" plurality rule or some version of proportional representation to elect legislators, there are other possible electoral vote aggregation methods, beyond those found in practice. Once a rule is in place, vested interests are a ready explanation for why they become so hard to change. Yet some countries do change their electoral systems, and it is not clear why the rules we observe came to be as they are. Given that the number of parties that choose to compete for office and legislative policy outcomes are deeply influenced by the rule in place, it seems important to develop theories of how rules emerge and how they might be changed to reflect changes in society, when appropriate.

28.5 REFERENCES

D. Acemoglu, G. Egorov, and K. Sonin. Dynamics and stability of constitutions, coalitions, and clubs. *American Economic Review*, 102:1446–1476, 2012.

P. Aghion, A. Alesina, and F. Trebbi. Endogenous political institutions. *Quarterly Journal of Economics*, 119:565–611, 2004.

R. Alonso and O. Camara. Persuading voters. *American Economic Review*, 106:3590–3605, 2016.

K. J. Arrow. *Social Choice and Individual Values*. New Haven: Yale University Press, 1951.

[16] Levy et al. (2022) and Eliaz and Spiegler (2020) adopt a "false model" approach to this issue in the context of understanding populism. Levy and Razin (2015) analyze an electoral model where voters have correlation neglect.

D. Austen-Smith. Sophisticated sincerity: Voting over endogenous agendas. *American Political Science Review*, 81:1323–1329, 1987.

D. Austen-Smith. Information transmission in debate. *American Journal of Political Science*, 34:124–152, 1990.

D. Austen-Smith. Allocating access for information and contributions. *Journal of Law, Economics and Organizations*, 14:277–303, 1998.

D. Austen-Smith and J. S. Banks. Elections, legislatures and legislative outcomes. *American Political Science Review*, 82:405–422, 1988.

D. Austen-Smith and J. S. Banks. Information aggregation, rationality, and the condorcet jury theorem. *American Political Science Review*, 90:34–45, 1996.

D. Austen-Smith and T. Feddersen. In Austen-Smith and J. Duggan, eds., *Social Choice and Strategic Decisions: Essays in Honor of Jeffrey S. Banks*. Berlin: Springer, 2005.

D. Austen-Smith and T. J. Feddersen. Deliberation, preference uncertainty and voting rules. *American Political Science Review*, 100:209–217, 2006.

J. S. Banks. Sophisticated voting outcomes and agenda control. *Social Choice and Welfare*, 1:295–306, 1985.

J. S. Banks. A model of electoral competition with incomplete information. *Journal of Economic Theory*, 50:309–325, 1990.

J. S. Banks and J. Duggan. Probabilistic voting in the spatial model of elections: The theory of office-motivated candidates. In D. Austen-Smith and J. Duggan, eds., *Social Choice and Strategic Decisions: Essays in Honor of Jeffrey S. Banks*. Berlin: Springer, 2005.

J. S. Banks, J. Duggan, and M. L. Breton. Bounds for mixed strategy equilibria and the spatial model of elections. *Journal of Economic Theory*, 103:88–105, 2002.

S. Barbera and M. Jackson. Choosing how to choose: self-stable majority rules and constitutions. *Quarterly Journal of Economics*, 119:1011–1048, 2004.

P. Barelli, S. Bhattacharya, and L. Siga. Full information equivalence in large elections. Working paper, Social Science Research Network (SSRN), 2021.

D. Baron and D. Diermeier. Elections, governments and parliaments in proportional representation systems. *Quarterly Journal of Economics*, 116:933–967, 2001.

M. Battaglini, R. Morton, and T. R. Palfrey. The swing voter's curse in the laboratory. *Review of Economic Studies*, 77:61–89, 2010.

S. Bhattacharya. Preference monotonicity and information aggregation in elections. *Econometrica*, 81:1229–1247, 2013.

L. Bouton. A theory of strategic voting in runoff elections. *American Economic Review*, 103:1248–1288, 2013.

L. Bouton and M. Castanheira. One person, many votes: divided majority and information aggregation. *Econometrica*, 80:43–87, 2012.

J. Chan, A. Lizzeri, W. Suen, and L. Yariv. Deliberating collective decisions. *Review of Economic Studies*, 85:929–963, 2018.

S. Coate and M. Conlin. A group rule-utilitarian approach to voter turnout: Theory and evidence. *American Economic Review*, 94:1476–1504, 2004.

M. d. Condorcet. *Essai sur l'application de l'analyse a la probabilite des decisions rendues a la pluralite des voix*. Trans. I. McLean and F. Hewitt. Paris: Imprimerie Royale, 1785.

G. Cox. Electoral equilibrium under alternative voting institutions. *American Journal of Political Science*, 31:82–108, 1987.

G. Cox. Centripetal and centrifugal incentives in electoral systems. *American Journal of Political Science*, 34:903–935, 1990.

A. Downs. An economic theory of political action in a democracy. *Journal of Political Economy*, 65(2):135–150, 1957.
J. Duggan. Endogenous amendment agendas. *Social Choice and Welfare*, 27:495–530, 2003.
J. Duggan and M. Jackson. Mixed strategy equilibrium and deep covering in multidimensional electoral competition. Working Paper, Department of Political Science, University of Rochester, 2005.
K. Eliaz and R. Spiegler. A model of competing narratives. *American Economic Review*, 110:3786–3816, 2020.
R. Farqhuarson. *Theory of Voting*. New Haven: Yale University Press, 1969.
T. J. Feddersen. A voting model implying duverger's law and positive turnout. *American Journal of Political Science*, 36:938–962, 1992.
T. J. Feddersen. Rational choice theory and the paradox of not voting: A literature review. *Journal of Economic Perspectives*, 18:99–112, 2004.
T. J. Feddersen and W. Pesendorfer. The swing voter's curse. *American Economic Review*, 86:408–424, 1996.
T. J. Feddersen and W. Pesendorfer. Voting behavior and information aggregation in elections with private information. *Econometrica*, 65:1029–1058, 1997.
T. J. Feddersen and W. Pesendorfer. Convicting the innocent: The inferiority of unanimous jury verdicts. *American Political Science Review*, 92:23–35, 1998.
T. J. Feddersen and W. Pesendorfer. Abstention in elections with asymmetric information and diverse preferences. *American Political Science Review*, 93:381–398, 1999.
T. J. Feddersen and A. Sandroni. Ethical voters and costly voting. *Quarterly Journal of Political Science*, 11:1–26, 2006.
D. Gerardi and L. Yariv. Deliberative voting. *Journal of Economic Theory*, 134:317–338, 2007.
J. K. Goeree and L. Yariv. An experimental study of collective deliberation. *Econometrica*, 79:893–921, 2011.
R. J. Gretlein. Dominance elimination procedures on finite alternative games. *International Journal of Game Theory*, 12:107–113, 1980.
C. Hafer and D. Landa. Deliberation as self-discovery and institutions for political speech. *Journal of Theoretical Politics*, 19:329–360, 2007.
J. Harsanyi. Rule utilitarianism and decision theory. *Erkenntnis*, 11:25–533, 1977.
G. Laffond, J.-F. Laslier, and M. L. Breton. The bipartisan set of a tournament game. *Games and Economic Behavior*, 5:182–201, 1993.
J.-F. Laslier. *Tournament Solutions and Majority Voting*. Berlin: Springer, 1997.
J. Ledyard. The pure theory of large two-candidate elections. *Public Choice*, 44:7–43, 1984.
G. Levy and R. Razin. Correlation neglect, voting behaviour and information aggregation. *American Economic Review*, 105:1634–1645, 2015.
G. Levy, R. Razin, and A. Young. Misspecified politics and the recurrence of populism. *American Economic Review*, 112:928–962, 2022.
A. Lindbeck and J. W. Weibull. Balanced-budget redistribution as the outcome of political competition. *Public Choice*, 52:273–297, 1987.
M. Mandler. The fragility of information aggregation in large elections. *Games and Economic Behavior*, 74:257–268, 2012.
R. D. McKelvey. General conditions for global intransitivities in formal voting models. *Econometrica*, 47:1086–1112, 1979.

R. D. McKelvey. Covering, dominance and institution-free properties of social choice. *American Journal of Political Science*, 30:283–314, 1986.

R. D. McKelvey and R. G. Niemi. A multistage game representation of sophisticated voting for binary procedures. *Journal of Economic Theory*, 18:1–22, 1978.

A. Meirowitz. Designing institutions to aggregate preferences and information. *Quarterly Journal of Political Science*, 1:373–392, 2006.

A. Meirowitz. In defense of exclusionary deliberation: communication and voting with private beliefs and values. *Journal of Theoretical Politics*, 19:329–360, 2007.

N. R. Miller. A new solution set for tournaments and majority voting. *American Journal of Political Science*, 24:68–96, 1980.

N. R. Miller. *Committees, Agendas and Voting*. Chur, Switzerland: Harwood Academic Publishers, 1995.

R. B. Morton. Groups in rational turnout models. *American Journal of Political Science*, 35(3):758–776, 1991.

D. P. Myatt. A theory of voter turnout. Working paper, London Business School, 2015.

R. B. Myerson. Large Poisson games. *Journal of Economic Theory*, 94:7–45, 2000.

R. B. Myerson and R. Weber. A theory of voting equilibria. *American Political Science Review*, 87:102–114, 1993.

P. C. Ordeshook and T. R. Palfrey. Agendas, strategic voting, and signaling with incomplete information. *American Journal of Political Science*, 32:441–466, 1988.

T. R. Palfrey and H. Rosenthal. A strategic calculus of voting. *Public Choice*, 41:7–53, 1983.

C. R. Plott. A notion of equilibrium and its possibility under majority rule. *American Economic Review*, 57:787–806, 1967.

W. H. Riker. *The Theory of Political Coalitions*. New Haven: Yale University Press, 1962.

W. H. Riker. *Liberalism against Populism*. San Francisco: W. H. Freeman, 1982.

W. H. Riker. The entry of game theory into political science. *History of Political Economy*, 24:207–223, 1992.

N. J. Schofield. Generic instability of majority rule. *Review of Economic Studies*, 50:695–705, 1983.

N. J. Schofield. Classification theorem for smooth social choice on a manifold. *Social Choice and Welfare*, 1:187–210, 1984.

L. S. Shapley and M. Shubik. A method of evaluating the distribution of power in a committee system. *American Political Science Review*, 48:787–92, 1954.

K. A. Shepsle and B. R. Weingast. Uncovered sets and sophisticated voting outcomes with implications for agenda institutions. *American Journal of Political Science*, 28:49–74, 1984.

J. von Neumann and O. Morgenstern. *Theory of Games and Economic Behavior*. Princeton, NJ: Princeton University Press, 1944.

29

Game Theory and Explanations for Armed Conflict

James D. Fearon

29.1 INTRODUCTION

In his 1921 article Émile Borel noted that problems of military tactics were "not without analogy" to the zero-sum game that he analyzed there. John von Neumann and a number of early game theorists working before and during World War II pursued the analogy with more enthusiasm, sometimes using as an example the problem of finding a best (or good) strategy in Colonel Blotto–type problems where two generals decide how to allocate their forces across multiple battlefields. Thomas Schelling (1960) argued that in the real world, essentially no strategic interaction, including armed conflict, is well represented as a zero-sum game. Rather, even adversaries in war have common as well as conflicting interests – all the more so, and in an extreme fashion, when nuclear war is a possible outcome (Schelling, 1966).

Nuclear weapons have not been used in war again since 1945, but these last seven decades have seen a great deal of highly destructive armed conflict. There has been much less interstate war than in the century before 1945, particularly between the most powerful states. There have been similar or greater levels of civil war and internal conflict, especially in low-income countries. Interstate wars in this period have tended to be relatively brief, intense, and end more often with negotiated settlements. Compared to interstate wars, civil wars tend on average to have a *much* longer duration and to end far more often with something close to a complete military victory for one side.

Given strong common interests in avoiding mass killing and economic devastation – or even the relatively small negative economic effects of some low-level internal conflicts – why do these conflicts occur?

Human affairs are too complex, messy, and interesting for any one angle to provide a fully satisfactory answer, and particularly an angle as schematic and bloodless as game theory. Even so, work using game-theoretic methods has developed answers that provide useful insights into important strategic dimensions and that provide plausible explanations for some of the more striking empirical patterns concerning armed conflicts in this period. This note reviews game-theoretic models of the outbreak and prosecution of large-scale armed conflict as they have developed in particular over the last forty years.

29.2 TWO CLASSES OF MODELS

Most work in this area develops one of two types of models, although there is sometimes overlap and recent research combines the approaches. In the first type, which I will call *arming models*, the focus is on inefficiency stemming from decisions to arm or exert other costly effort, while decisions to actually use the arms (violence) are not represented or are implicit. In the second type, which I will call *violence models*, the focus is on inefficiency stemming from the use of force – acts that cause death and destruction – with decisions to use or continue using force explicitly represented while decisions to use resources to build the capability for violence are not modeled (usually).

Arming models are more typical of work by economists. They employ and build on the tradition of contest models begun by Haavelmo (1954) and Tullock (2001 [1980]). Players choose arms levels or predatory effort, and this translates into allocations of a resource via a *contest success function* that is increasing in own effort and decreasing in other's effort. The application of contest models to explaining armed conflict was pioneered by Brito and Intriligator (1985), Hirshleifer (1988, 1989, 1995), Garfinkel (1990), Grossman (1991), Grossman and Kim (1995), Skaperdas (1992, 1996), and Skaperdas and Syropoulos (1996). Contest success functions provide a kind of reduced-form "engine" in a large range of applications.[1]

Although there is substantial overlap, violence models have been more typical in work by political scientists, particularly in the subfield of international relations. These are usually extensive-form games with Rubinstein(ish) bargaining or discrete war-of-attrition structures. Players often alternate in decisions to initiate, or to continue using, violent attacks. In many models they have options to make settlement offers as well (i.e., bargaining). Using violence is costly for both sides and thus inefficient if it occurs and while it lasts. Violent moves in these games almost always generate a military lottery with given probabilities of winning, losing, or stalemate. These "costly lotteries" are in effect a simple kind of contest success function, in which chances of winning the prize are not the result of previous, explicitly modeled arming investments. In some models the conflict odds are fixed over time. In others they may change over time, either exogenously or endogenously as a result of prior choices.

This research tradition was initiated by Nalebuff (1986), Powell (1987, 1990), and Morrow (1989), who took advantage of recently developed solution concepts for extensive-form games with incomplete information. Later, Fearon (1995, 1998, 2004), Powell (2004b, 2006), and others analyzed dynamic games

[1] For instance, see Esteban and Ray (2008) on ethnic conflict, or Besley and Persson (2011) on state strength, conflict, and economic development. See Garfinkel and Skaperdas (2007) for an excellent overview.

in which armed conflict could occur without any private information but instead due to commitment problems occasioned shifting power, in a manner that has parallels with the "hold-up problems" studied in the theory of the firm (Klein et al., 1978). Both the incomplete-information and commitment-problem approaches have generated a range of applications in diverse contexts where armed conflict sometimes occurs.

A smaller literature studies simultaneous-move games in which players have the option to attack or take some sort of violent action, and violence may occur in equilibrium due to first-strike fears and, in some cases, uncertainty about the other side's type (Schelling, 1960; Jervis, 1978; Baliga and Sjöström, 2004, 2012, 2020; Chassang and Padró i Miquel, 2009a, 2010; Fearon, 2020).

29.3 ARMING MODELS

In a basic contest model applied to armed conflict, players $i = 1, 2$ simultaneously choose arms levels $a_i \in [0, 1]$ with payoffs $u_i(a_i, a_j) = v_i/(1+(a_j/a_i)^n)-a_i$, and letting $u_i(0, 0) = v_i/2$. $v_i > 0$ is i's value for the prize relative to (here) a constant marginal cost of arms or effort. $n > 0$ is the "decisiveness" of this "ratio-form contest success function." n is known as an index for the *offense-defense balance* in the international relations literature (Jervis, 1978). Greater decisiveness or offensive advantage means that a marginal change in relative capabilities away from equality has a bigger effect on the advantaged side's chance of winning or their share of the prize obtained.

Inefficient diversion of resources to arms or "conflict" is explained here as the result of a Prisoners' Dilemma problem. The parties would like to contract on $a_1 = a_2 = 0$, but each would then do better by "defecting" to positive arms. The model represents the core logic of Thomas Hobbes' (1651) argument for why anarchical situations – that is, situations with no reliable third-party enforcement of agreements – are prone to inefficient investments in means for self-defense and predation.

In this most basic and common form, it is not clear that contest models provide a satisfactory explanation for either inefficient arming or the use of arms (violence). With repeated play and sufficiently patient players, it will be possible to solve the problem as described, in what would look like an arms control agreement (Garfinkel, 1990). Second, concerning violence, if the a_i choices are arms levels, why wouldn't the parties be able to bargain to an agreement after observing them, without any conflict risk (Skaperdas, 1992; Garfinkel and Skaperdas, 2007)?[2]

[2] If the players choose arms levels first, observe (a_1, a_2) and then choose whether to attack the other; then quite generally undominated equilibria will be in mixed strategies with positive probability of attack (Jackson and Morelli, 2009; Fearon, 2018). I struggle to think of a reasonable or natural "purification" story about mixing on arms levels, and the question remains as to why they aren't allowed to bargain. Meirowitz and Sartori (2008) allow the arms decisions to be private. Subsequent bargaining is then with private information about military capability,

If the choices (the a_i's) are understood to be the use of violence against the other rather than an arming investment, why aren't i's costs primarily a function of the other side's violence level? We can modify the model to have this feature – in the extreme, with a_j rather than a_i as the cost term – but doing so pushes in the direction of maximum violence being a dominant strategy. This is perhaps consistent with an interpretation of Hobbes' pessimism about the "condition of meer Nature," but depends on what seems like, for most situations, a strong assumption about first-strike advantage.

29.4 VIOLENCE MODELS: DYNAMIC COMMITMENT PROBLEMS

Why isn't the problem of armed conflict easily dealt with by repeated-game strategies? For many settings a plausible and interesting answer is that the use of force in one period (e.g., violent attack) allows a player to permanently change the other player's capacity to use force in the future and thus their future bargaining power. In the extreme, war may eliminate the other as a player. If so, then the situation should be modeled as a nonstationary dynamic game, not a standard repeated game.

Similarly, what if the players' capacity and prospects for violence are changing over time for (largely) exogenous reasons, such as differential economic growth? Again, the situation is now nonstationary, not a standard repeated game to which the standard folk theorems apply.

These observations motivate a literature using violence models to explain armed conflict with dynamic complete-information bargaining games in which the value for players' fight options can shift. Change may occur exogenously, as in models of the preventive war problem where relative power is shifting due to differential economic growth or other shocks (Fearon, 1994b, 1995; Powell, 2004b, 2006; Krainin, 2017; Schram, 2021). Or change in relative power may occur endogenously, as a result of territorial transfers (Fearon, 1996; Chadefaux, 2011), state consolidation (Fearon, 1994b, 2004; Powell, 2012, 2013), or investments in new military capabilities, such as nuclear weapons (Bas and Coe, 2012, 2016, 2018; Debs and Monteiro, 2014; Coe, 2018). Or relative power may change simply as a result of players' ability to use force to eliminate a competitor or reduce its violence capability in the future (Powell, 1993; Skaperdas and Syropoulos, 1996; Leventoglu and Slantchev, 2007; Coe, 2018; Fearon, 2018).[3]

When costly conflict occurs in these models, it is the result of a dynamic commitment problem: A player whose coercive power would increase in the future if the other does not initiate or continue using costly force would like

which can generate a positive risk of bargaining failure and violence (as discussed later in this chapter).

[3] In a model of civil war onset, Chassang and Padró i Miquel (2009b) show how random variation in players' opportunity costs for fighting, when combined with first-strike advantages, can occasion a similar dynamic commitment problem.

to promise not to exploit its future bargaining power. But (using an anarchy assumption about the strategic context) it cannot make the commitment credible. To avoid future exploitation or the costs of deterrence, the other player may prefer to use force.[4]

This class of models is helpful for explaining some of the major patterns regarding civil wars and how they differ from interstate wars. Civil wars frequently start with a shock to the relative coercive capabilities of the state versus potential challengers – challengers obtain a "window of opportunity" to seize power or get an insurgency going. The government can't buy off the rebels due to a liquidity constraint and its inability to commit to continued transfers or other policies desired by the opposition after the window of opportunity closes. For example, rebel groups anticipate that if they agree to a deal and disarm and come out of hiding, the government will renege and they will be dangerously exposed. Sharing power is difficult to arrange because neither side trusts the other not to use retained coercive capability to coup or otherwise seize all power when it has an opportunity. Many civil conflicts are of long duration because first of all these dynamic commitment problems make mutually preferable deals unenforceable, and second guerilla "technology" can be very robust in the right conditions, so that stalemates persist (Fearon, 2004, 2017).

Interstate wars are less often "about" this kind of commitment problem, as the sides can remain armed and so able to enforce a deal if they can agree on a new division of territory or policies (Walter, 1997, 2002). The implication is that interstate wars are more often "about" private information about willingness or capability to fight, which gets resolved relatively quickly (see the following discussion). There are important exceptions, however. The Entente in World War I could not accept a peace deal that left Germany in control of Belgium, as this would shift future military power too much against them. The Allies in World War II refused any thought of a deal with Hitler and sought unconditional surrender, as they did not trust that any satisfactory peace deal would be enforceable. Similar considerations were relevant for the George W. Bush administration concerning Saddam Hussein's regime in 2003, and probably also for Vladimir Putin's decision to invade Ukraine in February 2022 (where he sought regime change and imposed demilitarization, in part due to the difficulty of arranging credible commitments in Kiev against Ukraine moving out of Russia's sphere of influence, a development his government dislikes for a number of reasons). Weisiger (2013) develops and empirically evaluates the argument that interstate wars fall roughly into "private information" and "commitment problem" types, with the latter being less common, far more destructive, aimed at regime change, and of longer duration (parallel to civil wars).

4 These results also depend on an assumption of a liquidity constraint that prevents the "rising power" from paying the "declining power" enough today to compensate for the worse outcome tomorrow. This also means that when players are sufficiently able to use transfers to adjust the trajectory of relative power, they may be able to undo the conflict-causing effects of other forces.

Daron Acemoglu and James Robinson's models of democratic transitions, popular rebellions, and coups are based on the same kind of dynamic commitment problem as in the models of civil and interstate war discussed previously (Acemoglu and Robinson, 2000, 2001, 2006). In their context, random events may occasion mass protests in the capitol, giving the opposition a transitory window of opportunity to extract concessions from an autocratic regime. They argued that policy concessions were not credible, whereas institutional change (extending the franchise or other forms of democratization) could be. Acemoglu and colleagues (2008, 2012, 2015) analyze a more general class of dynamic models in which Pareto-improving reforms may be blocked by the ruling coalition's anticipation that these will lead to shifts in power that will reduce their future payoffs.

Schultz (2010), Yared (2010), and Padró i Miquel and Yared (2012) model situations in which violence is explained as the result of different kind of dynamic commitment problem – namely as a punishment strategy in an ongoing relationship with repeated moral hazard. For example, state B agrees to carry out certain policies – such as constraining terrorist groups who would like to attack in state A – but state A cannot perfectly observe state B's effort. Optimal second-best regimes involve periodic use of violence, even though state B is in fact complying. There are interesting connections to work on the problem of threatening to use force against a possible nuclear weapons program (Debs and Monteiro, 2014; Coe, 2018) and on the question of why agreements that significantly restrict arms levels are so rare (Coe and Vaynman, 2020).

29.5 VIOLENCE MODELS: ARMED CONFLICT FROM BARGAINING WITH INCOMPLETE INFORMATION?

In the political science field of international relations, incomplete-information explanations for costly conflict initially generated more interest and were given more empirical credit than commitment-problem accounts. This view has shifted over time, with one reason being that it seems difficult to explain long duration civil wars as a result of genuine private information about resolve or capabilities. The dynamic commitment problem models also better match the absence of serious bargaining in most civil wars (and for interstate wars that are plausibly driven by commitment issues), the extreme or total war aims typical of civil wars, and the dearth of negotiated settlements in which the combatants retain significant coercive capabilities.[5]

Nonetheless, it is surely not all one or the other, and exploration of incomplete-information approaches continues apace.[6]

[5] In contrast to civil wars over the control of a central government, secessionist or autonomy-seeking wars tend more often to end in negotiated deals with partial autonomy, because these are more similar to interstate conflicts where territorial separation makes power sharing of coercive capabilities less necessary.

[6] See Ramsay (2017) and Baliga and Sjöström (2013) for excellent analytic reviews of work in this area. The former goes into more detail than I do here on recent research on "mutual optimism"

The earliest models that sought to explain armed conflict using incomplete-information games were developed in the late 1980s and 1990s, mainly in international relations. They were models of what that field calls "crisis bargaining," which refers to intense, militarized disputes between states – for example, the Cuban Missile Crisis; the crisis over Czechoslovakia that ended with the Munich agreement between Hitler and Chamberlain in 1938; or the demands, talks, and military buildup that preceded Russia's 2022 invasion of Ukraine.

In standard crisis bargaining models there is an indivisible political stake, and two players (usually states) sequentially decide whether to concede this prize or to "stand firm" for another round, which could mean actual fighting or just not backing down in a tense standoff. Nalebuff (1986) and Powell (1987, 1988, 1990) showed how international crises between nuclear-armed states could be analyzed as second-price all-pay auctions in which states bid by running "autonomous risk" of nuclear disaster.[7] These models drew on Schelling's (1960, 1966) argument that the risk of accidents, first-strike panics, and irrationality produces pressure on leaders to settle in nuclear crises despite the incredibility of a threat to deliberately initiate all-out nuclear war. And as in Schelling's analysis, they produce the implication that secure second-strike forces turn intense conflicts between nuclear-armed states into "competitions in risk taking." But whereas Schelling tended to understand this as a competition decided by luck and tactical cleverness, Nalebuff's and Powell's auction-like models see the competition as decided by intensity of preferences over the political issues at stake, which determine willingness to run nuclear risk (that is, how much to "bid" for the prize).

For nonnuclear crisis bargaining, it is less clear how to think about the costs of continuing a crisis and thus what causes leaders to update the other side's true willingness to use force. Fearon (1994a) considered an auction-like model in which states choose how much to escalate in a crisis and whether to attack or back down at each moment. Backing down after more escalation produces greater "audience costs," meaning reputational damage and political criticism from domestic or international political audiences. Schultz (1998, 2001) adds explicit domestic politics to a crisis bargaining model, introducing an opposition party with access to private information about resolve but some desire also to see the party in power lose in the next election. The possibility of opposition signaling constrains bluffing by the government to some degree, suggesting a reason why democracies may be more able to signal credibly in crises.

Crisis bargaining models are perhaps unfortunately named, as they assume an indivisible good and are structured more like second-price auctions than bargaining in the sense of exchanging offers on a divisible good (or a price

and armed conflict, and the latter focuses on the factors working against Coase-conjecture-type results in armed conflict bargaining, discussed briefly later in this chapter.

[7] Powell (1989) showed that "counterforce wars of attrition" – in which states exchange limited nuclear strikes – could be understood in the same way.

in exchange for an indivisible good). The indivisible-good assumption seems like an empirically defensible approximation for many real-world international crises. Why this is so, however, is an interesting question. We would like to see leaders choosing to treat issues as indivisible emerging endogenously in genuine bargaining models that allow continuous division.[8]

Fearon (1995) examined a take-it-or-leave-it, continuous-demand bargaining model in which one state chooses how much territory to grab in a fait accompli attempt and the other state decides whether to go to war in response. With uncertainty about the second state's costs or fighting ability, the first state faces a "risk-return tradeoff" (Powell, 2002) and may choose to run some risk of war. It is unclear, however, why the first state would not be able to adjust its demand (or land grab) once it sees that the second state will fight, so why wouldn't settlement come quickly?[9]

Wagner (2000) modeled war (and the decision to go to war) as a Rubinstein bargaining model in which states exchange offers while they are fighting, which is costly. Offers are separated by an exogenous chance of "breakdown," meaning that one side disarms the other on the battlefield and can then impose its preferred settlement. To get costly conflict rather than immediate settlement, he assumes that the states can agree to disagree about their (prior) odds of winning in battle but that observing battlefield results leads them to update using Bayes' rule (see also Smith and Stam, 2004; Ramsay, 2017). Along the lines argued by Blainey (1988), war is thus explained by initial mutual optimism about military prospects, with battlefield outcomes gradually educating the parties in the true balance of power and so ultimately enabling a deal.

In a fully Bayesian game setup, the states should be able to draw inferences not only from battlefield outcomes but also from the other side's willingness to fight. As in the example provided, if state A guesses wrong and makes a demand or land grab that causes state B to use force, then why not quickly revise the demand down? Of course, if this was expected by state B, it can have a reason to fight a little to get the better offer quickly, in which case state A may think it needs to see "enough" fighting to be really convinced of B's capability or resolve. Parallel to crisis bargaining models' use of nuclear risk or audience costs, in this approach costly fighting is by itself a way to credibly signal low costs or high capability, and thus a "tough type's" need to receive in a negotiated settlement at least as much as its value for *more* fighting (Filson and Werner, 2002; Slantchev, 2003; Powell, 2004a). The core idea in

[8] This happens in dynamic commitment – problem models where parties make extreme demands because they see intermediate deals as unenforceable. It also happens, arguably, in incomplete-information bargaining models where the players believe the other could be a type who is committed for some reason to a particular strategy (Abreu and Gul, 2000).

[9] Powell (1996b,a) and Leventoglu and Tarar (2008) consider bargaining models with incomplete information about fighting costs in which parties exchange offers – a la Rubinstein (1982) – but can also go to war, which is represented as a costly lottery that also ends strategic interaction. Results depend on extensive-form specifics.

these arguments is that costly armed conflict is an attempt by tough types to credibly separate themselves from weak types so as to get a better deal.

If the private information is about costs (or value for the issues at stake) and these are uncorrelated across adversaries, then there is a tendency to get Coase conjecture-type results (Coase, 1972; Gul et al., 1986). That is, as the amount of time between offers and/or battles gets small, expected war duration goes to zero (or one could say that the duration of the war is determined roughly by the time it takes fight battles and generate offers following a battle; Powell, 2004a; Fearon and Jin, 2018). The intuition is that state A's inability to commit itself not to reduce its demands in the future undermines its current bargaining power, leading to rapid settlement.

If, by contrast, the private information is about factors that influence military prospects, then armed conflict bargaining is an interesting variant on bargaining with interdependent (or correlated) values (Ausubel et al., 2002; Deneckere and Liang, 2006). In buyer–seller settings with correlated values – the classic lemons problem (Akerlof, 1970) – it is natural to assume that values for the good are positively correlated through its quality and that the buyer can learn about quality only by inferences from the seller's behavior. By contrast, for armed conflict settings with private information bearing on military prospects, the parties' values for the "inside option" of bargaining (which here entails fighting) are negatively correlated, and the fighting itself can directly reveal at least some information as it proceeds. For the case of private information about costs, Powell (2004a) obtained a Coase-conjecture result in a model where arbitrarily many offers could be made in between battles separated by discrete amounts of time; he also showed that at least one battle may be necessary in equilibrium with private information about military capability. Fearon and Jin (2018) allow fighting to happen approximately continuously while offers are exchanged (as in Wagner's 2000 interpretation). As time between offers gets small, the Coase conjecture obtains when private information is on costs of fighting (that is, the duration of any "war" approaches zero), whereas they find that surprisingly long duration wars can occur when the private information affects military odds.[10] In a variant where the state making offers cannot commit itself to implement an accepted offer – so that it can ratchet up its demand if the other side reveals weakness by making a concession – in equilibrium the parties just fight rather than bargain in the sense of making serious offers (offers that have a positive chance of being accepted).

These results for specific incomplete-information games are consistent with results from mechanism-design analysis of armed conflict bargaining (as they must be). Banks (1990) applied Myerson and Satterthwaite's (1983) approach

[10] A partial intuition: Let x_S be the smallest offer large enough to satisfy a tough type of state B. With private information about military prospects, state A may prefer fighting against a weak type of state B to conceding x_S to that type. This reduces state A's incentive to "accelerate trade" (Deneckere and Liang, 2006) by increasing its offers, because there is no surplus to gain against the weak type with offers large enough to attract the tough type.

to "crisis bargaining," drawing out the implications from monotonicity that in any of a large class of bargaining games, tougher types run weakly higher war risk and obtain weakly more in any negotiated settlement. Bester and Wärneryd (2006) and Fey and Ramsay (2011) apply the approach to bargaining with conflict as the disagreement option and private information about chances of winning, showing that for a large class of games the most peaceful mechanism must have positive risk of war if war costs are low enough. Several recent articles have applied a mechanism-design approach to study the possibilities and limitations for third-party mediation in conflict settings, interpreting the mechanism designer as a mediator (Fey and Ramsay, 2010; Hörner et al., 2015; Meirowitz et al., 2019).

29.6 SOME FRONTIERS

The losses and damage due to arming and violence can both be very large. To illustrate, if the US annual defense budget were the gross domestic product of a country, it would be the twenty-third largest economy in the world (2021 estimates). And as I write, more than 10 percent of Ukraine's population are refugees and another 15 percent have been internally displaced.

Models that jointly examine decisions about arming and the use of force are less developed but are an active area of research. Powell (1993) identified a key linkage: The cost of arming to maintain deterrence effectively lowers one's value for living with the status quo, making use of force to eliminate the threat more attractive. If you want peace – or, really, if you want not to be coerced – prepare for war. But the defensive need to prepare for war can make war more attractive if winning may reduce the need for costly arms in the future. Several articles explore this strategic dynamic in both general and more specific contexts, including the question of war to prevent nuclear proliferation (Skaperdas and Syropoulos, 1996; Jackson and Morelli, 2009; Coe, 2018; Fearon, 2018).

In one of the first "modern" game-theoretic models of international conflict, Brito and Intriligator (1985) joined an arming phase to a bargaining phase with incomplete information, so that there can be an incentive to arm not only by the Prisoners' Dilemma logic already noted but potentially as a costly signal of resolve to affect negotiations (see Baliga and Sjöström 2013 for a version of this model that is easier to follow). Signaling implications of armament choices remain relatively unexplored, but see Kydd (1997, 2000, 2005) and Baliga and Sjöström (2004).

With only a few exceptions, the work reviewed in this chapter does not investigate explanations in which armed conflict is explained by strategic dynamics that operate primarily *within* one or the other parties to the conflict. There is important research in this area (and some examples include Hess and Orphanides, 1995; Smith, 1996; Bueno de Mesquita et al., 2005; Schultz, 2001, 2005; Jackson and Morelli, 2007; Baliga et al., 2011; Acharya et al., 2019). But the conflict remains underexplored, both theoretically and empirically.

29.7 REFERENCES

D. Abreu and F. Gul. Bargaining and reputation. *Econometrica*, 68(1):85–117, 2000.

D. Acemoglu, G. Egorov, and K. Sonin. Coalition formation in non-democracies. *Review of Economic Studies*, 75(4):987–1009, 2008.

D. Acemoglu, G. Egorov, and K. Sonin. Dynamics and stability of constitutions, coalitions, and clubs. *American Economic Review*, 102(4):1446–76, 2012.

D. Acemoglu, G. Egorov, and K. Sonin. Political economy in a changing world. *Journal of Political Economy*, 123(5):1038–1086, 2015.

D. Acemoglu and J. A. Robinson. Why did the West extend the franchise? Democracy, inequality, and growth in historical perspective. *Quarterly Journal of Economics*, 115(4):1167–1199, 2000.

D. Acemoglu and J. A. Robinson. A theory of political transitions. *American Economic Review*, 91(4):938–963, 2001.

D. Acemoglu and J. A. Robinson. *Economic Origins of Dictatorship and Democracy*. Cambridge: Cambridge University Press, 2006.

A. Acharya and E. Grillo. A behavioral foundation for audience costs. *Quarterly Journal of Political Science*, 14(2):159–190, 2019.

G. A. Akerlof. The market for "lemons": Quality uncertainty and the market mechanism. *Quarterly Journal of Economics*, 84(3):488–500, 1970.

L. M. Ausubel, P. Cramton, and R. J. Deneckere. Bargaining with incomplete information. In R. J. Aumann and S. Hart, eds., *Handbook of Game Theory with Economic Applications*, vol. 3, ch. 50, pp. 1897–1945. New York: Elsevier, 2002.

S. Baliga, D. O. Lucca, and T. Sjöström. Domestic political survival and international conflict: Is democracy good for peace? *Review of Economic Studies*, 78(2):458–486, 2011.

S. Baliga and T. Sjöström. Arms races and negotiations. *Review of Economic Studies*, 71(2):351–369, 2004.

S. Baliga and T. Sjöström. The strategy of manipulating conflict. *American Economic Review*, 102(6):2897–2922, 2012.

S. Baliga and T. Sjöström. Bargaining and war: A review of some formal models. *Korean Economic Review*, 29(2):235–266, 2013.

S. Baliga and T. Sjöström. The strategy and technology of conflict. *Journal of Political Economy*, 128(8):3186–3219, 2020.

J. S. Banks. Equilibrium behavior in crisis bargaining games. *American Journal of Political Science*, 34:599–614, 1990.

M. A. Bas and A. J. Coe. Arms diffusion and war. *Journal of Conflict Resolution*, 56(4):651–674, 2012.

M. A. Bas and A. J. Coe. A dynamic theory of nuclear proliferation and preventive war. *International Organization*, 70(4):655–685, 2016.

M. A. Bas and A. J. Coe. Give peace a (second) chance: A theory of nonproliferation deals. *International Studies Quarterly*, 62(3):606–617, 2018.

T. Besley and T. Persson. *Pillars of Prosperity*. Princeton, NJ: Princeton University Press, 2011.

H. Bester and K. Wärneryd. Conflict and the social contract. *Scandinavian Journal of Economics*, 108(2):231–249, 2006.

G. Blainey. *Causes of War*. New York: Simon and Schuster, 1988.

E. Borel. La théorie du jeu et les équations intégrales à noyau symétrique. *Comptes rendus de l'Académie des Sciences*, 173:1304–1308, 1921.

D. L. Brito and M. D. Intriligator. Conflict, war, and redistribution. *American Political Science Review*, 79(4):943–957, 1985.

B. Bueno de Mesquita, A. Smith, R. M. Siverson, and J. D. Morrow. *The Logic of Political Survival*. Cambridge, MA: MIT Press, 2005.

T. Chadefaux. Bargaining over power: When do shifts in power lead to war? *International Theory*, 3(2):228–253, 2011.

S. Chassang and G. Padró i Miquel. Defensive weapons and defensive alliances. *American Economic Review*, 99(2):282–286, 2009a.

S. Chassang and G. Padró i Miquel. Economic shocks and civil war. *Quarterly Journal of Political Science*, 4(3):211–228, 2009b.

S. Chassang and G. Padró i Miquel. Conflict and deterrence under strategic risk. *Quarterly Journal of Economics*, 125(4):1821–1858, 2010.

R. H. Coase. Durability and monopoly. *Journal of Law and Economics*, 15(1):143–149, 1972.

A. J. Coe. Containing rogues: A theory of asymmetric arming. *Journal of Politics*, 80(4):1197–1210, 2018.

A. J. Coe and J. Vaynman. Why arms control is so rare. *American Political Science Review*, 114(2):342–355, 2020.

A. Debs and N. P. Monteiro. Known unknowns: Power shifts, uncertainty, and war. *International Organization*, 68(1):1–31, 2014.

R. Deneckere and M.-Y. Liang. Bargaining with interdependent values. *Econometrica*, 74(5):1309–1364, 2006.

J. Esteban and D. Ray. On the salience of ethnic conflict. *American Economic Review*, 98(5):2185–2202, 2008.

J. D. Fearon. Domestic political audiences and the escalation of international disputes. *American Political Science Review*, 88(3):577–592, 1994a.

J. D. Fearon. Ethnic war as a commitment problem. *Annual Meetings of the American Political Science Association*, 1994b.

J. D. Fearon. Rationalist explanations for war. *International Organization*, 49(3):379–414, 1995.

J. D. Fearon. Bargaining over Objects That Influence Future Bargaining Power. Stanford, CT: Stanford University Press, 1996.

J. D. Fearon. Commitment problems and the spread of ethnic conflict. In *The International Spread of Ethnic Conflict*, pp. 269–305. Princeton, NJ: Princeton University Press, 1998.

J. D. Fearon. Why do some civil wars last so much longer than others? *Journal of Peace Research*, 41(3):275–301, 2004.

J. D. Fearon. Civil war and the current international system. *Dædalus*, 146(4):18–32, 2017.

J. D. Fearon. Cooperation, conflict, and the costs of anarchy. *International Organization*, 72(3):523–559, 2018.

J. D. Fearon. *Coups, Police Shootings, and Nuclear War*. Stanford, CT: Stanford University Press, 2020.

J. D. Fearon and X. Jin. Armed Conflict Bargaining. Stanford, CT: Stanford University Press, 2018.

M. Fey and K. W. Ramsay. When is shuttle diplomacy worth the commute? Information sharing through mediation. *World Politics*, 62(4):529–560, 2010.

M. Fey and K. W. Ramsay. Uncertainty and incentives in crisis bargaining: Game-free analysis of international conflict. *American Journal of Political Science*, 55(1):149–169, 2011.

D. Filson and S. Werner. A bargaining model of war and peace: Anticipating the onset, duration, and outcome of war. *American Journal of Political Science*, 46(4): 819–837, 2002.

M. R. Garfinkel. Arming as a strategic investment in a cooperative equilibrium. *American Economic Review*, 80(1): 50–68, 1990.

M. R. Garfinkel and S. Skaperdas. Economics of conflict: An overview. In T. Sandler and K. Hartley, eds., *Handbook of Defense Economics*, vol. 2, ch. 22, pp. 649–709. Amsterdam: Elsevier, 2007.

H. I. Grossman. A general equilibrium model of insurrections. *American Economic Review*, 81(4):912–921, 1991.

H. I. Grossman and M. Kim. Swords or plowshares? A theory of the security of claims to property. *Journal of Political Economy*, 103(6):1275–1288, 1995.

F. Gul, H. Sonnenschein, and R. Wilson. Foundations of dynamic monopoly and the coase conjecture. *Journal of Economic Theory*, 39(1):155–190, 1986.

T. Haavelmo. *A Study in the Theory of Economic Evolution*. Amsterdam: North-Holland Publishing, 1954.

G. D. Hess and A. Orphanides. War politics: An economic, rational-voter framework. *American Economic Review*, 81(4):828–846, 1995.

J. Hirshleifer. The analytics of continuing conflict. *Synthese*, 76(2):201–233, 1988.

J. Hirshleifer. Conflict and rent-seeking success functions: Ratio vs. difference models of relative success. *Public Choice*, 63(2):101–112, 1989.

J. Hirshleifer. Anarchy and its breakdown. *Journal of Political Economy*, 103(1):26–52, 1995.

T. Hobbes. *Leviathan*. New York: Penguin Classics, 2017 (1651).

J. Hörner, M. Morelli, and F. Squintani. Mediation and peace. *Review of Economic Studies*, 82(4):1483–1501, 2015.

M. O. Jackson and M. Morelli. Political bias and war. *American Economic Review*, 97(4):1353–1373, 2007.

M. O. Jackson and M. Morelli. Strategic militarization, deterrence and wars. *Quarterly Journal of Political Science*, 4:279–313, 2009.

R. Jervis. Cooperation under the security dilemma. *World Politics*, 30(2):167–214, 1978.

B. Klein, R. G. Crawford, and A. A. Alchian. Vertical integration, appropriable rents, and the competitive contracting process. *Journal of Law and Economics*, 21(2):297–326, 1978.

C. Krainin. Preventive war as a result of long-term shifts in power. *Political Science Research and Methods*, 5(1):103–121, 2017.

A. Kydd. Game theory and the spiral model. *World Politics*, 49(3):371–400, 1997.

A. Kydd. Arms races and arms control: Modeling the hawk perspective. *American Journal of Political Science*, 44(2):228–244, 2000.

A. H. Kydd. Trust and Mistrust in International Relations. Princeton, NJ: Princeton University Press, 2005.

B. Leventoglu and B. L. Slantchev. The armed peace: A punctuated equilibrium theory of war. *American Journal of Political Science*, 51(4):755–771, 2007.

B. Leventoglu and A. Tarar. Does private information lead to delay or war in crisis bargaining? *International Studies Quarterly*, 52(3):533–553, 2008.

A. Meirowitz, M. Morelli, K. W. Ramsay, and F. Squintani. Dispute resolution mechanisms and strategic militarization. *Journal of Political Economy*, 127(1):378–418, 2019.

A. Meirowitz and A. E. Sartori. Strategic uncertainty as a cause of war. *Quarterly Journal of Political Science*, 3(4):327–352, 2008.

J. D. Morrow. Capabilities, uncertainty, and resolve: A limited information model of crisis bargaining. *American Journal of Political Science*, 33:941–972, 1989.

R. B. Myerson and M. A. Satterthwaite. Efficient mechanisms for bilateral trading. *Journal of Economic Theory*, 29(2):265–281, 1983.

B. Nalebuff. Brinkmanship and nuclear deterrence: neutrality of escalation. *Conflict Management and Peace Science*, 9(2):19–30, 1986.

G. Padró i Miquel and P. Yared. The political economy of indirect control. *Quarterly Journal of Economics*, 127(2):947–1015, 2012.

R. Powell. Crisis bargaining, escalation, and mad. *American Political Science Review*, 81(3):717–735, 1987.

R. Powell. Nuclear brinkmanship with two-sided incomplete information. *American Political Science Review*, 82(1):155–178, 1988.

R. Powell. Nuclear deterrence and the strategy of limited retaliation. *American Political Science Review*, 83(2):503–519, 1989.

R. Powell. *Nuclear Deterrence Theory: The Search for Credibility*. Cambridge: Cambridge University Press, 1990.

R. Powell. Guns, butter, and anarchy. *American Political Science Review*, 87(1):115–132, 1993.

R. Powell. Bargaining in the shadow of power. *Games and Economic Behavior*, 15(2):255–289, 1996a.

R. Powell. Stability and the distribution of power. *World Politics*, 48(2):239–267, 1996b.

R. Powell. Bargaining theory and international conflict. *Annual Review of Political Science*, 5(1):1–30, 2002.

R. Powell. Bargaining and learning while fighting. *American Journal of Political Science*, 48(2):344–361, 2004a.

R. Powell. The inefficient use of power: Costly conflict with complete information. *American Political Science Review*, 98(2):231–241, 2004b.

R. Powell. War as a commitment problem. *International Organization*, 60(1):169–203, 2006.

R. Powell. Persistent fighting and shifting power. *American Journal of Political Science*, 56(3):620–637, 2012.

R. Powell. Monopolizing violence and consolidating power. *Quarterly Journal of Economics*, 128(2):807–859, 2013.

K. W. Ramsay. Information, uncertainty, and war. *Annual Review of Political Science*, 20:505–527, 2017.

A. Rubinstein. Perfect equilibrium in a bargaining model. *Econometrica*, 50(1):97–109, 1982.

T. C. Schelling. *The Strategy of Conflict*. Cambridge, MA: Harvard University Press, 1960.

T. C. Schelling. *Arms and Influence*. New Haven, CT: Yale University Press, 1966.

P. Schram. Hassling: How states prevent a preventive war. *American Journal of Political Science*, 65(2):294–308, 2021.

K. A. Schultz. Domestic opposition and signaling in international crises. *American Political Science Review*, 92(4):829–844, 1998.

K. A. Schultz. *Democracy and Coercive Diplomacy*, vol. 76 of Cambridge Studies in International Relations. Cambridge: Cambridge University Press, 2001.

K. A. Schultz. The politics of risking peace: Do hawks or doves deliver the olive branch? *International Organization*, 59(1):1–38, 2005.

K. A. Schultz. The enforcement problem in coercive bargaining: Interstate conflict over rebel support in civil wars. *International Organization*, 64(2):281–312, 2010.

S. Skaperdas. Cooperation, conflict, and power in the absence of property rights. *American Economic Review*, 82(4):720–739, 1992.

S. Skaperdas. Contest success functions. *Economic Theory*, 7(2):283–290, 1996.

S. Skaperdas and C. Syropoulos. Can the shadow of the future harm cooperation? *Journal of Economic Behavior & Organization*, 29(3):355–372, 1996.

B. L. Slantchev. The principle of convergence in wartime negotiations. *American Political Science Review*, 97(4):621–632, 2003.

A. Smith. Diversionary foreign policy in democratic systems. *International Studies Quarterly*, 40(1):133–153, 1996.

A. Smith and A. C. Stam. Bargaining and the nature of war. *Journal of Conflict Resolution*, 48(6):783–813, 2004.

G. Tullock. Efficient rent seeking. In G. Tullock and A. Lockhard, eds., *Efficient Rent-Seeking*, pp. 3–16. Boston: Springer, 2001 (1980).

R. H. Wagner. Bargaining and war. *American Journal of Political Science*, 44:469–484, 2000.

B. F. Walter. The critical barrier to civil war settlement. *International Organization*, 51(3):335–364, 1997.

B. F. Walter. *Committing to Peace: The Successful Settlement of Civil Wars*. Princeton, NJ: Princeton University Press, 2002.

A. Weisiger. *Logics of War: Explanations for Limited and Unlimited Conflicts*. Ithaca, NY: Cornell University Press, 2013.

P. Yared. A dynamic theory of war and peace. *Journal of Economic Theory*, 145(5):1921–1950, 2010.

30

Applications of Game Theory in the Political Economy of Trade Policy

Gene M. Grossman

Game theory has a long history in the political economy of trade policy. Beginning with Johnson (1953), trade economists have used these tools to study strategic interactions between governments, between interest groups representing industries or factors of production, between political parties, and between legislators representing different voting districts. Research has focused both on trade policies that have been set noncooperatively, sometimes in response to internal political pressures, and on the negotiation and features of cooperative trade agreements.

30.1 GAMES BETWEEN GOVERNMENTS

Johnson (1953) challenged Scitovszky's (1941–1942) claim that a country would necessarily lose from implementing its "optimum tariff" after retaliation by other governments. Johnson supposed that "retaliation takes the form of the imposition of an optimum tariff under the assumption that the other country's tariff will remain unchanged" (p. 142). He formulated policy choices as a game between the governments and provided an early application of a Nash equilibrium.

Dixit (1987) and others considered tariff setting in the context of a repeated game, pointing out that free trade might not be sustainable in a repeated game between impatient governments, even if prohibitive tariffs are used as the strongest, credible punishments. Bagwell and Staiger (1990) extended Dixit's analysis to allow for volatile swings in trade volumes, showing that maximum cooperation can be sustained by a tacit agreement to allow "special protection" during periods of especially high trade volume. In this way, they rationalized observed patterns of liberal trade during "normal" times and "managed trade" in the face of import surges. Bond and Park (2002) offered a rationale for gradual trade liberalization in a stable economic environment by considering the minimum sustainable tariffs in a repeated interaction between countries of different sizes.

Nash equilibrium – static and dynamic – has been applied frequently to other sorts of government-versus-government policy interactions. For example, Grossman and Lai (2004) considered unilaterally optimal choices of international protection of intellectual property by countries at different stages of development, showing that the static Nash equilibrium involves too little protection and thus too little innovation relative to the globally efficient levels. Grossman and colleagues (2021) studied noncooperative choices of product standards in a world of globally efficient trade policies to understand the unilateral incentives that governments have to use regulatory policy in the service of production delocation.

Brander and Spencer (1984, 1985) invoked Selten's (1965) notion of subgame perfection to explain the strategic use of export promotion and import protection in support of domestic firms that face oligopolistic competition. When firms engage in international Cournot competition, an export subsidy lends credibility to a *threat* of aggressive behavior by domestic firms that steals profits away from foreign rivals. But when two governments engage in such behavior, the winner might be a third country that imports from the two exporting countries. Eaton and Grossman (1986) offered a caveat: When competition involves firms setting prices instead of quantities, an export tax (or an import subsidy) is warranted. The tax makes credible firms' *promises* not to undercut their rivals. The alternative conclusions reflect the difference between games with "strategic complements" and "strategic substitutes"; see Bulow and colleagues (1985). In Bertrand competition, an aggressive move by one player (e.g., a price cut) invokes an aggressive response by the other. In Cournot competition, by contrast, an aggressive move (e.g., an expansion in quantity) instead brings forth a conciliatory response.

30.2 GAMES BETWEEN INTEREST GROUPS

Organized groups representing industry or factor interests play a central role in the politics of trade policy. Interest groups compete for favorable government treatment of their industries or factors at the expense of others. Their strategic tools include "contributions," interpreted broadly to mean not only monetary donations but also the labor inputs that politicians value for their electoral campaigns.[1]

The earliest work on the role of special interest groups in the determination of trade policy focused on an *electoral motive* for campaign giving. In a scenario proposed by Magee and colleagues (1989), two political parties contest

[1] Interest groups also provide information and expertise to politicians, which falls under the rhubric of "lobbying." Lobbying models have not been applied frequently to the political economy of trade policy per se, although see Blanga-Gubbay and colleagues (2021) for an exception. For a broader discussion of political games involving informational lobbying, and drawing on the Crawford and Sobel (1982) and Krishna and Morgan (2001) analyses of cheap-talk games and the Spence (1973) model of signaling, see Austen-Smith (1995), Lohmann (1995), and Grossman and Helpman (2001), among many others.

a winner-takes-all election. One party commits to a protectionist platform; the other commits to policies that promote exports. A group representing import-competing interests contributes to the former party in order to bolster its chances of winning the election. At the same time, a group representing export interests contributes to the rival party. In a Nash equilibrium, each group maximizes the effect of its giving on expected utility, considering the impact on the expected policy outcome net of the cost of the gift. In a prior stage, the parties choose their respective protectionist and exporting-promoting policies, trading off a direct (reduced-form) negative effect of inefficient policies on election odds against the greater contributions that such policies will elicit. The equilibrium of the two-stage game features policies that depart from free trade in a setting where any such interventions are bound to be inefficient.

Grossman and Helpman (1994) appreciated the focus on interest groups but questioned whether an electoral motive can be operative. In the work of Magee and colleagues (1989), the association of one party with import interests and the other with export interests is taken as given. The model cannot explain a structure of protection with different tariffs for different industries, and in fact a many-industry version of the model predicts pervasive free riding. It also cannot explain the frequent practice of industry interest groups contributing to both sides in an election. And the size of the contributions that would be needed to alter election odds sufficiently to justify the giving far exceeds the size of contributions that are actually observed.

Instead, Grossman and Helpman (1994) suggest an *influence motive* for campaign giving. Drawing on the work by Bernheim and Whinston (1986a,b) on menu auctions and common agency, they formulate a game between industry interests in which each organized group proposes a contribution *schedule* to the policy maker that links different vectors of trade policies to different amounts of giving, and the policy maker sets trade policies to maximize a weighted sum of total campaign contributions and aggregate welfare. With their contribution schedules, the groups compete for influence (i.e., trade policies that benefit their members, perhaps at the expense of others). In "Protection for Sale" (PFS), Grossman and Helpman derive a "modified Ramsey rule" that predicts the structure of trade protection as a function of inverse elasticities (that presage deadweight loss) but modified for indicators of political "power," such as the fraction of the population represented by an organized group, the weight that the policy maker places on aggregate welfare, and the ratio of industry output to imports.[2]

[2] Grossman and Helpman (1996) extend PFS by incorporating electoral competition between political parties. They posit a two-stage game in which organized interests offer contributions to one or both of two parties, and the parties subsequently choose their policy platforms to maximize their expected vote counts. Such a model can rationalize giving to both sides in an election but admits multiple equilibria with the sizes of the contributions as a function of the probabilities of election supposed by the groups and the contributors in turn inducing election odds that validate their expectations.

A shortcoming of the PFS model is that it takes the organization or lack thereof of industry interest groups as given, thereby side stepping the thorny problems of free riding on collective action raised by Olson (1965). Mitra (1999) addresses this issue.[3] He adds to PFS an initial stage in which agents with common interests decide whether to bear the fixed cost of becoming organized so as to be able to participate in the influence game. Unlike the results in PFS for an exogenous set of organized industries, Mitra finds that the magnitude of the departure from free trade need not increase monotonically with the policy maker's taste for campaign contributions. Rather, a high affinity for contributions might lead to the formation of a large number of opposing groups, whose efforts at influence roughly cancel one another in the contribution stage of the game.

30.3 GAMES BETWEEN POLITICAL PARTIES AND POLITICIANS

Trade policies can be used as instruments in political parties' and legislators' competition for power. Dixit and Londregan (1996) distinguish fundamental policy positions that define a party's identity and ideology and pliable positions that they adopt instrumentally to woo voters.[4] In a setting of probabilistic voting, two parties that differ in ideology compete for support from groups of voters that benefit asymmetrically from the pliable policies while differing also in their heterogeneous predispositions to the parties' fundamental positions. The model predicts convergence of the parties' pliable platforms, which seems to fit with the similarity of the trade policies pursued by different parties in many democracies. The equilibrium policies, which can be interpreted as industry tariffs, maximize a weighted sum of group utilities, where the weights are the densities of "swing voters" – that is, the number of voters in the group that are indifferent about the fundamental positions of the parties. Dixit and Londregan point to the large numbers of swing voters in the textile and apparel industries and the history of high protection for this industry as evidence in favor of their model.[5]

Trade policies can also be influenced by competition between elected legislators who attempt to deliver favorable policies to their own constituents. Baron and Ferejohn (1989) developed a well-known model of legislative bargaining in which a randomly chosen agenda setter proposes a bill that replaces the status quo if it can garner a majority of support in the law-making body. The bill initially proposed may be subject to amendment, depending on institutional rules. In any case, if a bill fails in a legislative session, the status quo persists

[3] See also Bombardini and Trebbi (2012), who study the choices by firms to form coalitions for influencing trade policy or to go it alone.

[4] Dixit and Londregan draw on a version of the probabilistic voting model developed by Lindbeck and Weibull (1987).

[5] See also Fajgelbaum and colleagues (2019), who find that the Trump tariffs levied on imports from China in 2018 and 2019 protected swing counties relative to those that leaned heavily to the Republicans or Democrats.

and a new agenda setter is selected in the next session. Thus the legislator designated as agenda setter must be forward looking, as in the Rubinstein (1982) bargaining model. Celik and colleagues (2012) applied this model of legislative bargaining to study trade policy bills negotiated by representatives of electoral districts comprising different industries. The model can rationalize a link between the structure of protection and the history of committee leadership, and it introduces randomness into policy outcomes not only due to the vagaries in the choice of agenda setter but also because the equilibrium of the model typically entails mixed strategies as the agenda setter seeks to attract a winning coalition at minimum cost.

Helpman and Persson (2001) examine the interaction between influence seeking via contributions, as in PFS, and legislative bargaining, as in Baron and Ferejohn (1989). Interest groups use their contingent contributions to influence both the agenda setter's proposal and the lawmakers' voting on the proposed bill. In this setting, the equilibrium outcome need not be a convex combination of the outcome predicted by a model of influence seeking and a model of legislative bargaining. Moreover, the model can rationalize the empirical observations that special-interest contributions seem to have a significant influence on policy outcomes, even though they are typically small in relation to the industry gains from protection. Grossman and Helpman (2005) also study a setting in which legislators represent the interests of their local industries. In their three-stage model of political campaigns, district elections, and legislative deliberation, each national party has an ex ante objective to win a majority of seats, but individual representatives have an ex post objective to deliver trade policies that benefit their local constituents. They identify a protectionist bias in majoritarian politics in settings in which districts differ in their ownership of industry-specific favors, national parties' leaders cannot fully commit their candidates to support efficient policies if elected, and members of minority delegations cannot fully compensate the majority to induce nationally efficient policy choices.

30.4 TWO-LEVEL GAMES

Putnam (1988) coined the term "two-level games" to describe situations in which domestic actors compete for intranational influence while their leaders vie for favorable international outcomes. Thinking about trade policy this way, two-level games link the contests between interest groups with those between national governments.

Grossman and Helpman (1995) extend the PFS model to incorporate an international level. Organized interest groups in each of two countries tender contribution offers as a function of the national vector of tariffs, as in PFS. Then the two governments set their tariffs, as in Johnson (1953), taking the foreign tariffs as a given. The contribution schedules induce a set of preferences for each government that combines the nation's aggregate welfare and the interests of its organized interests. The formula for each country's Nash equilibrium tariff vector has a term that reflects the government's efforts to manipulate its terms of trade, as in Johnson (1953), and a term that reflects the political power of the various interest groups, as in PFS.[6]

30.5 TRADE AGREEMENTS AS COOPERATIVE GAMES

The generic inefficiency of the noncooperative Nash equilibria suggests a motivation for international trade agreements. Trade economists have used tools of noncooperative and cooperative game theory to establish common features of negotiated trade agreements and other trade institutions.

Mayer (1981) characterized the tariff rates that would be Pareto efficient for two welfare-maximizing leaders and would leave neither country worse off than in the noncooperative Nash equilibrium described by Johnson. Efficiency requires similar relative prices of the two goods in each country. This can be achieved by free trade (zero tariffs), but also by a positive ad valorem tariff t in one and a negative tariff t^* in the other such that $(1 + t)(1 + t^*) = 1$. Zero tariffs might not be attainable, however, because as Johnson argued, the Nash equilibrium that serves as the threat point might leave one country better off than it would be with free trade.

Some might question whether governments still have an incentive to negotiate a trade agreement if their policy objectives reflect the political influence of interest groups. Grossman and Helpman (1995) argue that the Nash equilibrium in their two-level game also is generically inefficient from the point of view of the two policy makers. They study a two-stage game in which, in the first stage, interest groups offer contributions to leaders contingent on the protection that is retained by their government in the negotiated agreement, as well as the tariff concessions wrung from the foreign government. In the second stage, the two governments negotiate an agreement that is efficient from their own (political) perspective. The outcome is a pair of tariff vectors that do not incorporate any terms-of-trade considerations but instead depend only on the internal political forces. Specifically, policy shifts international prices in favor of the national industry that is more powerful in its internal political competition, where power is measured by the forces that determine equilibrium tariffs in the PFS game.

Bagwell and Staiger (2002) offer a more general observation. Suppose the home government has as its objective to maximize $G(p, p^w)$, where p is the internal relative price in the home country of the country's import good and p^w is the price that the country's consumers pay to the foreign suppliers of this good. The function $G(\cdot)$ can take any form, to reflect any model of domestic politics, except that the second partial must be negative; given domestic prices that determine domestic incomes and consumption choices, the policy

[6] Ossa (2014) estimates the size of equilibrium tariffs in a many-sector, many-country quantitative model of politically motivated trade policies.

makers should always prefer better terms of trade. Meanwhile, the foreign government maximizes $G(p^*, p^w)$, where p^* is the internal relative price and the second partial is positive, because the home country's import is the foreign country's export. In this general setting that accommodates, in reduced form, a broad set of political-economy models, the Nash equilibrium pair of tariffs is inefficient from the perspective of the two national leaders. Moreover, a trade agreement that generates Pareto gains for the governments must involve trade *liberalization* by both.[7]

Feenstra and Lewis (1991b) provide a different insight. They suppose that a government's preferences at any time are influenced in some way by internal political pressures that are not observed by its foreign counterparts. In a negotiation between the governments to avoid the inefficiencies of the Johnson equilibrium, the home government is tempted to claim that it faces unusually severe political pressure as an excuse for invoking something closer to its optimal tariff. To eliminate the incentive to misrepresent the state of the world, Feenstra and Lewis draw on the analysis of bilateral bargaining under asymmetric information by Myerson (1979). If all the gains from the agreement accrue to the home country, efficiency can be achieved by an agreement that stipulates a "tariff-quota"; that is, duty-free imports up to a designated level, with a positive tariff on imports beyond this level. By specifying an appropriate level for the tariff to kick in, the home government's incentives to misrepresent the state of its domestic politics can be eliminated. If instead the agreement must deliver some gains relative to the status quo to the foreign country, it must allocate to that country some of the rents created by trade restrictions. This can be accomplished by an agreement that calls for "voluntary export restraints" (VERs) in some states of the world.

Maggi (1999) investigates whether world efficiency can be promoted by a *multilateral* trade agreement, compared to what can be achieved by a web of bilateral agreements between pairs of countries. His starting point is the tacit cooperation in a repeated tariff game between impatient governments, as described by Dixit (1987), that eliminates to some extent the incentives countries have to exploit their monopoly power in trade. As noted previously, tacit cooperation requires punishments for deviations from the agreed tariffs. Maggi assumes that a multilateral agency, such as the World Trade Organization (WTO), plays the role of informing third parties when deviations from the tacit agreement have occurred. If the noncooperative equilibrium would feature bilateral imbalances of power – where one country stands to lose less (or gain) from a trade war with a particular trade partner – then a multilateral agreement may be beneficial, because it facilitates a transfer of enforcement power across relationships and thus supports greater cooperation than can be

[7] The Bagwell and Staiger (2002) book uses game-theoretic tools to rationalize a host of institutional features of the world trading system, including, for example, the role of the most-favored-nation clause in multilateral trade agreements.

achieved with punishments applied only by the country that is directly affected by the deviation.

Most of the literature on trade agreements finds the motivation for cooperation in the inefficiencies of a noncooperative Nash equilibrium between governments. But Maggi and Rodriguez-Clare (1998) draw on another game-theoretic insight attributed to Kydland and Prescott (1977) to explain why a government might wish to enter a trade agreement to tie its own hands when it is being pressured by its domestic interests. If a policy maker accepts "gifts" from a special interest in exchange for tariff favors, why would it wish to constrain itself and eschew that opportunity? Kydland and Prescott explained the value of (commitment) rules versus discretion in a multistage game with requirements for time consistency. Maggi and Rodriguez Clare import this idea into the realm of trade agreements. Suppose a government anticipates that it will later be tempted to protect an industry in exchange for political contributions. If private agents also anticipate a time-consistent trade policy, then they will overinvest in the industries they expect to be protected. This anticipation generates an ex ante misallocation of capital across sectors. A commitment under a trade agreement affords the policy maker a more efficient ex ante allocation of capital in exchange for a loss of any surplus it could otherwise gain by acceding to an industry's ex post demands. Depending on the anticipated distribution of rents in the ex post relationship, a commitment by the government might dominate the option to behave ex post with discretion.

30.6 REMAINING QUESTIONS

Game-theoretic tools have been invaluable for understanding the trade policies that emerge from political processes and the outcomes that might be achieved with greater cooperation. A number of questions remain, especially when seen in the light of the recent apparent reversal of long-standing trends toward more liberal trade, such as,

(1) What mechanisms might be designed to ensure greater participation in the national surplus created by liberal trade? The recent work of Autor and colleagues (2013) and others reminds us that trade often creates losers alongside the winners. The losers are a natural source of political opposition to a liberal trade regime. Some researchers have considered schemes to redistribute the gains from trade; see, for example, Dixit and Norman (1981) and Feenstra and Lewis (1991a, 1994). But these schemes have not been implemented or, in some cases (e.g., trade adjustment assistance), have not accomplished their goals. Would it be possible to design schemes to include in laws authorizing trade negotiations that might forestall the subsequent political opposition to trade agreements?

(2) What is the role of identity politics in the formation of trade policy? Social identities have featured in recent political-economic theorizing

about trade and migration policies by Bonomi and colleagues (2021), Grossman and Helpman (2021), Besley and Persson (2021), and Abramson and Shayo (2022). But much remains to be known about how identities are formed and evolve. What role do political parties and political entrepreneurs play in this process? When might trade issues become salient as determinants of identity? What is the relationship between special interest politics and identity politics?

(3) Relatedly, what is the relationship between globalization and the rise of populism? Globalization has occurred alongside skill-biased technical change and recurring financial crises – both of which have contributed to an increased income inequality in many countries – and yet, as Rodrik (2021) has argued, trade and migration have played an outsized role in populist rhetoric and politics. What are the mechanisms by which globalization fuels populism, and how are they different from those for other sources of spreading incomes? To what degree do gains for populist parties stem from the political demands of those hurt by trade and immigration, and to what extent do they stem from the opportunistic response of political actors to economic shocks? Game theoretic analysis of political competition between populists and those with a more cosmopolitan viewpoint in the face of economic shocks (see, for example, Levy et al., 2021) might help us gauge the likelihood that antiglobalization attitudes and policies will continue on their recent course.

(4) How might we design a system of dispute settlement in trade relations that respects national sovereignty and garners political legitimacy, while effectively policing opportunistic behavior by national governments? The WTO Dispute Settlement Procedure has been neutered by the United States' opposition to the appointment of Appellate Body members. The US opposition seems a response to political resentment on the part of certain interest and identity groups in the country. What sort of scheme could gain greater acceptance and support?

30.7 REFERENCES

B. Abramson and M. Shayo. International integration and social identity. *Journal of International Economics*, 137:103577, 2022.

D. Austen-Smith. Campaign contributions and access. *American Political Science Review*, 89(3):566–581, 1995.

D. H. Autor, D. Dorn, and G. H. Hanson. The China syndrome: Local labor market effects of import competition in the United States. *American Economic Review*, 103(6):2121–2168, 2013.

K. Bagwell and R. W. Staiger. A theory of managed trade. *American Economic Review*, 80(4):779–795, 1990.

K. Bagwell and R. W. Staiger. *The Economics of the World Trading System*. Cambridge, MA: MIT Press, 2002.

D. P. Baron and J. A. Ferejohn. Bargaining in legislatures. *American Political Science Review*, 83(4):1181–1206, 1989.

B. D. Bernheim and M. D. Whinston. Common agency. *Econometrica*, 54(4):923–942, 1986a.

B. D. Bernheim and M. D. Whinston. Menu auctions, resource allocation, and economic influence. *Quarterly Journal of Economics*, 101(1):1–31, 1986b.

T. Besley and T. Persson. *The Rise of Identity Politics: Policy, Political Organization, and Nationalist Dynamics*. Unpublished, London School of Economics, 2021.

M. Blanga-Gubbay, P. Conconi, and M. Parenti. Lobbying for globalization. Discussion paper, CEPR, 2021.

M. Bombardini and F. Trebbi. Competition and political organization: Together or alone in lobbying for trade policy? *Journal of International Economics*, 87(1):18–26, 2012.

E. W. Bond and J.-H. Park. Gradualism in trade agreements with asymmetric countries. *Review of Economic Studies*, 69(2):379–406, 2002.

G. Bonomi, N. Gennaioli, and G. Tabellini. Identity, beliefs, and political conflict. *Quarterly Journal of Economics*, 136(4):2371–2411, 2021.

J. A. Brander and B. J. Spencer. Tariff protection and imperfect competition. In H. Kierzkowski, ed., *Monopolistic Competition and International Trade*, pp. 194–207. Oxford: Clarendon Press, 1984.

J. A. Brander and B. J. Spencer. Export subsidies and international market share rivalry. *Journal of International Economics*, 18(1–2):83–100, 1985.

J. I. Bulow, J. D. Geanakoplos, and P. D. Klemperer. Multimarket oligopoly: Strategic substitutes and complements. *Journal of Political Economy*, 93(3):488–511, 1985.

L. Celik, B. Karabay, and J. McLaren. When is it optimal to delegate: The theory of fast-track authority. Working Paper 17810, National Bureau of Economic Research, 2012.

V. P. Crawford and J. Sobel. Strategic information transmission. *Econometrica*, 50(6):1431–1451, 1982.

A. K. Dixit. Strategic aspects of trade policy. In T. Bewley, ed., *Advances in Economic Theory*. New York: Cambridge University Press, 1987.

A. K. Dixit and J. Londregan. The determinants of success of special interests in redistributive politics. *Journal of Politics*, 58(4):1132–1155, 1996.

A. K. Dixit and V. Norman. *Theory of International Trade*. London: Cambridge University Press, 1981.

J. Eaton and G. M. Grossman. Optimal trade and industrial policy under oligopoly. *Quarterly Journal of Economics*, 101(2):383–406, 1986.

P. Fajgelbaum, P. K. Goldberg, P. J. Kennedy, and A. K. Khandelwal. The return to protectionism. *Quarterly Journal of Economics*, 135(1):1–55, 2019.

R. C. Feenstra and T. R. Lewis. Distributing the gains from trade with incomplete information. *Economics and Politics*, 3(1):21–39, 1991a.

R. C. Feenstra and T. R. Lewis. Negotiated trade restrictions with private political pressures. *Quarterly Journal of Economics*, 106(4):1287–1307, 1991b.

R. C. Feenstra and T. R. Lewis. Trade adjustment assistance and Pareto gains from trade. *Journal of International Economics*, 36(1):201–222, 1994.

G. M. Grossman and E. Helpman. Protection for sale. *American Economic Review*, 84(4):833–850, 1994.

G. M. Grossman and E. Helpman. Trade wars and trade talks. *Journal of Political Economy*, 103(4):675–708, 1995.

G. M. Grossman and E. Helpman. Electoral competition and special interest politics. *Review of Economic Studies*, 63(2):265–286, 1996.

G. M. Grossman and E. Helpman. *Special Interest Politics*. Cambridge, MA: MIT Press, 2001.

G. M. Grossman and E. Helpman. A protectionist bias in majoritarian politics. *Quarterly Journal of Economics*, 120(4):1239–1282, 2005.

G. M. Grossman and E. Helpman. Identity politics and trade policy. *Review of Economic Studies*, 88(3):1101–1126, 2021.

G. M. Grossman and E. L.-C. Lai. International protection of intellectual property. *American Economic Review*, 94(5):1635–1653, 2004.

G. M. Grossman, P. McCalman, and R. W. Staiger. The "new" economics of trade agreements: From trade liberalization to regulatory convergence? *Econometrica*, 89(1):215–249, 2021.

E. Helpman and T. Persson. Lobbying and legislative bargaining. *The B.E. Journal of Economic Analysis and Policy*, 1(1):1–33, 2001.

H. G. Johnson. Optimal tariffs and retaliation. *Review of Econoic Studies*, 21(2):142–153, 1953.

V. Krishna and J. Morgan. A model of expertise. *Quarterly Journal of Economics*, 116(2):747–775, 2001.

F. E. Kydland and E. C. Prescott. Rules rather than discretion: The inconsistency of optimal plans. *Journal of Political Economy*, 85(3):473–491, 1977.

G. Levy, R. Razin, and A. Young. *Misspecified Politics and the Recurrence of Populism*. Unpublished, London School of Economics, 2021.

A. Lindbeck and J. W. Weibull. Balanced-budget redistribution as the outcome of political competition. *Public Choice*, 52:273–297, 1987.

S. Lohmann. Information, access and contributions: A signaling model of lobbying. *Public Choice*, 85(3–4):267–284, 1995.

S. P. Magee, W. Brock, and L. Young. *Black Hole Tariffs and Endogenous Policy Theory*. Cambridge: Cambridge University Press, 1989.

G. Maggi. The role of multilateral institutions in international trade cooperation. *American Economic Review*, 89(1):190–214, 1999.

G. Maggi and A. Rodriguez-Clare. The value of trade agreements in the presence of political pressures. *Journal of Political Economy*, 106(3):574–601, 1998.

W. Mayer. Theoretical considerations on negotiated tariff adjustments. *Oxford Economic Papers*, 33(1):135–153, 1981.

D. Mitra. Endogenous lobby formation and endogenous protection: A long-run model of trade policy determination. *American Economic Review*, 89(5):1116–1134, 1999.

R. Myerson. Incentive compatibility and the bargaining problem. *Econometrica*, 47(1):61–73, 1979.

M. Olson. *The Logic of Collective Action*. Cambridge, MA: Harvard University Press, 1965.

R. Ossa. Trade wars and trade talks with data. *American Economic Review*, 104(12):4104–4146, 2014.

R. D. Putnam. Diplomacy and domestic politics: The logic of two-level games. *International Organization*, 42(3):427–460, 1988.

D. Rodrik. Why does globalization fuel populism? Economics, culture, and the rise of right-wing populism. *Annual Review of Economics*, 13:133–170, 2021.

A. Rubinstein. Perfect equilibrium in a bargaining model. *Econometrica*, 50(1):97–109, 1982.

T. Scitovszky. A reconsideration of the theory of tariffs. *Review of Economic Studies*, 9(2):89–110, 1941-42.

R. Selten. Spieltheoretische Behandlung eines Oligopolmodells mit Nachfragetragheit: Teil I Bestimmung des dynamischen Preisgleichgewichts. *Zeitschrift für die gesamte Staatswissenschaft*, 121:301–324, 1965.

M. Spence. Job market signaling. *Quarterly Journal of Economics*, 87(3):355–374, 1973.

PART VIII

HUMAN SOCIETY

31

Introduction to Part VIII

Kaushik Basu

Starting in the mid eighteenth century, the Industrial Revolution had left the discipline of economics floundering. Rapid technological change expanded the potential, true, but changing nature of markets, transactions, and labor threatened stability, with skies laden with soot and working-class children toiling from dawn to dusk blighting their own futures. Economics and the social sciences were in tatters trying to deal with the changing landscape of economy and society.

Fortunately, the Industrial Revolution coincided with one of the most remarkable periods of creative research and theoretical breakthroughs, bookended by Adam Smith (1776) and Leon Walras (1874), with a remarkable cluster of works in between – by Augustin Cournot, David Ricardo, John Stuart Mill, Stanley Jevons, and others. This helped us understand the then new world we were inhabiting, and to create laws, regulations, and policies, which at that time appeared radical and novel, to ride over the turbulence and toward a more prosperous global society.

Advances in artificial intelligence and the dramatic rise of digital technology over the last few decades have brought today's world to a similar juncture. To make matters worse, the time that people would have taken to learn the new technology has been sharply cut by the COVID-19 pandemic. People have been compelled by the pandemic to a forced "learning-by-doing" exercise. The outcome is that change is upon us more rapidly than anyone imagined.

It is arguable that for the social sciences, this is a time to move some of our attention away from "normal science" to the exploration of paradigm shifts. It is time once again for fundamental research of the kind we saw in the late eighteenth and early nineteenth centuries, this time to understand the evolving structure of economics, culture, and strife in our contemporary world.

This conference is an invitation for fundamental research by marshalling game theory – a method of analysis unavailable to scholars even a hundred

This final version has benefited greatly, in both substance and style, from the comments of Mark Voorneveld.

years ago – to address the challenges of our time, spanning the social science and beyond. The cluster of three chapters in this part on "Human Society" epitomizes this. The chapters by, respectively, Daron Acemoglu, Avinash Dixit, and Joseph Henrich range over diverse disciplines, most notably economics, politics, and evolutionary biology. However, they have a common methodological binding; they are all rooted in ideas and concepts of game theory. They are also united by the fact that all three of them address some of the deepest questions posed by the changing landscape of our economy and society.

In much of economics, the assumptions that we use we write down explicitly as assumptions or axioms, the most celebrated work along these lines being Gerard Debreu's (1959) *Theory of Value*, written with an elegance reminiscent of Euclidean axiomatics and an aesthetic appeal one finds in great works of art. However, all disciplines also have assumptions that are unwritten and so much a part of the woodwork that often the practitioners are themselves unaware of them. This is true for Debreu; this is true for Euclid. Euclid wrote down most of his assumptions explicitly as axioms, but he did not specify the assumption that it was all being done on a plane. For 2,000 years, no one questioned this, so much so that Euclidean geometry did not need the adjective "Euclidean." No disaster happened because by the time rapid travel over our near-spherical globe began, we had realized that there was this implicit assumption used by geometricians for hundreds of years. Fundamental research had begun from the early nineteenth century, giving birth to non-Euclidean geometry.

The turmoil in the world today, from polarized politics, to a fracturing climate, to destabilizing economic inequalities, all partly related to the rise of new technology, is making us aware of the need to explore the assumptions in the woodwork of economics. Many of these assumptions pertain to culture, social norms, and institutions. Consider, for instance, the fact that agents are able to talk and communicate when they do trade and exchange. No textbook of economics, describing the theory of what leads to trade, exchange, and a Pareto optimal outcome, writes down, alongside the axioms of transitivity, completeness, and convexity, the axiom "Can talk and communicate." That is an assumption in the woodwork of economics. It is arguable that there are other such axioms, such as our ability to restrain self-interested behavior in certain situations, by using our norms or even sense of justice and fair play (Vanderschraaf, 2021).

Most of the time, leaving such axioms as unstated is harmless. When we go over stretches of time during which these assumptions are persistently valid, there is no harm in treating them as immutable, banishing them into the woodwork, and continuing with "normal economics." However, the axiom "Can talk and communicate" may need to be examined and modified when – as with the rise of digital technology and the arrival of social media – there are changes in the way we communicate and how our sentences are interpreted by people of different cultural backgrounds. To use it as an axiomatic truth will result in errors in the predictions we make and is as risky as flying airplanes over large stretches of the globe, based on Euclidean calculations assuming the world is flat.

To question and modify one of these fundamental assumptions, rooted in culture and deep-seated norms, is to shake up the discipline and attempt a paradigm shift. We are at a stage of history where this is needed. We have to examine some of the fundamental assumptions, peel them off, and create new paradigms.

I would in fact go further and suggest that each discipline has an infinite embedding in deeper and deeper assumptions, hidden from our view. Every time we hit a crisis of the discipline we may need to peel off some layers, unearth some assumptions, modify them to suit our needs, and use the new theory to create new laws, regulations, and policies. There is never a permanent resting place. As the drift of technology continues and occasionally speeds up, we will have to be ever vigilant for these hidden assumptions, which may periodically be thorns that must be taken out.

The three chapters in this part try to explore (1) how different institutions emerge as a result of within-society conflict, and how social and political innovations develop in order to deal with this (Acemoglu, Chapter 32); (2) the role of sanctions and enforcement, and strategies not just to play the game that society presents us with but to change the game itself (Dixit, Chapter 33); and (3) the role of equilibrium selection, endogenous preferences, and the evolution of culture in which the economy is inevitably embedded (Henrich, Chapter 34).

The chapters are best viewed not as presentations of new results and theorems to understand and grapple with the tectonic shifts occurring beneath our economy, but more modestly, and therefore more importantly, as a prelude to new research and prodding to discover new paradigms to make sense of the world around us.

It is becoming increasingly clear that this ambitious new venture, straddling the social and biological sciences, and also moral philosophy and law, has a common methodological need for the concepts and methods of analysis used in the discipline of game theory, which has a history of barely 100 years, dating back to the seminal work of Émile Borel. This method is what binds these three chapters' quest to analyze the world.

Conventional economics is founded on separating out exogenous and endogenous variables, with the former being treated as causally prior to the latter. They constitute the cause; the endogenous variables are the effect. This clear delineation is, however, often flawed. Causality is a more complex relation than economists make it out to be. In an interview to *The Paris Review* (1982, vol. 84, p. 57), the English poet, Philip Larkin, when asked if he was shy, replied, "I was and am extremely shy. Anyone who has stammered will know what agony it is, especially at school." He then went on to make a quizzical observation about causality: "I often wonder if I was shy because I stammered, or vice versa."

This is often treated as a jocular observation. It is more than that. If causality is hard to determine in an individual, as Larkin suggests, it is a vastly more difficult matter in complex systems, where many more variables are interdependent than we, for reasons of scientific convenience, assume. The institution of caste, referred to in the chapter by Henrich, is a good example of this.

We often treat the persistence of these institutions as caused by the interest of one group, in this case the dominant caste that benefits from the persistence. But as Akerlof (1976) had shown, this need not be. The system can be a trap of interactive behavior and sanctions, out of which no individual can exit without hurting oneself, a focal point of enmeshed beliefs (Schelling, 1960). This is the same argument Vaclav Havel (1986) used to explain "post-totalitarian" systems, where all individuals, from the ordinary citizen to the policy maker, the police, and the president, are trapped in a Kafkaesque equilibrium. The problem, in essence, is that of a large collective action problem, arising from individuals and groups with divergent interests (Ferguson, 2020).

Of course, individual behaviors of conformity are often subject to formalized enforcement (Acemoglu and Wolitzky, 2020; Dixit, 2007; Greif et al., 1994). As (Dixit, 2009, p. 6) observes, "government and governance" are not even "almost synonymous." In fact, in the very end, society, in its entirety, is an endogenous system. We need to understand the interaction between economics, politics, and culture as a "game of life." Once we have understood this, we can think in terms of how we can modify the game of life that we are engaged in, so as to achieve a better outcome and, minimally, to avert the existential risk that we are lurching toward, be that from climate change, which is an outcome of our collective behavior, or political conflict and war, once again an outcome of individual aspirations and collective failure to contain these. The need to change the game of life sounds like a contradiction in terms, because to change the game of life we need to step outside of it.

This is an unavoidable challenge that we will have to sort out and understand better in the future. I would in fact argue that there is no such thing as an actual "game of life" (Basu, 2018). A game of life is simply a convention among the analysts – an agreement that we shall not step beyond these bounds for the present analysis. In reality, the game we analyze at any point of time is best thought of as lodged inside an endless onion. We can step out to a larger and larger domain of actions by peeling off layers and creating an ever larger game.

I mention this because many of the discussions in these chapters wade into areas that are bound to be controversial. Thus, in his chapter, Acemoglu talks about how people value freedom and dislike being bossed around, and how rebellion against authority is never far from the surface. One has to pit against this the human propensity to accept one's own plight as natural. This is nothing but a psychological propensity to make life tolerable, even when it is objectively miserable. This explains why casteism and slavery persisted for such long stretches of time, and quite at peace with the oppressors.

Likewise, Henrich talks about the tension between economics and cultural evolution that arises from the nature of equilibrium selection (Henrich, 2004). In his chapter, he points to the plethora of stable equilibria that arise when non-payoff-based transmission mechanisms are recognized, and rightly conjectures that economists are likely to treat this as an annoying modeling issue. Yet, on reflection, this is heartening. Different disciplines should help us locate different sets of possible equilibria. Ultimately, we can then zero in on the intersection of these sets as the prediction of a truly multidisciplinary social science.

This collection of three chapters is of special interest to me because of my belief that just as game theory showed us with games like the Prisoner's Dilemma that there may be a deep disconnect between individual rationality and group behavior, we may have a similar problem in the moral domain. A player turning moral can make the group or the collective behave in a more immoral way, thereby giving rise to "Greta's Dilemma," and it is possible to go further and show that in a strategically intertwined world, every person being more concerned about the future generation may make us, collectively, behave in ways that end up hurting future generations (Baldassarri, 2020). This would not be unexpected if people's morals were diverse (Moehler, 2018). What is interesting is that these adverse moral fallouts can occur even with people having essentially homogenous moral intentions.

This takes us to the brink of a deep real-world problem – that of establishing prosperity and liberty in a world that may be fundamentally diverse. The problem can be solved in specific nations and also in clusters of nations with similar cultural backgrounds, such as the "West," which learned to trust and cooperate and became prosperous (Henrich, 2020). However, with globalization this has to be taken a step further because we may need to bring fundamentally diverse groups under a common order. The Hobbesian solution of an authoritarian state may create order, but it cannot solve the more fundamental problem of well-being. First, we may need to distinguish between "state's laws" and "actual order" (Dixit, 2009) and, further, as Acemoglu and Robinson (2019, p. 12) observe, "Life under the yoke of the state can be nasty brutish, and short too."

The outcome contradicts our individual moral intentions. This disconnect between individuals and groups is what Nietzsche was drawing attention to when in his *Beyond Good and Evil*, he wrote, in his characteristically flamboyant style, "In individuals, insanity is rare; but in groups, parties, nations and epochs, it is the rule."

Game theory is the key to understanding this disconnect between the individual and the group. (I am glad Nietzsche is not around to read this, for he would find this assertion infuriating.) The hope must lie in keeping alive the moral intention that may have been foiled by the strategic dynamics of the collectivity. The big game-theoretic challenge that arises from this is best viewed in the way Dixit puts it in the context of our "irrational" behavioral urges that can lead us to outcomes that we regret in retrospect. We need to be aware that despite our moral desires, the strategic nature of interpersonal interaction can lead us to precisely the outcome we do not want. We need to deliberate and act in advance, based on our moral intention, to prevent society from ending up where we least want it to be.

The tension that all three chapters are concerned with – that of desirable order in groups of heterogenous individuals – has been heightened in today's world because of globalization. This is bringing together people with different norms and cultures. We are beginning to see what happens when people who live peacefully on two islands, one in which they have developed the norm of driving on the left and one in which they follow the norm of driving on the right, come to inhabit the same space.

The kind of problems that we solved in the past, when human beings formed tribes and groups and began to live and work together, is arising now at the level of the globe, as the peoples of different islands come to inhabit a common space. The need today is that of a minimal global constitution – a set of minimal rules that we all collectively agree to abide by. This is the only way to convert our huge technological advances into greater human well-being, and away from strife and conflict. This will not be an easy task. The issues raised here and in these chapters are best viewed as a prelude to such an effort.

31.1 REFERENCES

D. Acemoglu and J. Robinson. *The Narrow Corridor: States Societies and the Fate of Liberty*. New York: Penguin Press, 2019.

D. Acemoglu and A. Wolitzky. Sustaining cooperation: Community enforcement vs. specialized enforcement. *Journal of European Economic Association*, 18:1078–1122, 2020.

G. Akerlof. The economics of caste, and of the rat race, and other woeful tales. *Quarterly Journal of Economics*, 90:599–617, 1976.

D. Baldassarri. Market integration accounts for local variation in generalized altruism in a nationwide lost-letter experiment. *Proceedings of the National Academy of Sciences*, 117:2858–2863, 2020.

K. Basu. *The Republic of Beliefs: A New Introduction to Law and Economics*. Princeton, NJ: Princeton University Press, 2018.

K. Basu. Conventions, morals and strategy: Greta's dilemma and the Incarceration Game. Synthese, 200: 58, 2022.

G. Debreu. *Theory of Value: An Axiomatic Analysis of Economic Equilibrium*. New Haven, CT: Yale University Press, 1959.

A. Dixit. *Lawlessness and Economics: Alternative Modes of Governance*. Princeton, NJ: Princeton University Press, 2007.

A. Dixit. Governance institutions and economic activity. *American Economic Review*, 99:5–24, 2009.

W. Ferguson. *The Political Economy of Collective Action, Inequality and Development*. Stanford, CT: Stanford University Press, 2020.

A. Greif, P. Milgrom, and B. Weingast. Coordination, commitment and enforcement: The case of the merchant guild. *Journal of Political Economy*, 102:745–776, 1994.

V. Havel. The power of the powerless. In J. Vladislav, ed., *Living in Truth*. London: Faber and Faber, 1986.

J. Henrich. Cultural group selection, coevolutionary processes and large-scale cooperation. *Journal of Economic Behavior & Organization*, 53:3–35, 2004.

J. Henrich. *The WEIRDest People in the World: How the West Became Psychologically Peculiar and Particularly Prosperous*. New York: Farrar, Straus and Giroux, 2020.

M. Moehler. Diversity, stability and social contract theory. *Philosophical Studies*, 176:3285–3301, 2018.

T. C. Schelling. *Strategy of Conflict*. Cambridge, MA: Harvard University Press, 1960.

A. Smith. *An Inquiry into the Nature and Causes of the Wealth of Nations*. Reprint. New York: Random House, 1776.

P. Vanderschraaf. Contractarianisms and markets. *Journal of Economic Behavior and Organization*, 181:270–287, 2021.

L. Walras. *Elements d'economie politique pure* (translated as Elements of Pure Economics). Lausanne, Switzerland: Corbaz, 1874.

32

Conflict, Cooperation, and Innovation in the Evolution of Human Societies

Daron Acemoglu

32.1 INTRODUCTION

Humans are not the only species capable of achieving large-scale cooperation. But they may be the only one that has created diverse societies, institutions, and norms, ranging from the egalitarian small-scale foragers to absolutist empires and (sometimes) functioning democracies. In this chapter, I argue that three sets of ideas need to be considered simultaneously in order to understand this rich history and the future of humanity. These are (1) the need for cooperation, (2) within-society conflict, and (3) institutional flexibility and innovations.

A large literature in economics and cultural evolution, expertly discussed by Avinash Dixit (Chapter 33) and Joe Henrich (Chapter 34) in this volume, focus on the first. Cooperation is a difficult problem, especially beyond kin groups. Humans have developed myriad to modulate strategic motives and achieve stable cooperation.

The latter two – within-society conflict and institutional flexibility and innovation – receive comparatively less attention. It is my contention that we cannot understand human societies and the games that they play without bringing all three of these ideas together. By within-society conflict, I mean the problem of divergent interests within a group about the allocation of resources and status. The most important implication of this conflict for my purposes here is that it underpins the emergence of institutions and norms that create an organization of society (and associated economic and social allocations) that favor a specific group of individuals. Within-society conflict is not confined to humans. Chimpanzee and gorilla groups are organized around dominance hierarchies. For example, "alpha males" (or "silverbacks" in gorillas) are more powerful

This chapter is a shortened version of a longer piece, which contains more extensive references, some of which I omitted here to save space. This work draws on my work with several coauthors, including David Autor, Simon Johnson, Pascual Restrepo, and Alex Wolitzky. Most importantly, it builds on my lifelong collaboration with James Robinson. I am deeply grateful to all of my collaborators, especially to Jim, for their generosity and the multitude of contributions to my education and thinking. I am grateful to James Robinson and Alex Wolitzky for suggestions, and Rebecca Jackson for research assistance. The errors in this chapter are of course mine and mine only.

than and benefit at the expense of other members of the group (Waal, 2007; Boehm, 2012). In human societies, the same behavior is common, even if it does not always take the form of alpha males.

An important implication of taking within-society conflict seriously is that we cannot and should not think of social arrangements, including culture broadly construed, as efficient adaptations to prevailing conditions. Each social arrangement creates winners and losers, and some are adapted to serve powerful groups while others will generate greater equality of economic benefits and status.

This brings me to the third idea: institutional flexibility and innovations. What makes game theory so central for understanding human societies is the huge range of arrangements humans have come up with over time. The reason I add "innovations" in this context is because these arrangements are not fixed, and some of the most important transformations in human history emerge because communities were able to innovate in terms of their institutions and norms.

Different institutional arrangements foster distinct modes of behavior. They may even induce different types of evolutionary selection, though this probably is less relevant for the rapidly changing institutional tapestry we observe over the last 10,000 years. In comparing humans to our closest relatives, such as chimps, a puzzling feature is humans' ability to cooperate in relatively egalitarian communities. Such communities appear to be a good approximation to how many human communities lived before transition to settled agriculture. Although it is possible to model egalitarian communities as the outcome of coordination on the Pareto dominant equilibrium in a repeated prisoner's dilemma, there are other fruitful approaches.

An important hypothesis was formulated by Christopher Boehm (1993): Humans form "reverse dominance hierarchies," meaning that they gang up to bring down any member of the community who attempts to become the alpha male or set up a hierarchy. I will refer to this type of behavior as "reverse dominance coalitions," both to prevent any confusion that the original term causes with actual hierarchies and to emphasize the critical aspect of coalition formation. Indeed, foraging societies have a range of "leveling mechanisms" aimed at limiting hierarchy and bringing down upstarts (Woodburn, 1982; Lee and Daly, 1999). Nevertheless, neither these ideas nor those based on reciprocity within small groups can provide an immediate account of how cooperation and other institutions are maintained in societies made up of millions, sometimes hundreds of millions, of people.

In this chapter, I draw on and extend the framework introduced by Acemoglu and Robinson (2023, 2019), and argue that to understand cooperation and conflict in large-scale societies, we need to blend these ideas with a systematic study of within-society conflict and the institutions and norms that structure these relations.[1]

[1] References to other work on which I am drawing are listed in the longer version of this chapter.

32.2 VARIETIES OF COOPERATION: SMALL-SCALE COLLABORATION

One mode of cooperation is illustrated by foraging societies, which are typically small scale and comprise a tight-knit group of individuals, sometimes linked by kinship. Foraging societies are those that engage in hunting, gathering of wild plants, and fishing, with limited or no domestication of plants and animals (Lee and Daly, 1999), and I will use *hunter–gatherer* and *forager* as synonyms.

Cooperation plays a central role in hunting and gathering, and of course in the social life of these communities. Collaboration may be particularly important for big game hunting. There are many archaeological sites illustrating how our ancestors may have killed large herds of bison or other big game, most likely with the collective work of dozens, perhaps hundreds, of people (Boyd and Richerson, 2022). Child-rearing is another area where collective work was likely central.

Cooperation in small-scale societies appears to have been sustained by both carrots and sticks, and more importantly by internalized values of cooperation. Individuals most active in the hunt are rewarded by status and other means, while those who systematically shirk may be ridiculed and in some cases ostracized. See, for example, the work of Hill (2005) for evidence from the Ache, and see the writings of Johnson and Earle (1987) and Gurven and colleagues (2000) for more general discussions. Notably, in contrast to the basic theory of repeated games, which suggests that "extremal punishments" are socially optimal, there is little evidence of such severe punishments (see Baumard, 2010, for an overview). For instance, there are few reported cases of systematic violence being triggered because somebody has engaged in free-riding behavior, even though these societies can often be quite violent in other domains (e.g., in the context of intergroup conflict).

More than these external inducements, evidence from hunter–gatherers indicates that norms of cooperation were internalized. Most members did not receive a huge payoff gain by shirking and making their fellow members worse off, because they internalized the benefits from helping members of their group (Gurven, 2005; Wiessner, 2005).

The striking commonality across most foraging societies in record is that they were fiercely egalitarian (Lee and Daly, 1999). Many did not have powerful chiefs. When chiefs, even "big men," existed, their egalitarian ethos implied that these had limited powers and could be deposed. The anthropologist Richard Lee famously recounts his encounter with !Kung Bushmen who told him, when asked about their headmen, "We're all headmen .... Each one of us is headman over himself!" (Lee, 1979, p. 348). In fact, these small-scale societies, as well as some larger-scale examples, were staunchly antihierarchy and had rich leveling mechanisms against would-be alpha males and strongmen, sometimes going so far as exiling or killing them. The evidence suggests that it was not just political hierarchy but economic inequality that was viewed as suspicious, because this was interpreted as part of what Boehm calls "upstartism."

To limit such inequality, these communities often restricted market exchange and new technologies (Acemoglu and Robinson, 2019). Broad-based egalitarianism appears fused with their mode of cooperation.

So why this egalitarianism? We do not know for sure. But the most convincing reason is within-society conflict. Hierarchy is a slippery slope: Once a chief's authority is the main conduit for cooperation, it is difficult to take it back and prevent the chief from hogging all the resources. Hierarchy tends to reduce other men's utility, resources, and ability to procreate. Among chimpanzees and gorillas, there might not be a recourse against such alpha-male behavior. In humans, whose greater intelligence, flexibility, and language enable complex coalitions among weaker parties, there is a powerful remedy.

There is also a cost to this egalitarianism, however, even among hunters and gatherers. While certain modes of cooperation are feasible without any hierarchy, others are not. The most important types of cooperative human behavior that depends on hierarchy are conflict resolution and public service provision. This is easy to see in the case of conflict resolution. Conflict between humans is ubiquitous, and the most straightforward way of resolving such conflicts is for a third party to decide who is right and who is wrong and impose remedies (such as compensation). But this requires some sort of hierarchy. If the third party's recommendations can be ignored by one of the sides, then they would be of no use. Throughout history, third-party conflict resolution accompanies hierarchy (Acemoglu and Robinson, 2019).

Lack of third-party enforcement can be very costly. It not only holds back complex economic transactions but also leads to bouts of violence. Although there are examples of peaceful small-scale societies, many foraging bands were quite violent, and this was related to failure of effective conflict resolution (Keeley, 1996). Those that avoid such endemic violence often do so via other costly means, for example, by creating constricting traditions and mores that diminish individual freedom and autonomy.

The same is true for public services. Every community provides certain collective services (defense, inculcation of communal values, care and insurance for the needy) to its members. But without some type of state institutions, which of course presume hierarchy, these take very rudimentary forms. Holding back hierarchy holds back public services. This may be less obvious in the case of small-scale societies, because some of these public services also require scale (an education system is infeasible in a community of just 100 people). But hierarchy-less societies remained small-scale partly because of their inability and unwillingness to form state-like institutions to provide public services at a larger scale.

Like other social institutions, the foraging way of life endured thanks to political, economic, and cultural channels of persistence. Politically, egalitarianism, in the form of reverse dominance coalitions and other leveling mechanisms, made it difficult for hierarchy to emerge. Once hierarchy was limited, this strengthened egalitarian practices, making hierarchy even more difficult to form. With limited hierarchy and strong egalitarian practices, it became easier to contain upstart individuals wishing to grab a larger share of resources and gain more status and power. This political dynamic created a self-reinforcing cycle of egalitarianism.

The economic channel also contributed to persistence of this mode of cooperation. The small-scale of the societies meant that institutionalized conflict resolution and public service provision would have been less feasible or perhaps even impossible. But, then, the type of collaboration these societies practiced meant that the they did not grow beyond a certain scale, did not develop economic activities that required extensive specialization, and did not trigger technological and productivity growth, thus reducing the need for more complex forms of cooperation. The small scale of the societies also meant that personalized enforcement of rules and norms was more feasible, because community members knew each other.

Finally, the cultural channel was pivotal as well. Foraging societies developed cultural configurations and social meanings that were, at least to some degree, adapted to their way of life. This strengthened egalitarian values and impacted the types of goods and services they sought. The anthropologist Marshall Sahlins (1972) famously called these hunter–gatherer groups the "original affluent society," because they worked few hours, achieved fairly nutritious diets, and were quite healthy, especially compared to the agriculturalists who would come to the scene after the Neolithic Revolution. Sahlins recognized that there were many other goods and services we depend on today, which were absent among foragers, but argued that this was not inconsistent with affluence, because their preferences and values had evolved in such a way that they did not particularly value or demand these items.

32.3 VARIETIES OF COOPERATION: DESPOTIC RULE

Inequality starts emerging systematically in human record around the Neolithic Revolution. Although there is a debate as to whether inequality increased significantly before agriculture based on permanent settlements, two types of changes seem well documented in the millennia following agriculture. With permanent settlements, accumulating assets became feasible, opening the way to economic inequality. Together with, and in several cases in fact even before, transition to agriculture, there is also evidence of social differentiation, whereby some individuals become shamans or political elites, and their graves contain evidence of luxury goods (Moore et al., 2000; Schmidt, 2010). Later civilizations, including Sumarian cities such as Ur and Uruk around 2000 BCE, the Babylonian Empire, and ancient Egypt, start exhibiting more deep-rooted levels of inequality, both in economics and politics.

What we see in these societies, and the subsequent empires that emerge in Greece, Rome, Persia, the Indian subcontinent, and China, is a very different mode of cooperation. It takes place on a much larger scale, and it is directed and coordinated by hierarchy. It is also bolstered by a system of conflict resolution and early forms of public service provision.

Not just institutions but the norms and beliefs supporting social organization are very different from those of foragers. Social relations now look nothing like reverse dominance coalitions and egalitarianism we see in foraging societies. Rather, one could simplify and say that they look much more similar to the dominance hierarchies of chimps and gorillas.

The much-larger-scale cooperation that these societies achieved is visible in war making; in infrastructure, including irrigation projects, road building, and other collective works; and in administrative capacity (e.g., via law codes, courts, and bureaucratic procedures). These changes, collectively, improved the productivity of economic activities and reduced violence. When heavily armed armies fought, casualties could and did skyrocket, but the evidence suggests that rates of overall violent deaths declined once states and third-party enforcement came on the scene.

State-building comes with significant costs, however. To start with, state institutions expand and bolster inequality, enabling those who command political and social power to use it for their benefits. Relatedly, with strong states and well-defined elites, participation in collective decision-making from nonelite members dwindled. Consultation and systematic deliberation in foraging societies came to be replaced with much more despotic decision-making. As a result, decisions on how to resolve conflicts, which types of public services to provide, and who should benefit from rules and regulations became the purview of the elite with little input from the rest of society. Finally, freedoms and autonomy were significantly diminished, which is costly to the extent that individuals prefer to make their own choices and enjoy the reality or perception of having agency. Lack of autonomy is also costly to the extent that economic and social decisions benefit from diversity of approaches and viewpoints.

The nature of economic activity in these societies bears the imprint of these arrangements. We see larger-scale investments, such as irrigation systems and road networks, more systematic regulation and taxation of economic production, and some examples of more complex cooperation, even in areas that go beyond defense. Trade flourished in some of these empires, often thanks to greater stability and more effective conflict resolution. But on the whole this flourishing was unequalizing. Greater opportunities were open to some people, but this was often at the expense of the freedom of many others, who were suppressed or at the very least strongly induced to remain subservient.

The most symbolic aspect of this change is the emergence of a huge complex of coercive labor relations in the majority of archaic states, including slavery. The growing role of coercion in economic activities highlights the central importance of within-society conflict. The economic structure of these archaic states simultaneously benefited the politically powerful elite while impoverishing and repressing the majority of the citizens. The available evidence suggests that in many instances, the majority of the population worked harder, was less nourished, lived shorter lives, and enjoyed much less autonomy after the transition to settled agriculture (Sahlins, 1972; Suzman, 2017). This was true both before and after the emergence of large empires. Clearly these empires should not be viewed as an efficient adaptation to changing cooperation needs or as the next step in human civilization. They often made some people better off and some others significantly worse off.

Another remarkable feature is the dramatic change in the norms and values of these societies, which moved in a direction that was almost diametrically opposed to those of their forager ancestors. There was now much less of the egalitarian ethos. Instead, hierarchy came to be accepted as natural. This can be seen in several distinct features of early empires. In most of these cases, rulers claimed and often were accepted to have supernatural powers and divinely ordained authority. This hierarchy did not just distinguish kings and emperors from the rest; it also enshrined several distinct "castes." The extreme example is the Indian caste system, which from the beginning created separate "varnas" or social orders. This included brahmins, in charge of religious rituals, and kshatriya, who formed the warrior aristocracy. Both of these groups stood apart and above other varnas, such as vaishya, consisting of those engaged in farming and commerce; shudras, making up the laboring class; and the dalits, or the untouchables, at the very bottom (Smith, 1994). Even if less rigid and less ritualized, similar hierarchies existed in many other early states, including throughout Europe during the Middle Ages.

Religious beliefs were transformed as well, especially during the axial age, between eighth and third centuries BCE. Polytheistic and more loosely organized religions were in most cases replaced by religions with a single, moralizing god and clear rules and ready justifications for hierarchy. Also noteworthy is the diversity of supernatural beliefs that have emerged during the axial age. Although this period witnessed the birth of many of today's most important monotheistic religions, many early states, including both pre–Bronze Age and post–Iron Age Greek civilizations and the Romans, did not adopt monotheism. Even among those who did, there is quite a bit of diversity, ranging from the much more hierarchical and unequal religions such as Hinduism, to more egalitarian ones such as Buddhism and to monotheistic ones without moralizing gods, as in the case of China.

This account underscores the importance of institutional flexibility. Ant or bee colonies adapt to different circumstances, for example, when soldier ants become food collectors, depending on specific challenges the colony is facing (Hölldobler and Wilson, 1990). But to the best of my knowledge, we have no evidence of wholesale changes of social roles and hierarchies.

Institutional innovation played a critical role in this process as well: Many of the institutions and arrangements that emerged during this time period had to be invented, and the differential evolution of some of the societies cannot be understood without recognizing that they came up with distinct innovations – some of them up to the task and some of them completely inadequate for what they were trying to achieve. This innovation is again illustrated by the changes in religious beliefs and the types of hierarchies they supported, which took place very rapidly during the axial age. My emphasis on innovation also distinguishes the approach here from those that simply highlight how technological or environmental conditions dictate the evolution of politics and culture (e.g., Morris, 2015).

Like small-scale collaboration, despotic rule was a stable and durable arrangement, bolstered by the same three channels: political, economic, and cultural. Politically, once states under the command of elites emerged, they tended to structure politics in order to suppress dissent and control society. Means of participation for nonelites were curtailed, further amplifying elites' despotic rule.

Elite-dominated societies achieved a much larger economic scale and also started a process of technological change and productivity growth, for example, because of greater specialization in occupations and industries. These changes, even though they were often slow, brought many new challenges, including the need to build new infrastructure, such as irrigation and transport systems, and to defend large settlements against outside forces. They also necessitated extensive cooperation, which was made feasible by the coordination and monitoring that states and hierarchy provided. The larger scale of the economy and productivity growth enriched the elite, making it easier for them to maintain their politically privileged position (and did not generate much benefit for most of the rest of the population; Acemoglu and Robinson, 2012).

All of this meant that once such centralized states entered the scene, they would tend to stick around, even when they were very far from being efficient adaptations to their environment. Within-society conflict played a central role in the structuring of despotic institutions in the form of cooperation, and their persistence was often rooted in the fact that they served the interests of powerful constituencies.

32.4 VARIETIES OF COOPERATION: DEMOCRATIC GOVERNANCE

Egalitarianism in small-scale societies neither erased selfishness nor completely removed upstartist instincts. Likewise, even the most stable despotic regimes did not alter the fact that people value freedom and autonomy, and dislike repression and being bossed around. Rebellion of one sort or another against hierarchy was therefore not too far from the surface under most despotic states.

In a few places, these egalitarian impulses managed to provide a counterweight to state power and hierarchies. When they succeeded in this way, they prepared the ground for the emergence of another type of social organization bolstering large-scale cooperation, which I will call *democratic governance*.[2]

[2] This term might be slightly misleading, since such governance is not confined to democratic institutions. For example, many African precolonial institutions, though not democratic, included important participatory elements. As emphasized in Acemoglu and Robinson (2019), Germanic tribes possessed norms and institutions that encouraged political participation, for instance in the form of people's assemblies, and often required fairly broad-based consensus for most collective decisions. Similar arrangements were also present in a number of pre-Columbian civilizations in the Americas (Blanton et al., 1993). It is for this reason that James Robinson and

I choose this term to emphasize the governance aspect and cooperation implications of these institutions.

Under democratic governance, there are fairly well-developed state institutions, which engage in conflict resolution and public service provision. These institutions also coordinate large-scale cooperation, and not just during periods of war. Building an education system or the interstate highway system in the United States are examples of large-scale cooperation that appear almost impossible to achieve on the basis of small-scale collaboration. Second, and in contradistinction to despotic rule, these decisions are not imposed from the top. Even when they are decided and implemented by political leaders, they need to be approved and legitimized by the broader population. Third, there is a greater degree of information exchange and at least tacit cooperation between society and the state.

Relatedly, cooperation takes a "bottom-up impersonal" form under democratic governance. In small-scale societies, cooperation is bottom-up because its objectives and organization are not dictated by leaders and elites. But it is personal in the sense that individual behavior is monitored and incentivized by the observations of acquaintances and neighbors. If an individual behaves in non-cooperative ways, this will reduce her social standing in the community or may lead to sanctions and ostracism. In contrast, under despotic states, we have "top-down impersonal cooperation," because the elite and state institutions dictate what the objectives are and how different sectors should be contributing to those objectives. Yet because of the greater scale of despotic states, cooperation is also largely impersonal: Tax collectors often do not know the tax payers, and bureaucrats do not know the people who they are supposed to monitor. The apogee of this type of impersonal relationship is in conflict resolution and law enforcement. Instead of the community collectively enforcing its norms and finding ways of defusing conflict, state institutions and employees are now tasked with enforcing laws and punishing infringements.

Things are different under democratic governance, which supports larger-scale and even more impersonal cooperation. But the objectives are set by a more consultative process. Bottom-up impersonal cooperation also opens the door to better communication between citizens and state institutions. For this reason, and also because this type of interaction can trigger further development of state institutions, state capacity under democratic cooperation may ultimately exceed what we see in despotic states (see Acemoglu, 2005; Acemoglu and Robinson, 2019).

Economic dynamics under the auspices of democratic governance are very different as well, and for the same reasons. Compared to coercive systems under

I previously referred to the state institutions that support this type of governance as "shackled Leviathan" governance. In other work (Acemoglu, 2005), I used the concept of "consensually strong states" to capture the related notion that the strength of the state in this case is rooted in society's consensus that the state should expand its powers into activities that were previously out of its sphere of control.

despotic institutions or to production relations organized around traditions and notions such as "moral economy" (Polanyi, 1944; Thompson, 1971), a significant fraction of labor transactions now take place at market-determined wages. Simultaneously, we also see more entry from new firms, more innovative activities, and greater experimentation with new sectors, ways of organizing production, and technologies. Notably, this more fluid business environment critically depends on bottom-up impersonal cooperation. Small-scale collaboration, bolstered by rigid traditions and norms, does not accommodate the entry of new businesses and technologies. These may sometimes emerge under despotic state institutions, but that is rare, and when it happens, it is quite fragile because political power is unequally distributed and there are no effective constraints against its exercise for the benefit of elites.

These dynamics create room for much more shared prosperity under democratic governance than under other arrangements. Foragers have very rarely achieved prosperity, because their small scales make specialization difficult, but equally because of their resistance to innovation and markets. Despotic rule creates room for investment and even some technological progress, but it favors those close to despotic power and is typically inimical to equal opportunities. Despotic states sometimes redistribute to legitimize their rule and stave off discontent; yet this seldom leads to shared prosperity.

There is no guarantee that democratic governance will lead to broadly shared prosperity either, because some people and businesses may be advantaged and can use this advantage to gain more than others. But at least it raises the possibility of shared prosperity that may go on for extended periods, as we experienced in much of the West in the three decades that followed World War II. Democratic institutions can achieve this type of growth both because they produce the conditions for technological change and productivity growth, and also because they provide the political tools to limit inequality and the misuse of the economic power of businesses and wealthy individuals. Just like small-scale and despotic cooperation, democratic governance tends to endure once it is in place, and this is again via political, economic, and cultural channels.

Politically, democracy engenders new institutions, ranging from political parties to civil society organizations and critical media, facilitating bottom-up cooperation and democratic participation. It also legislates new laws that enshrine the rights of citizens to participate in politics. Economically, when such societies generate shared prosperity, they also empower different segments of society to have a voice in politics, and when they restrict economic monopolies, they contribute to limiting political monopolies. Democratic institutions also create a sense of citizenship among the people, which is critical for their participation in democratic governance (Besley and Persson, 2019; Acemoglu et al., 2021).

Nevertheless, there is an element of continuity between small-scale bottom-up cooperation and the type of organization we see under the auspices of democratic governance. Although the egalitarian ethos that energized reverse dominance coalitions is part of human nature, in modern large-scale societies it cannot take the form of a group of men ganging up on upstarts. Yet institutions can channel this ethos into behaviors that encourage political participation and practices that limit the dominance of powerful agents, which now include not just typical alpha males but large firms, leading politicians, and powerful bureaucrats. It may even be creative entrepreneurs who emerge as the new upstarts when they are highly successful and become fabulously wealthy. If so, these entrepreneurs need be constrained by institutionalized reverse dominance coalitions as well. Put differently, we may want to think of democratic governance as an institutionalized form of the reverse dominance coalitions, adapted to larger societies.

32.5 DYNAMICS

Although all three modes of cooperation tend to persist once in place, most societies should be conceived as being located away from these limiting outcomes and, instead, evolving along dynamic trajectories. Moreover, democratic governance should be viewed as a process, not as a static outcome. In this process the balance between the powers of the state and the elite versus those of nonelites plays a critical role (Acemoglu and Robinson, 2019).

Dynamics of institutions and the mode of cooperation are continuously affected by changes in the economic, political, and social environment. Economically, new opportunities will change the balance of power and provide new pathways for some groups to enrich themselves and become empowered at the expense of others. An example is the rise of the English merchant class and industrialists in the seventeenth century, with the opportunities proffered by the Atlantic trade (Acemoglu et al., 2005). Politically, even in the most egalitarian groups, upstartist instincts are present and generate repeated attempts to form new hierarchies. Though many of these attempts are suppressed by reverse dominance coalitions and the norms and traditions of small-scale societies, some will succeed.

Shocks can take the form of structural ones, such as changes in demographic or environmental conditions (such as the collapse of population in the fourteenth century due to the Black Death, which led to the unwinding of the feudal order in some places; e.g., Brenner, 1976). They can result from some upstarts managing to change the balance of power in their favor (e.g., Flannery and Marcus, 2014). Or it could be because larger groups of people solve their collective action problem and demand better rights (e.g., Acemoglu and Robinson, 2000), or even develop new leveling mechanisms. Or they can be technological, altering the nature of production or the balance of military or informational power.

The most fragile mode of cooperation in response to such shocks may actually be the democratic one, because it requires a delicate balance between elites and nonelites (or, equivalently, between states and societies). It is almost inevitable that this balance will get disrupted from time to time. But there is another powerful reason why democratic governance may be more fragile than the alternatives: Because democratic governance offers the best environment for technological change and more complex economic relations to develop, it will continuously create new inequalities and new winners and losers, and sometimes even spearhead technologies that catapult existing balances. Today may be one such time.

32.6 CONCLUSIONS AND THE FUTURE OF COOPERATION

The fact that many societies today are in what I view as the better mode of cooperation should not make one think that there is some "Whig version of history" hidden here, whereby there are inexorable forces taking societies toward "progress." On the contrary, I have argued that nondemocratic modes of cooperation – small-scale collaboration and despotic rule – are quite stable and can emerge and persist for very long time, even when they create inefficiencies and misery. Worse, democratic governance can be particularly fragile. This is often because its economic dynamism produces new conflicts and inequalities, and may also generate new technologies that destabilize its very institutions.

The last several decades have been marked by tremendous advances in digital technologies and electronics. We are currently in the midst of further changes because these advances have enabled a large amount of data to be collected and processed, and have also paved the way for potential breakthroughs in artificial intelligence (AI).

New technologies mean new capabilities for humans. If they are used appropriately, they can improve our material standards of living and enrich our lives. But they are also tools in the hands of some groups to produce new inequalities, alter established balances, and create new dominances. This is exactly what we should be worried about today.

I see three types of threats to our existing mode of cooperation from new technologies. First, new digital technologies have generated huge inequalities. New inequalities produce new opportunities for upstartism and social inequality. They also weaken existing leveling mechanisms. This may threaten the essence of democratic governance, as well as the prerequisites for reciprocal exchange, especially if society becomes increasingly two-tiered – meaning that one segment of society commands both social status and economic resources, while the rest become increasingly subservient.

Second, a major driver of these new inequalities has been advances in automation technologies, which have used the digital platform for generating new ways of substituting machines and algorithms for tasks previously performed by humans (Acemoglu and Restrepo, 2022). Rising inequality is not the only challenge that automation poses to democratic governance. By making labor less essential in production, automation disrupts the political balance and neutralizes one of the most important modern leveling mechanisms – less-skilled workers' role in the production process (Acemoglu, 2022).

Third, new digital technologies are being used for collecting huge amounts of data about consumers and citizens, and this trend is accelerating with AI. These data are empowering companies and governments, disrupting the current political balance in favor of elites and against democratic governance.

Human societies are superbly flexible. But this flexibility does not mean that they can always adapt and respond effectively to changing circumstances. In fact, this flexibility may sometimes make us particularly vulnerable to new sweeping changes in technologies, because those that are empowered and enriched by these technologies can reshape society in ways that are pernicious. Confronting these challenges may require new institutional innovations.

32.7 REFERENCES

D. Acemoglu. Politics and economics in weak and strong states. *Journal of Monetary Economics*, 52:1199–1226, 2005.

D. Acemoglu. Harms of AI. In J. B. Bullock, Y.-C. Chen, J. Himmelreich, V. M. Hudson, A. Korinek, M. M. Young, and B. Zhang, eds., *The Oxford Handbook of AI Governance*, ch. 34, pp. 660–706. Oxford: Oxford University Press, 2022.

D. Acemoglu, N. Ajzenmán, C. Aksoy, M. Fiszbein, and C. Molina. Institutions shape social preferences. Mimeo, 2021.

D. Acemoglu, S. Johnson, and J. A. Robinson. The rise of Europe: Atlantic trade, institutional change and economic growth. *American Economic Review*, 95:546–579, 2005.

D. Acemoglu and P. Restrepo. Automation, tasks and the rise in US wage inequality. *Econometrica*, 90:1973–2016, 2022.

D. Acemoglu and J. Robinson. *The Narrow Corridor: States Societies and the Fate of Liberty*. New York: Penguin Press, 2019.

D. Acemoglu and J. A. Robinson. Why did the West extend the franchise? Growth, inequality and democracy in historical perspective. *Quarterly Journal of Economics*, 115:1167–1199, 2000.

D. Acemoglu and J. A. Robinson. *Why Nations Are: The Origins of Power, Prosperity, and Poverty*. New York: Crown Books, 2012.

D. Acemoglu and J. A. Robinson. Weak, despotic, or inclusive? How state type emerges from state versus civil society competition. *American Political Science Review*, 117:407–420, 2023.

N. Baumard. Has punishment played a role in the evolution of cooperation? A critical review. *Mind and Society*, 9:171–192, 2010.

T. Besley and T. Persson. Democratic values and institutions. *American Economic Review: Insights*, 1:59–76, 2019.

R. E. Blanton, S. A. Kowalewski, G. M. Feinman, and L. M. Finsten. *Ancient Mesoamerica: A Comparison of Change in Three Regions*. New York: Cambridge University Press, 1993.

C. Boehm. Egalitarian behavior and reverse dominance hierarchy. *Current Anthropology*, 32:411–412, 1993.

C. Boehm. *Moral Origins: The Evolution of Virtue, Altruism, and Shame*. New York: Basic Books, 2012.

R. Boyd and P. Richerson. Large-scale cooperation in small-scale foraging societies. *Evolutionary Anthropology*, 31:175–198, 2022.

R. Brenner. Agrarian class structure and economic development in pre-industrial Europe. *Past & Present*, 70:30–75, 1976.

K. Flannery and J. Marcus. *The Creation of Inequality: How Our Prehistoric Ancestors Set the Stage for Monarchy, Slavery, and Empire*. Cambridge, MA: Harvard University Press, 2014.

M. Gurven. Reciprocal altruism and food sharing decisions among Hiwi and Ache hunter–gatherers. *Behavioral Ecology and Sociobiology*, 56:366–380, 2005.

M. Gurven, W. Allen-Arave, K. Hill, and M. Hurtado. "It's a wonderful life": Signaling generosity among the Ache of Paraguay. *Evolution and Human Behavior*, 21:263–282, 2000.

K. Hill. Altruistic cooperation during foraging by the Ache, and the evolved human predisposition to cooperate. *Human Nature*, 13:105–128, 2005.

B. Hölldobler and E. O. Wilson. *The Ants*. Cambridge, MA: Harvard University Press, 1990.

A. Johnson and T. Earle. *The Evolution of Human Societies: From Foraging Groups to Agrarian State*. Stanford, CT: Stanford University Press, 1987.

L. H. Keeley. *The Myth of the Peaceful Savage: War Before Civilization*. New York: Oxford University Press, 1996.

R. Lee. *The !Kung San: Men Women, and Work in a Foraging Society*. Cambridge: Cambridge University Press, 1979.

R. B. Lee and R. Daly. *The Cambridge Encyclopedia of Hunters and Gatherers*. Cambridge: Cambridge University Press, 1999.

A. M. T. Moore, G. C. Hillman, and A. J. Legge. *Village on the Euphrates: From Foraging to Farming at Abu Hureyra*. Oxford: Oxford University Press, 2000.

I. Morris. *Foragers, Farmers, and Fossil Fuels: How Human Values Evolve*. Princeton, NJ: Princeton University Press, 2015.

K. Polanyi. *The Great Transformation: The Political and Economic Origins of Our Time*. Boston: Beacon Press, 1944.

M. Sahlins. *Stone Age Economics*. London: Routledge, 1972.

K. Schmidt. Göbekli Tepe: The Stone Age sanctuaries. New results of ongoing excavations with a special focus on sculptures and high reliefs. *Documenta Praehistorica*, 37:239–256, 2010.

B. K. Smith. *Classifying the Universe: The Ancient Indian Varna System and the Origins of Caste*. New York: Oxford University Press, 1994.

J. Suzman. *Affluence without Abundance: The Disappearing World of the Bushmen*. London: Bloomsbury, 2017.

E. P. Thompson. The moral economy of the English crowd in the eighteenth century. *Past & Present*, 50:76–136, 1971.

F. D. Waal. *Chimpanzee Politics*. Baltimore: Johns Hopkins University Press, 2007.

P. Wiessner. Norm enforcement among the Juhoansi Bushmen. *Human Nature*, 16:115, 2005.

J. Woodburn. Egalitarian societies. *Man*, 17:431–451, 1982.

33

Laws and Norms in Games Humans Play

Avinash Dixit

33.1 INTRODUCTION

Humans get together and interact to obtain several kinds of benefits, economic and noneconomic. My focus in this paper is mostly on the former. Even that has many dimensions – economies of scale, specialization according to comparative advantage, provision of public goods, promoting actions with positive externalities and discouraging those with negative externalities, risk pooling, reciprocal assistance, and so on. All these interactions have strategic or game-theoretic aspects, with some key characteristics:

1. The players in any one of these games come from different subsets of the population. Each person is a player in several games, and the games have overlapping sets of players. The games have different forms of partnerships (teams) and conflicts (contests), and occur among different groups (family, workplace, business, politics, ...). Players who are rivals in one game may be partners in another.
2. Most of these games are non-zero-sum (involving a mixture of conflict and cooperation), most are repeated (with same or changing sets of players), and most have some links with other games through payoffs or information transmission (recordkeeping and reputation).
3. In many of these games, large numbers of players are needed for feasibility of a good positive-sum outcome. In small family groups or villages, economies of scale in manufacturing cannot be adequately achieved; public goods cannot be provided in sufficiently large quantity; people are similar and face highly correlated risks so there isn't much scope to exploit comparative advantage and trade, or for risk sharing or risk pooling. In today's jargon, this makes for massively multiplayer games that go beyond any one person's close network. To achieve the potential benefits, one must deal with strangers.[1]

I thank participants in the symposium, especially Roger Myerson, for valuable comments.

[1] Seabright (2010) develops this theme in its large historical and evolutionary context.

4. Nash equilibria of these games are often worse for all (or too many) of the players than outcomes at other terminal nodes reachable only through nonequilibrium strategies. In many such cases, humans have developed ways to change the game so as to achieve the better outcome; in other cases (climate change?), the search for such a game changer continues. These game changers require various collectively devised rules and procedures, such as monitoring, rewards, or punishments, to change the players' motivations and incentives; this is the broad canvas of the concept of "governance."
5. As the games differ in their structure, so do the methods of governance. Those played by small stable groups of people can rely on trust in ongoing relationships, shared understanding of social norms, and internal sanctions. Other games with large and shifting sizes beyond the limits of trust networks need more formal structures of laws and their enforcement by some coercive power.[2] And as the multiple games played by individuals in society link and interact, the devices that attempt to achieve good outcomes from each game overlap and interact, sometimes complementing each other but at other times working in conflict. These modes of governance and their interactions are the focus of this paper.
6. When overlapping sets of players are simultaneously engaged in multiple games, the rules, norms, and governance that are needed in some games may conflict with those in others. Some overarching rules and institutions must then resolve such conflicts and make the whole complex of games operate to achieve the best feasible outcomes. This requires a hierarchy of governance institutions, for example successive levels of courts with the possibility of appeals from a lower-level to a higher-level court, or diamond industry tribunals in local communities of traders with a World Federation of Diamond Bourses above them, or coexisting mafia families (see Dixit, 2004b, for an analysis). At the highest level we have the national constitution or even some international treaties, protocols, and court-like institutions. Usually, the higher up this ladder, the more formal the institution and its enforcement mechanisms; more on this later.
7. Are the players in these games rational? Yes and no. In my view, the dichotomy proclaimed over the past two or three decades between rational-choice-based economic theory and behavioral economics is overblown and misleading. Kahneman's two systems are useful conceptual categories, but they are better seen as complements than as alternatives. Some of the fast and instinctive System 1 gets built in from experience of actions and outcomes in similar previous games, so System 2 calculations and deliberations don't have to be performed afresh each and every time. In turn, those deliberations and calculations can take place in advance, looking ahead to the instinctive reactions and impulses that are likely to take over when the need for action

[2] See Dunbar (2010) for evidence concerning the limits of friendship circles and trust networks. Dixit (2004a, chapter 3) models how the least-cost method of governance varies with the size of the group.

arises in the future.[3] And whatever the basis of individual players' choices, are outcomes of games in reality the equilibria that theory would predict? Again, yes and no. A nonequilibrium outcome is less likely to persist in frequent play, but there can be long and variable lags in players' perception and revision of nonequilibrium strategies. In short, our analysis of these games should take into account the actual modes of behavior and outcome generation processes, and institutions and organizations of governance should do likewise.[4]

Research literature on all these matters is huge, and I do not pretend to be comprehensive or offer any new theories or insights. Given the purpose of this symposium, I will overview some literature through a lens that highlights its game-theoretic aspects. These are implicit in the many institutionally or historically oriented papers that do not even mention game theory, let alone use any of its terminology or results. But in my view the subject gets better organized and our understanding of it is greatly improved by making the connections to game theory explicit.

I will organize my analysis by dividing the large body of issues into smaller categories along three dimensions. As usual, the categories are for conceptual clarity; in reality there are overlaps and gaps among them.

33.2 TYPES OF GAMES

When social interactions involve collective action, the game is often a prisoners' dilemma. But other types of games also arise, and different games need different devices of governance to achieve good outcomes. In the stylized analysis of these games, each player chooses between two actions.[5] The socially optimal pattern of actions across individuals may not arise from their independently

[3] Here is a well-known everyday example of this: When preparing for sleep in the evening, you keep your alarm clock on the other side of the room, so the next morning you cannot give in to the temptation to push the snooze button and be late for that day's commitments. Schelling (1984), and also to some extent Schelling (1978; and Schelling, 1996, with the perfect title), analyzed such games and gave many striking examples of them. In my opinion he was a brilliant pioneer of this eclectic approach to game theory, integrating traditional economic theories of rational behavior and insights from psychology, sociology, and so forth. In those pre-behavioral-economics times, he was already a postbehavioral economist.

[4] The rationality or otherwise of individual players' beliefs, preferences, and strategies is also influenced by the society and culture around them; Henrich (Chapter 34 in this volume) discusses the dynamics of evolution of these, and implications for the emergence of social norms of cooperation and peer punishment. In this paper I will largely take individual behaviors, rational or otherwise, as given, but make a few relevant remarks at the end.

[5] More generally, the choice may be among multiple discrete actions, or an action with a continuously variable magnitude. Most of the conceptual game-theoretic issues of governance are captured by the binary analysis in this paper, so I will not delve into the more general formulations.

made choices; that calls for devices to achieve and sustain better outcomes. I consider three prominent types of games, as listed in the following sections.

33.2.1 Going with the Crowd

The simplest such games are of pure coordination. It does not matter which of the two actions each player chooses so long as they all choose the same one; mismatches are costly. Driving on the left versus right is the best-known example. It is in each player's own interest to drive on the left if everyone else is driving on the left; likewise on the right. Therefore the game has two Nash equilibria, one where everyone drives on the left and the other where everyone drives on the right, and the two are equally good from the social perspective. But any one individual may not know what the others are choosing. An equilibrium may not be attained; there may be costly crashes. To avoid this, we need a convention and its common knowledge. The convention, in the form of a rule of the road, can be publicly announced, but ensuring that it is common knowledge – "everyone knows that everyone knows that ..." – may not be easy. Chwe (2001) discusses and illustrates how societies create common knowledge.

In a slightly more complex variant of coordination games, one of the two equilibria, say the one where everyone takes action A, may be better for every player than the other where everyone does B,[6] but the game may yield the B outcome because each player expects the other(s) to do B. Cooperation for hunting versus fishing when everyone prefers game to fish is a primitive example. Participation of all (or almost all) is needed for success in each venture, so it is important to avoid the situation where some go hunting and others go fishing. Of the two Nash equilibria, suppose the one with hunting is unanimously preferred. But the group may get stuck in the other: Everyone goes fishing because each expects the others to go fishing because of history or expectations, or the cost of mismatches is such that fishing is the risk-dominant equilibrium, even though hunting is Pareto dominant.[7] If that happens, coordinating a shift to the better equilibrium and sustaining it requires a major effort to promulgate a convention and to ensure that it becomes common knowledge. Sadly, collapse from a Pareto dominant equilibrium to a dominated one seems easier to occur

[6] Such asymmetry exists even in the driving example. When cars on highways whizz past each other at a combined speed of more than 300 kilometers per hour, the airflows around them meet to form tiny tornados that can grow and inflict damage. These are worse in one direction of spin than in the other because of the Coriolis effects of earth's rotation. But I have not found any solid evidence to support this, and do not know whether it would be better to drive on the left in the Northern Hemisphere and on the right in the Southern Hemisphere, or the other way around!

[7] If you go fishing while others go big-game hunting, you will catch few fish; if you go big-game hunting while others go fishing, you risk becoming the victim rather than the hunter. Of course, a small number of people going after a big fish may "need a bigger boat."

than the other way around; think of the bank run in the movie *Mary Poppins*. As Virgil (*Aeneid* 6:126) says, "*facilis descensus averno*."

33.2.2 Going against the Crowd

In games of this kind, if too many people in the group are taking one action (call it A), it is in the interest of the rest to take the other action (B). Unlike a prisoner's dilemma, however, neither A nor B is a dominant strategy; which is better for you depends on how many of the others are doing one or the other. These games then have an equilibrium in with a mixture in the population, some taking action A and others B.[8] Typically, the players in one of these two subsets (say those playing A) get higher payoffs than those in the other (those playing B), but if all choose A, the result is very bad for all. These are games of the Hawk–Dove (or Chicken) type: It is best for one player to be the Hawk (drive straight) when others are Doves (swerve), but if everyone tries to be the Hawk (drive straight), all suffer serious damage in the fight (car crash).

Then the question arises of who gets to be in which group. That decision and its enforcement needs some form of collective action. In harmonious well-functioning societies, some redistribution – either at each time the game is played or by alternating the assignment of better outcomes to different groups or people over time – can ensure that all share in the aggregate gains. But in many societies the elite – whether an aristocracy, oligarchs, political leaders, religious authorities, or some other small subset of society – seize the gains, leaving the poor masses to take the lower payoff.[9]

33.2.3 Prisoners' Dilemma

This is the most frequent type of game that arises in situations of collective action, both to achieve good "positive-sum" outcomes (provide public goods by contributing money or effort, take actions that convey positive externalities on others) and to avoid or mitigate bad "negative-sum" outcomes (reduce depletion of common resource pools, restrain from inflicting negative externalities on others). Governance in such games is difficult because taking the socially desirable action is a dominated strategy, going against the selfish interest of every player. But many mechanisms of governance exist and succeed. They have been studied in theoretical models, in case studies, and in laboratory and field experiments – indeed so many that recapitulating them in this paper would make it far too long and tedious for people who have delved into the subject even cursorily.

At a very general level, mechanisms of governance to resolve prisoners' dilemmas need two features: (1) a rule (variously a law, norm, or code of

[8] With just two or few players, the corresponding equilibria have mixed strategies for each player.

[9] Acemoglu (Chapter 32 in this volume) emphasizes such "within-society conflict" and its implications for the evolution of institutions to achieve cooperation while managing the conflict.

behavior) that tells individuals what action they should take, and (2) a set of incentives, typically a sanction for violating the rule but sometimes a reward for conforming to it, that changes the dominance of the rule-violating action. These mechanisms in effect change the game, so it is no longer a prisoners' dilemma. Depending on the nature and size of the incentives, the changed game can take one of two forms. If the sanction applies for violating the rule only when sufficiently many others are conforming to it, the game becomes one where the individual incentive is now to go with the crowd. This has the two equilibria mentioned previously, and the better one can be achieved by a suitable creation of common knowledge. If a sufficiently strong sanction applies regardless of what others are doing, then the socially desired action can become the dominant strategy for each individual and the good outcome achieved.

In the following two sections I discuss in somewhat greater detail the nature of these sanctions and their enforcement.

33.3 TYPES OF SANCTIONS

The form of sanction most studied is that within the game, where the victim or victims of a violation of the rule or norm of behavior pursue a strategy that holds the violator down to a punitively low payoff. This happens usually in repeated play of the same stage game; the theory of this, especially when the same two players interact repeatedly, is too well known to need repetition here; a good overview is provided by Kandori (2008). I will confine my remarks to a few relatively less-well-known matters.

Sanctions within the game are also feasible if multiple games are being played "almost" simultaneously, and a preplay stage allows communication of a threat to punish in one game for misbehavior in another. Schelling gives good examples of this (Schelling, 1960, pp. 50–51,140). If two or more stage games are being played repeatedly, then their dynamic incentive constraints can be pooled to achieve greater power to punish. The threat of such punishment sustains greater adherence to the prescribed equilibrium strategies that yield better payoffs to all; see the work of Bernheim and Whinston (1990).

Asymmetric information adds an interesting twist. Suppose information about some random event that affects strategies allowed within the game is available to one player but not others. A prominent example is a mutual insurance scheme where the adverse event that triggers a claim is observed only by the affected party. Then this party can make false claims. This can be deterred by reducing that player's right to make future claims just sufficiently to offset the gain from a current false claim. See the work of Atkeson and Lucas (1992) for a specific model and that of Jackson and Sonnenschein (2007) for the general theory.

Sanctions can come from outside the game of immediate interest. For example, suppose a feasible strategy in this game is to renege on a contractual commitment or to perpetrate a commercial fraud. The formal legal system can use its power to impose fines or imprisonment, and this threat can deter the players in the game from such behavior. In principle one should regard the whole process as one large game that combines this game and that of enforcement with the state as an additional player in the latter, but in practice it is often simpler to maintain the distinction between behavior within the game and the threat of external punishment. Such simplification can be justifiable in cases where the possibility of corruption or failure of the state is not a concern; then we can regard the state as an exogenous external monitor and enforcer. If bias or corruption is a problem, and if the state's agents with their natural human motives can conspire with one side in a dispute, then it is important to endogenize this in the analysis and also examine how the state's agents can be induced to act more reliably in the overall social interest.

33.4 TYPES OF ENFORCEMENT

Perhaps the most direct method to get players to take the socially desirable actions is to internalize the social benefits and costs into their own payoffs. This is conceptually simple but not so easy to implement in practice. The most basic reason for prosociality is genetic. All members, even in large groups of ants, bees, bats, and so forth, are very closely related, so their selfish genes will accept much self-sacrifice for sake of the whole. For example, sick vampire bats self-isolate and distance from others in their cave; see the work of Ripperger and colleagues (2020). Among humans sufficient genetic uniformity may exist in extended family groups,[10] but that effect decays rapidly in groups of size needed to realize most scale economies or public good benefits. When there is not enough genetic kinship, human societies can and do change individual preferences to instill prosociality through upbringing in the family, education and friendship formation in school, and so forth.[11] All these processes of socialization create a personal code of behavior, and instill feelings of guilt or shame for violating it.[12] This may not work perfectly, but it works better than what the old-school dogmatic followers of the fully rational and selfish "homo economicus" would have us believe. Beyond family and social groups, the state's legal system meets out punishments for certain violations. In addition to the direct cost of the fine or prison time, the convict may suffer an internalized cost of shame.[13]

[10] Remember J. B. S. Haldane's willingness to sacrifice his life to save the lives of two brothers or eight cousins.

[11] See Dixit and Levin (2017) for a model of this. See also Henrich (Chapter 34 in this volume) for a discussion of social and cultural dynamics more generally.

[12] The difference between guilt and shame is that you feel the former even if no one else finds out about your misbehavior, whereas you feel the latter as the result of being found out.

[13] When some countries started to impose mandatory prison sentences, even short ones, for driving while drunk, many people punished for these offenses were ashamed to admit that to their social circles and tried to get away with telling their friends that they were going on a three-week vacation to an unspecified resort.

Avoiding any violation of the rules or norms of socially desirable actions by modifying the player's payoff functions can be thought of as "first-party enforcement." Second-party enforcement is imposition of sanctions by others involved in the game (who would be harmed by a violation); in third-party enforcement, the enforcer is not a direct participant in the game. Let us consider these in turn.

Resolution of two-person prisoners' dilemmas (and some other games where Nash equilibrium without any intervention would be suboptimal) has been studied in detail, both in theory and in reality. Strategies such as tit-for-tat in repeated games are well known even to non-game-theorists. The general result of these models is that good behavior can be sustained if the players are sufficiently patient. Numerous results, called folk theorems, say that any efficient outcome can be sustained as an equilibrium in the limit of infinite patient or zero discounting of the future. Of more practical interest are results that tell us how much cooperation can be sustained for given positive discount rates; the general theory of this follows Abreu and colleagues (1990). I will take all this for granted and make just one brief remark.

Theoretical models often involve some variant of grim trigger strategies – any cheating leads to a complete collapse of cooperation in all future plays. In fact, there is a general presumption in theory that the harshest sustainable (subgame-perfect) punishment achieves the most cooperation. This is in stark contrast to numerous findings that successful cooperative or collective action in reality uses graduated punishments. For example, start by cautioning the violator, asking for restitution for the harm suffered, and then perhaps impose a short cutoff from participation with an open door if remorse is shown and a promise of better behavior is made.[14] Total ostracism is only the last resort for persistent violations. I have not seen a really good theoretical treatment of this, though I have participated in an effort (Abreu et al., 2005).

Third-party enforcement is where the active players in the game have, or appoint, or hire an outsider to enforce, and sometimes to adjudicate, any violations. The state's legal system of regulation, courts, police, and so forth is the standard mechanism and institution here. In much of economics or game theory, this was long assumed to have worked perfectly and costlessly. If any player violated the law or the contractual stipulation, the remedy was to "take it to the judge." All that was needed was verifiable information about the violation – proof meeting the legal standard. Unfortunately, in many countries and times such a judge is absent, lacks understanding of the context needed to interpret evidence, or is too slow, too error prone, or corrupt. In such cases,

[14] See, for example, Ostrom (1990, pp. 97–99) and Ellickson (1991, pp. 53–64). The other authors in this session, Acemoglu (Chapter 32 in this volume) and Henrich (Chapter 34 in this volume) also emphasize this, and offer many examples from history and anthropology of the variety of devices that are used to deter and punish selfish free-riding in collective action situations.

players in the game devise their own mechanisms and institutions.[15] These include the private judges at the medieval Champagne fairs (Milgrom et al., 1990), Gambetta's (Gambetta, 1993) mafioso enforcer Don Peppe, or "Godfather's justice" in the famous movie. Dixit (2004a, chapter 4) reviews and extends many of these analyses.

Between the second-party and third-party mechanisms outlined previously, we find a rich and varied territory. Here we have a large and stable group of players, from which two (or a small subset of) members will play a stage game each time, but different ones play at different times. No bilateral meetings are sufficiently frequent to sustain cooperative behavior at the rates of discounting likely to prevail in reality.[16] What the group needs is for other members to punish a violator "on behalf of the victim" in their own future meetings with the violator.[17] To do so, they must forgo their own potentially mutually beneficial dealings with the violator. A human instinct to punish social wrongdoers even when one is not the direct victim and even at a personal cost often serves the purpose (Fehr and Gächter, 2002, and many others).[18] The problem can also be circumvented when the punishment is ostracism from all future trade with members of the group. If someone is tempted to deviate from the group's sanction regime when everyone else is conforming to it, the violator, already under ostracism by others, fears no extra punishment by cheating the deviator in the "sanction-busting" deal. To keep the violator honest, the prospective deviator must pay him a sufficiently larger share of the total surplus. It would be cheaper for him to deal with someone without history of past cheating. Adhering to the sanctions regime is therefore a Nash equilibrium; that makes not cheating in the first place is a subgame perfect equilibrium (Greif, 2006, pp. 76–77).

33.5 INTERACTIONS

These types of sanctions and enforcement have ambiguities and overlaps. Most importantly, they interact, sometimes in a reinforcing or synergistic way, but at other times conflicting and interfering with one another. Many examples of such interactions have been observed, but to my knowledge there is little conceptual analysis of the circumstances and forces that determine whether they are likely

[15] Private governance may occur for good reasons (e.g., insiders have genuine information or interpretation advantages) or for bad reasons (e.g., they want to conceal some illegal or criminal activity from outside oversight). In assessing social consequences of private governance in any specific instance, we must weigh this balance.

[16] Sometimes pairs of players may be able endogenously to choose to meet more frequently, to establish an ongoing relationship in which bilateral or second-party enforcement can be sustained.

[17] A memorable instance where direct or bilateral punishment by the victim is infeasible in the very nature of the situation is Yogi Berra's saying, "Always go to other people's funerals. Otherwise they won't come to yours."

[18] If the initial proportion of altruistic enforcers in the population is above a threshold, then an equilibrium with good behavior all around can be stable in evolutionary dynamics; see the work of Sethi and Somanathan (1996).

to be mutually reinforcing or rivalrous. Here I offer a somewhat systematically organized account in the hope of spurring such theoretical research.

At its best, amicable synergistic interaction exploits comparative advantage to allocate governance of the multiple games people play, and different components of any one game – detection, adjudication, and enforcement – to the most efficient first, second, or third parties for each purpose. Here are a few examples.

The parties to many private contracts must agree to resolve any disputes by arbitration in an industry-based forum, giving up their rights to sue in formal courts. These forums have many advantages: They are familiar with industry practices and can interpret information more easily and accurately; they can render verdicts faster; and in many contexts they can impose better sanctions through their members' actions than what the courts could levy in the general legal framework. Bernstein (1992, 2001) and others have studied these institutions in detail.[19] Courts respect these arrangements and verdicts; they will not hear appeals save in very exceptional circumstances. In international trade and investment, there are forums named after the various cities in which they are based and using the legal system of that country – either common law or civil law or some mixture – and the contract stipulates where a dispute is to be taken. These forums lack many of the benefits of the industry-based forums mentioned previously: specialized knowledge of the industry's customs and practices, speed, accuracy, and so forth. Their sole advantage may be that they are not biased or corrupt in favor of one country's citizens. When they have issued their verdict, each member country's legal system is committed to enforcing it under the New York Convention. See the work of Dezalay and Garth (1996) for history and details of this.

Conversely, sometimes the formal legal system adjudicates disputes, but a private mechanism has advantage in enforcement. Two examples: (1) Court verdicts for repossession of automobiles for non-payment of the loan are enforced by private specialists who can find them more easily than the police. (2) The mafia could more easily and severely punish defaulting borrowers in footloose industries like garment-making than could banks using courts; see Repetto (2004).

Formal and informal institutions interact. A change in law can change in customs and norms over time; see Aldashev and colleagues (2012) on inheritance, marriage and divorce in sub-Saharan Africa and India. But rooted customs may prevail over changes in formal law. British and post-colonial property rights laws in east Africa were not acceptance by local chiefs or extended families; then banks would not accept formal land titles as collateral for loans to business startups; see Musembi (2007).

[19] This advantage of expertise and information may be offset by a bias in favor of one side; many contracts in business and finance involving consumers or clients on one side and industry insiders on the other insist on arbitration to resolve disputes, and there is suspicion of bias in favor of insiders in such situations.

33.6 HIERARCHIES

The multiple institutions of governance that handle the multiple and interacting games among overlapping sets of players also interact, and some overarching institutions are needed to balance interests and resolve conflicts. Therefore we have a hierarchy of institutions and governance mechanisms, and the rules, norms, and enforcement at a higher level in the hierarchy take precedence over those at lower levels. At the topmost level we have constitutions and supreme courts, then various legislatures and high courts, then local governments and local community associations, and so on.[20]

In this hierarchy, the institutions at the highest level are usually the most "formal," in the sense of being part of the state's system of constitution, laws, law enforcement, and regulations to which all citizens are subject, rather than the rules, norms or conventions, and sanctions within a business or community association whose membership is to some extent voluntary. As is usual with dichotomies, this distinction is ambiguous, and leaves gaps and overlaps, but it is useful for focusing thought and analysis.[21]

What ensures that an enforcement measure announced by a formal higher-level authority will actually get implemented? It is often said that the ultimate source of the power to enforce its verdicts is the state's monopoly of coercion or violence. But that is an inadequate explanation at best. The state's agents who are supposed to exercise this coercion or violence are themselves players in the whole game, and their obedience cannot be assumed or taken for granted. Ultimately it has to be based on some broadly accepted sense of the authority's legitimacy and respect for its decision processes. As US Supreme Court Justice Elena Kagan said in a speech at Princeton University: "I think all of us need ... to realize how precious the court's legitimacy is. The court doesn't have an army to enforce its rulings. The only way we get people to do what we say that they should do is because people respect us and respect out fairness."[22]

It is harder to earn such acceptance and respect for a formal institution than an informal one. The latter is closer to the daily lives and activities of the people and the community where the it operates; they see and monitor its functioning more easily. The formal institution is more distant and partakes of the citizenry's general suspicion of "big government." Therefore it has to

[20] The problem of devising the optimal division or allocation of functions and authority in such a hierarchy has some formal parallels with that of fiscal federalism. To my knowledge this has not been exploited in research.

[21] Merriam-Webster (www.merriam-webster.com/dictionary/formal) gives two relevant definitions of the word "formal": "2a : following or according with established form, custom, or rule; b : done in due or lawful form." This is itself not without ambiguity: The b concept is closer to what I have chosen; the a concept is closer to what I would call informal, but in neither case is the correspondence exact. Such ambiguities plague most attempts to dichotomize, but dichotomies remain useful as conceptual categories, even when they are not clearly true or clearly false; see Gould (1987, pp. 8–9,199–200).

[22] Reported in www.npr.org/2022/01/18/1073428376/supreme-court-justices-arent-scorpions-but-not-happy-campers-either.

make special effort, employ clear and transparent procedures, and hold itself accountable for its decisions, if it is to establish and maintain confidence, trust, and acceptance. These features are easier to achieve, or even automatic, for an informal system that operates at a smaller scale of local communities or associations whose members are in regular ongoing relationships, and share some common understanding of the issues that they must decide and conflicts they must resolve.

33.7 COEXISTENCE OR NO EXISTENCE?

What determines whether the interaction between formal and informal institutions, and between laws and norms, will prove mutually complementary or rivalrous? Are there any general principles, or is it all too context-specific? Here I indulge in a little speculative thinking. In my view a plausible necessary condition for good interactions is broad acceptance of a rule-based system, recognition of socio-legal-political legitimacy of the constitution and its components, and recognition of the concept of a "loyal opposition" – namely, that people and groups can oppose specific policies without their loyalty to the larger society or nation being called into question – by all participants in political and social activities. This makes the game at its topmost level cooperative – think of it as establishing the overall constitution – even though various subgames that are played under its umbrella may be noncooperative.

This can be restated in the terminology and using the classification of societies and states provided by Acemoglu and Robinson (2019). The condition stated previously is like being in their Narrow Corridor, where the powers and interests of the state (formal law) and society (norms and customs) are reasonably well balanced. If the formal state is too powerful and oppressive (their Despotic Leviathan), it has no interest in seeking to benefit the masses of society. If the state is too weak and leaves society to devise a pure norm-based system with its cage of customs and restrictions (their Absent Leviathan), there is no larger cooperative game. And in my review of the book (Dixit, 2021), I suggested a fourth type, a Shambolic Leviathan, which has oppressive aims but has very weak state capacity. It has no top cooperative game – only active interference with society's attempts to sustain a system of norms. None of these three types will permit a complementary or synergistic interaction between formal institutions and informal customs.

We can also link my discussion to the concept of the society's culture and its evolution, as discussed by Henrich (Chapter 34 in this volume). He defines culture broadly, comprising the individuals' "ideas, beliefs, strategies, values, preferences…, motivations (e.g., fairness with strangers), decision-heuristics, [and] judgment biases." These evolve in a process of social learning and imitation. Henrich offers an overview of issues, detailed discussion of research on each, and many examples.

In such a dynamic process, small differences in initial conditions can amplify into polarization of society; see for example Schelling's (1978, chapter 4) model of tipping and segregation. I fear that the natural dynamics of societies seems to conform to what might be called the Second Law of Sociodynamics: a tendency of entropy (disorder) to increase.[23] Special and concerted efforts are required to counter this, and to keep a society and its culture within boundaries of tolerance and acceptance that will allow governance of the multiple ongoing games with overlapping players to proceed in a harmonious and synergistic manner. Research on how this can be accomplished should be a matter of the highest urgency in these times of increasing polarization within and across nations.

33.8 REFERENCES

D. Abreu, D. Pearce, and E. Stacchetti. Toward a theory of discounted repeated games with imperfect monitoring. *Econometrica*, 58(5):1041–1063, September 1990.

D. Abreu, B. D. Bernheim, and A. Dixit. Self-enforcing cooperation with graduated punishments. Working paper, 2005.

D. Acemoglu and J. Robinson. *The Narrow Corridor: States Societies and the Fate of Liberty*. New York: Penguin Press, 2019.

G. Aldashev, I. Chaara, J.-P. Plateau, and Z. Wahhaj. Using the law to change the custom. *Journal of Development Economics*, 97(2): 182–200, March 2012.

A. Atkeson and R. E. Lucas Jr. On efficient distribution with private information. *Review of Economic Studies*, 59(3):427–453, 1992.

B. D. Bernheim and M. D. Whinston. Multimarket contact and collusive behavior. *Rand Journal of Economics*, 21(1):1–26, 1990.

L. Bernstein. Opting out of the legal system: Extralegal contractual relations in the diamond industry. *Journal of Legal Studies*, 21(1):115–157, 1992.

L. Bernstein. Private commercial law in the cotton industry: Creating cooperation through rules, norms, and institutions. *Michigan Law Review*, 99(7):1724–1788, 2001.

M. Chwe. *Rational Ritual: Culture, Coordination and Common Knowledge*. Princeton, NJ: Princeton University Press, 2001.

Y. Dezalay and B. G. Garth. *Dealing in Virtue: International Commercial Arbitration and the Construction of a Transnational Legal Order*. Chicago: University of Chicago Press, 1996.

A. Dixit. *Lawlessness and Economics: Alternative Modes of Governance*. Princeton, NJ: Princeton University Press, 2004a.

A. Dixit. Two-tier market institutions. *Chicago Journal of International Law*, 5(1):139–155, 2004b.

A. Dixit. Somewhere in the middle we can survive: Review of the narrow corridor by Daron Acemoglu and James Robinson. *Journal of Economic Literature*, 59(4):1361–1375, 2021.

A. Dixit and S. Levin. Social creation of pro-social preferences for collective action. In W. Buchholz and D. Rubbelke, eds., *The Theory of Externalities and Public Goods*, pp. 127–143. Amsterdam: Springer, 2017.

[23] This labeling is by a purely formal analogy with thermodynamics; I have no "first law" to offer.

R. I. M. Dunbar. *How Many Friends Does One Person Need? Dunbar's Number and Other Evolutionary Quirks*. London: Faber and Faber, 2010.

R. C. Ellickson. *Order without Law: How Neighbors Settle Disputes*. Cambridge, MA: Harvard University Press, 1991.

E. Fehr and S. Gächter. Altruistic punishment in humans. *Nature*, 415:137–140, January 2002.

D. Gambetta. *The Sicilian Mafia: The Business of Protection*. Cambridge, MA: Harvard University Press, 1993.

S. J. Gould. *Time's Arrow, Time's Cycle: Myth and Metaphor in the Discovery of Geological Time*. Cambridge, MA: Harvard University Press, 1987.

A. Greif. *Institutions and the Path to the Modern Economy: Lessons from Medieval Trade*. Cambridge: Cambridge University Press, 2006.

M. O. Jackson and H. F. Sonnenschein. Overcoming incentive constraints by linking decisions. *Econometrica*, 75(1):241–257, 2007.

M. Kandori. Repeated games. In S. N. Durlauf and L. E. Blume, eds., *New Palgrave Dictionary of Economics*. New York: Palgrave Macmillan, 2008.

P. R. Milgrom, D. C. North, and B. R. Weingast. The role of institutions in the revival of trade: The law merchant, private judges, and the Champagne fairs. *Economics and Politics*, 2(1):1–23, 1990.

C. N. Musebi. Breathing life into dead theories about property rights: De Soto and land relations in rural Africa. *Third World Quarterly*, 28(8): 1457–1478, 2007.

E. Ostrom. *Governing the Commons: The Evolution of Institutions for Collective Action*. Cambridge: Cambridge University Press, 1990.

T. Repetto. American Mafia: *A History of Its Rise to Power*. New York, NY: Holt, 2004.

S. P. Ripperger, S. Stockmaier, and G. G. Carter. Tracking sickness effects on social encounters via continuous proximity-sensing in wild vampire bats. *Behavioral Ecology*, 31(6):1296–1302, 2020.

T. C. Schelling. *Strategy of Conflict*. Cambridge, MA: Harvard University Press, 1960.

T. C. Schelling. *Micromotives and Macrobehavior*. New York: W. W. Norton & Company, 1978.

T. C. Schelling. *Choice and Consequence*. Cambridge, MA: Harvard University Press, 1984.

T. C. Schelling. Coping rationally with lapses from rationality. *Eastern Economic Review*, 22(3):251–269, 1996.

P. Seabright. *The Company of Strangers*. Princeton, NJ: Princeton University Press, 2010.

R. Sethi and E. Somanathan. The evolution of social norms in common property resource use. *American Economic Review*, 86(4):766–788, 1996.

34

Game Theory in Cultural Evolution

Joseph Henrich

34.1 INTRODUCTION

The purpose of this paper is to review the key contributions of game theory to the field of cultural evolution, focusing particularly on interfaces between cultural evolution and economics. Because many readers may not be familiar with the interdisciplinary field of cultural evolution, I begin with a brief orientation to this field as a scientific enterprise and then highlight the important ways that game theory has been deployed in both theoretical and empirical research within the field, noting spillovers and interactions with economics.

The academic label "cultural evolution" only emerged in the last decade to delineate a cluster of related lines of interdisciplinary research that draws heavily on anthropology, biology, psychology, and economics, as well as a broad swath of other fields. The field now has its own society along with an emerging repertoire of theoretical and empirical methods, which includes tools drawn from economics and psychology as well as anthropology and evolutionary biology (Henrich et al., 2004; Ensminger and Henrich, 2014; Schulz et al., 2019). Foundational works include theoretical treatises by two duos, Boyd and Richerson and Feldman and Cavalli-Sforza, as well as others (Pulliam and Dunford, 1980; Cavalli-Sforza and Feldman, 1981; Lumsden and Wilson, 1981; Boyd and Richerson, 1985; Durham, 1991). For recent reviews, see the work of Mesoudi (2011), Henrich (2016), Boyd (2017), and Laland (2017). I also recommend (Nunn, 2021) chapter in *The Handbook of Historical Economics*, which gathers a number of insights and approaches from the cultural evolutionary literature and translates them for economists.

Theoretically, this field's point of departure is the assumption that humans can be modeled as adaptive learners who rely heavily on various forms of social learning – on learning from other people using a broad range of psychological mechanisms, including those glossed as "imitation." These learning mechanisms permit individuals to acquire ideas, beliefs, strategies, values, preferences (e.g., both food and mate preferences), motivations (e.g., fairness with strangers), decision heuristics, and judgment biases. Notably, because this field digested a large body of empirical research on social learning at its founding, much of it done in the 1970s in psychology (Bandura, 1977; Rosenthal and Zimmerman, 1978; Birch, 1981), theorists have generally assumed that individuals could acquire motivations and preferences (e.g., food preferences) from others via imitation – endogenous preferences. From this gateway, theoretical work has gone in three directions:

1. *Cultural evolution*: First, the process of cultural evolution itself can be modeled by looking at the outcomes of such individual-level learning processes in populations over time, and often over generations – because social learning creates a form of intergenerational inheritance. This work has focused on the emergence of sociological phenomena like social norms, cooperation, social classes, ethno-linguistic groups, and innovation, among other topics. Game theory naturally entered as researchers sought to construct models that combined learning and social interaction. Cultural evolution considers both the dynamics of these evolutionary process as well as their equilibrium states (or lack thereof). The equilibrium concepts used by cultural evolutionists emphasize dynamic stability (often Evolutionary Stable Strategies, following Maynard Smith, 1982), and both analytical and simulation models are used, often in a complementary fashion. Many simple models take the form of payoff-biased imitation (replicator dynamics), but theorists also study continuous trait models and models that include vertical transmission (copy parents), prestige biased transmission (copy who others are copying), conformist transmission (copy the majority or plurality), and the use of CRedibility Enhancing Displays (CREDs, where actions speak louder than words) – see Acerbi and colleagues (2020) for a recent review of some formalizations. Here I will elaborate primarily on the use of game theory in understanding cultural evolution.
   This work developed in parallel with important work on evolutionary game theory within economics (Weibull, 1995; Fudenberg and Levine, 1998; Young, 1998), though in my view it benefited from a richer engagement with anthropology and psychology, a greater willingness to deploy numerical and simulation techniques in modeling, and the requirement to micro-found its assumptions about individuals' learning abilities in evolutionary theory.
2. *Evolutionary foundations of learning*: Second, the particular learning abilities that individuals are assumed to possess can be microfounded by asking how natural selection might have shaped human minds genetically to permit them to most effectively (adaptively) learn from others, given the serious energetic and processing constraints imposed by our species phylogenetic history. This has permitted researchers to both make bottom-up predictions about how infants, children, and adults should learn, as well as provide a theoretical foundation for what is assumed in building models of cultural evolution. These models have explored when and why individuals should rely on non-payoff-based forms of learning, including conformist transmission (Henrich and Boyd, 1998; Kendal et al., 2009; Nakahashi et al., 2012) and parent–child transmission (McElreath and Strimling, 2008).

This approach leads researchers to assume that learners and actors are rather constrained in both the information available to them and their information processing abilities.

Taking an evolutionary approach to the origins and nature of people's learning abilities has also encouraged researchers to consider how our species' social instincts, such as kin-based altruism, incest aversion, and prestige psychology, might influence the formation of institutions (Henrich et al., 2015; Henrich, 2020).

3. *Culture-gene coevolution*: Finally, because this approach focuses attention on the interaction between genetic and cultural evolution, there's a large body of formal theoretical work, begun in the 1970s, that examines the interaction between our genetic and cultural inheritance streams (Boyd and Richerson, 1976; Feldman and Cavalli-Sforza, 1976; Aoki, 2001). Today, drawing on the growing body of evidence derived from studying the human genome, the case that culture has driven much of our species genetic evolution is now central to our understanding of human evolution and contemporary genetic variation (Laland et al., 2010; Richerson et al., 2010; Henrich, 2016; Boyd, 2017; Laland, 2017).

I'll now review some of the major contributions associated with the use of game theory in cultural evolution, with an emphasis on exchanges with economics.

34.2 THEORETICAL CONTRIBUTIONS

This review covers four main topics: (1) equilibrium selection and the role of intergroup competition; (2) large-scale cooperation and mechanisms for sustaining costly social norms; (3) the emergence of castes, ethno-linguistic groups, and honor cultures; and finally (4) endogenizing preferences (also called "values" or "types").

34.2.1 Equilibrium Selection and Intergroup Competition

A central difference between the application of game theory within the fields of cultural evolution and economics is the question of equilibrium selection (Henrich, 2004; Richerson et al., 2016). Both evolutionary and classical game theory often produce multiple stable equilibria (Fudenberg and Maskin, 1986; Boyd and Richerson, 1990; Weibull, 1995; Fudenberg and Levine, 1998; Young, 1998), and cultural evolutionary game theory produces even more stable equilibria when non-payoff-based transmission mechanisms are included – for example, conformist transmission (Henrich and Boyd, 2001) and credibility-enhancing displays (Henrich, 2009).

My sense is that economists see this plethora of equilibria as a "bug" (an annoying modeling issue) while cultural evolutionists see it as a "feature." That is, cultural evolutionists see the emergence of multiple stable equilibria as telling us something about the world: Dynamic and often gradual learning processes occur simultaneously in different groups or populations, resulting in different stable outcomes. The variation we observe around the world and back into history represents different stable equilibria or cultural evolutionary trajectories toward different equilibria. Some equilibria may favor greater success in competition with other groups – for example, via warfare (Boyd and Richerson, 1990), attracting more migrants (Boyd and Richerson, 2009), differential copying (Boyd and Richerson, 2002), and so forth – or they may be less vulnerable to shocks or drift (e.g., larger basins of attraction; (Kendal et al., 2006). Over the long run, these processes tend to favor those behavioral equilibria that foster success in intergroup competition, often leading to stable equilibria that generate higher average payoffs.

When economists began drawing ideas from the field of cultural evolution and collaborating with cultural evolutionists (Henrich et al., 2001; Boyd et al., 2003; Fehr and Henrich, 2003; Henrich et al., 2003, 2004), intergroup competition as an equilibrium selection mechanism played a central role (Bowles and Gintis, 1998, 2004a,b, 2011; Fehr et al., 2002; Gintis, 2003, 2006; Bowles, 2005, 2006; Bernhard et al., 2006; Choi and Bowles, 2007).

34.2.2 Origins of Costly Social Norms, Including Cooperative Ones

Much work in cultural evolution is focused on understanding how humans are different from other animals (Richerson and Boyd, 1998; Bowles and Gintis, 2011; Boyd et al., 2011; Turchin, 2015). As a consequence, a central research line has been to explain our species' ability to cooperate in large groups with non-kin and sometimes in nonrepeated interactions. As a result, much theoretical work has focused on modeling the evolution of cooperation using the n-person Prisoner's Dilemma. The game seemed particularly well-suited to the small-scale, residentially fluid, acephalous communities in which our species likely evolved (Smith et al., 2018). Early theoretical work suggested that unlike in the dyadic version of the Prisoner's Dilemma, strategies that relied on reciprocity and/or kinship (Axelrod and Hamilton, 1981; Axelrod, 1984) in the n-person game were not likely to sustain cooperation among hundreds or thousands of individuals (i.e., the scales observed among foragers). Moreover, even when reciprocity and/or kinship could sustain cooperation theoretically, the predicted patterns didn't match those observed in many hunter–gatherer contexts (Axelrod, 1986; Joshi, 1987; Boyd, 1988; Hill et al., 2009; Hill and Hurtado, 2009; Henrich, 2016), where little reciprocity was expected in practice and cooperation often involved non-kin (Hill et al., 2011). Animated by this challenge, a large body of later work can be understood as providing a variety of alternative mechanisms for creating stable equilibrium near full cooperation, including those based on peer punishment, positive indirect reciprocity (and linked games), negative indirect reciprocity, and signaling.

Crucially, while this work was initially focused on explaining cooperation, the results of these models consistently suggested that these mechanisms could sustain costly norms regardless of any benefits delivered to others or the group as a whole. This was taken by many cultural evolutionists – including me (Henrich, 2004) – to suggest that these mechanisms might explain the plethora of costly but noncooperative and even maladaptive norms found across human societies. Canonical examples include funerary rites that entail the consumption of the brains of dead relatives (leading to the transmission of a deadly prion disease), female genital cutting, foot binding, skull deformation, and a variety of food taboos (Edgerton, 1992; Brown and Feldman, 2009; Majid, 2015; Vogt et al., 2016).

34.2.2.1 *The Role of Diffuse or Peer Punishment*

The most important early model of the evolution of large-scale cooperation, using the *n*-person Prisoner's Dilemma, studied the impact of punishing strategies on the emergence of cooperation: Boyd and Richerson (1992) found that costly equilibria, including cooperative ones, could be sustained via diffuse punishment if punishers used a meta-punishing strategy in which they punished nonpunishers. That is, meta-punishing strategies punish not only noncooperators but also anyone who fails to punish when they are supposed to (the punishment of nonpunishers). However, whenever such cooperative equilibria existed, there were also stable equilibria for full defection with no punishment.

Later work built on this by looking for ways to alleviate the need for the (arguably) implausible meta-punishing strategy. Let's consider four approaches. First, Henrich and Boyd (2001) demonstrate that if learners rely on a small amount of conformist transmission – an evolvable bias to copy the majority or plurality – in addition to pay-off biased imitation, stable cooperative equilibria can emerge without the need for meta-punishing strategies. Specifically, when a population has cooperators and punishers who only defect or fail to punish due to errors, the differences between the payoffs of behaving prosocially (cooperating or punishing) versus free riding (defecting or not punishing) declines geometrically as one moves from cooperation to the punishment of noncooperators and further up the hierarchy of punishment (e.g., the punishment of those who fail to punish those who fail to punish noncooperators). This means that even an arbitrarily small (but nonzero) amount of conformist transmission can stabilize punishment at some finite level in the hierarchy. Once punishing is stable at a higher level, this will then stabilize punishing strategies at lower levels and eventually cooperation. The upshot is that the combination of conformist transmission and punishing strategies generates multiple stable equilibria. Henrich and Boyd then argue that intergroup competition will favor the cooperative equilibrium over the defecting equilibria with lower average payoffs.

Second, Boyd and colleagues (2003) reveal the synergies between cooperation, punishment, and intergroup competition. Intergroup competition can sustain punishing strategies (without the meta punishing assumption), and in turn, punishment sustains cooperation. Notably, Guzman and colleagues (2007) show that in the model explored by Boyd and colleagues, selection will favor the emergence of conformist transmission alongside payoff-biased transmission – theoretically justifying Henrich and Boyd's assumption (although see Van Cleve, 2016).

Finally, to offset the cost of diffuse or third-party punishment, some cultural evolutionary models have considered games in which punishment could act as a signal of an otherwise hidden inclination toward cooperativeness or trustworthiness (Gintis et al., 2001; Jordan et al., 2016). Here, individuals signal their social-behavioral qualities by punishing noncooperators (or any norm violator), which both sustains costly norms (including larger-scale cooperation) and promotes beneficial future interactions for the signaler.

Finally, signals can be used to coordinate punishment and sustain cooperation. In this model, after a norm violation occurs, punishers signal their intent to punish and then punish if enough others also signal their punitive intentions (Boyd et al., 2010). If too few individuals signal, punishers withhold their sanctions. By coordinating punishment and compelling defectors into cooperation, this system can guarantee that punishers tend to end up in cooperative groups, and when they don't, they can still avoid the costs of punishment.

34.2.2.2 *Positive and Negative Indirect Reciprocity*

Large-scale cooperation can also be sustained by reputational systems, often termed *indirect reciprocity*, that tie different kinds of social interactions together via a shared roster of who is in good or bad standing. Notably, while standard versions of indirect reciprocity can sustain cooperation in dyads, these models don't readily extend to explain larger-scale cooperation (Boyd and Richerson, 1989; Leimar and Hammerstein, 2001). However, indirect reciprocity models do better when a two-person game is linked via reputation to the n-person interaction. In a classic model (Panchanathan and Boyd, 2004), individuals experience two kinds of interactions: an n-person Prisoner's Dilemma and a dyadic mutual aid interaction. Individuals decide whether to help based on their partner's contribution to the public good (e.g., paying taxes). If a player defects in the public good, their partner can abstain from helping them in the dyadic interaction when they are in the role of "donor" (without themselves getting a bad reputation for it). Essentially, the withdrawal of aid in the dyadic helping interaction, which benefits the person freed from the costs of helping, is used to sanction noncontributors to the public good.

Focusing on negative indirect reciprocity and motivated by ethnographic observations of village-level cooperation in the South Pacific (Henrich and Henrich, 2014), Bhui and colleagues (2019) have constructed a model that links an n-person Prisoner's Dilemma with a dyadic exploitation game, where individuals have a chance to harm another individual for a benefit (e.g., theft). Strategies that only harm individuals with a bad reputation can sustain stable equilibria in which most individuals cooperate and don't harm others. Bad reputations are acquired by harming those with good reputations and by failing to cooperate in the *n*-person Prisoner's Dilemma. Ethnographic reports suggest this may be a common mechanism to sustain costly social norms in small-scale societies, where diffuse or third-party punishment are rare. The dynamics of this model could be described as "ostracism," potentially creating the "outlaw" situation in which individuals are no longer protected from exploitation by others.

Currently, many cultural evolutionists would argue that empirically different stabilizing mechanisms and combinations of these—signaling, punishment, and reputation (indirect reciprocity) – are relevant in different societies and contexts. For example, some societies engage in diffuse or third-party punishment while others do not (Henrich et al., 2006), suggesting that the use of punishing strategies is itself culturally evolved. This is a significant step, since initially these were thought of as alternative hypotheses to explain human cooperation. This empirical inference is consistent with research that deploys economic games across societies (as discussed later).

34.2.3 Castes, Ethnic Groups, and Honor Cultures

Theorists have deployed a version of the battle of the sexes game, a simple coordination game, and the hawk–dove game within a cultural evolutionary context to illuminate, respectively, the emergence of stratified social classes or castes, symbolically marked ethnic groups, and "cultures of honor."

Recurrently, across continents, social classes or castes have emerged in many societies, usually a few millennia after the origins of agriculture (but not always). To address this, Henrich and Boyd (2008) studied how economic interactions in a battle of the sexes payoff structure involving two "cultural subpopulations" (the subpopulations are where learning occurs) might lead to stable equilibria in which members of one subpopulation generally played the high payoff strategy (and usually received the higher payoff) while members of the other subpopulation generally played the lower-payoff strategy. They also consider the impact of intergroup competition on the long-run equilibria. The results give the conditions that favor the emergence of social stratification, which depend on the surplus generated, the rate of adaptive change, and the degree of mixing between the cultural subpopulations. The analysis also suggests that intergroup competition will favor an equal division of the surplus – see Turchin (2009, 2010, 2015) for work exploring the tension between the forces created by elite extraction and intergroup competition (as in economics, many models of political economy ignore intergroup competition entirely).

Across all regions of the globe, human societies form ethno-linguistic or tribal groupings. These groups are generally symbolically marked by different languages or dialects, as well as markers of dress, adornment, and greeting customs. Such markers have substantial impacts on who associates with whom in a variety of ways, including in marriage, trade, and war, and they are generally associated with an array of stable and enduring social norms. To explain the origins of this common sociological pattern, McElreath (2003) studied the impact of interactions in a simple two-person coordination game among individuals in a structured population. Individuals learned strategies for interaction within their home subpopulation but then interacted either within their subpopulation or with members of other subpopulations. During cultural learning, individuals acquire both a marker trait (e.g., dialect) and social practice (e.g., pay dowry, not brideprice) based on their model's payoffs. The results show that chance variation in ethnic markers can be harnessed as a cue of unobservable norms (marking the strategies likely to be used in the coordination game). The cultural evolution process then (often) produces groups marked by observable traits (e.g., dialect) that are strong predictors of nonobservable social norms, allowing individuals to avoid coordination failures. Economists and cultural evolutionists have teamed up to test this model by creating a laboratory simulation of the process (Efferson et al., 2008) that confirms the basic findings of the model.

In light of the pattern produced by cultural evolution, the authors consider if natural selection will favor a bias to both preferentially learn from, and interact with, those who share one's marker trait. When cultural evolution favors the emergence of marked groups that share norms (the behavior used in the coordination game), natural selection will favor a learning bias that cues off of symbolic markers, like language or dialect. Interestingly, later work confirmed the existence of the predicted psychological bias in young children and infants (Shutts et al., 2010; Kinzler et al., 2011, 2012).

In societies known for their "culture of honor," men react aggressively to any threats to their independence and property (which they perceive as including their wives and daughters), and women celebrate those traits in men. Anthropologists have long documented these societies ethnographically, but psychologists didn't begin to systematically explore the behavioral consequences of honor cultures until the 1990s (Nisbett and Cohen, 1996). Recently, economists have explored the impact of honor cultures on murder rates in the United States (Grosjean, 2014) and on warfare in Africa (Moscona et al., 2017). To develop a theory for this common sociological phenomena, McElreath (2003) deployed a hawk–dove payoff structure to explore why, when, and how cultural evolution might create cultures of honor. In this simple model, individuals from an infinite population are selected at random to interact in a hawk–dove payoff structure, and this interaction repeats with a fixed probability. Individuals possess noisy information on the reputation or standing of their opponent/partner that they can use in choosing whether to fight or split a resource. The results highlight how the value of the resources and the quality of reputational information, and factors like the ecology and population size might influence when and where we see the motivations, norms, and strategies associated with honor cultures. Recent work by economists (Cao et al., 2021) using newly available data sets confirm several of McElreath's predictions.

34.2.4 Endogenizing Preferences and Modeling Culture

Both the formal machinery and empirical findings of cultural evolution strongly point to the importance of what economists call "endogenizing preferences." Of course, this is an old idea: Bowles (1998) lays out a vision for this by drawing heavily on cultural evolutionary theory, citing the foundational work discussed previously, and anticipates many subsequent developments in the social sciences, emphasizing the role of social norms, cultural transmission, conformist transmission, norm internalization, and the impacts of markets on psychology (including on preferences), as well as cultural differences in personality (lately a hot topic outside of economics). In a footnote, Bowles even anticipates cultural variation in the endowment effect based on market integration – a speculation later confirmed empirically by Apicella and colleagues (2014).

Today, when modeling culture or endogenizing preferences, economists frequently reference models by Bisin and Verdier (1998, 2000). Notably, however, Bisin and Verdier explicitly point out that they are building on the work of cultural evolutionists, generally citing the "seminal" work of Boyd and Richerson and Cavalli-Sforza and Feldman (Bisin and Verdier, 2001), but then depending on the paper, they also reference work by Bowles and Gintis within the domain of cultural evolution.

Picking up this line of work, Francois and Zabojnik (2005) endogenize preferences and explore the emergence of local social norms that influence the operation of formal institutions, leading to distinct and stable effects on welfare. Building on this, recent modeling efforts that integrate cultural evolution with existing approaches to political economy, rooted in strategic decision-making, have further enriched this integration by showing how preferences ("values") interlock and coevolve with formal institutions to create distinct cultural evolutionary trajectories and often substantial persistence (Besley and Persson, 2019).

34.3 EMPIRICAL CONTRIBUTIONS RELATED TO GAME THEORY

Beginning in the 1990s, work in the nascent field of cultural evolution began an exchange with economics, particularly behavioral economics (although today the strongest connections are with development economics, political economy, and economic history). Tools drawn from behavioral economics were deployed to test theoretical ideas from cultural evolution, and long-running collaborations began to enrich both fields. As the twenty-first century dawned, work drawing on this collaboration began to be published in leading journals within economics (Fehr and Gächter, 1998, 2000; Henrich, 2000; Henrich et al., 2001), although more commonly it found its way into general scientific journals like *Science* and *Nature* with much larger and broader impacts (Fehr and Gächter, 2002; Boyd et al., 2003; Fehr and Fischbacher, 2003a; Fehr and Rochenbach, 2003; Henrich et al., 2005b; Silk et al., 2005; Bernhard et al., 2006; Bowles, 2006; Henrich et al., 2006; Choi and Bowles,

2007; Efferson et al., 2008). Interpreting the empirical results of behavioral game theoretical experiments, often conducted in diverse populations from around the world (including among both children and chimpanzees), these papers introduced and began to test numerous ideas and concepts developed theoretically in the modeling literature discussed previously. This work immediately began to appear in textbook treatments of both behavioral economics and microeconomics (Camerer, 2003; Bowles, 2004).

There were three key empirical contributions that emerged initially from this interaction: (1) costly punishment as a potential mechanism to explain cooperation in humans, (2) the breath of behavioral variation across populations in game-theoretic experiments like the Ultimatum Game (and others), and (3) the importance of endogenizing preferences given the variation in game play across societies and the existing empirical evidence that people can acquire preferences via observational learning.

34.3.1 Costly Punishment

As noted, in 1992 Boyd and Richerson had modeled costly punishment as one mechanism for sustaining cooperation in an *n*-person Prisoner's Dilemma. Early experiments by Fehr and Gächter (2000, 2002) provided an important and powerful initial demonstration of the power of diffuse costly punishment in sustaining cooperation, at least in the laboratory. The evidence suggested that Swiss students were willing to pay costs to punish free riders and that this could increase cooperation under many conditions. In developing this work, and in considering what it might mean for economic and evolutionary thinking, Fehr and colleagues developed the concept of strong reciprocity (Gintis, 2000; Fehr et al., 2002) and *Homo reciprocans* (Fehr and Gächter, 1998; Bowles and Gintis, 2002), as well as a number of new experiments to explore these concepts, including the Third-Party Punishment Game (Fehr and Fischbacher, 2003b). These findings and formulations propelled a cottage industry of empirical work on social preferences but also immediately posed a theoretical question for those interested in evolution: Why would people be willing to engage in this "altruistic punishment" and where did this "strong reciprocity" come from (Gintis, 2000; Fehr and Henrich, 2003; Bowles and Gintis, 2004b, 2011)?

34.3.2 Culture Matters

At the same time these ideas about costly punishment were developing, an interdisciplinary team of anthropologists, psychologists, and economists began conducting behavioral experiments in diverse societies around the world (key economists included Bowles, Gintis, Fehr, Eckel, and Camerer). Circling the globe from New Guinea and Indonesia to Tanzania and Siberia, the team conducted Ultimatum Games and other experiments among populations of hunter–gatherers, herders, slash-and-burn horticulturalists, sedentary farmers, and urban dwellers. The first phase focused primarily on using the Ultimatum Game (Henrich et al., 2001; Henrich, 2004; Henrich et al., 2005a), but a second project replicated and extended this prior project using the Dictator, Ultimatum (strategy method), and Third-Party Punishment Games (Henrich et al., 2006, 2010; Ensminger and Henrich, 2014). In my experience, many economists are familiar with the first phase, published in the *American Economic Review* (Henrich et al., 2001) and *Behavioral and Brain Sciences* (Henrich et al., 2005a), but not with the second phase, published in *Science* (Henrich et al., 2006, 2010).

These results highlighted three important empirical facts that drove subsequent research in a few areas:

1. Substantial variation exists across human populations in how people play these games even when large stakes are used and great efforts ensure that people comprehend the instructions, payments, and so forth. My colleagues and I have made the case that this is because the experiments tap different social norms in different places (Henrich et al., 2005a). This work (1) inspired more such comparative projects (Herrmann et al., 2008; Lowes et al., 2017; Falk et al., 2018; Smith et al., 2018; Felipe, 2018), both within economics and beyond; (2) motivated much work on culture and social norms within economics (Nunn, 2009; Alesina and Giuliano, 2015; Nunn and Sanchez, 2017); and (3) led to behavioral game experiments becoming a routine tool for both development economists and anthropologists (Tracer, 2003; Gurven, 2004; Cronk, 2007; Voors et al., 2012; Cassar et al., 2013; Kosfeld and Rustagi, 2015; Lightner and Hagen, 2021).
2. The canonical predictions from classical game theory (assuming folks are income maximizers, etc.) fail everywhere, but in different ways in different places. The main exception to this comes from work among chimpanzees, where the canonical predictions are strikingly accurate in many experiments (Silk et al., 2005; Jensen et al., 2007a,b; Vonk et al., 2008). Since chimpanzees are smart but don't have social norms, this fits the interpretation offered by our team.
3. Across both phases of this enterprise, a community's degree of market integration was associated with higher offers in our one-shot bargaining experiments – a fact consistent with the venerable Doux Commerce hypothesis. In the second phase, we also showed that participation in a world religion was associated with higher offers, and with data on the prevalence of second- and third-party punishment, we found that small communities showed little willingness to engage in any sort of punishment. This motivated more empirical work, both within and outside of economics, on how market integration and religion might affect preferences or at least game behavior (Rustagi et al., 2010; Siziba et al., 2012; Cecchi and Bulte, 2013; Gurven et al., 2015; Kosfeld and Rustagi, 2015; Purzycki et al., 2016; Lang et al., 2019; Baldassarri, 2020; Lightner and Hagen, 2021).

34.3.3 Intergroup Competition Selects among Equilibria

Economists have contributed a few approaches that illuminate the role of intergroup competition. First, experimentalists have built on the tradition of putting groups into competition with each other within the laboratory context using behavioral experiments such as the public goods game (Bornstein and Erev, 1994; Bornstein, 2000). In one instructive experiment, Gürerk and colleagues (2006) created multiple groups who could select to play a regular linear, repeated (finite), public goods game, or one with peer punishment. After each round, players could choose to move to the other group. Most people made the wrong choice by selecting the group without punishment (little foresight). Cooperation levels immediately began to decline in the group without punishment and gradually everyone migrated to the group with punishment – a process captured by this cultural evolutionary model (Boyd and Richerson, 2009). Punishment continued to sustain cooperation even as the reluctant migrants entered the group. Later such laboratory experiments have revealed how intergroup competition can endogenously generate cooperative institutions (Fehr and Williams, 2018).

Complementing this laboratory work with natural experiments, Francois and colleagues (2018) show the power of intergroup competition to drive up generalized trust. In their first study, they show how the deregulation of the US banking sector, which began in different states at different times for idiosyncratic reasons, increased competition among firms and gradually drove up trust levels (based on the "trust question"). Second, using panel data from Germany, they showed that when people moved from less competitive to more competitive sectors of the economy, their trust levels increased, while when they moved from more competitive to less competitive sectors, their trust levels declined (again, measured using the "trust question"). Finally, working in the laboratory, they show how competition increases cooperative contributions in social dilemmas and that this can be measured using the trust question.

Finally, an emphasis on intergroup competition suggests that humans may be sensitive to conflict and violence in predictable ways. By studying post-conflict societies using both surveys and behavioral games, economists and cultural evolutionists have teamed up to show how the experience of conflict influences social behavior (Bellows and Miguel, 2009; Blattman, 2009; Blattman and Annan, 2010; Cassar et al., 2013; Bauer et al., 2014) and religious commitments (Henrich et al., 2019). Bauer and colleagues suggest this has important implications for understanding the reconstruction of societies after long-running conflicts.

34.4 CONCLUSIONS

By providing a language for thinking systematically about different kinds of social interactions, tools from game theory have permitted substantial progress, both empirically and theoretically, in the new field of cultural evolution. These developments have both influenced, and been influenced by, a rich and ongoing interaction and exchange between economists and the cadre of anthropologists, evolutionary biologists, and psychologists that have laid the foundations for a new and fully interdisciplinary approach to *Homo sapiens*.

34.5 REFERENCES

A. Acerbi, A. Mesoudi, and M. Smolla. Individual-based models of cultural evolution: A step-by-step guide using R. OSF Preprints, 2020.

A. F. Alesina and P. Giuliano. Culture and institutions. *Journal of Economic Literature*, 53:898–944, 2015.

K. Aoki. Theoretical and empirical aspects of gene-culture coevolution. *Theoretical Population Biology*, 59:253–261, 2001.

C. L. Apicella, E. M. Azevedo, N. A. Christakis, and J. H. Fowler. Evolutionary origins of the endowment effect: Evidence from hunter–gatherers. *American Economic Review*, 104:1793–1805, 2014.

R. Axelrod. *The Evolution of Cooperation*. New York: Basic Books, 1984.

R. Axelrod. An evolutionary approach to norms. *American Political Science Review*, 80:1095–1111, 1986.

R. Axelrod and W. D. Hamilton. The evolution of cooperation. *Science*, 211:390–396, 1981.

D. Baldassarri. Market integration accounts for local variation in generalized altruism in a nationwide lost-letter experiment. *Proceedings of the National Academy of Sciences*, 117:2858–2863, 2020.

A. Bandura. *Social Learning Theory*. Englewood Cliffs, NJ: Prentice Hall, 1977.

M. Bauer, A. Cassar, J. Chytilová, and J. Henrich. War's enduring effects on the development of egalitarian motivations and in-group biases. *Psychological Science*, 25:47–57, 2014.

J. Bellows and E. Miguel. War and local collective action in Sierra Leone. *Journal of Public Economics*, 93:1144–1157, 2009.

H. Bernhard, U. Fischbacher, and E. Fehr. Parochial altruism in humans. *Nature*, 442:912–915, 2006.

T. Besley and T. Persson. Democratic values and institutions. *American Economic Review: Insights*, 1:59–76, 2019.

R. Bhui, M. Chudek, and J. Henrich. How exploitation launched human cooperation. *Behavioral Ecology and Sociobiology*, 73:78, 2019.

L. L. Birch. Generalization of a modified food preference. *Child Development*, 52:755–758, 1981.

A. Bisin and T. Verdier. On the cultural transmission of preferences for social status. *Journal of Public Economics*, 70:75–97, 1998.

A. Bisin and T. Verdier. A model of cultural transmission, voting and political ideology. *European Journal of Political Economy*, 16:5–29, 2000.

A. Bisin and T. Verdier. The economics of cultural transmission and the dynamics of preferences. *Journal of Economic Theory*, 97:298–319, 2001.

C. Blattman. From violence to voting: War and political participation in Uganda. *American Political Science Review*, 103:231–247, 2009.

C. Blattman and J. Annan. The consequences of child soldiering. *Review of Economics and Statistics*, 92:882–898, 2010.

G. Bornstein. Intergroup conflict. *International Journal of Psychology*, 35:89, 2000.
G. Bornstein and I. Erev. The enhancing effect of intergroup competition on group-performance. *International Journal of Conflict Management*, 5:271–283, 1994.
S. Bowles. Endogenous preferences: The cultural consequences of markets and other economic institutins. *Journal of Economic Literature*, 36:75–111, 1998.
S. Bowles. *Microeconomics: Behavior, Institutions, and Evolution*. Princeton, NJ: Princeton University Press, 2004.
S. Bowles. Emulation, inequality, and work hours: Was Thorsten Veblen right? *The Economic Journal*, 90:363–412, 2005.
S. Bowles. Group competition, reproductive leveling, and the evolution of human altruism. *Science*, 314:1569–1572, 2006.
S. Bowles and H. Gintis. The moral economy of communities: Structured populations and the evolution of pro-social norms. *Evolution and Human Behavior*, 19:3–25, 1998.
S. Bowles and H. Gintis. Behavioural science: Homo reciprocans. *Nature*, 415:125–128, 2002.
S. Bowles and H. Gintis. Persistent parochialism: Trust and exclusion in ethnic networks. *Journal of Economic Behavior and Organization*, 55:1–23, 2004a.
S. Bowles and H. Gintis. The evolution of strong reciprocity: Cooperation in heterogeneous populations. *Theoretical Population Biology*, 65:17–28, 2004b.
S. Bowles and H. Gintis. *A Cooperative Species: Human Reciprocity and Its Evolution*. Princeton, NJ: Princeton University Press, 2011.
R. Boyd. Is the repeated prisoner's dilemma a good model of reciprocal altruism? *Ethology and Sociobiology*, 9:211–222, 1988.
R. Boyd. *A Different Kind of Animal: How Culture Transformed Our Species*. Princeton, NJ: Princeton University Press, 2017.
R. Boyd, H. Gintis, and S. Bowles. Coordinated punishment of defectors sustains cooperation and can proliferate when rare. *Science*, 328:617–620, 2010.
R. Boyd, H. Gintis, S. Bowles, and P. J. Richerson. The evolution of altruistic punishment. *Proceedings of the National Academy of Sciences of the United States of America*, 100:3531–3535, 2003.
R. Boyd and P. Richerson. Punishment allows the evolution of cooperation (or anything else) in sizable groups. *Ethology & Sociobiology*, 13:171–195, 1992.
R. Boyd and P. J. Richerson. Simple dual inheritance model of conflict between social and biological evolution. *Zygon*, 11:254–262, 1976.
R. Boyd and P. J. Richerson. *Culture and the Evolutionary Process*. Chicago: University of Chicago Press, 1985.
R. Boyd and P. J. Richerson. The evolution of indirect reciprocity. *Social Networks*, 11:213–236, 1989.
R. Boyd and P. J. Richerson. Group selection among alternative evolutionarily stable strategies. *Journal of Theoretical Biology*, 145:331–342, 1990.
R. Boyd and P. J. Richerson. Group beneficial norms can spread rapidly in a structured population. *Journal of Theoretical Biology*, 215:287–296, 2002.
R. Boyd and P. J. Richerson. Voting with your feet: Payoff biased migration and the evolution of group beneficial behavior. *Journal of Theoretical Biology*, 257:331–339, 2009.
R. Boyd, P. J. Richerson, and J. Henrich. Rapid cultural adaptation can facilitate the evolution of large-scale cooperation. *Behavioral Ecology and Sociobiology*, 65:431–444, 2011.

M. J. Brown and M. W. Feldman. Sociocultural epistasis and cultural exaptation in footbinding, marriage form, and religious practices in early 20th-century Taiwan. *Proceedings of the National Academy of Sciences of the United States of America*, 106:22139–22144, 2009.

C. Camerer. *Behavior Game Theory: Experiments in Strategic Interaction*. Princeton, NJ: Princeton University Press, 2003.

Y. Cao, B. Enke, A. Falk, P. Giuliano, and N. Nunn. *Herding, Warfare, and a Culture of Honor: Global Evidence*. Cambridge: National Bureau of Economic Research, 2021.

A. Cassar, P. Grosjean, and S. Whitt. Legacies of violence: Trust and market development. *Journal of Economic Growth*, 18:285–318, 2013.

L. L. Cavalli-Sforza and M. W. Feldman. *Cultural Transmission and Evolution: A Quantitative Approach*. Princeton, NJ: Princeton University Press, 1981.

F. Cecchi and E. H. Bulte. Does market experience promote rational choice? Experimental evidence from rural Ethiopia. *Economic Development and Cultural Change*, 61:407–429, 2013.

J.-K. Choi and S. Bowles. The coevolution of parochial altruism and war. *Science*, 318:636–640, 2007.

L. Cronk. The influence of cultural framing on play in the trust game: A Maasai example. *Evolution and Human Behavior*, 28:352–358, 2007.

W. H. Durham. *Coevolution: Genes, Culture, and Human Diversity*. Stanford: Stanford University Press, 1991.

R. B. Edgerton. *Sick Societies: Challenging the Myth of Primitive Harmony*. New York: Free Press, 1992.

C. Efferson, R. Lalive, and E. Fehr. The coevolution of cultural groups and ingroup favoritism. *Science*, 321:1844–1849, 2008.

J. Ensminger and J. Henrich, eds. *Experimenting with Social Norms: Fairness and Punishment in Cross-Cultural Perspective*. New York: Russell Sage Press, 2014.

A. Falk, A. Becker, T. Dohmen, B. Enke, D. Huffman, and U. Sunde. Global evidence on economic preferences. *Quarterly Journal of Economics*, 91:335–341, 2018.

E. Fehr and U. Fischbacher. The nature of human altruism. *Nature*, 425:785–791, 2003a.

E. Fehr and U. Fischbacher. Third party sanction and social norms. *Evolution and Human Behavior*, 25:63–87, 2003b.

E. Fehr, U. Fischbacher, and S. Gächter. Strong reciprocity, human cooperation and the enforcement of social norms. *Human Nature*, 13:1–25, 2002.

E. Fehr and S. Gächter. Reciprocity and economic: The economic implications of homo reciprocans. *European Economic Review*, 42:845–859, 1998.

E. Fehr and S. Gächter. Cooperation and punishment in public goods experiments. *American Economic Review*, 90:980–995, 2000.

E. Fehr and S. Gächter. Altruistic punishment in humans. *Nature*, 415:137–140, January 2002.

E. Fehr and J. Henrich. Is strong reciprocity a maladaption? In P. Hammerstein, ed., *Genetic and Cultural Evolution of Cooperation*. Cambridge, MA: MIT Press, 2003.

E. Fehr and B. Rochenbach. Detrimental effects of sanctions on human altruism. *Nature*, 422:137–140, 2003.

E. Fehr and T. Williams. Social norms, endogenous sorting and the culture of cooperation. Working paper, 2018.

M. W. Feldman and L. L. Cavalli-Sforza. Cultural and biological evolutionary processes, selection for a trait under complex transmission. *Theoretical Population Biology*, 9:238–259, 1976.

V. C. Felipe. The mission: Human capital transmission, economic persistence, and culture in South America. *Quarterly Journal of Economics*, 134:507–556, 2018.

P. Francois, T. Fujiwara, and T. van Ypersele. The origins of human pro-sociality: A test of cultural group selection on economic data and in the laboratory. *Scientific Advances*, 4(9):1–10, 2018.

P. Francois and J. Zabojnik. Trust, social capital, and economic development. *Journal of the European Economic Association*, 3:51–94, 2005.

D. Fudenberg and D. Levine. *The Theory of Learning in Games*. Cambridge, MA: MIT Press, 1998.

D. Fudenberg and E. Maskin. The folk theorem in repeated games with discounting or with incomplete information. *Econometrica*, 54:533–556, 1986.

H. Gintis. Strong reciprocity and human sociality. *Journal of Theoretical Biology*, 206:169–179, 2000.

H. Gintis. The hitchhiker's guide to altruism: Gene-culture coevolution, and the internalization of norms. *Journal of Theoretical Biology*, 220:407–418, 2003.

H. Gintis. The origin of wealth: Evolution, complexity, and the radical remaking of economics. *Journal of Economic Literature*, 44:1018–1031, 2006.

H. Gintis, E. A. Smith, and S. Bowles. Costly signaling and cooperation. *Journal of Theoretical Biology*, 213:103–119, 2001.

P. Grosjean. A history of violence: The culture of honor and homicide in the US south. *Journal of the European Economic Association*, 12:1285–1316, 2014.

O. Gürerk, B. Irlenbusch, and B. Rockenbach. The competitive advantage of sanctioning institutions. *Science*, 312:108–111, 2006.

M. Gurven. Economic games among the amazonian tsimane: Exploring the roles of market access, costs of giving, and cooperation on pro-social game behavior. *Experimental Economics*, 7:5–24, 2004.

M. Gurven, A. V. Jaeggi, V. Rueden, H. Chris, L. Paul, and H. Kaplan. Does market integration buffer risk, erode traditional sharing practices and increase inequality? A test among Bolivian forager-farmers. *Human Ecology*, 43:515–530, 2015.

R. A. Guzman, C. Rodriguez-Sickert, and R. Rowthorn. When in Rome, do as the Romans do: The coevolution of altruistic punishment, conformist learning, and cooperation. *Evolution and Human Behavior*, 28:112–117, 2007.

J. Henrich. Does culture matter in economic behavior? Ultimatum game bargaining among the machiguenga of the peruvian amazon. *American Economic Review*, 90:973–980, 2000.

J. Henrich. Cultural group selection, coevolutionary processes and large-scale cooperation. *Journal of Economic Behavior & Organization*, 53:3–35, 2004.

J. Henrich. The evolution of costly displays, cooperation and religion: Credibility enhancing displays and their implications for cultural evolution. *Evolution and Human Behavior* 30:244–260, 2009.

J. Henrich. *The Secret of Our Success: How Culture Is Driving Human Evolution, Domesticating Our Species, and Making Us Smarter*. Princeton, NJ: Princeton University Press, 2016.

J. Henrich. *The WEIRDest People in the World: How the West Became Psychologically Peculiar and Particularly Prosperous*. New York: Farrar, Straus and Giroux, 2020.

J. Henrich, M. Bauer, A. Cassar, J. Chytilová, and B. G. Purzycki. War increases religiosity. *Nature Human Behaviour*, 3:129–135, 2019.

J. Henrich, S. Bowles, E. A. Smith, H. P. Young, R. Boyd, K. Sigmund, P. J. Richerson, and A. Hopfensitz. The cultural and genetic evolution of human cooperation. In P. Hammerstein, ed., *Genetic and Cultural Evolution of Cooperation*. Cambridge, MA: MIT Press, 2003.

J. Henrich and R. Boyd. The evolution of conformist transmission and the emergence of between-group differences. *Evolution and Human Behavior*, 19:215–242, 1998.

J. Henrich and R. Boyd. Why people punish defectors: Weak conformist transmission can stabilize costly enforcement of norms in cooperative dilemmas. *Journal of Theoretical Biology*, 208:79–89, 2001.

J. Henrich and R. Boyd. Division of labor, economic specialization, and the evolution of social stratification. *Current Anthropology*, 49:715–724, 2008.

J. Henrich, R. Boyd, S. Bowles, C. F. Camerer, E. Fehr, and H. Gintis. *Foundations of Human Sociality: Economic Experiments and Ethnographic Evidence from Fifteen Small-Scale Societies*. New York: Oxford University Press, 2004.

J. Henrich, R. Boyd, S. Bowles, C. Camerer, E. Fehr, H. Gintis, and R. McElreath. In search of Homo economicus: Behavioral experiments in 15 small-scale societies. *American Economic Review*, 91:73–78, 2001.

J. Henrich, R. Boyd, S. Bowles, C. Camerer, E. Fehr, H. Gintis, R. McElreath, M. S. Alvard, A. Barr, J. Ensminger, N. S. Henrich, K. Hill, F. Gil-White, M. Gurven, F. W. Marlowe, J. Q. Patton, and D. Tracer. "Economic man" in cross-cultural perspective: Behavioral experiments in 15 small-scale societies. *Behavioral and Brain Sciences*, 28:795–815, 2005a.

J. Henrich, R. Boyd, S. Bowles, C. Camerer, E. Fehr, H. Gintis, R. McElreath, M. S. Alvard, A. Barr, J. Ensminger, N. S. Henrich, K. Hill, F. Gil-White, M. Gurven, F. W. Marlowe, J. Q. Patton, and D. Tracer. Models of decision-making and the coevolution of social preferences. *Behavioral and Brain Sciences*, 28:838–855, 2005b.

J. Henrich, M. Chudek, and R. Boyd. The big man mechanism: How prestige fosters cooperation and creates prosocial leaders. *Philosophical Transactions of the Royal Society B: Biological Sciences*, 370:20150013, 2015.

J. Henrich, J. Ensminger, R. McElreath, A. Barr, C. Barrett, A. Bolyanatz, J. C. Cardenas, M. Gurven, E. Gwako, N. Henrich, C. Lesorogol, F. Marlowe, D. P. Tracer, and J. Ziker. Market, religion, community size and the evolution of fairness and punishment. *Science*, 327:1480–1484, 2010.

J. Henrich and N. Henrich. Fairness without punishment: Behavioral experiments in the Yasawa Island, Fiji. In J. Ensminger and J. Henrich, eds., *Experimenting with Social Norms: Fairness and Punishment in Cross-Cultural Perspective*, ch. 9, pp. 225–258. New York: Russell Sage Press, 2014.

J. Henrich, R. McElreath, A. Barr, J. Ensminger, C. Barrett, A. Bolyanatz, J. C. Cardaroas, M. Gurven, E. Gwako, N. Henrich, C. Lesoronol, F. Marlowe, D. Tracer, and J. Ziker. Costly punishment across human societies. *Science*, 312:1767–1770, 2006.

B. Herrmann, C. Thöni, and S. Gächter. Antisocial punishment across societies. *Science*, 319:1362–1367, 2008.

K. Hill, M. Barton, and A. M. Hurtado. The emergence of human uniqueness: Characters underlying behavioral modernity. *Evolutionary Anthropology*, 18:187–200, 2009.

K. Hill and A. M. Hurtado. Cooperative breeding in south American hunter–gatherers. *Proceedings of the Royal Society B – Biological Sciences*, 276:3863–3870, 2009.

K. R. Hill, R. S. Walker, M. Bozicevic, J. Eder, T. Headland, B. Hewlett, A. M. Hurtado, F. Marlowe, P. Wiessner, and B. Wood. Co-residence patterns in hunter–gatherer societies show unique human social structure. *Science*, 331:1286–1289, 2011.

K. Jensen, J. Call, and M. Tomasello. Chimpanzees are rational maximizers in an ultimatum game. *Science*, 318:107–109, 2007a.

K. Jensen, J. Call, and M. Tomasello. Chimpanzees are vengeful but not spiteful. *Proceedings of the National Academy of Sciences of the United States of America*, 104:13046–13050, 2007b.

J. J. Jordan, M. Hoffman, P. Bloom, and D. G. Rand. Third-party punishment as a costly signal of trustworthiness. *Nature*, 530:473–476, 2016.

N. V. Joshi. Evolution of cooperation by reciprocation within structured demes. *Journal of Genetics*, 66:69–84, 1987.

J. Kendal, M. W. Feldman, and K. Aoki. Cultural coevolution of norm adoption and enforcement when punishers are rewarded or non-punishers are punished. *Theoretical Population Biology*, 70:10–25, 2006.

J. Kendal, L. A. Giraldeau, and K. Laland. The evolution of social learning rules: Payoff-biased and frequency-dependent biased transmission. *Journal of Theoretical Biology*, 260:210–219, 2009.

K. D. Kinzler, K. H. Corriveau, and P. L. Harris. Children's selective trust in native-accented speakers. *Developmental Science*, 14:106–111, 2011.

K. D. Kinzler, K. Shutts, and E. S. Spelke. Language-based social preferences among children in South Africa. *Language Learning and Development*, 8:215–232, 2012.

M. Kosfeld and D. Rustagi. Leader punishment and cooperation in groups: Experimental field evidence from commons management in Ethiopia. *American Economic Review*, 105:747–783, 2015.

K. N. Laland. *Darwin's Unfinished Symphony: How Culture Made the Human Mind*. Princeton, NJ: Princeton University Press, 2017.

K. N. Laland, J. Odling-Smee, and S. Myles. How culture shaped the human genome: Bringing genetics and the human sciences together. *Nature Reviews Genetics*, 11:137–148, 2010.

M. Lang, B. G. Purzycki, C. L. Apicella, Q. D. Atkinson, A. Bolyanatz, E. Cohen, C. Handley, K. Klocová, L. Eva, M. Carolyn, M. Sarah, A. Rita, C. Moya, C. D. Placek, M. Soler, T. Vardy, J. L. Weigel, A. K. Willard, D. Xygalatas, A. Norenzayan, and J. Henrich. Moralizing gods, impartiality and religious parochialism across 15 societies. *Proceedings of the Royal Society B: Biological Sciences*, 286:20190202, 2019.

O. Leimar and P. Hammerstein. Evolution of cooperation through indirect reciprocity. *Proceedings: Biological Sciences*, 268:745–753, 2001.

A. D. Lightner and E. H. Hagen. Acculturation and market integration are associated with greater trust among tanzanian maasai pastoralists. *Evolutionary Human Sciences*, 3:E15, 2021.

S. Lowes, N. Nunn, J. A. Robinson, and J. L. Weigel. The evolution of culture and institutions: Evidence from the Kuba Kingdom. *Econometrica*, 85:1065–1091, 2017.

C. Lumsden and E. O. Wilson. *Genes, Mind and Culture*. Cambridge, MA: Harvard University Press, 1981.

M. F. Majid. The persistent effects of in utero nutrition shocks over the life cycle: Evidence from Ramadan fasting. *Journal of Development Economics*, 117:48–57, 2015.

J. Maynard Smith. *Evolution and the Theory of Games*. Cambridge, MA: Cambridge University Press, 1982.

R. McElreath. Reputation and the evolution of conflict. *Journal of Theoretical Biology*, 220:345–357, 2003.

R. McElreath and P. Strimling. When natural selection favors imitation of parents. *Current Anthropology*, 49:307–316, 2008.

A. Mesoudi. *Cultural Evolution: How Darwinian Theory Can Explain Human Culture and Synthesize the Social Sciences*. Chicago: University of Chicago Press, 2011.

J. Moscona, N. Nunn, and J. A. Robinson. Keeping it in the family: Lineage organizations and the scope of trust in Sub-Saharan Africa. *American Economic Review*, 107:565–571, 2017.

W. Nakahashi, J. Y. Wakano, and J. Henrich. Adaptive social learning strategies in temporally and spatially varying environments: How temporal vs. spatial variation, number of cultural traits, and costs of learning influence the evolution of conformist-biased transmission, payoff-biased transmission, and individual learning. *Human Nature*, 23:386–418, 2012.

R. E. Nisbett and D. Cohen. *Culture of Honor: The Psychology of Violence in the South*. Boulder: Westview Press, 1996.

N. Nunn. The importance of history for economic development. *Annual Review of Economics*, 1:65–92, 2009.

N. Nunn. History as evolution. In A. Bisin and G. Federico, eds., *The Handbook of Historical Economics*, ch. 3, pp. 41–91. San Diego, CA: Academic Press, 2021.

N. Nunn and D. L. S. R. Sanchez. Why being wrong can be right: Magical warfare technologies and the persistence of false beliefs. *American Economic Review*, 107:582–587, 2017.

K. Panchanathan and R. Boyd. Indirect reciprocity can stabilize cooperation without the second-order free rider problem. *Nature*, 432:499–502, 2004.

H. R. Pulliam and C. Dunford. *Programmed to Learn: An Essay on the Evolution of Culture*. New York: Columbia University Press, 1980.

B. G. Purzycki, C. L. Apicella, Q. D. Atkinson, E. Cohen, R. A. McNamara, A. K. Willard, D. Xygalatas, A. Norenzayan, and J. Henrich. Moralistic gods, supernatural punishment and the expansion of human sociality. *Nature*, 530:327–330, 2016.

P. J. Richerson and R. Boyd. The evolution of ultrasociality. In Eibl-Eibesfeldt and F. K. Salter, eds., *Indoctrinability, Ideology and Warfare, Irenaus*. New York: Berghahn Books, 1998.

P. J. Richerson, R. Boyd, and J. Henrich. Gene-culture coevolution in the age of genomics. *Proceedings of the National Academy of Sciences*, 107:8985–8992, 2010.

P. J. Richerson, R. Baldini, A. Bell, K. Demps, K. Frost, V. Hillis, S. Mathew, E. Newton, N. Narr, L. Newson, C. Ross, P. Smaldino, T. Waring, and M. R. Zefferman. Cultural group selection plays an essential role in explaining human cooperation: A sketch of the evidence. *Behavioral and Brain Sciences*, 39:1–46, 2016.

T. L. Rosenthal and B. J. Zimmerman. *Social Learning and Cognition*. New York: Academic Press, 1978.

D. Rustagi, S. Engel, and M. Kosfeld. Conditional cooperation and costly monitoring explain success in forest commons management. *Science*, 330:961–965, 2010.

J. F. Schulz, D. Bahrami-Rad, J. P. Beauchamp, and J. Henrich. The church, intensive kinship, and global psychological variation. *Science*, 366:eaau5141, 2019.

K. Shutts, M. R. Banaji, and E. S. Spelke. Social categories guide young children's preferences for novel objects. *Developmental Science*, 13:599–610, 2010.

J. B. Silk, S. F. Brosnan, J. Vonk, J. Henrich, D. J. Povinelli, A. S. Richardson, S. P. Lambeth, J. Mascaro, and S. J. Schapiro. Chimpanzees are indifferent to the welfare of unrelated group members. *Nature*, 437:1357–1359, 2005.

S. Siziba, E. Bulte, and S. Siziba. Does market participation promote generalized trust? Experimental evidence from southern Africa. *Economic Letters*, 117:156–160, 2012.

K. M. Smith, T. Larroucau, I. A. Mabulla, and C. L. Apicella. Hunter-gatherers maintain assortativity in cooperation despite high levels of residential change and mixing. *Current Biology*, 28:3152–3157, 2018.

D. P. Tracer. Selfishness and fairness in economic and evolutionary perspective: An experimental economic study in Papua New Guinea. *Current Anthropology*, 44:432–438, 2003.

P. Turchin. A theory for formation of large empires. *Journal of Global History*, 4:191–217, 2009.

P. Turchin. Warfare and the evolution of social complexity: A multilevel-selection approach. *Structure and Dynamics*, 4:1–37, 2010.

P. Turchin. *Ultrasociety: How 10,000 Years of War Made Humans the Greatest Cooperators on Earth*. Chaplin, CT: Beresta Books, 2015.

J. Van Cleve. Cooperation, conformity, and the coevolutionary problem of trait associations. *Journal of Theoretical Biology*, 396:13–24, 2016.

S. Vogt, M. Zaid, N. Ahmed, E. F. Ahmed, F. E. Hilal, and C. Efferson. Changing cultural attitudes towards female genital cutting. *Nature*, 538:506–509, 2016.

J. Vonk, S. F. Brosnan, J. B. Silk, J. Henrich, A. S. Richardson, S. P. Lambeth, S. J. Schapiro, and D. J. Povinelli. Chimpanzees do not take advantage of very low cost opportunities to deliver food to unrelated group members. *Animal Behaviour*, 75:1757–1770, 2008.

M. J. Voors, E. E. M. Nillesen, P. Verwimp, E. H. Bulte, R. Lensink, and D. P. Van Soest. Violent conflict and behavior: A field experiment in burundi. *American Economic Review*, 102:941–964, 2012.

J. W. Weibull. *Evolutionary Game Theory*. Cambridge, MA: MIT Press, 1995.

H. P. Young. *Individual Strategy and Social Structure: An Evolutionary Theory of Institutions*. Princeton, NJ: Princeton University Press, 1998.

Index

Other Books in the Series (continued from page ii)

K. Samphantharak & R. Townsend, *Households as Corporate Firms: An Analysis of Household Finance Using Integrated Household Surveys and Corporate Financial Accounting*, 2009

I. Gilboa, *Theory of Decision under Uncertainty*, 2009

F. Vega-Redondo, *Complex Networks*, 2007

R. Blundell, W. Newey, & T. Persson (eds.), *Advances in Economics and Econometrics: Theory and Applications, Ninth World Congress, Vols. I, II, & III*, 2006

J. Roemer, *Democracy, Education, and Equality*, 2006

C. Blackorby, W. Bossert, & D. Donaldson, *Population Issues in Social Choice Theory, Welfare Economics and Ethics*, 2005

R. Koenker, *Quantile Regression*, 2005

C. Hsiao, *Analysis of Panel Data, 2nd edn*, 2003

M. Dewatripont, L. P. Hausen, & S. J. Turnovsky (eds.), *Advances in Economics and Econometrics: Theory and Applications, Eighth World Congress, Vols. I, II, & III*, 2003

E. Ghysels, N. Swanson, & M. Watson (eds.), *Essays in Econometrics: Collected Papers of Clive W. J. Granger, Vols. I & II*, 2001

S. Strøm (ed.), *Econometrics and Economic Theory in the 20th Century: The Ragnar Frisch Centennial Symposium*, 1999

A. C. Cameron & P. K. Trivedi, *Regression Analysis of Count-Data*, 1998

D. Jacobs, E. Kalai, & M. Kamien (eds.), *Frontiers of Research in Economic Theory: The Nancy L. Schwartz Memorial Lectures*, 1998

D. M. Kreps & K. F. Wallis (eds.), *Advances in Economics and Econometrics: Theory and Applications, Seventh World Congress, Vols. I, II, & III*, 1997

R. Guesnerie, *A Contribution to the Pure Theory of Taxation*, 1995

C. Sims (ed.), *Advances in Econometrics, Sixth World Congress, Vols. I & II*, 1994

H. White, *Inference, Estimation and Specification Analysis*, 1994

J.-J. Laffont (ed.), *Advances in Economic Theory, Sixth World Congress, Vols. I & II*, 1992

W. Härdle, *Applied Nonparametric Regression Analysis*, 1990

A. Roth & M. Sotomayor, *Two-Sided Matching*, 1990

T. Lancaster, *The Econometric Analysis of Transition Data*, 1990

L. G. Godfrey, *Misspecification Tests in Econometrics*, 1989

H. Moulin, *Axioms of Cooperative Decision-Making*, 1988

T. Bewley (ed.), *Advances in Economic Theory, Fifth World Congress, Vols. I, II, & III*, 1987

C. Hsiao, *Analysis of Panel Data*, 1986

J. Heckman & B. Singer, *Longitudinal Analysis of Labor Market Data*, 1985

A. Mas-Colell, *The Theory of General Economic Equilibrium: A Differentiable Approach*, 1985

R. J. Bowden & D. A. Turkington, *Instrumental Variables*, 1985

B. Peleg, *Game Theoretic Analysis of Voting in Committees*, 1984

F. M. *Fisher, Disequilibrium Foundations of Equilibrium Economics*, 1983

J.-M. Grandmont, *Money and Value*, 1983

G. Debreu, *Mathematical Economics*, 1983

G. S. Maddala, *Limited Dependent and Qualitative Variables in Econometrics*, 1983

W. Hildenbrand (ed.), *Advances in Economic Theory*, 1983

W. Hildenbrand (ed.), *Advances in Econometrics*, 1983

Made in United States
North Haven, CT
29 May 2026

11939581R00241